WOMEN AND HEALTH

POWER, TECHNOLOGY, INEQUALITY, AND CONFLICT IN A GENDERED WORLD

KATHRYN STROTHER RATCLIFF

University of Connecticut

ALLYN AND BACON

Boston • London • Toronto • Sydney • Tokyo • Singapore

Series Editor: Jeff Lasser
Series Editorial Assistant: Andrea Christie
Marketing Manager: Judeth Hall
Editorial-Production Service: Omegatype Typography, Inc.
Manufacturing Buyer: Suzanne Lareau
Cover Administrator: Kristina Mose-Libon
Electronic Composition: Omegatype Typography, Inc.

A Pearson Education Company
75 Arlington Street
Boston, MA 02116

Internet: www.ablongman.com

Library of Congress Cataloging-in-Publication Data

Ratcliff, Kathryn Strother.
Women and health : power, technology, inequality, and conflict in a gendered world / Kathryn Strother Ratcliff.
p. cm.
Includes bibliographical references and index.
ISBN 0-205-30597-0 (alk. paper)
1. Women—Health and hygiene—Sociological aspects. 2. Medical care—Sex differences. 3. Health—Sex differences. I. Title.

RA564.85 .R38 2002
362.1'082—dc21

2001018866

Printed in the United States of America

10 9 8 7 6 5 4 3 2 1 06 05 04 03 02 01

CONTENTS

FOREWORD

This book is a result of three decades of women's health movement activism. It is the fruit of activists' and scholars' seeking and learning, the incorporation of our knowledge into the academic, medical, and political worlds and into popular discourse.

Women and Health introduces a wide range of women's health issues. Its virtue is that it never loses sight of the larger picture. It details the extent to which social, economic, and political factors affect women's health and the ways health care and medical care are "delivered." *Women and Health* always places its discussions in the contexts of class, ethnic, and other dimensions of diversity among women, as well as societal power imbalances, and the tendency to embrace uncritically all new technology. It consistently makes the distinction between health care and medical care, between public health issues and privatized, individually oriented health practice. It clearly shows how the historic devaluation of women and women's lives prevails in the twenty-first century, affecting how women are perceived, and whether they receive (or do not receive) adequate holistic, preventive health care and societal support. The commonsense idea that health care should be a right for all, not a privilege for the wealthy few, runs throughout the chapters.

We urge readers to digest the information in this book and then go one step further: Think about yourselves and the world in which you have grown up. Which of these subjects attracts you more than the others? Adopt it as your own, look into it more extensively. Seek out other women and men to whom it has been important. Together, explore how it has affected your lives, your work, surroundings, families, and friends. Then decide what you can do individually and collectively to change the situation for the better. Spread the word via further study, public speaking, and writing letters, articles, and books. Enter the fray of health work and help to develop woman-centered health policy and practice on the local, national, or international scenes. Remember always to ground yourselves in the particularity and power of women's experiences, with the awareness that all issues are interconnected.

In sum, incorporate what you have learned into your own life, and then move outward again. The second wave of the women's health movement was so powerful, so dynamic because we quickly made connections between the personal and political. Each of us at the Boston Women's Health Collective had experienced some aspect of faulty medical care, such as unhealthy or ineffective birth control devices, life-threatening abortions, overmedicalized childbirth, or workplace hazards—the countless injustices of a patriarchal medical system in which we had little say at all. Immediately, whatever we had gone through, all that we discovered and the things that other women told us made their way into *Our Bodies, Ourselves* (we were lucky to have such a vehicle). Over the past thirty-one years, this kind of learning has continued to inform, direct, and inspire us in our current health work.

In the early 1970s, we believed that we could change the world simply by pooling our knowledge and making our needs known. Now, ever hopeful, we are less naïve. Our efforts have improved awareness of issues, delivery of care, and appropriateness of research. Yet, because medical, political, economic, and antiwoman gender-based structures hold firm, most women still experience too many insufficiencies, deficiencies, indignities, and dangers, as documented throughout this book. More than ever, we must work at changing our existing health care and medical systems—indeed, transforming our society—until everyone's needs are met and all of our lives are honored, nourished, and sustained.

—Jane Pincus, with Judy Norsigian,
for the Boston Women's Health Book Collective

PREFACE

Over the years of working on this book, I have grown to appreciate how vibrant the study of women's health is. It has become a flourishing arena of popular literature and social science research, with exciting new books, articles, journals, and newsletters appearing regularly. Given the scarcity of material in this field a few years ago, the sheer amount available now can seem overwhelming. This book adds to that growing scholarship by providing a map for the reader who may have limited knowledge of the breadth of women's health writings, and by offering a critical introduction to important issues.

This book provides an interdisciplinary perspective, drawing on scholarship in sociology, history, women's studies, anthropology, political science, psychology, and medical science, as well as on writings in the popular press. Throughout, the book challenges traditional viewpoints on women and health; questions the values, power, and politics embedded in women's health; and highlights the importance of gender, ethnicity, class, sexual orientation, and able-bodiedness.

Addressing issues of social justice, ethics, and public policy, this book is structured around understanding and critiquing the dominant biomedical model, analyzing the powerful for-profit forces and seductive new technologies in health care, and examining health decisions and practices in a gendered world. Each chapter includes an overview, an extensive bibliography, and the work of other writers on more specific issues. As a reader, you will hear the voices of scholars from many disciplines, as well as those of activists, a farm wife, a mother, doctors, lawyers, and journalists. Fighting the tendency of sociologists to write in an obscure way with needless jargon, I have worked to make this book accessible not only to undergraduate social science students, but also to a more general audience.

This book covers many topics in women's health, but inevitably excludes others. It only infrequently mentions women outside the United States; it is about women, not girls. It hardly touches on sexuality, STDs, alcohol and substance abuse, mental health, or eating disorders, among other things. Space considerations dictated the omission of these and other important topics.

I owe an indirect debt to the many women from the Boston Women's Health Book Collective and the National Women's Health Network who have been trailblazers in women's health. Several people helped me more directly: Jane Wilkie, Claire Healy, and Davita Silfen Glasberg gave feedback on several chapters, and Jayne M. Fargnoli changed the basic organization of the book by offering major suggestions on a first book proposal. Greg Williams and Sydney Plum made editorial suggestions. My husband, Richard, son, Charles, and daughter, Emily, also helped with the book, especially on Chapters 11 and 13, and References. Myra Marx Ferree has no idea what is in this book, but she has been a wonderful role model for nearly twenty years.

I am also indebted to graduate students Kim Yanoshik, Cindy Barerre, and Marita McComisky, and to undergraduates Stephanie Gladwin, Meredith Wells, Maggie Callahan, and Dena Marder, all of whom actively participated as students in my classes, teaching me as they learned. Many of these former undergraduates are now pursuing careers as nurses and doctors. And I honor the memory of Christine Guyon, whose persistent questions stimulated my thinking.

Finally, I dedicate this book to the memory of my parents, who taught me the importance of activism in health with their lifelong involvement in the Group Health Cooperative of Puget Sound and their take-control attitude at the end of their lives.

ACKNOWLEDGMENTS

I would like to thank the following reviewers: Heather Dillaway, University of Delaware; Elizabeth Jenner, University of Illinois at Urbana-Champaign; Jacquelyn Litt, Iowa State University; Jean Robinson, Indiana University; and Linda Whiteford, University of South Florida.

CHAPTER 1

INTRODUCTION

The topic of women's health is a cornucopia of questions. Why is so little known about women's health? What birth control is available and is it safe? Is premenstrual syndrome (PMS) real? What are the risk factors for heart disease, and why have doctors ignored the symptoms and incidence of heart disease in women? Why do doctors dismiss other symptoms women report and say it is "all in their heads"? What do midwives do, and why aren't more midwives active in childbirth? Why are so many unnecessary hysterectomies, episiotomies, and cesarean sections performed on women? How did small breasts become a disease?

This anthology provides a sociological framework for discussing these questions. Because of their importance for the health of women, these questions and others like them require an understanding that will serve us in the long run—when new and different questions are posed, and opportunities for change emerge. An adequate sociological answer to a birth control safety question is not a simple listing of currently available methods with their safety and effectiveness data. Rather, the answer requires considering concepts such as power, to understand who controls the choices available; race and class discrimination, to understand who is offered what choices, how coercive that offering is, and why some people see birth control less as individual freedom from unwanted pregnancy and more as a way for society to control unwanted population; and structural incentives, to understand both the motivation of pharmaceutical-company decision makers and the reasons for potential biases in the data on safety and effectiveness.

This book provides a foundation for discussing questions surrounding women's health by using an eclectic set of concepts primarily derived from four themes. We argue that women's health and health care are fundamentally influenced by (1) the dominance of the biomedical model that emphasizes finding a pathology, locating disease in the individual, seeking biological causes, and focusing on cure rather than prevention; (2) the technological favoritism in society, science, and medicine, which encourages new, fancy, specialized, and often untested solutions over less invasive ones; (3) the increasing for-profit intrusions into health and health care, which have encouraged some remedies more for profit than for health, and have redefined the incentive structure for caregivers; and (4) the gender-, race-, and class-based organization of society.

Each of these factors has parallels in understanding men's health as well, but understanding women's health also requires a woman-centered examination of the fourth theme, which asserts that the organization of society has different consequences for women. The powerful position of men in society, the male-centered assumptions about women; the gendered division of labor in society; the relative economic poverty of women; and the long-standing patterns of sexism, racism, and other systems of oppression affect women's health and health care in ways different from their effects on men's health and health care. For example, the reasons why our country spends billions of dollars on drug testing are partly understood by examining the influence of the biomedical model, the for-profit sector, and our love of technology. Yet these factors do not explain an important pattern in drug testing: For decades the conclusions about safety and effectiveness were based on male-only samples. Women were excluded from test groups or from analysis; women were "the Other." If we are to understand the faulty logic producing this lopsided knowledge, we need to understand the gender-based organization of society.

The gendering of health and health care is insidious. Even the federal Medicare system for elderly women and men provides evidence of bias: The government-established reimbursement to doctors for female-specific procedures is less than that for most (79 percent of) comparable male-specific procedures. The dollar value placed on a woman's health is literally less than that for a man's (Goff, Muntz, and Cain 1997).

Gender-patterned reasoning also affects end-of-life treatment. Courts that become evaluators of requests for refusal of life-sustaining treatment make decisions that more likely respect the man's treatment preferences than the woman's (Miles and August 1990).

These four ideas form the thematic core of this book and will reappear throughout the anthology, both in the overviews and the readings. In some chapters, each of these themes receives explicit coverage; in others, only some of the themes are highlighted. Each of these four themes deserves some orienting comments here.

THE BIOMEDICAL MODEL

The biomedical model has been the reigning paradigm in medical science and practice since the seventeenth century (Engel 1988). It is a complex, subtle, and intellectually invasive model that has focused popular attention, research grants, training curricula, medical reimbursement, and health care on certain aspects of health, and at the same time has neglected other aspects of health. What kinds of health care providers are available, why medical histories are done as they are, why doctors talk so little about prevention—we can understand these patterns in the context of a biomedical model. The biomedical model has taught us to see the physical body in a particular way, to ask a particular set of questions about disease, health, and health care, and not to ask other questions.

The biomedical model begins by defining health as the absence of disease. In this book, we will come to find that this is an inadequate definition of health, but for the time being we will examine where the biomedical model has taken this definition. To promote health, the biomedical model works to eliminate disease. To do so, professional health care providers learn to screen for and diagnose disease, and prescribe an appropriate cure, likely to be a pharmaceutical prescription or a surgical solution. With screening, diagnosis, and cure as the focus of the health care system, attention to *prevention* is neglected. Thus, we spend more time and money detecting and curing cancer than we do preventing it; we invest in fetal surgery rather than understanding the causes of infertility; we build expensive neonatal intensive care units rather than providing prenatal care to at-risk pregnant women; we provide hip replacements for elderly women who fall rather than making architectural changes to their homes, providing walkers, or teaching them balancing techniques. Prevention is largely relegated to the less prestigious and less well-funded field of public health.

Focusing on screening and diagnosing disease privileges *pathology.* When doctors are observing a natural and usually healthy process, their minds are trained to be vigilant to possible pathology. "Healthy and normal" are not typical words in their vocabulary (Kapsalis 1997:72). Childbirth is an excellent example. While nearly all births are the uncomplicated unfolding of the natural process of pregnancy, doctors refer to pregnancy as a disease, and to childbirth as the most dangerous day in a child's life, to be considered normal only in retrospect. A doctor's mind-set anticipates that something might go wrong, so he or she constantly monitors the woman for problems and is ready to respond with drugs for inducing labor, or with surgery by performing a cesarean section. Sitting and waiting, as a midwife would, and supporting the natural process by reducing the woman's fear, making her more comfortable, or proposing a body position more conducive to successful contractions, are not the behaviors for which a doctor is trained. The doctor is trained to distrust the natural process, and to come to its rescue. This medicalization of a natural process takes control away from women and puts it in the hands of doctors. What was "women birthing" children has become "doctors delivering" them.

In its mission to eliminate disease, the biomedical model not only privileges cure over prevention and pathology over healthy processes, but it also privileges objective and technical approaches over subjective ones. The technical emphasis is seen in the biomedical model's implicit assumption of the body as a machine:

> *The Cartesian model of the body as a machine operates to make the physician a technician, or mechanic. The body breaks down and needs repair; it can be repaired in the hospital as a car is in the shop; once "fixed," a person can be returned to the community. The earliest models in medicine were largely mechanical; later models worked more with chemistry, and newer, more sophisticated medical writing describes computerlike programming, but the basic point remains the same. Problems in the body are technical problems requiring technical solutions, whether it is a mechanical repair, a chemical rebalancing, or a "debugging" of the system. (Rothman 1991:34–35)*

Any examination of the typical medical school curriculum shows this age-old model of body as machine still being taught, with courses that emphasize mastery of technical skills and knowledge, not mastery of the art of interviewing a patient. After medical school, residents continue to learn technical skills, and how to perform and read tests, not how to interact with patients. (See Chapter 3.)

By focusing attention on the technical aspects of the problem, the body-as-machine metaphor ignores the subjective experience accompanying the disease. Often referred to as "the illness," this subjective experience includes the meanings a person attaches to the disease. Thus, a woman who has a mastectomy because of breast cancer, or a hysterectomy because of uterine cancer, grapples not just with the physical loss of a body part, but may grieve the loss of the breast or uterus as symbolically important to her sense of self and sexuality. The technical focus ignores this.

This body-as-machine metaphor also places boundaries on the object of concern, requiring that the doctor examine and treat only the individual. The model assumes that the disease is located in the individual and that the sole focus there is thus appropriate. The role of the family in successful treatment is often ignored, as is the context of the disease. Thus, in caring for women who have suffered domestic abuse, doctors record that an injury has occurred and may list the immediate cause—"blow to head by stick with nail in it" (Warshaw 1989:512; also, see Chapter 5). However, they often neglect to record the health threat, the abusive husband. In fact, they tend to fix the injuries (repair the machine) and then send the woman back to the same environment.

Criticisms of the Biomedical Model

Sociologists, feminists, and others critique the biomedical model as limited, and they propose alternative models, variously called sociocultural, sociomedical, or psychosocial models. These models see health in a broader context. Rather than focusing on physical causes as the biomedical model does (the classic biomedical model talked of one specific biological cause for each disease), these models incorporate social, psychological, cultural, economic, and political causes for disease. Thus, rather than stopping with the stick and nail in the preceding example, the sociomedical model would not only note the abusive husband as an immediate instrument of the injury, but trace the cause back to a patriarchal society that has privileged men and condoned such behavior as an appropriate method to control women. Stress, social support or its absence, poverty, discrimination, mass media influences (e.g., emaciated role models and diet advertisements), the neighborhood, community and ethnic context, and the power of corporations in producing an unhealthy situation (e.g., the tobacco industry targeting women) are important candidates in these alternative explanatory models.

The sociomedical perspective argues that diseases are social constructions. Although the biomedical model sees the naming of disease as the result of the objective discovery of physical conditions, the sociomedical model argues that social structure and culture shape our beliefs about our bodies and our health. What diseases get "discovered" and named, and what explanations of bodily processes and diseases are accepted, are not objective matters—they are shaped by society. Dominant beliefs once allowed lesbianism to be classified as a disease with symptoms including hostility, weakness, and an inability to face the responsibilities of adulthood. Similarly, masturbation was once accepted as a disease, causing one to become a physical, moral, and mental wreck (Freund and McGuire 1995:194). Changes in the political climate have caused these constructs to be discarded. But the politics of disease naming are still with us. A political battle raged within the American Psychiatric Association when the PMS diagnosis was proposed. Lobbying, picketing, and petitioning were all part of the process of arriving at a majority vote that this is a medical condition. (See Chapter 9.)

Diseases are often defined by the biomedical model as statistical deviations from the norm on a measurable biological variable, be it anatomical, hormonal, neurophysiological, genetic, or biochemical. Such a designation has the ring of objectivity, until one examines who decides what variables have "harmful variation." When is such variation simply a part of the diversity of human experience with no health consequences? Is having breasts that are "abnormally" small a disease? Plastic surgeons have defined them as such, labeling this condition "micromastia," a deviation on a biological variable of breast size. But what makes this a disease? The power of the plastic surgeons to declare it so. (See Chapter 8.)

TECHNOLOGICAL FAVORITISM

The biomedical model provides a strong foundation for the use of technology. The mechanistic view of the human body and the interventionist mentality of science encourage technical solutions. But technology is also encouraged by the education and socialization of health care providers (particularly doctors), the reward structure for scientists and clinicians, the growth of litigation concerns, the inadequacies in the systems that evaluate technology, and the growth of for-profit health care. All push for the use of more technology.

With the biomedical model accepted as the dominant paradigm, the training of medical researchers and medical students emphasizes technical proficiency. That such training occurs in highly specialized hospitals that have the latest technology further supports technology. Doctors-in-training are likely to choose the more valued and rewarded specialties taught by the leading professors at their schools. Specialty medicine begets more technology.

Feminists have extensively researched and criticized the training of doctors and their workplace practices. The education of specialists in obstetrics-gynecology has come under close scrutiny by feminists because women have so much contact with this specialty. Obstetrician-gynecologists are specialists who provide generalist care for women in their reproductive years and beyond, serving as their primary care physicians. As surgical specialists, obstetrician-gynecologists tend to provide surgical solutions to problems. They are, for instance, more likely to deliver by cesarean section than are generalists (Kasper 1985). The surgical mentality of obstetrician-gynecologists conflicts with the health needs of women who typically come with everyday nonsurgical problems. Because surgery is a major avenue for advancement in the profession (Guillemin 1981), "the situation is ripe for the proliferation of unnecessary operations" (Scully 1994:139–140).

Doctors are also influenced to use high-tech procedures due to factors in their work context. For example, because of the perceived threat of malpractice suits as well as the growing complexity of the body of medical knowledge, doctors tend to practice defensive medicine, which calls for more extensive diagnostic tests. The patient often undergoes a barrage of tests, many routine and most low in informational payoff, because the doctor is seeking documented evidence confirming the wisdom of treatment decisions that were made on the basis of limited information.

Tests, along with drugs, devices, and procedures, are in ample supply because, despite an evaluation system formidable in appearance, we have, at best, a severely flawed method of determining the effectiveness and safety of health care innovations. New technologies are supposed to be evaluated at many levels. The most basic level is represented by the direct health care provider. However, although doctors are taught to be competent users of the latest medical innovations, they are not taught to be critical consumers or evaluators of such innovations. Their bias in favor of high-tech treatments is combined with limited training in research methodology. Furthermore, many technologies receive no evaluation whatever, are widely used prior to any systematic assessment (Banta and Behney 1981; McKinlay 1981), or are used despite negative evaluations. The electronic fetal monitor (Kunisch 1989), ultrasound (National Institute of Child Health and Human Development et al. 1984), intrauterine devices (IUDs) (Ruzek 1980:337), oral contraceptives (Corea 1985), and diethylstilbestrol (DES) (Mintz 1985) are among the technologies that have been used despite being poorly, belatedly, or negatively evaluated. Negative evaluations sometimes include strong cautionary statements, yet use of the technology persists or even increases (Ratcliff 1989:188).

Additionally, a problem in the evaluation system is the fact that evaluators are often interested parties. Evaluations of drugs are often based on industry-supplied data or on industry-funded research. The Dalkon Shield (Chapter 5) was accepted in the clinical community based on the research of a professor who benefitted financially from the commercial success of the Shield. In this case, there was not just the *appearance* of potential bias in the research—the bias was real. A major design flaw in his evaluation model allowed women who were using the Shield to simultaneously use contraceptive foam. Therapies thus combined cannot lead to research conclusions about the effectiveness of one of them.

Finally, reports evaluating health care technologies use standards and language with a built-in bias favoring technology. In terms of standards, what constitutes a finding of "harmful" or "harmless"? Often, because the rates of very serious side effects are low (the side effect occurs, but not that often), because the appearance of the side effect is not immediate, or because it is influenced by other contributing factors, large differences between the treated group and the untreated one are not found. Depending on the level of statistical significance chosen and the size of the group studied, an investigator may not be able to reject the hypothesis of no difference between the two groups. It is therefore assumed that the new technology is harmless. However, the technology has not been shown to be harmless; rather, the study has simply failed to find it is harmful enough to be noticed, given the constraints imposed on the study. The new technology is given the benefit of the doubt, just as our legal system gives the benefit of the doubt to the accused (innocent until proven guilty). Although this is an admirable standard in criminal justice, it is a questionable standard for evaluation, given the track record of many new technologies (Ratcliff 1989).

The social forces resulting from the biomedical model, the education and socialization of health care providers, and the failure of our system of evaluation have produced a health care system with an abundance of technology. The easy availability of technology has greatly altered the health care experience. Technology is used when it is not necessary and even when alternatives exist. When in use, technology provides compelling information that distances the caregiver from the client. One doctor, speaking of intensive care units (ICUs), says, "Call to mind an ICU with monitors blinking and beeping, and remember how all eyes (even family members') go to the monitors—and away from the patient. It requires effort *not* to watch the monitors" (Cassell 1986a:192). Referring to electronic fetal monitors (EFMs), another doctor notes how monitoring has dehumanized obstetrics: "We cannot divert our eyes or ears from the E[F]M's alluring LEDs [light-emitting diodes], beeps, and stylus-chattering graphs. We no longer listen to, talk with, gaze upon, or touch our patient" (Munsick 1979:410). Some have argued that we have ended up with a health care system that values machine information more than that obtained by mere humans (Banta and Gelijns 1987). The machine, not the physician (and certainly not the patient), ends up dictating the treatment (Crawshaw 1983).

The use of technology raises many issues. For feminists, equity is a central issue. "Technology has everything to do with who benefits and who suffers, whose opportunities increase and whose decrease, who creates and who accommodates" (Bush 1983:163). Basic access questions emerge because women are denied a technology for reasons of class (they cannot afford it) or moral judgment (they are not "appropriate" recipients because of their lesbianism, unmarried status, or poor education). More complex issues have emerged with the development of some technologies, such as prenatal testing procedures. These technologies, which may lead to the decision not to have a particular type of baby, have raised serious ethical concerns about who decides "who shall inhabit the earth" (Hubbard 1990). (See Chapters 13 and 14.)

FOR-PROFIT INTRUSION IN HEALTH CARE

American medicine has long been an industry shaped by the profit and income orientations of key participants who have developed and promoted various technologies, including devices, procedures, and pharmaceuticals (Relman 1980), sometimes with little regard for the health of those using the technology. The Dalkon Shield (noted earlier and in Chapter 5) and the electronic fetal monitor are clear examples. The Shield was promoted because it was an incredibly inexpensive product that could bring large profits to the Robins company. The EFM, useful in the high-risk pregnancies it was developed for, became routine in the delivery room because a company saw profits and ignored the negative consequences of the EFM for low-risk women (Kunisch 1989).

In recent years, major organizational changes have altered and intensified the for-profit aspect of the health care system: Multistate chains of hospitals have emerged; health care institutions have adopted business orientations that stress economic returns and diminish service, and have increasingly put decision making into the hands of people concerned with the bottom line; and managed care has become the typical insurance-provider arrangement.

These trends further compromise health care because they provide incentives or guidelines for care that shape the quality and nature of the health care we receive. It is now typical for a hospital management team to look at cost centers and be concerned with recruiting patients who are profitable. The treatment of PMS and the growth of in vitro fertilization (IVF) clinics provide dramatic examples. In Chapter 9, we discuss the social construction of PMS and question its existence. Health care providers act as though PMS does exist, and hospitals have duly recognized the financial benefits of such a diagnosis to the hospital.

Whether or not a treatment is provided, how aggressively it is marketed, and how readily the diagnosis is accepted are questions asked and answered on a balance sheet. IVF clinics provide expensive and largely ineffective treatment for infertile, well-to-do couples. They are promoted as profit centers for hospitals and clinics, and they thrive in an unregulated environment in which the health costs and benefits of IVF are not carefully evaluated.

The growth of managed care is relatively new, but already consumers have voiced concerns about the priorities in medical care decision making. Consumers have loudly protested drive-through deliveries and outpatient mastectomy procedures. The form of for-profit influences is changing, such that overtreatment may become less of a problem, and undertreatment may become a major problem for all—not just for women with inadequate insurance or none at all. The enduring questions in this for-profit climate are, Who is making decisions? On what basis?

And who is looking out for our health, not just the bottom line?

THE GENDER-, RACE-, AND CLASS-BASED ORGANIZATION OF SOCIETY, HEALTH, HEALTH RESEARCH, AND HEALTH CARE

The fourth theme in this anthology is the gender-, race-, and class-based organization of society. Although this fourth theme focuses on gender as a ubiquitous system of oppression, understanding women and health requires an examination of other systems of oppression: racism, classism, ageism, and discrimination against lesbians and women with disabilities. (See Bayne-Smith 1996 and Adams 1995 for an overview of ethnicity and health.)

The organization of society influences women's health, health research, and health care. For example, the androcentric assumptions, gendered power differences, and pervasive sexism of our patriarchal society are replicated within the health domain. Statements made to rationalize the exclusion of women from medical research (men are the norm; women are the "other"); the words used to justify hysterectomies ("women have outlived their ovaries"); or the concern with women as vectors and vessels, not as victims, of AIDS do not come from the biomedical model. They come from a culture which permits a view of women as less valuable than men, and useful primarily as reproductive vessels.

First, the organization of society affects how healthy women are. Simply put, women's health is compromised by their status in society. Poverty, the lack of power, racial discrimination, the gendered division of labor, and the devaluing of women all affect a woman's health. Women are exposed to different occupational conditions than men are, encounter more violence in the home, and have an increased risk of various health problems due to their relatively greater impoverishment.

Second, the gender-, race-, and class-based organization of society affects health research, which is largely done by men; researchers' cultural ideas about women shape their research. Some research excludes women because they are seen as reproductive beings, forever in a potentially-pregnant state; other research includes women, but interprets the findings about women in stereotypical ways (women are dependent, emotional, and need to fulfill a biological destiny). Women with less power have been used as guinea pigs or ignored. Puerto Rican and poor women were subjects in early trials of drugs and devices that were dangerous (e.g., the Dalkon Shield, and birth control pills); and poor African American women were subjected to painful and experimental genital surgical techniques (Scully 1994). Lesbian women and women with disabilities, their problems deemed unimportant, have been little researched.

Third, the organization of society has influenced health care. The current stratification of health care practitioners by gender and ethnicity is dramatic, though changing. Doctors are predominately male and nurses female. Less-well-paid health care workers are also primarily female, and often from minority ethnic groups. Within the medical profession, women are disproportionately in particular fields, such as family medicine, and pediatrics. Furthermore, female health care providers encounter sexism and racism in training and on the job. (See Chapter 15.)

Female patients in the health care system have less power than male patients due to their gender, and communication is likely to be less satisfactory for female patients. Ethnic minority female patients and those who are poor, lesbian, or disabled have even less power. Research shows that health care providers treat female and male patients differently, interpret the reporting of symptoms in a gendered way, are more likely to dismiss a woman's symptoms as psychological, request tests based in part on the patients' gender, and diagnose differently for men and women. For instance, women and men reporting angina (chest pain associated with heart disease) to a doctor are often treated differently. Men have typical angina, whereas women don't. Only if women present symptoms that are just like men's are they treated the same as men, a phenomenon that Bernadine Healy, the first female head of the

National Institutes of Health (NIH), refers to as the "Yentl syndrome" (Healy 1991). (See Chapter 10.)

The gendering of health care has been a particular problem in obstetrics and gynecology. Reviews of obstetrical texts indicate a persistently paternalistic and sometimes condescending attitude toward the female patient (Scully 1994:107), and gynecologists have been characterized as treating women "as though they were children" (Scully 1994:19). The roots and consequences of this sexism (as well as other systems of oppression) in women's health care will be examined throughout this volume.

CHAPTER 2

SCIENCE AND VALUES

According to the popular image, scientists conduct their experiments objectively, making observations to be replicated by their peers in the dispassionate search for truth. In this image, personal values and cultural biases—as well as race, class, and gender relations—are rendered invisible.

Scientists and historians of science have demonstrated the naivete of this popular image (Fausto-Sterling 1985; Harding 1991; Hubbard 1990; Keller 1983; Rosser 1994). Clearly, what is studied, how it is studied, and how it is reported are not value-free. Scientific progress does not evolve linearly, driven solely by an internal dynamic of the subject matter. Rather, scientists make choices about their research based on reigning paradigms and their embedded assumptions, entrenched traditions of the scientific community, and their own world view developed from their culture, class, gender, ethnicity, and personal experiences (Bleier 1985). Scientists are not different from others; they, too, are a product of their culture and its biases. Although our concern in this volume is primarily clinical medicine, not science or scientists per se, we need to understand the close link between science and health. Doctors, other health care providers, and even the lay public read scientific findings and are influenced by them. Learning that science is often not very "scientific," but instead is influenced by the society in which it is done, alerts us to possible biases that might affect our health care system, particularly the health of women. This chapter explores three ways in which values influence science: the questions scientists ask, who is studied or excluded from study, and how research is reported in journal articles and medical textbooks.

CULTURAL VALUES INFLUENCE SCIENCE

Ruth Bleier, a neurophysiologist, began an article with the bold and broad statement that "biological theories have provided the scientific justification for ideologies that support, explain, mystify, and obfuscate patriarchal relationships of power, domination, and control" (Bleier 1985:19). Her evidence for that thesis covers several points. First of all, she examines metaphors used in science that are influenced by, and in turn influence, the language of the dominant social order. Thus, she makes a connection between the Darwinian idea of survival of the fittest and the related ideas of competitive capitalism and eugenics, and the minimal sympathy for poor people and other "underdogs." Second, her evidence includes the historical example of craniometry (brain measurement); and third, it includes the logic of sociobiology. In her analysis, each area of evidence illustrates that how the research questions were asked and how the results were interpreted was biased by the prejudged superiority of white males and their assumptions of gendered behavior patterns.

The historical example of craniometry is particularly interesting, because it is a "science" that was also used to demonstrate the supposed inferiority of blacks. In *The Mismeasure of Woman*, Carol Tavris notes the parallels:

> *In* The Mismeasure of Man, *the scientist Stephen Jay Gould showed how science has been used and abused in the study of intelligence to serve a larger social and political agenda: to confirm the prejudice that some groups are assigned to their subordinate roles "by the harsh dictates of nature." The mismeasure of woman persists because it, too, reflects and serves society's prejudices. Views of*

woman's "natural" differences from man justify a status quo that divides work, psychological qualities, and family responsibilities into "his" and "hers." Those who are dominant have an interest in maintaining their difference from others, attributing those differences to "the harsh dictates of nature," and obscuring the unequal arrangements that benefit them. (Tavris 1992:24)

Craniometry has an enduring legacy (Fausto-Sterling 1986). Research on sex differences in brain structure and cognitive abilities, ongoing as we write, is useful to examine because the research clearly engenders parts of the physical body. The craniometry research tradition essentially argues that biology is destiny by alleging that differences in the hemispheric structure of the female and male brains cause differences in cognitive abilities. Criticism of this research includes methodological weaknesses such as small samples and the use of poor measures for the main indicator of brain characteristics (lateralization/integration of the hemispheres); the lack of evidence of how the alleged brain structure characteristics would affect cognitive ability; and the lack of statistically significant sex differences (Bleier 1988:95–97).

Despite these shortcomings, which seem to invalidate the sex difference findings, researchers *keep asking* the question of difference—why can't women think like men?—and keep searching for biological reasons to explain the alleged differences. Significantly, the sex differences in cognitive functioning—mathematical ability, spatial processing, verbal ability—that researchers are trying to explain are in fact rather trivial in size when compared to the differences that occur among women or among men. Put differently, the overlap of the male and female distributions is so considerable that asking the question of sex *difference* on these variables misses the big story of variation of these characteristics *within* genders or, more appropriately, within the entire populace.

Furthermore, the more important story goes beyond the relatively *trivial* sex differences in math or verbal SAT scores, or any other measure of cognitive functioning, to the *significant* sex differences in life outcomes, such as the choice of occupation—for example, the percent of doctors or microbiologists who are women in contrast to the percent of nurses or medical technicians who are women. These consequential differences between women and men are not explained by brain structure differences. "Rather than biology, it is the culture we have created that limits, by its institutions, ideologies, and expectations, the full expression of that potential" (Bleier, 1985:38). It is the analysis of gender, not biological sex, that reveals the reasons for these important differences.

A striking example of values in the social construction of a disease is lesbianism. The history of lesbianism in medicine provides clear evidence of how the cultural attitudes toward lesbian behavior, not our scientific knowledge of lesbianism, affect whether lesbianism is referred to as a sin, crime, disease, sexual orientation, or a life choice (Stevens and Hall 1991; reproduced in this chapter as a reading). This is but one demonstration of how science reflects and reinforces existing hierarchies, power arrangements, and societal belief systems. We will see other examples throughout this book.

THE EXCLUSION OF WOMEN FROM RESEARCH

Cultural values embedded in science have produced the rationale justifying the exclusion of women from many research studies. In the 1980s, public awareness of this exclusion grew. A public health service task force examined the issue of gender bias in research subjects, as did a committee selected by the Institute of Medicine. The evidence from these and other studies indicated that women were *categorically excluded* from many research studies. A study of the effects of caffeine on heart disease included 45,589 men and no women. A study of aspirin therapy to lower the risk of myocardial infarction studied 22,071 men and no women (Rosser 1994:6). A pilot study on obesity and breast cancer excluded women (Dresser 1992). The first twenty years of the Baltimore Longitudinal Study included only men (Chapter 10), yet the resulting publication was entitled "Normal Human Aging." In heart research, women were excluded in part because heart disease was considered a male problem. Women were not in the Mr. Fit Study, the Coronary Drug Project, or the Physicians' Health Study (Mastroianni, Faden, and Federman 1994:65). Three out of four randomized clinical trials on cholesterol-lowering drugs were conducted using only middle-aged men, yet half of the prescriptions for these drugs were written for women over the age of 60 (Mastroianni, Faden, and Federman 1994:113). How safe and effective are the drugs for these women? No one asked, so we do not know. Women's health clearly has been compromised by this exclusion.

Various reasons have been used to justify the exclusion of women. First, researchers claim that hormonal fluctuations make women too complicated to study; men had to be the norm. The logic of such a rationale for exclusion is clearly faulty. Once approved, drugs so studied are then prescribed to women without any knowledge of how those hormones influence the effects. If the hormones are important in the drug reaction, they need to be studied. Second, researchers view women as "potentially pregnant," regardless of age or contraceptive decision, and see the possible fetus in need of protection. Yet eliminating women means we are singularly concerned with protecting the egg, not the sperm, and hence not the fetus. Such rationales are not only faulty, they see women first and foremost as reproductive vessels.

In 1986, the National Institutes of Health (NIH) responded to the public disclosure of the exclusion of women from many research protocols with a new federal grant policy. Researchers were asked to justify any categorical exclusion of research subjects. Little changed for some time because there was no serious attempt to implement the new policy. "The grant application booklet researchers use to draw up their funding requests had not been revised to reflect the new guidelines, so proposals that, without explanation, excluded women were still being received, reviewed, and ultimately funded. A revised form did not appear until April 1991, over four years after the policy was first introduced" (Nechas and Foley 1994:25).

REPORTING FINDINGS IN THE LITERATURE

One's values not only affect the choice of questions to ask and subjects to study, but also how scientific findings are reported in journal articles and textbooks. An illustrative example from two centuries ago is the skeletal representations in anatomy books. At first glance, it is hard to imagine how a drawing of the skeletons of men and women could be subjective. In fact, as an article with the delightful title of "Skeletons in the Closet" (Schiebinger 1986) shows, rather than using a scientific method of selecting a typical male and female skeleton to include, the medical artists produced "ideal" male and female skeletons by reflecting on the culturally desirable characteristics of men and women.

The original impetus for the gendering of anatomy (including craniometry, as noted earlier) came from political and social ideas about women in the mid 1700s. Women were seen as uniquely suited for their domestic and procreative roles. Since reproductive biology demonstrated a difference between women and men, the question then became, What were the *other* inherent physical differences between women and men? The bias in this search for difference is evident in the skeletal remains recorded in anatomy textbooks. Male skeletons were chosen based on their portrayal of "strength and agility," with care taken that they not be too delicate. In contrast, one anatomist reports representing the women's skeletons based on his judgments of womanly beauty: "I have always observed that the female body, which is the most beautiful and womanly in all its parts, is one in which the pelvis is the largest in relation to the rest of the body" (quoted in Schiebinger 1986:62). Gendered images of men and women led to the selected drawings in the anatomy books, which in turn supported the cultural views that women were destined to have very different social roles. It was literally in their bones.

Medical textbooks of our era show similar biases. The male is presented as the typical case to be understood and the female is regarded as a variation on the theme. Men are the norm; women the other. In anatomy textbooks, the majority of the text is devoted to the male, and it is impossible in most chapters to understand women's health without *first* understanding men's health (Lawrence and Bendixen 1992). Medical textbook chapters begin with headings (e.g., "The Perineum") which provide a general discussion of an organ or system and give details on *male* anatomy. Then a subheading (e.g., "The Female Perineum") appears, and the female difference from the general model is discussed. One cannot thus understand the female perineum without first reading the more "general" (i.e., male) information.

Sometimes the female is forgotten entirely in the medical textbooks. A shared anatomical region might be discussed in terms of male structures only. For instance, "The inguinal canal with its inlet...and its outlet...result from the descent of the testes from the abdominal cavity into the scrotum" (quoted in Lawrence and Bendixen 1992:931). Never do we learn of the process in the female or even that there is a comparable process. Or drawings appear to examine the human condition, but in fact the drawings are of men. A drawing of the posterior abdominal wall in a 1979 textbook of human anatomy (Lawrence and Bendixen 1992:931) appears to represent the human condition. After all, the label on the figure does not mention sex. Yet the small labeling of anatomical parts on the drawing itself includes *testicular* veins and arteries. The posterior abdominal wall is not shown—the *male* posterior abdominal wall is shown. Furthermore, when women are mentioned, they are often contrasted with men (information on the male is given, and then "in contrast to the male" we learn about the female), or women's anatomy is shown as homologous to men's. We learn that the clitoris is homologous with the penis, never that the penis is homologous with the clitoris (Lawrence and Bendixen 1992:925).

Such a pattern in reporting led an indexer of the popular 1980 *Williams Obstetrics* textbook to surreptitiously include an item in the index which read, "Chauvinism, male, voluminous amounts, pp. 1–1102" (quoted in Mitford 1992:95). Chauvinism is subtle and pervasive. An article by Emily Martin on the egg and the sperm (Martin 1991, reproduced as a reading in this chapter) discusses the language used in discussions of conception. The language is not driven by scientific evidence of the biological process; rather it reproduces at the microlevel the cultural understanding of the male as the initiator and the female as the docile recipient of the male's interest. New research, as she points out, changes the description in minor ways, but the gender stereotype of the masculinized sperm and femininized egg persists.

In important ways, medical science has accepted the belief that women have to accede to the harsh dictates of nature. Science reports profound biological differences between men and women without necessarily admitting that their questions imply the differences they report; they make their studies of difference without necessarily studying both genders; and publications contain subtle and not-so-subtle stereotypes of women and their place in society. The dictates of being born female have been harsh indeed, but they are socially constructed, not biologically ordained.

THE EGG AND THE SPERM: HOW SCIENCE HAS CONSTRUCTED A ROMANCE BASED ON STEREOTYPICAL MALE-FEMALE ROLES

EMILY MARTIN

The theory of the human body is always a part of a world-picture.... The theory of the human body is always a part of a fantasy.

—James Hillman[1]

As an anthropologist, I am intrigued by the possibility that culture shapes how biological scientists describe what they discover about the natural world. If this were so, we would be learning about more than the natural world in high school biology class; we would be learning about cultural beliefs and practices as if they were part of nature. In the course of my research I realized that the picture of egg and sperm drawn in popular as well as scientific accounts of reproductive biology relies on stereotypes central to our cultural definitions of male and female. The stereotypes imply not only that female biological processes are less worthy than their male counterparts but also that women are less worthy than men. Part of my goal in writing this article is to shine a bright light on the gender stereotypes hidden within the scientific language of biology. Exposed in such a light, I hope they will lose much of their power to harm us.

EGG AND SPERM: A SCIENTIFIC FAIRY TALE

At a fundamental level, all major scientific textbooks depict male and female reproductive organs as systems for the production of valuable substances, such as eggs and sperm.[2] In the case of women, the monthly cycle is described as being designed to produce eggs and prepare a suitable place for them to be fertilized and grown—all to the end of making babies. But the enthusiasm ends there. By extolling the female cycle as a productive enterprise, menstruation must necessarily be viewed as a failure. Medical texts describe menstruation as the "debris" of the uterine lining, the result of necrosis, or death of tissue. The descriptions imply that a system has gone awry, making products of no use, not to specification, unsalable, wasted, scrap. An illustration in a widely used medical text shows menstruation as a chaotic disintegration of form, complementing the many texts that describe it as "ceasing," "dying," "losing," "denuding," expelling."[3]

Male reproductive physiology is evaluated quite differently. One of the texts that sees menstruation as failed production employs a sort of breathless prose when it describes the maturation of sperm: "The mechanisms which guide the remarkable cellular transformation from spermatid to mature sperm remain uncertain.... Perhaps the most amazing characteristic of spermatogenesis is its sheer magnitude: the normal human male may manufacture several hundred million sperm per day."[4] In the classic text *Medical Physiology,* edited by Vernon Mountcastle, the male/female, productive/destructive comparison is more explicit: "Whereas the female *sheds* only a single gamete each month, the seminiferous tubules *produce* hundreds of millions of sperm each day" (emphasis mine).[5] The female author of another text marvels at the length of the microscopic seminiferous tubules, which, if uncoiled and placed end to end "would span almost one-third of a mile!" She writes, "In an adult male these structures produce millions of sperm cells each day." Later she asks, "How is this feat accomplished?"[6] None of these texts expresses such intense enthusiasm for any female processes. It is surely no accident that the "remarkable" process of making sperm involves precisely what, in the medical view, menstruation does not: production of something deemed valuable.[7]

One could argue that menstruation and spermatogenesis are not analogous processes and, therefore, should not be expected to elicit the same kind of response. The proper female analogy to spermatogenesis, biologically, is ovulation. Yet ovulation does not merit enthusiasm in these texts either. Textbook descriptions stress that all of the ovarian follicles containing ova are already present at birth. Far from being *produced,* as sperm are, they merely sit on the shelf, slowly degenerating and aging like overstocked inventory: "At birth, normal human ovaries contain an estimated one million follicles [each], and no new ones appear after birth. Thus, in marked contrast to the male, the newborn female already has all the germ cells she will ever have. Only a few, perhaps 400, are destined to reach full maturity during her active productive life. All the others degenerate at some point in their development so that few, if any, remain by the time she reaches menopause at approximately 50 years of age."[8] Note the "marked contrast" that this description sets up between male and female: the male, who continuously produces fresh germ cells, and the female, who has stockpiled germ cells by birth and is faced with their degeneration.

Nor are the female organs spared such vivid descriptions. One scientist writes in a newspaper article that a woman's ovaries become old and worn out from ripening eggs every month, even though the woman herself is still relatively young: "When you look through a laparoscope...at an ovary that has been through hundreds of cycles, even in a superbly healthy American female, you see a scarred, battered organ."[9]

To avoid the negative connotations that some people associate with the female reproductive system, scientists could begin to describe male and female processes as homologous. They might credit females with "producing" mature ova one at a time, as they're needed each month, and describe males as having to face problems of degenerating germ cells. This degeneration would occur throughout life among spermatogonia, the undifferentiated germ cells in the testes that are the long-lived, dormant precursors of sperm.

But the texts have an almost dogged insistence on casting female processes in a negative light. The texts celebrate sperm production because it is continuous from puberty to senescence, while they portray egg production as inferior because it is finished at birth. This makes the female seem unproductive, but some texts will also insist that it is she who is wasteful.[10] In a section heading for *Molecular Biology of the Cell,* a best-selling text, we are told that "Oogenesis is wasteful." The text goes on to emphasize that of the seven million oogonia, or egg germ cells, in the female embryo, most degenerate in the ovary. Of those that do go on to become oocytes, or eggs, many also degenerate, so that at birth only two million eggs remain in the ovaries. Degeneration continues throughout a woman's life: by puberty 300,000 eggs remain, and only a few are present by menopause. "During the 40 or so years of a woman's reproductive life, only 400 to 500 eggs will have been released," the authors write. "All the rest will have degenerated. It is still a mystery why so many eggs are formed only to die in the ovaries."[11]

The real mystery is why the male's vast production of sperm is not seen as wasteful.[12] Assuming that a man "produces" 100 million (10^8) sperm per day (a conservative estimate) during an average reproductive life of sixty years, he would produce well over two trillion sperm in his lifetime. Assuming that a woman "ripens" one egg per lunar month, or thirteen per year, over the course of her forty-year reproductive life, she would total five hundred eggs in her lifetime. But the word "waste" implies an excess, too much produced. Assuming two or three offspring, for every baby a woman produces, she wastes only around two hundred eggs. For every baby a man produces, he wastes more than one trillion (10^{12}) sperm.

How is it that positive images are denied to the bodies of women? A look at language—in this case, scientific language—provides the first clue. Take the egg and the sperm.[13] It is remarkable how "femininely" the egg behaves and how "masculinely" the sperm.[14] The egg is seen as large and passive.[15] It does not *move* or *journey,* but passively "is transported," "is swept,"[16] or even "drifts"[17] along the fallopian tube. In utter contrast, sperm are small, "streamlined,"[18] and invariably active. They "deliver" their genes to the egg, "activate the developmental program of the egg,"[19] and have a "velocity" that is often remarked upon.[20] Their tails are "strong" and efficiently powered.[21] Together with the forces of ejaculation, they can "propel the semen into the deepest recesses of the vagina."[22] For this they need "energy," "fuel,"[23] so that with a "whiplash-like motion and strong lurches"[24] they can "burrow through the egg coat"[25] and "penetrate" it.[26]

At its extreme, the age-old relationship of the egg and the sperm takes on a royal or religious patina. The egg coat, its protective barrier, is sometimes called its "vestments," a term usually reserved for sacred, religious dress. The egg is said to have a "corona,"[27] a crown, and to be accompanied by "attendant cells."[28] It is holy, set apart and above, the queen to the sperm's king. The egg is also passive, which means it must depend on sperm for rescue. Gerald Schatten and Helen Schatten liken the egg's role to that of Sleeping Beauty: "a dormant bride awaiting her mate's magic kiss, which instills the spirit that brings her to life."[29] Sperm, by contrast, have a "mission:"[30] which is to "move through the female genital tract in quest of the ovum."[31] One popular account has it that the sperm carry out a "perilous journey" into the "warm darkness," where some fall away "exhausted." "Survivors" "assault" the egg, the successful candidates "surrounding the prize."[32] Part of the urgency of this journey, in more scientific terms, is that "once released from the supportive environment of the ovary, an egg will die within hours unless rescued by a sperm."[33] The wording stresses the fragility and dependency of the egg, even though the same text acknowledges elsewhere that sperm also live for only a few hours.[34]

In 1948, in a book remarkable for its early insights into these matters, Ruth Herschberger argued that female reproductive organs are seen as biologically interdependent, while male organs are viewed as autonomous, operating independently and in isolation:

> *At present the functional is stressed only in connection with women: it is in them that ovaries, tubes, uterus, and vagina have endless interdependence. In the male, reproduction would seem to involve "organs" only.*
>
> *Yet the sperm, just as much as the egg, is dependent on a great many related processes. There are secretions which mitigate the urine in the urethra before ejaculation, to protect the sperm. There is the reflex shutting off of the bladder connection, the provision of prostatic secretions, and various types of muscular propulsion. The sperm is no more independent of its milieu than the egg, and yet from a wish that it were, biologists have lent their support to the notion that the human female, beginning with the egg, is congenitally more dependent than the male.*[35]

Bringing out another aspect of the sperm's autonomy, an article in the journal *Cell* has the sperm making an "existential decision" to penetrate the egg: "Sperm are cells with a limited behavioral repertoire, one that is directed toward fertilizing eggs. To execute the decision to abandon the haploid state, sperm swim to an egg and there acquire the ability to effect membrane fusion."[36] Is this a corporate manager's version of the sperm's activities—"executing decisions" while fraught with dismay over difficult options that bring with them very high risk?

There is another way that sperm, despite their small size, can be made to loom in importance over the egg. In a collection of scientific papers, an electron micrograph of an enormous egg and tiny sperm is titled "A Portrait of the Sperm."[37] This is a little like showing a photo of a dog and calling it a picture of the fleas. Granted, microscopic sperm are harder to photograph than eggs, which are just large enough to see with the naked eye. But surely the use of the term "portrait," a word associated with the powerful and wealthy, is significant. Eggs have only micrographs or pictures, not portraits.

One depiction of sperm as weak and timid, instead of strong and powerful—the only such representation in western civilization, so far as I know—occurs in Woody Allen's movie *Everything You Always Wanted To Know About Sex*: *But Were Afraid to Ask*. Allen, playing the part of an apprehensive sperm inside a man's testicles, is scared of the man's approaching orgasm. He is reluctant to launch himself into the darkness, afraid of contraceptive devices, afraid of winding up on the ceiling if the man masturbates.

The more common picture—egg as damsel in distress, shielded only by her sacred garments; sperm as heroic warrior to the rescue—cannot be proved to be dictated by the biology of these events. While the "facts" of biology may not *always* be constructed in cultural terms, I would argue that in this case they are. The degree of metaphorical content in these descriptions, the extent to which differences between egg and sperm are emphasized, and the parallels between cultural stereotypes of male and female behavior and the character of egg and sperm all point to this conclusion.

NEW RESEARCH, OLD IMAGERY

As new understandings of egg and sperm emerge, textbook gender imagery is being revised. But the new research, far from escaping the stereotypical representations of egg and sperm, simply replicates elements of textbook gender imagery in a different form. The persistence of this imagery calls to mind what Ludwik Fleck termed "the self-contained" nature of scientific thought. As he described it, "the interaction between what is already known, what remains to be learned, and those who are to apprehend it, go to ensure harmony within the system. But at the same time they also preserve the harmony of illusions, which is quite secure within the confines of a given thought style."[38] We need to understand the way in which the cultural content in scientific descriptions changes as biological discoveries unfold, and whether that cultural content is solidly entrenched or easily changed.

In all of the texts quoted above, sperm are described as penetrating the egg, and specific substances on a sperm's head are described as binding to the egg. Recently, this description of events was rewritten in a biophysics lab at Johns Hopkins University—transforming the egg from the passive to the active party.[39]

Prior to this research, it was thought that the zona, the inner vestments of the egg, formed an impenetrable barrier. Sperm overcame the barrier by mechanically burrowing through, thrashing their tails and slowly working their way along. Later research showed that the sperm released digestive enzymes that chemically broke down the zona; thus, scientists presumed that the sperm used mechanical *and* chemical means to get through to the egg.

In this recent investigation, the researchers began to ask questions about the mechanical force of the sperm's tail. (The lab's goal was to develop a contraceptive that worked topically on sperm.) They discovered, to their great surprise, that the forward thrust of sperm is extremely weak, which contradicts the assumption that sperm are forceful penetrators.[40] Rather than thrusting forward, the sperm's head was now seen to move mostly back and forth. The sideways motion of the sperm's tail makes the head move sideways with a force that is ten times stronger than its forward movement. So even if the overall force of the sperm were strong enough to mechanically break the zona, most of its force would be directed sideways rather than forward. In fact, its strongest tendency, by tenfold, is to escape by attempting to pry itself off the egg. Sperm, then, must be exceptionally efficient at *escaping* from any cell surface they contact. And the surface of the egg must be designed to trap the sperm and prevent their escape. Otherwise, few if any sperm would reach the egg.

The researchers at Johns Hopkins concluded that the sperm and egg stick together because of adhesive molecules on the surfaces of each. The egg traps the sperm and adheres to it so tightly that the sperm's head is forced to lie flat against the surface of the zona, a little bit, they told me, "like Br'er Rabbit getting more and more stuck to tar baby the more he wriggles." The trapped sperm continues to wiggle ineffectually side to side. The mechanical force of its tail is so weak that a sperm cannot break even one chemical bond. This is where the digestive enzymes released by the sperm come in. If they start to soften the zona just at the tip of the sperm and the sides remain stuck, then the weak, flailing sperm can get oriented in the right direction and make it through the zona—provided that its bonds to the zona dissolve as it moves in.

Although this new version of the saga of the egg and the sperm broke through cultural expectations, the researchers who made the discovery continued to write papers and abstracts as if the sperm were the active party who attacks, binds, penetrates, and enters the egg. The only difference was that sperm were now seen as performing these actions weakly.[41] Not until August 1987, more than three years after the findings described above, did these researchers reconceptualize the process to give the egg a more active role. They began to describe the zona as an aggressive sperm catcher, covered with adhesive molecules that can capture a sperm with a single bond and clasp it to the zona's surface.[42] In the words of their published account: "The innermost vestment, the *zona pellucida*, is a glycoprotein shell, which captures and tethers the sperm before they penetrate it.... The sperm is captured at the initial contact between the sperm tip and the *zona*.... Since the thrust [of the sperm] is much smaller than the force needed to break a single affinity bond, the first bond made upon the tip-first meeting of the sperm and *zona* can result in the capture of the sperm."[43]...

SOCIAL IMPLICATIONS: THINKING BEYOND

These revisionist accounts of egg and sperm cannot seem to escape the hierarchical imagery of older accounts. Even though each new account gives the egg a larger and more active role, taken together they bring into play another cultural stereotype: woman as a dangerous and aggressive threat. In the Johns Hopkins lab's revised model, the egg ends up as the female aggressor who "captures and tethers" the sperm with her sticky zona, rather like a spider lying in wait in her web.[44] The Schatten lab has the egg's nucleus "interrupt" the sperm's dive with a "sudden and swift" rush by which she "clasps the sperm and guides its nucleus to the center."[45] Wassarman's description of the surface of the egg "covered with thousands of plasma membrane-bound projections, called microvilli" that reach out and clasp the sperm adds to the spiderlike imagery.[46]

These images grant the egg an active role but at the cost of appearing disturbingly aggressive. Images of woman as dangerous and aggressive, the femme fatale who victimizes men, are widespread in Western literature and culture.[47] More specific is the connection of spider imagery with the idea of an engulfing, devouring mother.[48] New data did not lead scientists to eliminate gender stereotypes in their descriptions of egg and sperm. Instead, scientists simply began to describe egg and sperm in different, but no less damaging, terms.

Can we envision a less stereotypical view? Biology itself provides another model that could be applied to the egg and the sperm. The cybernetic model—with its feedback loops, flexible adaptation to change, coordination of the parts within a whole, evolution over time, and changing response to the environment—is common in genetics, endocrinology, and ecology and has a growing influence in medicine in general.[49] This model has the potential to shift our imagery from the negative, in which the female reproductive system is castigated both for not producing eggs after birth and for producing (and thus wasting) too many eggs overall, to something more positive. The female reproductive system could be seen as responding to the environment (pregnancy or menopause), adjusting to monthly changes (menstruation), and flexibly changing from reproductivity after puberty to nonreproductivity later in life. The sperm and egg's interaction could also be described in cybernetic terms. J. F. Hartman's research in reproductive biology demonstrated fifteen years ago that if an egg is killed by being pricked with a needle, live sperm cannot get through the zona.[50] Clearly, this evidence shows that the egg and sperm *do* interact on more mutual terms, making biology's refusal to portray them that way all the more disturbing.

We would do well to be aware, however, that cybernetic imagery is hardly neutral. In the past, cybernetic models have played an important part in the imposition of social control. These models inherently provide a way of thinking about a "field" of interacting components. Once the field can be seen, it can become the object of new forms of knowledge, which in turn can allow new forms of social control to be exerted over the components of the field. During the 1950s, for example, medicine began to recognize the psychosocial *environment* of the patient: the patient's family and its psychodynamics. Professions such as social work began to focus on this new environment, and the resulting knowledge became one way to further control the patient. Patients began to be seen not as isolated, individual bodies, but as psychosocial entities located in an "ecological" system: management of "the patient's psychology was a new entrée to patient control."[51]

The models that biologists use to describe their data can have important social effects. During the nineteenth century, the social and natural sciences strongly influenced each other: the social ideas of Malthus about how to avoid the natural increase of the poor inspired Darwin's *Origin of Species.*[52] Once the *Origin* stood as a description of the natural world, complete with competition and market struggles, it could be reimported into social science as social Darwinism, in order to justify the social order of the time. What we are seeing now is similar: the importation of cultural ideas about passive females and heroic males into the "personalities" of gametes. This amounts to the "implanting of social imagery on representations of nature so as to lay a firm basis for reimporting exactly that same imagery as natural explanations of social phenomena."[53]

Further research would show us exactly what social effects are being wrought from the biological imagery of egg and sperm. At the very least, the imagery keeps alive some of the hoariest old stereotypes about weak damsels in distress and their strong male rescuers. That these stereotypes are now being written in at the level of the *cell* constitutes a powerful move to make them seem so natural as to be beyond alteration.

The stereotypical imagery might also encourage people to imagine that what results from the interaction of egg and sperm—a fertilized egg—is the result of deliberate "human" action at the cellular level. Whatever the intentions of the human couple, in this microscopic "culture" a cellular "bride" (or femme fatale) and a cellular "groom" (her victim) make a cellular baby. Rosalind Petchesky points out that through visual representations such as sonograms, we are given *"images* of younger and younger, and tinier and tinier, fetuses being 'saved.'" This leads to "the point of visibility being 'pushed back' *indefinitely.*"[54] Endowing egg and sperm with intentional action, a key aspect of personhood in our culture, lays the foundation for the point of viability being pushed back to the moment of fertilization. This will likely lead to greater acceptance of technological developments and new forms of scrutiny and manipulation, for the benefit of these inner "persons": court-ordered restrictions on a pregnant woman's activities in order to protect her fetus, fetal surgery, amniocentesis, and rescinding of abortion rights, to name but a few examples.[55]

Even if we succeed in substituting more egalitarian, interactive metaphors to describe the activities of egg and sperm, and manage to avoid the pitfalls of cybernetic models, we would still be guilty of endowing cellular entities with personhood. More crucial, then, than what *kinds* of personalities we bestow on cells is the very fact that we are doing it at all. This process could ultimately have the most disturbing social consequences.

One clear feminist challenge is to wake up sleeping metaphors in science, particularly those involved in descriptions of the egg and the sperm. Although the literary convention is to call such metaphors "dead," they are not so much dead as sleeping, hidden within the scientific content of texts—and all the more powerful for it.[56] Waking up such metaphors, by becoming aware of when we are projecting cultural imagery onto what we study, will improve our ability to investigate and understand nature. Waking up such metaphors, by becoming aware of their implications, will rob them of their power to naturalize our social conventions about gender.

NOTES

1. James Hillman, *The Myth of Analysis* (Evanston, Ill.; Northwestern University Press, 1972), 220.

2. The textbooks I consulted are the main ones used in classes for undergraduate premedical students or medical students (or those held on reserve in the library for these classes) during the past few years at Johns Hopkins University. These texts are widely used at other universities in the country as well.

3. Arthur C. Guyton, *Physiology of the Human Body,* 6th ed. (Philadelphia: Saunders College Publishing, 1984), 624.

4. Arthur J. Vander, James H. Sherman, and Dorothy S. Luciano, *Human Physiology: The Mechanisms of Body Function,* 3d ed. (New York: McGraw Hill, 1980), 483–84.

5. Vernon B. Mountcastle, *Medical Physiology,* 14th ed. (London: Mosby, 1980), 2:1624.

6. Eldra Pearl Solomon, *Human Anatomy and Physiology* (New York: CBS College Publishing, 1983), 678.

7. For elaboration, see Emily Martin, *The Woman in the Body: A Cultural Analysis of Reproduction* (Boston: Beacon, 1987), 27–53.

8. Vander, Sherman, and Luciano, 568.

9. Melvin Konner, "Childbearing and Age," *New York Times Magazine* (December 27, 1987), 22–23, esp. 22.

10. I have found but one exception to the opinion that the female is wasteful: "Smallpox being the nasty disease it is, one might expect nature to have designed antibody molecules with combining sites that specifically recognize the epitopes on smallpox virus. Nature differs from technology, however: it thinks nothing of wastefulness. (For example, rather than improving the chance that a spermatozoon will meet an egg cell, nature finds it easier to produce millions of spermatozoa.)" (Niels Kaj Jerne, "The Immune System," *Scientific American* 229, no. 1 [July 1973]: 53). Thanks to a *Signs* reviewer for bringing this reference to my attention.

11. Bruce Alberts et al., *Molecular Biology of the Cell* (New York: Garland, 1983), 795.

12. In her essay "Have Only Men Evolved?" (in *Discovering Reality: Feminist Perspectives on Epistemology, Metaphysics, Methodology, and Philosophy of Science,* ed. Sandra Harding and Merrill B. Hintikka [Dordrecht: Reidel, 1983], 45–69, esp. 60–61), Ruth Hubbard points out that sociobiologists have said the female invests more energy than the male in the production of her large gametes, claiming that this explains why the female provides parental care. Hubbard questions whether it "really takes more 'energy' to generate the one or relatively few eggs than the large excess of sperms required to achieve fertilization." For further critique of how the greater size of eggs is interpreted in sociobiology, see Donna Haraway, "Investment Strategies for the Evolving Portfolio of Primate Females," in *Body/Politics,* ed. Mary Jacobus, Evelyn Fox Keller, and Sally Shuttleworth (New York: Routledge, 1990), 155–56.

13. The sources I used for this article provide compelling information on interactions among sperm. Lack of space prevents me from taking up this theme here, but the elements include competition, hierarchy, and sacrifice. For a newspaper report, see Malcolm W. Browne, "Some Thoughts on Self Sacrifice," *New York Times* (July 5, 1988), C6. For a literary rendition, see John Barth, "Night-Sea Journey," in his *Lost in the Funhouse* (Garden City, N.Y.: Doubleday, 1968), 3–13.

14. See Carol Delaney, "The Meaning of Paternity and the Virgin Birth Debate," *Man* 21, no. 3 (September 1986): 494–513. She discusses the difference between this scientific view that women contribute genetic material to the fetus and the claim of long-standing Western folk theories that the origin and identity of the fetus comes from the male, as in the metaphor of planting a seed in soil.

15. For a suggested direct link between human behavior and purportedly passive eggs and active sperm, see Erik H. Erikson, "Inner and Outer Space: Reflections on Womanhood," *Daedalus* 93, no. 2 (Spring 1964): 582–606, esp. 591.

16. Guyton (n. 3 above), 619; and Mountcastle (n. 5 above), 1609.

17. Jonathan Miller and David Pelham, *The Facts of Life* (New York: Viking Penguin, 1984), 5.

18. Alberts et al., 796.

19. Ibid., 796.

20. See, e.g., William F. Ganong, *Review of Medical Physiology,* 7th ed. (Los Altos, Calif.: Lange Medical Publications, 1975), 322.

21. Alberts et al. (n. 11 above), 796.

22. Guyton, 615.

23. Solomon (n. 6 above), 683.

24. Vander, Sherman, and Luciano (n. 4 above), 4th ed. (1985), 580.

25. Alberts et al., 796.

26. All biology texts quoted above use the word "penetrate."

27. Solomon, 700.

28. A. Beldecos et al., "The Importance of Feminist Critique for Contemporary Cell Biology," *Hypatia* 3, no. 1 (Spring 1988): 61–76.
29. Gerald Schatten and Helen Schatten, "The Energetic Egg," *Medical World News* 23 (January 23, 1984): 51–53, esp. 51.
30. Alberts et al., 796.
31. Guyton (n. 3 above), 613.
32. Miller and Pelham (n. 17 above), 7.
33. Alberts et al. (n. 11 above), 804.
34. Ibid., 801.
35. Ruth Herschberger, *Adam's Rib* (New York: Pelligrini & Cudaby, 1948), esp. 84. I am indebted to Ruth Hubbard for telling me about Herschberger's work, although at a point when this paper was already in draft form.
36. Bennett M. Shapiro. "The Existential Decision of a Sperm," *Cell* 49, no. 3 (May 1987): 293–94, esp. 293.
37. Lennart Nilsson, "A Portrait of the Sperm," in *The Functional Anatomy of the Spermatozoan*, ed. Bjorn A. Afzelius (New York: Pergamon, 1975), 79–82.
38. Ludwik Fleck, *Genesis and Development of a Scientific Fact*, ed. Thaddeus J. Trenn and Robert K. Merton (Chicago: University of Chicago Press, 1979), 38.
39. Jay M. Baltz carried out the research I describe when he was a graduate student in the Thomas C. Jenkins Department of Biophysics at Johns Hopkins University.
40. Far less is known about the physiology of sperm than comparable female substances, which some feminists claim is no accident. Greater scientific scrutiny of female reproduction has long enabled the burden of birth control to be placed on women. In this case, the researchers discovery did not depend on development of any new technology. The experiments made use of glass pipettes, a manometer, and a simple microscope, all of which have been available for more than one hundred years.
41. Jay Baltz and Richard A. Cone, "What Force Is Needed to Tether a Sperm?" (abstract for Society for the Study of Reproduction, 1985), and "Flagellar Torque on the Head Determines the Force Needed to Tether a Sperm" (abstract for Biophysical Society, 1986).
42. Jay M. Baltz, David F. Katz, and Richard A. Cone, "The Mechanics of the Sperm-Egg Interaction at the Zona Pellucida," *Biophysical Journal* 54, no. 4 (October 1988): 643–54. Lab members were somewhat familiar with work on metaphors in the biology of female reproduction. Richard Cone, who runs the lab, is my husband, and he talked with them about my earlier research on the subject from time to time. Even though my current research focuses on biological imagery and I heard about the lab's work from my husband every day, I myself did not recognize the role of imagery in the sperm research until many weeks after the period of research and writing I describe. Therefore, I assume that any awareness the lab members may have had about how underlying metaphor might be guiding this particular research was fairly inchoate.
43. Ibid., 643, 650.
44. Baltz, Katz, and Cone (n. 42 above), 643, 650.
45. Schatten and Schatten, 53.
46. Wassarman, "The Biology and Chemistry of Fertilization," 557.
47. Mary Ellman, *Thinking about Women* (New York: Harcourt Brace Jovanovich, 1968), 140; Nina Auerbach, *Woman and the Demon* (Cambridge, Mass.: Harvard University Press, 1982), esp. 186.
48. Kenneth Alan Adams, "Arachnophobia: Love American Style," *Journal of Psychoanalytic Anthropology* 4, no. 2 (1981): 157–97.
49. William Ray Arney and Bernard Bergen, *Medicine and the Management of Living* (Chicago: University of Chicago Press, 1984).
50. J. F. Hartman, R. B. Gwatkin, and C. F. Hutchison, "Early Contact Interactions between Mammalian Gametes *In Vitro*," *Proceedings of the National Academy of Sciences (U.S.)* 69, no. 10 (1972): 2767–69.
51. Arney and Bergen, 68.
52. Ruth Hubbard, "Have Only Men Evolved?" (n. 12 above), 51–52.
53. David Harvey, personal communication, November 1989.
54. Rosalind Petchesky, "Fetal Images: The Power of Visual Culture in the Politics of Reproduction," *Feminist Studies* 13, no. 2 (Summer 1987): 263–92, esp. 272.
55. Rita Arditti, Renate Klein, and Shelley Minden, *Test-Tube Women* (London: Pandora, 1984); Ellen Goodman, "Whose Right to Life?" *Baltimore Sun* (November 17, 1987); Tamar Lewin, "Courts Acting to Force Care of the Unborn," *New York Times* (November 23, 1987), A1 and B10; Susan Irwin and Brigitte Jordan, "Knowledge, Practice, and Power: Court Ordered Cesarean Sections," *Medical Anthropology Quarterly* 1, no. 3 (September 1987): 319–34.
56. Thanks to Elizabeth Fee and David Spain, who in February 1989 and April 1989, respectively, made points related to this.

A CRITICAL HISTORICAL ANALYSIS OF THE MEDICAL CONSTRUCTION OF LESBIANISM

PATRICIA E. STEVENS AND JOANNE M. HALL

Lesbians are in vulnerable positions as health care clients. In several U.S. investigations (1–6), lesbian clients describe encountering ostracism, invasive questioning, rough physical handling, derogatory comments, breaches of confidentiality, shock, embarrassment, unfriendliness, pity, condescension, and fear in health care situations. Some believe that health care providers' knowledge of their lesbianism could result in neglect, physical endangerment, infliction of pain, or withdrawal of concern should providers harbor negative moral judgments about lesbians. Survey evidence suggests that their fears are legitimate (7–12). Significant numbers of physicians and nurses still consider lesbianism a pathological condition, make attributions of immorality, perversion, and danger to lesbian women, are uncomfortable providing care for lesbian clients, and regularly refuse service to women who are lesbian. Lesbian clients' access to health care services is compromised. As a result of their negative experiences in health care encounters, many lesbians report hesitation in using health care systems and say they delay seeking treatment (6, 13–18)....

However, health care experiences of lesbian women cannot be understood apart from the historical construction of medical ideologies that have scapegoated lesbians or the discriminatory aspects of institutional structures that have sustained these ideas over the decades. Lesbianism has been pathologized by the medical profession and condemned by the general public. Lesbians' encounters with health care systems are fraught not only with the repercussions of gender, race, and class stratification, but specifically with the ideological construction of lesbianism as sin/crime/sickness....

MORAL CONDEMNATION

Moral condemnation of lesbian women has a long history. For centuries, same-sex sexual behavior was seen as a violation of God's nature, a dangerous diversion of energy from the task of human survival. Repression of gay and lesbian sexuality was sustained by an extreme moral fury that lay at the heart of Judeo-Christian cultural foundations. Christians hunted, tortured, and killed gay and lesbian people for 1400 years, from the 3rd through the 17th centuries....

American colonial attitudes toward male homosexuality and lesbianism are evident in the words of Thomas Jefferson, who in 1779 proposed that, "Whoever shall be guilty of sodomy shall be punished if a man by castration, if a woman by cutting through the cartilage of her nose a hole one-half inch in diameter" (quoted in 19, p. 187). In 19th century America, sodomy was equated with masturbation, both being construed as sinful deviations from procreation. Religious beliefs were incorporated wholesale into medical theories of the period; Benjamin Rush said both sins caused mental and physical illness. Clitoridectomy and blistering of the vulvar area were examples of treatments employed to "cure" masturbation and other "perversions" during this period (20)....

MEDICALIZATION OF LESBIANISM

At the end of the 19th century new medical-scientific definitions were imposed upon many moral categories of behavior, reinterpreting them as pathologies. A series of medical theories were developed at this time, proclaiming "homosexuality" to be a disease. The 20th century saw the development of technological societies that valued scientific solutions to social problems. Thus religion and state, as institutions of Western social control, relinquished some of their prerogatives to medicine (21, 22–24). Therapeutic response to aberrant same-sex sexual behavior was idealized as a more effective way to restore normality where punitive legal and moral attempts at social control had failed (25).

Medicine's power in the realm of social control stems from its authority to define which behaviors, persons, and things are "normal." Deviance from the normal refers to those behaviors that are defined in particular historical sociopolitical contexts as inappropriate to or in violation of certain powerful groups' conventions. Deviance designations serve political purposes and are created to support and buttress specific status interests at the expense of others (26).

As lesbianism began to be seen as a matter for the physician rather than as the exclusive territory of priests and judges, lesbians became ensnared in an ideological netherworld between immorality and madness. Perceptibly punitive medical interventions tended to "preserve" past moral overtones of "medicalized" problems (24). As Churchill suggested, "In the mass mind there was but a meager distinction, if any at all, between sinfulness and disease.... Originally the same devices were used to cleanse the body of illness that were used to purge the soul of sinfulness" (23, p. 29). Medical involvement in the lives of lesbians and gays did not stop religious and legal scrutiny nor make them immune from moral and punitive sanctions. Rather, the pronouncement of lesbianism as a sickness left its negative moral evaluation intact and created a powerful new tool by which to exact women's behavioral conformity.

Homosexuality As Pathology

The medical passion for classification and elaborate description of various forms of deviant sexual behavior served the purposes of making homosexual behavior more recognizable to society and the sanction of lesbians and gays more efficient (21). Late 19th century hereditary theories, such as those of Carl Westphal, Jean Martin Charcot, and Richard von Krafft-Ebing, claimed homosexuality to be a "congenital constitutional weakness," "inborn predisposition to perversion," and "hereditary taint" that could precipitate a full range of dangerous insane and "primitive" behaviors. Confinement in asylums was employed to contain lesbians' and gays' "moral insanity," to protect society from their violence and contaminatory evil (20, 27, 28)....

Medical writings during the first three-quarters of this century portrayed homosexuality as both a disease and a moral corruption. Health care providers and the general public were continually warned about the dangers posed by lesbians and gay men, who were said to be responsible for the rise in crime, murder, racism, societal chaos, and the weakening of the American family (29–33). Psychoanalysts' intellectual rationalizations were invoked to justify irrational hatred and fear and to legitimate discriminatory behaviors toward lesbians and gays (34, 35–37). Their theories of homosexuality provided justification for governmental and private policies of surveillance, blacklisting, and prosecution during the infamous McCarthy years (34). Medical proclamations were pressed into service to vindicate job discrimination (38–40), military exclusion (41–43), expulsion from government employment on the basis of "security risk" (44, 45), immigration and naturalization restrictions (37), and inequalities in housing, public accommodations, child custody, adoption, foster care, association and free speech, insurance coverage, and occupational licensing (46–50).

As Lewes concluded, "Physicians' attack on homosexuals was conducted with an intemperance, ferocity, and lack of empathy that is simply appalling.... Equally remarkable was the failure of other physicians to rebuke the offensive stance of more voluble colleagues" (34, p. 239). The sentiments of one psychoanalyst illustrate how objections were constrained. He attacked those advocating the normalcy of homosexuality on the ground that they "are themselves homosexuals" (51). Fear resulting from such "queer-baiting" has deterred many scholars from writing on gay and lesbian topics.

The Kinsey reports (52, 53) were islands of clarity amid a sea of psychoanalytic speculation about male homosexuality and lesbianism. In spite of the Kinsey findings about the prevalence of homosexuality among productive, well-adjusted, nonclinical populations, the psychoanalysts persisted in, and even intensified, their efforts to pathologize homosexuality during the 1950s, 1960s, and 1970s.

Specific Targeting of Lesbians

Lesbians were said to harbor the same sickness and evil found in gay men; however, several medical theories warned of even greater danger associated with female homosexuality. Bergler, who authored more than 300 articles and 24 books about homosexuality during his medical career (34), declared that the numbers of lesbians were far more staggering than those of male homosexuals. He contended that "camouflaged lesbians hiding in marriages" were surreptitiously spreading their "violent hatred," "pathological jealousy," and "masochistic injustice-collecting" (54, pp. 261–265).

Psychoanalytic case studies of lesbians concluded that the "feminine passive attitude" was incompletely developed in such women because of penis envy, hatred of the mother, suicidality, masochistic desires, "uterine fantasies," guilt, fear of disappointment, and sadism (55). Rado (56) claimed that fears of pregnancy and childbirth drove some women to homosexuality. Jones (57) characterized lesbian women as having "extreme oral eroticism." Other manifestations of lesbianism cited in the medical literature included: incapacitating fears of the opposite sex (58), aggressive hatred of a dominating mother (58), infantile fixation (57), and hostility (59). Its implied causes were: fear of responsibility, rape, incest, incest desires, "tomboy" behavior, seduction by older women, masturbation, and fear of dominance (60). Lesbians were specifically described as tragically unhappy and sexually unfulfilled (61). A "cure" for lesbianism suggested by many medical experts was "finding real love with a man" (62, p. 15)....

Many medical descriptions legitimated dreadful stereotypes of lesbian women (63), including the following contentions. Half of "female homosexuals" have concomitant schizophrenia, and the other half suffer obsessional phobias, character disorders, psychopathic personalities, or some variety of addiction (64, p. 90). Lesbians are aggressive, hostile, and domineering (30, 58, 59). Besides being "man-haters," homosexual women hate motherhood and children (65, 66). They are self-aggrandizing and behave like "pseudo-men" in order to shock others (51). Lesbians are "brutally sadistic," "blood thirsty," and seek "murderous revenge" (64, pp. 52–56). Lesbians have "violent, brutal sex" (30, p. 170). They fly into "homicidal rages" and sometimes commit murder (30, p. 170).

Why were lesbians perceived to be so dangerous? Ferguson (67) suggests that social and technological changes at the beginning of the 20th century offering women more freedom were perceived as threats to the patriarchy. Urbanization, increased wage and labor opportunities for women, cheap mass-produced birth control, availability of abortion, and liberalization of divorce allowed women to consider options that separated sexuality from marriage, child-rearing, and heterosexuality. Medical ideology was a powerful inhibitory force that sustained women's traditional heterosexual roles by pathologizing nonprocreative sexuality and nontraditional feminine behaviors (68–70).

Lesbianism represented the peril of women's freedom. It was declared a serious intrapersonal disease as well as a drastic social ill, believed to be increasing geometrically with the growing independence of wage-earning women and the rise of feminism (71, 30, 72). The feminist movement itself was accused of exacerbating the contagion of lesbianism. It was believed that "predatory lesbians" abounded in conditions of gender equality, "seducing young girls and causing them to give up the thought of marriage and family life for a life of homosexual enslavement" (30, p. 8). As one physician summed it up, "The real damage from homosexuality lies not in actual sex association but in homosexual attitudes toward life which influence how thousands of women think about men, marriage, and family life" (30, p. 9).

Moreover, emancipatory behaviors and appearances were labeled lesbian and classified as diagnostic signals. The taxonomy of medical symptoms indicative of lesbianism included: casual clothing, short haircut, lack of cosmetics and "feminine accessories," interest in the women's movement, competition with men, dedication to career, and "unwomanly" work such as skilled labor, business, law, politics, theater, art, science, and writing (73, 64, 71, 30, 33).

Physicians also claimed to be able to diagnose a lesbian based on morphological evidence (64, 29, 32, 74–77). Lesbians were characterized as having wider shoulders, bigger waists, firmer adipose tissue, greater height, firmer muscles, masculine distribution of body hair, smaller uteri, smaller breasts, unusually small or unusually large genitalia, and lower-pitched voices. These physical criteria were proferred as tools of detection, "marks of Cain" (78) constructed by medical science, extending social stereotypes to haunt lesbians at a bodily level.

Published "studies" of lesbianism often relied on speculation, nonscientific literature, and selected cases from psychiatric populations. Caprio's (30) medical treatise on female homosexuality, for instance, drew conclusions about lesbianism from the stories of women prisoners and prostitutes, novels, autobiographical confessions, and tabloid publications such as *My Confessions, Romance Magazine,* and *Coronet* (46). Thus, cross-pollination between professional and popular discourses perpetuated and amplified false, unseemly, bizarre images of lesbian women that continue to influence health care interactions experienced by lesbian clients today.

COLLECTIVE EFFORTS AT DESTIGMATIZATION

For most of the 20th century, lesbians and gay men suffered psychiatric confinement, electroshock treatment, genital mutilation, aversive therapy, psychosurgery, hormonal injection, psychoanalysis, and psychotropic chemotherapy aimed at "curing" their homosexuality (79, 26, 80, 81, 46). Their lives were circumscribed by oppressive medical, legal, political, and religious institutions. In their struggle to resist the exigencies of inferiorization, many lesbians and gays in the early decades of the century looked to the medical profession as a potential compassionate protector (79). They believed it was better to be viewed as sick than as criminal or evil. Therapeutic control initially appeared less coercive than incarceration and damnation (28, 82).

However, in the 1950s a visible emergent lesbian and gay movement, which had been forming in the United States for some decades (83), began to problematize its disenfranchised position. This movement crystallized in the formation of national homophile organizations. The Mattachine Society, One, Inc., and the Daughters of Bilitis attempted to end oppression by educating society about the respectability and competence of lesbians and gays. To an unprecedented extent, these early lesbian and gay rights groups served to unify the many lesbian and gay subcultures. They promoted a positive identity and symbolized a collectivity of lesbian women and gay men who had common concerns and experiences. They educated their constituents about how to cope with hostile environments and provided social support.

In the 1960s it became clearer that accommodation would not end the repression of lesbians and gays. Frank Kameny, an employee terminated in 1957 from his civilian position with the U.S. Army on charges that he was gay, was the first public opponent of the Army's anti-gay policies. He later was instrumental in convincing the homophile movement to adopt a more militant agenda (84). The civil rights movement, opposition to the Vietnam War, and the feminist movement provided a milieu conducive to lesbian and gay liberation efforts. The number of homophile organizations proliferated, and their major focus shifted to activism for civil rights for lesbians and gays (85–89). On June 27, 1969, an incident in a Greenwich Village bar ushered in the modern lesbian and gay liberation movement. Gay and lesbian bar patrons unexpectedly fought back against police during a "routine" gay bar raid. The three day "Stonewall Rebellion" marked a transition in lesbian/gay activism from accommodation to confrontation. This historic moment galvanized self-definition and self-love among lesbian and gay people (84, 86).

In the mid-1960s, the lesbian and gay movement targeted medical diagnostic authority as pivotal to societal exclusion and discrimination. Lesbians and gays began to articulate the burden of humiliation they faced at the hands of medicine's labeling (80, 84, 90–92). For instance, they identified the use of the term "homosexual" as a medical construction, an instrument of oppression, and insisted upon use of cultural terms such as lesbian and gay to designate themselves (93, 94).

With fresh confidence and solidarity, lesbian and gay political organizations in the early 1970s unified their attack on medicine's power over their lives. They utilized organized protests and advanced articulate spokespersons to place persistent and significant pressure upon the American Psychiatric Association (APA) to remove homosexuality from its *Diagnostic and Statistical Manual of Mental Disorders II (DSM II)* (25, 95, 96). They presented research evidence on the prevalence of homosexuality (52, 23, 53, 97) and documented the positive psychological adjustment found in nonclinical samples of lesbians and gays (98–101) to refute medical diagnosis of homosexuality. Fueled by lesbian and gay activism, the *DSM II* debate raged vociferously in professional journals and meetings from 1970 to 1974, splitting psychiatry into two camps. Psychiatrists vested in maintaining control over the "disease" of homosexuality charged the APA with capitulating to pressure from lesbian and gay rights groups. The other faction insisted that the conception of homosexuality as disease was based on inadequate science. The result was an unprecedented referendum of the entire APA membership. The mail-in vote succeeded in removing homosexuality per se from the nosology (25, 80, 72, 102).

Most accounts of these events heralded them as the demedicalization of homosexuality, suggesting that medicine had indeed surrendered its position of social control over lesbians and gays. Less well known, however, was the debate three years later during the drafting of the *DSM III,* in which "ego-dystonic homosexuality" was constructed as a psychiatric disorder. This compromise category allowed for the diagnosis of lesbians and gays who, in the clinical judgment of their physicians, appeared unhappy or distressed about their sexual orientation (96, 103–105). It also sanctioned reorientation therapy in which aversive and other techniques were used in order to produce a shift to heterosexuality (106). This development was protested on ethical grounds by many psychiatrists as well as lesbian and gay communities (107–109). The ego-dystonic label demonstrated lingering psychiatric hostilities toward homosexuality (110, pp. 363–364):

> *This new category of psychosexual disorder is restricted to homosexuals; by definition it does not apply to heterosexuals who find their sex lives with members of the opposite sex a source of persistent concern and wish them to be different.... The fact that 'ego-dystonic' heterosexuality is not a diagnosis reflects a continuing implicit belief that homosexuality is abnormal.*

This later nosological debate was confined to a small circle of physicians who resisted its exposure to public scrutiny and the risk of eroding psychiatry's territorial boundaries and its professional authority over social behavior. Even psychiatrists opposed to the inclusion of a disease category pertaining to lesbians and gay men hesitated to involve the general APA membership and lesbian and gay communities in the negotiations, because of burgeoning social conservatism in the United States and growing sympathy toward the traditional view of homosexuality within the profession. They feared publicity would reopen the dispute over the pathological basis of homosexuality itself (103). Through its quiet maneuverings, medicine once again: "resorted to the codification of social mores while masquerading as an objective science" (105, p. 26).

In May 1987, the APA removed ego-dystonic homosexuality from the revised edition of *DSM III* (111). It maintained a diagnosis, "sexual disorder not otherwise specified," which can be applied in cases where there is "persistent and marked distress about one's sexual orientation" (112, p. 296).

CONCLUSION

The cultural definition of lesbianism as a disease has influenced a long history of scientific inquiry that emphasizes etiology, diagnosis, and cure (113, 114). A relaxation of this perspective in health sciences research was not evident until the 1980s (115). Health and social sciences textbooks continue to label lesbians and gay men deviant and devote much of their discussion to etiological theories of homosexuality (116, 117). Any undertaking that seeks to discover or elaborate the causes of homosexuality prejudicially isolates the experience of being lesbian as an abnormality in need of explanation. It depicts lesbianism as an unhealthy disturbance that requires prevention and treatment (34, 104).

Clearly, the medicalization of lesbianism has been accomplished through its reinforcement of societal prejudices. Depicting behaviors of lesbian women to be both symptoms of disease and causes of social disorder answered institutional demands for social control of women. Indeed, lesbianism has yet to be effectively demedicalized. In the aftermath of the *DSM* debates, medicine simply closed ranks and reconsolidated its power base to prevent any further erosion of its boundaries (118). Psychiatrists became less accusatory about the psychosexual abnormality of homosexuality but retained status as acknowledged experts on the distress of "deviant" sexuality. The theory and research of the 1980s generally did not pathologize homosexuality per se but rather pinpointed developmental and relational aspects of lesbian "lifestyles" as appropriate foci for mental health therapies (119). This "gay-positive" approach tends to depoliticize lesbian identity as a coincidental aspect of the individual, having only to do with a "sexual preference." It also creates a new "pathology" within the heterosexual person, called "homophobia," which blames the individual heterosexual for holding prejudicial attitudes that are actually pervasive in the dominant culture (119).

Deeply entrenched stigmatized meanings about lesbian health remain influential in the education of health care providers, the quality of health care they deliver, their comfort in interacting with clients, and the institutional policies under which they work. The intensity of stigmatizing interactions experienced by lesbians over time has been fueled by moral condemnation, legal proscription, and medical diagnosis and intervention. For nearly a century, lesbians have been characterized by the medical profession as sick, dangerous, aggressive, tragically unhappy, deceitful, contagious, and self-destructive. They have been made to suffer exploitive treatments aimed at curing their homosexuality and have repeatedly been objects of research designed to confirm the pathology of their condition. Such a history underscores the vulnerable position lesbians occupy today as health care clients.

What are the questions clinicians, researchers, and theorists should be asking to demystify ideologies that place lesbians at risk of ostracism, discrimination, misdiagnosis, and attack? How can a more critical analysis of medicine's historical proclamations about lesbians enter into research about women's health, education of health care providers, and health care policy-making? When can a focal shift be made in scholarship and clinical practice so that barriers to and discrimination in health care delivery are problematized rather than blame placed on the gender, sexual orientation, or privatized "coping" skills of individual clients? Without critical investigation and emancipatory changes in health care practice and policy, health care providers will continue to rely on unexamined habits and emotional responses to guide their practices in caring for lesbian women, with all the potential pitfalls of myth, ignorance, and antipathy.

REFERENCES

1. Dardick, L., and Grady, K. E. Openness between gay persons and health professionals. *Ann. Intern. Med.* 93: 115–119, 1980.

2. Johnson, S. R., et al. Factors influencing lesbian gynecological care: A preliminary study. *Am. J. Obstet. Gynecol.* 140: 20–28, 1981.
3. McGhee, R. D., and Owen, W. F. Medical aspects of homosexuality. *N. Engl. J. Med.* 303: 50–51, 1980.
4. Paroski, P. A. Health care delivery and the concerns of gay and lesbian adolescents. *J. Adolesc. Health Care* 8: 188–192, 1987.
5. Smith, E. M., Johnson, S. R., and Guenther, S. M. Health care attitudes and experiences during gynecological care among lesbians and bisexuals. *Am. J. Public Health.* 75: 1085–1087, 1985.
6. Stevens, P. E., and Hall, J. M. Stigma, health beliefs and experiences with health care in lesbian women. *Image: J. Nurs. Scholarship* 20: 69–73, 1988.
7. Harvey, S. M., Carr, C., and Bernheine, S. Lesbian mothers: Health care experiences. *J. Nurse Midwifery* 34: 115–119, 1989.
8. Levy, T. The Lesbian: As Perceived by Mental Health Workers. Doctoral dissertation, California School of Professional Psychology, San Diego, 1978.
9. Mathews, W. C., et al. Physicians' attitudes toward homosexuality: Survey of a California county medical society. *West J. Med.* 144: 106–110, 1986.
10. Randall, C. E. Lesbian phobia among BSN educators: A survey. *J. Nurs. Educ.* 28: 302–306, 1989.
11. White, T. A. Attitudes of psychiatric nurses toward same sex orientations. *Nurs. Res.* 28: 276–281, 1979.
12. Young, E. W. Nurses' attitudes toward homosexuality: Analysis of change in AIDS workshops. *J. Continuing Educ. Nurs.* 19: 9–12, 1988.
13. Friend, R. A. Sexual identity and human diversity: Implications for nursing practice. *Holistic Nurs. Pract.* 1(4): 21–41, 1987.
14. Gonsiorek, J. C. Mental health issues of gay and lesbian adolescents. *J. Adolesc. Health Care* 9: 114–122, 1988.
15. Good, R. S. The gynecologist and the lesbian. *Clin. Obstet. Gynecol.* 19: 473–482, 1976.
16. Jones, R. With respect to lesbians. *Nurs. Times* 84(20): 48–49, 1988.
17. Raymond, C. A. Lesbians call for greater physician awareness, sensitivity to improve patient care. *JAMA* 259: 18, 1988.
18. Whyte, J., and Capaldini, L. Treating the lesbian or gay patient. *Del. Med. J.* 52: 271–280, 1980.
19. Abramson, H. A. The historical and cultural spectra of homosexuality and their relationship to the fear of being lesbian. *J. Asthma Res.* 17: 177–188, 1980.
20. Bullough, V. L. Homosexuality and its confusion with the 'secret sin' in pre-Freudian America. In *Sex, Society, and History,* edited by V. L. Bullough, pp. 112–124. Science History, New York, 1976.
21. Bullough, V. L., and Bullough, B. *Sin, Sickness, and Sanity: A History of Sexual Attitudes.* Garland, New York, 1977.
22. Bullough, V. L. Homosexuality and the medical model. *J. Homosex.* 1(1): 99–110, 1974.
23. Churchill, W. *Homosexual Behavior among Males: A Cross-cultural and Cross-species Investigation.* Hawthorn, New York, 1967.
24. Zola, I. K. Medicine as an institution of social control. *Social. Rev.* 20: 487–504, 1972.
25. Bayer, R. *Homosexuality and American Psychiatry: The Politics of Diagnosis.* Princeton University Press, Princeton, N.J., 1987.
26. Conrad, P., and Schneider, J. W. *Deviance and Medicalization: From Badness to Sickness.* C. V. Mosby, St. Louis, Mo., 1980.
27. Krafft-Ebing, R. V. *Psychopathia Sexualis.* F. A. Davis, Philadelphia, 1894.
28. Schmidt, G. Allies and persecutors: Science and medicine in the homosexuality issue. *J. Homosex.* 10(3/4): 127–140, 1984.
29. Henry, G. W., and Galbraith, H. M. Constitutional factors in homosexuality. *Am. J. Psychiatry* 14: 1249–1270, 1934.
30. Caprio, F. S. *Female Homosexuality: A Psychodynamic Study of Lesbianism.* Citadel, New York, 1954.
31. Chideckel, M. *Female Sex Perversion: The Sexually Aberrated Woman As She Is.* Eugenics, New York, 1935.
32. Henry, G. W. *Sex Variants: A Study of Homosexual Patterns.* Paul B. Hoeber, New York, 1948.
33. Morse, B. *The Lesbian: A Frank Study of Women Who Turn to Their Own Sex for Love.* Monarch, Derby, Conn., 1961.
34. Lewes, K. *The Psychoanalytic Theory of Male Homosexuality.* Simon & Schuster, New York, 1988.
35. Illich, I. *Medical Nemesis: The Expropriation of Health.* Random House, New York, 1976.
36. Shackle, E. M. Psychiatric diagnosis as an ethical problem. *J. Med. Ethics* 11: 132–134, 1985.
37. Szasz, T. S. *The Manufacture of Madness.* Dell, New York, 1970.
38. Bell, A. P., and Weinberg, M. S. *Homosexualities: A Study of Diversity among Men and Women.* Simon & Schuster, New York, 1978.

39. Chafetz, J., et al. A study of homosexual women. *Soc. Work* 19: 714–723, 1974.
40. Levine, M. P., and Leonard, R. Discrimination against lesbians in the work force. *Signs: J. Women Culture Society* 9: 700–710, 1984.
41. Berube, A. *Coming Out under Fire: The History of Gay Men and Women in World War II.* Macmillan, New York, 1990.
42. Berube, A., and D'Emilio, J. The military and lesbians during the McCarthy years. *Signs: J. Women Culture Society* 9: 759–775, 1984.
43. Williams, C. J., and Weinberg, M. S. *Homosexuals and the Military.* Harper & Row, New York, 1971.
44. Humphreys, L. *Out of the Closets: The Sociology of Homosexual Liberation.* Prentice-Hall, Englewood Cliffs, N.J., 1972.
45. McCrary, J., and Gutierrez, L. The homosexual person in the military and in national security employment. *J. Homosex.* 5(1/2):115–146, 1979/80.
46. Browning, C. Changing theories of lesbianism: Challenging the stereotypes. In *Women-identified Women,* edited by T. Darty and S. Potter, pp. 11–30. Mayfield, Palo Alto, Calif., 1994.
47. Hitchens, D. Social attitudes, legal standards and personal trauma in child custody cases. *J. Homosex.* 5(1/2): 89–95, 1979/80.
48. Reynolds, W. T. The immigration and national act and the rights of homosexual aliens. *J. Homosex.* 5(1/2): 79–87, 1979/80.
49. Solomon, D. M. The emergence of associational rights for homosexual persons. *J. Homosex.* 5(1/2): 147–155, 1979/80.
50. Vetri, D. The legal arena: Progress for gay civil rights. *J. Homosex.* 5(1/2): 25–34, 1979/80.
51. Aardweg, van den, G. J. M. *On the Origins and Treatment of Homosexuality: A Psychoanalytic Reinterpretation.* Praeger, New York, 1986.
52. Kinsey, A. C., et al. *Sexual Behavior in the Human Female.* W. B. Saunders, Philadelphia, 1953.
53. Kinsey, A. C., Pomeroy, W. B., and Martin, C. E. *Sexual Behavior in the Human Male.* W. B. Saunders, Philadelphia, 1948.
54. Bergler, E. *Homosexuality: Disease or Way of Life.* Hill & Wang, New York, 1957.
55. Deutsch, H. On female homosexuality. *Psychoanal. Q.* 1: 484–510, 1932.
56. Rado, S. Fear of castration in women. *Psychoanal. Q.* 2: 425–475, 1933.
57. Jones, E. The early development of female sexuality. *Int. J. Psychoanal.* 8: 459–472, 1927.
58. Fenichel, O. *The Psychoanalytic Theory of Neurosis.* W. W. Norton, New York, 1945.
59. Bene, E. On the genesis of female sexuality. *Br. J. Psychiatry* 111: 815–821, 1965.
60. Rosen, D. H. *Lesbianism: A Study of Female Homosexuality.* Charles C. Thomas, Springfield, Ill., 1974.
61. Wolff, C. *Love between Women.* Harper & Row, New York, 1971.
62. Robertiello, R. C. *Voyage from Lesbos: The Psychoanalysis of a Female Homosexual.* Citadel, New York, 1969.
63. Simpson, R. *From the Closets to the Courts: The Lesbian Transition.* Viking Press, New York, 1976.
64. Socarides, C. W. *The Overt Homosexual.* Grune & Stratton, New York, 1968.
65. Stekel, W. *The Homosexual Neurosis.* Emerson Books, New York, 1946.
66. Cory, D. W. [pseudonym]. *The Lesbian in America.* Citadel, New York, 1964.
67. Ferguson, A. Lesbian Identity: Beauvoir and History. *Women's Stud. Int. Forum* 8: 203–208, 1985.
68. Faderman, L. *Surpassing the Love of Men: Romantic Friendship and Love between Women from the Renaissance to the Present.* William Morrow, New York, 1981.
69. Smith-Rosenberg, C. The female world of love and ritual: Relations between women in nineteenth century America. *Signs: J. Women Culture Society* 1: 1–24, 1975.
70. Faderman, L. The morbidification of love between women by 19th-century sexologists. *J. Homosex.* 4(1): 73–90, 1978.
71. Stekel, W. *Bi-sexual Love.* Physicians and Surgeons Books, New York, 1933.
72. Marmor, J. Overview: The multiple roots of homosexual behavior. In *Homosexual Behavior: A Modern Reappraisal,* edited by J. Marmor, pp. 3–22. Basic Books, New York, 1980.
73. Berg, C., and Allen, C. *The Problem of Homosexuality.* Citadel, New York, 1958.
74. Dickinson, R. L. The gynecology of homosexuality. In *Sex Variants: A Study of Homosexual Patterns,* edited by G. W. Henry, pp. 1069–1130. Paul B. Hoeber, New York, 1948.
75. Dickinson, R. L., and Beam, L. *The Single Woman.* Williams & Wilkins, New York, 1934.
76. Griffith, P. D., et al. Homosexual women: An endocrine and psychological study. *J. Endocrinol.* 63: 549–556, 1974.

77. Kenyon, F. E. Physique and physical health of female homosexuals. *J. Neurol. Neurosurg. Psychiatry.* 31: 487–489, 1968.
78. Shoham, S. G., and Rahav, G. *The Mark of Cain: The Stigma Theory of Crime and Social Deviance.* St. Martin's Press, New York, 1982.
79. Katz, J. *Gay American History: Lesbians and Gay Men in the USA.* Avon Books, New York, 1976.
80. Adam, B. D. *The Rise of the Gay and Lesbian Movement.* Twayne, Boston, 1987.
81. Katz, J. N. *Gay/Lesbian Almanac: A New Documentary.* Harper & Row, New York, 1983.
82. Tripp, C. A. *The Homosexual Matrix.* McGraw-Hill, New York, 1975.
83. Lauritsen, J., and Thorstad, D. *The Early Homosexual Rights Movement (1864–1935).* Times Change Press, New York, 1974.
84. D'Emilio, J. *Sexual Politics, Sexual Communities.* University of Chicago Press, Chicago, 1983.
85. Bronski, M. *Culture Clash: The Making of Gay Sensibility.* South End Press, Boston, 1984.
86. Licata, S. J. The homosexual rights movement in the United States: A traditionally overlooked area of American history. *J. Homosex.* 6(1/2): 161–189, 1980/81.
87. Martin, D., and Lyon, P. *Lesbian Woman.* Bantam Books, New York, 1972.
88. Masters, R. E. L. *The Homosexual Revolution: A Challenging Expose of the Social and Political Directions of a Minority Group.* Julian Press, New York, 1962.
89. Weiss, A. *Before Stonewall: The Making of a Gay and Lesbian Community.* Naiad Press, New York, 1988.
90. Abbott, S., and Love, B. *Sappho Was a Right-on Woman: A Liberated View of Lesbianism.* Stein & Day, New York, 1972.
91. Altman, D. *Homosexual Oppression and Liberation.* Avon Books, New York, 1971.
92. Altman, D. *The Homosexualization of America: The Americanization of the Homosexual.* St. Martin's Press, New York, 1982.
93. Adam, B. D. *The Survival of Domination: Inferiorization and Everyday Life.* Elsevier, New York, 1978.
94. Hodges, A., and Hutter, D. *With Downcast Gays: Aspects of Homosexual Self-Expression.* Pomegranate Press, London, 1974.
95. Silverstein, C. Even psychiatry can profit from its past mistakes. *J. Homosex.* 2(2): 153–158, 1976/77.
96. Silverstein, C. The ethical and moral implications of sexual classification: A commentary. *J. Homosex.* 9(4): 29–38, 1984.
97. Ford, C. S., and Beach, F. A. *Patterns of Sexual Behavior.* Harper and Brothers, New York, 1951.
98. Freedman, M. *Homosexuality and Psychological Functioning.* Wadsworth, Belmont, Calif., 1971.
99. Hooker, E. The adjustment of the male overt homosexual. *J. Projective Techniques* 21: 18–31, 1957.
100. Hooker, E. Male homosexuality in the Rorschach. *J. Projective Techniques* 22: 33–54, 1958.
101. Saghir, M. T., and Robins, E. *Male and Female Homosexuality: A Comprehensive Investigation.* Williams & Wilkins, Baltimore, 1973.
102. Green, R. Homosexuality as a mental illness. *Int. J. Psychiatry* 10: 77–128, 1972.
103. Bayer, R., and Spitzer, R. L. Edited correspondence on the status of homosexuality in DSM III. *J. Hist. Behav. Sci.* 18: 32–52, 1982.
104. Goodman, G., et al. *No Turning Back: Lesbian and Gay Liberation for the '80s.* New Society, Philadelphia, 1983.
105. Suppe, F. Classifying sexual disorders: The Diagnostic and Statistical Manual of the American Psychiatric Association. *J. Homosex.* 9(4): 9–28, 1984.
106. Council on Scientific Affairs. Aversion therapy. *JAMA* 258: 2562–2566, 1987.
107. Begelman, D. A. Homosexuality and ethics of behavioral intervention: Paper 3. *J. Homosex.* 2(3): 213–219, 1977.
108. Davison, G. C. Homosexuality and the ethics of behavioral intervention: Paper 1. *J. Homosex.* 2(3): 195–204, 1977.
109. Silverstein, C. Homosexuality and the ethics of behavioral intervention: Paper 2. *J. Homosex.* 2(3): 205–211, 1977.
110. Davison, G. C., and Neale, J. M. *Abnormal Psychology: An Experimental Clinical Approach,* Ed. 3. Wiley, New York, 1982.
111. Harris, S. E. Aversion therapy for homosexuality. *JAMA* 259: 3271, 1988.
112. American Psychiatric Association. *Diagnostic and Statistical Manual of Mental Disorders Revised,* Ed. 3. APA, Washington, D.C., 1987.
113. Morin, S. F. Heterosexual bias in psychological research on lesbianism and male homosexuality. *Am. Psychol.* 32: 629–637, 1977.
114. Schwanberg, S. L. Changes in labeling homosexuality in health sciences literature: A preliminary investigation. *J. Homosex.* 12(l): 51–73, 1985.

115. Watters, A. T. Heterosexual bias in psychological research on lesbianism and male homosexuality (1979–1983): Utilizing the bibliographic and taxonomic system of Morin (1977). *J. Homosex.* 13(l): 35–58, 1986.

116. Adam, B. D. The construction of a sociological 'homosexual' in Canadian textbooks. *Rev. Can. Sociol. Anthropol.* 23: 399–411, 1986.

117. Newton, D. E. Representations of homosexuality in health science textbooks. *J. Homosex.* 4(3): 247–254, 1979.

118. Pasnau, R. O. The remedicalization of psychiatry. *Hosp. Community Psychiatry* 38: 145–151, 1987.

119. Kitzinger, C. *The Social Construction of Lesbianism.* Sage, Beverly Hills, Calif., 1987.

Chapter 3

POWER AND THE CLINICAL SETTING

In 1970, the Boston Women's Health Book Collective published the forerunner to *Our Bodies, Ourselves.* With sales now exceeding 4 million, *Our Bodies, Ourselves* has become a classic, having been revised numerous times and now published in almost 20 foreign languages. The impetus for this empowering book came from a workshop discussion of women and health. The women in the workshop discovered a commonality: Each had a doctor story to tell, filled with frustration toward "doctors who were condescending, paternalistic, judgmental, and uninformative" (Norsigian et al. 1999:35).

At that time, feeling anger toward the medical profession came easily. Doctors behaved like authoritarian father figures and were trained to make unilateral decisions for their patients. In medical school, they were taught to be disrespectful, even contemptuous, of women. One example of this was the widespread practice of teaching medical students how to do pelvic examinations by using anesthetized women (Kapsalis 1997:65), hardly a situation that would teach doctors-to-be to respect a woman's body or her wishes. The medical textbooks furthered the denigration of women by showing images of ashamed women and speaking of the naturalness of male power and female submission. Thus the cover of one 1970 textbook in its eighth edition shows a naked woman attempting to cover her pubic area and breasts with her hands, as she cried out in agony. The source is a famous painting of Eve trying to conceal her shame upon her expulsion from paradise (Fisher 1988:154–156 has photos of each). Another text asserts that the "traits that compose the core of the female personality are feminine narcissism, masochism, and passivity," and that a woman should acquiesce to a man, as in a wife allowing "her husband's sex drive to set their pace" by attempting "to gear hers satisfactorily to his" (quoted in Scully and Bart 1973:1048). In yet another textbook, the author goes so far as to claim divine qualities for the gynecologist: "If he is kind, then his kindness and concern for his patient may provide her with a glimpse of God's image" (quoted in Scully and Bart 1973:1048).

Though clinician–patient relations have changed as our health care system has evolved, many women are still dissatisfied with the process of talking with their doctors. Current comments sound much like those of the 1970s. A national survey reports that women feel "talked down to" by doctors (quoted in Elderkin-Thompson and Waitzkin 1999). A witness from the inside, a female doctor, notes the anger women feel at their doctors' arrogance (Legato 1992). Another female doctor writes about the pelvic examinations her patients had experienced with other doctors: They complained that these procedures were "insensitive, embarrassing, uncommunicative, and performed in a demeaning and patronizing fashion" (Wallis 1998:xxxvii). Even reports of unauthorized pelvic examinations on anesthetized women have not ended (Kapsalis 1997:65).

A major reason for this continued dissatisfaction is the entrenched power differences in the patient–clinician relationship. This chapter explores the bases on which these power differences rest, how such power differences affect the interaction between doctor and patient, how women have resisted the dominance of doctors, and what organizational changes have supported the evolution of a more egalitarian relationship.

In this discussion, the patient will be referred to as a woman, and the doctor as a man. Despite the growing number of female doctors and the importance of other types of caregivers, such a designation still reflects the majority of health care interactions, including those that are regarded by women as least satisfying.

DOCTORS' POWER ADVANTAGE

Doctors have enormous power in their interactions with patients. Their income, education, professional status in society, and often their social class and gender, are all valued social assets that confer an advantage over the typical female patient. The doctor's power also comes from his "turf" advantage. Patients come to see doctors in a setting that is completely familiar to the doctor, but often confusing and unsettling to the patient. The doctor's interactional edge grows because he is comfortable in his street clothes covered perhaps by a white lab coat, or surgical scrubs, while the patient is often awkwardly naked with a skimpy gown, or in a passive or supine position.

Power is also about who controls resources. A primary resource in the doctor–patient interaction is information. The patient comes in a time of need, seeking access to information held by the doctor, who serves as a gatekeeper regarding the dissemination of this information. If significant health problems exist, the attendant fear and anxiety on the part of the patient make the need for information greater, but even more difficult to obtain. The personal account of a medical encounter by one sociological expert on medical interactions and gynecology is telling. Stunned that she first met the doctor as she lay disrobed on the examining table, she found herself accepting the limited information offered. Diagnosed with an ovarian mass, she was told by the doctor that she needed immediate hospitalization for testing and surgery. She did not ask for a discussion of alternatives. She left the office feeling

> *a lot less confident about my ability to cope during medical interactions. I knew from my previous research that the institutional authority of the doctor's role provided an interactional edge for the physician that placed the patient at a disadvantage. But I had been totally unprepared for how great that disadvantage would be for me—a well-informed professional woman. (Fisher 1988:2)*

A woman could gain power in this situation if she had alternative strategies to choose from. Or, as a last resort, she could simply leave the interaction if no improvement in the discourse was forthcoming. Yet few women do so. Insurance coverage and managed care arrangements that specify access to particular doctors increasingly limit options. Time, too, may constrain the individual. Getting a second opinion and perhaps making a transfer to a new doctor requires time to research the availability of doctors with similar specialities, and then wait for an open appointment, which may be several weeks away. Work schedules and other commitments may make such shopping around burdensome at best.

When a woman enters the medical office and meets the doctor, his greater power translates into the likelihood that he will set the agenda for the interaction, determine what kind of information is exchanged on what time schedule, and make the decisions. Although his power would allow him to facilitate a shared agenda, to promote symmetry (an equal exchange) in conversation, and to encourage collaborative decision-making, these outcomes are unlikely for several reasons.

Barriers to Interactional Symmetry

The male-doctor/female-patient interaction persists as an interaction among unequal parties because it replicates the gender inequalities of our society. Although medical students no longer learn from textbooks with explicitly outrageous comments about women, medical education still embraces gendered concepts. Thus, as we saw in Chapter 2, research reports may contain subtle, sexually stereotypical images, such as those of the egg and the sperm. Or medical textbooks may present information implying that the man is the norm and the woman is "the other." Moreover, the gendered division of labor in society is duplicated in the medical setting, with men in the more powerful and prestigious positions. And doctors are trained in settings that are not exempt from sexual harassment. (See Chapter 15.) All of these factors lend support to the establishment and maintenance of an unequal playing field, one that encourages the preeminence of the doctor when interacting with women.

In addition, medical training and the culture of medicine have been physician-centered, teaching doctors that, regardless of the gender of their patients, they should be in control. Doctors spend years learning highly technical information and do so in a context that often silences the patient and treats her as an object. When doctors take medical students on rounds to make bedside visits to patients, they talk about the patients in the third person, as though the patient were not there (Mizrahi 1984). The medical model has them focus on the disease to the point where doctors may even refer to patients by their diseases, rather than by their names. They may refer to the "gall bladder in room 4," rather than to Mrs. Rhodes.

When doctors talk to patients, they also retain control by holding information back from the patient. A long-standing tradition in medicine supports the idea that the patient should not know everything; just as a doctor should not give a patient all medications in his bag, he should not give her all the information. Although doctors now share information with their patients about the diagnosis (a major change since 1960, when 90 percent of doctors did not even tell their patients of a cancer diagnosis), other information is often withheld, and doctors are of the mind-set that they should be the ones to make life and death decisions (Laine and Davidoff 1996).

Furthermore, it takes a skilled clinician to make an interaction between people of dissimilar power into a more symmetrical exchange. Yet medical school education and subsequent training as an intern and resident poorly prepare doctors in the art of medical communication. The people who plan the curriculum see time in short supply, necessitating the setting of priorities. They value biology, anatomy, and physiology courses over time spent learning bedside manners or how to interview a patient to gather maximally useful information. The emphasis on medicine as a science and on objective information as defining disease has meant that interpersonal skills are seen as so much fluff in the curriculum, with the result that the art of the interview is often neglected. As discussed later in this chapter, it was not until the 1980s that the training of medical school students in interviewing became even a small part of curricula at more progressive medical schools.

Upon leaving medical school, the doctor-in-training continues to be in situations that value and reward the learning of technical procedures. At each stage, the doctors who supervise the training of interns and residents judge them based on their technical expertise, not based on their interactional abilities. Medical students and interns become skilled in *minimizing* time with the patient so that they will have time to develop technical skills (Mizrahi 1986). They spend so much time with the technology and so little time with the patient that they learn to devalue the information they can get from a patient.

For some doctors, talking with patients is less about communicating with them than about finding opportunities to use and develop technical skills. Thus on a gynecological rotation, a resident may use his privileged position during intake to surreptitiously note which women patients are potential surgical candidates. Weeks or months later, when that resident has rotated to the surgical phase of the training, he can call up these women in order to try to convince them to have a hysterectomy (Scully 1994).

The Doctor–Patient Interaction

The powerful position of doctors, their training to focus on technical matters, and their lack of training in interviewing skills produce particular patterns of clinician–patient interactions. The doctor's goal is to discover a problem that he can diagnose and treat. He typically begins the conversation and controls it by asking closed-ended questions to elicit a yes or no answer, or a limited description. Doctors have mastered symptom lists that script much of the interaction with patients and serve the narrow goal of eliciting objective information that can either rule out or suggest particular diagnoses (Lazare, Putnam, and Lipkin 1995:3). Patients ask few questions and are often nervous when they do (West 1993:150–151).

If the patient speaks too long, the doctor quickly interrupts her. Said one doctor, "I used to get frustrated with people because patients rambled. Now I just don't give them a chance to ramble" (Mizrahi 1984:160). Estimates are that on average, the doctor jumps in after 18 to 23 seconds (Beckman and Frankel 1984; Marvel et al. 1999). Although most patients do not have time-consuming responses to an opening question, and if allowed to talk freely, most finish in 6 to 90 seconds (Beckman and Frankel 1984; Carlson and Skochelak 1998:36; Marvel et al. 1999), the doctor cuts them off. The quick interruption means that much is missed that the patient finds important. By interrupting, the doctor may not even elicit the real reason for the visit, nor find out how much information the woman wants, or what topics she wants to cover (Putnam and Lipkin 1995).

In one study, doctors underestimated patients' desire for information in 65 percent of their interactions (Waitzkin 1984). In another, 58 percent of genetic counselors (primarily doctors) were unaware of what patients wanted to discuss (Wertz noted in Todd 1989:20). In visits with menopausal women, doctors often do not learn that women are interested in hearing about the long-term consequences of low estrogen, not the short-term effects (Randall 1993). Sixty percent of women over the course of their pregnancy report they did not discuss all the topics concerning their babies or impending labors that they had wanted to (Shapiro et al. 1983).

Some patterns of doctor–patient interaction are clearly shaped by the gender of the patient. Doctors are more dismissive of women and more likely to doubt the authenticity of their health complaints. They are more likely to underestimate a woman's understanding of medical information than a man's (Carlson and Skochelak 1998:36) and more likely to give a woman an answer that is less technical. Although women ask more questions and get more answers, they do not get more time for those answers, which turn out to be more superficial than answers given to male patients (Wallen, Waitzkin, and Stoeckle 1979:145).

Doctors seeing women and men with similar symptoms appear suspicious of the women's reports of their symptoms. They are less likely to give women a physical diagnosis based on those symptoms, and are more likely to diagnose women as having psychosomatic problems (Robbins and Kirmayer 1991). Doctors of female patients are thus less aggressive in their pursuit of the typical treatment for the given symptoms. Heart disease, discussed in Chapter 10, is an excellent example. A research and clinical tradition has led doctors to see women who complain of chest pains as "moaning and groaning" about nothing. Thus doctors are unlikely to follow up on a woman's cardiac symptoms by pursuing further diagnostic procedures and treatment options.

Doctors' training to be gatherers of objective information ill prepares them for the feeling dimension that patients bring to the interaction. Since women are more expressive than men in their presentation of symptoms, the emphasis on finding the cold, hard, physical facts disadvantages them. Doctors miss many windows of opportunity for responding with empathy to a patient's fears and concerns (Suchman et al. 1997). The expression of emotion by female patients seems instead to confuse the doctor. A study of doctors' responses to patients with cardiac symptoms demonstrated the effect that a woman's expressiveness has on her doctor. The researchers used videotapes of a female actor portraying two types of patients: an unemotive, controlled, businesslike woman, and an emotive woman who used considerable voice inflection and gesticulation. The scripts used by the actress were identical, as were the positive lab results that accompanied each tape. Only half (53 percent) of the doctors who viewed the expressive woman recommended a cardiac workup, compared to nearly all (93 percent) of the doctors who viewed the woman with a more "professional" demeanor (Birdwell, Herbers, and Kroenke 1993). These differences in recommendations, based solely on presentation style, are dramatic.

Doctors' power has allowed them to encourage women to make health decisions based on only limited information. With pregnant patients, doctors suggest prenatal tests for fetal abnormalities as though they were routine procedures, without explaining the dangers of the tests and the implications of the findings. (See Chapter 14.) If an abnormality is detected, the doctor might use his position to suggest fetal surgery, appealing to the woman's "motherly duty" to do all she can for her child. The extent of risk for the mother is little discussed (Casper 1998). The duty to risk one's own health for the health of the fetus is left as an unexamined, presumptive expectation of appropriate maternal behavior.

At times doctors' recommendations move beyond powerful persuasion, and the relationship with the patient may become adversarial. Doctors have decided in some situations that women were not behaving in the best interests of their fetuses and turned to the court system to intervene on behalf of the fetuses. On the basis of such requests, courts have ordered women to have medical procedures, such as forcing pregnant women to have cesarean sections. This coercive power over women has been invoked primarily with women of low income or minority status. (See Chapter 14.)

Doctors have also used their power over patients and their views of women to perform unnecessary operations. For instance, hysterectomy, the removal of a woman's uterus and sometimes her ovaries, is the most common nonpregnancy operation for women. By age 65, about one-third of all women will have had a hysterectomy. Eleven percent of hysterectomies are performed as a lifesaving treatment for uterine, ovarian, or advanced cervical cancer (Dorin 1998). Most hysterectomies are elective. Some provide great symptom relief from benign problems such as fibroid tumors, excessive bleeding, or pain. But many hysterectomies are unnecessary and invasive operations that doctors persuade women to have. Doctors have had a very cavalier attitude toward hysterectomies:

> *I remember a common quip that I heard in medical school from the mouths of my esteemed professors.... "There seems to be no testicle bad enough to come out and no ovary good enough to stay in!" Although said with a twinkle and a smile, it captures the mind-set that makes this major procedure so overperformed. And indeed, it may well underlie the view of both women and their doctors that a hysterectomy is somehow a trivial procedure rather than the serious medical encounter that it is. (Healy 1995:186)*

Fisher's study of decision-making in hysterectomies found doctors quite willing to recommend a hysterectomy for the "benign diseases" of the nuisance of menstruation and the possibility of pregnancy. A doctor might say, "What you should do if you don't want any more children is have a hysterectomy. No more uterus, no more cancer, no more babies, no more birth control, and no more periods" (Fisher 1988:48). Influenced by the persuasive sell of the doctor and uninformed of the risks of surgery or the long-term impact, most women in her study accepted the treatment recommendations unquestioningly (Fisher 1988:44). Social class differences were apparent. Doctors were more likely to recommend hysterectomies to lower-class patients.

A doctor's power also means that any prejudices he has, whatever lack of empathy he may have for particular kinds of people, may be consequential for his patients. Women with devalued characteristics—elderly women, lesbians, women with disabilities, and minority women, among others—do not get the same kind of care and respect as other women, whose only devalued characteristic is their gender. Thus, a doctor may continue to relate to a lesbian patient as though she were heterosexual, asking inappropriate questions about sexuality and contraception (Stevens 1996), or otherwise display homophobic attitudes (Solarz 1999). A woman with physical disabilities may find the examination table incompatible with her mobility and postural restrictions (Welner

1998). An elderly woman may find that doctors' dislike of older women leads to inferior care. A woman of color may find herself excluded from decision making if her doctor is not of the same ethnic background (Cooper-Patrick et al. 1999). And a poor woman may discover that although she typically wants more information from the doctor than a middle-class woman does, she is given less (Shapiro et al. 1983) and may be forced to assume the role of "teaching material"—literally used to train future doctors rather than having her own health care be the central aspect of her visit (Fisher 1988:57). Clinic patients are routinely seen by doctors in training who are in need of experience on patients. The patients who must use clinics for medical care have little power to protest.

WOMEN RESISTING DOMINATING DOCTORS

Some women grant doctors considerable power in their interactions, acceding to a "paternalism with permission" (Allman et al. 1993), perhaps because they do not want responsibility for difficult decisions, or perhaps due to discomfort with the situation. Thus, a study of college women having pelvic examinations suggested that many decided that a passive role with no questions asked was a reasonable way to speed up an unpleasant procedure (Griffith 1997).

But many women show resistance to doctors' domination of the interaction (Todd 1993). Some women reject what the doctor says because their own relevant experiences contradict the advice (Abel and Browner 1998). If a doctor recommends exercise and limiting weight gain during pregnancy to a woman pregnant with a second child, that woman may use her experience with her first pregnancy to decide not to comply with the doctor.

Moving out of a passive interactional role with a doctor may require that women become more informed. Such was the philosophy of the Boston women who produced *Our Bodies, Ourselves.* They felt that knowledge was power, and that women should go to their doctors with a greater understanding of their bodies. Women do tend to be more active than men in the health care setting, perhaps because they are more informed, and also because they see doctors more often. They ask more questions than men do, which begins to challenge the doctors' power and may dramatically change the outcomes of the medical encounter. In a study of gynecological surgery, simply asking "Is it necessary?" generated a discussion in which a surgical solution changed from being the only option considered to one of several possibilities (Fisher 1988).

Women are increasingly armed with information. In addition to publications such as *Our Bodies, Ourselves* and newsletters from the National Women's Health Network and other groups, the Internet provides health information from medical encyclopedias, government health sites, and various organizations (see Chapter 17). Having the information is, however, not enough. To be effective with such information, women need to enter the doctor's office with specific questions in mind and resolve to get them answered. It takes hard work with one's doctor to have questions heard and answered. Active patients are still not the status quo, and doctors sometimes resist their approach, viewing them as inappropriately demanding (Carlson and Skochelak 1998; Ainsworth-Vaughn 1998).

STRUCTURAL AND LEGAL CHANGES

Important though the empowerment and resistance of individual women is in making the interaction with doctors more symmetrical and satisfying, doctors' power endures because of structural supports. Changes in medical education and culture, in organizational arrangements, and in laws are critical in facilitating a more egalitarian relationship. Fortunately, some of those changes have occurred and have established a solid foundation for more.

A 1972 case (*Canterbury v. Spence*) was an important first step, changing the doctor–patient relationship by redefining informed consent. Prior to 1972, a *physician-centered* perspective defined informed consent as what a reasonable physician was expected to tell a patient, and was often interpreted as requiring the physician to provide little or no information. The 1972 case changed the definition of informed consent to a *patient-centered* perspective of what a reasonable patient had the right to know (Laine and Davidoff 1996). This and subsequent court rulings affirmed the duty of physicians to share information. In 1991, patients were further empowered when the federal government passed the Patient Self-Determination Act, which requires institutions to provide written information to patients on treatment options and advance directives, thus enabling their greater participation in health care decisions. (See Chapter 10.)

Impressive though these legal and administrative edicts were on paper, huge gaps continued to exist between the law and the real world of patient care. The change they asked of doctors was dramatic. Some doctors, skeptical of a patient's ability to participate in decision making in a meaningful way or uncomfortable with talking about terminal illness, complied only with the letter of the law (Macklin 1993). Yet these regulations and proclamations had important effects: They defined a more egalitarian ideal in the doctor–patient relationship and opened up discussion of a more patient-centered model of care.

The medical establishment has reinforced these ideals, albeit slowly, with pronouncements from committees of esteemed professionals, and changes in the medical education curriculum: An international panel of experts convened in Canada in 1991 to discuss the doctor–patient relationship; in 1993, the American College of Obstetricians and Gynecologists agreed to rethink its relationships with patients; articles in the *Journal of the American Medical Association (JAMA)* spoke of a "professional evolution" toward patient-centered care (Laine and Davidoff 1996); and prominent doctors wrote books for clinicians committed to forming more effective relationships with patients (Lipkin, Putnum, and Lazare 1995).

There are two messages from such efforts. One is pessimistic—it laments how far the profession still needs to go. Thus, although experts did get together in 1991 to discuss the doctor–patient relationship, the panel ended up with a consensus report making rather pedestrian suggestions: Avoid interrupting patients, allow patients to speak about their feelings and expectations, and listen to them to develop a clear understanding of the nature of the patient's problem (Carlson and Skochelak 1998). Part of the problem is that established doctors were trained in the old physician-centered model, and find altering their habits to be very difficult. They need to be told not to interrupt and not to impose their judgment of the situation.

The other message is optimistic. A major philosophical shift has occurred: Doctors are talking constructively about doctor–patient relationships (Carlson and Skochelak 1998). Moreover, new models of medical education that incorporate the ideas of patient-centered care move us beyond mere talk. At several medical schools, such as Wayne State (Frankel and Beckman 1993), and at Harvard's "New Pathways" program, there is training in humanistic medicine, in basic clinical interviewing skills, and in how to establish a supportive relationship with patients. This training gives medical students much earlier and more extensive contact with patients, as well as a mechanism to receive feedback on their interactional skills.

Given the importance of the pelvic examination to women's health, it is notable that improved methods of teaching pelvic examinations were an early focus of curriculum innovators (Bell 1979). The once-radical model employing gynecological teaching associates (GTAs) is now in use at most medical schools. A GTA is a woman who works as a simulated patient at the same time that she instructs medical students on the manual and communication skills essential for a proper pelvic examination (Kapsalis 1997). The GTA may tell the medical student that his technique hurts or that she is uncomfortable with the interaction. The student not only learns better techniques, but may also learn that patients have a voice.

Some of the receptivity both in medical schools and among practicing doctors to the new patient-centered model has come from a growing body of research findings attesting to the importance of physician–patient relationships. Patients who ask more questions have better medical outcomes and greater satisfaction with care, and those patients who are able to communicate about their feelings have better medical outcomes. (See review in Carlson and Skochelak 1998.) Those who have more support and information are likely to have reduced hospital stays and recovery time (Mumford, Schlesinger, and Glass 1982). Overall, the conclusion is that more egalitarian decision making leads to better functional outcomes, greater satisfaction, and fewer malpractice suits.

Such collaboration of the doctor and the patient is not easy. Both parties to the interaction must participate, and old habits must be changed. The doctor must agree to having the patient participate, inform her sufficiently to make that participation real, and relinquish whatever remaining allegiance he has to concentrating solely on the objective, physical disease. The woman's "life world" needs to be part of the discussion. The woman must agree to become informed about her body and her health, be assertive in asking questions, and be willing to participate in making decisions about her health care.

The current health care system does not make such collaboration easy. Managed care, the relatively new third party to the doctor–patient interaction, has changed the rules of engagement. Certainly some of the early effects have been negative, with bottom line considerations causing doctors to spend less time with patients, and restricting the options they are able to offer to patients. One must hope that recent changes in the financial structure of the American health care system will not undo thirty years of improving the treatment of women in clinical settings. More doctors have now been trained in patient-centered care, which at least establishes a ground. It will be up to a new generation of activists—both doctors and patients—to see that a healthy doctor–patient relationship is part of the evolution of managed care.

CADAVERS, DOLLS, AND PROSTITUTES: MEDICAL PEDAGOGY AND THE PELVIC REHEARSAL

TERRI KAPSALIS

> *My first question, as I suspect yours may be, was, "What* kind *of woman lets four or five novice medical students examine her?"*
>
> —James G. Blythe, M.D.[1]

FEARING THE UNKNOWN

In a paper entitled "The First Pelvic Examination: Helping Students Cope with Their Emotional Responses," printed in the *Journal of Medical Education* in 1979, Julius Buchwald, M.D., a psychiatrist, shares his findings after ten years of conducting seminars with medical students starting their training in OB/GYN.[2] He locates six primary fears associated with a first pelvic examination: (1) "hurting the patient"; (2) "being judged inept"; (3) the "inability to recognize pathology"; (4) "sexual arousal"; (5) "finding the examination unpleasant"; and (6) the "disturbance of the doctor–patient relationship" (when a patient reminded them of somebody they knew, e.g., mother or sister).

Because the pelvic exam produces fear and anxiety in medical students, numerous methods have been used to offer them a pelvic exam "rehearsal." This practice performance is meant to help soothe or disavow student fears while allowing them to practice manual skills. The types of practice performances adopted reveal and promote specific ideas about female bodies and sexuality held by the medical institution. The use of gynecology teaching associates (GTAs), trained lay women who teach students using their own bodies, is a relatively new addition to pelvic exam pedagogy that will be examined at length. Previous to and contemporaneous with this practice, medical schools have cast a variety of characters as subjects of this pelvic exam rehearsal, including actual patients, cadavers, anesthetized women, prostitutes, and plastic manikins.... The ways medical students have been taught to perform pelvic exams illustrate the predicament of the gynecological scenario, a situation in which a practitioner must, by definition, examine a woman's genitals in a clinical and necessarily nonsexual manner. The array of pedagogical methods used to teach pelvic exams reveals how the medical institution views female bodies, female sexuality, and the treatment of women....

Many medical students have encountered their first performance of a pelvic exam on an actual patient. Oftentimes a group of students on rounds would repeat pelvic exams one after another on a chosen patient while the attending physician watched. If we consider that the pelvic exam is often sexualized by novice practitioners, this pedagogical situation resembles a "gang rape." Many times there is little communication with the woman being examined, nor is her explicit consent necessarily requested. Due to the intimidation of the medical institution, a woman may not resist repeated examination, even if she is adamantly against the use of her body for pedagogical purposes. This actual patient situation is one that Buchwald locates as anxiety provoking for the medical student (he fails to mention the anxiety this may cause the woman being examined).[3] This situation adds to what Buchwald refers to as the student's "fear of being judged inept": "a frequent remark was, 'if the resident sees the way I'm going about it, he'll think I'm stupid.' In some respects what began to evolve was the image of the experienced, wise, worldly, and sexually competent adult (the resident or attending physician) sneering at the floundering explorations of an adolescent (the medical student) who is striving to become a 'man.'"[4] Buchwald's reading of this situation is gendered inasmuch as he compares the pelvic exam to an adolescent male rite of passage. This gendered reading is telling. The medical apparatus, particularly this 1970s version, incorporates specifically gendered male positions of physician and medical student. Even though there are increasing numbers of women medical students, physicians, and medical educators, the structures of this apparatus, specifically the structures of medical pedagogy, are in many instances unchanged or slow in changing and require a female medical student to fit into this masculinized subject position....

Other than the attending physician, one person within the pelvic equation who might also judge the student as inept or whose presence might distract the student from performing a proper first exam and therefore cause the student anxiety, is the patient herself. Cadavers, anesthetized women, and anthropomorphic pelvic models like the plastic manikins "Gynny," "Betsi," and "Eva" are pelvic exam subjects who, for a variety of reasons, are rendered absent and therefore cannot talk back or have an opinion about the medical student's performance. These female models alleviate anxiety regarding inappropriate patient performance since they cannot possibly act out. The pedagogical use of these models may also have been developed in order to avert other student fears. If the woman's body is anesthetized, dead, or replaced altogether by a plastic model certainly there can be no fear of causing her pain. However, this logic is questionable in the case of the anesthetized patient: How might repeated pelvic exams under anesthestic affect how a woman "feels" both psychologically and physically when she wakens?

More importantly, the legality of this practice is extremely questionable. How many women would actually consent to this practice? Many women are anxious at the thought of a single pelvic exam, let alone multiple exams. Furthermore, the fear of a pelvic exam is often associated with feeling vulnerable and out of control; under anesthetic, a woman is particularly vulnerable and out of control. And yet teaching medical students how to do pelvic exams on anesthetized women appears to be widely practiced, although public discussion of this method outside (and inside) the medical community is relatively scarce.[5] At a 1979 conference sponsored by the Women's Medical Associations of New York City and State, New Jersey, and Connecticut held at Cornell University Medical College, this issue was discussed and found its way into the *New York Times,* where the conference recommendation was quoted: "If examined in the operating room, patients must be told prior to anesthesia that they will be examined by the members of the operating team, including the medical student."[6] Decades later this recommendation is often unheeded. For example, a surgical nurse I interviewed provided a common scenario: "While doing an exam on a woman who is sedated for a urological procedure, a physician may discover that she has a prolapsed uterus. The student or students observing the procedure will then be invited to perform a bi-manual exam on the woman [inserting two fingers in her vagina while pressing on her abdomen] in order to feel her uterus." I have overheard physicians at a prestigious Chicago medical school encouraging students to "get in surgery as much as possible to get pelvic exam practice." The assumption is that students will not be intimidated by an unconscious woman and that the patient will, in addition, have relaxed abdominal muscles, thus permitting easy palpation of her ovaries and uterus. Many physicians have not heard about such "practicing" and are outraged at the suggestion, maintaining that this is medically sanctioned sexual assault. Some physicians who are aware of the practice dodge the questionable issues, maintaining that for some students it is the only way they will learn.

But what *are* students learning in this scenario? By using anesthetized women, cadavers, or plastic models as pelvic exam subjects students are being taught that a model patient (or patient model) is one who is essentially unconscious or backstage to the performance of the pelvic exam; she should be numb to the exam, providing no feedback and offering no opinions. In the tradition of Sims's experiments, passive and powerless female patients are considered ideal "participants" in the learning process. In addition, students practicing on essentially silent and lifeless models are learning that the manual skills associated with completing a pelvic exam are more important than the fundamental skills needed to interact with the patient—skills that ideally would help the patient relax and participate in the exam.

Perhaps these rehearsal methods are used under the assumption that an anesthetized, dead, or plastic model is unerotic and will thus relieve students of Buchwald's fear #4, "a fear of sexual arousal." And yet the rendering of the object of manipulation or the gaze as passive simply heightens the power differential between examiner and examined that can in effect tap into an altogether different system of erotics. Necrophilia may be coded into a pelvic examination on a cadaver. Similarly, there have been noted cases of sexual abuse when patients are under anesthetic.[7] Likewise, the anthropomorphically named pelvic manikins "Gynny," "Betsi," and "Eva," with their custom orifices for medical penetration, could be recognized as the medical correlates to inflatable sex dolls.[8]

In the late 1970s, numerous medical pedagogues were reexamining what one physician referred to as "the time-honored methods" of pelvic exam pedagogy: students examining anesthetized women, conscious patients, cadavers, or plastic models.[9] The problems with these methods were discussed in a number of articles. The authors of the 1977 article "Professional Patients: An Improved Method of Teaching Breast and Pelvic Examination" in the *Journal of Reproductive Medicine* found that training medical students on actual patients "has many disadvantages, including infringement of patients' rights, inadequate feedback and moral and ethical concerns. Another approach that is widely used is the anesthetized preoperative patient. Again, problems include informed consent, increased cost and/or risk and lack of an interpersonal exchange. The introduction of the 'Gynny' and 'Betsi' models has been an attempt at improvement, but not without drawbacks, which include a lack of personal communication, unreal exposure and difficulty with 'live' correlation."[10] Where was the medical community to find these living models? Some went to what must have seemed a very natural source. In the early 1970s a number of schools, including the University of Washington Medical School and the University of Oklahoma Physician's Associate Program, hired prostitutes to serve as "patient simulators."[11] What other women would accept payment for spreading their legs? Logically, these educators felt that a prostitute would be the most fitting *kind* of woman for the job. In a sense, the patriarchal medical establishment took the position of a rich uncle, paying for his nephew, the medical student, to have his first sexual experience with a prostitute. This gendered suggestion assumes that female medical students are structurally positioned as masculinized "nephew" subjects as well.

Although lip service has been paid to the supposed importance of desexualizing the pelvic patient, in choosing prostitute patient models, medical educators inadvertently situated the exam as a sexualized act. They must have thought that only a prostitute would voluntarily submit to exams repeatedly and for nondiagnostic purposes. Or perhaps the underlying assumption was that a lady *pays* to get examined whereas a whore *gets paid* for the same exam. It may have also been assumed that prostitutes are more accustomed to and have a higher tolerance for vaginal pain than other women and would thus be more fitting practice models for novice students. In choosing to hire prostitutes as patients the boundaries of pornographic and medical practice were collapsed. Within this scenario of a hired prostitute, the student physician was put in the position of medicalized lover or "john." Certainly Buchwald's fear #3, "a fear of sexual arousal," was confirmed and even encouraged by hiring prostitutes. Buchwald notes that certain students "appeared to project their anxiety by asking, 'what should I do if the patient starts responding sexually?'"[12] By hiring prostitutes as pelvic patients, the medical establishment not only enforced the trope of the "seductive patient," but also paid for it. "Playing doctor" in this pelvic rehearsal cast with patient prostitutes threatened to translate the pelvic exam into an act of sexualized penetration and bodily consumption.

In many cases when prostitutes were hired, the medical student was led to believe that the woman being examined was a clinical outpatient rather than a prostitute. Thus the prostitute still had a relatively passive position in the training of medical students. In order to properly perform her role as clinical outpatient, she could offer the student little feedback. In addition, the working logic of the medical educators remained relatively opaque inasmuch as the student was not directly learning about the medical establishment's opinion of model patients. And yet these attitudes undoubtedly found their way into medical practice. Years later, students are still told by certain unaware medical faculty that GTAs are prostitutes. Today certain faculty still conclude that no other *kind* of woman would submit her body to multiple exams in exchange for a fee. This points to the importance of understanding the recent history of pelvic pedagogy. Those physicians trained in the 1970s are the same physicians practicing and educating today. . . .

THE GTA PROGRAM

In 1968 at the University of Iowa Medical School's Department of Obstetrics and Gynecology, Dr. Robert Kretzschmar instituted a new method for teaching junior medical students how to perform the pelvic exam.[13] For the pelvic model he used a "simulated patient," first defined in the medical literature as a "person who has been trained to completely simulate a patient or any aspect of a patient's illness depending upon the educational need."[14] Many simulated patients were actresses and actors hired by the medical establishment to realistically portray a patient. Their critical feedback was not traditionally requested. They simply served as a warm body for the practicing student. This stage of Kretzschmar's program was not dissimilar to the other programs that hired prostitutes. Initially, Kretzschmar adhered to this simulated patient model. He hired a nurse for the role of patient. She agreed to repeated exams by medical students; "however, it was necessary to compromise open communication with her, as she was draped at her request in such a way as to remain anonymous."[15] The curtain rose but the nurse's knowledge, thoughts, feelings, and face remained backstage. All that was revealed was the object of the exam: the woman's pelvic region. The logic behind draping the simulated patient presumed that if "only a whore gets paid" for a nondiagnostic exam, perhaps the nurse could avoid whore status by becoming faceless and silent.

In many gynecology textbooks, as will be examined in the following chapter, a similar logic prevails. Photographs picturing women are cropped so that faces are not shown or bands are placed across eyes to maintain the model's anonymity. If the woman's face and eyes are pictured, the photo could enter the realm of pornography; the woman imaged cannot be soliciting or meeting the medical practitioner's gaze, a potentially sexualized act. If the nurse who served as simulated patient was draped to maintain her anonymity she was in effect attempting to desexualize her body for the medical gaze. But is this an effective strategy for the desexualization of the exam? Is a faceless, vulnerable female body less erotic? In addition, although this professional patient model rehearsal did save actual patients from the task of performing the role of pelvic model, it did little to encourage communication between student and patient. Maintaining such anonymity taught the students that it was acceptable and even preferable for them to ignore the woman backstage behind the drape. They were also shown that a modest woman, unlike a prostitute, would need to disassociate her face from her body. And therefore, a modest woman preferred to be treated as though she were anonymous and invisible.

In 1972, Kretzschmar instituted a different program. The new simulated patient, now named the gynecology teaching associate (GTA), would serve as both patient and instructor, stressing the importance of communication skills in addition to teaching the manual skills required to perform a proper pelvic exam. Unlike the nurse clinician who was first hired as a simulated patient in 1968, the GTA would actively teach and offer feedback to medical students, forsaking any anonymity through draping. The GTAs first hired by Kretzschmar were women who were working on or had received advanced degrees in the behavioral sciences but who had no formal medical training. The women had normal, healthy anatomy and were willing to undergo multiple exams. They then received elaborate instruction in female anatomy and physiology, pelvic and breast examination, self-breast-examination and abdominal examination, with an emphasis on normal anatomy. They worked in pairs, one GTA serving as "patient" TA, one as "instructor" TA. They were assigned a small group of medical students and conducted the educational session in an exam room. The "patient" TA received the exam, role-playing as patient and co-instructor, while the "instructor" TA remained alongside the students, helping and instructing them during the exam. After receiving two exams the "patient" TA changed from gown to street clothes and became "instructor" TA, and the "instructor" TA changed from street clothes to gown to become the "patient" TA. The teaching session was then repeated with a new group of medical students, thus assuring that one TA of each pair would not receive all the exams.

Kretzschmar's GTA model provided a radically new way of teaching medical students how to do pelvic and breast exams. No longer was the simulated patient a teaching tool; now she was both teacher and patient. The women's movement undoubtedly influenced this model. In the 1960s and '70s women were demanding better health care and some took matters into their own hands by establishing self-help groups and feminist clinics. In fact, many early GTAs were directly associated with these groups and clinics and believed their new position within the medical establishment as GTA could allow them to bring their alternative knowledge to the heart of the beast.

Kretzschmar received a variety of critical responses from the medical community for his new GTA program. Some were positive, applauding him for his innovative method and his success in avoiding a "men's club" attitude by hiring women as teachers.[16] Some, however, were skeptical at best. They were particularly cautious regarding the GTAs' motives for participating in such a perverse endeavor. The epigraph to this chapter—"What *kind* of woman lets four or five novice medical students examine her?"—was a question asked by many physicians, according to Kretzschmar. Some human subjects committee members who reviewed the GTA concept "felt that women who were willing to participate must be motivated by one or more of several questionable needs, such as desperate financial circumstances (in which case exploiting their need would be unethical). Others fear the women would be exhibitionists or that they would use the pelvic exam to serve some perverse internal sexual gratification (in which case portraying them as normal to medical students would be irresponsible)."[17] Once again, the pelvic exam was compared to a sexual act by the medical establishment. Cultural fears regarding female sexuality and its perversions surface in these objections to the GTA program. Only a nymphomaniac would seek out multiple exams, enjoying repeated penetration with speculums and fingers. Also, poor women might lower themselves to such embodied work out of desperation, thereby aligning the GTA with the prostitute in an explanatory narrative. Furthermore, the committee questioned the psychological stability of the GTA, with the assumption "that women who are emotionally unstable might be attracted to the program, or that undergoing repeated examination might be psychologically harmful."[18] These human subject committee members reveal their nineteenth-century ideas about (white) women: frail female psychological health and sexual health are seen as mutually dependent and delicate partners. If their equilibrium is tipped by the "pleasure" or pain incurred by the excessive sexualized act of multiple pelvic exams, then who knows what horrors will take place.

Unquestionably, teaching female genital display and manipulation has been the cause of a great deal of anxiety. These fears are much more reflective of the medical institutions constructions of the female psyche and female sexuality than of any actual threat to women posed by the role of GTA. One reason the role of GTA could seem threatening to these critics is that they were faced with a new and potentially powerful position for women in the predominantly male medical establishment. Their attempt at pathologizing the GTA could have been propelled by a desire to maintain the status quo: that *normal* women are passive, quiet, disembodied recipients of a hopelessly unpleasant but necessary pelvic exam. For them, perhaps this was the least threatening alternative.

Despite its early critics, Kretzschmar's model has become the pedagogical norm in the vast majority of institutions. Over 90 percent of North American medical schools employ this instructional method, recognized as "excellent" by the Association of Professors of Gynecology and Obstetrics Undergraduate Education Committee.[19] Many GTA programs throughout the country maintain the same basic form as Kretzschmar's 1972 incarnation, though there is some variation. For example, some schools have GTAs working alone, rather than in pairs; a few schools still hire the more passive live pelvic model or "professional patient" to be used in conjunction with an instructing physician. The use of pelvic manikins, anesthetized women, cadavers, and actual patients continues to supplement some student learning....

THE TEACHING SESSION

The students enter the exam room, where the GTA wears a patient gown. She is both their teacher and the object of their examination. The GTA explains the purpose of the teaching session. She is a healthy woman with normal anatomy who is there to help the students learn how to perform a proper breast and pelvic exam. Medical students, however, have been indoctrinated into a system that privileges pathology. They have learned that what is normal and healthy is not as interesting as what is abnormal and unhealthy. Some students seem disappointed when they are told that the GTA session is one part of their medical education in which they will not be presented with pathology.

The GTA explains that the patient, performed by herself, is there for a yearly exam. She has no complaints. Rather, they are there to have the experience of examining a normal, healthy woman and thus should offer the "patient" feedback after each part of the exam, letting her know that "everything appears healthy and normal." The GTA emphasizes that no woman can hear the phrase "healthy and normal" too much. For many medical students "healthy" and "normal" are new additions to their medical script. Often, these second- and third-year medical students admit that the GTA session is the first time they have been encouraged to use these words. In a moment that struck me as simultaneously encouraging and tragicomic, one student, upon hearing me discuss the phrase "healthy and normal," pulled a 3 × 5 notecard and pen out of his pocket. He then said, "Tell me those words again. I want to write them down so I can remember them." In medical pedagogy, pathology is the norm, and normalcy is often viewed as mundane or unremarkable. For a woman in need of her yearly pap smear, the clinician's preoccupation with pathology can have sad consequences, both adding to the woman's anxiety about the possibility of the clinician finding that something is wrong and leaving her with the feeling that something is wrong regardless of actual clinical findings.

During the GTA session, other aspects of the students' scripts are rewritten and relearned. They are taught to use words that are less sexually connotative or awkward. For example, "I am going to *examine* your breasts now" as opposed to "I'm going to *feel* your breasts now." A number of script adjustments are made: "insert" or "place" the speculum as opposed to "stick in"; "healthy and normal" as opposed to "looks great." Changes are encouraged with regard to tool names: "footrests" as opposed to "stirrups"; "bills" rather than "blades" of the speculum.

When I was working as a "professional patient" with a young white woman physician as instructor, she kept referring to the "blades" of the speculum while teaching the students. I explained to her that many people within the medical community were replacing the term "blades" with "bills" because of the obvious violent connotations of the term, especially given that it refers to that part of the speculum placed inside the woman's body. The physician replied, agitated, "Well, we don't say it to the *patient*." Her assumption was that words that circulate within the medical community do not affect patient care or physician attitudes toward patients as long as those words do not reach the patient's ears. This is naive and faulty thinking, resistant to change, disabling the idea that language does indeed help structure attitudes and practice. . . .

The GTA offers many tips on how the clinician may help the patient feel more powerful and less frightened during an exam. "Talk before touch" is a technique used in the pelvic exam by which the clinician lets the patient know that she or he is about to examine the patient: with the phrase "You'll feel my hand now," the clinician applies the back of her or his hand to the more neutral space of the insides of a patient's thighs. Since the patient cannot *see* where the clinician's hands are, this technique offers her important information about where and when she will be touched.

Eye contact is another important and often ignored part of the pelvic exam. The GTA reminds the student to maintain eye contact with her throughout most parts of the exam. Many women complain that oftentimes clinicians have spoken at their genitals or breasts rather than to them. Eye contact not only offers the clinician another diagnostic tool, since discomfort and pain are often expressed in a patient's face, but it also makes the patient feel as though she is being treated as a person rather than as fragmented parts. In order to facilitate eye contact, the students are taught to raise the table to a 45-degree angle rather than leaving it flat. This has the added benefit of relaxing the woman's abdominal muscles. Specific draping techniques are taught so that the student-clinician cannot hide in front of the drape, ignoring the parts of the woman that reside backstage behind the curtain....

Similarly, the GTA encourages students to continuously communicate with the patient, informing her as to what they are doing, how they are doing it, and why they are doing it. For example, the student must show the woman the speculum, holding it high enough so that she can see it (without aiming it at her like a gun), while explaining, "This is a speculum. I will insert this part, the bills, into your vagina, opening them so that I can see your cervix, the neck of your uterus. I do this so that I can take a pap smear, which is a screening test for cervical cancer." Many women have had dozens of pelvic exams without ever having had the opportunity to see a speculum. More often, they hear the clanking of metal as the speculum is snuck out of its drawer and into their vagina.

Clinicians should not use words that patients will not understand, nor should they patronize patients; rather, they should piggyback medical terms with simpler phrases. In addition, students are taught that women should be given verbal instruction when they need to move or undress. For example, the woman should not be handled like a limp doll as a clinician removes her gown for the breast exam; instead the woman should be asked to remove her own gown. This helps her feel a little more in control of her own body and space. Ideally, the pelvic exam can become an educational session and the patient a partner in her own exam.

Lilla Wallis, M.D., an OB/GYN professor at Cornell University Medical School and a strong advocate of the GTA program, promotes this idea of "the patient as partner in the pelvic exam,"[20] and in addition encourages the use of many techniques popular within the women's health movement. Wallis adopts what some institutions might consider radical techniques. For instance, she urges clinicians to offer patients a hand mirror so that they might see what is being done to them. The patient is encouraged to look at her own genitals and not feel as though this were a view limited to the practitioner. Wallis also questions the draping of the patient: "This separates the patient from her own body. It suggests that the genitals are a forbidden part of her body that she should modestly ignore. It also isolates the doctor."[21] Instead, she believes that patients should have the choice of whether to be draped or not. She refers to the use of GTAs as "a quiet revolution" in American medical schools, believing that GTA programs will lead to better, more thoughtful care by physicians....

The pelvic exam is in itself a pedagogical scenario. The woman receiving the exam, despite the political or philosophical orientation of the clinician, is taught attitudes about female bodies. In this respect, the physician is as much a pedagogue as a healer, if the two roles can be separated. In teaching medical students, one is therefore teaching teachers, transferring knowledge, methods, and attitudes to those practitioners who will in turn conduct private tutorials with individual women who seek their care. Thus the methods used to teach medical students how to do pelvic exams significantly structure how these physicians-to-be will educate their future patients. The various ways medical students have been taught to do pelvic exams are intimately related to the medical institution's attitudes toward women and in turn structure how future practitioners perceive and treat their women patients.

The use of GTAs alters the normal pelvic scenario to some degree. Here the "doctor" is being educated by the "patient," a potentially powerful role for the GTA. As an educator, she may critique the student from the patient's perspective (e.g., "Use less pressure," "you're not palpating the ovary there"). One would think that the medical student would not argue with the woman who is experiencing the exam. And yet, because the GTA is not a physician, the student is sometimes skeptical of her expertise, doubting her advice even if it is based on her bodily experience. The very fact that her experience is bodily may serve to deny the importance of her role. Her embodiment of the exam makes her a curious and suspect educator in the eyes of many since she is being *paid* for the use of her body in addition to her teaching skills. Her role continually elicits question about what *kind* of woman she must be to undergo multiple exams.

In the GTA's educational performance there is no hypothetical signified, no abstract female body; rather the GTA is a fleshy referent with her own shape, anatomical variation, and secretions. At the site of the GTA, medicine, pornography, and prostitution mingle, highlighting medical attitudes regarding female sexuality, vulvar display, and genital manipulation. The teaching session may be a "representation" of a "real" exam, but for the GTA, as well as the medical student, it is simultaneously representation *and* practice.

It is curious, but not surprising, that the medical institution has focused so much attention on the GTA's role. Instead of focusing on what *kind* of woman would allow multiple exams to be performed on her, physicians might be more justified in asking how the medical establishment perceives the proper pelvic model or model patient. Or to turn the question back onto the medical institution itself, one might ask what *kind* of man or woman will *give* multiple exams. Unless there is a continued investigation of the medical structures that construct and reflect attitudes about female bodies and sexuality, the answer to this question might indeed be something to really fear.

NOTES

1. Quoted in Robert M. Kretzschmar, M.D., "Evolution of the Gynecology Teaching Associate: An Education Specialist," *American Journal of Obstetrics and Gynecology* 131, no. 4 (June 15, 1978): 373; italics added.
2. Julius Buchwald, M.D., "The First Pelvic Examination: Helping Students Cope with Their Emotional Reactions," *Journal of Medical Education* 54 (September 1979): 725–28.
3. See Louis Vontver, M.D., et al., "The Effects of Two Methods of Pelvic Examination Instruction on Student Performance and Anxiety," *Journal of Medical Education* 55 (September 1980): 778–85. Here elaborate methods are used to monitor student stress—researchers employed EKGs—whereas little consideration is paid to patient's comfort. Shouldn't EKGs have been used to monitor the patients' stress levels?
4. Buchwald, "First Pelvic Examination," p. 726.
5. I did find mention of the use of anesthetized women in teaching students how to do pelvic exams. See Ralph W. Hale, M.D., and Wilma Schiner, R.N., "Professional Patients: An Improved Method of Teaching Breast and Pelvic Examination," *Journal of Reproductive Medicine* 19, no. 3 (September 1977): 163; Gerald B. Holzman, M.D., et al., "Initial Pelvic Examination Instruction: The Effectiveness of Three Contemporary Approaches," *American Journal of Obstetrics and Gynecology* 129, no. 2 (September 15, 1977): 128.
6. Nan Robertson, "Panel Faults Breast, Pelvic Test Methods," *New York Times,* March 26, 1979.
7. See Audrey W. Mertz, "Sexual Abuse of Anesthetized Patients," in *Sexual Exploitation of Patients by Health Professionals,* ed. Ann W. Burgess, R.N., D.N.Sc., and Carol R. Hartman, R.N., D.N.Sc. (New York: Praeger, 1986), pp. 61–65. Mertz offers a case study of a male anesthesiologist "who had orally copulated with [anesthetized] women, while surgery was in process, many times during a two-year period." Nurses had reported incidences numerous times to various supervisors, but their reports had been ignored. It is interesting that in this edited volume chapters are dedicated to anesthesiology, gynecology, and pediatrics. One could maintain that in these three specialties, patients are in particularly vulnerable positions (due to unconsciousness, youth, and direct genital contact) and the doctor-patient power differential is potentially greater than in most other specialties.
8. Not surprisingly, "Betsi," "Gynny," and "Eva" are sectioned pelvises. Unlike eighteenth-century wax models with faces, hair, and even pearls, these plastic pelvic models provide only the necessary anatomy. Perhaps this is another place in which female volition is policed. (See chapter 4 for a discussion of how sectioning and cropping function in gynecology textbook images.) For a discussion of eighteenth-century wax models, see Ludmilla Jordanova, "Body Image and Sex Roles," in *Sexual Visions: Images of Gender in Science and Medicine between the Eighteenth and Twentieth Centuries* (Madison: University of Wisconsin Press, 1989), pp. 43–65. Apparently "dummies" were also used in American medical schools to teach medical students obstetrics. See R. W. Wertz and D. W. Wertz, *Lying-in: A History of Childbirth in America* (New Haven: Yale University Press, 1977), p. 5.

9. Dr. Robert A. Munsick uses this phrase in a discussion following Kretzschmar's article. See Kretzschmar, "Evolution," p. 373.
10. Hale and Schiner, "Professional Patients," p. 163.
11. Thomas R. Godkins, Daniel Duffy, M.D., Judith Greenwood, and William D. Stanhope, "Utilization of Simulated Patients to Teach the 'Routine' Pelvic Examination," *Journal of Medical Education* 49 (December 1974): 1175–76.
12. Buchwald, "First Pelvic Examinntion," p. 726.
13. Kretzschmar, "Evolution," p. 368.
14. See H. S. Barrows, "The Development and Use of a New Technique in Medical Education," in *Simulated Patients (Programmed Patients)* (Springfield: Charles C. Thomas Publisher, 1971), pp. 3–42.
15. Kretzschmar, "Evolution." p. 368.
16. J. Andrew Billings, M.D., and John D. Stoekle, M.D., "Pelvic Examination Instruction and the Doctor-Patient Relationship," *Journal of Medical Education* 52 (October 1977): 838.
17. Robert M. Kretzschmar, M.D. and Deborah S. Guthrie, M.A., "Why Not in Every School?" *Journal of the American Medical Women's Association* 39, no. 2 (March/April 1984): 44.
18. Ibid.
19. C. R. B. Beckmann, M.D., et al., "Training Gynaecological Teaching Associates," *Medical Education* 22 (1988): 124. Many medical schools also employ men to teach medical students rectal and male genital exam. This program would be a fascinating topic for critical investigation.
20. Lilla A. Wallis, M.D., "The Patient as Partner in the Pelvic Exam," *The Female Patient* 7 (March 1982): 28/4–28/7. Dr. Joni Magee touched on some of Wallis's points in her important essay, "The Pelvic Examination: A View from the Other End of the Table," *Annals of Internal Medicine* 83 (1975): 563–64.
21. Wallis, "Patient as Partner," p. 28/4.

CHAPTER 4

POVERTY

Most Americans have had no significant contact with fellow citizens who are poor. Television sometimes does provide a glimpse, but that brief moment of coverage is likely to be about poverty in a poor nation far removed from ours, not Appalachian rural poverty, New York City poverty, nor homeless people in Seattle. American poverty differs from poverty in a poor nation; it isn't characterized by large numbers of unbelievably thin people dying of starvation. Nonetheless, it is a cruel and often demoralizing fate in an affluent society. The contrasts between rich and poor in our country are particularly glaring during a time when many middle- and upper-class women and men make more money just sitting back and watching their pensions and investments grow, than poor people can earn working a full-time job.

Poverty impacts women's health disproportionately by exposing women to a myriad of hazards in the home, in the neighborhood, in the work setting, and in life. Moreover, poverty is associated with limited access to health care and exposure to a chaotic nonsystem that provides a lower quality of health care to poor people. This chapter examines the links between poverty and women's health.

POVERTY IN THE UNITED STATES

The government has given poverty an official definition. It has established the income needed for a modest food budget, and, based on studies suggesting that poor people spend one-third of their income on food, multiplies that number by three to arrive at an "official" poverty line. With adjustments for size of family and adult-child composition, the government then declares people below that line to be "in poverty." In 2000, a single person with a monthly income below $695, or a family of four with a monthly income below $1,420, was, according to this standard, said to live in poverty (U.S. Department of Health and Human Services 2000: 7555–7557).

The official poverty line is not only arbitrary—it is stingy. Trying to subsist on the established amounts and cover rent, electricity, heat, phone, food, transportation, clothes, and health care is close to impossible. Consider heading a family of four with $1,392 a month to live on, and the inadequacy of the amount becomes clear. The government's definition becomes farcical if one adds expenses that would begin to allow a person a minimal level of participation in our society (what might be said to be guaranteed by the Declaration of Independence as a universal right to "life, liberty, and the pursuit of happiness"), such as access to a television, occasional entertainment, and a meal at a restaurant.

> *Pay the gas bill, and they'll shut off the phone. Do the laundry, and the car fare to the dentist is gone. Buy the baby's diapers—and tell your older girl she'll have to skip her class trip because you can't give her the bus money.... [E]veryday life is a series of small Sophie's Choices, a painful, bitter, humiliating juggling act. (Dujon and Withorn 1996:155)*

Although an understanding of poverty cannot be limited to the government's definition because it is so restrictive, this definition is important because it has major consequences for individuals, families, and our society. Eligibility for government programs providing cash assistance and health insurance depend on the poverty-line definition, although many programs set maximum allowable incomes somewhat higher (e.g., at 133 percent of the poverty line).

Based on this definition of poverty, 12.7 percent of Americans were in poverty in 1998, and a disproportionate number of these are minorities. The percent of African Americans (26 percent) and Hispanics (26 percent) in poverty is nearly double the percent of the overall population that is in poverty. Among women who head households, 30 percent are in poverty, with the figures for African American women (41 percent) and Hispanic women (44 percent) again about twice that of non-Hispanic whites (21 percent) (Dalaker 1999:Table A).

POVERTY AS A CAUSE OF ILL HEALTH

Poverty in America is unhealthy. Not having enough money to make ends meet places poor people in substandard and overcrowded housing, or perhaps a homeless shelter, which is likely to expose them to peeling lead paint, unsafe electrical wiring, hazardous and inadequate heating systems, cockroaches, rats, and infectious diseases. Their dwellings are typically in neighborhoods with abandoned buildings, high rates of crime, and other violence. Toxic waste is more likely to be close to poor neighborhoods, exposing poor people disproportionately to environmental pollutants. Individually, poor people lack the resources to change these conditions, and poor communities typically lack the resources and networks to challenge them. Sometimes, out of economic need, poor communities will even promote unsafe conditions. Thus, poor communities have approved toxic waste dumps in their neighborhoods because of the potential for employment opportunities and economic payoff for the community. On a very different level, poverty in America means that meals lack the combination of fresh fruits and vegetables—foods rich in needed vitamins, minerals, and fiber—that nutritionists advocate. Such foods are expensive and often are not even available in the grocery stores serving poor neighborhoods.

If a poor woman has a job, her workplace is more likely than middle-class workplaces to be characterized by toxic exposures, high levels of stress, and other unsafe conditions (Chapter 6), while at the same time her job is less likely to offer any economic security, pension benefits, or health insurance. Work is also less healthy for poor people because their employers make it difficult for them to take time off for illness or health care visits. The lack of unionization means poor people have fewer resources in any effort to make work less hazardous to their health.

These physical conditions of home, neighborhood, and the workplace are consequential for the health of poor people, as is exposure to social stresses such as class or ethnic discrimination, fear of violence, anguish over economic insecurity or inability to provide for one's children, and lack of a vision for a better future. Although many poor women maintain a proud and resilient spirit in the face of these discouraging conditions, and many women successfully struggle to move out of poverty, others experience poverty as all-enveloping. Now, as in the 1960s when Michael Harrington first wrote his expose of American poverty, for many people in poverty, "[e]verything about them, from the condition of their teeth to the way in which they love, is suffused and permeated by the fact of their poverty" (Harrington, 1997:16).

Poverty is clearly a health hazard. Poverty is associated with an overall poorer health status and an increased risk of specific illnesses. Economically disadvantaged women are more likely to report only fair or poor health status; be hospitalized for preventable problems; have heart disease, diabetes, hypertension, cervical cancer, asthma, anemia, and ulcers; and have other chronic health problems (Rowland, Feder, and Keenan 1999; Hoffman 1998). Women in poverty are more likely to birth babies who die, or babies whose problems require extra days in the hospital. Poverty also exposes women to potentially injurious medical research and procedures. The sterilization of poor women, birth control experiments performed on poor women without their consent, and hysterectomies performed on poor women as "teaching material" all happen because poor women are less powerful and treated as less worthy. (See Chapters 2 and 16.)

There is a paucity of health research that examines the combined effect of class, gender, and ethnicity on health (Lillie-Blanton et al. 1993). Women of color do have higher rates of certain diseases and higher rates of death from some diseases than white women. For instance, African American women and Hispanic women have higher rates of diabetes, hypertension, maternal mortality, and infectious diseases than do non-Hispanic white women. African American women have higher death rates for cardiovascular disease and cancer, and Mexican-born Hispanics and Native Americans have higher death rates from diabetes and homicide (Lavizzo-Mourey and Grisso 1994). Although some of these ethnic differences are primarily accounted for by class differences (Lillie-Blanton et al. 1993), research does show that in some cases ethnicity can have an effect above and beyond class and insurance coverage (Roetzheim et al. 1999). More research is clearly needed to clarify the complex class–ethnicity connections to health.

Poverty and AIDS: The Intersection of Race, Class, and Gender

In recent years, a major health problem for women of color in poverty has been AIDS. Three-quarters (76 percent) of women diagnosed with AIDS in the twelve months ending in June, 1995, were African American or Hispanic. African American women were 16.5 times as likely to have AIDS as non-Hispanic white women; Hispanic women were 6.4 times as likely; and Native American women were 1.2 times as likely (CDC 1995).

The manner in which the government, researchers, and clinicians have responded to AIDS in women has been strongly criticized for its racism, classism, and sexism (Rosser 1994; Farmer 1996). Although first identified in gay men in 1981, a case of female AIDS was discovered a mere two months later. Yet the official definition of AIDS based on male symptoms persisted for over a decade, until 1993, when the Centers for Disease Control (CDC) finally included gynecological complications (cervical cancer and recurrent pelvic inflammatory disease) in the definition. In addition, women were not included in clinical trials until 1993.

Women with AIDS are very different from gay men with AIDS. The men are white, educated, and well-networked; they lobby for government action on their behalf. The women are not so lucky. Similar to male drug users with AIDS, women with AIDS are primarily from an ethnic minority and in poverty. This intersection of class, ethnicity, and gender is literally deadly. The government and researchers kept failing to recognize that these women had a problem, despite the fact that the most rapid rate of increase in AIDS in the United States was among African American and Hispanic women. Researchers did see these women as vectors (prostitutes) and vessels (pregnant women) who caused problems for others, and thus they directed most of their research on AIDS in women to studies of prostitutes and pregnancy (Rosser 1994:22–24; Nechas and Foley, 1994).

Yet the health of the women themselves went unnoticed. When researchers finally did study AIDS and HIV among women, they seemed unable to connect it to the realities of poverty and racism. Thus, a study in the *New England Journal of Medicine* examined heterosexual transmission of AIDS and concluded that "a sizable proportion of all women of reproductive age are at risk for infection through heterosexual transmission" (quoted in Farmer 1996:25). Nowhere did the words *poverty* or *racism* appear in the article, although these concepts, along with despair and powerlessness, are clearly the basis of the women's greater risk (Farmer 1996). Similarly, a study reported in the *American Journal of Public Health* concluded that the African American women and Latinas they recruited from homeless shelters and drug treatment centers needed "culturally sensitive education programs." Yet the women already knew about AIDS transmission. What they didn't know was how to solve the problem of being poor, minority women. In reviewing these two studies, this same author concludes:

> *[T]he most frequently encountered and easily circulated theories about women and AIDS are far more likely to include punitive images of women as purveyors of infection—prostitutes, for example, or mothers who "contaminate" their innocent offspring—than to include images of homelessness, barriers to medical care, a social-service network that doesn't work, and an absence of jobs and housing. (Farmer 1996:33)*

POVERTY AND ACCESS TO HEALTH CARE

When South Africa decided to provide free primary health care for everyone in 1996, the United States became the only industrialized country in the world that lacked some type of comprehensive health care for all of its citizens. The poorest citizens in every other industrialized country can walk into a health care facility and be entitled to receive care. In the United States, such access is not assured and is often denied. An extreme example of the latter is the way hospitals have refused to serve patients—so-called "patient dumping." Horror stories of patient dumping, such as the case of a high-risk woman in active labor who was transferred to a distant hospital, led the federal government, in 1987, to outlaw transfers of patients who were not medically stable. Although the intent was good, enforcement was lax and problems persist. In 1997, the Public Citizen's Health Research Group reported that nearly seven hundred hospitals (one in ten acute-care hospitals) had violated the patient-dumping law in its first ten years (Public Citizen's Health Research Group 1997).

Clearly health care in the United States is not a universal entitlement. Rather, health care access in the United States most typically is obtained through job-based insurance. To have a good job is to have a good benefit package that provides private health insurance. Poor people are not likely to have good jobs. Rather, they have part-time jobs, nonunionized jobs, or low-wage jobs, all of which are much less likely to provide health insurance. As a result of this employer-based method of providing health insurance, many people are not covered. Thus, in 1995, nearly one-fifth (19 percent) of women below the poverty line were uninsured, as were nearly one-fourth (25 percent) of the near-poor—those whose incomes are between 100 and 199 percent of the poverty line (Hoffman 1998:72). Hispanics (especially Mexican-born) are particularly likely to lack health insurance (De la Torre et al. 1996).

Medicaid

These strikingly high percentages of Americans without health insurance would be much higher were it not for Medicaid, a federally supported health insurance program for the poor established in the 1960s. Medicaid has dramatically improved the health care of poor women. Basic access and care statistics demonstrate this: Women with Medicaid are more likely than uninsured women to have a usual source of care, to have had a Pap smear in the last year, blood pressure screenings, and mammography (Rowland, Salganicoff, and Keenan 1999).

Although Medicaid has greatly improved poor people's access to health care, its coverage is severely limited by restrictive rules of eligibility and what have often been arbitrary administrative practices (and state variations). To be eligible, one must have a poverty-level income (a definition that excludes many who are clearly poor) and fit into a defined category. In its original design, for a poor, nonelderly woman to be covered by Medicaid, she had to be both officially poor and also had to be either pregnant or have children, which made her eligible for Aid to Families with Dependent Children (AFDC, the welfare system until the welfare reforms of 1996). Such a definition left out childless poor women unless they became disabled or were elderly, and it left out the near-poor. Furthermore, coverage for many women can be transitory, as with pregnancy-related care, which ends 60 days after the child's birth (Rowland, Salganicoff, and Keenan 1999). As is true with many social programs, the rules for eligibility, the bureaucracy, and the application forms are all complex and confusing enough to discourage many women from applying. Furthermore, they may even bewilder social service workers, who may misadvise clients or not even make them aware of programs for which they are eligible (Abraham 1993; Families-USA 1999).

Medicaid coverage became even more limited and uncertain due to the welfare reforms of 1996. The reforms meant that the old link between welfare and Medicaid, which had made Medicaid coverage automatic for those on welfare, was severed, which led many—an estimated 675,000 in 1997—to lose Medicaid benefits (Families-USA 1999; Houppert 1999; Chavkin, Wise, and Elman 1998). This unintentional effect of the reforms happened for several reasons. First, many of those who, due to the encouragement or mandates of the reforms, left welfare to take a job ended up losing Medicaid, even when their new job had *no* health benefits. Second, the old connection of welfare to Medicaid has persisted in the minds of caseworkers, and even in the computer software, so that when a woman left welfare, she could erroneously lose Medicaid. Third, sometimes arbitrary welfare practices hurt the poor. In some areas, welfare workers, often under pressure to show reductions in welfare costs, made it nearly impossible to apply for Medicaid. In 1999, a federal court determined that "New York City's Job Center staff illegally discouraged and denied needy people from applying for Medicaid" (Families-USA, 1999:10).

Although, as noted earlier, Medicaid has significantly improved health access and health for poor women, having Medicaid does not mean that one's health needs are going to be well addressed. A number of substantial problems exist. First, Medicaid does not cover some kinds of health care visits, procedures, health devices, and drugs: States have discretion over pharmaceutical coverage, dental coverage, and vision care; abortion is not usually covered (Haas-Wilson 1993); prenatal testing may be only partially reimbursed or subject to restrictive situations (Nsiah-Jefferson 1994); and state-of-the-art cancer treatment may not be available. Second, women on Medicaid may be required to reestablish their eligibility frequently, and coverage may be subject to repeated cancellations. If a woman's income is slightly above the eligibility threshold, then each month she may need to spend a set amount on medical expenses (similar to a deductible with other insurance) in order to qualify for Medicaid that month. Here, the greater complexity in health care coverage for the poor is apparent. A poor woman must keep detailed records so as to document every health cost she incurs. A woman may begin a month as ineligible for Medicaid, but then she could meet the "spend-down" level on the 20th of the month and thus become eligible for Medicaid for the rest of the month. The whole process, with the responsibility always on the shoulders of the poor person, would then begin again the following month (Abraham 1993:51).

Third, many providers refuse to treat Medicaid patients. Although social prejudice may play a role, government "reimbursement schedules" certainly are a major factor. These schedules indicate the amount the government will pay a health care provider or facility for treating a Medicaid recipient with a particular diagnosis. Since these payments are less than the reimbursement for providing the same treatment to a privately insured patient, the disincentive for treating Medicaid patients is clear. Thus, doctors turn away many poor patients. One study found only one-third (37 percent) of obstetricians would accept new Medicaid patients (Gifford 1997), echoing the findings of another study showing that only one-third of self-employed physicians in solo or small-group practices would accept all Medicaid patients who came to them (Perloff, Kletke, and Fossett 1995).

Finding a doctor who will take a Medicaid patient does not ensure good treatment. Medicaid recipients seeking office-based care may be dependent on doctors who have high-volume Medicaid practices. Sometimes referred to as "Medicaid mills" because of the high numbers of patients and concentration on people who have Medicaid, these practices "confront strong financial incentives to develop practice styles which differ in significant ways from those of mainstream physicians, [namely, to] see as many patients as possible and to limit preventive care and counseling, which lengthen visit times without providing additional revenue" (Fossett et al. 1990:127–128).

NAVIGATING A NONSYSTEM

In important ways, Medicaid recipients face problems similar to those faced by people without any insurance. They must find a health care provider within a health care system designed not for people like themselves, but for those with adequate resources. An irony is that most of the nonpoor, who have many more resources for dealing with complexities, are tied to a system that is visible and understandable, whereas the poor, whose lesser educational and financial resources ill equip them to deal with complexities, confront a system that at best seems chaotic and arbitrary and at worst is a *nonsystem.* The response to health and illness in the United States is aptly termed a nonsystem because, rather than being a coordinated strategy to promote the health of all Americans, it is a poorly networked arrangement of providers and facilities that fails to match an individual's need for care with the type and sophistication of care supplied. For many problems, those people *least* in need are given easy access to the most technologically advanced facilities with the most well credentialed providers, whereas those *most* in need are denied such access. For example, an economically advantaged low-risk pregnant woman has easy access to prenatal care, top medical providers, and a well-equipped hospital for delivery, while an economically disadvantaged, high-risk pregnant woman does not have access to these resources. The literature refers to this as the "inverse care law."

A thorough understanding of why this mismatch has occurred is beyond the scope of this chapter, requiring as it would a historical examination of the political economy of health—namely, the role of the government in health care, particularly its lack of leadership in promoting health care for all and its willingness to help construct a patchwork of programs and facilities for health; and the role of for-profit health interests. Health care is not treated as a public good, but as a commodity that is sold to those who can afford it. Simply put, producing and selling medical care in a market environment means that it is distributed along class lines (Brown 1979), and our government has done little to affect this distribution.

Ample evidence of the class-based distribution of health care exists. It can be seen in the geographical distribution of doctors. Market forces, not health planning, determine where their practices are located. Doctors are more likely to locate in upper-income areas where patients are likely to have good health insurance coverage (Fossett et al. 1990). Class-based distribution can also be seen in the quality of care received by poor people. We have allowed vulnerable people to have inadequate or nonexistent health insurance which greatly restricts their access to care, as already discussed, and we have allowed a second tier of care to exist. For reasons of proximity and a willingness to treat, public facilities (e.g., state- or county-run hospitals) and emergency rooms have become the usual source of care for poor women, whether the women have Medicaid or are uninsured. Public facilities are generally underfunded, understaffed, and overcrowded. Waits may be long and doctors are disproportionately doctors-in-training or doctors with less prestigious credentials.

Women served in such facilities typically do not have the choice of seeing the same health care provider over a period of time. They must deal with the consequences of records that have become lost in the transfer between overly busy and understaffed facilities. Similarly, they find that providers fail to communicate important patient care issues with each other; or they are not made aware of programs that would help them; or they are treated in hospitals lacking appropriate protocols defining standard treatment for particular symptoms. A deadly example of the latter is the finding that most (eight out of eleven) hospitals in New York City serving the poor and uninsured had no policy on the early detection of breast cancer.

As a result, in these hospitals, 65 percent of cancers detected were at a late stage, versus a national average of 25 percent (Lee 1990; and see Ayanian et al. 1993). If they do receive treatment for breast cancer, they are more likely to receive substandard care (Hand et al. 1991), and they experience a greater risk of dying (Ayanian et al. 1993). For these reasons, public facilities are considered a less-adequate second tier of health care in the United States.

In addition, publicly funded health facilities used by poor women may become too costly for cities to keep them open. In 1991, three publicly supported family planning clinics in New York City, serving the boroughs of Manhattan, Brooklyn, and Queens, closed. Ten thousand women had to find new places to receive their care, with the expectation that increased travel times to care would further complicate their lives (Brozan 1991).

The problems with Medicaid in particular, and with health care for the poor in general, have not gone unnoticed by policy makers, but attempts to address the problems have often been less than adequate. In recent years, as managed care has become the dominant model in health care in general, policy makers have sought ways to draw the poor into managed care systems. Thus, pointing to the costs of providing Medicaid (and Medicare) coverage and the unsatisfactory health results, the government has in recent years moved many Medicaid patients to managed care arrangements. Managed care providers, initially pleased to enroll new groups of patients, agreed to establish Medicaid-managed care, accept Medicaid enrollees, receive a set dollar amount for each, and guarantee coverage of their health care needs.

Although some plans have greatly improved the health of poor people—by, for instance, identifying at-risk pregnant women and giving them excellent prenatal care—many have failed, providing what one critic called "managed neglect instead of managed care." According to this critic, "bureaucracy and profiteering have thrived, as have marketing scams and incompetent or just plain mean medical management" (Anders 1996:193–194). A Florida state fraud investigator testified that "Medicaid HMOs have made obscene profits and have not delivered the services they offered" (quoted in Anders 1996:195). In Ohio, Medicaid HMOs excluded 45 percent of pregnant women from adequate prenatal care (Anders 1996:196). The appearance of success that some Medicaid HMOs report may be due to "cream skimming," covering only the healthiest of the poor. Some observers argue that vulnerable populations, such as poor and minority women, are not well served by a managed care system (Pearlman 1998). Managed care is changing rapidly, so the ultimate result of this attempt to merge health care for at least some of the poor with managed care cannot be determined. It is clear, however, that serious problems will have to be overcome if the system is to meet its goals.

THE ILL-CURE FOCUS

In addition to facing a nonsystem that provides them with inadequate care, poor women are disproportionately hurt by the bias in the U.S. health care system in favor of curing illness. Thus, instead of health promotion and disease prevention, our health care providers, facilities, and insurance reimbursement formulas focus on finding acute diseases in individuals and curing them. This emphasis, derived from the biomedical model (as noted in Chapter 1), is problematic for all women (and men). It is especially troublesome for women in poverty.

We have long known that poverty is a cause of ill health. The early evaluations of public health initiatives made it clear that overcrowded and unsanitary living conditions and poor nutrition were major contributors to ill health, and that alleviating those conditions did more to promote health than fancy technological advances (McKinlay and McKinlay 1977). This basic public health truth on the importance of prevention is largely forgotten in our ill-cure nonsystem. A clear sign of this is the hospitalization of many poor people for preventable illnesses (Weissman, Gatsonis, and Epstein 1992).

A public-health orientation holds another truth: Health and illness are not just individual matters. Finding disease in the individual and curing it there is inadequate—health and illness are embedded in the community. Just as public health campaigns around the turn of the century successfully changed community conditions by establishing sanitary garbage and sewage disposal systems and access to clean water, so the 1960 War on Poverty's focus on communities was critical in its success. Under the health initiatives of the War on Poverty, the Office of Economic Opportunity funded Neighborhood Health Centers (now called Community Health Centers) and empowered people to participate in the identification of problems and the search for solutions. One health center diagnosed malnutrition as a community health problem and not only prescribed food, but encouraged the founding of cooperatives for growing and distributing food. It is hard to imagine a more community-based and preventive health strategy (Geiger 1984).

Such an approach follows the wisdom of a metaphor often repeated in public health circles. The American way has been to save the drowning people in the river, and to do so with increasingly sophisticated, more successful, and more expensive methods. A more humane way would be to walk upstream to find out why people are falling into the river in the first place: The answer would be poverty. What is needed is not a rescue plan for drowning victims, but a guarantee that people won't fall into the river—by making sure they live in healthy communities, have safe jobs, earn adequate incomes, can afford nutritious food, and have access to quality health care when they need it.

Those who would most benefit from a revisioning of health care to include more preventive public health care and from changing social policy priorities are those least likely to be able to influence the powerful economic and political interests that have cast our health system into this mold. To the contrary, our stereotypes of the poor as undeserving people have led us, as a political nation, to both blame the victim for her illness and to deny her adequate care.

FITFUL PRIMARY CARE FAILS MRS. JACKSON

LAURIE KAYE ABRAHAM

[Mrs. Jackson is the grandmother of Jackie Banes. Jackie is in charge of securing health care for four generations in her African American family in Chicago.]

A few days after Rose's visit, Mrs. Jackson saw her internist at Mount Sinai, Dr. Boris Gurevich.

"Can you feel this?" asked Dr. Gurevich. He was examining Mrs, Jackson's remaining leg, poking the top of her blackening left toe with his index finger. Mrs. Jackson did not reply immediately.

"No...," she began.

"...or does it feel like it's dead?"

Dr. Gurevich, Jackie, and her grandmother were squeezed tightly into a small medical suite at Mount Sinai, where on Thursday mornings, between about 8:30 and 10, the physician sees patients from the West Side.

Jackie watched the exchange between Dr. Gurevich and her grandmother carefully. After prodding at her dark toe, he looked at the sore on Mrs. Jackson's heel. He did not ask about her diabetes, or check the deepening, half-dollar-size bedsore on her buttocks, which Jackie brought to his attention.

"Bring her back in two weeks," he said.

"Why can't we admit her today before it gets worse?" Jackie demanded. "We have to pay for the medicar, and we may not be able to come back."

Dr. Gurevich did not respond to Jackie's plea. Instead, he picked up the phone and rang Mrs. Jackson's podiatrist, Dr. Robert I. Steinberg. Then he called Mount Sinai's admitting office.

Irregular primary care had been a problem for Mrs. Jackson from the start, when diabetic gangrene was first diagnosed in her right foot in February. That infection, of course, had led to the amputation of her right leg, and Jackie feared that events were about to repeat themselves. Diabetics who lose one leg have a 50–50 chance of losing the other.[1]

Back in the waiting room, Mrs. Jackson leaned forward to take pressure off her bedsore....

Mrs. Jackson's lips were pressed tightly together. She began to moan softly every minute or so. "I wish they'd hurry up," she said in the first sentence she had spoken all morning. "My poor back is hurting me." Though Jackie had told her that it confuses doctors, Mrs. Jackson prefers to call her buttocks her back.

A half hour passed before the admitting clerk arrived. The wait was not overly long, but Jackie had become increasingly agitated as she watched her grandmother grimace in pain. "This ain't no hotel," Jackie said finally.

Worried about her grandmother's foot and not wanting to miss the appointment, Jackie had been stewing all week about how to scrape together the money to get her grandmother back and forth to see Dr. Gurevich. Finally, the day before the appointment, Public Aid's computer registered that she had met her spend-down. With Mrs. Jackson's name in the computer, the medicar companies would transport her to Mount Sinai without requiring cash up front, as they trusted that Public Aid would pay the bill. Otherwise, Mrs. Jackson probably would have missed the appointment because Jackie could not spare seventy dollars for the two-mile roundtrip ride to Mount Sinai. For that reason, Mrs. Jackson had missed an appointment earlier in the week with the podiatrist, Dr. Steinberg.

Jackie had inquired about scheduling all of her grandmother's doctors' appointments on the same day, but that did not fit the physicians' schedules. Neither Dr. Steinberg nor Dr. Gurevich have offices at Mount Sinai; they only see outpatients there for a couple of hours each week. Dr. Steinberg's office is in Oak Park, a suburb on the western border of Chicago, fairly close to the Baneses' home in North Lawndale. But seeing Dr. Gurevich at his office was out of the question. He is based far from the hospital in a Russian-Jewish enclave on the northwest side of Chicago, a trip of at least a half-hour each way by car. Dr. Gurevich bases his practice there because many of his patients are Russian-Jewish immigrants, as he is; the physician came to the United States in 1978.

As an attending physician at Mount Sinai, Dr. Gurevich gets additional patients when he is on call in the hospital's emergency room one day a month. Patients who are admitted to the hospital through the emergency room on that day but who do not have a doctor may be referred to him. These patients are almost always blacks and Hispanics from the neighborhood. He picks up a few additional West Side patients through referrals from other physicians, which is how he came to be Mrs. Jackson's doctor.

Dr. Steinberg had been the first doctor at Mount Sinai to examine Mrs. Jackson, when she visited him at his Monday-morning clinic four months before in February. "We put her in the hospital right away," Dr. Steinberg said, remembering her gangrenous foot. "Her big toe and part of her foot were as black as coffee." As a podiatrist, Dr. Steinberg does not have the training to treat Mrs. Jackson's significant medical problems—diabetes, high blood pressure, and peripheral vascular disease—so he asked Dr. Gurevich to accept her as a patient.

Some of the most fundamental deficiencies in Mrs. Jackson's care can only be found by going back to this time, to the events that led to the amputation of her right leg in April, and even further back, to the years when she lacked the basic care necessary to prevent the crippling complications of diabetes. There, little support can be found for the notion that Medicare assures the same quality and quantity of care to the middle-class and poor elderly. The episodic, uncoordinated nature of Mrs. Jackson's treatment conspired against her health, until, as Jackie would say, "It look like Mama going to have to get just about everything cut off."…

The big toe on her right foot was infected and had become progressively painful and dark over the course of several weeks. "It was very foul," Jackie said. "But her being Miss Doctor, she thought it was a bad bruise." Mrs. Jackson's diabetes was not severe enough to require insulin injections, but she had known she was diabetic and had taken medication for the condition for some years. Despite that, she evidently did not know that foot problems often accompany diabetes. Even if she had, she may not have realized that without prompt treatment infections can quickly turn gangrenous and require amputation.

She was not putting off the doctor's appointment for lack of insurance. Then as now, Mrs. Jackson was covered by Medicare, which paid for her visit when she finally decided to seek help from Dr. Hector Marino, a general practitioner whom the family had visited for all manner of problems since Jackie was a girl.

Dr. Marino had been prescribing medication in a not too successful effort to control Mrs. Jackson's diabetes for about a decade. When he saw her foot one Friday in February, he decided to refer her to another doctor. Jackie said he told her grandmother to visit a podiatrist but did not recommend anyone in particular, so Jackie planned to take her to one the next Monday. But by Saturday, her grandmother was in such pain that Jackie called 911 for a Chicago Fire Department ambulance. She spoke to a dispatcher. "I was telling them my grandmother's toe was messed up and she needed to get to the hospital. They said they was no cab service for somebody who got a hurt toe."…

Later, Jackie would hone the skill of making her grandmother's illness "sound a little more impossible than it is." In November, months after the above incident, when the old woman was vomiting and refusing to eat, Jackie again called the fire department, which does not require payment up front. "My grandmother had a fall," Jackie lied, "and her stomach is paining her." The fall did the trick; the paramedics promptly arrived to take Mrs. Jackson to Mount Sinai, where she was sick enough to be admitted.

But back in February, Jackie was still a novice at working the system. So the Monday morning after the paramedics refused to transport her grandmother, she called a couple of foot doctors whose offices were relatively close to the house but none could see her grandmother that day. This was not a simple task: although the Yellow Pages has a one-page display advertisement of podiatrists according to neighborhood, no poor neighborhoods are included. The individual listings are ten pages long and in small type; Jackie went through, skimming the addresses after each doctor's name. With the morning wearing on, she decided to call Mount Sinai directly, where Mrs. Jackson's sister Eldora went for her diabetes. Here her luck changed, at least for a moment.

Fortunately, it was a Monday, because Mount Sinai's podiatry clinic is only held once a week, for three hours on Monday mornings. Dr. Steinberg was working the clinic and agreed to see Mrs. Jackson right away. He told Jackie to get her grandmother to the hospital's outpatient Kling building by 12:30 P.M.

Jackie returned to the Yellow Pages. Since she didn't think her grandmother could make it on the bus, she called several private ambulance services. The first two quoted prices of $100 to take her grandmother one way to Mount Sinai. Finally, a smaller outfit said they would carry her for $35.

Dr. Steinberg hospitalized Mrs. Jackson immediately. Over a two-week stay, most of her right foot was amputated and surgeons inserted a synthetic blood vessel in her thigh to route blood around her own obstructed vessel. They hoped to increase circulation to the remainder of her foot so that any leftover infection could be cleared away. Mrs. Jackson went home in early March, under the care of a home nurse who was to visit once a day for the first week and twice a week for eight weeks thereafter.

From here on, Mrs. Jackson would be cared for through Mount Sinai's outpatient department. Dr. Marino did not follow her at Mount Sinai, though he had when she was admitted to Saint

Anthony Hospital in 1987 after suffering a stroke, from which she recovered almost completely. Jackie did not push for Dr. Marino to come to Mount Sinai because she had the impression from doctors there that he should have immediately hospitalized her grandmother when he saw her gangrenous foot. For his part, Dr. Marino said that for convenience's sake he prefers to restrict his practice to one Chicago hospital, Saint Anthony.

Both hospitals border Douglas Park, Saint Anthony to the south, and Mount Sinai to the east. The Catholic institution traditionally has been the hospital of choice for South Lawndale residents, most of them Hispanic. Mount Sinai, on the other hand, has drawn more of its patients from the all-black North Lawndale. These boundaries do not hold tight because of doctors' practice patterns and other factors. Were it not for Jackie, for example, Mrs. Jackson easily could have ended up at Saint Anthony several times, despite her connections at Mount Sinai. Fire department rules say ambulances must take people to the closest hospital, and paramedics sometimes decide that, from Jackie's apartment, located on the border between North and South Lawndale, Saint Anthony is closer. "I would beg for them to take her to Mount Sinai, and they'd look at each other and say, 'OK,' Jackie said. Doctors who practice in Chicago's inner city say that because of paramedics' rules, it is not unusual to be assigned to a case only to discover several weeks later that the patient recently had been hospitalized at a different institution. Because the patient was too sick or docile to relay the information, the new doctors had to start from scratch—which wastes time and money and sometimes delays proper treatment.

With Jackie as her advocate, that did not happen to Mrs. Jackson. Nonetheless, two decades worth of Mrs. Jackson's medical history were never transferred from Dr. Marino to Mount Sinai, as would be routine for middle-class patients. Her new physicians may have assumed that, like many other poor blacks, she did not have any regular source of primary care, or that the information from a "storefront doctor" would not have been reliable. Another reason may be that since Dr. Gurevich and Dr. Steinberg saw Mrs. Jackson at the hospital instead of at their offices, a secretary was not available to track down her medical history.

Generally considered less desirable than private doctors' offices because of the lack of continuity, hospital outpatient departments are used much more commonly by poor minorities than others. Before Medicaid and Medicare were introduced in the 1960s, there was a substantial difference in the number of annual doctors' visits for rich and poor, black and white. That gap has narrowed because of the two government insurance programs[2] (though many health experts contend that minorities and the poor still are not getting enough primary care, that they should in fact be visiting doctors *more* often because national surveys continually show they are the sickest Americans).[3] What has not changed is that race and class still determine the setting in which people get care, and, not surprisingly, separate is not equal.

In 1989, 20 percent of blacks, compared to 12 percent of whites, reported in an annual federal health survey that their last contact with a physician had been at a hospital outpatient department. The gap between rich and poor was similar: 18 percent of survey respondents from families with incomes lower than $14,000 reported a hospital outpatient department as their last physician contact, compared to 11 people with incomes higher than $50,000. . . .[4]

A pioneering study of hospital discharge data in New York found that while elderly New Yorkers in the poorest areas use emergency rooms one and one-half times more than their counterparts in affluent areas, they visit hospital outpatient departments four times as often.[5]

There is no obvious reason for hospital outpatient departments to offer poorer primary care than private doctors' offices. And, in fact, the clinical quality of the care in hospitals may be no different, and even better. The problems at hospitals are more subtle. Typically, patients see medical residents who spend only a few months in one clinic before rotating to the next. "People who go to outpatient departments don't have a physician who is really in charge. There seems to be a sense that there is some institutional responsibility for the patient, but that's really kind of hollow," explained Melvin I. Krasner, senior director of research for the United Hospital Fund of New York, which conducted the hospital discharge study. "The poorer patients need even more than the middle-class patient in terms of continuity and management, but they get less."

Mrs. Jackson's situation was somewhat different since Dr. Gurevich, an attending physician rather than an intern or resident, became her physician, but the continuity and coordination problems remained. Dr. Gurevich's home base on the other side of town meant that he spent only a few hours each week seeing outpatients at Mount Sinai. When he was there, Jackie often could not afford a medicar to take her grandmother to see him. In sum, nobody was aggressively steering Mrs. Jackson's care.

The problems of getting Mrs. Jackson to the doctor were especially acute after she went home in March with a partially amputated right foot. During that delicate time, she had to be followed carefully if she were to have any chance of keeping the remainder of her foot and her leg.

Mrs. Jackson had appointments with Dr. Steinberg on Mondays and Dr. Gurevich on Thursdays. Jackie never took her grandmother to both because she was unaware that she could get her to them for anything less than a $70 roundtrip. "I didn't know that ASC [a medicar company] and them take Medicaid," Jackie said later. "I had to hear that from the nurse. I thought they were cash-only people." To her chagrin, about the same time she made that discovery, she realized her grandmother had been put on the spend-down program, which meant she was not eligible for Medicaid every month.

So four days after Mrs. Jackson was discharged from the hospital following the amputation of her foot, Jackie paid $70 to get her grandmother to and from an appointment with Dr. Steinberg. She skipped Dr. Gurevich's Thursday morning appointment three days later, deciding to wait until the next week. She figured she would alternate; Steinberg one week, Gurevich the next. It was not a bad strategy given the circumstances, but a strategy nobody would willingly choose.

The following week, on a Thursday morning in late March, the medicar was a little late, so Jackie called the outpatient suite at Mount Sinai to let Dr. Gurevich know she was on her way. She was assured that the physician would still be around, but when Jackie hurriedly pushed her grandmother in her wheelchair into the clinic at about 9:30, he had gone.

"I was so mad," Jackie said. "I rolled her right over to the emergency room. I told them they had to see her."

Mount Sinai cannot locate the medical records from this encounter. All that is left to document it is a large red emergency room logbook. It shows that Mrs. Jackson was brought to the emergency room at 9:39 A.M. suffering from "leg edema," a swollen right leg, and was sent home eight long hours later at 5:40 P.M.

There are also laboratory tests from that day, evidently ordered by the emergency room staff. They show that Mrs. Jackson was beginning to have a dangerous reaction to Coumadin, a drug she was taking to keep her blood from coagulating and thus allow it to flow to her leg and what was left of her foot.[6] The drug was prescribed in an attempt to prevent further amputation, but while Coumadin can be beneficial, it has a very narrow therapeutic margin. It's easy for a patient to overdose on it and bleed uncontrollably.

A test called a prothrombin time (PT) measures patients' coagulation levels. A normal level is about 11, but Dr. Gurevich did not want Mrs. Jackson's level to be normal, he wanted to prevent her from developing blood clots, which were more likely to form in her sluggish circulatory system. To do the job, her Coumadin level needed to be one and one-half to two times the normal reading. Accordingly, the ideal level for Mrs. Jackson would have been between 16 and 22. That day in the emergency room, however, Mrs. Jackson's PT level registered 35—more than three times the normal level—so high that her coagulation level needed to be monitored closely in the next few days, lest she begin to bleed to death. Yet, according to medical records, no such monitoring took place. How that happened shows how a primary care system made from fraying cloth can rip apart, leaving patients exposed to dangerous illness, even death.

Mrs. Jackson supposedly stopped taking Coumadin the day after her emergency room visit, on doctor's orders. The next week, however, she missed her appointments with both Dr. Gurevich and Dr. Steinberg because Jackie did not have the money to get her there and did not understand the gravity of the situation. The problem could have been solved had the home health nurse drawn Mrs. Jackson's blood for a PT test during that week, but presumably because of inadequate communication between Dr. Gurevich, the emergency room staff, and the nurse, that never happened. Judging from the nurse's notes, she did not seem to be aware that Mrs. Jackson was regularly missing doctors' appointments where her coagulation level might have been measured.[7]

The inevitable happened. On a Saturday morning, after two missed doctors' appointments, a private ambulance took Mrs. Jackson to the emergency room. Her nose had bled all night. The diagnosis: "Coumadin toxicity." Her PT level was 40, higher than it had been the last time she visited the emergency room, suggesting that somehow Mrs. Jackson had mistakenly continued to take Coumadin.

Medicare paid for this ambulance trip because it resulted in a hospitalization and was thus deemed "medically necessary." The federal health insurer would not have paid to get Mrs. Jackson to the doctor earlier in the week, when her high Coumadin level might have been detected and brought under control. Not only would an earlier visit have been better for Mrs. Jackson's health, but it could have saved the government several thousand dollars for the week-long hospital stay needed to treat the Coumadin poisoning. But even such minimal "prevention" does not comport with Medicare policy, which again, summarily defines nonemergency trips to the doctor's office as medically unnecessary.

Dr. Gurevich visited Mrs. Jackson the day after she was admitted to the hospital. "Patient supposed to see me as out-patient ten days ago, but she missed the appointment," his notes say. "Was [warned] about the Coumadin risk."

The hospital record also included a note from Dr. B. S. Iyer, the surgeon who had inserted a synthetic blood vessel into Mrs. Jackson's thigh during her first hospital stay. Evidently, Dr. Iyer had examined her in the emergency room the day she missed her appointment with Dr. Gurevich. As a surgeon, he would not be the physician responsible for monitoring her Coumadin level, but he, too, noted in the hospital record that she had not followed doctor's orders. "I had seen this patient in ER 10–12 days ago. She was to come back and see me in 1 week, which she never did," Dr. Iyer wrote.

Without the emergency-room medical record, it is impossible to know what arrangements the ER staff made for Mrs. Jackson's follow-up care. Dr. Iyer speculated that she was discharged from the overburdened emergency room before the equally overburdened hospital lab processed the tests showing her high PT level. "That's always a problem at Mount Sinai," he said. "It can take eight to ten hours to get labs."

The chief of emergency medicine, Dr. Karen O'Mara, conceded that Mrs. Jackson may have been discharged before her lab results came back. (Because of the constant delays, Dr. O'Mara had checked into setting up a satellite lab for the ER, but the $50,000 start-up cost was beyond Mount Sinai's shoestring budget.) Even so, normal emergency-room procedure would have been to contact Mrs. Jackson's doctor with the results once they were completed so that someone could order a PT test. Whatever the exact chronology of events, Dr. O'Mara said it was evident that there was a communication breakdown somewhere along the line. Perhaps Dr. Gurevich was not informed of the lab results, or he received them but neglected to order the nurse to perform a PT test. Dr. Gurevich declined to be interviewed....

After a week in the hospital, Mrs. Jackson was stable enough to go home. But not for long. A week later she was back in the emergency room....

It was during this hospitalization that Mrs Jackson's right leg was amputated up to the thigh. The infection in her partially amputated foot had not healed and was beginning to spread. Doctors had no choice but to amputate.

No one knows the exact cause of noninsulin-dependent diabetes, the kind that afflicts Mrs. Jackson, her sister Eldora, who was blinded by the disease, and more than 90 percent of all diabetics. It seems to be triggered by obesity and runs in families, which suggests a genetic link....[8]

While poverty and the fragmented primary care system that accompanies it may not explain why blacks get diabetes more often, it may explain why they suffer such serious complications. The amputation rate among blacks is twice as high as among whites; diabetes-related kidney failure is three times as frequent; and black women are three times as likely to be blinded by the condition.[9]

Another provocative finding of the United Hospital Fund's study was that, despite many similarities in the reasons that rich and poor elderly are hospitalized, diabetes and other chronic diseases stand out as exceptions. In poor areas, diabetes ranks as the sixth most common reason for admission, whereas it barely makes the top twenty in neighborhoods where less than 10 percent of the population is poor. The report concluded that although Medicare puts rich and poor elderly on more equal footing than younger people who do not have the benefit of government-sponsored insurance, disparities in access and "ability to make the dietary and lifestyle changes necessary to manage the disease" persist.[10]

Dr. Paula Butler, an endocrinologist who runs a clinic for diabetics at Mount Sinai, pointed to one simple example of the access gap. Since Medicare does not cover medications, poor diabetics with erratic secondary insurance, or none at all, may not be able to afford the drugs and equipment necessary to control their disease. "The medicines are expensive, the home blood-sugar tests are expensive," she said....

The real fight against Mrs. Jackson's encroaching peripheral vascular disease should have begun in the years before she showed up at Mount Sinai with a gangrenous foot. But, once again, having insurance is not a guarantee of good care for the poor; the skills and training of many doctors who practice in their neighborhoods may be substandard. Mrs. Jackson saw Dr. Marino regularly, but he said he had trouble bringing her blood sugar under control. When her blood sugar levels became increasingly high, he said he urged her to replace the oral diabetes medication she was taking with more potent insulin, but she refused because she did not want to give herself injections. Mrs. Jackson considered her high blood pressure—the probable cause of her 1987 stroke—to be her most serious problem. And it was, until, as the years passed, her blood sugar levels began to rise, too.

A general practitioner whose patients range from old women to pregnant girls to adolescent boys, Dr. Marino was a trusted family doctor for Mrs. Jackson and the Baneses. He saw Jackie when she was a little girl, and he delivered DeMarest. Mrs. Jackson first began to visit Dr. Marino in the early 1970s when his office was located in the heart of North Lawndale on Madison Street. When that office burned down a decade later, Dr. Marino moved a few miles west to a small storefront on the border of Chicago and suburban Oak Park, and Mrs. Jackson followed him. These facts paint a picture of a Norman Rockwellian doctor of the kind that health planners say are in desperately short supply in the inner city: a family practitioner who over two decades provided basic primary care for three generations of poor people.

What Mrs. Jackson and her family had no way of knowing was that Dr. Marino had failed a peer review by the Department of Public Aid's Medical Quality Review Committee. The five-doctor panel investigated fifteen cases beginning in 1988 and concluded that Dr. Marino had over-prescribed narcotics, prescribed antibiotics without documenting a need for them, failed to order appropriate laboratory studies, and had not consistently provided proper checkups for children.[11] In one case, a forty-six-year-old alcoholic died from kidney and liver failure twenty-three days after his last visit with Dr. Marino, yet nowhere in the physician's records was "there any indication of an illness of this severity," the reviewers wrote. "Even an abbreviated physical exam would have found the jaundice, ascites [a swollen abdomen often associated with alcoholic liver failure] and peripheral edema [swollen extremities that may be caused by cirrhosis or renal failure]."

The peer review team recommended that Dr. Marino revise his practices in accordance with their findings and take ten hours of Continuing Medical Education in pediatrics. He was put on "continuous monitoring status," which meant his performance would be reviewed after nine months. To put Dr. Marino's case into perspective, the physicians' panel found such serious quality-of-care deficiencies with only sixty-seven of twenty-one thousand doctors who accepted Medicaid during 1991. Twenty-three of those physicians were terminated from the Medicaid program altogether; one was suspended and forty-three (including Dr. Marino) were put on "continuous monitoring status."[12]

Dr. Marino has what is considered a large Medicaid practice; he treated more than one thousand Medicaid recipients in both 1989 and 1990, earning $65,217 the first year and $80,976 the second.[13] Practices consisting mostly of Medicaid patients—often called "Medicaid mills"—are worrisome because they have been associated with short visits and inadequate preventive care. A dramatic example of the segregation of Medicaid patients was reported by former University of Illinois political scientist James Fossett and public health researcher Janet Perloff. They found that in 1986 fewer than two dozen obstetrician/gynecologists cared for more than one-third of all Medicaid patients in Cook County and St. Clair County, also a poor, urban area in Illinois.[14]

Another charge against Medicaid mills is that they do not provide steady, reliable care, partly because the doctors who run them may not be allowed to work in hospitals. Hospital privileges are usually reserved for doctors who have had residency training and who are certified by a medical specialty board, which, although not a prerequisite to practice medicine, is an easily quantifiable measure of competence. But doctors who establish solo practices in poor neighborhoods often lack one or both of these credentials, a common reason being that they earned their medical degrees in foreign countries and did not pursue further training here.

Dr. Marino, for one, graduated from medical school in the Philippines in 1972 and started but did not finish a residency at a Chicago hospital. Although he is not certified by a medical specialty board, he does have privileges at Saint Anthony and a suburban hospital. Nevertheless, Mrs. Jackson's care still lacked continuity. Dr. Marino said he referred her to a specialist, but he did not remember who it was, and he did not note the doctor's name in his chart. He even wavered on what kind of specialist he would have chosen for her, a vascular surgeon, perhaps, but he was not sure. Mrs. Jackson, of course, told Jackie she was supposed to see a podiatrist. Such vague referrals are a problem in a medical system where specialists hesitate to take patients who have not been referred by another doctor. The problem is worse in poor neighborhoods where medical specialists are scarce.

Mrs. Jackson could have received something closer to state-of-the-art diabetic care at Mount Sinai's outpatient department, which adds another complicating piece to the puzzle of health care in ghettos. The revolving door for medical residents may interfere with continuity at outpatient departments, but young physicians' knowledge of current diagnostic techniques and treatments is often significantly better than that of doctors who practice in the city's poor neighborhoods.

The diabetic outpatient clinic may offer the best of both worlds. It is regularly staffed by two full-time physicians who supervise residents but also have close contact with patients. Held two mornings a week, the clinic is run more like a traditional office-based practice than is usual for hospital-based primary care.

Patients make appointments and generally visit their doctors every two months. The clinic tries to get all of its diabetics to use home test kits, so that when they detect a significant fluctuation in their blood-sugar levels, they can call the clinic for an appointment or a medication adjustment. This helps to prevent the wild swings in blood-sugar levels that doctors believe contribute to the development of kidney failure, blindness, and peripheral vascular disease. Patients also get another bonus that a general practitioner like Dr. Marino could not afford to provide: a diabetic health educator.

Clinic director Dr. Butler said the health educator was invaluable. "He spends a lot of time talking about what they should be doing, with their diets and everything else. We really badger them a lot, though at some point, you tell them it's in their hands." Perhaps the health educator could have taught Mrs. Jackson to take proper care of her feet before it was too late. Jackie said her grandmother's feet had been tender for years. "She'd grab people by the collar who stepped on her feet on the bus."

The amputation of Mrs. Jackson's right leg the last week of April had not, of course, put an end to her medical worries. She seemed destined to spend the summer going in and out of the hospital.

The day that Mrs. Jackson was admitted to Mount Sinai by a seemingly reluctant Dr Gurevich, Jackie escorted her to a room on the sixth floor. The room had a nice view of Douglas Park, though it was a dreary, unseasonably cold summer day. As two nurses started to prepare Mrs. Jackson's bed—she needed a special mattress for her bed sores—Jackie took the elevator back downstairs for a cup of coffee and doughnut in the hospital cafeteria.

She was pleased that she had persuaded Dr. Gurevich to admit her grandmother, as opposed to simply having her foot examined again at her next appointment. "In two weeks [the infection] would have done gone through her whole foot," Jackie said. "I know what they would have told me. It's gotten so bad, we're going to have to..." Jackie made a chopping motion with her hand.

Upstairs, Mrs. Jackson was getting settled in,...

The rest of the afternoon Mrs. Jackson was rarely alone; a series of medical professionals came by to check her in.

First was senior resident Dr. Mark Angel....

The next visitor was a dietician....

After the dietician came a technician pushing an electrocardiogram machine. "Going to do an EKG on you, Mrs. Jackson," she said, as she helped Mrs. Jackson slip out of her hospital gown....

A nurse arrived to take her medical history....

The nurse asked about her bowel movements, and Mrs. Jackson said they were "doing well," though she had told a doctor earlier that she had not had one for a week. Taking Mrs. Jackson's medical history without Jackie around was an arduous task, rife with imprecision.

The most painful moment of the afternoon came during a visit from medical resident Dr. Kyu-Jang Oh.

"Can we start your IV?" Dr. Oh asked.

"Hmmmm," Mrs. Jackson replied. She had learned by now that in hospitals, questions and statements are the same thing.

With Dr. Oh was a medical student, Nancy Church.... They probed with the needle. Mrs. Jackson's eyes squeezed shut and she raised her free fist to the sky.

No luck. Dr. Oh left for another needle.

"Sorry about this. Sorry we have to stick you again," Church consoled.

The second time, Church grabbed Mrs. Jackson's free hand in a gesture of support. She held it in her own plastic-gloved one until the needle took. The ritual of Mrs. Jackson's fourth hospital stay in five months had begun.

NOTES

1. Randi S. Most and Pomeroy Sinnock, "The Epidemiology of Lower Extremity Amputations in Diabetic Individuals," *Diabetes Care* 6, no. 1 (January/February 1983): 87.

2. National Center for Health Statistics, *Health, United States, 1990* (Hyattsville: Public Health Service, 1991), p. 139. In 1964, 42 percent of blacks but only 32 percent of whites had not seen a doctor in the past year. In 1989, the comparable figures were 23 percent and 22 percent. In 1964, 41 percent of people in families with incomes under $14,000 had not seen a doctor in the past year, compared to 26 percent of people in families with incomes greater than $50,000. In 1989, the comparable figures were 24 percent and 18 percent.

3. The Robert Wood Johnson Foundation, *Special Report 1986.*

4. National Center for Health Statistics, *Health, United States, 1990,* p. 137.

5. Emily J. Goodwin et al., "Access to Health Care: Medicare and the Poor Elderly," in *Poverty and Health in the United States,* ed. Melvin I. Krasner (New York: United Hospital Fund, 1989), p. 124.

6. I reviewed all available inpatient and outpatient medical records for Mrs. Jackson kept at Mount Sinai Hospital. The chronology of her experience on Coumadin is based on those records, as well as interviews with several physicians who participated in her care.

7. Mount Sinai home health nurses write progress notes each time they visit a patient; I reviewed Mrs. Jackson's notes.

8. William H. Herman et al., "Diabetes Mellitus," in *Closing the Gap: The Burden of Unnecessary Illness,* ed. Robert W. Amler and H. Bruce Dull (New York: Oxford University Press, 1987), p. 72.

9. Maureen I. Harris, "Non-Insulin Dependent Diabetes Mellitus in Black and White Americans," *Diabetes/Metabolism Reviews* 6, no. 2 (1990): 71–90.

10. Goodwin, "Access to Health Care: Medicare and the Poor Elderly," pp. 111–12

11. Letter to Hector Marino, M.D., from Mabel Patterson, manager, Health Care Standards Section, Bureau of Medical Quality Assurance, Illinois Department of Public Aid, 11 December 1991. Letter included findings of peer review and informed Dr. Marino that he would be placed on "continuous monitoring status."

12. Physician peer review data obtained through Freedom of Information Act request to Illinois Department of Public Aid, 24 March 1992.

13. Physician financial data obtained through Freedom of Information Act request, 24 March 1992.

14. James W. Fossett et al., *Medicaid Patients' Access to Office-Based Obstetricians* (Chicago: The Institute of Government and Public Affairs, 1989), p. 5.

CHAPTER 5

VIOLENCE AGAINST WOMEN

In April, 1999, the weekly magazine *Newsweek* devoted an issue entirely to women's affairs with a feature titled "Health For Life: What Every Woman Needs to Know." Seventy-one pages in length, it focused on topics ranging from cancer, pregnancy, and menopause, to mental health, exercise, and eating. But totally missing was any coverage of the biggest health threat to women—domestic violence. This curious absence of any coverage of violence as a women's health issue, which is unfortunately not unusual, directs resources and public concern to other health topics, while simultaneously contributing to the exclusion of domestic violence from public discussion.

Ironically, a woman is least safe in her own home. Domestic violence is the leading cause of injury for women between the ages of 15 and 44 (Grisso et al. 1991). National leaders have called it a public health problem (Novello et al. 1992) that knows no class, ethnicity, or sexual preference boundaries (Crenshaw 1991). Not even pregnant women are safe (Gazmararian et al. 1996).

Violence against women takes many forms, including murder, rape, battering and other physical injuries, emotional abuse, psychological manipulation, stalking, fondling, grabbing, insults and humiliation, obscene phone calls, restriction of activities, forced sterilization, unnecessary gynecological operations, sexual harassment in the workplace, and corporate violence.

Domestic violence against women occurs within a relationship with a friend or partner (current or former), which may or may not be a marriage, may be heterosexual or lesbian. Examples of domestic violence within a marriage are primarily used in this chapter, because historical and current legislation, case law, and public statements about the marital situation have enabled researchers to provide a well-documented and cohesive study on the subject. Since acquaintance rape is so closely related, it is also included in this chapter.

DOMESTIC VIOLENCE AGAINST WOMEN

Domestic violence is everywhere. Ordinary people in an ordinary neighborhood may suddenly have the tranquility of the day cut short.

> *On a glorious April morning, one year ago, as I stood in my driveway packing the car for a trip, I heard my neighbor, Alison, scream. I froze. More screams, three funny sounding pops, breaking glass, then silence. On her front step, thirty minutes after our daughters had left for school, the abusive boyfriend whose relationship she had severed the previous day, ended her life.*
>
> *...Yesterday morning, almost a year after Alison's murder, in the next town, a young woman was shot to death by her boyfriend, two days after she ended the relationship. On Thursday, he sent her roses, the paper said. On Friday, he killed her. (Furey 1997:viii)*

Although the above events are not typical—most women who are victims of domestic violence are not actually killed by their husbands and boyfriends—beginning our discussion with the death of women alerts us to the seriousness of a pervasive situation. Recent surveys estimate women suffer five million violent assaults and 500,000 rapes annually (Bachman and Saltzman 1995). Up to one third (22 to 35 percent) of women who go to the emergency room do so because of injury or stress from living in an abusive situation (Randall 1990). Feminists and others who understand these crimes know that they do not result from individual pathology, but rather from the structure of a social order that condones the exercise of power of men and their control over women.

Historical Roots

The laws in use during colonial times were largely English common law, and these were kept in place after the formation of the republic of the United States. The common-law doctrine of coverture, referring to the status of a woman under the cover (the protection) of a man, defined the legal status of a woman during marriage as follows:

> *According to the logic of coverture, women must be (or need to be) supported; in order to ensure that support, women marry and engage in household services for their husbands. "Marriage obligates a wife to perform household services in return for benefit of her husband's duty of support, thus absorbing the wife's entire worth into the marital unit while requiring the husband's economic participation in that unit only to the extent of support." (Johnson quoted in Marcus 1994:19)*

As such, coverture "confirmed and validated a sex-based locus of virtually unaccountable power and control in a marital relationship" (Marcus 1994:20). The husband was essentially granted permission to discipline his wife through the use of violence, and this allowance thereby "upheld the principle that sex-based power and control in the home was desirable as a matter of law and public policy" (Marcus 1994:21). By using common law as a legal precedent, some states passed laws specifically approving wife-beating. The first law in the United States to recognize a husband's right to control his wife with physical force was upheld in 1824 in a ruling by the Supreme Court of Mississippi. It permitted the husband "to exercise the right of moderate chastisement in cases of great emergency" (quoted in Kurz 1989:496). Other courts, such as those in Maryland and Massachusetts, followed with laws giving husbands the right to "correct" their wives, albeit in moderation (Kurz 1989:496).

Although in the 1800s some states began to pass reform measures that prohibited husbands from physically disciplining their wives, these laws had limited effect. They also unintentionally exposed how horrendous conditions had been. In 1871, an Alabama court ruled that "the privilege, ancient though it be, to beat her with a stick, to pull her hair, choke her, spit in her face or kick her about the floor, or to inflict upon her like indignities, is not now acknowledged by our law" (quoted in Kurz 1989:496). In 1874, North Carolina nullified the right of a husband to chastise his wife under any circumstances, but then in effect "nullified the nullification" (Jones 1994:20). The ruling helped to institutionalize a noninterference approach to violence by adding, "If no permanent injury has been inflicted, nor malice, cruelty nor dangerous violence shown by the husband, it is better to draw the curtain, shut out the public gaze, and leave the parties to forgive and forget" (quoted in Kurz 1989:496). Beating one's wife finally became illegal in all states in 1920 (Marcus 1994:22). However it took another sixty-one years for the first states (New Jersey and Massachusetts) to criminalize the rape of one's wife. Unfortunately, a huge gap often existed between what the law said and what was actually allowed to continue to happen, as is discussed next.

Institutional Support for Domestic Violence

With the passage of reform measures that outlawed the use of violence by husbands, how did domestic violence manage to continue during the twentieth century? The answer lies in the "persistence of patriarchal biases" of many state and social institutions that normalized, encouraged, and hid violence against women (Bart et al. 1989:434).

Religious and Social Service Agencies. If a woman turned to her pastor or religious counselor for support after being beaten, instead of hearing outrage about the situation and support for her point of view, she might hear about the importance of forgiveness, the role of a woman in the family, and learn of the religious view of sacrifice and the social view of woman as sacrificial (Adams 1993:70).

If the woman turned instead to a social service agency, she might find herself blamed for causing her beating. A study of social work in Massachusetts in the mid-1900s (Gordon 1988) found that social workers often faulted women for behaving in a way that encouraged wife-beating. Social work agency procedures were changed in the 1930s in ways that required the social worker to "map the problem onto the client who was present and influenceable" (Gordon 1988:281). This policy meant that the woman, who was obviously more likely than the man to seek help, became the client onto whom the problem was "mapped." Social workers found women "more introspective and self-critical—more productive in casework" (Gordon 1988:281). Men, in contrast, were defensive about their behavior and rarely willing to meet with social workers. Seemingly by default, marital violence became the burden the wife had to bear. In short, "instead of encouraging her laments about her husband, efforts were made to help her understand his needs and the strains he was under" (quoted in Gordon 1988:282). By the late 1940s in New York, this same sentiment was expressed in an agency manual on women in marital conflict when it "categorized problems under the headings: excessive dependence, the need to suffer, rejection of femininity, sex response, interfering relatives, cultural differences, and economic factors; four of the seven referred to women's faults, none to men's faults, and three to extramarital pressures" (Gordon 1988:282).

Women were up against a double bind: If they sought help by going to agencies that specialized in the dispensation of assistance, they were told to change their behavior—in essence, to accept their suffering as a part of the marriage covenant. If they chose instead *not* to seek help, their suffering continued unabated, although privately, out of the eyes of state and religious bureaucracies. Choosing the former route often ended up in humiliation, and opting for the latter route only served to make domestic violence all the more difficult to document; away from the public eye, it remained a shameful secret behind closed doors.

Social Science Research. Understanding domestic violence against women fared no better in the social science literature, or in other clinical settings. For thirty years—between 1939 and 1969—a major journal in the social science arena, *Journal of Marriage and the Family,* had not published one single article on family violence (Pleck 1987:182). When psychiatrists did conduct research on domestic violence, they found that the women, *not the men,* were the ones with psychiatric problems. At one clinic, psychiatrists were supposed to examine men referred by the court after being charged with assault and battery on their wives. The psychiatrists, like the social workers discussed earlier, found that the wives were more willing to talk than their husbands were. The psychiatrists' gaze thus was diverted to a "direct interest in exploring the wives' roles in the marital strife" (Snell, Rosenwald, and Robey 1964:108). They found that women who are beaten are typically ones who assumed all responsibility for managing money, paying bills, and disciplining children while resisting their drunken husbands' sexual advances. Their conclusion? "One cannot hope to understand the offender and his offense without having some understanding of the people with whom he has to deal" (Snell, Rosenwald, and Robey 1964:112). Instead of validating the valiant measures adopted by housewives who not only coped with abusive, drunk husbands, but also managed to successfully run a family, they found that the women who came to them displayed "aggressiveness, masculinity, frigidity, and masochism" (Snell, Rosenwald, and Robey 1964:111). In a stunning tour de force of twisted logic, the clinician-researchers were guilty of blaming the victim. Sadly, their mistakes were compounded by other researchers who declared battered women to be of low intelligence or mentally retarded (Pleck 1987:193).

Insights into domestic violence were further thwarted by the adoption of misleading terms due to the use of faulty methodologies to examine the problem. The terminology many social scientists used when describing assaults against women needlessly muddied the waters by "erasing" or "gender-neutralizing" these experiences with such concepts as "*family* violence" (Bart et al. 1989:431). This misnaming came about by the use of a highly controversial scale to measure violence, which found that women and men were equally violent and thus warranted the new phrase. The scale social scientists employed was controversial because it combined three different categories of violence—threatened, attempted, and actual violence—despite the obvious disparities. Furthermore, no data on actual injuries were included, and offensive behaviors were not distinguished from acts of self-defense (Dobash and Dobash 1988; Yllo 1988). These peculiar choices in methodology resulted in the conclusion that women were every bit as violent as men.

Health Care Settings. When battered women went to hospitals and clinics, they found health care providers misdiagnosing their problems due to a seeming blindness to any evidence of abuse. A study of one hospital emergency service found that doctors had labeled a fifth of the battered women with "quasi-psychiatric designations such as 'hysteric,' 'neurotic female,' 'well-known woman with vague complaints,' 'crock,' 'depressed, anxious lady' and 'hypochondriac'" (Kurz and Stark 1988:253) In one specific case of a woman who had been shot at by her husband, the health care system's response was to admit her to a psychiatric ward for anxiety. She was tested there by the resident psychiatrist who found her to rank high on the paranoia scale. The woman recalls, "I asked what that meant, and he said, 'It means you have an irrational fear that someone is out to get you.' My anxiety turned to depression. I was released to go back home a week later with a prescription for Valium" (quoted in Jones 1994:149).

Other studies have come to the same conclusion: Health care providers are very reluctant to categorize battered women as such. One doctor's audit of medical room records left him "astounded at the improbable stories his doctors were buying. The record was replete with accounts of mysterious seizures and falls" (Glazer 1993:173). In another examination of emergency room procedures, researchers found physicians using "disembodied language" to record what happened. The record would read, "was beaten to face and head with fist," "blow to head by stick with nail in it," "hit on left wrist by a jackhammer" (Warshaw 1989:512). Missing was "who hit her, what her relationship to the person was, what the circumstances of the attack were, or why she waited five hours to seek medical help" (Warshaw 1989:512). The medical model focuses on diagnosis, ignores social causes, and then releases the woman back into the same environment in which they were battered. "[D]ata from emergency department records show that a majority of women who are victims of domestic abuse are discharged without any arrangements made for their safety" (Randall 1990:939). The prevailing medical model, with its cyclopean focus on diagnosis, ignores social causes and does nothing to prevent future injury. Worse, clinical mistreatment becomes the second trauma for the battered woman (Stark and Flitcraft 1996).

Police and Court System. Women who turned to the police and the legal system found attitudes and procedures which often ignored, trivialized, or normalized the violence they had experienced. They encountered police departments that were "male-dominated and, especially among the rank and file, steeped in a 'macho style' masculinity" (Sparks 1997:38). The police officers themselves had a high rate of domestic abuse (Mignon and Holmes 1995). Many police believed that a marriage license was a "hitting license," detested going to "domestic disputes," delayed doing so, felt they were wasting their time, assumed the woman was also at fault, and believed that if it were really serious, the woman would leave (Binder and Meeker 1992:11; Ferraro 1989; Chaney and Saltzstein 1998:747–748).

Supported by federal grants, the police force in New York was trained in crisis intervention techniques. They were told not to treat domestic violence against women as a criminal matter so much as a problem of interpersonal communication, which was, of course, a private matter.

> *In practice, these changes had* negative *consequences for women victims of violent husbands and boyfriends. A victim became the subject to the same "cooling out" techniques as the assailant; she might be encouraged to "think about the good time" in the relationship, or about "how hard it would be on her own with the kids." Where this approach was used, women were given the message that they were equal participants in the dispute, and that they too were responsible for the violence. (Wermuth 1982:33)*

If the woman's complaint was taken to the prosecutor to be pursued by the criminal justice system, she could find herself revictimized, retelling her story to a prosecutorial staff more interested in hearing the sexual descriptions than in recording the needed evidence. Numerous studies, including those undertaken by the states of Minnesota, Nevada, and Utah, have shown that prosecutors, who have considerable discretion in deciding which cases warrant being brought to trial, choose not to pursue incidents of domestic violence that come to their attention. Prosecutors readily admit that they do not take domestic violence against women as seriously as other crimes, and many believe "that women provoke abuse against them, or even that women like being beaten" (Cahn 1992:162–163). According to state commission studies, prosecutors' attitudes and behavior actually inhibit prosecution because prosecutors "misunderstand legal options available to a victim, discourage the filing of complaints, and encourage mediation or reconciliation" (Cahn 1992:162).

On the occasions that domestic violence reports actually appeared before the court, there was no guarantee that the woman would be treated seriously. The Supreme Court of Georgia reported that one judge "'mocked,' 'humiliated,' and 'ridiculed' a female victim of repeated assaults and 'led the courtroom in laughter as the women left.' The woman's assailant—her estranged husband—subsequently murdered her" (cited in Jones 1994:36–37). A 1986, Boston, Massachusetts, case made front page news when the judge gave a battered woman a restraining order, then told her she did not need an escort to recover her belongings from her apartment, and commented that the woman's fears were "trivial." "The court has a lot more serious matters to contend with," he said. Five months after the hearing, the woman was brutally murdered by her husband. "Judicial harrassment of battered women" became a public issue (Ptacek 1999:4–5).

Whatever difficulties white, middle-class women had in being taken seriously, the same problems are geometrically compounded for minority and lesbian women. Access to legal recourse is absolutely dependent on the will of those in power who make judgments about the worthiness and credibility of those who face them (Frohmann, 1997). Furthermore, the victim must be willing to come forward. Lesbians, minority women, and the economically disadvantaged have many reasons to distrust police and the legal system, since "police have historically been agents in the oppression of people of color, poor people, and homosexuals" (Sparks 1997:39). They are less likely to report violence possibly because of a fear that the publicity could backfire on their community. For instance, lesbians may fear that discussions of lesbian rape may only solidify the community's marginalization of homosexuals. Minorities may worry that any media attention to domestic violence in their community may only serve to strengthen stereotypical views of sexuality and violence. This, in turn, may also lead to unusually harsh treatment of the perpetrator, especially if he is black (Richie and Kanuha 1993), since black men have never fared well in the criminal justice system.

Although the attitudes of the police and of the court system concerning domestic violence have arguably changed little since the time of these studies in the 1980s and early 1990s, the procedural protocols certainly have changed. In 1984, the actions of an abused wife, Tracey Thurman, made police take women's complaints more seriously, both in her hometown of Torrington, Connecticut, as well as in departments nationwide.

Tracey Thurman had a violent husband who publicly threatened to kill her and had already physically abused her to the point that she was able to get a court order restraining him from contacting her. When he again threatened her, she called the police, who repeatedly refused to offer assistance. When they finally did respond, they chose not to intervene, and instead stood idly by and watched as her husband slashed and stabbed her repeatedly with a knife, leaving her permanently disfigured and partially paralyzed. As paramedics lifted her into the ambulance, her husband attacked yet again. The police finally decided that his last action went beyond the pale, and so they belatedly took him into custody. Tracey Thurman sued the police for failing to give her equal protection under the law and was awarded nearly two million dollars. The Torrington police department woke up to what they considered a major problem—ignoring domestic violence could be costly (Sparks 1997).

The Thurman suit, combined with the widely quoted social science research by Sherman and Berk, which evaluated the effectiveness of varied police responses to domestic violence cases, led to the enactment of laws allowing police officers to arrest suspects without the victim's consent, or laws actually mandating police to make arrests. These laws and policy changes did not immediately change the behavior of police, however. In some jurisdictions, law enforcement officers were not pleased with the changes and only reluctantly and slowly altered their procedures (Mignon and Holmes 1995). Many other police agencies found they could still exercise discretion, even with so-called mandatory-arrest laws (Stalans and Lurigio 1995), because the police could declare that the conditions requiring mandatory arrest had not been met.

The mandatory-arrest laws clearly signaled a change in the level of tolerance for domestic violence and increased the number of arrests for this offense. But opinions differ over the effectiveness of the laws in stemming violent behavior (Buzawa and Buzawa 1996). The crackdown on violence in the home has had many unforeseen ramifications, such as an increased likelihood that the police will arrest *both* parties to the dispute (Martin 1997). Moreover, the early enthusiasm for the effectiveness of new laws has waned with the recognition of the complexity of certain scenarios that were, again, unforeseen. It appears that mandatory arrests reduce domestic violence primarily among married and employed batterers, but may backfire among those who are not squarely set in the middle of the status quo. Women who are minorities or economically disadvantaged may actually be placed in increased danger (Buzawa and Buzawa 1993). The mandatory arrest laws appear to be more effective in communities with feminist activists (Pence and Shepard 1988) who are closely involved in overseeing the actions of the police and courts. Finally, mandatory arrests may disempower battered women, giving them no voice in deciding what will happen (Sparks 1997).

The policy changes in police departments were accompanied by changes in the prosecutor's office. Whereas previously women had typically been required to sign a complaint against the abuser if prosecution were to proceed, policy changes in the criminal justice system led the prosecutor (rather than the victim) to sign off on the complaint, and made the victim a witness who could be summoned with subpoena power (Stalans and Lurigio 1995:393). All of these changes reduced the amount of discretion police and prosecutors had, and increased their power in handling domestic violence cases, but they did not completely eliminate discretion. Enduring attitudes about domestic violence continue to shape the actions of police and criminal justice agencies.

Popular Culture. Popular culture adds another layer of insensitivity to violence against women. Some analysts refer to a "rape culture" that encourages male sexual aggression and supports violence against women. "A rape culture condones physical and emotional terrorism against women *as the norm*" (Buchwald, Fletcher, and Roth 1993:vii; emphasis theirs).

A direct confirmation of the rape culture can be seen in the publishing world, which promotes domestic violence against women with sex manuals that conflate sex and violence. For instance, in a popular sex manual that saw forty-five printings in the United States between 1930 and 1965, the author wrote,

> *What both man and woman, driven by obscure primitive urges, wish to feel in the sexual act, is the essential force of* maleness, *which expresses itself in a sort of violent and absolute* possession *of the woman. And so both of them can and do exult in a certain degree of male aggression and dominance—whether actual or apparent—which proclaims this essential force. (quoted in Jones 1994:107)*

Music, movies, video games, and now chat rooms on the Internet glorify male violence. A not-atypical rap song's lyrics state that seeing a beautiful woman's body causes the speaker to think about committing a violent rape, using a knife to force submission (Jones 1994: 118).

The use of violence as a training device for American servicemen seems appropriate until one hears the lyrics of a popular marching chant at the U.S. Naval Academy at Annapolis. Midshipmen run in formation during their training exercises while chanting, "Rape, Maim, Kill babies. Rape, Maim, Kill Babies, Oorah!" (Burke 1997:146).

Naming the Problem

This social construction of violence against women was little contested until the feminist movement of the 1970s. Feminists and others were responsible for creating an antirape movement that in turn provided crisis centers, education programs, and advocacy for women throughout the United States (Schechter 1982). The first rape crisis center opened in Washington, D.C., in 1972 (Donat and D'Emilio 1992), and the first battered women's shelter opened a year later in Arizona (Britton 1997:487). As women met and talked about their experiences, they realized that rapists were not usually men who jumped out from behind bushes, as depicted on television, but acquaintances and husbands (Warshaw 1994). Buttons saying "87% know" refer to the fact that 87 percent of the assailants in rape and sexual assault cases are known to the victim (Bachman and Saltzman 1995).

As women examined the reasons for their oppression, they began to realize that "the personal is political." The violence women were experiencing was not personal—not peculiar only to themselves—but political, "constructed socially as a result of the hierarchical gender system in our culture" (Donat and D'Emilio 1992:14), and provided a means for men to control women (Bart et al. 1989:435). Although today these statements may sound obvious, they came as a revelation back in 1972 (Schechter 1982:34).

The antirape movement served to raise the consciousness of women throughout the social spectrum and provided a platform that added cohesiveness to the women's movement. The "parameters of what women would individually and collectively tolerate" (Schechter 1982:34) were redefined. Women's problems were collectively addressed for perhaps the first time in terms everyone understood. The problems were named. Women could now speak of and understand rape, date rape, domestic violence against women, wife-beating, and, later, marital rape and separation assault (Mahoney 1991). People were now able to talk about and treat their experiences with legitimacy, challenging other social constructions that had obfuscated the problem with euphemistic language that bore little semblance to reality.

The antirape movement and the battered-women's movement were incredibly successful social movements. Women not only provided safe places for other women and raised consciousness, but they also pressured legislatures to pass laws that served the interests of women, and they made the police, the courts, and the health care settings adopt a more proactive stance in their treatment of women. In 1994, the Violence Against Women Act became law. It established a civil rights remedy for gender-based violence, allowing the victim to sue for compensatory and punitive damages and injunctive relief.

The very term *domestic violence against women* still sits uneasily with many women (Naranch

1997). Some argue that the inclusion of the word "domestic" fails to convey the horror of the event (Jones 1994:81). It softens the blow of the violence, in much the same way the phrase "ethnic cleansing" understates genocide. Furthermore, the term fails to name the aggressor (just as the emergency room doctors did). For the time being, however, domestic violence against women is the most widely accepted label for this heinous behavior.

Feminists also made it clear that asking the question, "Why doesn't she leave?" was not really a question, but a judgment (Jones 1994) about what the woman should have done. Moreover, it assumed that leaving was a possibility. Research on the separation period illustrates how tragically mistaken that assumption is—separating can be a very dangerous act (Mahoney 1991). Equally important, the question also deflected attention from the real issue: Why did he batter?

Complex problems that are deeply rooted in the social fabric are not easily resolved by simply pushing through a rash of new legislation. Despite the newfound visibility of domestic violence, the funding for shelters, and the reform measures enacted in many institutions, many activists claim that the state has not addressed the real sources of domestic violence. Thus, while "the state funds battered women's shelters, it has failed to provide women with the economic resources needed for their long-term empowerment" (Daniels 1997:1).

Some of the stereotypical images of battered women refuse to go away. People still ask, "Why doesn't she leave?" The reading included in this section provides an excellent example of how people have been conditioned to think in this fashion (Jones 1994). Women are still blamed as being psychologically defective for the beatings they receive. The battered-women's syndrome, used as a defense by some women accused of killing their abusive husbands, portrays a passive woman of diminished capacity and low self-esteem because of being beaten. Thus, this syndrome is constructed more as an excuse, a pathology, than as a justification for self-defense. It reinforces "traditional patriarchal assumptions that women are unable or unwilling to take care of themselves" (Daniels 1997:1).

Controversy surrounds many of the so-called gains in protecting battered women. Though these issues are beyond the scope of this chapter, it is important to note them. Debates about mandatory arrest policies (noted above) persist, as do debates over mandatory reporting by health care providers. The role of pornography as a causal factor in the rape of women remains a heatedly discussed topic. On a more philosophical level, writers argue about the appropriateness of depending on the "oppressor state" for protection from male violence, and the wisdom of allowing the state to enter the private space of the home (Collective 1997).

SEXUAL HARASSMENT IN THE WORKPLACE

Nearly simultaneous with antirape and domestic violence actions in the 1970s, major strides were made in defining sexual harassment in the workplace. In 1974, a legal scholar, Catharine MacKinnon, began work on her book *Sexual Harassment of Working Women,* in which she argues that sexual harassment is a form of sex discrimination that should be actionable under Title VII of the 1964 Civil Rights Act. This act prohibits discrimination based on race, color, religion, sex, or national origin. The resulting regulations, which went into effect after the publication of her book and the attendant publicity it received, were passed in 1980 by the Equal Employment Opportunity Commission (EEOC). The EEOC defines illegal behaviors as unwelcome sexual advances, requests for sexual favors, and other verbal or physical conduct of a sexual nature "when submission to or rejection of this conduct explicitly or implicitly affects an individual's employment, unreasonably interferes with an individual's work performance or creates an intimidating, hostile, or offensive work environment" (EEOC 1999).

Under these guidelines, sexual harassment is much more than, say, a woman being whistled at by a construction worker as she passes by on her way to the office. It is the eroticization of domination, an aggressive behavior toward women that clearly shows they are being treated as sexual objects (Greenberg, Minow, and Roberts 1998a:285). And yet, because the culture at large tolerates such actions, similar behavior in the workplace is often made out to seem trivial (Estrich 1991).

Once this behavior was named, studies of sexual harassment against women showed how ubiquitous it was. Over 50 percent of women reported sexual harassment in the workplace (Paludi and Barickman 1991). Allegations of harassment occurred in all types of work settings, from the law offices of a future United States Supreme Court justice, to the White House. The first United States Supreme Court case involved a bank teller; however, women in blue collar jobs reported sexual harassment, as did professional women, including female doctors (Frank, Brogan, and Schiffman 1998; and see Chapter 15 on medical students and doctors). Sexual harassment of women in the military came to light with reports of the horrendous actions at the 1991 Tailhook convention of naval fighter pilots, where women were groped and fondled as they were passed down a gauntlet of drunken, male, naval aviators (Pope 1993).

CORPORATE VIOLENCE AGAINST WOMEN

The third form of violence against women is corporate violence, defined here as the marketing of products targeted at women when those products have known or suspected harmful effects. Most of the examples of such corporate violence are products having to do with reproduction. Although men, too, suffer from callous decisions of corporate policy makers who are more concerned with the bottom line than with the health of Americans, the history of tort litigation suggests that products made for women have generated the most problems (Steinman 1992).

The list is long. We will examine two in some detail, but first, some other products deserve a brief note. Early birth control pills contained high concentrations of hormones that caused blood clots, depression, and death. These product flaws went unacknowledged by the major pharmaceutical companies until Barbara Seaman, then a writer for *Ladies Home Journal* and *Brides Magazine,* made the connection between women's complaints and their use of the pill. She wrote a book detailing the pill's danger to women, and lobbied for change. Another harmful product was diethylstilbestrol (DES), a synthetic estrogen. DES was enthusiastically promoted as a preventative for miscarriage by companies who were fully aware of its potential dangers when used by pregnant women and of prior research showing it was potentially carcinogenic (Dutton 1988). Doctors and pharmaceutical companies have promoted other products, such as diet pills, (e.g., the recent Phen Fen), despite health concerns; and they promoted silicone breast implants, despite internal company memos suggesting caution (Chapter 8).

The two products we will examine in some detail are Rely tampons and the Dalkon Shield. Rely tampons were introduced in the early 1970s by Procter & Gamble. Already dominant in the diaper business, Procter & Gamble set out to capture the tampon sector with the new superabsorbent Rely tampons, the competitive answer to the leading brand, Tampax. Rely was so powerful that it "could absorb an entire menstrual flow in one tampon" (quoted in Swasy 1996:280). Almost immediately, Rely users complained to Procter & Gamble of vomiting and diarrhea. The company should have anticipated that its new synthetic approach to menstruation control would generate complaints; one internal company memo discussed Rely's cancer-causing components and also noted that "Rely affected the natural microorganisms and bacteria found in the vagina" (Swasy 1996:282). Complaints escalated with reports of toxic shock syndrome (high fever, vomiting, rash, difficulty breathing, low blood pressure) reaching the Center for Disease Control (CDC). Despite these clear indications of serious problems, Procter & Gamble continued to aggressively market Rely, distributing millions of free samples. At one point, it considered placing a warning label on the package, but did not follow through. Increasing pressure from the CDC and the Food and Drug Administration (FDA), together with reports of users of Rely who had died, belatedly led to a recall of Rely tampons (Swasy 1996).

The Dalkon Shield provides a second example of corporate violence. The Dalkon Shield was an intrauterine birth control device (IUD) produced by the A.H. Robins Company, Inc., in the 1960s and 1970s. Company records and interviews indicate that male, corporate decision makers pushed to produce the Shield quickly and at the lowest possible price. Like Procter & Gamble, A.H. Robins wanted to capture a highly profitable niche in the marketplace for contraceptives. In the process, it disregarded early evidence that the device was hazardous to the health of women. The company's indifference was particularly disturbing since the company was fully aware of the source of the danger—the type of string attached to the shield, a feature designed to minimize the discomfort experienced by male partners during intercourse. The result was the widespread distribution of a product that caused serious physical harm to thousands of women. An estimated 235,000 American women were injured by the device, including women who suffered permanent infertility and had to undergo complete hysterectomies. Twenty American women died. The judge who presided over the class-action suit brought against A.H. Robins clearly noted the connections between for-profit motives and antifemale sentiments:

> *Gentlemen, the results of these activities and attitudes on your part have been catastrophic.... [N]one of you has faced up to the fact that more than nine thousand women have made claims that they gave up part of their womanhood so that your company might prosper.... I dread to think what would have been the consequences if your victims had been men rather than women, women who seem through some strange quirk of our society's mores to be expected to suffer pain, shame, and humiliation.... [Y]ou planted in the bodies of these women instruments of death, of mutilation, of disease.... The only conceivable reasons you have not recalled this product are that it would hurt your balance sheet and alert women who already have been harmed that you may be liable for their injuries. You have taken the bottom line as your guiding beacon, and the low road as your route. This is corporate irresponsibility at its meanest. (Mintz 1985:265–267)*

Robins stopped sales of the device in 1974, though it did not recall Dalkon Shields that were already on the market. A tide of lawsuits by injured women led the company to file for bankruptcy protection. Settlements were meager and slow in coming. Most women who sued received $725 or less. The final payments came in 1996 ("Dalkon" 1996).

Despite media attention that gives the impression that cancer, eating disorders, and depression are the major health problems of women, violence is actually the biggest health threat women face. As this chapter has demonstrated, violence comes in many forms: physical and psychological abuse by a friend, partner, or stranger; sexual harassment on the job; and injuries from the callous behavior of corporations. The injuries caused by violence are profound both for the individual women affected and for the community. The violence is not personal with meaningful solutions on the individual level; rather, it is embedded in our culture and political structure and requires more fundamental changes.

SEXUAL TERRORISM

CAROLE J. SHEFFIELD

The right of men to control the female body is a cornerstone of patriarchy. It is expressed by their efforts to control pregnancy and childbirth and to define female health care in general. Male opposition to abortion is rooted in opposition to female autonomy. Violence and the threat of violence against females represent the need of patriarchy to deny that a woman's body is her own property and that no one should have access to it without her consent. Violence and its corollary, fear, serve to terrorize females and to maintain the patriarchal definition of woman's place.

The word *terrorism* invokes images of furtive organizations of the far right or left, whose members blow up buildings and cars, hijack airplanes, and murder innocent people in some country other than ours. But there is different kind of terrorism, one that so pervades our culture that we have learned to live with it as though it were the natural order of things. Its targets are females—of all ages, races, and classes. It is the common characteristic of rape, wife battery, incest, pornography, harassment, and all forms of sexual violence. I call it *sexual terrorism* because it is a system by which males frighten and, by frightening, control and dominate females.

The concept of terrorism captured my attention in an "ordinary" event. One afternoon I collected my laundry and went to a nearby laundromat. The place is located in a small shopping center on a very busy highway. After I had loaded and started the machines, I became acutely aware of my environment. It was just after 6:00 p.m. and dark; the other stores were closed; the laundromat was brightly lit; and my car was the only one in the lot. Anyone passing by could readily see that I was alone and isolated. Knowing that rape is a crime of opportunity, I became terrified. I wanted to leave and find a laundromat that was busier, but my clothes were well into the wash cycle, and besides, I felt I was being "silly," "paranoid." The feeling of terror persisted, so I sat in my car, windows up, and doors locked. When the wash was completed, I dashed in, threw the clothes into the dryer, and ran back out to my car. When the clothes were dry, I tossed them recklessly into the basket and hurriedly drove away to fold them in the security of my home.

Although I was not victimized in a direct, physical way or by objective or measurable standards, I felt victimized. It was, for me, a terrifying experience. I felt controlled by an invisible force. I was angry that something as commonplace as doing laundry after a day's work jeopardized my well-being. Mostly I was angry at being unfree: a hostage of a culture that, for the most part, encourages violence against females, instructs men in the methodology of sexual violence, and provides them with ready justification for their violence. I was angry that I could be victimized by being "in the wrong place at the wrong time." The essence of terrorism is that one never knows when is the wrong time and where is the wrong place.

Following my experience at the laundromat, I talked with my students about terrorization. Women students began to open up and reveal terrors that they had kept secret because of embarrassment: fears of jogging alone, dining alone, going to the movies alone. One woman recalled feelings of terror in her adolescence when she did child care for extra money. Nothing had ever happened and she had not been afraid of anyone in particular, but she had felt a vague terror when being driven home late at night by the man of the house.

The men listened incredulously and then demanded equal time. The harder they tried the more they realized how very different—qualitatively, quantitatively, and contextually—their fears were. All agreed that, while they experience fear in a violent society, they did not experience terror; nor did they experience fear of rape or sexual mutilation. They felt more in control, either from a psychophysical sense of security that they could defend themselves or from a confidence in being able to determine wrong places and times. All the women admitted fear and anxiety when walking to their cars on the campus, especially after an evening class or activity. None of the men experience fear on campus at any time. The men could be rather specific in describing when they were afraid: in Harlem, for example, or in certain parts of downtown Paterson, New Jersey—places that have a reputation for violence. But these places could either be avoided or, if not, the men felt capable of self-protective action. Above all, male students said that they *never* feared being attacked simply because they were male. They *never* feared going to a movie or to dinner alone. Their daily activities were not characterized by a concern for their physical integrity.

As I read the literature on terrorism it became clear that both sexual violence and nonviolent sexual intimidation could be better understood as terrorism. For example, although an act of rape, an unnecessary hysterectomy, and the publishing of *Playboy* magazine appear to be quite different, they are in fact more similar than dissimilar. Each is based on fear, hostility, and a need to dominate women. Rape is an act of aggression and possession, not of sexuality. Unnecessary hysterectomies are extraordinary abuses of power rooted in man's concept of woman as primarily a reproductive being and in his need to assert power over reproduction. *Playboy,* like all forms of pornography, attempts to control women through the power of definition. Male pornographers define women's sexuality for their male customers. The basis of pornography is men's fantasies about women's sexuality.

COMPONENTS OF SEXUAL TERRORISM

The literature on terrorism does not provide a precise definition.[1] Mine is taken from Hacker, who says that "terrorism aims to frighten, and by frightening, to dominate and control."[2] Writers agree more readily on the characteristics and functions of terrorism than on a definition. This analysis will focus on five components to illuminate the similarities of and distinctions between sexual terrorism and political terrorism. The five components are: ideology, propaganda, indiscriminate and amoral violence, voluntary compliance, and society's perception of the terrorist and the terrorized.

An *ideology* is an integrated set of beliefs about the world that explains the way things are and provides a vision of how they ought to be. Patriarchy, meaning the "rule of the fathers," is the ideological foundation of sexism in our society. It asserts the superiority of males and the inferiority of females. It also provides the rationale for sexual terrorism. The taproot of patriarchy is the masculine/warrior ideal. Masculinity must include not only a proclivity for violence but also all those characteristics necessary for survival: aggression, control, emotional reserve, rationality, sexual potency, etc. Marc Feigen Fasteau, in *The Male Machine,* argues that "men are brought up with the idea that there ought to be some part of them, under control until released by necessity, that thrives on violence. This capacity, even affinity, for violence, lurking beneath the surface of every real man, is supposed to represent the primal untamed base of masculinity."[3]

Propaganda is the methodical dissemination of information for the purpose of promoting a particular ideology. Propaganda, by definition, is biased or even false information. Its purpose is to present one point of view on a subject and to discredit opposing points of view. Propaganda is essential to the conduct of terrorism. According to Francis Watson, in *Political Terrorism: The Threat and the Response,* "Terrorism must not be defined only in terms of violence, but also in terms of propaganda. The two are in operation together. Violence of terrorism is a coercive means for attempting to influence the thinking and actions of people. Propaganda is a persuasive means for doing the same thing."[4] The propaganda of sexual terrorism is found in all expressions of the popular culture: films, television, music, literature, advertising, pornography. The propaganda of sexual terrorism is also found in the ideas of patriarchy expressed in science, medicine, and psychology.

The third component, which is common to all forms of political terrorism, consists of "indiscriminateness, unpredictability, arbitrariness, ruthless destructiveness and amorality."[5] Indiscriminate violence and amorality are also at the heart of sexual terrorism. Every female is a potential target of violence—at any age, at any time, in any place. In her study of rape, Susan Brownmiller argues that rape is "nothing more or less than a conscious process of intimidation by which all men keep all women in a state of fear."[6] Further, as we shall see, amorality pervades sexual violence. Child molesters, incestuous fathers, wife beaters, and rapists often do not understand that they have done anything wrong. Their views are routinely shared by police officers, lawyers, and judges, and crimes of sexual violence are rarely punished in American society.

The fourth component of the theory of terrorism is "voluntary compliance." The institutionalization of a system of terror requires the development of mechanisms other than sustained violence to achieve its goals. Violence must be employed to maintain terrorism, but sustained violence can be costly and debilitating. Therefore, strategies for ensuring a significant degree of voluntary compliance must be developed. Sexual terrorism is maintained to a great extent by an elaborate system of sex-role socialization that in effect instructs men to be terrorists in the name of masculinity and women to be victims in the name of femininity.

Sexual and political terrorism differ in the final component, perception of the terrorist and the victim. In political terrorism we know who is the terrorist and who is the victim. We may condemn or condone the terrorist depending on our political views, but we sympathize with the victim. In sexual terrorism, however, we blame the victim and excuse the offender. We believe that the offender either is "sick" and therefore in need of our compassion or is acting out normal male impulses....

CONCLUSION

Sexual terrorism is a system that functions to maintain male supremacy through actual and implied violence. Violence against the female body (rape, battery, incest, and harassment) and the perpetuation of fear of violence form the basis of patriarchal power. Both violence and fear are functional. Without the power to intimidate and to punish, the domination of women in all spheres of society—political, social, and economic—could not exist.

NOTES

1. Yonah Alexander, "Terrorism and the Mass Media: Some Considerations," in Yonah Alexander, David Carlton, and Paul Wilkinson, eds., *Terrorism: Theory and Practice* (Boulder, Colo.: Westview Press, 1979), 159; Ernest Evans, *Calling a Truce to Terrorism: The American Response to International Terrorism* (Westport, Conn.: Greenwood Press, 1979), 3; Charmers Johnson, "Perspectives on Terrorism," in Walter Laquer, ed., *The Terrorism Reader* (Philadelphia: Temple University Press, 1978), 273; Thomas P. Thornton, "Terror as a Weapon of Political Agitation," in H. Eckstein, ed., *The Internal War* (New York: Free Press, 1964), 73; Eugene Walter, *Terror and Resistance* (New York: Oxford University Press, 1969), 6; Francis M. Watson, *Political Terrorism: The Threat and the Response* (Washington, D.C.: R. B. Luce Co., 1976), 15; Paul Wilkinson, *Political Terrorism* (New York: John Wiley and Sons, 1974), 11.

2. Frederick R. Hacker, *Crusaders, Criminals and Crazies: Terrorism in Our Time* (New York: W. W. Norton and Co., 1976), xi.

3. Marc Feigen Fasteau, *The Male Machine* (New York: McGraw-Hill Book Co., 1974), 144.

4. Watson, 15

5. Wilkinson, 17.

6. Susan Brownmiller, *Against Our Will: Men, Women and Rape* (New York: Simon and Schuster, 1975), 5.

THE "RAPE" OF MR. SMITH

ANONYMOUS

The law discriminates against rape victims in a manner that would not be tolerated by victims of any other crime. In the following example, a holdup victim is asked questions similar in form to those usually asked of a victim of rape:

INTERVIEWER: Mr. Smith, you were held up at gunpoint on the corner of 16th and Locust?

VICTIM: Yes.

INT: Did you struggle with the robber?

V: No.

INT: Why not?

V: He was armed.

INT: Then you made a conscious decision to comply with his demands rather than resist?

V: Yes.

INT: Did you scream? Cry out?

V: No. I was afraid to.

INT: I see. Have you ever been held up before?

V: No.

INT: Have you ever given money away?

V: Yes, of course.

INT: And you did so willingly?

V: What are you getting at?

INT: Well, let's put it like this, Mr. Smith. You've given away money in the past—in fact, you have quite a reputation for philanthropy. How can we be sure that you weren't *contriving* to have your money taken from you by force?

V: Listen, if I wanted—

INT: Never mind. What time did this holdup take place, Mr. Smith?

V: About 11:00 P.M.

INT: You were out on the streets at 11:00 P.M.? Doing what?

V: Just walking.

INT: Just walking? You know that it's dangerous being out on the street that late at night. Weren't you aware that you could have been held up?

V: I hadn't thought about it.

INT: What were you wearing at the time, Mr. Smith?

V: Let's see. A suit. Yes, a suit.

INT: An *expensive* suit?

V: Well, yes.

INT: In other words, Mr. Smith, you were walking around the streets late at night in a suit that practically *advertised* the fact that you might be a good target for some easy money, isn't that so? I mean, if we didn't know better, Mr. Smith, we could even think that you were asking for this to happen, mightn't we?

V: Look, can't we talk about the past history of the guy who *did* this to me?

INT: I'm afraid not, Mr. Smith. I don't think you would want to violate his rights, now would you?

WHY DOESN'T SHE LEAVE?

ANN JONES

When we look again at the facts—millions of women battered every year, a woman battered every few seconds, thousands of women murdered every year by the men they live with—and when we consider what a fundamental right it is to be able to live, just to *be,* free of harm inside one's own skin, then the next question should be obvious: why hasn't this violence been stopped? Any reasonable person has to ask: What can we do to prevent it?

But as it turns out, that's not the question reasonable people ask. We ask instead: *Why doesn't she leave?*

Take Dan Rather, for example. For the CBS network show "48 Hours" he interviewed Tracey Thurman in her kitchen in Torrington, Connecticut, in 1988. Charles Thurman, who had been sentenced to twenty years for his attempt to kill Tracey, was scheduled to become eligible for parole in 1990, and Tracey Thurman explained to Rather how she felt about the possibility of his release. "I know that he's going to come back after me, and that frightens me," she said.

> *And it just scares me to think that I'm going to have to live like I lived for eight months, when I was going through the separation. I mean, a nervous wreck; my child I didn't allow to go outside...for his own protection. And I know one day I'm going to have to go through all that again. Hopefully this time they'll be there on time, and they'll be able to protect me. Hopefully. But I know that he's determined, and I know he has stated right in the courtroom, and his father got on the stand and said that he said that he will finish the job. And he has stated in several things that both of us can't live in this world, and he's not going to be the one to go. What frightens me most is the fear that—him ever hurting my child. That scares me. Just the thought of...If he was ever to get to me, I would rather him just—I mean, then finish the job then, because I could never deal with another beating like this. You know, I mean, I—how much more handicapped could I be?*[1]

Since that interview Tracey Thurman has learned to live with fear, for Buck Thurman was released in April 1991 to a Connecticut halfway house, having served seven years and ten months of his twenty-year sentence. He was placed on closely supervised probation for five years.[2] His parental rights were terminated. Tracey Thurman, who still lives in Torrington, has become a compelling and articulate voice for battered women in Connecticut, but she can no longer travel freely around the state as she could when Buck was behind bars. Testifying before the Senate judiciary Committee in December 1990 on behalf of the proposed Violence Against Women Act, Tracey Thurman said, "Because of what I've experienced with him, I know he's going to find me."[3] Now, day in, day out, with her second husband and her son, Tracey Thurman Motuzick must plan always for her safety.[4]

But when Dan Rather interviewed Tracey Thurman, he had a suggestion, one he perhaps guessed would occur to thousands of his viewers. "Why not move away?" he asked. "Why not get a long, long way?"[5]

The familiar question. Why doesn't she just walk away?—this disfigured and terribly handicapped woman whom the television viewers have watched struggling with her physical therapy exercises and the monumental task of frying an egg? Why doesn't she take her little boy and just leave? Again.

Tracey Thurman had an answer. She said: "Why should I? You know...I grew up here.... My family is here, my support is here.... I can go to another state, but even if I was in Hawaii and I had heard that he was getting out, my son would still be glued to me. I mean I would be scared to death. I mean, if he really wants me that bad—it's awful morbid—but if he really wants me that bad, he's that determined, he's going to find me no matter where I go. And I feel as though here, the Torrington police department don't want to mess up again. They don't want to look like they made themselves look the first time."[6]

But of course it's the question, not the chilling and sensible answer, that sticks in the mind. It suggests that Tracey Thurman's life is entirely in her own hands, that the violence of the man she once married, the man she left, is *her* problem, *her* responsibility. What does it mean to "leave"? How far does a woman have to go? And how many times?

Despite the immense achievements of the battered women's movement in the past fifteen years, those who work to stop violence against women—those who staff the hotlines and the shelters and the legal service centers, those who press to make law enforcement and criminal justice act responsibly, those who lobby for legislative reform—know that the next time a woman is battered in the United States (which is to say within the next twelve seconds) few people will ask: What's wrong with that man? What makes him think he can get away with that? Is he crazy? Did the cops arrest him? Is he in jail? When will he be prosecuted? Is he likely to get a serious sentence? Is she getting adequate police protection? Are the children provided for? Did the court evict him from her house? Does she need any other help? Medical help maybe, or legal aid? New housing? Temporary financial aid? Child support?

No, the first question, and often the only question, that leaps to mind is: *Why doesn't she leave?*

This question, which we can't seem to stop asking, is not a *real* question. It doesn't call for an answer; it makes a judgment. It mystifies. It transforms an immense social problem into a personal transaction, and at the same time pins responsibility squarely on the victim. It obliterates both the terrible magnitude of violence against women and the great achievements of the movement against it. It simultaneously suggests two ideas, both of them false: that help is readily available to all *worthy* victims (which is to say, victims who leave), and that *this* victim is not one of them.

So powerful and dazzling is this question that someone always tries to answer it. And the answer given rarely is the simple truth you find in the stories of formerly battered women: She does leave. She is leaving. She left. No, so mystifying is the question that someone always tries to explain why she doesn't leave even *after she has left.* This exchange takes place remarkably often on television talk shows and news programs—as it did on "48 Hours"—heavily influencing the way the public thinks about battered women. Let me give you another example.

In October 1987 the local New York City affiliate of the CBS television network included in the nightly news a segment on the case of Karen Straw, a twenty-nine-year-old woman about to stand trial for murder. Karen Straw had left her husband Clifton in 1984, after a three-year marriage, and moved with her two children to a welfare hotel. She wanted a divorce, but she couldn't afford one. For more than two years, her husband harassed and beat her although she obtained orders of protection from the court and tried at least ten times to have him arrested and prosecuted. In December 1986 he broke into her room, beat her, raped her at knifepoint in front of the children, and threatened to kill her. She got hold of a kitchen knife and stabbed him. She was charged with second degree murder, the heaviest charge the state could bring against her since New York reserves first degree murder charges for murders of police officers and prison guards.[7] The WCBS report filed by reporter Bree Walker, a woman, showed footage of Karen Straw, the Queens courthouse where she was to be tried, and short bites of three interviews prerecorded separately with Michael Dowd, a prominent attorney who had volunteered to defend Straw; Madelyn Diaz, a woman previously acquitted of all charges after killing her assaultive husband (a police officer);[8] and me. Introduced by Jim Jensen, the anchorman, the segment went like this.

JIM JENSEN: This is a problem society has never really learned to deal with: women who are physically abused by their husbands. This evening we take a closer look at this problem and the way some women are finally getting some help. Bree Walker has more.

BREE WALKER (*REPORTER*): Jim, it's a painful closer look at this black eye on society, how the cuts and bruises suffered by women with abusive husbands are usually overlooked, but when women finally stop suffering in silence and turn to desperate measures like murder, no one can overlook that, especially in court where once again the plea of self-defense will be tested.

Tomorrow this woman, Karen Straw, faces the trial of her life. The charge: second degree murder. The penalty: life in prison. Karen Straw allegedly killed her husband after escaping to a shabby welfare apartment where she lived with her two children. She says she turned a knife on him after he broke in and raped her at knifepoint. After two years of repeated attacks, her attorney says she had no other way out.

MICHAEL DOWD (*ATTORNEY*): She went to the family court. She had him arrested in the criminal court. She called the police numerous times. She moved away from him. And nothing that she did stopped him from coming back, beating her, threatening her, hospitalizing her, raping her.

ANN JONES: She'd done everything a battered woman can do to get out of that situation and to get the criminal justice system to be responsive and responsible for her safety. But it still didn't work. They still didn't protect her.

WALKER: …Both [Jones] and Straw's attorney agree: the only protection our society provided Karen was a flimsy paper shield.

DOWD: She was given a piece of paper—what we call an order of protection. It's as if we gave her a crucifix to defend herself against a vampire.

WALKER: The story of Karen Straw begins to unfold here tomorrow at her trial in Supreme Court. But it's a story that's hardly unique. She's only one of many battered wives who turn to violence as a last defense. A common thread ties many of these women together. They are victims not only of abusive husbands but of weak criminal justice, of a system that again and again failed them until finally it was too late. We've seen it in newspapers and on television. A movie called "The Burning Bed" told the story of Francine Hughes, a Michigan housewife who poured gasoline around the bed of her husband and lit a match, leaving him to die in the flames. And two years ago a Bronx woman said her husband left her no alternative.

MADELYN DIAZ: I just remembered what he had threatened me. He said if I didn't change my mind in the next few hours that he would kill me and the baby.

WALKER: Sympathetic juries in both cases found these women not guilty, but experts say cases like these shouldn't have to even go that far.

JONES: Battered women are denied protection. Battering men are not arrested. They're not locked up for any substantial length of time.

DOWD: There's no question in my mind that Karen Straw was acting justifiably. She defended herself in her own home. Hopefully twelve honest people will give her something that the professionals couldn't—and that's some fairness and justice and a chance to live her life.

WALKER: The one positive note to this tragic song that plays too often is that support [systems] like victim service agencies, hospitals, and church outreach groups seem to be making a difference. The numbers show women murdering husbands and boyfriends is the only type of homicide that has in fact decreased in the last ten years. So perhaps we can say that where the courts have left off, individuals have picked up.

That ended Walker's prerecorded report. Wrapping it up, anchorman Jensen leaned toward reporter Walker, sitting beside him in the studio, and asked the standard question, the one everybody always asks: Why didn't she leave? Jensen phrased it this way: "Why would one murder her husband instead of just walking away?" The question was particularly remarkable, for it didn't match Bree Walker's report or the circumstances of Karen Straw's life at all.

But even more remarkable was reporter Walker's reply. As though the facts lay not in her own report but in the anchorman's irrelevant question, Bree Walker began to explain why Karen Straw, a woman who *had* walked away, had not. "There are a lot of different reasons psychologists say—helplessness, dependence, a lot of different reasons. A lot of women feel…"

Jensen interrupted: "Well, if they're dependent on them, when they kill 'em, they've lost their dependence, haven't they?" He sounded angry, as if he were scolding Walker for her point of view.

Walker, looking startled, responded, "Well, certainly. Yes. It's an ugly, ugly confusing problem." There was a moment's awkward airspace before anchorwoman Carol Martin jumped in. "Well, from that subject we'll move on," she said. "Still ahead, we'll talk about the rain...."[9]

But Jensen's question still hung in the air: "Why would one murder her husband instead of just walking away?" It enveloped the story in a fog of mystification. Clifton Straw's violence and terrorism disappeared in that puff of rhetoric, utterly overlooked. Vanished too was the public issue reporter Walker had presented, magically replaced by the personal problem of another dumb woman. Viewers did not have to question the failure of the police and courts to protect this woman; they could think instead that Karen Straw might simply have walked away. Just when viewers were beginning to feel indignant on her behalf, they could say to themselves instead: "How stupid of her. Why didn't she think of that?"

I told this story about the TV program to a very smart, very successful network television producer, a woman, of my acquaintance. "Don't you think Jim Jensen's comments were outrageous?" I asked.

"You're too hard on men," she said. "You can't expect men who've never been that scared of another person to understand why battered women can't leave. You have to be patient and explain to them that it was fear, or just dependence, that made her stay with him."

"Wait a minute," I said, taken aback. "You didn't *hear* the story either. The point is that this woman *didn't* stay. She was outta there. Gone. Goodbye. She *left*."

My friend looked puzzled. "Then how did she get raped?"

Karen Straw was acquitted of all charges against her by jurors who heard the whole story; and she was released to gather up the tatters of her life.[10] But that familiar, trivializing question—the question that obscures both the extent of violence against women and the immense individual and collective efforts of women to overcome it—doesn't go away. It contains the whole history of woman beating in America. And our response to it shapes the future....

FRATERNITIES AND RAPE ON CAMPUS

PATRICIA YANCEY MARTIN AND ROBERT A. HUMMER

Rapes are perpetrated on dates, at parties, in chance encounters, and in specially planned circumstances. That group structure and processes, rather than individual values or characteristics, are the impetus for many rape episodes was documented by Blanchard (1959) [long ago]....

Many rapes, far more than come to the public's attention, occur in fraternity houses on college and university campuses, yet little research has analyzed fraternities at American colleges and universities as rape-prone contexts (cf. Ehrhart and Sandler 1985)....

...Ehrhart and Sandler (1985) identify over 50 cases of gang rapes on campus perpetrated by fraternity men, and their analysis points to many of the conditions that we discuss here. Their analysis is unique in focusing on conditions in fraternities that make gang rapes of women by fraternity men both feasible and probable. They identify excessive alcohol use, isolation from external monitoring, treatment of women as prey, use of pornography, approval of violence, and excessive concern with competition as precipitating conditions to gang rape (also see Merton 1985; Roark 1987).

The study reported here confirmed and complemented these findings by focusing on both conditions and processes. We examined dynamics associated with the social construction of fraternity life, with a focus on processes that foster the use of coercion, including rape, in fraternity men's relations with women. Our examination of men's social fraternities on college and university campuses as groups and organizations led us to conclude that fraternities are a physical and sociocultural context that encourages the sexual coercion of women. We make no claims that all fraternities are "bad" or that all fraternity men are rapists. Our observations indicated, however, that rape is especially probable in fraternities. because of the kinds of organizations they are, the kinds of members they have, the practices their members engage in, and a virtual absence of university or community oversight. Analyses that lay blame for rapes by fraternity men on "peer pressure" are, we feel, overly simplistic (cf. Burkhart 1989; Walsh 1989). We suggest, rather, that fraternities create a sociocultural context in which the use of coercion in sexual relations with women is normative and in which the mechanisms to keep this pattern of behavior in check are minimal at best and absent at worst. We conclude that unless fraternities change in fundamental ways, little improvement can be expected.

METHODOLOGY

Our goal was to analyze the group and organizational practices and conditions that create in fraternities an abusive social context for women. We developed a conceptual framework from an initial case study of an alleged gang rape at Florida State University that involved four fraternity men and an 18-year-old coed. The group rape took place on the third floor of a fraternity house and ended with the "dumping" of the woman in the hallway of a neighboring fraternity house. According to newspaper accounts, the victim's blood-alcohol concentration, when she was discovered, was .349 percent, more than three times the legal limit for automobile driving and an almost lethal amount. One law enforcement officer reported that sexual intercourse occurred during the time the victim was unconscious: "She was in a life-threatening situation" (*Tallahassee Democrat*, 1988b). When the victim was found, she was comatose and had suffered multiple scratches and abrasions. Crude words and a fraternity symbol had been written on her thighs (*Tampa Tribune*, 1988). When law enforcement officials tried to investigate the case, fraternity members refused to cooperate. This led, eventually, to a five-year ban of the fraternity from campus by the university and by the fraternity's national organization.

In trying to understand how such an event could have occurred, and how a group of over 150 members (exact figures are unknown because the fraternity refused to provide a membership roster) could hold rank, deny knowledge of the event, and allegedly lie to a grand jury, we analyzed newspaper articles about the case and conducted open-ended interviews with a variety of respondents about the case and about fraternities, rapes, alcohol use, gender relations, and sexual activities on campus. Our data included over 100 newspaper articles on the initial gang rape case; open-ended interviews with Greek (social fraternity and sorority) and non-Greek (independent) students (N = 20); university administrators (N = 8, five men, three women); and alumni advisers to Greek organizations (N = 6). Open-ended interviews were held also with judges, public and private defense attorneys, victim advocates, and state prosecutors regarding the processing of sexual assault cases. Data were analyzed using the grounded theory method (Glaser 1978; Martin and Turner 1986). In the following analysis, concepts generated from the data analysis are integrated with the literature on men's social fraternities, sexual coercion, and related issues.

FRATERNITIES AND THE SOCIAL CONSTRUCTION OF MEN AND MASCULINITY

Our research indicated that fraternities are vitally concerned—more than with anything else—with masculinity (cf. Kanin 1967). They work hard to create a macho image and context and try to avoid any suggestion of "wimpishness," effeminacy, and homosexuality. Valued members display, or are willing to go along with, a narrow conception of masculinity that stresses competition, athleticism, dominance, winning, conflict, wealth, material possessions, willingness to drink alcohol, and sexual prowess vis-à-vis women.

Valued Qualities of Members

When fraternity members talked about the kind of pledges they prefer, a litany of stereotypical and narrowly masculine attributes and behaviors was recited and feminine or woman-associated qualities and behaviors were expressly denounced (cf. Merton 1985). Fraternities seek men who are "athletic," "big guys," good in intramural competition, "who can talk college sports." Males "who are willing to drink alcohol," "who drink socially," or "who can hold their liquor" are sought. Alcohol and activities associated with the recreational use of alcohol are cornerstones of fraternity social life. Nondrinkers are viewed with skepticism and rarely selected for membership.[1]

Fraternities try to avoid "geeks," nerds, and men said to give the fraternity a "wimpy" or "gay" reputation. Art, music, and humanities majors, majors in traditional women's fields (nursing, home economics, social work, education), men with long hair, and those whose appearance or dress violate current norms are rejected. Clean-cut, handsome men who dress well (are clean, neat, conforming, fashionable) are preferred. One sorority woman commented that "the top ranking fraternities have the best looking guys."...

Certain social skills are valued. Men are sought who "have good personalities," are friendly, and "have the ability to relate to girls" (cf. Longino and Kart 1973). One fraternity man, a junior, said: "We watch a guy [a potential pledge] talk to women...we want guys who can relate to girls." Assessing a pledge's ability to talk to women is, in part, a preoccupation with homosexuality and a conscious avoidance of men who seem to have effeminate manners or qualities. If a member is suspected of being gay, he is ostracized and informally drummed out of the fraternity. A fraternity with a reputation as wimpy or tolerant of gays is ridiculed and shunned by other fraternities. Militant heterosexuality is frequently used by men as a strategy to keep each other in line (Kimmel 1987)....

The Status and Norms of Pledgeship

A pledge (sometimes called an associate member) is a new recruit who occupies a trial membership status for a specific period of time. The pledge period (typically ranging from 10 to 15 weeks) gives fraternity brothers an opportunity to assess and socialize new recruits. Pledges evaluate the fraternity also and decide if they want to become brothers....

...Brotherhood often plays itself out as an overriding concern with masculinity and, by extension, femininity. As a consequence, fraternities comprise collectivities of highly masculinized men with attitudinal qualities and behavioral norms that predispose them to sexual coercion of women (cf. Kanin 1967; Merton 1985; Rapaport and Burkhart 1984). The norms of masculinity are complemented by conceptions of women and femininity that are equally distorted and stereotyped and that may enhance the probability of women's exploitation (cf. Ehrhart and Sandler 1985; Sanday 1981, 1986).

Practices of Brotherhood

Practices associated with fraternity brotherhood that contribute to the sexual coercion of women include a preoccupation with loyalty, group protection and secrecy, use of alcohol as a weapon, involvement in violence and physical force, and an emphasis on competition and superiority.

Loyalty, Group Protection, and Secrecy. Loyalty is a fraternity preoccupation. Members are reminded constantly to be loyal to the fraternity and to their brothers. Among other ways, loyalty is played out in the practices of group protection and secrecy. The fraternity must be shielded from criticism. Members are admonished to avoid getting the fraternity in trouble and to…

…Our interviews indicated that individual members knew the difference between right and wrong, but fraternity norms that emphasize loyalty, group protection, and secrecy often overrode standards of ethical correctness.

Alcohol As Weapon. Alcohol use by fraternity men is normative. They use it on weekdays to relax after class and on weekends to "get drunk," "get crazy," and "get laid." The use of alcohol to obtain sex from women is pervasive—in other words, it is used as a weapon against sexual reluctance. According to several fraternity men whom we interviewed, alcohol is the major tool used to gain sexual mastery over women (cf. Adams and Abarbanel 1988; Ehrhart and Sandler 1985). One fraternity man, a 21-year-old senior, described alcohol use to gain sex as follows: "There are girls that you know will fuck, then some you have to put some effort into it.… You have to buy them drinks or find out if she's drunk enough.…"

A similar strategy is used collectively. A fraternity man said that at parties with Little Sisters: "We provide them with 'hunch punch' and things get wild. We get them drunk and most of the guys end up with one." "'Hunch punch,'" he said, "is a girls' drink made up of overproof alcohol and powdered Kool-Aid, no water or anything, just ice. It's very strong. Two cups will do a number on a female." He had plans in the next academic term to surreptitiously give hunch punch to women in a "prim and proper" sorority because "having sex with prim and proper sorority girls is definitely a goal." These women are a challenge because they "won't openly consume alcohol and won't get openly drunk as hell." Their sororities have "standards committees" that forbid heavy drinking and easy sex.

In the gang rape case, our sources said that many fraternity men on campus believed the victim had a drinking problem and was thus an "easy make." According to newspaper accounts, she had been drinking alcohol on the evening she was raped; the lead assailant is alleged to have given her a bottle of wine after she arrived at his fraternity house. Portions of the rape occurred in a shower, and the victim was reportedly so drunk that her assailants had difficulty holding her in a standing position (*Tallahassee Democrat,* 1988a). While raping her, her assailants repeatedly told her they were members of another fraternity under the apparent belief that she was too drunk to know the difference. Of course, if she was too drunk to know who they were, she was too drunk to consent to sex (cf. Allgeier 1986; Tash 1988).

One respondent told us that gang rapes are wrong and can get one expelled, but he seemed to see nothing wrong in sexual coercion one-on-one. He seemed unaware that the use of alcohol to obtain sex from a woman is grounds for a claim that a rape occurred (cf. Tash 1988). Few women on campus (who also may not know these grounds) report date rapes, however; so the odds of detection and punishment are slim for fraternity men who use alcohol for "seduction" purposes (cf. Byington and Keeler 1988; Merton 1985).

Violence and Physical Force. Fraternity men have a history of violence (Ehrhart and Sandler 1985; Roark 1987). Their record of hazing, fighting, property destruction, and rape has caused them problems with insurance companies (Bradford 1986; Pressley 1987). Two university officials told us that fraternities "are the third riskiest property to insure behind toxic waste dumps and amusement parks." Fraternities are increasingly defendants in legal actions brought by pledges subjected to hazing (Meyer 1986; Pressley 1987) and by women who were raped by one or more members. In a recent alleged gang rape incident at another Florida university, prosecutors failed to file charges but the victim filed a civil suit against the fraternity nevertheless (*Tallahassee Democrat,* 1989).

Competition and Superiority. Interfraternity rivalry fosters in-group identification and out-group hostility. Fraternities stress pride of membership and superiority over other fraternities as major goals. Interfraternity rivalries take many forms, including competition for desirable pledges, size of pledge class, size of membership, size and appearance of fraternity house, superiority in intramural sports, highest grade-point averages, giving the best parties, gaining the best or most campus leadership roles, and, of great importance, attracting and displaying "good looking women." Rivalry is particularly intense over members, intramural sports, and women (cf. Messner 1989).

FRATERNITIES' COMMODIFICATION OF WOMEN

In claiming that women are treated by fraternities as commodities, we mean that fraternities knowingly, and intentionally, *use* women for their benefit. Fraternities use women as bait for new members, as servers of brothers' needs, and as sexual prey.

Women As Bait. Fashionably attractive women help a fraternity attract new members. As one fraternity man, a junior, said, "They are good bait." Beautiful, sociable women are believed to impress the right kind of pledges and give the impression that the fraternity can deliver this type of woman to its members.

Fraternities compete in promising access to beautiful women. One fraternity man, a senior, commented that "the attraction of girls [i.e., a fraternity's success in attracting women] is a big status symbol for fraternities." One university official commented that the use of women as a recruiting tool is so well entrenched that fraternities that might be willing to forgo it say they cannot afford to unless other fraternities do so as well....

In displaying good-looking, attractive, skimpily dressed, nubile women to potential members, fraternities implicitly, and sometimes explicitly, promise sexual access to women. One fraternity man commented that "part of what being in a fraternity is all about is the sex" and explained how his fraternity uses Little Sisters to recruit new members:

> *We'll tell the sweetheart [the fraternity's term for Little Sister], "You're gorgeous; you can get him." We'll tell her to fake a scam and she'll go hang all over him during a rush party, kiss him, and he thinks he's done wonderful and wants to join. The girls think it's great too. It's flattering for them.*

Women As Servers. The use of women as servers is exemplified in the Little Sister program. Little Sisters are undergraduate women who are rushed and selected in a manner parallel to the recruitment of fraternity men. They are affiliated with the fraternity in a formal but unofficial way and are able, indeed required, to wear the fraternity's Greek letters. Little Sisters are not full-fledged fraternity members, however; and fraternity national offices and most universities do not register or relate them.

Our observations and interviews suggested that women selected by fraternities as Little Sisters are physically attractive, possess good social skills, and are willing to devote time and energy to the fraternity and its members. One undergraduate woman gave the following job description for Little Sisters to a campus newspaper:

> *It's not just making appearances at all the parties but entails many more responsibilities. You're going to be expected to go to all the intramural games to cheer the brothers on, support and encourage the pledges, and just be around to bring some extra life to the house. [As a Little Sister] you have to agree to take on a new responsibility other than studying to maintain your grades and managing to keep your checkbook from bouncing. You have to make time to be a part of the fraternity and support the brothers in all they do. (*The Tomahawk, *1988)*

The title of Little Sister reflects women's subordinate status; fraternity men in a parallel role are called Big Brothers....

Women As Sexual Prey. Little Sisters are a sexual utility. Many Little Sisters do not belong to sororities and lack peer support for refraining from unwanted sexual relations. One fraternity man (whose fraternity has 65 members and 85 Little Sisters) told us they had recruited "wholesale" in the prior year to "get lots of new women." The structural access to women that the Little

Sister program provides and the absence of normative supports for refusing fraternity members' sexual advances may make women in this program particularly susceptible to coerced sexual encounters with fraternity men.

Access to women for sexual gratification is a presumed benefit of fraternity membership, promised in recruitment materials and strategies and through brothers' conversations with new recruits. One fraternity man said: "We always tell the guys that you get sex all the time, there's always new girls.... After I became a Greek, I found out I could be with females at will." A university official told us that, based on his observations, "no one [i.e., fraternity men] on this campus wants to have 'relationships.' They just want to have fun [i.e., sex]." Fraternity men plan and execute strategies aimed at obtaining sexual gratification, and this occurs at both individual and collective levels.

Individual strategies include getting a woman drunk and spending a great deal of money on her. As for collective strategies, most of our undergraduate interviewees agreed that fraternity parties often culminate in sex and that this outcome is planned. One fraternity man said fraternity parties often involve sex and nudity and can "turn into orgies." Orgies may be planned in advance, such as the Bowery Ball party held by one fraternity. A former fraternity member said of this party:

> *The entire idea behind this is sex. Both men and women come to the party wearing little or nothing. There are pornographic pinups on the walls and usually porno movies playing on the TV. The music carries sexual overtones.... They just get schnockered [drunk] and, in most cases, they also get laid.*

When asked about the women who come to such a party, he said: "Some Little Sisters just won't go.... The girls who do are looking for a good time, girls who don't know what it is, things like that."

Other respondents denied that fraternity parties are orgies but said that sex is always talked about among the brothers and they all know "who each other is doing it with." One member said that most of the time, guys have sex with their girlfriends "but with socials, girlfriends aren't allowed to come and it's their [members'] big chance [to have sex with other women]." The use of alcohol to help them get women into bed is a routine strategy at fraternity parties.

CONCLUSIONS

In general, our research indicated that the organization and membership of fraternities contribute heavily to coercive and often violent sex. Fraternity houses are occupied by same-sex (all men) and same-age (late teens, early twenties) peers whose maturity and judgment is often less than ideal. Yet fraternity houses are private dwellings that are mostly off-limits to, and away from scrutiny of, university and community representatives, with the result that fraternity house events seldom come to the attention of outsiders. Practices associated with the social construction of fraternity brotherhood emphasize a macho conception of men and masculinity, a narrow, stereotyped conception of women and femininity, and the treatment of women as commodities. Other practices contributing to coercive sexual relations and the cover-up of rapes include excessive alcohol use, competitiveness, and normative support for deviance and secrecy (cf. Bogal-Allbritten and Allbritten 1985; Kanin 1967).

Some fraternity practices exacerbate others. Brotherhood norms require "sticking together" regardless of right or wrong; thus rape episodes are unlikely to be stopped or reported to outsiders, even when witnesses disapprove. The ability to use alcohol without scrutiny by authorities and alcohol's frequent association with violence, including sexual coercion, facilitates rape in fraternity houses. Fraternity norms that emphasize the value of maleness and masculinity over femaleness and femininity and that elevate the status of men and lower the status of women in members' eyes undermine perceptions and treatment of women as persons who deserve consideration and care (cf. Ehrhart and Sandler 1985; Merton 1985).

Androgynous men and men with a broad range of interests and attributes are lost to fraternities through their recruitment practices. Masculinity of a narrow and stereotypical type helps create attitudes, norms, and practices that predispose fraternity men to coerce women sexually, both individually and collectively (Allgeier 1986; Hood 1989; Sanday 1981, 1986). Male athletes on campus may be similarly disposed for the same reasons (Kirshenbaum 1989; Telander and Sullivan 1989).

Research into the social contexts in which rape crimes occur and the social constructions associated with these contexts illumine rape dynamics on campus. Blanchard (1959) found that group rapes almost always have a leader who pushes others into the crime. He also found that the leader's latent homosexuality, desire to show off to his peers, or fear of failing to prove himself a man are frequently an impetus. Fraternity norms and practices contribute to the approval and use of sexual coercion as an accepted tactic in relations with women. Alcohol-induced compliance is normative, whereas, presumably, use of a knife, gun, or threat of bodily harm would not be because the woman who "drinks too much" is viewed as "causing her own rape" (cf. Ehrhart and Sandler 1985).

Our research led us to conclude that fraternity norms and practices influence members to view the sexual coercion of women, which is a felony crime, as sport, a contest, or a game (cf. Sato 1988). This sport is played not between men and women but between men and men. Women are the pawns or prey in the interfraternity rivalry game; they prove that a fraternity is successful or prestigious. The use of women in this way encourages fraternity men to see women as objects and sexual coercion as sport. Today's societal norms support young women's right to engage in sex at their discretion, and coercion is unnecessary in a mutually desired encounter. However, nubile young women say they prefer to be "in a relationship" to have sex while young men say they prefer to "get laid" without a commitment (Muehlenhard and Linton 1987). These differences may reflect, in part, American puritanism and men's fears of sexual intimacy or perhaps intimacy of any kind. In a fraternity context, getting sex without giving emotionally demonstrates "cool" masculinity. More important it poses no threat to the bonding and loyalty of the fraternity brotherhood (cf. Farr 1988). Drinking large quantities of alcohol before having sex suggests that "scoring" rather than intrinsic sexual pleasure is a primary concern of fraternity men.

Unless fraternities' composition, goals, structures, and practices change in fundamental ways, women on campus will continue to be sexual prey for fraternity men. As all-male enclaves dedicated to opposing faculty and administration and to cementing in-group ties, fraternity members eschew any hint of homosexuality. Their version of masculinity transforms women, and men with womanly characteristics, into the out-group. "Womanly men" are ostracized; feminine women are used to demonstrate members' masculinity. Encouraging renewed emphasis on their founding values (Longino and Karl 1973), service orientation and activities (Lemire 1979), or members' moral development (Marlowe and Auvenshine 1982) will have little effect on fraternities' treatment of women. A case for or against fraternities cannot be made by studying individual members. The fraternity qua group and organization is at issue. Located on campus along with many vulnerable women, embedded in a sexist society, and caught up in masculinist goals, practices, and values, fraternities' violation of women—including forcible rape—should come as no surprise.

NOTE

1. Recent bans by some universities on open-keg parties at fraternity houses have resulted in heavy drinking before coming to a party and an increase in drunkenness among those who attend. This may aggravate, rather than improve, the treatment of women by fraternity men at parties.

REFERENCES

Allgeier, Elizabeth. 1986. "Coercive Versus Consensual Sexual Interactions." G. Stanley Hall Lecture to American Psychological Association Annual Meeting, Washington, DC, August.

Adams, Aileen and Gail Abarbanel. 1988. *Sexual Assault on Campus: What Colleges Can Do.* Santa Monica, CA: Rape Treatment Center.

Blanchard, W. H. 1959. "The Group Process in Gang Rape." *Journal of Social Psychology* 49:259–66.

Bogal-Allbritten, Rosemarie B. and William L. Allbritten. 1985. "The Hidden Victims: Courtship Violence Among College Students." *Journal of College Student Personnel* 43:201–4.

Bradford, Michael. 1986. "Tight Market Dries Up Nightlife at University." *Business Insurance* (March 2): 2, 6.

Burkhart, Barry. 1989. Comments in Seminar on Acquaintance/Date Rape Prevention: A National Video Teleconference, February 2.

Byington, Diane B. and Karen W. Keeter. 1988. "Assessing Needs of Sexual Assault Victims on a University Campus." Pp. 23–31 in *Student Services: Responding to Issues and Challenges.* Chapel Hill: University of North Carolina Press.

Ehrhart, Julie K. and Bernice R. Sandler. 1985. *Campus Gang Rape: Party Games?* Washington, DC: Association of American Colleges.

Farr, K. A. 1988. "Dominance Bonding Through the Good Old Boys Sociability Network." *Sex Roles* 18:259–77.

Glaser, Barney G. 1978. *Theoretical Sensitivity: Advances in the Methodology of Grounded Theory.* Mill Valley, CA: Sociology Press.

Hood, Jane. 1989. "Why Our Society Is Rape-Prone." *New York Times,* May 16.

Kanin, Eugene J. 1967. "Reference Groups and Sex Conduct Norm Violations." *The Sociological Quarterly* 8:495–504.

Kimmel, Michael, ed. 1987. *Changing Men: New Directions in Research on Men and Masculinity.* Newbury Park, CA: Sage.

Kirshenbaum, Jerry. 1989. "Special Report, An American Disgrace: A Violent and Unprecedented Lawlessness Has Arisen Among College Athletes in all Parts of the Country." *Sports Illustrated* (February 27): 16–19.

Lemire, David. 1979. "One Investigation of the Stereotypes Associated with Fraternities and Sororities." *Journal of College Student Personnel* 37:54–57.

Longino, Charles F., Jr., and Cary S. Kart. 1973. "The College Fraternity: An Assessment of Theory and Research." *Journal of College Student Personnel* 31:118–25.

Marlowe, Anne F. and Dwight C. Auvenshine. 1982. "Greek Membership: Its Impact on the Moral Development of College Freshmen." *Journal of College Student Personnel* 40:53–57.

Martin, Patricia Yancey and Barry A. Turner. 1986. "Grounded Theory and Organizational Research." *Journal of Applied Behavioral Science* 22: 141–57.

Merton, Andrew. 1985. "On Competition and Class: Return to Brotherhood." *Ms.* (September): 60–65, 121–22.

Messner, Michael. 1989. "Masculinities and Athletic Careers." *Gender & Society* 3:71–88.

Meyer, T. J. 1986. "Fight Against Hazing Rituals Rages on Campuses." *Chronicle of Higher Education* (March 12):34–36.

Muehlenhard, Charlene L. and Melaney A. Linton. 1987. "Date Rape and Sexual Aggression in Dating Situations: Incidence and Risk Factors." *Journal of Counseling Psychology* 34:186–96.

Pressley, Sue Anne. 1987. "Fraternity Hell Night Still Endures." *Washington Post* (August 11):Bl.

Rapaport, Karen and Barry R. Burkhart. 1984. "Personality and Attitudinal Characteristics of Sexually Coercive College Males." *Journal of Abnormal Psychology* 93:216–21.

Roark, Mary L. 1987. "Preventing Violence on College Campuses." *Journal of Counseling and Development* 65:367–70.

Sanday, Peggy Reeves. 1981. "The Socio-Cultural Context of Rape: A Cross-Cultural Study." *Journal of Social Issues* 37:5–27.

———. 1986. "Rape and the Silencing of the Feminine." Pp. 84–101 in *Rape,* edited by S. Tomaselli and R. Porter. Oxford: Basil Blackwell.

Sato, Ikuya. 1988. "Play Theory of Delinquency: Toward a General Theory of 'Action.'" *Symbolic Interaction* 11: 191–212.

Tallahassee Democrat. 1988a. "FSU Fraternity Brothers Charged" (April 27):1A, 12A.

———. 1988b. "FSU Interviewing Students About Alleged Rape" (April 24):1D.

———. 1989. "Woman Sues Stetson in Alleged Rape" (March 19):3B.

Tampa Tribune. 1988. "Fraternity Brothers Charged in Sexual Assault of FSU Coed." (April 27):6B.

Tash, Gary B. 1988. "Date Rape." *The Emerald of Sigma Pi Fraternity* 75(4):1–2.

Telander, Rick and Robert Sullivan, 1989. "Special Report, You Reap What You Sow." *Sports Illustrated* (February 27):20–34.

The Tomahawk. 1988. "A Look Back at Rush, A Mixture of Hard Work and Fun" (April/ May):3D.

Walsh, Claire. 1989. Comments in Seminar on Acquaintance/Date Rape Prevention: A National Video Teleconference, February 2.

CHAPTER 6

OCCUPATIONAL HEALTH

In 1911, a fire at the Triangle Shirtwaist Company, a New York City garment industry sweatshop employing primarily young Jewish and Italian immigrant women, led to the deaths of 145 workers. Unable to escape the flames because their employer had locked or blocked exit doors, workers burned to death or died jumping from the building. The enormity of the tragedy generated an awareness of dangerous working conditions and prompted a major investigation of chemicals and fire protection in the workplace.

Since then the federal government has assumed a more active role in protecting workers, including the passage of the Occupational Safety and Health Act in 1970, which led to the creation of the Occupational Safety and Health Administration (OSHA), within the U.S. Department of Labor. OSHA promoted safe and healthy working conditions by establishing and enforcing safety standards, and by inspecting work sites. Most importantly, OSHA had the teeth to enforce its decisions by fining those who didn't comply. Like many other political creations, however, OSHA was dependant on future political administrations for its continued funding, and it suffered from twelve years of attrition during the Reagan and Bush presidencies.

In 1991, eighty years after the Triangle Shirtwaist disaster, a fire at the Imperial Products poultry plant in North Carolina—which employed primarily African American women—led to the deaths of twenty-five workers because management, fearing workers would steal chickens, had locked the doors. Though impressive in its initial mission statements, an underfunded OSHA had never sent an inspector to the poultry factory during its eleven years of operation.

When these two tragedies, spaced eight decades apart, occur with an eerie similarity, workplace safety seems at first glance to have been sadly ignored. Despite instance after instance of needless deaths caused by employers interested only in saving a few dollars—or, in the case of the poultry factory, a few chickens—dangers have been left unaddressed. Although in truth many important safety procedures have been initiated in male-dominated occupations, safety for women has sadly been ignored for a number of reasons that will be discussed in this chapter.

We begin with an examination of the gendered workplace, to understand why women's exposure to workplace hazards differs from men's. Then we examine how the government, corporate America, and even researchers respond to workplace hazards in a gendered way—that is, based on normative conceptions of men's and women's lives. We will see that occupational health is quite clearly a women's health issue.

THE GENDERED WORKPLACE

Despite the media's attention to women's advances into previously male-dominated occupations, such as law and medicine, the great majority of working women do not have access to these positions. For all the rhetoric about equal opportunity in the marketplace, women are still grouped into occupations that are predominately female. Over 28 million women, 47 percent of the female work force, are found in job categories in which 75 percent or more of the employees are female. Twelve million of these women (21 percent of all working women) work in almost exclusively female occupations (over 90 percent of employees are female): They are nurses, secretaries, bookkeepers, kindergarten teachers, private child-care workers, private household cleaners, and hairdressers (Bureau of the Census 1999).

Even when men and women are in the same occupation, assigned tasks within those occupations may be gendered. Males and females in a poultry plant have different jobs, with women more likely than men to use knives and scissors. Similarly, men and women who are gardeners do different things, with women more likely to plant and weed, while men prune (Messing 1997:43). This gendering of both occupations and jobs within occupations means that men and women have different exposures to health hazards. These differences are reflected in occupational injury statistics (Toscana, Windau, and Knestaut 1998; Collins et al. 1997). For instance, women are more likely than men to be injured by repetitive motion, inhalation of harmful substances, and assaults and violent acts. Other general gendered differences include the greater likelihood that women will be exposed to the stress of "emotional" labor (Hochschild 1983) in clerical, sales, and service jobs, where a smile must remain on the employee's face, and the customer is always right; the need for women to contend with what for them are poorly designed workplaces and tools, such as the height of a work area or the size of a handgrip, based on average male measurements; and, importantly, women's exposure to sexual harassment in the workplace, a topic covered in Chapter 5.

For many injured workers, the link between their health problems and the work setting is never made. As a result of underdiagnosis and underreporting, most (estimated at 60 to 90 percent) new cases of work-related disease and/or injury are not properly classified as occupational (Friedman-Jimenez et al. 1994a:48). In part, this results from the limited training of doctors. Most schools do not expose medical students to occupational health issues, limiting the chances that a primary care doctor will ask appropriate, if any, questions about possible occupational links. And occupational medical specialists are rare.

Despite this underreporting, it is clear that, in addition to their gender, women face unusual problems in the workplace for two principal reasons—the low levels of unionization in the jobs they hold (Bureau of Labor Statistics 2000), and the false designation of their work as being "safe."

LACK OF UNIONIZATION

The first implication of a nonunion job is that it is less likely to provide health insurance for workers. In our country, health care insurance is extremely difficult and costly to obtain other than through an employer. Without insurance, one's health is in great jeopardy. Second, without a union, employers are likely to provide less information about occupational hazards (Kemp and Jenkins 1992). As important as right-to-know legislation is, many women are still left uninformed about toxic chemicals in the workplace because they lack union advocates.

Working in a nonunion environment presents other problems as well. Employees have a much-decreased chance of engaging in a unified action to address safety issues to management. Employees may understandably be unwilling to act on their own to redress such issues for fear of losing their jobs, regardless of how unsafe and unhealthy it may be.

The plight of the women at the Albuquerque, New Mexico, plant of Lenkurt, a subsidiary of General Telephone and Electric Corporation (GTE), which specialized in telephone switching and transmission equipment, provides a striking example of what horrendous health problems nonunion employees will endure. These women were not only reluctant to complain to their employers, but also were hesitant to inform their families of the problems, knowing that the families depended on their income. Employers are well aware of the greater power they have when a union is not around. GTE explicitly chose the Albuquerque area because it was nonunion, and the workers were primarily minorities (Fox 1991:4; see the reading at the end of this chapter).

Other important health hazards associated with nonunion or lower-level jobs include problems associated with demands for speed on the job (e.g., small-parts assembly lines), lack of control over the pace of work, and a low level of decision latitude (Messing 1997:53).

Unions have traditionally been slow to approach the "pink collar" (female-dominated) workplace, and their efforts will be further hindered by the recent phenomenon of temporary help—workers hired through an agency on a per-day basis. The recent tendency of employers to hire increasing numbers of "temps" in lieu of full-time employees in order to avoid paying job benefits has an unpleasant ramification: It undercuts the efforts of full-time employees to unionize. Temporary workers have little interest in collective action, since they have little commitment to the workplace and are unlikely to benefit from changes.

JOBS ASSUMED TO BE SAFE

An ironic impediment to securing safety reforms for women is the commonly held belief that their jobs are already safe—that their workplaces are safe, clean environments. Most women are not hard at work in traditionally dangerous and dirty jobs such as construction, coal mining, or steel manufacturing/smelter work—jobs that immediately evoke concerns about occupational health and safety. Women can instead be found in "clean" industries such as health care, electronics, teaching, secretarial and clerical work, and retail, nearly all of which take place in environments that are accessible to the public. Visitors to such places, no matter how brief their stay, tend to come away with the impression that such workplaces are clean and therefore safe. Often these images are misleading. Four types of work settings are instructive: office work, the electronics industry, health care work, and housework. Important hazards in these so-called clean workplaces include ergonomic hazards, toxic exposures, and assaults.

Office Work

Some occupations retain the image of a healthy work environment because their hazards have only recently been recognized. A particularly good example is the office workplace, which is considered "safe" despite the presence of numerous ergonomic hazards. These hazards are due to poor equipment design, jobs that require awkward or constrained postures, or jobs that demand a series of repetitive movements. Some ergonomic hazards seem invisible. "A chair the wrong height or a counter the wrong width may cause constant oversolicitation of the same tendons or joints, yet the observer sees no problem" (Messing 1997:50). With repetitive motions or awkward stances, each instance may individually "make trivial demands on the human body" (Messing 1997:50) and appear to the observer as safe because the cumulative effect over time is not considered. Computer data entry and secretarial work are prime examples of occupations with ergonomic hazards, and women are more likely to be in such jobs.

Ergonomic hazards can cause a variety of disabling and painful musculoskeletal disorders, such as carpal tunnel syndrome, tension neck syndrome, and low back pain. Repetitive trauma disease (illness or injury caused by repetitive motion or holding a position for a long period of time) increased from under 20 percent to over 50 percent of reported occupational diseases in the 1980s (Friedman-Jimenez et al. 1994b).

Occupations typically have some hazards that are intrinsic to the required tasks, and some hazards that are not. Many of the latter dangers may be easily remedied if anyone had a mind to do so. Although voice recognition technology may make the typist's risk for carpal-tunnel syndrome nonexistent, at present the repetitive motion of striking one's fingers against the keyboard remains a necessary part of the job. The fit of the chair, the height of keyboard, the position of the mouse, the number of breaks the person has, the diversity of tasks in the job—all of these could easily be altered to the worker's benefit without undue expense and loss of productivity. And yet these dangers persist, due to the lack of a collective voice to demand job safety.

OSHA has, since its inception, paid special attention to the hazards of the construction site and of heavy industry, both of which are male-dominated occupations. In response to these dangers, it mandated the use of hardhats, protective gloves, and eyewear. OSHA also established safety guidelines, such as setting weight limits on lifting in general, and dispensed safety instructions, such as how to lift objects properly, and tips on how to safely climb ladders or how to avoid back injury. But where are the guidelines for chair height or how frequently a motion can be repeated? These hazards do not fit the typical model of a workplace problem that stimulates government or organizational response. An OSHA rule on ergonomics was not published until November 14, 2000 (Jeffress 1999).

Electronics Industry

Women, particularly low-income and minority women, are the primary workers in the manufacture and assembly of silicon chips, disk surfaces, disk-drive heads, circuit board assembly for computers, and in the production of solid state devices for telecommunications switching and transmission equipment. This industry is associated with the most current information technology and appears far removed from dangerous or dirty jobs. In Silicon Valley, an area of California synonymous with the computer industry and the new information technology, workers don gloves, facial masks, and special gowns to work in an environment designed to keep the tiniest piece of dust from the semiconductor chip. Yet these so-called "clean rooms" are neither clean nor safe for workers. Electronics workers are exposed to the gases

> *arsine, phosphine, diborane, and chlorine, the latter internationally abhorred over 60 years ago after its use as a weapon on the Western front. These gases are prized by the semiconductor industry because they impart electrical properties to microchips. They are among the most toxic substances in the biosphere. When mixed and released under pressure at high temperatures and in extreme environments, they combine to hazardous effect—effects modern medicine studiously ignores. (Hayes 1989:64)*

The lack of vigilance for the health and safety of these workers stems in part from the power of the industry and the weakness of OSHA. OSHA often is left to accept what the industry tells it. If OSHA could make surprise visits and levy large fines when the workplace endangers workers, then the workplace would be much safer. But OSHA is not that powerful; it often must accept the industry's definition of the situation. For instance, after OSHA raised concerns about the industry's illness rate, the Semiconductor Industry Association played a semantics game, redefining one-time or instantaneous chemical exposures as injuries—which do not have to be reported to the state if they do not result in lost work time—instead of referring to them as illnesses, which must be reported (Bass 1984:31). OSHA's reaction was to accept this redefinition, which clearly benefitted the employers and jeopardized the workers. The result was an underreporting of occupational illness and injury in the semiconductor manufacturing industry (McCurdy, Schenker, and Samuels 1991).

When the day-to-day exposure of workers in the electronics industry is described, the conditions of work seem more appropriate to the age of Dickens than the enlightened computer-telecommunications age. A chapter from *Toxic Work,* which examines the health hazards of work at the Lenkurt–GTE plant that employs primarily Hispanic women, is a reading at the end of this chapter. Working at Lenkurt exposed workers to an unbelievable multitude of poorly tested toxic chemicals. In this minimal testing, these chemicals were not tested for their effects on women, nor were they tested in the context in which they were used at GTE–Lenkurt—a context of exposure to multiple chemicals in a poorly ventilated room with little or no safety equipment available for the worker. Workers with health problems contacted either doctors who were connected to the company, and thus predisposed to find no occupational link to their illnesses, or doctors who had little training in making such a connection.

Health Care

The health care industry is important to examine because many women (more than 10 percent of all working women) work in health care, and because it is a predominately female industry. More than three-fourths of the health care workers are women.

Despite the fact that health care workers are in an industry that by definition focuses on health, to have a job in this industry can be a health hazard. Occupational risks for health care workers are many and varied: puncture wounds, back injuries, needle sticks, chemical hazards (e.g., drugs used for cancer treatment, anaesthetic waste gases, and chemicals for sterilizing and disinfecting), and infectious diseases lead the list. And the rate of occupational health hazards is high. Referred to as an epidemic by some (Charney and Fragala 1999), the rate of nonfatal occupational injuries and illness was recently 11.8 per 100 full-time hospital workers, and 17.3 for workers in nursing and personal care facilities, far in excess of the 8.5 rate for private industry (Rogers 1999:12).

Reasons for the high level of health problems for workers in the health industry are many and include the introduction into the workplace of "chemicals, treatments, and medical technology without first testing for occupational risk" (Charney, 1999:3); the pressures from managed care, which have increased patient load and reduced the skill level of workers; and the lack of occupational health training in both nursing and medical school curricula (Charney 1999:3–4). The Joint Commission on Hospital Accreditation Organization (JCHAO) establishes standards for the workplace, yet has developed no standards "that deal with needle stick prevention or management, the most prevalent risk. No standards exist for ergonomics or back injury, the most expensive risk. There is no mention of ethylene oxide, one of the most toxic chemicals used in hospitals" (Charney 1999:4).

Some health care workers are more at risk than others. "The hazards for nonprofessional, so-called indirect care and auxiliary personnel, who are more likely to be women and persons of color, are seldom addressed in research on direct care-givers" (Kemp and Jenkins 1992:145). Health care is a rapidly changing industry, with "nursing and personal care in patients' homes adding jobs faster than any other segment of the U.S. economy" (Bureau of Labor Statistics 1997:1). For health workers in the home, their work site is invisible and unregulated. This situation has a popular image of being "clean;" working in a private home doing "women's work" does not evoke images of a dangerous work environment. Home health care workers may be called on to lift or move a large person singlehandedly and with no lifting equipment, as one might use for the same work in the hospital or nursing home setting. These injuries from overexertion add up to a category of ill health for home health care workers that is 2.4 times the national rate for private industry (Bureau of Labor Statistics 1997). Back pain has become the most common reason for filing worker's compensation claims. In other contexts, notably among men who lifted heavy objects all day, back pain was taken seriously, and safety guidelines were developed. One could calibrate items lifted and standardize maximum weights. But this is obviously impossible with patients. Furthermore, just standing for long periods of time also causes lower back pain, and women in occupations such as nursing (as well as personal care, hairdressing, and retail) experience a particularly high rate of this injury (Guo et al. 1999). There are no government standards for how long one can stand.

The health care industry also exposes women to nonfatal workplace assaults and violent acts. Over two-thirds of the nonfatal assaults against women in the workplace were assaults by patients on service workers in hospitals, nursing homes, and social service industries (Toscano, Windau, and Knestaut 1998:18; Collins et al. 1997:17).

Housework

The most commonly overlooked workplace is one's own home. Homeworkers engage in a full-time occupation that is just as strenuous and filled with hazards as any of the other occupations discussed in this chapter. The only difference is that housework is unpaid and unregulated—no benefits, no vacation time, no sick time, and no OSHA. Surprisingly, even in one's own home, one is surrounded by a special set of hazards, many of which are potentially life-threatening.

Homes have an smorgasbord of chemicals. Look in your cupboards at home, and you are likely to find many of the following: air fresheners, bleaches, carpet shampoo, dishwasher detergents, drain cleaners, furniture polish, mold and mildew cleaners, oven cleaners, laundry detergents and stain removers, toilet bowl cleaners, flea powders, and, for gardens, various pesticides and herbicides. Examine the labels: Many contain dire warnings, and some are known carcinogens. One estimate is that the average household has over two hundred chemicals "toxic enough to require medical attention if ingested" (Doyal 1995:35).

Little is known about the health effects of these household hazards. Sometimes we are cautioned not to ingest the chemical or get it in our eyes, but little is said about the fumes, or long-term effects of exposure through the skin. We are not trained in the use of these products, as we might be in a paid work site, nor are we educated about their toxicity. The paucity of information about household hazards and our cavalier use of them are alarming. Scientific studies of the danger of household chemicals are difficult to conduct: People do not use household chemicals in dose-regulated ways; they are likely to be exposed sporadically, at low levels, over long periods of time, and in combination with other chemicals; and they don't show symptoms indicating problems for years or even decades after exposure. Obviously, because women continue to carry the burden of household cleaning, their exposure is, in general, higher than that of men.

Work in the home also exposes women to any environmental toxicity in the neighborhood. The dosage may be low, but the years of exposure may have profound effects. With women generally spending more time in the home than men, their exposure is greater. In Chapter 16, we explore women in the environmental health movement. Another major hazard in the home, domestic violence, is considered in Chapter 5.

STUDIES OF WOMEN'S OCCUPATIONAL HEALTH

We have already seen how OSHA, the federal government's job safety watchdog, has shown a lack of concern for gender-specific health effects (Pottern 1994) by concentrating on hazards in predominately male occupations, not on hazards in women's jobs, which are commonly thought of as being safe. If an occupation does not attract the interests of researchers, its health risks can only be guessed at, not documented and taken seriously (Mergler et al. 1987:417).

Exclusion from Research

Women's occupational health issues are also ignored due to their exclusion from relevant research. Early studies of occupations and heart disease focused on male subjects (Messing 1997:53). Decades of studies on radiologists were conducted before studies of X-ray technicians, nurses, or other technologists working with nuclear therapy were conducted (Erickson 1987:34). Studies of occupations and cancer have focused on white males (Zahm et al. 1994). An even greater omission is the near "invisibility of minority women in the occupational health literature" (Kemp and Jenkins 1992:147).

When studies do include women, there is typically little examination of potential sex differences, and, if found, little analysis of why that difference occurs. Less than 20 percent of the epidemiological studies of occupational cancer done between 1971 and 1990 included data analyzed by gender. In several studies, the sample included sufficient numbers of women, but the opportunity for a cross-gender analysis was overlooked (Zahm et al. 1994).

Another example of gender bias is to be found in a review of twelve air-pollution studies. The reviewers were dismayed to find that the researchers dutifully noted but didn't bother to analyze why women reported two to four times the number of symptoms that men did. In only one of the twelve studies did the researchers try to understand gender differences. In that one study, researchers reported that the gendered work setting (e.g., women doing more photocopying and more office-sharing) might account for the differences found (Messing 1997:45). Gender differences might also result from dissimilar responses to exposures because of genetic, hormonal, metabolic, or anatomical differences between women and men.

Gender Stereotypes

When researchers do attempt to understand women's occupational health issues, all too often the analysis is based on gender stereotypes. One recurrent stereotype in occupational health has been to claim that women's complaints were all in their heads—that no real health threat existed. Thus, although we know that workplace exposure to organic solvents (in adhesives, paints, lubricating agents, and cleaning agents) has acute, toxic effects, many investigations of the complaints of women working with organic solvents led to the conclusion that "mass psychogenic illness" or "workplace hysteria" was the cause of the symptoms. Not only were the women working with a known toxic agent, but the symptoms they reported were "symptoms already shown to be associated with solvent exposure in experimental and occupational field studies of *male* workers" (Dew et al. 1989:329). Fortunately, more recent research is exposing this bias, by documenting a dose–symptom connection in women (Dew et al. 1989; Bowler et al. 1992; and see Messing 1997:52). But this tendency to deny rather than examine women's complaints remains an easy out for the gender-biased researcher.

A chilling example of how ludicrous gender stereotyping can become occurred in 1994. Paramedics brought a woman to the emergency room of a California hospital. Twenty-three of the thirty-seven emergency medical staff treating her experienced unusual symptoms—including fainting, retching, and a burning sensation on the skin. Five were hospitalized overnight, including one who stayed in the hospital for two weeks. The initial conclusion of mass hysteria came from the "[l]ack of evidence for a poison and the fact that women were more likely to suffer severe symptoms, both hallmark signs of mass hysteria" (Stone 1995:71). Entertaining a diagnosis of mass hysteria under these circumstances indicates an enduring sexism.

A second recurrent stereotype in occupational health has been to claim that women are the weaker sex. "When women workers suffer from health problems in what are popularly considered to be 'easy' jobs, this is explained by differential susceptibility due to women's biologic 'weakness'" (Mergler et al. 1987:417). However, under serious consideration, male–female differences often disappear when working conditions are controlled for. Thus, in poultry slaughterhouses, women report more problems with their backs, upper and lower limbs, and their nervous systems than the men working in the same workplace. But jobs within the slaughterhouse are very different—women are more likely to be engaged in repetitive motion, to stand still, and to use knives and scissors. When these job differences are taken into account, symptom "overreporting" by women disappears (Mergler et al. 1987).

POWER AND OCCUPATIONAL HEALTH

Improving women's occupational health has clearly not been part of the national agenda. Rather, hazards have been ignored or dismissed.

Some might point to the protective policies developed to keep women out of hazardous jobs as evidence that there are conditions under which women's health is protected. For instance, employers developed policies to protect women from chemical exposure at the American Cyanamid Company, and from lead exposure at Johnson Controls, by simply barring them from certain jobs.

On closer examination, a different picture emerges. In these industries, the protection of women's health occurred under the guise of "fetal protection," a subset of the more general paternalistic "protective" legislation for women in the workplace that has greatly limited women's workplace participation and delayed efforts to improve the working conditions for all people.

The American Cyanamid Company imposed a policy excluding all women aged fifteen to fifty from almost all jobs at its plant. The exclusion applied to all women, "regardless of their marital status, sexual orientation, or childbearing intentions. The only ones not affected would be those who could present medical verification of sterility. Birth control, even a spouse's vasectomy, would not suffice" (Bertin 1989:289). The resulting "your fertility or your job" choice led five women to submit to surgical sterilization. In 1982, four years after American Cyanamid began its policy of exclusion, the battery-making division of Johnson Controls established a "fetal protection" policy (FPP) barring all fertile women from jobs exposing them to lead, and as a result virtually precluded career paths to the better-paying jobs at the plant. An implicit message of these policies is that it is not women who matter, but women as potentially childbearing people who need to be protected.

These gender-based exclusions lay bare the power of the industry to manipulate information, ignore OSHA, and make its own rules about exposure to health hazards. These industries have a long history of indifference to hazards in the workplace. The Manufacturing Chemists Association hid the link between vinyl chloride exposure and angiosarcoma, a fatal form of liver cancer; the Lead Industries Association has argued for permissible levels of lead in the blood that OSHA sees as leading to "severe lead intoxication" (quoted in Bertin 1989:293). Furthermore, both industries have been in noncompliance with OSHA regulations (Bertin 1989:290, 293).

In implementing FPPs, these industries made assumptions about occupational health in direct opposition to scientific findings. They assumed that exposure of the fetus was the problem, when studies clearly indicated that both the egg and the sperm were at risk (Bertin 1989:292). Thus, excluding women did not protect the fetus; it merely kept women out of the workplace.

Exclusions of women by use of FPPs did occur in other industries. The types of industries that developed such policies is instructive. "Despite known reproductive hazards in the clothing/textile industry, in laundry/drycleaning establishments, for migrant workers, and for hospital workers, FPPs are uncommon in these work areas. In fact, FPPs have been adopted almost exclusively in unionized industries with rigid pay scales, where the increased costs of hiring women cannot be offset by paying women less" (Blank 1993:100).

The power of industry to socially construct the work situation by defining risk, using a rhetoric of protection, and excluding women from well-paying jobs ended when litigation against Johnson Controls reached the United States Supreme Court in 1991. The court held that the employers' actions were unlawful sex discrimination. Rather than understanding the toxicity of the environment and correcting it for all affected workers, a single category of worker, the woman, had been eliminated.

HEALTH COMPLAINTS AND THE DEATHS OF FRIENDS

STEVE FOX

Despite liking their jobs and the money they made, many GTE Lenkurt production workers began having illness symptoms they had never had before, usually within a year of beginning work. The women in the following six case studies reflect the age, ethnicity, marital and family status, and tenure of employment of the group that would later become plaintiffs against GTE: they began work at the plant near the year 1973 at an average age of thirty-two, and worked an average of nine and a half years in production and assembly. They are among the more articulate and assertive of that group, but their health complaints are not more serious than most who became plaintiffs.

SADIE MIERA

Sadie Miera came to work at Lenkurt in May 1973 at the age of thirty-one. She was married and had children ten, nine, and three years old. It was her first and only job. She began in Department 320, Component Assembly, and stayed there ten years. Her first task was "potting," filling transformers with a sealer. She poured the potting compound through paper funnels, varying the flow by putting a pencil in the hole, on trays holding 35 transformers at a time, 4,000 transformers per day. The term *potting* may have sounded vaguely domestic, like washing pots or potting plants, but what she was handling every day was a combination of hydrocarbons, polyolefins, styrene–ethylene, and butylene styrene, a brew of epoxy resins and several types of solvents.

She got rashes and white spots from the potting resin during her first year: "We girls used to say we'd get immune to the potting rash." Some of the spotting was permanent. For the first two years she worked at Lenkurt, Sadie also did all the housework at home, either before or after work, the "double shift" familiar to all employed women. Actually, Sadie had a triple shift, because at work, there was more housework to do:

> *Every time they delivered my drum of hardener there would be spills. The handle was always broken, so I used a piece of pipe and a funnel sort of like the kind you pour gasoline with. It got sticky all over the floor. I couldn't stand on it, and the fumes from the hardener were horrible. I asked for the maintenance people to clean it, but my supervisor and foreman said to clean it myself.*

From then on, she put cardboard down on her floor and changed it every other week. Her shift mates recall seeing Sadie often on her knees at her work station, cleaning resin hardener with a red can of alcohol, itself a form of solvent known to cause dizziness, irritability, and narcosis when inhaled. The vents over her work tables were always clogged with sticky resin and dust and hair, slowing the air flow to nothing. "The foreman said to clean that ourselves, but there was no vacuum cleaner. So I brought mine from home."

Three years after the plant opened, management changed the policy on worker assignment. Instead of emphasizing maximum worker and management flexibility by moving all workers from task to task whenever rush orders needed filling, management began to identify good workers and keep them at particular tasks. The underlying reason for both policies, which will be illustrated by Sadie's case, was production efficiency, not worker benefit.

After three years of handling epoxy-solvent combinations, Sadie was chronically sick. She suffered constant nasal and sinus congestion, headache, dizziness, dry cough, sores in nostrils, wheezing, shortness of breath, loss of taste, and nausea. She began having heavy menstrual periods every fourteen days, with considerable discomfort, but felt pressure not to take sick leave or complain: "The reason I never took off is I was the only one who could do that lousy job." When she finally got a helper, the woman got sick and told her doctor she worked with resin hardener; "her doctor asked Lenkurt for a sample of the chemical, and when they refused, I figured there was no use mentioning it to my doctors."

After another two years, Sadie had an enigmatic brush with an engineer from the front office, George Kerr, and her foreman, Jack Wiggins. One day the two men appeared together, watching her work, and asked her, "Don't you think you need a change? Your limit in here should be three to five years." Sadie did not know what to reply; she did not know what they meant by "limit." Kerr offered to help her find another job in the plant. Sadie said in her deposition, "I didn't know if they were joking with me or wanted somebody else in there. If I took a transfer, they could say I refused my other job, and if I refuse a job, I'll be thrown out the door." Wiggins and Kerr made no attempt to explain what they meant or to discover how Sadie felt.

Sadie Miera pressed on with her triple shift, cleaning up at home and at work. Although she had a family doctor she saw between 1973 and 1984, her various problems caused her to be referred to six others before she left GTE in 1984.

MARY LOU C DE BACA

Mary Lou C de Baca started at Lenkurt in 1972 at the age of thirty-three. She was married, with children twelve and fourteen, and had worked for about four years as a waitress and a sales and billing clerk. Her first two years were spent in Department 345, Crystal Filters, and the next nine in Department 320, Component Assembly. After she had been at Lenkurt seven months, she began having heavy menstrual bleeding and wearing a sanitary pad every day all month long. In 1974 she had a hysterectomy.

In Department 320, Mary Lou sat across from Sadie Miera, near a tank of heated Chlor-Trimetron solvent. She experienced several of the same symptoms Sadie had, though at different times. She complained to supervisors that solvents ate through the rubber finger cots (fingertip covers) she wore. They issued her more finger cots. In 1978, her work accounting procedure changed to an incentive system, with a required quota and bonuses for production beyond that total. Her health got worse. "I was embarrassed to go to the dispensary every time, because they would say, 'You again?'"

Her husband, a painter, developed a drinking problem and entered Alcoholics Anonymous; a son and his wife had a retarded baby; Mary Lou tried to support them all emotionally while keeping her house spotless. The GTE incentive system offered more money, but more stress as well:

> *You had to sit there with your neck like this, and I mean you had to work. If you got out of your seat you'd have to rush to the bathroom, back again, sit back down, and I mean with your head like this, and I mean, just eight, ten hours straight, if you wanted to…get any money. [We were] always prodded to make more, because if you made a little bit of money that week, it seemed like right away they would bring somebody else to [adjust] the rates, because you were making money and they wanted you to go even faster.… I thrived on good attendance. I had only four tardies in fourteen years.… [*Did your machinery ever break down?*] No, because…I mean, I was the machine, you know? I mean, when I broke down, was when I went to the doctor.*

Throughout the 1970s Mary Lou repeatedly went to her doctor, Arturo Garcia, for sore throats, sinus infections, earaches, fevers, gastrointestinal problems, chronic headaches, chronic coughs, rundown feelings, and bleeding gums. In 1975 she was referred to a specialist for thyroid problems, including the constant colds and flus, weight gain and loss, sleepiness, nervousness, hypertension, high blood pressure, mood swings, loss of memory, decline in cognitive ability, and paresthesia (numbness and tingling). Finally, in 1980, she reluctantly accepted a physician's suggestion that she needed psychological help, because he could find no reason for her symptoms. She was given a prescription for Librium, which she used off and on. She had been repeatedly told by supervisors that the chemicals were known to be harmless. Her doctors did not inquire about her working environment. She was examined by fourteen doctors of various specialties between 1976 and 1984.

MERCY CHAVEZ

Mercy Chavez started work at Lenkurt two months after the plant opened. She had been married five years and had children one and three years old. She had four years' experience working at a medical lab in Oregon. Assigned to Department 320, she was loaned out to every production department in the plant except Crystal Filters. Working at a heated freon tank, she began getting nosebleeds, breathing problems, sore throats, and constant mucous drainage. She had septum surgery in 1974 and again in 1976 to relieve the congestion and nosebleeds.

Mercy later worked near Mary Lou and Sadie, mixing the Lencast epoxy and gluing components. In 1974, "there was always fumes that you could see when you walked inside the plant...a gray, smoky mist, you know...like when a lot of people were smoking." Employees were allowed to smoke on the job in many areas until after 1980. The Lencast epoxy added fumes to that haze:

> *I would say it was strong. It wasn't so bad when we had the little fans going, because [they] would pull it out directly away from our face, and the Lencast, once it started to heat, that smelled like a sulfur. Before then, it didn't have an odor, but once it started to warm up, then it would throw this smoke and it would smell. We would all complain, and then like all humans we would come in early and steal fans from people that had them. Little fans, eight inches, maybe ten inches across. Maybe there were ten in the whole department. And at night when we got ready to leave, we would hide them, you know, because people who could get them would lock them up for tomorrow. That's terrible.*

Mercy worked over a heated freon tank and was issued a rubber apron and face shield. She complained of the rash that traveled up her arms, and after several months GTE supplied a barrier cream to protect the skin from the solvent and retard solvent absorption through the skin. The cream was kept in a supply area and given only to those who asked for it. GTE had done a time and motion study that was later produced to Josephine Rohr. The study timed each step of applying the barrier cream, in tenths of a second: unscrewing the lid of the jar or tube, applying cream, spreading cream, replacing the lid, putting gloves on over the cream, repeating the process after lunch. GTE's analysis found that the use of a barrier cream took fifteen minutes per day from production—an hour a week, five hours a month, sixty hours a year. Therefore, it was not cost effective.

In October 1980, while working with Lencast epoxy glue, Mercy developed severe blistering of her eyelids, nose, and mouth. Her gums swelled and bled. Her friend Ellen Kayser testified that Mercy looked as if she had measles or skin poisoning; Lucille Guernsey, who had the same reaction, said, "We looked like something out of 'Weird Theater.'" The company physician at Lovelace Medical Center verified her allergic reaction to Lencast, using patch tests; GTE put her on medical leave and began paying her workers' compensation weekly. She asked to be given any other job in the plant, but the company interpreted union rules as prohibiting reassignment unless there was another position of her grade open, even under health criteria.

Management settled her case in May 1982, after she had been on unpaid medical leave for eighteen months, with a lump-sum payment of $20,000 and two years of medical coverage. Lenkurt's workers' compensation insurer, Kemper Insurance, supplied her with a lawyer, whom she met for the first time in the corridor outside the courtroom. She never caught his name. Like many lump-sum settlements, it included clauses releasing GTE from any future liability and declaring that Mercy considered the payment just and fair compensation. Mercy thought it was limited specifically to her lost work time, said yes to all questions, and accepted the settlement, which included $100 for the lawyer who represented her at the hearing. Aside from the Lencast episode, Mercy had consulted nine other physicians over her years at GTE.

JANET M. CAUDILL

Janet M. Caudill went to work for GTE at the age of twenty-eight in 1974. She had two children, aged three and eight. According to her medical records and her own recollection, she had not had a single health problem prior to her employment at the plant. Caudill worked in Crystal Filters, making little devices tuned to resonate at a certain frequency. She used a lot of trichloroethylene, freon, and isopropyl alcohol at her work station, and sat near a boiling freon tank. She and her friends often had "rotten-egg burps" from upset stomachs.

> *They kept upping our quotas. There was this fantastic and constant pressure to produce. We had to get creative to handle the quotas—when we were doing okay, we hid extra crystals behind the machine that we could get and put in our quotas on bad days when the pressure got too high.*

A year after she started work at Lenkurt, Caudill hemorrhaged for eight to ten days; she got anemia from the blood loss. She saw a gynecologist, who could find no reason for the bleeding and took her uterus out. He told her afterward, "It was too bad we had to do that, because your uterus was pink and perfectly healthy. But the heavy bleeding gave us no choice." Janet says she "felt bad for all the women who wanted babies and couldn't have them, and there was my good uterus being thrown away." Solvents had been known since the early 1960s to affect the endocrine system, which in women regulates the hormonal functions, including the menstrual cycle, but no Albuquerque doctor made the connection between disturbed menstruation and toxic chemicals.

There were about thirty-five workers on Janet's shift, and several other women in their twenties and thirties had hysterectomies after beginning work there. As the women who had had the operation found out about the others, they joked, "We all get spayed in this department." After two more years, Janet's sinus problems were constant, and she developed high blood pressure. She had to take medication for a heart arrhythmia, another effect of solvent overexposure reported in the literature of toxicology. "I had just tolerated the job because we were buying a house and needed the money," Caudill said. "Then, for a while, I thought I'd just die in that job. But one day, I felt so bad I just quit and went home. I'd had it with feeling so bad." Caudill was in the minority of GTE production workers who could afford to quit and go home. Most lived from paycheck to paycheck, a form of economic powerlessness enforced by management prerogatives to "adjust the work force" at will.

Over the four years that passed after she quit Lenkurt and before the lawsuits became publicized in 1984, Caudill began to see former coworkers at church and at the shopping malls. She began to realize that a lot of them had had serious illnesses. One of them became a plaintiff, and convinced Caudill to go see Josephine Rohr. Before she did, Caudill sat down and made a list of coworkers on the day shift and their health problems. She was shocked to see the total—eleven women out of the approximately thirty-five who had worked there as long as she did, had had hysterectomies. There were miscarriages, thyroid tumors, nasal operations, and blackout spells sprinkled around the group. National trends in performing unneeded hysterectomies have given women in the United States a 50 percent chance of losing reproductive organs by the age of sixty-five. But Janet Caudill's co-workers had a 30 percent rate, by her count, before they were forty.

ELLEN KAYSER

Ellen Kayser was one of the few who came to the new GTE plant with previous electronics experience. She was also one of the older workers, starting at GTE in November 1972 at age forty-seven. Her mother was full-blooded Mescalero Apache, her father Scotch-Irish. Her children were grown by the time she started work at the plant. Before coming to Albuquerque, she had toured southern California as the singer for a country and western band, and she still has an outgoing, country talkativeness.

After some brief electronics training at a local Skills Center, Kayser went to work at the new Singer-Friden plant, helping uncrate the tables, shelves, and machinery and set it all up. Managers immediately spotted her skill in solving mechanical problems on the production lines, and made her a head troubleshooter and inspector. Her ideas broke a bottleneck on the line that made heat sinks used in large adding machines, upping production from 25 to 229 heat sinks a day. Her pride in excellent work clashed with a supervisor who asked her to let defective circuit boards be sent out of her department. After taking time off to recover from a heart attack, she decided not to return to Singer and applied at Lenkurt.

A GTE supervisor noticed Kayser's speed and skill in soldering diodes during the mandatory beginner's electronics course at Lenkurt and asked for her in Department 341. There Kayser made two-inch hybrid circuit boards and installed chip capacitors, inductors, integrated circuits, thermistors, and other components on the boards. Ellen excelled at this detail work, but when borrowed for two weeks by the plastics department, where incentive pay seemed easier to get, she asked to remain there even though it was much rougher work:

> *It was hard, dirty, dangerous work but it kept me good and busy. And I'm a workaholic, I guess, I enjoy working.... We made boxes, spools, tubs, injection moldings, compression moldings, connectors, blocks, face plates, shields, and panels and all sorts of things. It was very interesting work to me, and I did enjoy working in there.*

Moving a heavy upright tool cabinet, with drawers of tools open on the side away from her vision, Ellen broke her wrist: "And the box tipped over, and that handle on there caught my wrist where I couldn't turn loose, and it just twisted on around." She had the GTE nurse put an Ace bandage on it and continued operating power tools for three days. "It finally swolled so bad they sent me to the doctor. It hurt like the mischief, but I and the nurse didn't realize it was broken." She also cut off a finger on a table router:

> *And this I blamed on the engineer that had us do this job, and I told him at the time, I says, "Kelly, someone is going to get hurt seriously with that, because you have no safety device to hold that part." They didn't fix it, and it was me that got it, and I had been warning him that that's what would happen. And as you can see, it's way shorter than the other one because of the piece that was buggered up right bad in the joint. And I do have a pin in it yet from that.*

In 1976 Kayser was transferred to Department 320. She sat near barrels with disturbing labels:

> *It says, "Can Cause Death." I mean, just that simple, "Can Cause Death." I worked as far as from you to me from those barrels all the time.* [What was in the barrels?] *I don't know, but when it runs over the top of the tank, it peels the paint right off the tank.*

In 1979, Kayser became "deathly ill":

> *I kept losing my voice and losing my voice, and at first it was periodically. The nurse referred to it as laryngitis, but I had no sign of cold or anything that remotely resembled a cold...and the last time it happened was on a Friday, we were heading back to the plant from the bank...and she and I were talking, and right in the middle of the conversation, I mean, my words just shut off, I couldn't get a sound out. And she said, "Well, finish telling me." And I couldn't...and it wasn't five minutes later that this pain hit my throat, if you can feature in your mind or imagination what it would feel like to have a giant claw grab ahold of your throat and rip it out...it was excruciating. I couldn't even catch my breath to scream. I couldn't have screamed if I'd wanted to, I had no voice.*

The illness was thyroid cancer, for which she had surgery and radiation treatment that year. Divorced, with no alimony or insurance, she returned to work almost immediately, unable to afford to take a longer recovery without income.

> *I was out exactly a month with that [surgery]. I had to go along there [at work] holding on to things to walk because of the weakened condition I was in. A size ten pant was big and baggy on me, if you can feature that in your mind. But I still continued working.... The following February 29th, I started again getting so deathly sick, and I had this feeling like I was plugged into the wall and somebody had pulled the plug. I just felt like if I was to relax for one instant that I would just literally melt into the floor. I didn't feel like there was a bone in my whole structure, and the hurt was terrible, all in my upper chest and in my throat, the side of my neck, and in behind what I guess is the mastoid there...and it seemed like it just radiated back in behind this eye. And that continued—I lost a total of fifty-eight pounds from February 29th to March 28th...and through it all I have kept going to work. I try not to miss any at all. I try to do my job to the best of my ability. Like I said, as long as the Lord loans me breath, I want to work and earn my way.... I fluctuate from a size eighteen pant to a size ten, back and forth, and it's really miserable, I'll tell you.... And the headaches are always there, and the dizziness and nausea.*
>
> [Do you think these problems are connected?]
>
> *It set us all to wondering why so many from that general area started getting so ill. Several people died. One woman died in my arms at St. Joseph Hospital, Isabel Romero, she died in my arms. And she died in April, prior to my going into the hospital in September.... And the supervisor that used to be on the line working with Isabel was Lupe Luna, and she lost a breast to cancer right after I had the thyroid cancer. And right across the aisle from us was the maintenance department, and Steve—I can't think of Steve's name, bless his soul. But Steve died of cancer. Jim Kelly in the tool crib right directly across from where I was working has lost a leg, or maybe his life by now, I don't know. Cammie Wright used to work in that area when it was Department 390. She was a supervisor. She died. She went into the hospital the same time I went into the hospital. Dot Tuma worked right alongside of us in the Lencast and Plastisol and them other things...but Dot is no longer with us. She died of a brain tumor. And Mary Anaya, she's dead too. And then there was Margie, they removed a brain tumor from her too, but she's still with us. There is Ruby Shannon, and she's all crippled up with cancer. There was so many people. There is Ed Wooten, used to work in 390 with Cammie Wright, and they removed a tumorous growth from his shoulder. And there has been several people that worked with chemicals in the PC lab, the wet area, nine out of ten of these people have had problems of some kind. And I cannot speak for them, and I'm not trying to, but you asked how did I connect all of this.... Irene Baddy, she used to be in charge of moving those chemicals, those barrels and drums with a forklift. And I walked in the bathroom one time and this lady was frantically washing her hands and shaking like a leaf. And I said, "My gosh, Irene, what's wrong?" And she couldn't hardly get any words out. I put my arms around her and calmed her down, and she said, "They're making me change all the labels on all those barrels out there because OSHA is coming to check." And I says, "Well, Irene, surely they won't make you do anything that would harm you." And she says, "Yes, but some of that spilled on me." That woman couldn't calm down and was removed from the plant, taken to a mental institute. The last I heard of her they had taken her to some sanitarium or something. She wasn't exactly the smartest person in the world, but she knew that something was radically wrong, or why would they have her change the labels?*

Ellen Kayser was devastated by the death of Isabel Romero, a quiet Pueblo woman. Though Apache and Pueblo peoples were historically enemies, there was special closeness between the Native Americans of any tribes at the factory.

> *One day at work she was looking as gray as death, and I said, "Isabel, my Lord, are you all right?" She said she had cancer and would only be able to work a few more days. She went out to her mother's at Santa Ana Pueblo when she couldn't work any more. Then, one day when they had brought her in to town to the hospital, I went to visit her there, it was a Wednesday. She asked me to sit her up. She looked at the clock, and said, "One more day." I looked at the clock, and it said five 'til six.*

Next day at work, I asked another Indian friend, Inez, to come with me to see Isabel again right after work. We hurried over there—it was nearly six when we got there. Isabel was rational 'til the last minute. She said, "Oh, Ellen, you're here." I was standing beside the bed; she asked me to sit her up. I took ahold of her one hand, and her sister Lucy took the other. She looked out the window; it was clear as could be. She said, "The clouds will come to take me." Then she said, "I'm so tired." I asked the Lord to take her right then. [Ellen is weeping, her strong voice choked into falsetto.] She was looking straight up at the ceiling. I took and closed her eyes. And we laid her back down. When her mother realized what had happened, her mom grabbed me and clung to me and said, "You're my daughter now." That was April 26, 1979.

CHAPTER 7

CANCER

Cancer is the number two killer of women. Breast and lung cancer lead the cancer incidence list and the cancer mortality list. In part due to earlier detection, women living longer, and increases in environmental carcinogens, the known prevalence of cancer and the known mortality from cancer are increasing among women.

Cancer in women is important to understand because of the number of women it affects. It is also important because it is a disease that scares people: It is invisible, largely asymptomatic, and discovered suddenly when test results are returned. Breast cancer looms especially large; it is something constantly in our consciousness—we are, after all, told to check monthly for signs of breast cancer. One does not cure breast cancer so much as beat the statistics—remaining cancer-free for enough years following treatment to become "potentially cured" (Horton 1992:50).

Cancer research and treatment illustrate the power of the biomedical model; the influence of for-profit actors; and the omnipresence of sexism, racism, and other systems of oppression. Understanding the ways these forces have shaped cancer research and treatment not only provides sociological enlightenment, but also provides the tools to fight for change.

The biomedical model, described in Chapter 1, is a belief system that determines how we think about disease, its causes, and its remedies. Among other things, this model stresses cures over prevention and biological causes over social ones. Research on and treatment of cancer, particularly on breast cancer, testify to the dominance of this approach.

CANCER AND THE BIOMEDICAL MODEL

The biomedical model's mandate to diagnose and treat sick individuals translates into an emphasis on cure, not prevention, in cancer research and clinical trials. Research monies have focused on the development of surgical, chemical, and radiation treatments. With respect to breast cancer, the emphasis on cure has focused on early detection, primarily through the use of mammograms and self-examination. However, for all the stress placed on mammograms, they represent technology that is belatedly and ineffectively regulated (the Mammography Quality Standards Act was not passed until 1992), and more enthusiastically promoted than the reliability of radiologists' interpretations would warrant (Elmore et al. 1994). Furthermore, although researchers agree on the general usefulness of mammograms for women aged 50 and older, there is considerable disagreement about a public policy endorsement of mammograms for women aged 40 to 50 and for even younger cohorts (Love 1993). Furthermore, mammograms are often misrepresented in the popular press and academic literature as being *preventive* measures; they are discussed as "secondary prevention" (Bowen et al. 1993). Yet a mammogram does not prevent cancer; it allows early detection and more effective treatment for people who already have a disease. It is a part of the cure, not prevention. Real prevention stops cancer before it starts.

At the highest levels of policy making and research grant approval, there is strong affirmation of this curative approach. Policy is set by the National Cancer Institute (NCI), a part of the

National Institutes of Health (NIH). The NCI has shown little commitment to prevention research. "In February 1995, the NCI's on-line database for clinical trials listed 173 clinical trials of 'active' treatments for breast cancer, compared with only eight trials focusing on prevention" (Weijer 1995:42). A critic of the "cancer establishment"—which consists of the NCI; the American Cancer Society (ACS), a charity organization; and twenty comprehensive cancer treatment centers—notes that the NCI, among others, shows an "indifference to and ignorance of cancer cause and prevention" in part because the representatives on the various policy bodies have only minimal expertise in occupational and environmental causes (Epstein 1998:72).

A serious concern with prevention would focus our attention on a variety of environmental causes of cancer. For instance, lifetime exposure to estrogen—from early menstruation, longer periods of time on birth control pills, late childbearing, late menopause, and more exposure to estrogen replacement—is associated with cancer (Davis et al. 1999). Such a connection suggests that synthetic estrogenic compounds found in some plastics, pesticides, and fuels may amplify the estrogen effect (Davis and Bradlow 1995), and should be considered as prime candidates in cancer causation. In addition, radiation from X rays, nuclear power, and nuclear weapons testing are potentially carcinogenic (Arditti and Schreiber 1994). And organochlorines, a combination of chlorine and carbon used to manufacture plastics and pesticides, are suspected carcinogens. Greenpeace has published a report entitled "Chlorine, Human Health, and the Environment—The Breast Cancer Warning" discussing the effect of organochlorines (including dioxin, DDT, and PCBs) on cancer; and a Harvard Medical School report in the *Women's Health Watch* indicates that DDT is a prime suspect in breast cancer. Evidence of environmental causes of cancer suggests the possibility of prevention, if we could stop the production of hazardous chemicals.

A concern with prevention would also turn attention to occupational settings. As we note in Chapter 6, occupational health issues have been little researched, and here, too, there is reason to suspect carcinogenic hazards. Industry has been, in the past, quick to exclude women from the workplace to "protect the fetus," but slow to discover the true risks. An even less well-researched area is that of domestic exposure to carcinogens from household cleaning chemicals (Doyal 1995).

Another focus for cancer prevention is the avoidance of tobacco. Although the proximate disease agent is recognized, and women are encouraged by health care providers to stop smoking, if there is to be prevention of cancers caused by tobacco use, we need to go beyond the biological disease agent and focus on the cause of its existence—the power of tobacco companies. The business decisions made by these multinational companies, and their deceit about the addictive properties of nicotine, are the real cause of lung and related cancers. Their actions have affected both men and women, but women have been specifically targeted in advertisements through the years. In the 1930s, tobacco was implicitly advertised to women as a remedy for weight control (Chapter 8). Women are still a targeted tobacco market here and abroad. Virginia Slims has, with its name, found a way to remind us of the weight-control claims of yesteryear and, with its sponsorship of women's sporting events, has worked to be associated with the image of vibrant healthy females. The American Heart Association has taken particular exception to the techniques of one tobacco company:

> *One of the most egregious examples of the tobacco industry's targeting of women was the introduction of "Dakota" by R. J. Reynolds in 1990. An internal Reynolds marketing plan revealed that Dakota was to be marketed to "virile females" between the ages of 18 and 24 who have no education beyond high school and who watch soap operas and attend tractor pulls. At a 1990 Interagency Committee on Smoking and Health meeting chaired by the Surgeon General, the Dakota marketing plan was called a "deliberate focus on young women of low socioeconomic status who are at high risk of pregnancy." (American Heart Association 1999:2)*

Prevention of tobacco-caused cancer will require governmental action against these companies that have become "agents of death."

All of the potential cancer causes noted here thus far are largely ignored by the medical community, and suggest that cancer is socially constructed. Production and profit-making decisions by corporations have put us in contact with carcinogenic compounds. These corporations' economic power, and the ties that they have developed with the cancer-research establishment, have muted concerns about the possibility of environmental hazards. The major cancer-policy decision makers are not neutral players. The chair of the President's Cancer Panel in the early 1980 was Armand Hammer, whose corporation was implicated at Love Canal for toxic dumping. The world's largest private cancer center, Memorial Sloan Kettering, has a board dominated by heads of the oil, chemical, automobile, pharmaceutical, and tobacco industries. An increasing proportion of the budget for the ACS has come from the pharmaceutical industry—which produces drugs for cancer treatment—and other large corporations (Epstein 1999). The potential for conflict of interest is apparent (Paulsen 1994; Arditti and Schreiber 1994). Manifestations of the conflict include ACS's defense of the agrichemical industry when the Public Broadcasting Service (PBS) aired a segment on the health hazards of pesticides in the diets of children, and ACS's "resistant, if not frankly hostile" reactions to the U.S. Office of Technology Assessment's recommendations to test alternative therapies for cancer (Epstein 1999).

When attention and research money have supported attempts to understand the causes of cancer, the focus has been almost exclusively on genetic causes, which is consistent with the biomedical model. Research on breast cancer illustrates this tendency. Two breast cancer genes, BRCA1 and BCRA2, were identified in 1994 and announced to an academic conference and to the public with great fanfare (Davies and White 1996). Research money is now disproportionately targeted to further our knowledge of the action of these genes. Thus, a $100 million donation to a cancer research center at the University of Utah will attempt "to attract 50 new senior researchers, who will focus their work on the genetic aspects of the disease" (Arenson 1995:A12).

Yet, on close examination we find that these two genes account for only a small percent of breast cancer (5 to 10 percent is a typical estimate). Despite all the money and research time focused on the biological basis of breast cancer, "most women who get breast cancer have no known risk factors at all" (Hubbard 1995:91), other than being a woman. Focusing on the two genes will lead to a commercial payoff for the companies involved in screening women for these genes (Hubbard and Lewontin 1996), although the resultant knowledge is of questionable use for women. Not only would a woman not learn how to prevent her cancer, but she would also be left with disturbing genetic knowledge. Already, some women fearful of familial cancer have chosen one option in response to this knowledge: prophylactic removal of the breast. Hubbard, a biologist who has written extensively on women and health, suggests that we have entered an era of "genomania" in which the search for genetic connections "draws our attention away from the major problems that needlessly threaten the health of large segments of the world's population" (Hubbard 1995:14).

FOR-PROFIT VENTURES

Cancer, like many other areas of health, is big business. Sales of drugs for the treatment of cancer alone exceed $12 billion annually (Epstein 1999). For-profit involvement includes the relatively straightforward development and promotion of products, but it also includes cases in which the for-profit connection is more complex and sinister. The mammography industry and the cancer drug tamoxifen are interesting examples.

Early detection through mammography has been a mainstay in the official fight against breast cancer. Why has the mammography industry assumed such a prominent role, and who benefits from the success of this industry? Mammography became prominent in part because it is well connected to the cancer establishment: five presidents of the ACS have been radiologists (Epstein 1999). When policy is decided, the voices of the ACS and the mammography industry, not those of epidemiologists who might advocate for prevention rather than early detection, are well represented. Moreover, a main beneficiary of the profits from the mammogram industry is a corporate polluter. General Electric (GE), a polluter of New York's Hudson River valley, also makes mammography machines. Thus, in effect, GE causes cancer, then profits from attempts to detect it (Batt and Gross 1999).

GE's dual role as profitable polluter and profitable problem solver is similar to that of the Zeneca corporation, which manufactures chlorinated chemicals and has dumped carcinogenic wastes, and then profited from developing a cancer treatment—Nolvadex, a trade name for tamoxifen. In addition, Zeneca has been a force in determining the discourse around breast cancer. It has been able to define the cancer problem in ways beneficial to its own interests because, as the primary financial backer for National Breast Cancer Awareness Month (NBCAM), it can literally censor the discussion of environmental causes of cancer (Paulsen 1994). A coalition of activist organizations in the Bay Area, the Toxic Links Coalition (TLC), have called NBCAM's

> *discourse of early detection and its refusal to speak of carcinogens and prevention...as a campaign of miseducation, obfuscation, and shameless profiteering. Therefore, as part of their project of reeducation, the TLC declared that October was no longer National Breast Cancer Awareness Month but was instead renamed Cancer Industry Awareness Month. TLC's first collective action was to set up an informational picket at the 1994 Race for the Cure in Golden Gate Park. They targeted the Race because its sponsor, the Komen Foundation, was a participant in NBCAM and because the Komen Foundation, like NBCAM, avoided any mention of causality, carcinogens, or the environment in its publicity. (Klawiter 1999:118)*

Further controversy surrounds Zeneca because of the Tamoxifen Breast Cancer Prevention Trial begun in 1992. In this study, tamoxifen, a drug sometimes given to former breast-cancer patients in the hopes of preventing recurrence, was given to healthy women in order to test its prevention potential. Although admirable in its focus on prevention, this was prevention at great risk—tamoxifen is known to be associated with an increased risk of uterine cancer and other health problems. Such a study represents a movement toward the medicalization of prevention (Fugh-Berman and Epstein 1992), rather than realizing prevention through a societal reduction of environmental carcinogens. (Arditti and Schreiber 1998, reproduced here).

SEXISM

The major focal points of the discussion of women and cancer are the emphasis placed on cure rather than prevention, the focus on genetic causes above others, and the entanglement of for-profit actors with both policy-making organizations and seemingly neutral charity organizations such as the ACS. It is also important to note, however, that the discourse on cancer has included a subtle sexism. When the Women's Health Trial, a nutritional study of the hypothesis that the percent of fat in one's diet affected breast cancer, was first proposed in the 1980s, it was thwarted by researchers who had much to lose if nutritional causes of cancer were taken seriously (Rennie 1993). A movement toward such studies would bring in a cadre of new researchers from different specialties, and would limit monies to the currently active research labs. One mode of attack against the study included claims that women's allegedly unreliable memories of diet made the proposed study weak (even though using men's memories in similar studies of heart disease had not been questioned); and that women were incapable of changing their diets (despite evidence to the contrary) (Rennie 1993).

The research on cervical cancer provides another illustration. A century-old study of cervical cancer compared cloistered nuns to the general population and found that nuns did not have cervical cancer (Darby 1992). The study has had a profound influence on cervical cancer research and treatment; it has led to a characterization of the disease as a disease of promiscuity, causing doctors to ask young women with positive Pap smears questions about the number of sexual partners they have, and to blame their sexuality for their health problem. In her book *In the Patient's Best Interest,* Fisher writes of two conversations she had with doctors reacting to their patient's abnormal Pap smears. The first doctor told her

> *that an unmarried, sexually active young woman was promiscuous and getting what she deserved.... [Another doctor] commented that they (young women) think they are all grown up when they do it (engage in sexual intercourse) but they cry like babies when they have to pay the consequences (again the consequences are an abnormal Pap smear). Like many physicians, these doctors drew a causal inference: sexual intercourse with multiple partners at an early age caused cervical cancer. (Fisher 1988:27–28)*

This misplaced emphasis has meant that many promising leads about the cause of cervical cancer have been neglected, including the effects of both birth control pills and the male partner's occupational exposure to carcinogens on cervical cancer. Possible causes in their own right, many times these other variables are seen primarily as correlates of promiscuity (Darby 1992).

Another example of sexism in the medical profession's detection and treatment of cancer is the fact that lesbian women often encounter discriminatory attitudes from health care providers, which reduces the chances of early detection (O'Hanlan 1995).

RACE, CLASS, AND CANCER

One's race and class influence the likelihood that one will have cancer: One's economic resources, nutritional habits, occupation, living conditions, and residential location—all linked to race and class in our society—affect the predisposition to cancer. Race and class are also related to access to health care and treatment options, which influences mortality.

Black women are more than twice as likely as white women to die of breast cancer, in large part because their disease more often reaches an advanced stage before it is diagnosed (Eley et al. 1994). Minority women and poor women have less access to screening for cancer because screening programs do not have effective strategies to enroll underserved populations (Vellozzi, Romans, and Rothenberg 1996). One reason for the racial differences in mortality is that protocols in public clinics often do not define a policy for breast cancer detection, and once detected, minority women receive inadequate treatment (Chapter 4). There are treatment differences by race and social class. For instance, black women are less likely to be treated surgically for breast cancer than white women, and more likely to have no treatment at all (McWhorter and Mayer 1987). Clinical follow-up after an abnormal mammography is slower for a minority woman than for a white woman (Chang et al. 1996).

RESPONDING TO CANCER

A growing literature on women with cancer has highlighted feminist concerns and made evident the contribution of a qualitative approach that seeks to hear the voices of affected women. Women who have had a mastectomy have not merely had a medical procedure that has removed a cancerous growth. In addition to the medical dimension of their illness, they face social and psychological issues. They encounter a public claiming they are disfigured, mutilated, and lopsided in a society in which women's attractiveness to men is a key measure of their social worth. Such a characterization "is clearly influenced by the cultural emphasis on breasts as objects of male sexual interest and male sexual pleasure" (Wilkinson and Kitzinger 1993:230). The resultant socially defined need to reconstruct the breast is then heavily marketed. Yet this focus on the appearance of the breast may relate little to the woman's psychological needs at the time. Issues of mortality may be more important. Some women do not mourn the loss of the breast nor value its surgical replacement (Kasper 1994:272); some attend more to hair loss, perhaps as symbolic of the assault on their self-concepts and social isolation (Kasper 1994:274). Others may refuse breast reconstruction, seeing reconstruction as unnecessary for moving forward with their lives

(Kasper 1994:276), and be resentful of the ACS's Reach for Recovery program, which requires volunteer workers who have had mastectomies to wear a prosthesis so they will look "normal" (Batt 1994; reproduced as a reading in this chapter). For some, coping with a mastectomy is more than a cosmetic concern. Rather, it raises issues about social norms of body image, puts women at risk of commercial exploitation, and silences their experiences.

WOMEN'S VOICES

Women's voices are important in changing cancer research, policy, and treatment. At the individual level, support groups have been important resources for women with cancer, and some recent evidence would even suggest that they confer some increase in survival time (Spiegel et al. 1989; Spiegel 1995; Waxler-Morrison et al. 1991). Women's voices are also important in the doctor's office. Asking questions during an exam has been shown to be an important way for women to provide options for themselves. In decisions about a hysterectomy, a woman who simply asks if there are other options is less likely to have an unnecessary operation (Fisher 1988:50–55; Bickell et al. 1994).

Women's voices, coming together, have been important in building organizations effective in questioning the power of the biomedical model's emphasis on genetic cause and the near exclusion of research on environmental causes and prevention (Chapter 16). Consumer groups and books by women have pushed for informed-consent laws that question the routinization of radical mastectomies (Montini and Ruzek 1989). Local groups have been important in bringing attention to cancer issues. The National Women's Health Network (NWHN) has produced fact sheets, testified in Congress for more attention to environmental causes of cancer and for more safeguards in the Tamoxifen Breast Cancer Prevention Trial, questioned the routine use of mammograms for premenopausal women, and successfully petitioned federal government agencies to conduct research on the relationship between oral contraceptive use and breast cancer (Pearson 1995). Numerous local, breast-cancer activist groups exist, as do more focused groups such as the African American Breast Cancer Alliance and the Project for Lesbians with Cancer.

The voices of these groups and the voices of individual women question the current emphasis in cancer research and treatment, which relies almost exclusively on the biomedical model's concern with genetic causes and cure over prevention; responds to profit interests rather than the interests of women; and continues to devalue women.

"PERFECT PEOPLE": CANCER CHARITIES

SHARON BATT

Some readers may be startled to learn that the overall mortality rate from carcinoma of the breast remains static. If one were to believe all the media hype, the triumphalism of the profession in published research, and the almost weekly miracle breakthroughs trumpeted by the cancer charities, one might be surprised that women are dying at all from this cancer.

—Editorial, *Lancet,* Feb. 6, 1993

...The period of my cancer treatments was an intensely inward-looking time. I counted the days to the end of my chemotherapy and radiation treatments, and watched my athletic looks give way to pallor, weight gain and ghoulish baldness. I struggled with my fear of death. And I wondered: how could I have been so oblivious to a disease that claims the lives of so many women—5,500 in Canada and 45,000 in the U.S. in 1992; 570,000 world wide in 1980. Breast cancer claims women at an age considered young in industrialized counties; [on average] age 62, compared to age 82 for women who die of cardiovascular disease. Many who die are women like me, who believed themselves healthy, well informed, and somewhere in the mid-region of their life. When I learned these facts, I felt tricked, as if I had stumbled into a chamber of horrors kept secret behind a veil of cheerful platitudes. *Do breast self-exams. Have regular mammograms. See your doctor at the first sign of a lump. Breast cancer can be cured!* I needed to know where these slogans had come from....

After my diagnosis I became very curious about the Cancer Society. What I had assumed was a worthy organization devoted to aiding people who had cancer took on the appearance of an extremely odd beast which lumbered in incomprehensible ways. As a cancer patient, I was struck most of all by the Society's absence in my time of need. No volunteer had visited me in the hospital. After my surgery, in the long hours of waiting for chemotherapy treatments and check-ups, I sometimes perused the stacks of brochures in the hospital waiting room. Most were published in the U.S. and simply reprinted with a Canadian Cancer Society logo. For the most part they gave the standard advice on breast self-exams and explained the conventional treatments. One that caught my eye was titled "The Woman with Breast Cancer as a Single Woman." I picked it up, wondering why we singles needed our own special leaflet. Inside, a text that would do Ann Landers proud explained that a woman does not have to mention her cancer surgery to a man on a casual first date, but she would want to tell him soon, "if he is someone she cares about."

A few years later, I got another glimpse of the Cancer Society at a meeting of the National Coalition of Cancer Survivors (NCCS) in Denver. I joined the American advocacy group because I wanted to meet others with cancer and no Canadian organization existed to give a voice to our concerns. The conference had a slot set aside for networking and a group of about 12 of us with breast cancer squeezed into someone's hotel room to exchange experiences.

Elaine Hill, a slender Black woman in her early 50s, gave a frank account of her frustration with the American Cancer Society. Her first disappointment with the Society had come shortly after her diagnosis. She decided she needed something more than her conversations with doctors, friends and family could provide. "I'd reached the point where I wanted to talk to another woman who had the disease." She called the American Cancer Society in her Tennessee community and explained her situation. The receptionist told her about Reach to Recovery. She could send Elaine a visitor, but she needed a doctor's referral.

Elaine was incredulous. "You mean you don't believe I have breast cancer?" she asked.

"Oh, no," said the receptionist, "You just have to have a doctor's referral."

At that point Elaine was looking for another surgeon. She didn't want the same doctor who had done her biopsy to perform the rest of her surgery and she had no physician who could make the referral. "So I struggled along without another woman to talk with, until I finally pinned down a neighbour and said to her, "You've lived here all these years, surely you must know *one* woman with breast cancer I can talk to!"

"And that was my first experience with Reach to Recovery."

I considered Elaine's experience little short of emotional abuse, but it wasn't the first disturbing story I'd heard about Reach to Recovery. Rose Kushner waged a long battle with the American Cancer Society over its Reach to Recovery program. The problems started in 1974 when Kushner, who was convinced that women who had mastectomies suffered long-term physical and psychological trauma, asked the Society to help her document women's reactions to breast surgery long after the operation. No way, said a Reach to Recovery rep in the ACS' Washington office. Kushner's idea ran counter to the whole philosophy of Reach to Recovery, namely, "to convince women they do not have a disabling handicap." When setting up the program, the Cancer Society had explicitly rejected the idea of a "mastectomy club" although such long-term support groups exist for people who have had bowel, bladder and larynx operations. "Having a mastectomy is not a permanent handicap," the woman informed Kushner, "and even the worst of scars can be hidden by a well-fitting prosthesis and the right clothes. So we decided we would help the woman for just a few weeks and then leave her to her own psychological recovery."[1]

This made no sense to Kushner. "What good was a 'recovery' program that left women stranded after a hospital visit and a few weeks of telephone service?" she asked. Her own mastectomy, although expertly done and not a radical, left her numb for five months in the area around the incision, and so tender in other places that "any fondling from the waist up was simply out of the question." Anywhere near the left arm was "strictly no touch." And a day of Caribbean sun left her with a temporary case of lymphedema—her arm "began to develop strange swollen curves and to twist and grind."[2] As for her psychological adjustment, she firmly believed for several years that she had no hang-ups about being one-breasted, until a fire in a hotel where she was staying forced her to admit that she could not venture out in public looking lopsided, even if her life was in danger.

I had also read an essay by the poet Audre Lorde about her encounter with a Reach to Recovery volunteer. Lorde felt "outraged and insulted" after the woman's visit to her hospital room, and "even more isolated than before." The volunteer, says Lorde, was "quite admirable and even impressive in her own right." But she did not speak to Lorde's concerns, which were not about "what man I could capture in the future, much less whether my two children would be embarrassed by me in front of their friends." Lorde's questions had to do with her chances of survival, the effects of a possibly shortened life upon her work and her priorities, whether the cancer could have been prevented, and how she could keep it from recurring. As a 44-year-old Black lesbian feminist, she did not expect the woman to be a role model but she did attempt to discuss with her the task of integrating the experience into the whole of her life. The woman glossed over her questions, chided her for not looking "on the bright side of things" and gave her a lambswool puff to fill out her bra.

The volunteer's response gathered resonance when Lorde went to her doctor's office 10 days later. This was her first trip out since coming home from the hospital and she had groomed and dressed herself carefully. She felt beautiful and glad to be alive. She was surprised when the nurse, rather than complimenting her on how well she looked, remarked instead ("a little anxiously and not at all like a question") that she was not wearing a prosthesis. "No," said Lorde, "It doesn't really feel right."

The nurse, usually sympathetic, continued to press the point. Even if the temporary prosthesis didn't look exactly right, it was "better than nothing" and would do until she was ready for a "real form." She informed Lorde that she would "feel so much better with it on" and that they really would like her to wear something when she came for her appointments, "otherwise it's bad for the morale of the office."[3] Lorde was outraged by this "assault on my right to define and to claim my own body."

In a newspaper article, I'd read about a Canadian Cancer Society volunteer named Darlene Betteley in Waterloo, Ontario. Darlene's story was so odd I made a detour to her modest bungalow in the community outside Toronto, to hear her full account.

After Betteley's cancer diagnosis in 1986, she had both breasts removed. A few years later, she became a Reach to Recovery volunteer. When one of the convenors (the woman who matches visitors with patients) discovered that Betteley did not wear breast prostheses, Betteley was advised that she would have to get a bustline or give up her visits. "We like our volunteers to look normal," the convenor explained.

Betteley has all the letters and newspaper clippings from the dispute neatly organized in a big blue binder. The opening page has two full-length, colour photos of her, standing erect in her back yard—Before and After Surgery. "Now

I ask you, Sharon," she prompts me, "Do I look normal?"

An unlikely rebel, Betteley is in her mid-50s, a mother of grown children and a devout believer. She loved making hospital visits. She enjoys people and when she recovered from her two operations she was so happy to be alive that she wanted to share her zest for life with others. She had modelled as a teenager and she still loves clothes. She took pride in her ability to dress becomingly after the two mastectomies. She had been a Reach to Recovery volunteer for over a year when her convenor, who knew she didn't wear a prosthesis, called her to "talk things over." It happened that the head convenor for Ontario had called the local convenor in search of a suitable visitor for a woman who was having a double prophylactic mastectomy. Darlene's name was suggested. Did she wear a prosthesis? the Ontario convenor wanted to know.

"No."

"Well," the provincial convenor said, "We like our volunteers to look normal."

The local convenor, a woman Betteley knew well, presented her with the senior convenor's verdict. Faced with the prospect of losing her volunteer status, Betteley almost capitulated, but something in her rose up in protest. "Why should I have to go against something I really believe?" she asked. "I am happy with myself. You have to like yourself before you can share your happiness and your love with other people."

In that case, the convenor said, Betteley could no longer make hospital visits.

"Well, there were tears and there was anger," explained Betteley, "because visiting was very important to me." She began asking question that had never occurred to her before. "I thought, 'does the Cancer Society have anything to do with all these companies that make prostheses? And what do they do with the money they raise?'" Betteley's daughter Cathy was particularly incensed by her mother's dismissal. Cathy worked as a personnel officer and she urged her mother to complain to the Human Rights Commission. Betteley demurred. She would rather put the whole thing behind her. "There'll be another door opening," she said, with her characteristic aplomb.

Cathy wrote a letter to the chairman of the volunteer unit at the local Cancer Society office. Betteley also wrote to the Society, explaining that "after discussions with my doctor and my husband, I decided, for my own physical comfort, not to wear a prosthesis." Cathy sent yet another letter to the editor of the local newspaper and the paper decided to run a story. At a nearby university, a sociology student was so indignant when he read the article, he fired off letters to every major newspaper in the country. The first to pick up on it was the *Globe and Mail.* By now, Betteley had lost her reticence about speaking out. A male volunteer, she pointed out in the front page story, "is not required to shove a golf ball down his pants before meeting people." The policy, she said, was sexist ("a word I didn't even have in my vocabulary until these students brought it to mind"). "I'm wondering how many men sit on the board of the Cancer Society who need to see a woman with a bustline," she told the reporter. The *Globe and Mail* story opened the media floodgates. First the Toronto *Star* phoned for an interview, then a Florida tabloid, which ran its version of the story under the headline, "Whatta Bunch of Boobs!" The same day, reporters from her local TV station crowded into her small living room with lights and cameras while another TV crew waited in the driveway to get in. Next Betteley guested on a noon hour radio phone-in program from Montreal. "It was awesome," she recalls.

The Canadian Cancer Society's public response did little to shed light on the organization's thinking. "There is a lot of misinformation and confusion about our policy," said the local convenor, Maryann Istiloglu. "Women who are about to undergo breast surgery, or who have just had the procedure, don't want to be reminded of how they are going to end up looking,"she said.[4] Mark Sikich, co-chairman of patient services for Betteley's local unit explained that breast cancer patients are usually emotional after surgery, "Most patients are very concerned with body image and looking so-called normal. It's best to send someone in wearing a prosthesis." An Ontario representative said that since one aspect of a volunteer's visit was to provide a temporary prosthesis, and information about purchasing a permanent prosthesis, "To be not wearing a prosthesis herself would appear to be a contradiction of the message she is bringing." Not all Society personnel agreed. One said the policy made her angry and she would never enforce it.[5] Most of the eight volunteers working for the Society's Kitchener-Waterloo office resigned after the incident.

Wear casual clothes. Must be well-fitted over the bustline. Darlene Betteley points to the offending line in the handbook she was given when she trained as a Canadian Cancer Society volunteer. In later editions the grooming instructions were changed (*Be nicely groomed and dressed. Don't wear heavy cologne or jangly jewelry.*) but the policy stood as an unwritten rule, at least in the minds of some Cancer Society officials. Other rules clearly circumscribe the volunteer's scope for discussion. "*Never* give medical advice or interfere with the patient's relationship with the doctor," says one; "Do not be persuaded to show your scar, or look at the scar of the person you are visiting," instructs another. Among the qualifications for volunteers is "a positive attitude toward conventional treatment methods." As well, the volunteer "does not promote unconventional therapies."...

Elaine Hill's second experience with the Cancer Society in Tennessee was a variation on the same theme. Elaine's surgery left her with lymphedema ("milk-arm"), a permanent and debilitating result of breast surgery which is not uncommon. Both surgery and radiation can damage the circulatory system of lymph fluid in the arm so that the fluid flows down the arm but not up. One result is a lowered resistance to infection in that arm; another is swelling which can be extremely painful and impair movement. An elastic post-mastectomy sleeve is one method of damage control, while severe cases may require a lymphedema pump.

Elaine wears a lymphedema sleeve. When I met her in Denver, she described a rejection not unlike Darlene Betteley's. People at the local branch of the ACS knew that Elaine had worked as a social worker and approached her about working as a Reach to Recovery visitor. She agreed, she says, "because I thought it was a very good thing."

Shortly before the training session started, Elaine developed lymphedema. She decided she should let the Cancer Society know about this development before the training started. "In the back of my mind" she says,"I guess I thought they would say, 'well gee, you're so great, come on and do it anyway.' Instead, they said they would get back to me." Three weeks passed without a word, so Elaine called the office. "After hemming and hawing," Elaine recalls, "the lady told me they couldn't use me because of the sleeve. They needed 'perfect people,' people with no sign of cancer to go to talk to the women. That was their policy."

"Well, lymphedema *is* a common side effect of breast cancer surgery," Elaine responded. The woman wouldn't bite on that one, but suggested perhaps Elaine could take off the sleeve, or come in when the lymphedema got better. "I have no real hope that I can ever go without the sleeve," Elaine told her, "and I can't do exercises without the sleeve on."

Elaine didn't let on how hurt she felt. "I assured them I had no hard feelings—though I really did feel badly. I said, 'I understand, I certainly don't want to frighten anyone or raise their anxiety level.'" In fact, she felt rejected. "First I had surgery, then three months later they found cancer in the other breast so I had surgery again. This seemed like another knock in the face—and from the American Cancer Society!"[6]

Far from overhauling its "get-on-with-it" view of breast cancer recovery, in recent years the American Cancer Society has redefined the cosmetic problem. In 1988, the ACS launched a new initiative called Look Good, Feel Better (LGFB), in collaboration with a charitable foundation set up by cosmetics manufacturers and people employed in the beauty industry. Women having treatment are now invited to come to their local hospital for a group makeover "workshop" where they receive tips on beauty techniques and a package of free cosmetics. The idea caught fire in the U.S., spread to Australia, and soon had its copycat program in Canada, sponsored by the Canadian Cancer Society and a similar consortium from the beauty industry....

The PR and marketing appeal of LGFB for the beauty industry is fairly straightforward, but the gusto with which medical professionals have taken up the cause of make-up for cancer patients warrants scrutiny. Oncology is, after all, the same specialty that rains scepticism on meditation, visualization, support groups, and other "soft" feel-good adjuncts to medical treatment. Yet in no time, with funding from the cosmetic industry's Foundation, Yale University's Comprehensive Cancer Center undertook a two-year study "to evaluate the effectiveness of Look Good, Feel Better on quality of life for women breast cancer patients undergoing chemotherapy treatment."[7]

The intense romance between medical experts and cosmeticians is less bizarre than it seems at first glance. The same magnet that pulled surgeons to Reach to Recovery now has oncologists stuck on Look Good, Feel Better. In the days of the Halsted radical, surgeons used to worry that terror of surgical mutilation would keep women from having a lump investigated. Bedside visits by "perfect people," they hoped, would soothe fears about surgery. These fears were firmly rooted in reality—the operation was sexually devastating, often caused permanent physical disability and frequently failed to arrest the disease—but that was of no matter. Reach to Recovery was tailored precisely to deflect these fears, not to meet the woman's deep emotional needs. Part of Reach to Recovery's current crisis stems from the fact that the Cancer Society can't figure out how to adapt the program to women who look no different after surgery than before.

Enter Look Good, Feel Better. The treatment that most often affects a breast cancer patient's appearance today is chemotherapy. Now it's the oncologist who frets that a patient might not show up for her appointment. Chemotherapy's most dramatic effect is hair loss, but the circulating poisons can also cause weight loss or weight gain and turn glowing skin into a splotchy mess. In the early stages of the disease, when most women are diagnosed, the illness itself is much less likely to affect the woman's appearance than are the treatments. Radiation, which is standard therapy after breast conserving therapy, has some of the same effects on one's looks. Reach to Recovery gained entrée as a Cancer Society's program in the late 1960s, just when the Halsted radical was going down for the last count. Now, with chemo cocktails on the ropes, make-up companies are welcomed in many leading cancer centers.

Coincidence or not, both programs have the timely effect of diverting our attention from the main drama being played out in the medical arena. In the current debate over chemotherapy, as in the earlier debate over radical surgery, critics within the profession are asking defenders of an orthodox treatment whether the benefits really justify making the woman Look Bad, Feel Worse.

Audre Lorde faulted Reach to Recovery for encouraging nostalgia in women with breast cancer. While the urge to go back to the pre-cancer state is a natural reaction (Lorde felt its pull herself), it is regressive, she says. Rather than facing the full dimensions of the diagnosis, Reach to Recovery encourages the woman to concentrate on breast cancer as a cosmetic problem, "one which can be solved by a prosthetic pretence."[8]

Rose Kushner also deplored Cancer Society policies that forced women to go underground with their pain. She welcomed the famous coming-out of Betty Ford and Happy Rockefeller in 1974, but was uneasy that the women and the media coverage steered away from the subject of physical and emotional aftereffects. "Pain? Swelling? Not a word. The only problems either woman would admit to were some fatigue and discomfort. As far as the psychological aspects of losing their breasts were concerned, neither woman admitted having any emotional problems whatsoever." Mrs. Ford was quoted as saying the mastectomy involved only a "little foam rubber." She had no patience with women who said they would rather lose an arm than a breast, "I can't imagine such talk," she said, "It's so stupid." Her advice to women was the classic, "Once it's done, put it behind you and go on with your life."[9] Mrs. Rockefeller wrote in *Reader's Digest* that she, too, was "putting breast cancer behind her." In the coverage of the Ford and Rockefeller diagnoses, Kushner complained, "the grim side of breast cancer was somehow understated. The media seemed to concentrate only on the cosmetics of breast cancer."

When Kushner revised her book in 1984, she reported that a whiff of reality appeared to have seeped into the American Cancer Society. Several women she regarded highly had risen in the Society's hierarchy. Kushner predicted "new and valuable programs" would be put in place and "archaic traditions" would be abandoned. She was particularly eager to see the ACS abandon a long-standing philosophy that all information must reach patients through their physicians. "The words M.D. no longer stand for Medical Deity in the minds of women today," she declared. "While menfolk may still be timid and trusting about their medical/surgical problems, we women want to know. What's more, we want to have more than a tip of our fingers in deciding our own destinies. Current ACS standards prohibit giving women anything other than predigested information that has been approved by a board of physicians."[10] Kushner, of course, was a leading fountain of "non-approved" information. In addition to writing a popular book, she set up a non-profit information hotline and mail service, the Breast Cancer Advisory Center, which she ran with a nurse.

My assessment, in the early 1990s, is that the changes Kushner hoped for have not occurred. If anything, the Cancer Societies, both Canadian and American, are more removed than ever from women's desire to know and to control their destinies. Incidents like Darlene Betteley's expulsion (in 1990) and Elaine Hill's exclusion (in 1991) dramatize the attitudes that make Reach to Recovery an object of anger and ridicule among women with cancer. They are not isolated incidents, but part of the underground lore now developing among women with breast cancer who are speaking out....

When your life is at risk, play-acting that you are well exacts an emotional price. It creates barriers of communication between the woman with cancer and those she loves. Attempting to look "beautiful," "normal" or "perfect" drains money from our bank accounts at a time when we may be unable to work. Most important, these tricks to keep surgery and baldness secret make us invisible to each other and to society at large. Astonishingly, it took activists speaking out in large numbers to alert the North American public that the "advances" of modern medicine have not lowered the death rate of women in our most prosperous societies from breast cancer. Women, and the public at large, had swallowed the lie that breast cancer is a piffling disease, easily treated and relegated to one's past.

Naomi Wolf argues that the idea of an objective quality called "beauty" is a myth that is not about women at all. "It is about men's institutions and institutional power."[11] The experiences of Audre Lorde, Darlene Betteley, Rose Kushner and Elaine Hill illustrate how the beauty myth is used against women with cancer to reinforce the power of the institutions of medicine and medical technology. Inner confidence in her own beauty allowed each woman to buck the coercion. Rather than conforming to the norm of silence, they spoke out. The same assurance permits a growing number of women, like Ellen Hobbs, to live with breast cancer on their own terms, and to challenge these oppressive institutions.

The changes in my appearance when I was having cancer treatments affected me in a way that was not trivial. My altered appearance was an integral part of a profound change in my life. Just after my diagnosis, I recall glimpsing myself in the washroom mirror at the office and observing a woman with dishevelled hair and wild eyes. The Madwoman of Shallot, I thought with a shock… and I continued out into the office without bothering to comb my hair. I was a madwoman at that moment and if it bothered my co-workers, so be it. As the months wore on, I lost my hair and became increasingly fatigued. When my friend Jeannie commented that I looked tired, I snapped in anger that I was not at all tired, I'd just been to the gym. Later I admitted to myself that her remark, meant caringly, was extremely threatening. Maybe the treatments weren't doing me any good. Maybe I was dying. My appearance was an imperfect barometer to my prospects of recovery but it was more real to me than a blood test. I also remember shocks of pleasure, like examining the contours of my bald head in the mirror and marvelling at its shapeliness. These experiences, and many more, were part of reconciling myself to the changed person I was—no longer a woman whose health was "perfect."

The beauty myth subverts women's power, says Naomi Wolf.[12] A woman with cancer who confronts the world with her baldness or breastlessness has tremendous power to effect change. Audre Lorde captured this in her oft-quoted image, "For instance, what would happen if an army of one-breasted women descended upon Congress and demanded that the use of carcinogenic, fat-stored hormones in beef feed be outlawed?" Gradually women with cancer are beginning to harness the power Lorde held out to us. Artist Matushka used it when she revealed her mastectomy scar on the cover of the *New York Times Magazine.* With one unforgettable image, she obliterated the pretence that women look "normal" after breast surgery.

Seeing my own photo, hairless, in the newspaper gave me strength. I had faced my own human vulnerability and exposed my tenuous grip on life to others. I felt the power of my act when I arrived for a doctor's appointment and learned that a nurse had posted the article in the staff room. Again, when a stranger who heard me say my name in the post office accosted me to tell me that she had given my article to a newly diagnosed friend. And once more when a shy woman approached me at a public meeting holding the crumpled three-year-old clipping in which I had voiced her own feelings.

"There is nothing wrong, per se, with the use of prostheses, if they can be chosen freely for whatever reason after a woman has had a chance to accept her new body," says Audre Lorde.[13] Nor is there any reason why a woman with cancer shouldn't wear make-up or a wig. I know women who thoroughly enjoyed a Look Good, Feel Better session, who were happy to have a free bag of expensive cosmetics to take home. (Not the least of their pleasure came from the opportunity to meet with other women with cancer.) But the intense promotion of prostheses and cosmetics, coupled with the coercive tactics used on those who eschew them, signal that these accessories are not really meant for our benefit.

The myth that medical treatments transform women with breast cancer back into "perfect people" nurtures a dependence on the medical profession and related technologies. We turn their inadequacies against ourselves, believing that if we die of the disease, it is because we failed to do breast self-exams the "right" way; or we didn't have mammograms often or soon enough; or our uncooperative bodies "failed to respond to treatment." If each woman with breast cancer understood medicine's limited ability to control the disease, our reliance on physicians, tests and medical interventions would be enormously reduced. The power of these institutions over us would dwindle accordingly. Without the Rosy Filter, women with breast cancer would gain the right to map our own futures, within the very real constraints imposed by a life-threatening disease.

NOTES

1. Rose Kushner, 1986. *Alternatives: New Developments in the War on Breast Cancer.* New York: Warner: 314–315.
2. Kushner: 325.
3. Audre Lorde, 1980. *The Cancer Journals.* San Francisco: Spinsters Ink: 59.

4. Robert MacLeod, 1990. "Cancer Society Aide Attacks 'Sexist Policy,'" *Globe and Mail.* Dec. 6: Al.
5. Margaret Mironowicz, 1990. "Ex-Cancer Patient Is Eager to Share Gained Confidence," *Kitchener-Waterloo Record.* Aug. 24: C 1.
6. Interview with Elaine Hill, Tennessee, Jan. 4, 1992.
7. Barbara Aarsteinsen, 1993. "Don't Make Do... Makeup: The Look Good, Feel Better Program," *Chatelaine,* Oct: 8.
8. Lorde: 55.
9. James T. Patterson, 1987. *The Dread Disease: Cancer and Modern American Culture.* Cambridge: Harvard University Press.
10. Kushner: 380–381.
11. Naomi Wolf, 1991. *The Beauty Myth.* Toronto: Vintage: 12–13.
12. Wolf: 46.
13. Lorde: 63.

BREAST CANCER: THE ENVIRONMENTAL CONNECTION, A 1998 UPDATE

RITA ARDITTI AND TATIANA SCHREIBER

Today in the United States we live in the midst of a cancer epidemic. Cancer is currently the second leading cause of death; one out of every three people will get some kind of cancer, and one out of four will die from it. Twenty-seven years have gone by since the National Cancer Act was signed, yet the treatments offered to cancer patients are the same ones as those offered fifty years ago: surgery, radiation, and chemotherapy (or slash, burn, and poison, as they are called bitterly by both patients and increasingly disappointed professionals). And in spite of sporadic pronouncements from the cancer establishment, survival rates for the three main cancer killers—lung, breast, and colorectal cancer—have remained virtually unchanged and depressingly low.

In the 1960s and 1970s environmental activists and a few scientists emphasized that cancer was linked to environmental contamination, and their concerns began to make an impact on the public awareness of the disease.[1] In the 1980s and early 1990s, however, with an increasingly conservative political climate and concerted efforts on the part of industry to play down the importance of chemicals in causing cancer, we were presented with a new image of the disease. It was portrayed as an individual problem that could be overcome only with the help of experts and then only if one had the money and the know-how to recruit them for one's personal survival efforts. The emphasis on personal responsibility, lifestyle, and genetic factors has reached absurd proportions. People with cancer are asked "why they brought this disease on themselves" and why they don't work harder at "getting well." Testing for "cancer genes" is presented as one of the most important new developments in cancer research, with little or no evidence of the usefulness of this testing for the vast majority of the population.

While people with cancer should be encouraged not to fall into victim roles and to do everything they can to strengthen their immune systems (our primary line of defense against cancer), the sociopolitical and economic dimensions of cancer have been pushed almost completely out of the picture by the conservative backlash of our times. "Blaming the victim" is a convenient way to avoid looking at the larger environmental and social issues that frame individual experiences. This retrenchment has happened in spite of the fact that many lines of evidence indicate that cancer *is* an environmental disease. Even the most conservative scientists[2] agree that approximately 80 percent of all cancers are avoidable and in some way related to environmental factors (this includes smoking). Support for this view relies on four lines of evidence: (1) the dramatic differences in the incidence of cancer between communities (the incidence of cancer among people of a given age in different parts of the world can vary by a factor of 10 to 100); (2) changes in the incidence of cancer (either lower or higher rates) in groups that migrate to a new country; (3) changes in the incidence of particular types of cancer over time; and (4) the actual identification of specific causes of certain cancers (such as beta-naphthylamine, responsible for an epidemic of bladder cancer among dye workers employed at DuPont factories in the 1930s).[3] Other well-known environmentally linked cancers are lung cancer (linked to asbestos, arsenic, chromium, several other chemicals, and, of course, smoking); endometrial cancer, linked to estrogen use; thyroid cancer, often the result of childhood exposure to irradiation; and liver cancer, linked to exposure to vinyl chloride.

The inescapable conclusion is that if cancer is largely environmental in origin, it is largely preventable. "Environment" as we use it here includes not only air, water, and soil, but also our diets, medical procedures, and living and working conditions. This means that the food we eat, the water we drink, the air we breathe, the radiation to which we are exposed, where we live, what kind of work we do, and the stress that we suffer are responsible for up to 80 percent of all cancers. In this article we discuss some of the recent research on possible environmental links to breast cancer, the controversies that surround it, and the need for prevention-oriented research and political organization around cancer and the environment.

BREAST CANCER AND CHEMICALS

In the United States breast cancer has reached epidemic proportions: in 1998, estimates are that 178,700 women will develop breast cancer and 43,900 will die from it.[4] In other words, in 1998 nearly as many women will die from breast cancer as the number of American lives lost in the entire Vietnam War. Cancer is the leading cause of death among women of ages thirty-five to fifty-four, and approximately one-third of these deaths are due to breast cancer. African American women occupy a special place in this picture: in spite of the fact that their breast cancer incidence rate is lower than white women's, African American women have a higher breast cancer mortality rate and are more likely to get breast cancer at an earlier age. [5] Evidence indicates that breast cancer fulfills three of the four lines of reasoning regarding its nature as an environmental disease: (1) the rates of incidence of breast cancer between communities can vary by a factor of 7, (2) the rate for breast cancer among populations that have migrated conforms to that of their new residence within one generation, and (3) the lifetime incidence of breast cancer in the United States has increased from one in twenty in 1950 to one in eight in the 1990s.

A number of factors have been linked to breast cancer: age (the risk of breast cancer increases with age), a first blood relative (parent, sibling, or child) with the disease, early onset of menstruation, late menopause, no childbearing or late age at first full-term pregnancy, and higher education and socioeconomic status. However, for the overwhelming majority of breast cancer patients (70 to 80 percent), their illness is not clearly linked to any of these factors. Furthermore, only 5 to 7 percent of breast cancer is hereditary, making the discovery of the so-called breast cancer genes, BRCA1 and BRCA2, irrelevant to the vast majority of breast cancer patients. As for those women who may carry one of these genes, Kay Dickerson, an epidemiologist who has had breast cancer and is herself a likely carrier of the gene, has put it clearly: "We have nothing to offer women who test positive."[6]

In the early 1990s work began to appear focusing on the chemical–breast cancer connection. Elihu Richter and Jerry Westin reported that Israel had seen a real drop in breast cancer mortality in the decade of 1976–1986, despite a worsening of all known risk factors.[7] Westin and Richter could not account for the drop solely in terms of demographic changes or improved medical intervention. Instead, they suspected that the change may have been related to the 1978 ban on three carcinogenic pesticides (benzene hexachloride, lindane, and DDT) that heavily contaminated milk and milk products in Israel. These pesticides are known as inducers of a superfamily of enzymes called the cytochrome P450 system. These enzymes can promote cancer growth, can weaken the immune system, and are capable of destroying anticancer drugs. The researchers suspected that these induced enzymes could have increased the virulence of breast cancer in women and thereby increased the mortality rates. They speculated that the removal of the pesticides from the diet resulted in much less virulent cancer and reduced mortality from breast cancer. Other researchers then began to directly measure chemical residues in women who had breast cancer and compare them with those who didn't. Mary Wolff and Frank Falk did a case-controlled study of fifty women in which a number of chemical residues, including DDE (a DDT metabolite) and PCBs, were measured, and they found that these were significantly elevated in cases of malignant disease as compared with nonmalignant cases.[8] A follow-up study by Wolff, Paolo Toniolo, and colleagues examined DDE and PCB residues in stored blood samples of women enrolled in the New York University Women's Health Study between 1985 and 1991. The study matched 58 women who developed breast cancer with 171 similar women who did not. After controlling for confounding factors (such as first-degree family history of breast cancer, lifetime lactation, and age at first full-term pregnancy), the data showed a fourfold increase in the risk of developing breast cancer for women who had a higher level of DDE in their blood sera.[9] Another study compared data among women in different racial groups[10] and looked at the level of DDE and PCBs in the stored blood of white, Asian American, and African American women who developed breast cancer, as compared with matched controls. At first glance, this study did not reveal statistically significant differences. However, reanalysis of the data showed that the white and African American subjects with the highest level of exposure to the chemicals were two to three times more likely to acquire breast cancer than those with lower levels.[11]

A critical point to bear in mind in assessing these studies is that DDE and PCBs in our bodies may be associated with other chemicals that have not yet been identified. Also, in the real world we are exposed to dozens of chemicals, many of which have effects on our metabolism and may potentiate each other. So although these studies are important, they hardly reflect the conditions in which we live.

Additional research has implicated plastics in breast cancer development because of their ability to leach substances that have estrogenic effects. Ana Soto and Carlos Sonneschein discovered this effect unexpectedly while studying the role of estrogen on the development of breast cancer cells in the lab. Using methods they had long successfully employed to remove all estrogen from their blood samples, they were surprised to find one day that their samples continued to show estrogenic activity. The reason turned out to be that a new type of centrifuge tube they were using was leaching *p*-nonyl-phenol into the cultures, causing the estrogenic effect. Nonyl-phenols are part of a group of compounds, alkylphenols, that are widely used in plastics, as lubricants in condoms, and in spermicides and vaginal foams. While many of these chemicals are individually present in the environment at levels too low to produce an effect of their own, Soto reports that "when you take the 10 estrogenic chemicals and combine each of them at one-tenth of their effective dose, you now have an effective dose."[12]

Out of these (and other) studies a hypothesis started to emerge. It is a generally accepted fact that estrogen, a hormone produced by the ovaries, is a risk factor for breast cancer. The hormone influences cell growth by binding to an intracellular protein known as the estrogen receptor. Complexes of the hormone and receptor can bind to DNA in the nucleus and activate the genes that direct cell division, increasing the likelihood that a carcinogenic mutation will take place. The new hypothesis suggested that certain substances that are introduced into the body from the environment mimic the action of estrogen produced in cells or alter the hormone's activity. These substances were named xenoestrogens (foreign estrogens), and some of them, found in pesticides, drugs, fuel, and plastics, could amplify the effects of estrogen and promote breast cancer. However, other xenoestrogens (phytoestrogens), found in plant foods such as soy, cauliflower, and broccoli, could alter the hormone's activity and protect against breast cancer. This helps to explain the lower breast cancer incidence of Asian women whose diets are rich in phytoestrogens.[13] Timing of exposure may also be an important factor in breast cancer development. According to Devra Lee Davis and Leon Bradlow, "Various investigations suggest that unusually high exposure to estrogen during prenatal development, adolescence, or the decade or so before menopause primes breast cells to become malignant. At those times, the estrogen presumably programs the cells to respond strongly to stimulation later in life."[14]

The work on xenoestrogens and other endocrine-disrupting materials suggests that they may also be contributing to abnormal development in animals and to a range of reproductive disorders in men worldwide, such as testicular cancer, undescended testis, urinary tract defects, and lowered sperm counts. For some researchers, the disruption of the hormonal balance of many species and the transgenerational effects are, in the long run, even more frightening than their carcinogenic effects. Carlos Sonneschein believes that "the effect of these pollutants can wipe out the whole species.... It's not that one species disappears and that's it; the disappearance of one species affects others, for example, when we don't have bees, fruits and vegetables are affected.... One has to have a strategy that concerns both the short-term and the long-term effects of these compounds."[15]

BREAST CANCER AND RADIATION

Another area that demands urgent investigation is the role of radiation in breast cancer development. It is widely accepted that high doses of ionizing radiation cause breast cancer, whereas low doses are generally regarded as safe. Questions remain, however, regarding the shape of the dose-response curve, the length of the latency period, and the significance of age at time of exposure. These questions are of great importance to women because of the emphasis on mammography for early detection. Few voices dare challenge mammography screening. One of them is Rosalie Bertell, who criticized the breast cancer screening program of the Ontario Health Minister in Canada in 1989. Bertell argued that the program would "increase breast cancer death by increasing breast cancer incidence" and presented a risk-benefit assessment of the program to support her criticism.[16]

According to Bertell, the present breast cancer epidemic is a direct result of "above ground weapons testing" carried out in Nevada between 1951 and 1963, when two hundred nuclear bombs were set off and the fallout dispersed across the country. Because the latency period for breast cancer peaks at about 40 years, this is an entirely reasonable hypothesis. Chris Busby in the United Kingdom has recently come up with results that support Bertell's hypotheses. In the UK the increases in cancer incidence began in areas of high rainfall, such as Wales, Scotland, and the west country; cancer incidence did not increase in the dry areas. A good explanation for this is that the cancers were the result of atmospheric nuclear bomb testing in the period 1955 to 1963 by the nuclear superpowers in Kazakhstan, Nevada, and the South Pacific. The explosions drove "large quantities of radioactive material into the stratosphere, and this was circulated globally, falling to Earth everywhere, but particularly in high rainfall areas." At the peak of the testing (1961–1963) infant mortality began to rise and there was concern that strontium-90, accumulating in the milk, might be affecting babies. At the World Conference on Breast Cancer in 1997, in Ontario, Canada, Busby reported that this cohort of women, the nursing mothers exposed at the peak of testing, have shown the largest increase in breast cancer.[17]

Questions have also been raised about the possible effect of electromagnetic fields (EMFs).

Studies on telephone company and electrical workers have raised the possibility of a connection between EMF exposure and breast cancer in *males.* Genevieve Matanoski of Johns Hopkins University studied breast cancer rates on male New York Telephone employees from 1976 to 1980 and observed a dose-response relationship to cancer and two cases of male breast cancer.[18] Another study, by Paul Demers of the Hutchinson Cancer Research Institute in Seattle, Washington, also found a strong correlation between breast cancer risk for men and jobs that involved exposure to EMFs. [19] Finally in 1994, a study appeared on *female* electrical workers in the United States. It showed excessive breast cancer mortality relative to other women workers.[20] While this study has limitations because it is based on mortality statistics, which do not include information on other known risk factors, its results are consistent with the work of David Blask and others concerning melatonin. This work has shown that exposure to low-frequency electromagnetic fields, as well as exposure to light at night, reduces the pineal gland's production of its main hormone, melatonin. Melatonin, when given in normal physiological doses, is able to inhibit the growth of breast cancer cells in culture and in animals; it does so by decreasing the production of the cell's estrogen receptors.[21] Clearly, further investigation is strongly warranted in this area.

THE PRECAUTIONARY PRINCIPLE

The importance of environmental factors to the current breast cancer epidemic is often dismissed; their contribution is considered too small to worry about. But as Rachel Carson succinctly explained in her groundbreaking work in 1962, repeated small doses of a carcinogen can be more dangerous than a single large dose. She wrote, "The latter may kill cells outright, whereas the small doses allow some to survive, though in a damaged condition. These survivors may then develop into cancer cells. This is why there is no 'safe' dose of a carcinogen."[22]

In November 1996 the Harvard Center for Cancer Prevention released a report claiming to summarize the current knowledge about the causes of human cancer. Shockingly, the report claimed that only 2 percent of U.S. cancer deaths can be attributed to environmental pollution. However, the definition of "environmental pollution" used in the report was extremely limited ("air pollution and hormonally active aromatic organochlorines") and has been sharply criticized by other scientists and environmental activists. All other environmental hazards were covered under separate categories. For example, adding the percentage of risk that the report attributed to factors we would consider "environmental," such as occupational factors, radiation, and food additives and contaminants, brings the figure to 10 percent, and since a half million deaths are caused by cancer in the United States each year, that means that 50,000 deaths are due to environmental factors. The report suggests that an additional 30 percent of cancer mortality is due to diet and obesity, but it does not discuss the issue of environmental carcinogens in food, particularly those stored in fat. Water contamination (a significant source of pesticide residues in the diet) was not included in the environmental pollution section. The report also discusses socioeconomic status as a risk factor without clarifying that money or education does not *cause* cancer and that socioeconomics is always a surrogate for something else. Minimizing environmental factors through this kind of manipulation of statistics, while emphasizing "lifestyle" factors instead, obstructs real progress in the struggle against cancer.

"It's a blame-the-victim perspective," said Peter Montague, the editor of *Rachel's Environment and Health Weekly.* "You can make a choice about eating spinach or not. It's more difficult to choose not to eat pesticides, or to control what's in your water or what's in your food. The choice just isn't available to most people to pick clean or contaminated food."[23] Cancer activists saw the report as a backlash against the small inroads being made on the topic of cancer and the environment, and pointed out that the Harvard School of Public

Health, which sponsored the report, lists in its 1996 annual report dozens of major chemical manufacturers among its large donors. These include ARCO Chemical Company; Asarco, Inc.; Chevron; CIBA-GEIGY, Ltd.; Dow Chemical; DuPont; Eastman Chemical Company; General Electric; Monsanto; Shell Oil; Texaco; Union Carbide; and Procter & Gamble. DuPont and Asarco were among the companies reporting the highest release of toxic substances in 1994, according to an Environmental Protection Agency report. CIBA-GEIGY is the brains behind Atrazine and Simazine (widely used herbicides that have been classified as possible human carcinogens), and Monsanto is the maker of bovine somatropin (also called BGH), the growth hormone given to cows to increase milk production.[24] Clearly, it is not in the interest of chemical manufacturers to support a major report that would accurately name environmental pollution as a significant causal factor in cancer risk.

The question that screams to be addressed is, what should be considered sufficient proof to take action to eliminate potentially harmful substances from the environment? Or, as the Ontario Task Force on the Primary Prevention of Cancer put it in their March 1995 report,

> *The central issue facing those involved in the primary prevention of cancer attributable to environmental sources is how much evidence is required and how strong the evidence must be before remedial action is taken to reduce or eliminate exposures.* [25]

The Precautionary Principle is a public health guideline requiring that we act to prevent illness and death. Framing an issue from a public health perspective means that we recognize the existence of other factors apart from personal habits—such as economic, political, and cultural factors—that determine the parameters of the problem. We do not need to wait for absolute proof of harm. The Precautionary Principle emphasizes prevention and puts the burden of proof on those who risk the public health by introducing potentially harmful chemicals into the environment. As a public health principle, it has an honorable history and has been incorporated into several international agreements. The case of the Great Lakes is a good example of its application in North America. For more than forty years the Great Lakes have been a dumping ground for toxic chemicals produced by industry. More than eight hundred chemicals have been identified in the Great Lakes, many of them implicated in cancer, birth defects, and damage to the nervous and immune systems. An outpouring of concern forced the United States and Canada to sign a sweeping document requiring an end to the discharge of toxic substances. A binational commission responsible for monitoring and assessing the progress made after the agreement took a responsible view and came down clearly on the side of the Precautionary Principle. They wrote, "It is first necessary to shift the burden of responsibility for demonstrating whether substances should be allowed in commerce. The concept of reverse onus, or requiring proof that a substance is not toxic or persistent before use, should be the guiding philosophy of environmental management agencies, in both countries."[26] The Precautionary Principle takes a "weight of evidence" approach to assessing environmental health risks. It synthesizes the evidence gathered from epidemiological and biochemical research, wildlife observation, and other approaches, taking into account the cumulative weight of the studies that focus on the question of injury (or the likelihood of injury) to life, instead of narrowly focusing on one type of study alone. It brings an interdisciplinary and much needed holistic perspective to the sciences, and it introduces an important value: prudence. If there is not enough evidence, let's err on the side of caution!

The Precautionary Principle is necessary in order to protect public health and the environment, since the regulation of toxic chemicals in the United States is ineffective and out of date. The Toxic Substances Control Act (TSCA) was established in 1976 to determine which chemicals are dangerous and how the public can be protected from them. There are some 70,000 chemicals now in use, and every year about 1000 new chemicals enter the commercial market. During a typical year, the National Toxicology Program—a consortium of eight federal agencies—studies the cancer effects of one or two dozen chemicals. It is impossible, given the resources allocated to the program, to evaluate the dangers of all the chemicals now in circulation. A corporate self-regulation provision of the law proved completely ineffective, with chemical corporations failing to report scientific data on adverse health effects from chemicals. The overall outcome of twenty-one years of work under the TSCA has been to remove nine chemicals from the market.[27]

In her recent book *Living Downstream,* ecologist Sandra Steingraber writes that we all live downstream from toxic wastes dumped into the environment, and that to end cancer we need to go upstream and stop the pollution that is poisoning our lives.[28] In practice, however, national cancer policies emphasize early diagnosis and treatment, with minimal attention directed toward prevention. The recent highly publicized Breast Cancer Prevention Trial using tamoxifen (an antiestrogen synthetic hormone) on healthy volunteers considered to be at high risk for breast cancer raises troubling questions about what prevention really means for the medical establishment. In this study, although breast cancer incidence decreased among those taking tamoxifen, the number of deaths was the same between the treated and untreated groups because of other life-threatening conditions that developed among the group taking tamoxifen.[29] It is estimated that 29 million healthy women would be "potentially eligible" for preventive treatment with tamoxifen. At a cost of $80 to $100 for a month's supply, this is truly a "big deal" for Zeneca, the company that manufactures the drug under the name Nolvadex.

Biochemist Ross Hume Hall's analysis of the reasons we are making so little progress on cancer is compelling.[30] In discussing who directs cancer policy, he takes a look at a coalition of shared interests, which he calls the "medical industrial complex," that conducts research, develops drugs and medical equipment, and provides treatment. The medical part of the complex controls a vast number of cancer institutes, all focusing on diagnosis, treatment, and the search for a cure; the industrial part of the complex, on the other hand, has no interest in prevention because healthy people do not need their products or services. The hugely powerful chemical industry fights every initiative that would reduce the number of pollutants in the environment and funds much of cancer research. A striking example of this conflict of interest is offered by the case of Zeneca, the company mentioned previously. Zeneca owns and manages eleven cancer treatment centers in the United States; it is also the primary sponsor of October as Breast Cancer Awareness Month and has veto power over any materials produced in connection with this month of activities. Not surprisingly, the literature of Breast Cancer Awareness Month never mentions the word carcinogen, and it relentlessly emphasizes mammography as the "best protection" for women. Given the results of the Breast Cancer Prevention Trial, it is likely that tamoxifen will be included in their list of recommendations for breast cancer prevention. Zeneca is also the producer of a carcinogenic herbicide, acetochlor, and has been involved in litigation stemming from environmental damage to California harbors. Thus, Breast Cancer Awareness Month reveals the close connection between the chemical industry and the cancer research establishment.

Women's cancer groups at both the local and international levels have been at the forefront of criticism of the medical-industrial complex and have asked for the development of a true prevention approach, summarized by the phrase "Stop cancer before it starts." At the 1997 World Conference on Breast Cancer, delegates from fifty-four countries emphasized that breast cancer not only is a medical issue, but is also a social problem that needs to be addressed by international activism. Environmental factors were discussed in depth. Nancy Evans, a delegate from California, was clear about the need for environmental activism: "We are losing the war on cancer because we are fighting the wrong enemies," she said. "The cancer establishment has taught us to look for the enemy within—within our genes, our unwise reproductive choices or our stressful lifestyle. Although these factors may contribute to breast cancer and other cancers, our real enemies are faceless transnational corporations that spread their poisons around the globe in the name of free trade.... Prevention activism means understanding who these enemies are."[31]

Indeed, if we want to stop not just breast cancer but all cancers, we need to think in global terms and link across nations and disciplines, building a perspective that incorporates the knowledge gained from public health science, grassroots environmental groups, and people living with cancer. Only then will we be able to reverse the trend that has resulted in the present epidemic, and set the basis for a healthy future for ourselves and the following generations.

NOTES

1. See, for instance, Epstein, Samuel. *The Politics of Cancer.* Garden City, NY: Anchor Press/Doubleday, 1979; and Agran, Larry. *The Cancer Connection.* New York: St. Martin's Press, 1977.
2. Doll, Richard, and Richard Peto. *The Causes of Cancer: Quantitative Estimates of Avoidable Risks of Cancer in the United States Today.* New York: Oxford University Press, 1981.
3. Proctor, Robert N. *Cancer Wars: How Politics Shapes What We Know and Don't Know about Cancer.* New York: Basic Books, 1995, p. 38. See also Clayson, D. B., "Occupational Bladder Cancer," *Preventive Medicine,* Vol. 5, 1976, p. 228–244.
4. American Cancer Society. *Cancer Facts & Figures—*1998. Atlanta, GA: American Cancer Society, 1998.
5. Moormeier, Jill. "Breast Cancer in Black Women," *Annals of Internal Medicine,* Vol. 124, No. 10, May 15, 1996, pp. 897–905.
6. Quoted in Batt, Sharon. *Patient No More.* Charlottetown, PEI, Canada: Gynergy Books, 1994, p. 169.
7. Westin, Jerome B., and Elihu Richter. "The Israeli Breast-Cancer Anomaly," *Annals of the New York Academy of Science,* "Trends in Cancer Mortality in Industrial Countries," edited by Devra Davis and David Hoel. 1990, p. 269–279.
8. Falk, Frank, Andrew Ricci, Mary S. Wolff, James Gobold, and Peter Deckers. "Pesticides and Polychlorinated Biphenyl Residues in Human Breast Lipids and Their Relation to Breast Cancer," *Archives of Environmental Health,* Vol. 47, No. 2, March/April 1992, pp. 143–146.
9. Wolff, Mary S., Paolo G. Toniolo, Eric W. Lee, Marilyn Rivera, and Neil Dubin. "Blood Levels of Organochlorine Residues and Risk of Breast Cancer," *Journal of the National Cancer Institute,* Vol. 85, No. 8, April 21, 1993, pp. 648–652.
10. Krieger, Nancy, Mary S. Wolff, Robert A. Hiatt, Marilyn Rivera, Joseph Vogelman, and Norman Orentreich. "Breast Cancer and Serum Organochlorines: A Prospective Study Among White, Black, and Asian Women," *Journal of the National Cancer Institute,* Vol. 86, No. 8, April 20, 1994, pp. 589–599.
11. Davis, Devra Lee, and H. Leon Bradlow. "Can Environmental Estrogens Cause Breast Cancer?" *Scientific American,* October 1995, pp. 166–172.
12. Soto, Ana M., Honorato Justicia, Jonathan W. Wray, and Carlos Sonneschein. "*p*-Nonyl-Phenol: An Estrogenic Xenobiotic Released from 'Modified' Polysterene," *Environmental Health Perspectives,* Vol. 92, 1991, pp. 167–173; and personal communication with Ana Soto and Carlos Sonneschein, October 1994.
13. See note 11, p. 170.
14. See note 11, p. 168. See also vom Saal, Frederick. "Getting to the Truth: What We Know and Don't Know about the Hazards of Endocrine Disrupting Chemicals," *Pesticides and You,* Vol. 17, No. 3, 1997, pp. 9–16.
15. Arditti, Rita, and Tatiana Schreiber. "Breast Cancer: Organizing for Prevention," *Resist,* Vol. 3, No. 9, November 1994, p. 4. See also Colborn, Theo, Dianne Dumanoski, and John Peterson Myers. *Our Stolen Future.* New York: Dutton, 1996.
16. The paper can be obtained by writing to Dr. Rosalie Bertell, President, International Institute of Concern for Public Health, 830 Bathurst Street, Toronto, Ontario, Canada, M5R 3Gl. See also Bertell, Rosalie. "Breast Cancer and Mammography," *Mothering,* Summer 1992, pp. 949–957.
17. Busby, Chris. "Cancer and the 'Risk-Free' Radiation," *The Ecologist,* March/April 1998, Vol. 28, No. 2, p. 54–56.
18. Matanoski, G. M., P. N. Breysse, and E. A. Elliott. "Electromagnetic Field Exposure and Male Breast Cancer," *Lancet,* No. 337, 1991, p. 737.
19. Demers P. A., D. B. Thomas, K. A. Rosenblatt et al. "Occupational Exposure to Electromagnetic Fields and Breast Cancer in Men." *American Journal of Epidemiology,* Vol. 134, 1991, pp. 340–347.

20. Loomis, Dana P., David A. Savitz, and Cande V. Ananth. "Breast Cancer Mortality among Female Electrical Workers in the United States," *Journal of the National Cancer Institute,* Vol. 86, No. 12, June 15, 1994, pp. 921–925.
21. Personal communication with Dr. David E. Blask, September 1994. See also Hill, Steven M., and David E. Blask. "Effects on the Pineal Hormone Melatonin on the Proliferation and Morphological Characteristics of Human Breast Cancer Cells (MCF-7) in Culture," *Cancer Research,* No. 48, November 1, 1988, pp. 6121–6126.
22. Carson, Rachel. *Silent Spring.* Boston: Houghton Mifflin, 1962, p. 232.
23. Schreiber, Tatiana. "Misleading and Irresponsible: Cancer Activists Decry Harvard Report," *Resist,* Vol. 6, No. 3, April 1997, p. 5.
24. See note 23.
25. *Recommendations for the Primary Prevention of Cancer.* Report of the Ontario Task Force on the Primary Prevention of Cancer, Ministry of Health, March 1995, p. 33. See also Arditti, Rita. "The Precautionary Principle: What It Is and Why We Should Embrace It," *Women's Community Cancer Project Newsletter,* Summer 1997, pp. 1–2.
26. *Seventh Biennial Annual Report on Great Lakes Water Quality.* International Joint Commission, Windsor, Ontario, 1994, pp. 1–2.
27. Montague, Peter. "Is Regulation Possible?" *Ecologist,* Vol. 28, No. 2, March/April 1998, pp. 59–61.
28. Steingraber, Sandra. *Living Downstream: An Ecologist Looks at Cancer and the Environment.* Reading, MA: Addison-Wesley, 1997.
29. Arditti, Rita. "Tamoxifen: Breast Cancer Prevention That Is Hard to Swallow," *Sojourner,* July 1998, p. 32.
30. Hume Hall, Ross. "The Medical-Industrial Complex," *Ecologist,* Vol. 28, No. 2, March/April 1998, pp. 62–68.
31. John, Lauren. "World Conference Calls for Global Action Plan," *Breast Cancer Action Newsletter,* No. 44, October/November 1997, p. 9.

CHAPTER 8

WOMEN AND BODY IMAGE

DENISE ANTHONY AND KATHRYN STROTHER RATCLIFF

Beginning around the tenth century and continuing for a thousand years, the practice of foot-binding in China grossly distorted a girl's foot, subjected her to unbearable pain, and made walking nearly impossible. Yet it made her marriageable. Photos of a bound foot show a close approximation to a high-heeled shoe made out of living flesh (Freedman 1986: see photograph p. 179). To contemporary eyes, the image is grotesque and unbelievable.

In a very different era and culture, we have reports from the 1800s of the torture women went through to wear a corset. One mother, interested in enhancing her daughter's marriageability, laced her daughter up too tightly and killed her; the lacing had caused her ribs to grow into her liver and crushed other internal organs (Hesse-Biber 1996:25). These practices are behind us, but new ones have replaced them. Log onto the Internet and search using the term *cosmetic surgery.* You are likely to find hundreds of sites offering face-lifts, liposuction possibilities, tummy tucks, and chemical peels. Each culture and each epoch have defined the desirable female body, demanding that women do incredible things to achieve the current ideal. As these examples attest, cultural ideals of beauty often impel women to be "at war with their bodies" (Seid 1989), and, like any war, that war is not healthy.

Concern with body appearance and adornment of the body is not necessarily bad. The visual delights of decoration, shape, and form are part of any culture. Rather, it is when attention to skin quality, facial features, or body shape becomes an obsession; when the definition of the ideal woman stamps out diversity among women and choice for women; or when attempts to conform to the ideal lead to behaviors (starving, dangerous drugs, and surgery) that harm our physical and mental selves, that concern with body appearance becomes unhealthy. Although some behaviors clearly cross the line into extreme risk and characterize the women who engage in them as "sick," it is increasingly problematic that most women in our society engage in behaviors with some degree of risk at some time in their lives in order to affect their appearance (Szekely 1988). Understanding why so many women subject their bodies to these practices requires understanding the complex interaction among cultural influences, socioeconomic factors, and individual choices.

BEAUTY STANDARDS

Women are evaluated against a dominant cultural standard of beauty that is present everywhere. Discussions of weight and appearance are constant fare in women's magazines. Go to the supermarket, especially just after the December holidays or just before the summer, and you will be bombarded with magazine covers headlining articles on how to lose weight and look better. The images on TV are of thin, conventionally attractive women. Actresses who are below average in weight get more positive comments from male characters about their appearance (Fouts and Burggraf 1999). Successful models in the 1990s, such as Kate Moss, were typically ultrathin—representing the underfed waif look. These conventional standards are even reproduced in toys, such as Barbie dolls.

Although men are under increasing pressure to conform to a narrowly defined cultural ideal for body image, it is women who are constantly evaluated on physical appearance no matter the cultural domain or social situation. It is not surprising that women are evaluated on appearance in the dating and marriage market. A "major manifestation of patriarchy is the primary image of women as good wives and mothers and objects of decorative worth" (Hesse-Biber 1996:5). More surprising is the observation that women are evaluated superficially in other domains. The acceptance of women as decorative is so pervasive, we even see such imagery used in medical discussions of healthy weight. In the journal *Nutrition Action,* public health practitioners begin a discussion of weight by saying, "It's spring, when a young man's fancy turns to love…and everyone else's turns to how they're going to look in a bathing suit" (quoted in Austin 1999:262). Such imagery "positions the fictional 'young man' as the agent in love and judge of 'everyone else' (read women), who must be concerned with their self-presentation in order to become the object of his affections" (Austin 1999:262).

The obsession with appearance has been exploited by industry, which has found many profitable niches. The $50 billion fitness industry has made money—home exercise equipment, gyms, health clubs, and personal trainers have become commonplace (Hesse-Biber 1996:44–50). The diet industry profits from pills, weight-loss programs, diet books, videos, and speciality foods.

As if the power of corporate America might be insufficient in making beauty standards evident, the government and medical professions add their voices. Early in the last century, the state of Massachusetts produced a pamphlet asking the reader, "Are you as attractive as nature intended you to be?" If the reader answered "No," the state suggested that action be taken for improvement of skin, hair, and figure (Brumberg 1997:83). The president of the American Society of Plastic and Reconstructive Surgeons saw serious problems with the appearance of Americans. In his 1955 outgoing address to the society he noted, "One has only to walk a block down a busy city street; probably one of every five persons one meets will have some defect which could be improved or completely corrected by plastic surgery" (quoted in Haiken 1997:138). Contemporary advertisements in newspapers and magazines by cosmetic surgeons leave no doubt that there are many areas of the body needing surgical attention.

Standards for appearance are particularly powerful because enforcement comes from so many sources. The standards are part of the language of a woman's everyday life. "When a friend phones and says, 'God, I was bad this weekend,' we don't expect to hear about sexual licentiousness or about cruel temper and behavior. Instead, we expect to hear about how much our friend ate" (Seid 1989:7).

Judging one's appearance against these standards can be depressing. Surveys document the dissatisfaction women feel with their appearance. At puberty, boys celebrate their adult growth in hair and their body muscle, whereas girls try to remain slim and unchanged. More than half of the women in one survey reported globally negative evaluations of their appearance, a negativism that did not change as they aged. Not surprisingly, women have a more negative view of their body image than men (Muth and Cash 1997).

Clearly, self-evaluation and the response to cultural standards does vary. Some resist the mandate to conform to culturally imposed standards, instead celebrating their natural body features and contours, their inner strengths and character. In general, African American women are more satisfied with their appearance than Hispanic or Anglo women (Cash and Henry 1995). However, the racism that privileges light skin and "European" hair has had its effects, both in encouraging attempts to alter one's appearance and, alternatively, in resisting oppressive images (Mercer 1990; Zones 1997).

The discontent that often results from a failure to live up to these standards must be situated in the recognition that these standards are socially constructed. There is no objective standard of beauty. There have been times when what we would now refer to as "chubby" women were considered the most beautiful of all. Even within the last century, a span of time rather consistently associated with thinness as an ideal, there was in fact a moving target of the "ideal" woman's appearance. Although the standards have been unremittingly western, youthful, and able-bodied, popular portrayals of appropriate weight changed dramatically, as have standards for shape. Miss America contestants and winners over the years have become increasingly slender (Wiseman et al. 1992). The reigning Miss America in 1922 was 5 feet 7 inches and weighed 140; the 1954 winner was taller but lighter (5 foot 8 and 132 pounds); by the early 1980s the average contestant of that height was down to a mere 117 pounds (Seid 1989:97, 136). The overall change from 1922 to 1995 was a height increase of 2 percent and a body weight decrease of 12 percent (Rubinstein and Caballero 2000).

The shift in the standard for women's body shape becomes evident by contrasting the 1920s, 1950s, and 1990s. In the 1920s, the standard was the thin flapper girls, with their bound breasts. In the 1950s there was a brief interruption in the celebration of thinness (Hesse-Biber 1996:27), as the voluptuous and curvaceous images of Marilyn Monroe and Jayne Mansfield defined a new beauty. The "mammary fixation" of the 1950s was heard at local high schools, where girls exercised to the chant of "I must. I must. I must develop my bust" (Brumberg 1997:117).

The attraction of thinness returned in the mid-1960s, when Twiggy, at five foot six and ninety-seven pounds (Hesse-Biber 1996:28), moved the standard. The century ended with the "cult of thinness" in full control. It was a new thinness, in great contrast to the flapper girls. Breasts were to be celebrated, pushed up and augmented, and made conspicuous. For body shaping, no external aides like girdles were used, but rather hard work was required to achieve a muscular body, with abs and buns of steel. The emphasis was increasingly on having slender legs and bottom. Even Miss America contestants stressed out over their perceived "thunder thighs" (Brumberg 1997:126).

Not only did the standards move, but they were not even based on real people. Images in magazines are likely to be airbrushed and computer enhanced. And even top models could not achieve their looks without unhealthy habits, such as lousy eating patterns, anorexia, bulimia, or cosmetic surgery. One model reported eating a head of lettuce as her only sustenance for the day. Her supermodel roommate came home, horrified at the scene: "You're eating a *whole* head of lettuce? How could you?" (Sporkin 1993:82).

Though the standards are artificial, they are clearly real in their consequences. Women who are conventionally attractive get more of the valued resources, and this is true even from an early age. "Cute babies are cuddled more than homely ones; attractive toddlers are punished less often. Teachers give special attention to better-looking pupils, strangers offer help more readily to attractive people, and jurors show more sympathy to good-looking victims" (Freedman 1986:7–8). Even health care professionals treat attractive patients better (Nordholm 1980). In contrast, women who are fat face a stern moral evaluation. Americans hate fat people, finding them sinful, sloppy, lazy, weak-willed, and morally lax (Hesse-Biber 1996:4).

Women certainly suffer severe consequences for being overweight. One study showed that overweight women had lower levels of educational attainment and higher rates of poverty than non-overweight women (Gortmaker et al. 1993). It even appears that women are evaluated physically in occupational assessments. For example, one study found that obesity had a significantly negative effect on earnings for women, but not for men, even after controlling for education and experience (Register and Williams 1990). Similarly, in a study of women's career payoffs in a large aerospace organization, Haskins and Ransford (1999) find that overweight women suffer lower income in entry-level managerial positions, and that overweight women have lower occupational status.

And the standards are also real in their consequences because many women do respond by battling with their bodies: They obsess about hair removal by shaving, waxing, and resorting to laser surgery to remove the tiniest unwanted hair; they try to rigidly control their weight and reshape their bodies through diets, exercise, and surgery. All of this takes time and may escalate to become an overwhelming obsession in the pursuit of the perfect body (Wolf 1991). Instead of developing sensible, enjoyable, and health-promoting exercise activities, many women develop rigid running routines, let nothing stop their workout time on the Stairmaster or Nordic track, and otherwise allow their addiction to fitness to take over their lives. "People are in bondage," comments one fitness trainer (quoted in Hesse-Biber 1996:46).

Although many responses of those trying to conform to the standards for beauty are worthy of examination, for the purposes of this chapter, only two will be discussed: weight loss and cosmetic surgery. Each has a long history in women's health, and each has led to serious health consequences.

WEIGHT AND WEIGHT LOSS

To understand issues of women's health regarding weight loss, it is important first to examine what we know about the health problems of carrying excess weight. Yet there are difficulties both in defining what is excess weight and in determining who defines it as such. The notion that any and all excess weight is bad is such a taken-for-granted idea that it is hard to accept it as socially constructed. We may feel that the cultural standards for weight are silly, but feel that the underlying science justifies a concern with weight. Though the weight charts currently used appear to be quantitative, objective standards, their history tells a different story.

It was, in fact, not medical science that developed the first accepted standards for excess weight, but Metropolitan Life Insurance Company (MLIC), which wanted to know how much to charge people for insurance coverage. To evaluate the risks of being overweight, MLIC used a sample of its own policyholders, a self-selected segment not representative of all classes and ethnic groups in America. Importantly, it also overrepresented the less healthy among the most overweight people (Seid 1989:118), and thus overestimated the mortality rates for being overweight. Findings correlating overweight and mortality were further compromised by policyholders' typical underreporting of their weight (Seid 1989:118–119); simply put, the mortality of a person who was really 20 pounds overweight became the reported risk for a person only 10 pounds overweight. Thus the consequences of moderate overweight were exaggerated. The medical community did not protest the inaccuracies in the MLIC analysis: instead, it accepted and promoted the standards (Seid 1989:120). So thorough was the medical community's indoctrination that when its own studies in the 1950s showed little association between weight and mortality, medical scientists still did not question the MLIC dogma, but instead became "perplexed by their own data" (quoted in Seid 1989:121).

Through the years, MLIC's definition of appropriate weight standards fluctuated dramatically. In the 1940s, it began by promoting "ideal" weights that were below the average weight, pushing the idea that "what was average and so, normal, was not healthy" (Seid 1989:117). Even pregnant women were subject to these guidelines. Doctors told them they were to gain only 15 to 20 pounds over their "ideal weight." If a pregnant woman was overweight when she got pregnant, her doctor might have even prescribed diet pills.

In the 1950s, new studies at MLIC produced a revised chart. "Ideal weights" were changed to "desirable weights" (Seid 1898:139), with the desirable weights even lower than the ones they replaced. At the same time, MLIC exposed the cultural and gendered influences on its standards. In 1952, MLIC's *Statistical Bulletin* listed the "handicaps" of being overweight: "(E)mployers preferred normal-weight applicants; children ostracized obese youngsters; the obese girl's chances for marriage were poorer than her thinner rivals" (Seid 1989:131).

During the 1980s, researchers began using the body-mass index rather than overall weight in studies of the effect of weight on health. The body-mass index is calculated as weight in kilograms divided by the square of height in meters. The way the body-mass index is used to measure overweight and obesity varies, however. Some studies define overweight as a body-mass index above the ninety-fifth percentile for age and sex (e.g., Gortmaker et al. 1993). Others use the body-mass index to create categories roughly analogous to the MLIC weight tables (e.g., Manson et al. 1995; Stevens et al. 1998).

By 1990, the federal government had begun to issue its own weight charts. Again, the definition of excess weight was elusive. Discarding prior conventions using gender or frame size to list ideal weights, the government developed a unisex table of "healthy" weights. The decade began with recommended weights higher than those of the MLIC charts, with weight gain allowed as one grew older (Marwick 1991). In 1995, the government revised the standards to recommend that people should weigh less and not gain weight as they aged ("New Weight" 1995b).

The quantification of excess weight clearly has been in turmoil, but is there a health (versus a cultural) justification for a concern with overweight? Has science found health risks of being overweight? The simple answer is: No. Despite strong pronouncements about weight and health, the over 80 years of actuarial and scientific concern with weight shows little if any evidence that weight is a health problem for most people. A study in 1995 based on a cohort of 115,195 women in the Nurses' Health Study found that only among the very overweight (i.e., body mass index at or above 27, or those considered obese) was early death substantially increased (Manson et al. 1995:682). Yet the final paragraph of the article left the reader with a different impression, stating, "These prospective data indicate that body weight is an important determinant of mortality among middle-aged women.... The increasingly permissive U.S. weight guidelines may therefore by unjustified and potentially harmful" (Manson et al. 1995:683–684). No wonder that the popular press began its coverage with an unqualified endorsement of thinness. Referring to the Manson study, the first sentence in the *New York Times* coverage read, "The evidence continues to accumulate: For health and longevity, it pays to be thin" (Brody 1995:A1).

Some doctors took exception to the spin that was put on the results. One wrote: "From the perspective of public policy, this report inadvertently fuels the obsession with thinness and the devotion to altering body shape that beset women in our culture" (Hamburg 1996:732). Others, trying to understand the medical attention given to weight and weight loss in the face of ambiguous findings of adverse health effects (except for the obese), suggested that the campaign against weight is an example of the

> *tendency to medicalize behavior we do not approve of. In this age of political correctness, it seems that obese people can be criticized with impunity, because the critics are merely trying to help them. Some doctors take part in this blurring of prejudice and altruism by overstating the dangers of obesity and the redemptive powers of weight loss. (Kassirer and Angell 1998:53)*

The voices of popular culture, science, and the government appear to speak in unison: Weight is a problem. Being constantly bombarded with variations on this theme, no wonder many individuals buy the rhetoric that overweight is bad in so many ways, and make unfavorable self-judgments at each of their frequent trips to the bathroom scale. Damaging though such self-judgments might be, the greater damage comes from the methods used to combat this so-called problem.

Weight loss is often an unhealthy endeavor involving desperate attempts to achieve impossible goals eagerly promoted by corporate interests. Early methods of weight control promoted cigarette smoking. In 1930, tobacco advertisements explicitly promoted the use of tobacco as a means to retain an attractive figure:

> *We do not represent that smoking Lucky Cigarettes will bring modern figures or cause the reduction of flesh. We do declare that when tempted to do*

yourself too well, if you will "Reach for a Lucky" instead, you will thus avoid over-indulgence in things that cause excess weight and, by avoiding over-indulgence, maintain a modern, graceful form. (Lucky Cigarettes advertisement in Literary Digest *April 5, 1930)*

Sixty-six years later, the tobacco industry conveys the same message, with a bit more subtlety. Putting a reference to weight in their name, Virginia Slims loudly proclaims the connection between smoking and a good figure. Accompanying a picture of a woman in a swimsuit, the advertisement text reads, "When we're wearing a swimsuit, there is no such thing as 'constructive criticism.' Virginia Slims. It's a woman thing." (advertisement on back cover of *Home Magazine,* June, 1996)

The tobacco industry continues to promote and attempt to profit from an obviously unhealthy method of weight loss. And what about the other methods? The options of the slimming industry, a diversified $30 to $50 billion dollar enterprise (Kassirer and Angell 1998:52), include special foods, such as low-calorie foods and drinks, fat-free foods, liquid diets such as Metrecal in the 1960s and Slimfast in the 1990s, and prepared meals; diet plans (just eat grapefruit, or avoid carbohydrates); weight-loss programs such as Jenny Craig and Weight Watchers; diet pills; and exercise equipment and programs. To say that most of these methods are expensive, ineffective, and unsafe, but profitable for the industry is a generalization with considerable truth.

It is estimated that at any time about forty percent of women in the United States are trying to lose weight (Cleland et al. 1997:8). Some attempt to control their weight by use of laxatives, diuretics, and vomiting. More complete diet plans promoted by doctors and others have a long history. For example, early in the last century, Dr. Hay promoted eating one category of food per meal and using one enema a day; in the 1960s, Dr. Taller promoted a high-fat diet; and in 1970, Dr. Linn promoted a syrup that was a "loathsome blend of crushed animal horns, hooves and hides mixed with enzymes" (Jackson 1994:151). Today, the large number of weight loss books offers a wide variety of poorly tested and ineffective methods doctors and others have concocted.

More ambitious, more expensive, and similarly ineffective are the weight-loss programs developed by companies such as Jenny Craig and Weight Watchers. In 1992, a panel at the National Institutes of Health examined such programs and other components of the diet industry, and found profits for the companies but failure for the consumers. Most dieters either never lost weight or gained it back. The claims made by the weight-loss programs, however, have suggested otherwise. The Federal Trade Commission (FTC) worked out an out-of-court settlement with three major diet programs to change their advertising techniques (Rosenthal 1992).

A more dangerous method of weight loss is prescription diet pills. Although in the 1960s and 1970s doctors liberally prescribed addictive amphetamines to women who wanted to lose weight, the widespread acceptance of diet pills did not occur until the early 1990s. The increasing acceptance of pharmaceuticals accompanied a changed view of obesity and excess weight as a chronic disease due to genetic, biological, and other factors (Cleland et al. 1997). One recent episode in American public health demonstrates the health risks associated with our obsession to control our weight. In 1997, the FDA approved three appetite suppressants (fenfluramine, dexfenfluramine, and phentermine) for short-term, single-drug use—not in combination with each other (Rheingold 1998).

One obscure study suggesting that the combination of two of the drugs (fen-phen) was particularly effective for weight reduction led to a huge demand for them (see Rheingold 1998). "Fueling the demand was extensive coverage in the popular press and saturation advertising campaigns by programs, obesity clinics, and individual physicians offering access to these 'miracle' drugs" (Cleland et al. 1997:22). In their overexuberance, doctors prescribed the drugs to people who wanted to lose only a few pounds (not the obese patients they were originally intended for), neglected to do thorough patient examinations, and sometimes failed to tell patients of the potential risks of the drugs (Rheingold 1998). "(M)any physicians established overnight diet-pill clinics and attracted a vulnerable public into their offices with advertisements exclaiming medical breakthroughs with quick, safe and permanent results"(Cleland et al. 1997:22).

Concerns about the safety of prescribing these drugs in combination, against the FDA's approved use, came swiftly. A 1997 study by the Mayo Clinic found that women who had taken fen-phen had an unusually high rate of heart valve damage and pulmonary hypertension (Connolly et al. 1997). The FDA acted swiftly, asking the manufacturers to withdraw two of the three drugs from the market. A subsequent health concern is the possibility that these drugs may have affected brain function, including cognition, memory, and aggression (McCann et al. 1997).

With popular acceptance of weight watching as healthy and the sense that there is scientific evidence that any excess weight is a health problem for many people, doctors easily assumed a role in prescribing pills and otherwise helping people with their weight-reduction plans. Weight control and weight loss became tied to health, and that was a doctor's turf. Next, we examine interactions among medicine, cosmetic surgery, and women's health. Cosmetic surgery, in contrast to weight control, is clearly much more about women as decorative objects.

COSMETIC SURGERY

Medical science moves beyond the realm of its usual mandate (Dull and West 1991:55) when it makes a large nose, skin tone, droopy eyelids, wrinkles of aging, or small breasts the object of the medical gaze. Doctors entered the world of aesthetic standards primarily through the respected route of plastic surgery, with its ability to correct disfigurements from birth defects, disease, accidents, and war.

Plastic surgery was originally closely tied to efforts to reconstruct facial and other injuries of veterans returning from the First and Second World Wars, but the supply of such clients was not inexhaustible, nor were they replaced by other individuals requiring reconstruction:

> *During the war, some surgeons had expressed confidence that civilian casualties from accidents and burns would keep them busy in the postwar years, but not even large-scale industrial catastrophes would have generated enough patients to keep busy the increased number of surgeons the war produced.... In the years after World War II, plastic surgeons led what would become a widespread trend toward marketing medical techniques and technologies to particular groups. The first problem they targeted was aging, and the first audience they targeted was female—specifically, middle-aged, middle-class women. (Haiken 1997:134)*

With the media forever extolling the beauty of young women, some doctors were able to identify a niche and exploit it. They used familiar biomedical model phraseology to turn the effects of aging—loose and sagging skin, wrinkles, and creases—into pathology. They would "routinely use words like 'deformity' and 'pathology' to describe such conditions, further encouraging their patients to view aging as a medical problem" (Haiken 1997:172). Cosmetic surgery became not an issue of wanting a change, but of needing it. Thus, "surgeons often refer to the face-lift as something that is needed rather than desired, that may be delayed but not escaped" (Haiken 1997:172).

And like the MLIC statistician for whom weight was a problem in part because of its gendered cultural consequences, disadvantaging one in the marriage market vis á vis one's "rivals," surgeons also articulated the centrality of gendered cultural ideas in their treatment of female patients. For instance, aging had very different consequences for men and women. One surgeon said, "Our society has got a very strange double standard and it can be summarized that when a man gets old, he gets sophisticated, debonair [and] wise; but when a woman gets old, she gets old. A man with a wrinkly face doesn't necessarily look bad in our society. A woman with a wrinkly face looks old" (quoted in Dull and West 1991:65).

Cosmetic surgery has grown far beyond the facelifts for aging women of the post–World War II era. Women are now able to transform their bodies with focused fat removal using liposuction, rhinoplasties (nose jobs), breast reduction or augmentation, and lip augmentation, to name only a few. As they had with aging, doctors used biomedical language to justify the further expansion of cosmetic surgery. Talking about cosmetic surgery as they would talk about any disease treatment, they used words such as "'flaws,' 'defects,' 'deformities,' and 'correctable problems' of appearance" (Dull and West 1991:63). In a study of Asian American women seeking cosmetic surgery, doctors used medical terms such as *excess fat* to "problematize the shape of their eyes so as to define it as a medical condition" (Kaw 1993:63). This pathologizing of aesthetic variations helps to blur the line between the respected reconstructive surgery and the more frivolous cosmetic surgery (Dull and West 1991:63).

Intertwined with the pathologizing of appearance in general is a very particular view of female beauty—an aesthetic of beauty defined by people with medical training. Cosmetic surgeons working with Asian American clientele present a glaring example. "Their description of Asian features verges on ideological racism," by connecting the creaseless upper eyelid with a dullness, passivity, and weakness of personality (Kaw 1993:81). More generally, studies find cosmetic surgeons "united in the view that women's concerns for their appearance are *essential* to their nature as women" (Dull and West 1991:64). Gendered content was glaringly evident when the gaze of the cosmetic surgeon turned to the breast. The American Society of Plastic and Reconstructive Surgeons (ASPRS) used its power to declare the breast a suitable object of their concern by naming a normal occurrence, small breasts, a disease. The ASPRS wrote, "There is a substantial and enlarging body of medical information and opinion to the effect that these deformities [small breasts] are really a disease" (quoted in Ehrenreich 1992:88). With some humor, one observer noted, "Not a fatal disease, perhaps, to judge from the number of sufferers who are still hobbling around untreated, but a disease nonetheless" (Ehrenreich 1992:88). They named the disease micromastia. Never once did the ASPRS indicate that micromastia presented any physical health risk. Rather, just by having "statistically small" breasts, the woman had a problem with her breast image that medicine could and should address (Haiken 1997:272). Difference became deformity, and deformity became disease.

Women responded by eagerly seeking out doctors to augment their breasts. One million American women had breast implants by 1990 (Zuckerman 1998). The procedure became controversial because of early press reports of problems women had with their implants, particularly those that ruptured, and the decreased reliability of breast cancer detection. Legal suits inflamed the controversy. Damaging evidence was uncovered: The major manufacturer, Dow Corning, admitted to not following up on early safety concerns documented in internal memos; and congressional staff members found that the government had been concerned about the potential risks of the implants for many years, but had done nothing (Zuckerman 1998). Following hearings in 1991 and 1992, the FDA restricted breast implants to women requiring reconstruction, and insisted that they be enrolled in a clinical study. Dow Corning stopped selling silicone breast implants.

At this writing, the final evaluation of the health risks of the implants is in doubt. The juries which awarded millions did so not based on clear scientific evidence of a problem, nor did the FDA's regulatory ruling rely on a wealth of scientific findings (Angell 1996). Most of the studies since that time have found no relationship between implants and connective-tissue diseases or other health problems, but the studies are based on very small samples (Zuckerman 1998). The study with the largest sample (Hennekens et al. 1996) did report an increased risk of connective-tissue disease for women with breast implants. Given this contradictory information, the FDA concludes that the "studies do not resolve the question of whether the variety of symptoms some women report might be related to their implants" (FDA 1998:2 of "Illness and Conditions" section of Internet site). Women who developed unusual health problems following a breast implant are angry and disillusioned, feeling that their problems have largely been dismissed (Zimmerman 1998).

As with any type of surgery, all forms of cosmetic surgery have documented dangers. The Physician Insurers Association of America reports thirty deaths in a ten-year period from operations ranging from nose jobs to liposuction, an increasingly popular procedure (Podolsky 1996). Despite the risks, the cosmetic surgery business has grown rapidly. In 1985, the American Association of Cosmetic Surgeons was formed to include practitioners not only in plastic and reconstructive surgery, but also dermatology, ophthalmology, oral surgery, cosmetic dentistry, and other medical specialties. The 1998 statistics from the Association show 3,892,149 cosmetic surgeries for women, versus just under a million that year for men. Not all cosmetic surgeons belong to this organization, so these figures are an underestimate.

The growth of cosmetic surgery is a particular problem because, as an unregulated industry, any licensed doctor may perform cosmetic surgery, and as an elective procedure it is an attractive option for doctors tired of managed care oversight. Some doctors have moved their operations to facilities that more resemble cosmetic boutiques and spas than doctors' offices (Hayt 1999). Even nonphysicians have recognized the money-making potential of cosmetic surgery and have opened facilities, hired doctors, and aggressively marketed procedures by making questionable claims of safety and effectiveness. Minimal state regulation of surgery in private offices (outside of hospitals) increases the risk to patients and hides abuses (Sullivan 2001:Chapter 8).

The striking feature of the health problems linked to women's body image is that they are overwhelmingly socially created. This realm of "medical care" for women has a profoundly negative impact on women. There are minimal, at best, health reasons for most women to be concerned about their weight, yet they engage in behaviors to control their weight that often seriously endanger their health. The vast profits gained by pharmaceutical companies that develop and market diet drugs, and the high incomes of doctors who specialize in supplying such drugs, are based much more on doing harm to women's health than on improving it. Similarly, the cosmetic surgeons who promote such medical interventions as liposuction and breast implants are seldom providing treatments that will improve the health of their patients. In fact, in many cases their work carries both immediate and long-term risks.

The medical industry, including corporations, hospitals, and doctors, is not alone, of course, in promoting women's use of medical interventions to shape their bodies. Cultural forces, stressing constructed images ranging from thinness to particular skin tones, create a demand for such interventions. These forces are replicated, focused, and intensified in many ways, from printed and electronic media to the most direct kinds of peer and family pressures. All of these factors working together create a sector of health care as far removed from promoting improved health as one could imagine.

THE CARE AND FEEDING OF THE DIET INDUSTRY: IMPLICATIONS FOR WOMEN'S HEALTH

DENISE ANTHONY

Stand in the checkout line of any grocery store, and scan the many magazines and tabloid offerings on display. You will be bombarded with messages such as "How to have the body you want," "Diet wars: Which diet is best for you," and "10 best ways to lose those unwanted pounds." Tune-in to daytime television talk shows and even news magazine programs, and the focus on weight continues. Books promoting new diet regimens regularly make the best-seller lists. Indeed, over 26,000 diets and diet programs have been published in the past century (Schwarcz 1999). Americans seem to be obsessed with body size and weight control. Feeding our obsession is the vast diet industry, which encompasses everything from diet drinks and foods, such as Slimfast, to over-the-counter diet pills, such as Dexatrim; from weight-loss clinics such as Jenny Craig, to prescription drugs, such as Xenical. Growing ever fatter, the diet industry has exploded into a $50 billion-dollar industry, used by over 65 million people a year.

Who are the 65 million people who use diet products, and why? Some may consider the answer to the latter part of that question to be simple: People diet for their health, their appearance, or both. Sociologists, however, typically want to go beyond looking simply at individual explanations for some behavior, to understand the broader social forces that, in this case, encourage more and more people to patronize the diet industry.

As we will discuss, dieting has increased because social forces beyond the ubiquitous advertising of the diet industry have helped to fuel its growth. Two reasons stand out as causes for increased dieting. First, the cultural and medical standards for "appropriate" or ideal body weight have become slimmer over time, and second, dieting has been socially constructed as the solution to the health problem of obesity.

WHO DIETS?

Attempting to control one's weight is indeed a common behavior of Americans, who consider dieting to be the best way to control body weight (Horm and Anderson 1993). Weight loss through restrictive dieting includes everything from simply eating less, to self-starvation and induced vomiting, from use of over-the-counter diet pills, diuretics and laxatives, to prescription drugs and the use of commercial weight-loss centers and their products. At any given time, two-thirds of adult women and one-half of adult men are actively attempting to control their weight. Among high school students, the gender gap is greater: nearly three-quarters of females and over one-third of males are attempting to lose or keep from gaining weight (Serdula et al. 1993).

Not only is dieting behavior especially prevalent among females, but female dieters are more likely to diet in ways that seriously endanger their health. Female dieters, especially adolescents, are more likely to report using unhealthy weight-loss practices such as self-induced vomiting or taking diet pills (Neumark-Sztainer et al. 1998). And many female dieters diet even though they are not actually overweight. Studies have found that 25 percent of female adolescents and 20 percent of adult women who consider themselves to be the "right weight" continue to actively diet (Public Health Service 1991b; Serdula et al. 1993).

WHY DO WE DIET?

Restrictive weight-loss practices reflect the specific cultural context within which they occur.

For decades, feminist scholars have analyzed and called attention to the important problems associated with beauty standards for women and girls in society (e.g., Bordo 1989; Brumberg 1989; Millman 1980). Regarding body size, studies have found that the current standards of slimness portrayed on television and in magazines are, on average, slimmer for women than for men, and that these standards for women are slimmer now than in the past (Silverstein et al. 1986). More exposure to the cultural standards of beauty increases attempts to conform to those standards. For example, girls who are frequent readers of fashion magazines are two to three times more likely than infrequent readers to diet to lose weight (Field et al. 1999).

In addition to the increasingly slim cultural standard, medical standards have changed over the years to advocate slimmer bodies. Prior to the mid 1990s, studies defined overweight as a body-mass index (BMI, measured as weight in kilograms divided by height in meters squared) greater than or equal to 27, making an estimated 25 to 33 percent of American adults overweight or obese (Public Health Service 1991a; Kuczmarski et al. 1994). A major government report (NHLBI 1998) now advocates defining overweight as BMI > 25, making over 50 percent of American adults overweight.

Given this cultural and medical context that promotes extreme thinness standards, especially for women, it is not surprising that many more women than men overestimate their weight, that more women than men diet and use commercial weight-loss programs, or that most women diet at some point in their lives, whether or not they are overweight. Because the ideal standards of weight are unattainable for most women, many seek help to reach and maintain those standards. For this, they turn to diet programs and products in an industry that thrives, despite few if any successful results. The disproportionate practice of dieting and use of diet products by women engenders real consequences for women's health.

The second major reason the diet industry is expanding is the response to the widely promoted and accepted idea that *any* excess weight is unhealthy. To be sure, actual obesity, as opposed to mere excess weight, has been shown to be associated with increased risk of disease and death. Controlling weight among the obese is argued to have health benefits for some. The National Institutes of Health's National Heart, Lung and Blood Institute (NHLBI 1998) states in its report on obesity that there is evidence that weight loss in some overweight and obese individuals reduces their risk for certain diseases.

Both the medical and lay presses, however, often go far beyond a focus on obesity to promote the claim that thinner is always better. For example, an article published in the *New England Journal of Medicine* (Manson et al. 1995) claimed that *all* increases in body weight are directly related to increased risk of death for all women. This research received widespread coverage in major newspapers throughout the United States (e.g., Brody 1995; Monmaney 1995). Despite these claims, however, there is no simple relationship between excess weight and morbidity or mortality. (See Chapter 8.) Most people of "average weight" (technically, BMI between 21 and 27) face *no* increased health risks associated with their weight, even though by cultural (and now, even medical) standards, they may appear or feel overweight.

The constant focus on excess weight and ways to control it has produced serious health risks. The emergence and increase of eating disorders such as bulimia and anorexia nervosa, diseases much more prevalent among women than men, highlight the dangers of extreme dieting practices (Szekely 1988; Foreyt, Poston, and Goodrick 1996). However, obsessive weight control does not have to reach these extremes for dieting to be dangerous. Rapid weight loss and use of over-the-counter diet pills can cause serious risks to dieters (Morgan, Kagan, and Brody 1985; Wilson 1993), especially adolescent dieters. Even the use of prescription weight-loss drugs under medical supervision often entails serious health risks (Curfman 1997).

Yet the health risks caused by dieting rarely receive equal attention because of the focus on obesity. To the extent that the health risks of excess weight, and therefore the health *benefits* of *losing* weight, dominate social discourse on health and weight control, the health risks of dieting are minimized. Moreover, because many of the individuals who actively diet are not overweight or obese, the possible health benefits of dieting largely disappear. Clearly the risks of dieting, particularly for women's health, are discounted so long as the primary focus of social discussion of weight control is on the health risks of excess weight.

CONGRESSIONAL HEARINGS ON THE DIET INDUSTRY

Concerns about the claims made by the diet industry, as well as the recognized dangers of some dieting practices promoted by the diet industry, prompted federal legislators to inquire into the standards and consequences of the diet industry in the early 1990s by holding a series of four hearings titled "Deception and Fraud in the Diet Industry" (U.S. House of Representatives 1990a–c, 1992). These hearings are useful not just as a record of the dispute, but also as a microcosm of contemporary views of weight and dieting, illustrating how some issues are dominant while others get minimized or overlooked entirely. My treatment of these hearings thus has two levels—as a record of the public dispute, and as an analysis of the alternative conceptions of the issues, and how some conceptions are more central and others are more marginal whenever the topic emerges.

Prior to these hearings, the diet industry received only limited regulation regarding the safety and effectiveness of its products, despite being regulated by at least three federal agencies. The Food and Drug Administration (FDA) has jurisdiction over the content and labeling of foods, drugs, and medical devices, while the Federal Trade Commission (FTC) is responsible for regulating fraudulent advertising and commerce, and the U.S. Postal Service deals with mail fraud. Nevertheless, the diet industry has produced more products making fraudulent claims, with questionable safety, than any other industry, save producers of aphrodisiacs and baldness remedies. During the twentieth century, the FTC has brought nearly 150 cases against purveyors of weight-loss products for making fraudulent or exaggerated claims. For example, as early as 1927 the FTC brought a case against a company for selling a product advertised to "quickly and permanently dissolve away excess flesh from certain parts of the body" (Cleland 1997). Anyone who believes that either producers or consumers have become more knowledgeable or sophisticated about health care since 1927 should consider two cases the FTC brought in 1997: one against the "Svelt-PATCH transdermal skin patch for weight loss," and the other against "Slimming Insoles for shoes, for weight loss based on reflexology" (Cleland 1997).

The hearings began with the committee chair, Representative Wyden (D-OR), boldly characterizing the "fast-growing health care industry" as fueled by "hard-sell advertising," "riddled by hucksters" with their "dubious wares" offering "miracle cures, while the government regulators sit snoozing on the sidelines." Referring specifically to weight loss clinics, he suggested that "a new mix of questionable products, untrained providers, and deceptive advertising is exposing our citizens to unexpected and unnecessary health risks" (U.S. House of Representatives 1990a:1).

In order to understand the power of the social construction of obesity as a social problem and dieting as its solution, I examined the speakers and the speeches given at the hearings. Despite the very critical attention implied by the opening words of Representative Wyden, a close analysis of the discourse during the hearings and the resulting regulatory actions suggests that the social construction of obesity is powerful: Even critics of the diet industry buy into the notion that dieting to lose weight is a social good. By conceding that point, the focus remains on the health problems of obesity, not the health problems engendered by an industry and culture that promote the constant need for dieting.

The distribution of witnesses at the hearings can be seen as reflective of the way dieting was viewed, even when under critical scrutiny. On the one hand, the industry itself was well represented (18% of speakers), with ample opportunity to provide its view of the need for diet products. The largest group were representatives of governmental agencies (39%), followed by medical experts (25%). Additionally, five consumers (11%) were asked to tell of their individual experiences with dieting, and three representatives of advocacy groups (7%) also testified. Only one of the three advocacy groups, the National Association for the Advancement of Fat Acceptance (NAAFA), can be identified as being outside of the mainstream medical establishment (the other two being the American Dietetic Association [ADA] and the National Association of Anorexia Nervosa and Associated Disorders [ANAD]). No feminist or women's group testified.

While women's groups were perhaps not purposely excluded, their absence shows that, despite the actual social context of dieting in which women are the majority consumers of diet products, and most American women diet, dieting is not considered to be associated with women's health in particular. Nevertheless, many of the hearing participants are very aware that women are the primary consumers of diet products. A representative from the diet company Jenny Craig International, for example, stated that women comprise 85 percent of their client base. Yet, rather than explicitly recognize and address the gendered nature of the diet industry, most participants merely made claims about the health of generic individuals. One notable exception came in the final hearing when a representative from the National Institutes of Health (NIH) stated up-front the paradox that many of the people who diet are women who are not overweight: "It was disturbing to find out that many persons not overweight, particularly young women, were trying to lose weight" (U.S. House of Representatives 1992:7).

To analyze the testimony, I coded and classified all statements made during the hearings using a technique called cognitive mapping, a highly reliable method for graphically summarizing written or verbal texts (Axelrod 1976; Carley and Palmquist 1992). Cognitive mapping yields frequencies of words and phrases in a text, and also provides a way to examine the relationships between them. The analysis revealed three very distinctive views about the health issues associated with dieting: what I refer to as pro-diet, anti-diet, and weight-control discourses. One third of all statements made in the hearings were *pro-diet discourse,* providing a simple and straightforward view of dieting and weight: Dieting is an admirable behavior in and of itself, and it is desirable because it reduces obesity, a serious health problem. Essentially this view claims that obesity is very harmful, self-control is important for reducing obesity, and dieting practices are good because they encourage self-control, reduce obesity, and are beneficial to overall well-being. For example, a typical statement was, "It is clear that dieting is a two-way street. There are no miracle cures.... We need a little discipline imposed from outside.... So, weight-loss programs, when followed responsibly, can produce satisfied, healthier customers" (U.S. House of Representatives 1990b:4).

Not surprisingly, the major proponents of a pro-diet discourse are members of the diet industry. All members of the diet industry who testified at the hearings promoted a pro-diet view, which is to be expected given their economic interests. Less expected are the others, such as government officials and medical doctors, who also advocated dieting as the best solution to obesity.

In direct contrast to the pro-diet view is an *anti-diet discourse* that makes one dominant claim: Dieting and diet products are harmful. For example, a speaker decrying the impact for adolescents said, "The practice of dieting alone and the subsequent use of diet aids or other weight-altering pharmaceutical products can be dangerous as well as deadly habits for adolescents" (U.S. House of Representatives 1990c:24). In contrast to the other two views found in the hearings, anti-diet discourse makes very different claims regarding the effect of obesity and the relationship between dieting and obesity. Some speakers claimed that in the great majority of instances, dieting practices had no effect on obesity, while others said that dieting actually contributes to obesity. Most speakers promoting an anti-diet view, however, made no assertions about the effects of obesity; that is, they did not discuss obesity as a health problem at all. One physician stated, "There is no reason on earth why we should all be an ideal weight or the same weight any more than there is any reason why we should all be the same height" (U.S. House of Representatives 1990a:41). Moreover, many proponents of the anti-diet discourse strongly and explicitly claimed that diet products are harmful, especially to women's health. Two proponents of anti-diet discourse represent advocacy groups, ANAD and NAAFA, two groups founded on the negative consequences of dieting. The anti-diet view, however, was clearly a minority view at the hearings, comprising only approximately one-quarter of the overall discourse.

In comparison to both the pro-diet and anti-diet discourse, the *weight-control discourse* is more complicated. Nearly half of all speakers at the hearings promoted this view, defining the weight-control problem as twofold: (1) Obesity is a major health problem that requires urgent attention (often through dieting of some kind), but (2) unscrupulous members of the diet industry prey on the public's lack of knowledge about appropriate weight-loss mechanisms and desire for easy, get-thin-quick schemes. For example, a typical statement was, "Obesity robs the individual of their productivity and health and the nation of needed health care resources.... However, make no mistake, abuse, incompetence, and irresponsibility is present throughout the weight-loss [industry]" (U.S. House of Representatives 1990b:91). Notice that dieting is problematic not because it poses a health risk, but because the diet industry is incompetent or irresponsible. Most speakers espousing this view claimed that both obesity and dieting are harmful, with many emphasizing that obesity is the far bigger problem. For example, one speaker claimed that, although some diet products pose some risk to health, it is "not as much risk as the citizen's obesity itself has placed them at in the first place for disease, disability, and death" (U.S. House of Representatives 1990c:92). This statement not only places dieting and obesity in context together, it also demonstrates that many advocates of this view believe that obesity, and not mistaken body images or diet industry practices, is the major health problem. Although claiming that both obesity and dieting are harmful, the weight-control discourse is somewhat ambivalent regarding diet products because dieting in itself is considered both detrimental and yet important for weight control.

It should not be surprising then that some of these speakers address the health problems associated with weight control merely by advocating "better" weight-control products. That is, they encourage the government to (1) control diet-industry claims about effectiveness and ensure diet-industry products are safe, and (2) help consumers make informed choices about the best, healthy ways to lose weight. For example, "Concerning the issues of obesity, weight-loss, and public health policy, the basic concern should focus on the underlying problem of obesity as well as on the imperfections of those efforts designed to treat it" (U.S. House of Representatives 1990b:92).

Overall, despite the challenge of anti-diet discourse and the strident opening comments of Representative Wyden, claims that excess weight is extremely harmful to health were the most powerful message to emerge from the hearings. The pro-diet and weight-control discourses both claim that obesity is extremely harmful not merely to individuals who "suffer" from it, but to the entire society as well. It is considered such a dangerous social problem that it must be controlled and prevented. "Prevention" rhetoric is an attractive kind of political rhetoric for policy makers because advocating prevention always means decrying what is "bad" and promoting the "good." Prevention rhetoric is especially prevalent within the realm of health care and health policy for two reasons. First, state officials favor prevention through health education because it is typically cheap and uncontroversial. Employing education programs aimed at individuals, officials can claim credit when programs are successful, while blaming failure on the lack of commitment in the target population

(Stone 1989). Second, individualized prevention approaches fit well with the individualized consumption of health care. Various commercial interests can construct prevention strategies as a series of individual transactions, whereas policies aimed more broadly at public health have no comparable methods for commercializing interventions (Freeman 1992). Diet products fit the general requirements of prevention rhetoric in that they are directed at individuals through commercial products and services, ensuring that lack of individual commitment and will-power can be blamed when dieting fails to control obesity.

Hearing Outcomes

The congressional hearings were important as a basis for reform because they exposed some of the most egregious fraudulent practices and claims about effectiveness made by the diet industry. Federal regulation did increase significantly in the 1990s following the congressional hearings. For example, the FTC has brought sixty-three cases of fraud since the first congressional hearing in 1990, this after bringing a total of only nine cases throughout the entire decade of the 1980s. Similarly, after decades of inaction by the FDA, it finally banned over 100 ingredients once found in over-the-counter diet products, either because they were ineffective or unsafe.

In addition, following the congressional hearings, both the FTC and the FDA published brochures for consumers to communicate information regarding questionable practices and claims by the diet industry (see the FTC website http://www.ftc.gov/bcp/conline/pubs/health/diets.htm, and see U.S. Dept. of Health and Human Services pub. no. FDA 92–1189). The NIH also issued a report on obesity, providing information and recommendations to both consumers and health providers (see NHLBI 1998, or the NHLBI website http://www.nhlbi.nih.gov/health/public/heart/obesity/lose_wt/index.htm). Essentially, the hearings' outcomes followed directly the solutions posed by the dominant view espoused during the hearings—the weight-control discourse. That is, government regulators became more diligent in ensuring the accuracy and safety of some diet products, and they provided more information about dieting and weight loss directly to consumers. The hearings, however, did not reexamine the social context of who is dieting, nor did they address how the promotion and support of dieting as a treatment for obesity may contribute to a health problem at least as much as it solves one.

DIETING DISCOURSE AND WOMEN'S HEALTH

Defining the problem as the threat of obesity to health means none of the complex issues of weight have to be acknowledged or addressed. In this view, important facts get ignored, including that most of the people who diet are women, that many (possibly the majority) of those who use commercial diet products are not obese, and that distorted concerns about weight contribute to eating disorders and dangerous weight-loss practices, which disproportionately affect females. These complex realities require bringing more than just simple concerns about obesity to the fore. They raise cultural, political, and economic issues of the underlying gender structure that are far more troubling than those issues policymakers are willing to confront. Because the rhetoric of prevention gives the appearance of taking action against a social or health problem, policymakers have no reason to deal with the more complex, underlying issues.

The discourse on dieting and obesity found in the hearings also fits within the culture of American individualism because it is the individual dieter who is responsible for success and blamed for failure. Similarly, individual health problems resulting from diet products are isolated as individual events, resulting from individual mistakes. The powerful frame of individualism obscures recognition of the gendered nature of dieting. Hence the millions of women who diet have no way of connecting their individual experiences with broader political and cultural issues related to gender. More important, a women's health issue is obscured by gender-blind dieting discourse.

Whether intended or not, discourse that places dieting in the context of a solution to the health problem of obesity promotes the growth of the diet industry, while at the same time it obscures the women's health problems that a dieting culture promotes.

REFERENCES

Axelrod, Robert. 1976. *Structure of Decision: The Cognitive Maps of Political Elites.* Princeton: Princeton University Press.

Bordo, Susan. 1989. "The body and the reproduction of femininity: A feminist appropriation of Foucault." Pp. 13–33 in *Gender/ Body/Knowledge,* ed. Alison Jagger and Susan Bordo. New Brunswick, NJ: Rutgers University Press.

Brody, Jane E. 1995. "Moderate weight gain risky for women, a study warns." *The New York Times* (14 September): section A1, column 1.

Brumberg, Joan Jacobs. 1989. *Fasting Girls: The History of Anorexia Nervosa.* Cambridge, MA: Harvard University Press.

Carley, Kathleen, and Michael Palmquist. 1992. "Extracting, representing, and analyzing mental models," *Social Forces* 70: 601–636.

Curfman, Gregory. 1997. "Diet pills redux." *NEJM* 337(9): 629–630.

Field, Alison, Lilian Cheung, Anne Wolf, David Herzog, Steven Gortmaker, and Graham Colditz. 1999. "Exposure to the mass media and weight concerns among girls." *Pediatrics* 103(3): 660.

Foreyt, John, Walker Carlos Poston, and G. Ken Goodrick. 1996. "Future directions in obesity and eating disorders." *Addictive Behaviors* 21(6): 767–778.

Freeman, Richard. 1992. "The idea of prevention: A critical review." Pp. 34–56 in *Private Risks and Public Dangers,* ed. Sue Scott, Gareth Williams, Stephen Platt, and Hilary Thomas. Brookfield, VT: Ashgate.

Horm, John, and Kay Anderson. 1993. "National Institutes of Health Technology Assessment Conference: Who in America is trying to lose weight?" *Annals of Internal Medicine* 119:672–676.

Kuczmarski, Robert J., Katherine M. Flegal, Stephen M. Campbell, and C. L. Johnson. 1994. "Increasing prevalence of overweight among U.S. adults: The National Health and Nutrition Examination Surveys, 1960 to 1991." *JAMA* 272: 205–211.

Manson, JoAnn E., Walter C. Willett, Meir J. Stampfer, Graham A. Colditz, David Hunter, Susan Hankinson, Charles Hennekens, and Frank Speizer. 1995. "Body weight and mortality among women." *NEJM* 333(11): 677–685.

Millman, Marcia. 1980. *Such a Pretty Face.* New York: Berkely Books.

Monmaney, Terence. 1995. "Study finds thin women have lowest risk of death." *Los Angeles Times.* (14 September): part A1.

Morgan, John P., Doreen V. Kagan, and Jane S. Brody (eds.). 1985. *Phenylpropanolamine: Risks, Benefits and Controversies.* New York: Praeger Press.

National Heart, Lung and Blood Institute (NHLBI). 1998. *Clinical Guidelines on the Identification, Evaluation, and Treatment of Overweight and Obesity in Adults.* NIH pub. no. 98–4083. Washington, DC: National Institutes of Health.

Neumark-Sztainer, Dianne, Mary Story, Lori Beth Dixon, and David Murray. 1998. "Adolescents engaging in unhealthy weight-control behaviors: Are they at risk for other health-compromising behaviors?" *American Journal of Public Health* 88(6):952–955.

Public Health Service. 1991a. *Healthy People 2000: National Health Promotion and Disease Prevention Objectives.* Dept. of Health and Human Services pub. no. (PHS) 90–50212, Washington, DC: U.S. Government Printing Office.

———. 1991b. "Body-weight perceptions and selected weight-management goals and practices of high school students—U.S., 1990." *Morbidity and Mortality Weekly Report* 40(43): 741–750.

Schwarcz, Joe. 1999. "Feeding the diet industry." *The Montreal Gazette Magazine* (11 July): C3.

Serdula, Mary, Elizabeth Collins, David Williamson, Robert Anda, Elsie Pamuk, and Time Byers. 1993. "National Institutes of Health Technology Assessment Conference: Weight-control practices of U.S. adolescents and adults." *Annals of Internal Medicine* 119(7S): 667–671.

Silverstein, Brett, Lauren Perdue, Barbara Peterson, and Eileen Kelly. 1986. "The role of the mass media in promoting a thin standard of bodily attractiveness for women." *Sex Roles* 14(9/10): 519–532.

Stone, D. 1989. "Upside down prevention." *Health Service Journal* 20: 890–891.

Szekely, Eva. 1988. *Never Too Thin.* Toronto: The Women's Press.

U.S. House of Representatives. 1990a. Committee on Small Business, Subcommittee on Regulation, Business Opportunities and Energy. *Deception and Fraud in the Diet Industry (Part I)* 101st Congress, 2nd session. Serial 101–50. Washington, DC: Government Printing Office.

———. 1990b. Committee on Small Business, Subcommittee on Regulation, Business Opportunities and Energy. *Deception and Fraud in the Diet Industry* (Part II) 101st Congress, 2nd session. Serial 101–57. Washington DC: Government Printing Office.

———. 1990c. Committee on Small Business, Subcommittee on Regulation, Business Opportunities and Energy. *Juvenile Dieting, Unsafe Over-the-Counter Diet Products, and Recent Enforcement Efforts by the Federal Trade Commission.* 101st Congress, 2nd session. Serial 101–80. Washington, DC: Government Printing Office.

———. 1992. Committee on Small Business, Subcommittee on Regulation, Business Opportunities and Energy. *Deception and Fraud in the Diet Industry* (Part IV) 102nd Congress, 2nd session. Serial 102–78. Washington, DC: Government Printing Office.

Wilson, GT. 1993. "Relationship of dieting and voluntary weight loss to psychological functioning and binge eating." *Annals of Internal Medicine* 119: 727–730.

DISCOURSE OF RULES: WOMEN TALK ABOUT COSMETIC SURGERY

REBECCA WEPSIC ANCHETA

Cosmetic surgery, by its very nature, requires some explanation. It is the act of taking a healthy body and causing harm for the sake of surgically altering appearance. The need for explanation increases within a feminist sociopolitical belief system: How do women, particularly feminist women, choose to have cosmetic surgery? As a feminist studying cosmetic surgery, there is a central paradox I must address: How can I study women who have cosmetic surgery, without undermining the decisions of these very women? Feminist research on women's experiences conforming to dominant beauty practices has historically been divided into two conflicting positions (Dellinger and Williams 1997). While each side supports feminist beliefs, and believes it represents the best interests of women, they hold opposing views of some appearance practices as either empowering or oppressive.

At one end is the "beauty-as-oppression" position (Davis 1995), where researchers view women as oppressed victims and women's beauty practices are seen as further propagating their oppression (Faludi 1991; Wolf 1991). This theoretical standpoint is supported by Foucault's (1979) theory of the "docile body," which maintains that power relationships are expressed and reproduced in the body. The work of Susan Bordo (1991, 1993, 1997) is an example of this perspective, in that she examines how women are influenced and shaped by cultural images in ways that reinforce gender hierarchies.

Attempts to recognize women's agency in beauty practices compose the other end of the continuum, constituting the "beauty-as-liberation" position. Women's choices to undergo cosmetic surgery can be explained using a rational-choice model (Gillespie 1996), by stating that cosmetic surgery can be empowering for women on an individual level in a market-economy model where women are valued for conforming to cultural standards of appearance.[1] In Dellinger and Williams' (1997) study of women's makeup use at work, Judith Butler's (1990) theory of subversion and parody is utilized as an attempt to recognize women's agency in beauty practices. Although Dellinger and Williams look for ways women might use makeup to resist and subvert dominant norms of appearance, they found no evidence of such use. Their research participants used makeup to conform, rather than rebel.

A primary problem with framing the question of cosmetic surgery as either oppressive or empowering is that it tends to reify the dualistic and competing images of women as either "dopes" or "agents" (Davis 1991, 1995). These two models oversimplify and polarize women's experiences of cosmetic surgery. By forcing this complex multileveled issue of women's relationships to beauty practices into a dualistic model, neither position adequately represents the relationship of women's individual choices to the position of women on a sociopolitical level. In this paper I present a third possibility for a feminist analysis of women choosing cosmetic surgery. Through a qualitative analysis of women's discourses of their experiences with cosmetic surgery, I explore how women are able to reframe and redefine the questions of oppression. Women use language—and, more specifically, *a set of rules*—for describing their cosmetic surgery experiences. These rules allow women to reframe questions of oppression and avoid conflict between their beliefs and their cosmetic surgery practices. By focusing on the discursive practices of women engaging in cosmetic surgeries, I am able to develop a feminist criticism that takes into account women's active participation in their decisions to have cosmetic surgery.

METHODS AND DESCRIPTION OF THE SAMPLE

The data for this paper are drawn primarily from in-depth, qualitative interviews with twenty-one women who have had cosmetic surgeries (Ancheta 2000). Participants were recruited through a combination of snowball sampling and physician referrals. Each interview was structured around a set of open-ended questions, audiotape recorded and transcribed. I then analyzed the interviews using a grounded theory method (Strauss and Corbin 1990). Analysis began with open coding and proceeded through a series of analytic memos.

The sample includes women from age 34 to 71. Half of the women were in their late fifties or early sixties. As a group, the participants were highly educated and reported high household incomes. The types of cosmetic surgeries participants had included facelifts, eyelid lifts, breast implants, breast lifts, nose jobs, facial acid peels and laser peels, neck lifts, tummy tucks, and liposuction of the body and neck. It was common for participants to have had more than one surgery. Roughly 75 percent of the sample (16 women) had undergone two or more surgeries. Of these, seven had had three or more surgeries.

FINDINGS: (I LEARN THE RULES)

Women's discourse about their choices and experiences with cosmetic surgery is characterized by a set of rules. Rules are largely unspoken and learned as one enters the domain of cosmetic surgery. I discovered and learned these rules by unknowingly breaking them.

It was my second interview, and the research participant was describing for me the reasons she had seven cosmetic surgeries. Using her "before" pictures laid out on the table in front of us, she pointed out various facial flaws. She cited that her earlier nose job had left her nose crooked with cartilage poking out, that she had bags under her eyes, and deep lines in her forehead. Amy[2] said to me, "And I was most concerned about my nose, which is initially why I went to see him."

I agreed with her, responding, "And you can really see that it's crooked there, and you can see the cartilage poking through, and how you have that line in the middle there."

Amy, caught off guard, responded with an excuse as to why she looked so poorly in the picture:

> *Yeah. So anyway, he took these photographs just before surgery, and in fairness to the photographer, they'd already given me Valium, so I probably looked a little more gork than I normally would.*

A few sentences later she cued me in to the rules by saying,

> *But what the surgeon did was very undrastic, I thought. He just smoothed out the bone of my nose and tried to give me a little more nostril, which I lacked.*

She minimized the results, calling them "undrastic," and used minimizing language of "smoothed out the bone" and giving her "a little more nostril." I, however, was not yet knowledgeable of the rules of cosmetic surgery discourse, and replied, "That made a very big difference." Finally, Amy firmly responded by correcting me:

> *Well, it wasn't a lot, and as far as I was concerned, I didn't look very different. Nobody ever mentioned it or knew....*

This interchange is an example of how rules of discourse can be taught to new members of the cosmetic surgery community. It was clear I did not know the culturally accepted way to respond to her surgeries, and she was doing her best to correct my comments. Amy tried to make my comments rule-appropriate and instructed me on the right ways to judge a cosmetic procedure. I, on the other hand, had no idea that subtle results are a valued quality, and thought a drastic makeover was an optimal result. After all, she spent a lot of money and time, and endured pain, to achieve this "subtle" result. While throughout the interview I believed I was validating her experience of the difference surgery made, instead she experienced my comments as criticism. I had learned my first rule—the rule of minimizing.

The Rule of Minimizing

There are two primary analytic themes in women's discourse about their cosmetic surgery experiences: minimization and self-authorization. The rule Amy taught me was the rule of minimizing, present in participants' discussion of their motivations, surgeries, and results. Patty used the minimizing rule to describe her friend's laser surgery and her own post-op recovery. Although the friend had a complication, the story is told to minimize her difficulties.

PATTY: My one friend had a very bad experience with Dr. Wolf, even though she loves him, with the laser. And she didn't want to have the laser and then she later said it's the best thing she ever did, but the process was awful. What happened is she went away for the weekend. And it [the bandage] stuck to her face, and the truth is, she went too long, and so she tried to take it off, it was just a mess. But now she says it's the best thing that ever happened to her. Everyone has a different post-op tale.

INTERVIEWER: How was your post-op?

PATTY: It was a piece of cake.

INT: You didn't have a lot of bruising?

PATTY: Down here, the only thing I remember, in fact, all the blood went down and it hung right here in my neck. And it took me a long time for that purple bruise to go away. Then the other day I had a flu shot, and I have a bruise that is two weeks old that is just horrible up here. So I had a great experience. I was very motivated, I was very pleased.

Calling her own recovery a "piece of cake" and stating that laser surgery was "the best thing that ever happened" to her friend, Patty simultaneously minimized the difficult recoveries they both experienced and exaggerated the positive effects of the surgery. Later in the interview, Patty made an overt reference to the importance of minimizing. She described disclosing her surgery to others, specifically describing that she does *not* say, "well, I look so great because I've been slashed and diced." While Patty made it clear that she has been "slashed and diced," she was also explaining that she would be breaking the rules if she described it that way. Thus she doesn't tell people about the extent of her surgeries.

Laura minimized the surgery itself, through her use of minimizing words. Describing her surgery, she recalls that the surgeon,

> *just stuck a little sack, and then re-stitched it.... All I had done was, they took extra skin off my breasts and just kind of tightened underneath. There was no implant or anything.*

Describing her surgery in this way, Laura is minimizing her breast reduction. Her words of "just," "little," and "kind of" are minimizing. Even when she talks more specifically about the incisions, she describes these in minimizing ways:

> *They made like a half-moon under the breast, then a T up to the nipple, and they actually did go around the nipple because they had to move the nipple up. And then took off like a pie shape underneath and then just tightened it altogether.*

It is striking how Laura is able to downplay the extent of her surgery, even while graphically describing the incisions. Downplaying the invasiveness of surgery is common in the cosmetic surgery community, where surgeries are described as a "nip and a tuck" and often compared with other everyday beauty practices, such as having one's haircut and using makeup. By minimizing the extent of surgery, research participants avoided discussion of the severity of surgery. The discourse of minimizing thus serves as a tool, allowing women to have cosmetic operations yet not recognize their seriousness. Because cosmetic surgery may appear severe to people who are outside of the surgery arena, telling minimizing stories is an important way to negotiate the deviance and horror associated with surgery. Communicating their surgery stories as "normal" takes the edges off the deviance and horror of cosmetic surgery, thereby socially placing cosmetic surgery—and the research participants' socially communicated selves—in an acceptable category.

The Rule of Self-Authorization: "I Did It for Myself."

Women gave a variety of reasons for having cosmetic surgery. Some women cited wanting to look differently in clothing, while others sought to regain a more youthful appearance. While the reasons varied, women consistently pointed out that they did not have surgery to please other people. Versions of the phrase "I did it for myself" were common in interviews. However, this phrase does not mean participants were not referencing a social self or social selves. Rather, "doing it for myself" is a fully social reason related to cultural and sexual norms of attractiveness and youthfulness. While the phrase "doing it for myself" implies solely individual action, women are certainly aware of the cultural mandates around youthful attractiveness. Rather, their comments sustain a rule of self-authorization.

"Doing it for myself" is a discourse that the women repeat frequently in their stories, claiming autonomy in their decision making. Doctors also use the phrase "doing it for themselves" (Dull and West 1991, p. 61) to describe good patients. "Through these means, surgeons located the impetus for aesthetic improvement within patients themselves" (Dull and West 1991, p. 61). However, participants' motivations are clearly socially situated. Dull and West note their data show a range of outside influences (family, friends, etc.), and that doctors expressed preferences contradicted other reasons patients seek surgery (such as for a job or relationship). Good patients are thus "*created* as well as 'found'" (p. 62). Dull and West point out that the interactions which make a good patient are part of our gender accomplishment. Thus, women are "naturally" good candidates for cosmetic surgery.

From the participants' perspectives, women are trying to be "good patients" by upholding and subscribing to the "doing it for myself" rule. It is a rule that helps them to ignore social influences and minimizes external pressures in their decision-making process. Carol, a forty-one-year-old secretary, elected to have a tummy tuck and liposuction body contouring after losing over one hundred pounds. Recounting an initial consultation with her surgeon, she describes the importance of having surgery for the "right reasons":

> *He interviewed me—"Why do you want to have this done?"—to make sure you're doing it for the right reasons, not because you want to catch a husband or whatever.... I told him about the weight loss, that I wanted to do that for me, it wasn't for my husband, it wasn't for anybody else but me.*

Carol later adds that having surgery is like a gift to herself:

> *That's how I view all the surgeries. Like when I get a massage. This is for me. And we all need that; there's nothing wrong with it.*

Emily, a thirty-four year old hair stylist had breast implants and liposuction. As the youngest participant in this study, she faced an extra burden when describing why she chose to have cosmetic surgery at a young age. Her husband questioned her decision to have surgery, and her response was that she's "doing it for myself."

> *"Why do you want to do that? You look fine." I'm doing it for myself, you know. I feel better about myself. When you find that perfect dress and you put it on and it just doesn't fit right.*

Emily consciously tells me that surgery is for herself, reminding herself to cite the right reason for surgery. By adding "I should say" to her description, the importance of self-authorization as a rule of discourse is highlighted.

> *Well, we all can't look like supermodels. But we can try. I think we do it—for myself,* I should say*—it makes me feel better about myself. This is how I see myself. This is who I want to be. This is the way I want other people to see me. That's probably the best way to describe it. But I'm pretty much doing it for myself. When you get out of the shower, you look at yourself in the mirror.*

A major exception to the rule of self-authorization was the importance of one's employment in the decision to have cosmetic surgery. Women talked about wanting to look younger for their careers as one reason for having cosmetic surgery. This was the case with Jean, an executive secretary, who told me that she had facial cosmetic surgery at age 67 because of her job.

> *I feel in my job situation, I'm 67 as you probably know, but almost everybody where I work is much younger...and I just felt that it made me feel like I belonged more.... And in that situation it kind of behooves you to look as—it's not necessary to look young, but to feel youthful.*

She later adds that although her male boss is older, as a woman she is aware that a youthful appearance is important to her career.

> *But it's still a man's world when it comes to looks. I think women think more about staying youthful than men do; it's more acceptable for men not to, see.... I felt that as long—and it was a gift to myself, kind of. If I'm gonna be working at this age, and I'm still working and vital and active.... But I felt that it was important to me, and also, it was kind of like a gift to myself. If I'm going to work at this age, past 65, then I've gotta give myself a present. So I did.*

Thus, while Jean initially talks about the importance of having surgery to maintain a youthful appearance for her employment, she returns to the rule of self-authorization. In a version of "I did it for myself," she says that having cosmetic surgery was "kind of" a "gift" to herself.

With the exception of their employment relationships, research participants often claimed autonomy in making their cosmetic surgery decisions, thus abiding by the rule of self-authorization. Rarely did research participants question standards of appearance. For example, when Laura, a fifty-four-year-old public health nurse, talks about her decision to have breast-reduction surgery, she tells me it is because she was "really drooping."

> *I could never wear something like a halter-top or anything without looking like I was really drooping....*

She never questions why "really drooping" is a physical state requiring surgery. Similarly, Laura had earlier described how she decided to have surgery as a result of taking care of a friend post-operatively and being exposed to the friend's physician. She tells me,

> *I was very impressed with the work that she had done and with the physician himself. So then I decided to go ahead and do it.*

By referencing only the physician as a factor in her decision for surgery, Laura is avoiding any discussion of an appearance-related reason. Other research participants described that they were beginning to look old or tired, but not one research participant ever discussed *why* looking old or looking tired warrants having surgery.

Occasionally a research participant would acknowledge the importance of social relationships in her decision for surgery. This was the case with Diane, who reluctantly connected her decision to have breast implants with her recent divorce:

DIANE: I probably never would have done that if I were not divorced. But I just figured....
INT: Was that around when you were divorced?
DIANE: Mm hmm. I just thought, well, to attract another man I'd better look good.
INT: So it was related.
DIANE: Yes it was. *I hate to say it,* it was.

Diane expresses her reluctance to recognize her divorce as a factor in her decision when she states, "I hate to say it." By admitting to the influence of her intimate relationships in her surgery decisions, she is breaking the rule of self-authorization. Having "surgery for myself" ensured that women abided by the rule of self-authorization, thereby upholding their claim that cosmetic surgery decisions are made autonomously. By abiding by the rule for self-authorization, women individualized their decisions to have cosmetic surgery, and internalized the motivation for seeking surgery.

Learning the Rules

Although I began my research as an outsider to the social world of cosmetic surgery, I quickly learned to navigate the rules of discourse. The experience of learning the rules is not unique to researchers. Rather, research participants occasionally made overt references to learning the rules themselves. Heather described a story of learning the rule of minimizing when she first entered the domain of cosmetic surgery, by caring for a friend after a face-lift. She recounted the first time she saw her friend post-operatively:

> *That was the first time I had seen her. And I think I hurt her feelings, because I didn't tell her I thought she looked terrific. I just sort of looked at her and she was discolored, she was swollen, and she expected me, I think, to say 'Oh, you look wonderful and beautiful!' and I didn't say that right at the very beginning, and then I realized later on afterwards, I really* should *tell her she looks great.*

Heather's use of the word "should" highlights that this is a rule of discourse—not a response she sincerely feels, but one that is expected. Heather is learning a discourse to minimize the severity of cosmetic surgery recoveries.

Abiding by rules minimizes cosmetic surgery experiences and avoids the harder questions of what social and cultural themes brought the women to the knife. By ruling these out and emphasizing the individualistic aspects, the women act agentically but without reference to themes that in other literatures have been called oppressive. By utilizing a discourse of minimizing, women's cosmetic surgery experiences are effectively minimized in interactions, becoming through discourse less serious, less dangerous, and less painful. This minimization makes cosmetic surgery seem to be a "natural" part of women's everyday worlds, making it an often unquestioned practice by those engaging in it. Similarly, the discourse of "doing it for myself" supports the rule of self-authorization. By professing that they are individually motivated for surgery, and minimizing external social pressures, participants were able to describe their choices for surgery as an act of self-care, thus sustaining the continuing practice of cosmetic surgery. This rule also locates the desire for surgery within each woman, supporting Dull and West's (1991) findings that it is through the accomplishment of gender that cosmetic surgery is practiced.

IMPLICATIONS

The findings described here reflect and amplify our understandings of the critical role of the body in articulation of socially and culturally situated selves and identities. This exploration of the cultural construction of women's bodies goes beyond previous work on cosmetic surgery, to focus on how the social importance of age and gender is culturally constructed through practices of cosmetic surgery and the meanings and interpretations attached to those practices by the women. The findings reveal processes that are implicated in the multiple articulations of women's bodies and in how those bodies are configured with plastic surgery, and that are realized through meanings the women attach to the experience of the surgery.

The analysis of the intensely social aspects of the decision to undertake cosmetic surgery and the experience of it lifts our understanding of women opting for cosmetic surgery from the narrow binary views in some feminist literature (oppression vs. liberation) to a more complex grasp of dynamic, not static, social and cultural pressures. Women's exercise of choice and agency in the decision and the experience are always culturally and materially situated. This work problematizes that binary view and opens new realms with which to interpret this phenomenon much more closely in line with the women's own lived "everyday and everynight experiences" (Smith 1979).

These social and phenomenological processes are imbedded in the cultural norms for youthfulness and sexual attractiveness. Hence the sculpting of the women's bodies is more than the application of the cosmetic surgeon's knife—it is the sculpting, or construction, of social and cultural process in which, it must be clearly understood, the women participate fully. These are not cultural dopes; they are making reasoned decisions within a framework of choices and pressures. More than anything else, this research speaks to the continuing situation of women in a society, where, in spite of economic, social, racial, ethnic, and sexual gains, women are still beholden to antiquated norms and unrealizable ideals—perpetually young, valued more for their appearance than their ideas, and where maintaining a wrinkle-free face and fat-free body are expected signs of good womanhood.

REFERENCES

Ancheta, Rebecca Wepsic. 2000. "Saving face: Women's experiences with cosmetic surgery." University of California, San Francisco. Unpublished dissertation.

Bordo, Susan. 1991. " 'Material girl': The effacements of postmodern culture." Pp. 106–130 in *The Female Body: Figures, Styles, Speculations,* ed. L. Goldstein. Ann Arbor: The University of Michigan Press.

———. 1993. *Unbearable Weight: Feminism, Western Culture, and the Body.* Los Angeles: University of California Press.

———. 1997. *Twilight Zones: The Hidden Life of Cultural Images from Plato to O. J.* Berkeley: University of California Press.

Butler, Judith. 1990. *Gender Trouble: Feminism and the Subversion of Identity.* New York: Routledge.

Davis, Kathy. 1991. "Remaking the she-devil: A critical look at feminist approaches to beauty." *Hypatia* 6:21–43.

———. 1995. *Reshaping the Female Body: The Dilemma of Cosmetic Surgery.* New York: Routledge.

Dellinger, Kirsten, and Christine L. Williams. 1997. "Makeup at Work: Negotiating Appearance Rules in the Workplace." *Gender and Society* 11:2: 151–177.

Dull, Diana, and Candace West. 1991. "Accounting for cosmetic surgery: The accomplishment of gender." *Social Problems* 38:54–70.

Faludi, Susan. 1991. *Backlash: The Undeclared War on American Women.* New York: Crown Publishers.

Foucault, Michel. 1979. *Discipline and Punish: The Birth of the Prison.* New York: Vintage.

Gillespie, Rosemary. 1996. "Women, the body and brand extension in medicine: cosmetic surgery and the paradox of choice." *Women & Health* 24:4: 69–85.

Smith, Dorothy. 1979. *The Everyday World as Problematic: A Feminist Sociology.* Boston: Northeastern University Press.

Strauss, Anselm, and Juliet Corbin. 1990. *Basics of Qualitative Research.* Newbury Park, CA: Sage Publications.

Wolf, Naomi. 1991. *The Beauty Myth: How Images of Beauty Are Used against Women.* New York: Doubleday.

NOTES

1. However, Gillespie (1996) does recognize that the practice of cosmetic surgery also contributes to women's further oppression, thus creating a "paradox of choice."

2. In order to preserve the confidentiality of participants, all names used are pseudonyms.

Chapter 9

RAGING HORMONES

For about thirty-five years of their lives, women have monthly reproductive cycles which indicate their potential for gestating new life. Yet, rather than being celebrated, this monthly reassurance that the continuation of life is possible has been met with fear and repugnance by many cultures, including our own. Medical researchers and practitioners in the United States have, to a greater or lesser degree, managed to declare the menstrual cycle as dirty, denigrating—a disease. This chapter explores the social construction of menstruation, the premenstrual period, and menopause as negative processes, in the sense that they are all liable to be treated as unhealthy and pathological.

Embedded in the prevailing medical declarations of PMS and of menopause as diseases—in essence the medicalization of normal female bodily processes—is a gender bias that runs so deeply and is so firmly entrenched that women have suffered needlessly. Curiously, the corresponding changes in life that men experience are rarely remarked upon as being anything other than normal. For example, it is unheard of in medical circles to discuss male castration if a man is moody or depressed, although the removal of a woman's ovaries has, until recently, been considered reasonable medical treatment for her psychological problems. One aspect of the medicalization of these female processes is the definition of women as emotionally unstable and so performance-impaired that they are precluded from full participation in life. The conflation of biology and ideology is glaringly apparent.

MENSTRUATION

Many cultures have traditionally ritualized the time of the month when women pass blood. Their taboos around menstruation are clear indicators of the awe and power in which this cycle is held. Although in centuries past our cultural forebears have associated menstrual blood with some positive powers—such as curing leprosy, birthmarks, and hemorrhoids—they primarily have seen it as a negative force. Men have believed that women who were menstruating could turn wine sour, kill seedlings, and rot meat, sometimes just by looking at the objects in question (Golub 1992; Delaney, Lupton, and Toth 1988). Because of their perception of this dual nature of menstruation, many cultures have excluded women from normal social activities during their periods by enforcing taboos to isolate them physically in menstrual huts, keep them from handling food, and make them abstain from sex.

Beliefs concerning menstruation have been slow to change over the course of time. Ancient and outdated though the ideas about wine, seedlings, and menstrual huts may be, they have been evident over the past century and a half in the negative images of the menstrual cycle, in the continuation of restrictions societies assert are necessary for women, and in the claims that women are ruled by their biology. For instance, in 1873, Prof. Edward H. Clarke of Harvard University argued that between the ages of twelve and twenty, the female reproductive system was at a critical point in its development. That development would be irreparably harmed if the woman did not carefully nurture it. His theory was that the body had a set amount of energy, and for women to expend that energy on mental work, particularly by getting an education, would do great damage to their reproductive potential. The clear conclusion was that women should not pursue higher education. According to Clarke, even if a woman successfully navigated these early years, she would still need complete rest from mental activity during her days of menstruation (Bullough and Voght 1973).

Following Clarke's ideas, doctors and others offered advice for the next sixty years to avoid singing during menstruation and warned against dancing, athletic exercise, and travel (noted in Bullough and Voght 1973). They later suggested that women should avoid long showers, swimming, or overexertion. Coupled with these restrictions was a growing tendency in the nineteenth and twentieth centuries to view the menstrual period as not just a time of physical limitations, but as a medically pathological phenomenon. Medical texts at the end of the 1900s increasingly use words such as "disintegration," "diminished," "regression," "debris," and "degenerate" when describing menstruation, terms that are far from neutral (Martin 1987:48–49). Rather than being viewed as part of a normal and necessary process, bleeding has been portrayed as negative, even harmful. (Recall our discussion in Chapter 2 of the sperm and the egg.)

PREMENSTRUAL DISORDERS

Although the dominant image of a woman's period remains negative, it is the image of another aspect of the menstrual cycle that has become controversial and disturbingly harmful. The current manifestation of the negativism and diseasing of the menstrual cycle focuses not on the bleeding phase, but on the premenstrual phase of the month. Researchers first drew attention to the premenstrual phase and gave it a negative connotation when, in 1931, Robert T. Frank, an American gynecologist, coined the term *premenstrual tension* and recommended treatment of severe cases by removal of the ovaries or radiation (X-ray) therapy. Then in 1950, Katharina Dalton, a British physician, defined a more inclusive category with the term *premenstrual syndrome,* or PMS, by referring to "any symptoms or complaints which regularly come just before or during early menstruation but are absent at other times of the cycle" (quoted in Figert 1996:5). Although discussed in the popular, medical, and psychological literature in the 1960s and 1970s, PMS did not became a household term until the 1980s (Rittenhouse 1991). During that time, in a British trial, a woman accused of murdering her lover successfully used PMS as a defense and received a lesser sentence as a result.

Problems with Research on PMS

Interest in PMS generated considerable research, although one reviewer later concluded, "We can look, in vain, for credible research that defines and analyzes PMS" (Fausto-Sterling 1985:94). Credible research requires strong research designs that analyze the relationships between carefully defined variables. For the most part, PMS research has lacked these attributes. First, researchers have failed to define the premenstrual period in a consistent way. Some use the two days before the menstrual flow, whereas others, by referring to cases in a three-week time period—two weeks before the menses and one week after—make women premenstrual for most of their waking hours (Fausto-Sterling 1985).

Another obstacle to a clear definition of PMS is the overwhelming number of symptoms that have been attributed to this syndrome. Over one hundred symptoms are listed for PMS (Fausto-Sterling 1985), including physical changes (such as bloating and headaches), emotional problems (such as mood swings and depression), and behavior changes (such as sleep disturbance and crying spells). "Mercy!" says one psychologist. "With so many symptoms, accounting for most of the possible range of human experience, who wouldn't have 'PMS'?" (Tavris 1992:136). To add to the disarray, some checklists "include mutually contradictory symptoms (such as 'was less interested in sex' *and* 'was more sexually active,' or 'had less energy' *and* 'couldn't sit still')" (Tavris 1992:136). The result of using such catchall lists to define the major variables in the study is that researchers estimate widely different percentages of women who suffer from PMS. Perhaps it is 30 to 50 percent (Miller 1998) or between 5 and 97 percent (Gurevich 1995). With an all-inclusive definition, it is indeed likely to be, as Dalton suggests, "the world's commonest disease" (quoted in Rome 1986:145).

Lay people, academics, feminists, and others have critiqued the use of the word *syndrome* to describe these assorted physical changes, behaviors, and moods (Choi 1995:759). The common meaning of a syndrome in a medical context is a group of symptoms typical of a *disease* or disturbance. Yet this is a list of symptoms that includes all of the usual changes experienced by women going through a healthy, normal, monthly cycle.

Another critique of the research on PMS is the way it was conducted. Much of the research has used a retrospective design in which women were asked to recall symptoms they had during prior premenstrual times. The resulting findings supported the idea that moods and cycle went together. However, retrospective reporting is prone to error, and when people know (and perhaps even believe) the expected connection (in this case between their premenstrual phase and the list of problems), their memories are likely to support such a connection. Such a possibility of bias seems quite likely when prospective and blind studies have very different results from the retrospective ones. Thus, if women are asked to keep a diary of their moods, and are not made aware that the research is about menstrual cycles until the end of the study, the connections between cycle and mood disappear (Fausto-Sterling 1985:102–103; Tavris 1992:145–146).

Research that *did* attempt to measure the symptoms prospectively and blindly did not find the expected relationship between mood and cycle (Choi 1995). Moreover, indirect evidence of a connection could have come from the evaluation of hormone-based treatments for PMS. If prescribed hormones could fix so-called PMS problems, then a connection between PMS hormones and mood would seem more likely. Yet these evaluations, too, produced anomalous results. Placebos were often as effective as active substances (Tavris 1992:144–145).

Defining PMS as a Psychiatric Disorder

In the mid 1980s, the American Psychiatric Association (APA) decided to consider if there was some aspect of PMS that should be defined as a psychiatric disorder. Periodically, the APA reviews research and clinical findings and publishes a revision of its official manual, the *Diagnostic and Statistical Manual (DSM)*. The manual defines all accepted psychiatric diagnoses, and provides a corresponding code number for each diagnosis to be used by psychiatrists and other mental health professionals when they seek reimbursement for their services. If the Association is unsure of the validity of a diagnosis, but feels that further research on it is warranted, it can include suggested research criteria in an appendix. The hope is that additional research will have resolved the ambiguities by the time the *DSM* comes under subsequent revision.

The American Psychiatric Association appointed a committee to examine PMS. Anyone needing to be convinced that science is politically influenced should read an account of this committee and the subsequent decisions that were made to include a PMS disorder in the *DSM* (e.g., see Figert 1996 and Caplan 1995). The committee's work immediately became controversial, with charges that such a diagnosis would stigmatize all women. Opponents organized pickets, letter-writing campaigns, and a computer-based solicitation of signatures on a petition of protest; produced radio spots; and mobilized twenty-one professional organizations, such as the American Psychological Association, the National Association of Social

Workers, and the National Coalition for Women's Mental Health to register their objections to the diagnosis (Figert 1996:44, 87, 104).

In letters of protest to the APA, gynecologists argued that taking care of endocrinologic problems of women "is our province, not yours" (quoted in Figert 1996:76). They argued that making premenstrual problems into a psychiatric diagnosis meant that women would be told that society and their doctors thought of them as "disordered," a characterization that "does not seem helpful" (quoted in Figert 1996:77). The APA response, voiced by the head of the work group revising the *DSM* was, "Gynecologists are totally irrelevant. This is purely a mental disorder. It is not a physical or neurological disease" (quoted in Figert 1996:78).

The result was a controversial decision in 1987 by the American Psychiatric Association to include "late luteal phase dysphoric disorder" in the *DSM,* version *III-R.* The APA's committee on women said the research was inadequate and the head of the work group acknowledged that the "causes and optimal therapy are unknown" (quoted in Figert 1996:93). Thus it was no surprise that the APA did not place the diagnosis in the body of the manual, but in an appendix under the heading "Proposed diagnostic categories needing further study." Although this placement in the appendix gave the disorder less status than a regular diagnosis, the profession gave it a diagnostic code, making it more "real" and encouraging doctors and others to actually use it as a clinical diagnosis. In 1993, the name of the diagnosis was changed to "premenstrual dysphoric disorder" and was included, again amidst considerable protest, in the body of the *DSM-IV.*

Proponents of the diagnosis argue that the APA's actions define an entity very different from the more inclusive and ambiguous PMS. Estimates are that only about five percent of women meet criteria for the diagnosis, because the definition is tighter than the 100-plus symptoms of PMS and requires a report of "significant" interference with work or other activities. By having a diagnosis that applies to so few women, it "curbs the abuse" of PMS (Figert 1996:133). Proponents also feel that women who do suffer in the premenstrual phase receive some affirmation by having a diagnosis that says their symptoms are real. Tired of hearing from doctors and others that their problems are imaginary, these women at last have a diagnosis that legitimizes their complaints.

Criticism of the Disorder

Critics continue to object to the APA's diagnosis, feeling that the potential for stigmatizing all women by turning a normal biological cycle into a psychiatric problem outweighs any benefits. Many agree with the arguments the gynecologists used in their debate with the psychiatrists: A woman's reproductive cycle is a gynecological issue. It is usually healthy, but when it isn't, the gynecologist is the one to understand the anatomical or hormonal dysfunction and correct it. Treatment of many other mood changes uses this logic: A person with mood swings coming from a thyroid abnormality doesn't go to a psychiatrist. Why would mood changes from the menstrual cycle be treated differently (Tavris 1992:142)?

Premenstrual dysphoric disorder might have generated less of an uproar were it not for the long history of linking women's reproductive capacity to mental problems. Saying that reproductive hormones can cause depression sounds a lot like saying that the uterus causes hysteria, a belief dating back to the fifth century, when a restless womb was characterized as wandering through the body, causing disease. By the 1800s, some doctors felt the resulting condition, called hysteria (the Greek word for the uterus), was a "wastepaper basket of medicine where one throws otherwise unemployed symptoms" (Goldstein 1987:324), including vivid emotional states, tears and sobs, and fainting. But a French doctor systematized the definition in the 1880s and gave it more respectability. The result was that many more women were labeled as hysterics. At about the same time, American doctors turned their attention to a milder form of nervous problems that they linked to the uterus, and proposed a new diagnosis—

neurasthenia. Charlotte Perkins Gilman, a famous feminist writer, was treated for neurasthenia and given the popular "rest cure," which required living "as domestic a life as possible"—in her case, limiting her intellectual pursuits and keeping her from writing (Gilman 1935:96). Gilman's short story, "The Yellow Wallpaper," is a critique of the rest cure that nearly caused her to lose her mind.

Popular culture has echoed these historical ideas and taken them to extremes, creating a PMS "media monster" (Chrisler and Levy 1990). Companies produce calendars, mugs, bumper stickers, postcards, and greeting cards representing the premenstrual phase as a time when women are crazy, bitchy, aggressive, and downright dangerous. "What's the difference between a PMS woman and a terrorist? You can reason with a terrorist," reads a typical greeting card (See Figert 1996 for reproductions.) Movies and television contribute similarly unpleasant visions of the PMS woman. A popular culture filled with such images encourages everyday comments and jokes about PMS and becomes a way to control and dismiss women in general. An example is the use of a phrase such as, "Don't listen to her, she's PMSing."

Premenstrual dysphoric disorder also would be a less contentious diagnosis were it not for a culture that characterizes women in the premenstrual phase as persons who are unable to perform adequately, if at all. Prominent individuals have made bold public statements about women's raging hormones. Edgar Berman, the personal physician of former Vice President Hubert Humphrey, said,

> *Even a congresswoman must defer to scientific truths...[that] there just are physical and psychological inhibitants that limit a female's potential.... I would still rather have a male John F. Kennedy make the Cuban missile crisis decisions than a female of the same age who could possibly be subject to the curious mental aberrations of that age group. (quoted in Fausto-Sterling 1985:91)*

This statement is based on a long-standing assumption of impaired performance during a woman's premenstrual phase. Yet there is no evidence suggesting that this is true (Choi 1995). Although some researchers would have us accept the idea of a woman's diminished performance until proven otherwise, an equally logical (and fairer) assumption is to assume there is no diminished performance, until proven otherwise. But the cultural bias that the reproductive cycle throws women out of control reverses the usual burden of evidence.

The belief that the premenstrual phase causes difficulties in the workplace is present not only in scientific research, but also in the mass media. The *Wall Street Journal* claims that PMS-related absenteeism costs U.S. industry 8 percent of its total wage bill (Tavris 1992:136–137). However, some analysts argue that this idea of premenstrually caused decreased work performance receives prominent attention only during times when women are competing with men for jobs—during depressions and after wars—and is not brought up when women are needed in the workforce (Martin 1987:120).

Emboldened by the action of the APA, which states that hormones *do* influence mood, a huge PMS industry has emerged. Clinics specializing in the treatment of PMS abound, and remedies have proliferated, due in part to a recognition of the profit-potential of PMS. In one book, a group of hospital consultants argue that the development of women's health care services can generate business for a hospital, and that PMS is particularly lucrative. "In the short term, a premenstrual syndrome (PMS) program, for example, can generate additional revenue through diagnostic and X-ray work. Research has shown that the average PMS patient presents with twenty-eight different symptoms; thus ancillary services become an important tool in the initial work-up of these patients." The authors/consultants go on to discuss the long-term payoff. If a woman is happy with the PMS services she receives, "she is more likely to refer members of her family to that facility should the need arise" (Dearing et al. 1987:202). The *New England Journal of Medicine* editorialized that clinics for PMS were "being merchandized like many of the fast-food chains. Such clinics frequently provide unproved or ineffective forms of therapy" (Vaitukaitis 1984:1372). Needless to say, women with severe problems associated with the premenstrual phase need better treatment. They must have their problems correctly diagnosed and appropriately and effectively treated.

An unfortunate consequence of all the attention given to the more severe problems of the premenstrual phase is that we have all but ignored the normal cycle. Many women experience only minor physical problems in the premenstrual phase, such as water retention. Likewise, they suffer only minor "emotional" problems, such as "feeling under the weather." Despite PMS lists that define such signs as part of a syndrome (symptoms typical of a disease), they are the normal discomforts of a natural body cycle. To better understand these prosaic problems, and thus develop remedies to ease them and bring relief, would contribute considerably to women's health.

MENOPAUSE

Menopause occurs when a woman is about fifty years old. Ovarian estrogen declines from age 25 on, dropping off more rapidly in one's late forties, finally reaching a level too low to support continued menstruation. After a year of no menstrual periods, a woman in effect postdates her menopause to the date of her last menstrual period. The short-term effects of lowered estrogen include hot flashes, a thinning and drying of tissues (such as vaginal tissue and skin), and insomnia, primarily the result of nighttime hot flashes. For most women, these effects are mild; for about 10 percent they are severe (Wallis and Barbo 1998). Cultural variations in reports of menopausal symptoms suggest that some of these differences are due to diet. Thus, in Japan the low incidence of hot flashes may result from a diet rich in plant estrogens (phytoestrogens) from soy products (Finkel 1998). Cultural differences in women's ideal weight, the number of children women have, mothers' age at their birth, and the status of aging women may influence the type and severity of symptoms. The long-term effects of lowered estrogen include increased risk of heart disease and osteoporosis (thinning of the bones).

Images of Menopause

Although physicians and other health providers have updated their views of menopause over the years, their views remain consistently negative, having an embedded image of the culturally defined proper social role of the woman as a bearer of children, and suggest an inherent emotional instability of women. Nineteenth-century physicians saw menopause as a time of sin and decay; the early twentieth century brought images of neurosis and "moral insanity" (McCrea 1983; Barbre 1993:29). Twentieth-century psychiatrists developed a diagnosis of "involutional melancholia," an agitated depression at the time of menopause, and they hospitalized women who were going through a normal change in the life cycle (Dickson 1993:50). These professional actions contributed to the development of cultural myths of "menopausal madness." This myth continues to linger on, although contemporary research shows that depression is no more common among menopausal women than it is for women in general (Elias 1993). One study found the occurrence of menopausal depression equal to that of female Yale students, the preponderance of whom are in their late teens and early twenties (reported in Wallis and Barbo 1998).

Promotion of Estrogen Replacement Therapy

In the 1960s, a major transformation occurred in the way menopause was viewed. Gynecologists "'discovered' that menopause was a 'deficiency disease'" (McCrea 1983:111). This "discovery" *followed* the development of a cure, estrogen replacement therapy (ERT). The cure was based on scientific advancements that found external sources of estrogen: namely, the production of a synthetic form of estrogen, and the extraction of estrogen from pregnant mares' urine (which formed the basis of the trade name Premarin).

The history of the promotion of ERT and its widespread acceptance is not a story of dispassionate scientists offering proven remedies to patients with diagnosable problems. Rather, it was the crusade of one gynecologist, Dr. Robert A. Wilson, whose decidedly unscientific images of menopausal problems were "crucial to the acceptance of menopause as a 'deficiency disease'" (McCrea 1983:112). Wilson wrote of menopause as a "malfunction threatening the 'feminine essence' [and] described menopausal women as 'living decay' but said that ERT could save them from being 'condemned to witness the death of their womanhood'" (quoted in McCrea 1983:112–113). In his influential best-seller, *Feminine Forever,* he made his argument for ERT. Menopausal women, and all those around her, were clearly in crisis:

> *The transformation, within a few years, of a formerly pleasant, energetic woman into a dull-minded but sharp-tongued caricature of her former self is one of the saddest of human spectacles. This suffering is not hers alone—it involves...all others with whom she comes into contact. Multiplied by millions, she is a focus of bitterness and discontent in the whole fabric of our civilization. (Wilson 1966:97)*

Some of the early advertisements for ERT even suggested that it be used "for the menopausal problems that bother *him* the most" (quoted in McCrea 1983:114. Italics added).

Others echoed Wilson's ideas and popularized them. In another best-seller, *Everything You Wanted to Know about Sex,* the author proclaimed that menopausal women were in a state of sexual limbo: "Not really a man but no longer a functional woman, these individuals live in a world of intersex. Having outlived their ovaries, they have outlived their usefulness as human beings" (quoted in McCrea 1983:114). Similarly, Wilson referred to menopausal women as "castrates" (Wilson 1966:40).

It is hard to imagine any clearer statement of the belief that a woman's reason for existing is to display feminine qualities and to have children. When menopause strips women of these qualities, she becomes the "saddest of human spectacles," a useless human being. Use of such dramatically hostile, limiting, and sexist visions of women by ERT proponents led feminists and others to oppose its use (McCrea 1983).

Other concerns also arose regarding the medical efficacy of administering estrogen to women. By the mid 1970s, accumulating evidence suggested that ERT could cause endometrial cancer, a possibility long suspected but little researched. Yet this finding only briefly derailed the ERT crusade. "[D]rug companies had tasted the potential of marketing products to menopausal women: In the US more than 28 million prescriptions for oestrogen had been filled in 1975" (Worcester and Whatley 1992:4). Pharmaceutical companies were not ready to give up such a lucrative market, so they advertised aggressively, changing the promises of ERT as new possibilities arose. Advertisements for replacement therapy evolved from an early (1966–1975) stress on eternal beauty and femininity to promises of short-term symptom relief (1975–1981), and from there (starting in 1980) to promises of the prevention of chronic diseases, most notably osteoporosis and heart disease (MacPherson 1993). Furthermore, despite controversy over the safety and effectiveness of ERT, a pharmaceutical company sponsored a public relations campaign in the mid 1980s that used fear tactics to encourage *all* menopausal and postmenopausal women to take estrogens. Ads showed women their two grim choices: medication for the silent killer, osteoporosis, or life in a wheelchair (Worcester and Whatley 1992:11).

Deciding Whether to Have Hormone Replacement Therapy

Menopausal therapies are currently in a state of change. Hormone replacement therapy (HRT), which adds progestogen to the estrogen, is now more typical than "unopposed" estrogen, despite women's nearly universal experience of breakthrough bleeding with the combined hormones. While this addition of progestogen eliminates the endometrial cancer side effect found with ERT (Healy 1995:197), it has not produced a therapy with unambiguous effectiveness and safety, or a therapy with clear superiority over other approaches to reducing risks of osteoporosis and heart disease.

Although research results do show that HRT is effective in postponing the bone loss of osteoporosis (Wallis and Barbo 1998), questions persist concerning when treatment should start, how long it should last, and what the appropriate dosage should be. Evidence suggests that women who are above average in bone mass before menopause are unlikely to experience a drop in bone mass to a dangerous level, so some researchers argue against these women using HRT at all (Heaney 1998:450). Safe and effective alternatives, such as exercise (especially weight training) and abstinence from smoking or heavy drinking, are rarely promoted by doctors (BWHBC 1998:561).

In addition, the research results on heart disease vary widely. One can find studies stating that HRT does not reduce the chances of a heart attack (Hulley 1998), and others that state the opposite (Wallis and Barbo 1998). Although differences in research results are not unusual in science and are often due to random error, the confusion in the HRT–heart disease research results clearly come from identifiable sources: sample bias, changes in therapy, and the need for longitudinal research.

Sample bias is a problem because HRT users are typically better educated, more health-conscious, good compliers, and under close medical supervision. Each of these characteristics is associated with better health outcomes. Thus, to find that HRT users do well may merely be a restatement of the effects of these other characteristics, not evidence that HRT has been beneficial (Rifkind and Rossouw 1998). Changes in therapy are a problem because many of the studies quoted as showing effectiveness are based on ERT therapy, not HRT. The suspicion is that HRT is less effective than ERT (NWHN 1993:7). Finally, longitudinal research is needed to assess an outcome such as heart disease. With therapies changing, studies started a decade ago produce only marginally relevant results. Assessing the effect of a current therapy requires patience while waiting for a significant passage of time to elapse before one can come to any meaningful conclusions.

Safety concerns with respect to HRT no longer focus on endometrial cancer, but the possible increase in hysterectomies, breast cancer, and gall bladder disease (NWHN 1993). These issues are not resolved. Thus, an article in the *Journal of the American Medical Association* says that the question of an increased risk of breast cancer from ERT or HRT is "still being asked today, even though more than 5 decades of experience with this therapy and scores of epidemiological studies addressing the issue are available" (Bush and Whiteman 1999:2140). In January of 2000, this same journal published an article suggesting that HRT increases the risk of breast cancer (Schairer et al. 2000). And again, as with osteoporosis, easy alternative preventive measures such as exercise, not smoking, and heart-smart eating are not promoted as much as they could be.

Because of the decades of controversy over ERT and HRT, the inconclusive results of recent studies, and the expectation that the results of ongoing studies will provide more definitive answers, the decision whether to use a hormone replacement therapy is difficult. The National Women's Health Network (NWHN) has argued that it is poor public health practice to "attempt to prevent chronic disease conditions which will occur in *some* women by using drugs of unknown safety and effectiveness on *all* women in the population" (NWHN 1993:3). Most women have neither serious enough short-term menopausal symptoms nor such a high risk of long-term problems to require a strong hormonal remedy that may in itself have risks. The final decision on whether to take HRT must ultimately rest on each individual woman. She needs to weigh her own personal risk factors for osteoporosis, heart disease, and cancer in making her decisions, and also bring into the decision making her own personal values and risk preferences. One woman may want to do all she can to avoid osteoporosis; another may wish to minimize the risk of cancer.

These women would make very different decisions about HRT.

Decision making on health issues of this magnitude is not easy, and they are made more difficult because of pressures from the pharmaceutical industry to make HRT a prescription for nearly all women. By 1998, Wyeth-Ayerst reported sales of $1 billion a year for HRT (Winslow 1998). As with other medicines that generate a healthy revenue, Wyeth-Ayerst invests much of its profit in advertising, generating slick advertisements, producing videos, and hiring attractive spokeswomen to spread the word.

Continuing Criticism of the Deficiency-Disease Model

In addition to their concerns over the effectiveness and safety of HRT, feminists have voiced objections to the dominant "deficiency" model of menopause, which gives power to doctors and takes it away from women by making every menopausal woman a menopausal patient. Many women become passive participants in the process, particularly because the research results are so confusing. By naming menopause a deficiency disease, doctors have marginalized subjective interpretations of this life transition.

What happens and what is expected to happen are defined by doctors, not by the firsthand experiences of women. In fact, the menopausal experience is quite varied. Women who say "it was nothing" (Martin 1987:173) are not the women whom the doctors have treated for menopause. Some women even feel that menopause is a positive transition giving them freedom from the nuisance of menstrual periods and the possibility of an unwanted pregnancy, or perhaps even clearly marking the transition to a new, creative period of life.

GENDER AND HORMONES

The lives of the members of only one gender are characterized and circumscribed by their hormones. No parallel theory for men corresponding to female "hysteria"—one that suggests that "testicles break free and relocate to other parts of the body," causing aggression—was ever put forth (Meyer 1997:2). Scientists give scant attention to any correlation between testosterone levels and acts of aggression, such as assaults, wife-beatings, and murder rates. In fact, studies of testosterone and mood more frequently target *women* than men (Tavris 1992:149). Men's testosterone levels fluctuate and vary between individuals, yet it has not been seriously proposed that men's lives are ruled by their hormones.

The gendered treatment of hormones has declared that for women, biology is destiny, and that this destiny is to be restricted from full participation in life, prone to incapacitating emotional instability, and so altered by menopause that only physically endangering medical treatments can restore them to normalcy. Although a woman's monthly cycle and her menopausal transition do cause impressive bodily changes, and some women do experience serious problems, most women experience only minor problems. The medicalization of normal female bodily processes is based less on scientific research—which has been limited and flawed—than on social constructs. Still, medical and popular literature continue to focus attention on pathology and on medical cures.

What is missing is any normative viewpoint and treatment of a woman's typical monthly cycle and passage through menopause, although it is known that natural remedies—such as exercise and good nutrition—alleviate the symptoms of these processes without medical intrusion into women's minds and bodies. In addition, women scholars and researchers have suggested innovative conceptions of menstruation, the premenstrual phase, and menopause that are much more positive. One dramatically different concept of menstruation has been proposed by Margie Profet, a recipient of a MacArthur genius grant. She sees menstrual blood as a cleansing agent, protecting the body from impurities such as those brought in with the sperm and seminal fluid (Profet 1993). Other works construct the premenstrual time as one of creativity (Choi 1995). Chapter 10, on aging, will show how the image of menopause and the postmenopausal woman are undergoing positive revision.

IF MEN COULD MENSTRUATE—A POLITICAL FANTASY

GLORIA STEINEM

A white minority of the world has spent centuries conning us into thinking that a white skin makes people superior—even though the only thing it really does is make them more subject to ultraviolet rays and to wrinkles. Male human beings have built whole cultures around the idea that penis-envy is "natural" to women—though having such an unprotected organ might be said to make men vulnerable, and the power to give birth makes womb-envy at least as logical.

In short, the characteristics of the powerful, whatever they may be, are thought to be better than the characteristics of the powerless—and logic has nothing to do with it.

What would happen, for instance, if suddenly, magically, men could menstruate and women could not?

The answer is clear—menstruation would become an enviable, boast-worthy, masculine event:

Men would brag about how long and how much.

Boys would mark the onset of menses, that longed for proof of manhood, with religious ritual and stag parties.

Congress would fund a National Institute of Dysmenorrhea to help stamp out monthly discomforts.

Sanitary supplies would be federally funded and free. (Of course, some men would still pay for the prestige of commercial brands such as John Wayne Tampons, Muhammad Ali's Rope-a-dope Pads, Joe Namath Jock Shields—"For Those Light Bachelor Days," and Robert "Baretta" Blake Maxi-Pads.)

Military men, right-wing politicians, and religious fundamentalists would cite menstruation ("*men*struation") as proof that only men could serve in the Army ("you have to give blood to take blood"), occupy political office ("can women be aggressive without that steadfast cycle governed by the planet Mars?"), be priests and ministers ("how could a woman give her blood for our sins?"), or rabbis ("without the monthly loss of impurities, women remain unclean").

Male radicals, left wing politicians, mystics, however, would insist that women are equal, just different, and that any woman could enter their ranks if only she were willing to self-inflict a major wound every month ("you *must* give blood for the revolution"), recognize the pre-eminence of menstrual issues, or subordinate her selfness to all men in their Cycle of Enlightenment.

Street guys would brag ("I'm a three-pad man") or answer praise from a buddy ("Man, you lookin good!") by giving fives and saying, "Yeah, man, I'm on the rag!"

TV shows would treat the subject at length. ("Happy Days": Richie and Potsie try to convince Fonzie that he is still "The Fonz," though he has missed two periods in a row.) So would newspapers. (SHARKS SCARE THREATENS MENSTRUATING MEN. JUDGE CITES MONTHLY STRESS IN PARDONING RAPIST.) And movies. (Newman and Redford in "Blood Brothers"!)

Men would convince women that intercourse was *more* pleasurable at "that time of the month." Lesbians would be said to fear blood and therefore life itself—though probably only because they needed a good menstruating man.

Of course, male intellectuals would offer the most moral and logical arguments. How could a woman master any discipline that demanded a sense of time, space, mathematics, or measurement, for instance, without that in-built gift for measuring the cycles of the moon and planets—and thus for measuring anything at all? In the rarefied fields of philosophy and religion, could women compensate for missing the rhythm of the universe? Or for their lack of symbolic death-and-resurrection every month?

Liberal males in every field would try to be kind: the fact that "these people" have no gift for measuring life or connecting to the universe, the liberals would explain, should be punishment enough.

And how would women be trained to react? One can imagine traditional women agreeing to all these arguments with a staunch and smiling masochism. ("The ERA would force housewives to wound themselves every month": Phyllis Schlafly. "Your husband's blood is as sacred as that of Jesus—and so sexy, too!": Marabel Morgan.) Reformers and Queen Bees would try to imitate men, and *pretend* to have a monthly cycle. All feminists would explain endlessly that men, too, needed to be liberated from the false idea of Martian aggressiveness, just as women needed to escape the bonds of menses-envy. Radical feminists would add that the oppression of the nonmenstrual was the pattern for all other oppressions ("Vampires were our first freedom fighters!") Cultural feminists would develop a bloodless imagery in art and literature. Socialist feminists would insist that only under capitalism would men be able to monopolize menstrual blood....

In fact, if men could menstruate, the power justifications could probably go on forever.

If we let them.

MENOPAUSE: THE STORM BEFORE THE CALM

ANNE FAUSTO-STERLING

An unlikely specter haunts the world. It is the ghost of former womanhood..., "unfortunate women abounding in the streets walking stiffly in twos and threes, seeing little and observing less.... The world appears [to them] as through a grey veil, and they live as docile, harmless creatures missing most of life's values." According to Dr. Robert Wilson and Thelma Wilson, though, one should not be fooled by their "vapid cow-like negative state" because "There is ample evidence that the course of history has been changed not only by the presence of estrogen, but by its absence. The untold misery of alcoholism, drug addiction, divorce and broken homes caused by these unstable estrogen-starved women cannot be presented in statistical form.[1]

Rather than releasing women from their monthly emotional slavery to the sex hormones, menopause involves them in new horrors. At the individual level one encounters the specter of sexual degeneration, described so vividly by Dr. David Reuben: "The vagina begins to shrivel, the breasts atrophy, sexual desire disappears.... Increased facial hair, deepening voice, obesity... coarsened features, enlargement of the clitoris, and gradual baldness complete the tragic picture. Not really a man but no longer a functional woman, these individuals live in the world of intersex."[2] At the demographic level, writers express foreboding about women of the baby-boom generation, whose life span has increased from an average forty-eight years at the turn of the century to a projected eighty years in the year 2000.[3] Modern medicine, it seems, has played a cruel trick on women. One hundred years ago they didn't live long enough to face the hardships of menopause but today their increased longevity means they will live for twenty-five to thirty years beyond the time when they lose all possibility of reproducing. To quote Dr. Wilson again: "The unpalatable truth must be faced that all postmenopausal women are castrates."[4]

But what medicine has wrought, it can also rend asunder. Few publications have had so great an effect on the lives of so many women as have those of Dr. Robert A. Wilson who pronounced menopause to be a disease of estrogen deficiency. At the same time in an influential popular form, in his book *Feminine Forever,* he offered a treatment: estrogen replacement therapy (ERT).[5] During the first seven months following publication in 1966, Wilson's book sold one hundred thousand copies and was excerpted in *Vogue* and *Look* magazines. It influenced thousands of physicians to prescribe estrogen to millions of women, many of whom had no clinical "symptoms" other than cessation of the menses. As one of his credentials Wilson lists himself as head of the Wilson Research Foundation, an outfit funded by Ayerst Labs, Searle, and Upjohn, all pharmaceutical giants interested in the large potential market for estrogen. (After all, no woman who lives long enough can avoid menopause.) As late as 1976 Ayerst also supported the Information Center on the Mature Woman, a public relations firm that promoted estrogen replacement therapy. By 1975 some six million women had started long-term treatment with Premarin (Ayerst Labs' brand name for estrogen), making it the fourth or fifth most popular drug in the United States. Even today, two million of the forty million postmenopausal women in the United States contribute to the $70 million grossed each year from the sale of Premarin-brand estrogen.[6] The "disease of menopause" is not only a social problem: it's big business.[7]

The high sales of Premarin continue despite the publication in 1975 of an article linking estrogen treatment to uterine cancer.[8] Although in the wake of that publication many women stopped taking estrogen and many physicians became more cautious about prescribing it, the idea of hormone replacement therapy remains with us. At least three recent publications in medical journals seriously consider whether the benefits of estrogen might not outweigh the dangers.[9] The continuing flap over treatment for this so-called deficiency diseases of the aging female forces one to ask just what *is* this terrible state called menopause? Are its effects so unbearable that one might prefer to increase, even ever-so-slightly, the risk of cancer rather than suffer the daily discomforts encountered during "the change of life"?

Ours is a culture that fears the elderly. Rather than venerate their years and listen to their wisdom, we segregate them in housing built for "their special needs" separated from the younger generations from which we draw hope for the future. At the same time we allow millions of old people to live on inadequate incomes, in fear that serious illness will leave them destitute. The happy, productive elderly remain invisible in our midst. (One must look to feminist publications such as *Our Bodies, Ourselves* to find women who express pleasure in their postmenopausal state.) Television ads portray only the arthritic, the toothless, the wrinkled, and the constipated. If estrogen really is the hormone of youth and its decline suggests the coming of old age, then its loss is a part of biology that our culture ill equips us to handle.

There is, of course, a history to our cultural attitudes toward the elderly woman and our views about menopause. In the nineteenth century physicians believed that at menopause a woman entered a period of depression and increased susceptibility to disease. The postmenopausal body might be racked with "dyspepsia, diarrhea...rheumatic pains, paralysis, apoplexy...hemorrhaging...tuberculosis...and diabetes," while emotionally the aging female risked becoming irritable, depressed, hysterical, melancholic, or even insane. The more a woman violated social laws (such as using birth control or promoting female suffrage), the more likely she would be to suffer a disease-ridden menopause.[10] In the twentieth century, psychologist Helene Deutsch wrote that at menopause "woman has ended her existence as a bearer of future life and has reached her natural end—her partial death—as a servant of the species."[11] Deutsch believed that during the postmenopausal years a woman's main psychological task was to accept the progressive biological withering she experienced. Other well-known psychologists have also accepted the idea that a woman's life purpose is mainly reproductive and that her post-reproductive years are ones of inevitable decline. Even in recent times postmenopausal women have been "treated" with tranquilizers, hormones, electroshock, and lithium.[12]

But should women accept what many see as an inevitable emotional and biological decline? Should they believe, as Wilson does, that "from a practical point of view a man remains a man until the end," but that after menopause "we no longer have the 'whole woman'—only the 'part woman'"?[13] What is the real story of menopause?

THE CHANGE: ITS DEFINITION AND PHYSIOLOGY

In 1976 under the auspices of the American Geriatric Society and the medical faculty of the University of Montpellier, the First International Congress on the Menopause convened in the south of France. In the volume that emerged from that conference, scientists and clinicians from around the world agreed on a standard definition of the words *menopause* and *climacteric*. "Menopause," they wrote, "indicates the final menstrual period and occurs during the climacteric. The climacteric is that phase in the aging process of women marking the transition from the reproductive stage of life to the non-reproductive stage."[14] By consensus, then, the word *menopause* has come to mean a specific event, the last menstruation, while *climacteric* implies a process occurring over a period of years.*...

What happens to the intricately balanced hormone cycle during the several years preceding menopause is little understood, although it seems likely that gradual changes occur in the balance between pituitary activity (FSH and LH production) and estrogen synthesis.[16] One thing, however, is clear: menopause does not mean the *absence* of estrogen, but rather a gradual lowering in the availability of *ovarian* estrogen.... The other estrogenic hormones, as well as progesterone and testosterone, drop off to some extent but continue to be synthesized at a level comparable to that observed during the early phases of the menstrual cycle. Instead of concentrating on the notion of estrogen deficiency, however, it is more important to point out that: (1) postmenopausally the body makes different kinds of estrogen; (2) the ovaries synthesize less and the adrenals more of these hormones; and (3) the monthly ups and downs of these hormones even out following menopause.

While estrogen levels begin to decline, the levels of FSH and LH start to increase. Changes in these hormones appear as early as eight years before menopause.[17] At the time of menopause and for several years afterward, these two hormones are found in very high concentrations compared to menstrual levels (FSH as many as fourteen times more concentrated than premenopausally, and LH more than three times more). Over a period of years such high levels are reduced to about half their peak value, leaving the postmenopausal woman with one-and-one-half times more LH and seven times more FSH circulating in her blood than when she menstruated regularly.

It is to all of these changes in hormone levels that the words such as *climacteric* and *menopause* refer. From these alterations Wilson and others have chosen to blame estrogen for the emotional deterioration they believe appears in postmenopausal women. Why they have focused on only one hormone from a complex system of hormonal changes is anybody's guess. I suspect, however, that the reasons are (at least) twofold. First, the normative biomedical disease model of female physiology...looks for a simple cause and effect. Most researchers, then, have simply assumed estrogen to be a "cause" and set out to measure its "effect." The model or framework out of which such investigators work precludes an interrelated analysis of all the different (and closely connected) hormonal changes going on during the climacteric. But why single out estrogen? Possibly because this hormone plays an important role in the menstrual cycle as well as in the development of "feminine" characteristics such as breasts and

*There is also a male climacteric, which entails a gradual reduction in production of the hormone testosterone over the years as part of the male aging process. What part it plays in that process is poorly understood and seems frequently to be ignored by researchers, who prefer to contrast continuing male reproductive potency with the loss of childbearing ability in women.[15]

overall body contours. It is seen as the quintessential female hormone. So where could one better direct one's attention if, to begin with, one views menopause as the loss of true womanhood?

Physical changes do occur following menopause. Which, if any, of these are caused by changing hormone levels is another question. Menopause research comes equipped with its own unique experimental traps.[18] The most obvious is that a postmenopausal population is also an aging population. Do physical and emotional differences found in groups of postmenopausal women have to do with hormonal changes or with other aspects of aging? It is a difficult matter to sort out. Furthermore, many of the studies on menopause have been done on preselected populations, using women who volunteer because they experience classic menopausal "symptoms" such as the hot flash. Such investigations tell us nothing about average changes within the population as a whole. In the language of the social scientist, we have no baseline data, nothing to which we can compare menopausal women, no way to tell whether the complaint of a particular woman is typical, a cause for medical concern, or simply idiosyncratic.

Since the late 1970s feminist researchers have begun to provide us with much-needed information. Although their results confirm some beliefs long held by physicians, these newer investigators present them in a more sophisticated context. Dr. Madeleine Goodman and her colleagues designed a study in which they drew information from a large population of women ranging in age from thirty-five to sixty. All had undergone routine multiphasic screening at a health maintenance clinic, but none had come for problems concerning menopause. From the complete clinic records they selected a population of women who had not menstruated for at least one year and compared their health records with those who still menstruated, looking at thirty-five different variables, such as cramps, blood glucose levels, blood calcium, and hot flashes, to see if any of these symptoms correlated with those seen in postmenopausal women. The results are startling. They found that only 28 percent of Caucasian women and 24 percent of Japanese women identified as postmenopausal "reported traditional menopausal symptoms such as hot flashes, sweats, etc., while in non-menopausal controls, 16% in Caucasians and 10% in Japanese also reported these same symptoms."[19] In other words, 75 percent of menopausal women in their sample reported no remarkable menopausal symptoms, a result in sharp contrast to earlier studies using women who identified themselves as menopausal.

In a similar exploration, researcher Karen Frey found evidence to support Goodman's results. She wrote that menopausal women "did not report significantly greater frequency of physical symptoms or concern about these symptoms than did pre- or post-menopausal women."[20] The studies of Goodman, Frey, and others[21] draw into serious question the notion that menopause is generally or necessarily associated with a set of disease symptoms. Yet at least three physical changes—hot flashes, vaginal dryness and irritation, and osteoporosis—and one emotional one—depression—remain associated in the minds of many with the decreased estrogen levels of the climacteric. Goodman's work indicates that such changes may be far less widespread than previously believed, but if they are troublesome to 26 percent of all menopausal women they remain an appropriate subject for analysis.

We know only the immediate cause of hot flashes: a sudden expansion of the blood flow into the skin. The technical term to describe them, *vasomotor instability,* means only that nerve cells signal the widening of blood vessels allowing more blood into the body's periphery. A consensus has emerged on two things: (1) the high concentration of FSH and LH in the blood probably causes hot flashes, although exactly how this happens remains unknown; and (2) estrogen treatment is the only currently available way to suppress the hot flashes. One hypothesis is that by means of a feedback mechanism, artificially raised blood levels of estrogen signal the brain to tell the pituitary to call off the FSH and LH. Although estrogen does stop the hot flashes, its effects are only temporary; remove the estrogen and the flashes return.

Left alone, the body eventually adjusts to the changing levels of FSH and LH. Thus a premenopausal woman has two choices in dealing with hot flashes: she can either take estrogen as a permanent medication, a course Wilson refers to as embarking "on the great adventure of preserving or regaining your full femininity,"[22] or suffer some discomfort while nature takes its course. Since the longer one takes estrogen the greater the danger of estrogen-linked cancer, many health-care workers recommend the latter.[23]

Some women experience postmenopausal vaginal dryness and irritation that can make sexual intercourse painful. Since the cells of the vaginal wall contain estrogen receptors it is not surprising that estrogen applied locally or taken in pill form helps with this difficulty. Even locally applied, however, the estrogen enters into the bloodstream, presenting the same dangers as when taken in pill form. There are alternative treatments, though, for vaginal dryness. The Boston Women's Health Collective, for example, recommends the use of non-estrogen vaginal creams or jellies, which seem to be effective and are certainly safer. Continued sexual activity also helps—yet another example of the interaction between behavior and physiology.

Hot flashes and vaginal dryness are the *only* climacteric-associated changes for which estrogen unambiguously offers relief. Since significant numbers of women do not experience these changes and since for many of those that do the effects are relatively mild, the wisdom of ERT must be examined carefully and on an individual basis. Both men and women undergo certain changes as they age, but Wilson's catastrophic vision of postmenopausal women—those ghosts gliding by "unnoticed and, in turn, notic[ing] little"[24]—is such a far cry from reality that it is a source of amazement that serious medical writers continue to quote his work.

In contrast to hot flashes and vaginal dryness, osteoporosis, a brittleness of the bone which can in severe cases cripple, has a complex origin. Since this potentially life-threatening condition appears more frequently in older women than in older men, the hypothesis of a relationship with estrogen levels seemed plausible to many. But as one medical worker has said, a unified theory of the disease "is still non-existent, although sedentary life styles, genetic predisposition, hormonal imbalance, vitamin deficiencies, high-protein diets, and cigarette smoking all have been implicated."[25] Estrogen treatment seems to arrest the disease for a while, but may lose effectiveness after a few years.[26]

Even more so than in connection with any physical changes, women have hit up against a medical double bind whenever they have complained of emotional problems during the years of climacteric. On the one hand physicians dismissed these complaints as the imagined ills of a hormone-deficient brain, while on the other they generalized the problem, arguing that middle-aged women are emotionally unreliable, unfit for positions of leadership and responsibility. Women had two choices: to complain and experience ridicule and/or improper medical treatment, or to suffer in silence. Hormonal changes during menopause were presumed to be the cause of psychiatric symptoms ranging from fatigue, dizziness, irritability, apprehension, and insomnia to severe headaches and psychotic depression. In recent years, however, these earlier accounts have been supplanted by a rather different consensus now emerging among responsible medical researchers.

To begin with, there are no data to support the idea that menopause has any relationship to serious depression in women. Postmenopausal women who experience psychosis have almost always had similar episodes premenopausally.[27] The notion of the hormonally depressed woman is a shibboleth that must be laid permanently to rest. Some studies have related irritability and insomnia to loss of sleep from nighttime hot flashes. Thus, for women who experience hot flashes, these emotional difficulties might, indirectly, relate to menopause. But the social, life history, and family contexts in which middle-aged women find themselves are more important links to emotional changes occurring during the years of the climacteric. And these, of course, have nothing whatsoever to do with hormones. Quite a number of studies suggest that the majority of women do not consider menopause a time of crisis. Nor do most women suffer from the so-called "empty nest syndrome" supposedly experienced when children leave home. On the contrary, investigation suggests that women without small children are less depressed and have higher incomes and an increased sense of well-being."[28] Such positive reactions depend upon work histories, individual upbringing, cultural background, and general state of health, among other things.

In a survey conducted for *Our Bodies, Ourselves,* one which in no sense represents a balanced cross section of U.S. women, the Boston Women's Health Collective recorded the reactions of more than two hundred menopausal or postmenopausal women, most of whom were suburban, married, and employed, to a series of questions about menopause. About two-thirds of them felt either positively or neutrally about a variety of changes they had undergone, while a whopping 90 percent felt okay or happy about the loss of childbearing ability![29] This result probably comes as no surprise to most women, but it flies in the face of the long-standing belief that women's lives and emotions are driven in greater part by their reproductive systems.

No good account of adult female development in the middle years exists. Levinson,[30] who studied adult men, presents a linear model of male development designed primarily around work experiences. In his analysis, the male climacteric plays only a secondary role. Feminist scholars Rosalind Barnett and Grace Baruch have described the difficulty of fitting women into Levinson's scheme: "It is hard to know how to think of women within this theory—a woman may not enter the world of work until her late thirties, she seldom has a mentor, and even women with life-long career commitments rarely are in a position to reassess their commitment pattern by age 40," as do the men in Levinson's study.[31]

Baruch and Barnett call for the development of a theory of women in their middle years, pointing out that an adequate one can emerge only when researchers set aside preconceived ideas about the central role of biology in adult female development and listen to what women themselves say. Paradoxically, in some sense we will remain unable to understand more about the role of biology in women's middle years until we have a more realistic *social* analysis of women's post-adolescent psychological development. Such an analysis must, of course, take into account ethnic, racial, regional, and class differences among women, since once biology is jettisoned as a universal cause of female behavior it no longer makes sense to lump all women into a single category.

Much remains to be understood about menopause. Which biological changes, for instance, result from ovarian degeneration and which from other aspects of aging? How does the aging process compare in men and women? What causes hot flashes and can we find safe ways to alleviate the discomfort they cause? Do other aspects of a woman's life affect the number and severity of menopausally related physical symptoms? What can we learn from studying the experience of menopause in other, especially non-Western cultures? A number of researchers have proposed effective ways of finding answers to these questions.[32] We need only time, research dollars, and an open mind to move forward.

CONCLUSION

The premise that women are by nature abnormal and inherently diseased dominates past research on menstruation and menopause. While appointing the male reproductive system as normal, this viewpoint calls abnormal any aspect of the female reproductive life cycle that deviates from the male's. At the same time such an analytical framework places the essence of a woman's existence in her reproductive system. Caught in her hormonal windstorm, she strives to attain normality but can only do so by rejecting her biological uniqueness, for that too is essentially deformed: a double bind indeed. Within such an intellectual structure no medical research of any worth to women's health can be done, for it is the blueprint itself that leads investigators to ask the wrong questions, look in the wrong places for answers, and then distort the interpretation of their results.

Reading through the morass of poorly done studies on menstruation and menopause, many of which express deep hatred and fear of women, can be a discouraging experience. One begins to wonder how it can be that within so vast a quantity of material so little quality exists. But at this very moment the field of menstrual-cycle research (including menopause) offers a powerful antidote to that disheartenment in the form of feminist researchers (both male and female) with excellent training and skills, working within a new analytical framework. Rejecting a strict medical model of female development, they understand that men and women have different reproductive cycles, *both* of which are normal. Not binary opposites, male and female physiologies have differences *and* similarities. These research pioneers know too that the human body functions in a social milieu and that it changes in response to that context. Biology is not a one-way determinant but a dynamic component of our existence. And, equally important, these new investigators have learned not only to *listen* to what women say about themselves but to *hear* as well. By and large, these researchers are not in the mainstream of medical and psychological research, but we can look forward to a time when the impact of their work will affect the field of menstrual-cycle research for the better and for many years to come.

If women are seen as emotional slaves of their reproductive physiologies, men do not get off scot-free: *their* "problem hormone" is testosterone. In normal amounts it is seen as the source of many positive traits—drive, ambition, success. But too high a quantity, so the theory goes, can cause antisocial behavior—crime, violence, and even war. In contrast, women's lower testosterone levels mean they are less likely to make it in the world of the hard-driving professional, although they can derive pride from their more peaceable manner. This tale of testosterone and aggression forms yet another subplot in the collection of biological stories about male and female behavior. The chapter that follows analyzes its text.

REFERENCES

1. Robert A. Wilson and Thelma A. Wilson, "The Fate of the Nontreated Postmenopausal Woman: A Plea for the Maintenance of Adequate Estrogen from Puberty to the Grave," *Journal of the American Geriatric Society* 11 (1963):352–56.

2. David Reuben, *Everything You Always Wanted to Know about Sex but Were Afraid to Ask.* (New York: McKay, 1969), 292.

3. Wulf H. Utian, *Menopause in Modern Perspectives* (New York: Appleton-Century-Crofts, 1980).

4. Wilson and Wilson, "The Fate of the Nontreated Postmenopausal Woman," 347.

5. Robert A. Wilson, *Feminine Forever* (New York: M. Evans, 1966).

6. Marilyn Grossman and Pauline Bart, "The Politics of Menopause," in *The Menstrual Cycle,* vol. 1, ed. A. Dan, E. Graham, and C. P. Beecher. (New York: Springer, 1980).

7. Kathleen MacPherson, "Menopause as Disease: The Social Construction of a Metaphor," *Advances in Nursing Science* 3(1981):95–113; A. Johnson, "The Risks of Sex Hormones as Drugs," *Women and Health* 2(1977):8–11.

8. D. Smith et al., "Association of Exogenous Estrogen and Endometrial Cancer," *New England Journal of Medicine* 293(1975):1164–67.

9. H. Judd et al., "Estrogen Replacement Therapy," *Obstetrics and Gynecology* 58(1981):267–75; M. Quigley, "Postmenopausal Hormone Replacement Therapy: Back to Estrogen Forever?" *Geriatric Medicine Today* 1(1982):78–85; and Thomas Skillman, "Estrogen Replacement: Its Risks and Benefits," *Consultant* (1982):115–27.

10. C. Smith-Rosenberg, "Puberty to Menopause: The Cycle of Femininity in 19th Century America," *Feminist Studies* 1(1973):65.

11. Helene Deutsch, *The Psychology of Women* (New York: Grune and Stratton, 1945), 458.

12. J. H. Osofsky and R. Seidenberg, "Is Female Menopausal Depression Inevitable?," *Obstetrics and Gynecology* 36(1970):611.

13. Wilson and Wilson, "The Fate of the Nontreated Postmenopausal Woman," 348.

14. P. A. vanKeep, R. B. Greenblatt, and M. Albeaux-Fernet, eds., *Consensus on Menopause Research* (Baltimore: University Park Press, 1976), 134.

15. Marcha Flint, "Male and Female Menopause: A Cultural Put-on," in *Changing Perspectives on Meno-*

pause, ed. A. M. Voda, M. Dinnerstein, and S. O'Donnell (Austin: University of Texas Press, 1982).
16. Utian, *Menopause in Modern Perspectives.*
17. Ibid.
18. Madeleine Goodman, "Toward a Biology of Menopause," *Signs* 5(1980):739–53.
19. Madeleine Goodman, C. J. Stewart, and F. Gilbert, "Patterns of Menopause: A Study of Certain Medical and Physiological Variables among Caucasian and Japanese Women Living in Hawaii," *Journal of Gerontology* 32(1977):297.
20. Karen Frey, "Middle-Aged Women's Experience and Perceptions of Menopause," *Women and Health* 6(1981):31.
21. Eve Kahana, A. Kiyak, and J. Liang, "Menopause in the Context of Other Life Events," in *The Menstural Cycle,* vol. 1, ed. Dan, Graham, and Beecher, 167–78.
22. Wilson, *Feminine Forever,* 134.
23. A. Voda and M. Eliasson, "Menopause: The Closure of Menstrual Life," *Women and Health* 8(1983): 137–56.
24. Wilson and Wilson, "The Fate of the Nontreated Postmenopausal Woman," 356.
25. Louis Avioli, "Postmenopausal Osteoporosis: Prevention vs. Cure," *Federation Proceedings* 40(1981): 2418.
26. Voda and Eliasson, "Menopause: The Closure of Menstrual Life."
27. G. Winokur and R. Cadoret, "The Irrelevance of the Menopause to Depressive Disease," in *Topics in Psychoendocrinology,* ed. E. J. Sachar (New York: Grune and Stratton, 1975).
28. Rosalind Barnett and Grace Baruch, "Women in the Middle Years: A Critique of Research and Theory," *Psychology of Women Quarterly* 3(1978):187–97.
29. Boston Women's Health Collective, *Our Bodies, Ourselves.*
30. D. Levinson et al., "Periods in the Adult Development of Men: Ages 18–45," *The Counseling Psychologist* 6(1976):21–25.
31. Barnett and Baruch, "Women in the Middle Years," 189.
32. Ibid.; Goodman, "Toward a Biology of Menopause"; and Voda, Dinnerstein, and O'Donnell, eds., *Changing Perspectives on Menopause.*

THE BITTER PILL: BOMBARDED BY PROPAGANDA ON PREMARIN, WE CAN'T TRUST OUR DOCTORS AND WE CAN'T TRUST OURSELVES

LEORA TANENBAUM

Barbara Dworkin, 61, is one of eight million American women taking Premarin, an estrogen replacement that eases menopausal symptoms such as hot flashes and dry skin. Dworkin started on Premarin 15 years ago and plans to take the drug for the rest of her life. Although studies have shown that Premarin may increase the risk of breast cancer by 30 percent, as well as cause fatal blood clots, the drug also offers protection against osteoporosis and decreases the risk of fatal heart disease by 53 percent. Besides, as a 911 operator living on Long Island, NY, she leads stressful days fielding emergency calls and feels thankful for Premarin because it "makes my life much more pleasant and secure."

But Premarin costs between $15 and $25 a month. If there were a generic version, Suffolk County, New York (which covers Dworkin's drug plan) could cut its costs by 30 percent—over $3,000 for her lifetime. If you consider that millions of other women lack health insurance or prescription drug coverage, a generic could save them more than $300 million a year.

But economizing isn't the only reason to push for a generic. Premarin is derived from the urine of pregnant horses, a fact that concerns animal rights supporters—and repulses many users. People for the Ethical Treatment of Animals (PETA) claims that the collection methods on "urine farms" are barbaric: some 80,000 pregnant mares are confined to stalls for six months out of the year so that their urine can be collected; the 65,000 foals born to them are slaughtered as unusable byproducts of these pregnancies. PETA advises women to switch to an alternative hormone treatment that doesn't harm animals.

An alternative, however, will not be forthcoming. The FDA announced in May that it will not approve a recently manufactured, affordable, plant-based generic form of Premarin, even though FDA research has shown the generic to be just as effective as the brand-name drug. Rather than heed the recommendation of its own Office of Pharmaceutical Science, the FDA appears to have bowed to political pressure—at the expense of women. While there are several plant-derived, FDA-approved estrogen regimens such as Estrace and Estraderm, they have not been proven to offer long-term health benefits. Only those who can afford Premarin—or whose insurance will pay—will be able to relieve their menopausal symptoms, ward off heart attacks and avoid bone fractures.

It's no surprise that the common interests of Premarin's manufacturer, Wyeth-Ayerst, have superseded health considerations, but the tactics involved are particularly outrageous. Wyeth-Ayerst cultivated influential supporters through financial contributions. Then, when the company needed them, it prodded its beneficiaries to take a stand against their competition. The result? Several highly visible politicians and advocacy groups—who knew nothing about the issues involved—testified before the FDA against the generic form of Premarin. In the end, the consumer's ability to get the best drugs for the lowest price was sacrificed. The saddest part of this whole incident? Feminist politicians and women's groups were key players.

"DOCTOR, I WANT MY PREMARIN"

You don't have to be menopausal to recognize the brand-name Premarin. No doubt you've seen the drug's fear-inducing magazine ads, which suggest that midlife women who don't take estrogen will be crippled by osteoporosis—if they don't die from a heart attack first. The ads also intimate that midlife women who don't take estrogen can never hope to achieve the carefree, wrinkle-free look of the models depicted.

Premarin, of course, is merely one of dozens of prescription drugs aggressively advertised in magazines such as *Newsweek, Redbook, Mirabella,* and *The New Yorker.* In recent years, drug companies have bypassed physicians and marketed their products directly to consumers. Eli Lilly's multimillion dollar campaign for Prozac, for instance, includes ads in more than 20 magazines. Some magazines, like *Good Housekeeping* and the *Ladies' Home Journal,* contain so many drug ads you might be tempted to double-check the cover to make sure you're not reading a professional medical journal. Which is precisely the point: drug manufacturers want consumers to play doctor by asking their physicians to prescribe particular drugs. And 99 percent of physicians do comply with patients' requests, market research confirms. In this era of "managed care," when physicians are pressed to see as many patients as possible in the shortest amount of time, educated patients who know how they want to be treated are a dream come true.

A dream come true, that is, for physicians and drug companies—but not necessarily for the patients. We may believe that by asking our physicians for Premarin or Prozac we are empowering ourselves by being more assertive in our relationships with our physicians, because only we really know our bodies and what's best for our health. But in reality, the drug companies are taking advantage of our adherence to this *Our Bodies, Ourselves* credo. We are intermediaries in a loop of influence that originates in magazine ads and culminates in a prescription.

Last year alone, pharmaceutical companies spent nearly $600 million advertising prescription drugs directly to consumers—twice as much as they spent in 1995 and almost 10 times more than they spent in 1991, according to Competitive Media Reporting, a company that tracks ad spending. None of that money, however, seems to be spent on factual research: more than half of the drug ads scrutinized last year by the Consumers' Union advocacy group contained misleading information on risks and benefits and false claims about efficacy.

POLITICS VS. SCIENCE

But as the case of the massively popular Premarin shows, the influence of drug companies goes far beyond false advertising. Wyeth-Ayerst Laboratories is a pharmaceutical Goliath that garners $1 billion a year in revenue from Premarin, the most commonly prescribed drug in America. Owned by American Home Products, Wyeth-Ayerst has maintained a monopoly on Premarin ever since it began manufacturing the estrogen replacement in 1942. Even though the patent expired over 25 years ago, Wyeth has gotten the FDA to change its guidelines in determining bioequivalence in generics, making it difficult for competitors to match Premarin. A lot is at stake: sales could reach $3 billion within five years, with more than one-third of all women in the United States currently over the age of 50, and another 20 million entering the menopausal years within the next decade.

Because of the size of that market, two small generic drug companies have decided to compete with Wyeth. After the FDA concluded in 1991 that an effective generic requires only two active ingredients (estrone and equilin), Duramed Pharmaceuticals Corp. and Barr Laboratories Inc. teamed up to develop a urine-free generic according to FDA guidelines. In response, Wyeth filed a citizens petition requesting that one of Premarin's ingredients (an obscure estrogen called delta 8,9 dehydroestrone sulfate or DHES) be reclassified as a necessary component. Duramed has not been able to replicate an equivalent of DHES and Wyeth holds the patent on the estrogen. Furthermore, in 1995 the FDA found that based on clinical trials, there was no evidence that DHES was anything other than an impurity.

And so Wyeth shrewdly lined up the support of several influential women's and health groups by making donations to Business and Professional Women/USA, the American Medical Women's Association, the National Consumers League, and the National Osteoporosis Foundation, among others. Representatives of these groups testified before the FDA on the drug company's behalf, saying that they opposed the approval of a generic that lacks DHES, despite the FDA's own contention that the estrogen wasn't essential. The president of the Women's Legal Defense Fund also testified although this group did not accept money from Wyeth. None of these groups had taken a position on DHES prior to being contacted by Wyeth.

The company also developed close ties to the White House and the Senate. John Stafford, chairman and CEO of Wyeth-Ayerst's parent company, American Home Products, attended an intimate 17-person White House "coffee klatsch" with President Clinton in November 1995. And in June 1996, according to the Federal Elections Commission, American Home Products made a $50,000 contribution to the Democratic National Committee. Several months later, Democratic senators Barbara Mikulski (Md.) and Patty Murray (Wash.) wrote the FDA for assurance that "it has no intention of approving a generic version of Premarin that lacks the 'same' active ingredient as the innovator." According to her press secretary, Murray became involved in this issue after she "was contacted by women's groups. As a result, our office spoke with the manufacturer, who was in contact with the same women's groups."

Lo and behold, the FDA reversed its stance. Janet Woodcock, M.D., director of the FDA's Center for Drug Evaluation and Research, announced on May 5 that "based on currently available data, there is at this time no way to assure that synthetic generic forms of Premarin have the same active ingredients as the [urine-based] drug." Or, put another way "Perhaps everything in this pool of animal waste could have benefits for human females," in the words of Duramed CEO and president E. Thomas Arington.

No matter how you look at it, the FDA flip-flop appears to be the result of Wyeth-Ayerst's considerable lobbying muscle. Of course, just because a decision is politically influenced doesn't mean it's wrong. But an internal FDA memo dated May 3 (two days before the decision was announced) supports the generic, saying that DHES is not a necessary component. Even the vice president of Wyeth-Ayerst's regulatory affairs department admitted to *The Wall Street Journal* that there's "probably nothing" special about DHES, and that "it's but one of many components in Premarin."

Consumer health is clearly the last thing on the minds of everyone involved in the Premarin debacle. "This decision is pure politics," fumes Cynthia Pearson, executive director of the National Women's Health Network, the only women's organization that publicly supports the generic. Coincidentally, the network does not accept donations from drug companies. The decision "was not backed up by science," says Pearson. "This never would have happened without political pressure orchestrated by Wyeth-Ayerst."

Duramed has challenged the FDA decision in an administrative appeal; the company intends to file a court appeal if it is turned down. But Wyeth is already a step ahead: it is busily working to ensure that no matter what happens, it will continue to dominate the estrogen replacement market. After all, Wyeth is the sole sponsor of an important "memory study" on Premarin's effectiveness in warding off Alzheimer's disease, a study conducted under the aegis of the government-sponsored Women's Health Initiative. If a correlation is found, physicians and consumers alike will naturally turn to Premarin as a preventative for Alzheimer's....

A MATTER OF TRUST

The growing power of pharmaceutical companies is troubling on a number of levels. It is frightening how poorly we are informed about the appalling treatment of animals in drug manufacturing. It is wasteful to pay for needlessly expensive medications. Forget about President Clinton's 1992 plea to the drug companies to control their prices. In the last few years, big-name drug companies such as Merck and Hoechst have withdrawn from the generics field because they realized they could make far more money selling brand-name drugs. But the real bottom line is that the drug companies have robbed consumers of the ability to trust anyone in the area of drug research: commercialism has infected everyone involved. We can't trust those companies to which we entrust our health to accurately represent their products. We can't assume that the FDA has weighed all of the scientific research fairly. We can't even take for granted that the scientists who perform drug research are working independently.

Savvy consumers, of course, realize that drug companies are motivated by profit. But what about advocacy groups, including women's and health organizations? Aren't they supposed to be looking out for the public good? It's in this arena that consumers are really misled. "I can't understand how any woman in a position of influence would deliberately deny a high-quality, low-cost alternative [the Premarin generic] to postmenopausal women who need this important drug," says Duramed's Arington. It seems that advocates, in the public or private sphere, will do anything for the right price. Even the American Medical Association, whose own internationally respected journal previously disclosed the Synthroid saga, agreed in August to endorse Sunbeam health products in exchange for royalties until, stung by charges of conflict of interest and commercialism, it decided to abandon the plan.

"All medical organizations receive money from the pharmaceutical companies," rationalizes Debra R. Judelson, M.D., president of the American Medical Women's Association, one of the organizations that accepted money from Wyeth and testified before the FDA on the same issue. "There are no virgins. We've all been lobbied by the pharmaceuticals on all the issues." The National Women's Health Network, the lone women's advocacy group to support the Premarin generic, must be the only virgin at the orgy.

But perhaps the ever-increasing power and determination of certain drug companies to quash their competition isn't so terrible. Look, if we all just took Prozac, it wouldn't seem so bad.

CHAPTER 10

GROWING OLDER

What is it like to be a woman growing old in America? Media representations, gerontology texts, and popular opinion suggest it is a time of brittle bones, shortening stature, incontinence; a time of forgetting and being forgotten; of progressive decline into disability and disease; a time when one becomes an increasing burden on one's family and friends.

The sources of such a negative portrayals are twofold: our societal worship of youth, and our fear of death. These two powerful forces make us reluctant to study aging, and when we do study it, the dominant medical model focuses on disease and disability, rather than on methods by which one can successfully make the transition into old age. "The conventional psychology of aging is almost completely devoted to a study of its discontents: aging as depletion, aging as catastrophe, aging as mortality. At best the aged are deemed barely capable of staving off disaster" (quoted in Friedan 1993:71). Aging is something to be fought off, as indicated by the new subspecialty of "anti-aging" medicine.

In this chapter, we begin by examining why we know so little about the health of elderly women. We will then critique our health care system, focusing on how inadequately older people in general, and women in particular, are served. Finally, we will examine innovative views of aging that challenge its negative image. We will see that aging can be fulfilling, and that women can find great pleasure and new strengths as they gain in years.

OUR LIMITED KNOWLEDGE

Our limited knowledge of health and the aging woman come from a dearth of general information on aging. In the world of medical, sociological, and psychological research, gerontology has been understudied and underfunded. The little we do know is necessarily based on earlier birth cohorts and falls short in helping us to understand the aging process of people today. Today aging women enjoy a wider variety of resources than did earlier cohorts, thus giving them enhanced health and health care opportunities. But the biggest hindrance to our understanding the aging process is due to an entrenched sexism within the medical field. Researchers have systematically excluded women from many research protocols on aging and have made assumptions based on stereotypes of female behavior. As a result, our understanding of the health of women as they age is often uninformative about, or harmful to, them.

The Baltimore Longitudinal Study of Aging is an excellent example of exclusion. Begun in 1958, the study focused on the normal processes of aging. Despite the fact that women live substantially longer than men and therefore do more aging than men, only men were chosen as research participants during the first twenty years of the study's existence. The excuse given at the time for the lack of female participants was that the single bathroom on the premises could not be used by both men and women; therefore, one sex had to be excluded (Nechas and Foley 1994:107). The published results from the early years of the study were titled *Normal Human Aging,* which gives no clue to the fact that women were excluded. Men were allowed to define "normal."

What is distressing about this incident is that researchers were then well aware that the social context of aging is gendered. Women live longer and are more likely to spend their last years in poverty, or to be left widowed and alone, or to be institutionalized in nursing homes. All of these facts have a definite and pronounced effect on women's health. As a result of the skewed selection process in research studies such as the Baltimore Longitudinal Study, we are only now just beginning to learn about the differences between men and women as they age.

Recent research on heart disease illustrates these differences and also underscores the prevailing sexism in the medical field. The underlying assumption of most early research was that heart disease was a "widow maker," a male disease. Although a conference sponsored by the American Heart Association in 1964 was advertised "for women only," the promotion was unintentionally ironic. The sponsors were actually trying to attract women who would be tending to their husband's heart problems. Another twenty-five years elapsed before the American Heart Association, in 1989, held its first conference that focused on women's heart disease (Laurence and Weinhouse 1994:85–88).

The source of the myth that heart disease was restricted to men was the Framingham study, a huge National Institutes of Health (NIH) research project that started in 1948. Although both men and women were included, at the twelve-year follow up, the researchers allowed their results to be influenced by the stereotypical notions that women were prone to be hypochondriacs. When examining the predictive value of early signs of heart problems, the researchers found that 70 percent of the men who had shown early signs had died, whereas for women who experienced the same early signs, the predictive value was negligible. In fact, 69 percent of the women with early symptoms actually did well—the early signs appeared benign. Initially at a loss to explain these very different outcomes for men and women, researchers resorted to invoking stereotypes of female behavior. Women were seen "moaning and groaning about nothing, turning small annoyances into large, unwarranted fears of heart disease" (Healy 1995:332). This powerful dismissal of women's heart problems with the sexist assumption of "hysterical and hypochondriacal" women shaped a long tradition of research studies.

The Framingham study misled doctors for years into dismissing female complaints of chest pain (angina) because they believed that, for women, angina was not indicative of anything more serious. Years later, further research resulted in very different conclusions. Doctors should not lightly dismiss chest pain in women. Dr. Healy, a cardiologist and former director of the NIH, comments:

> *We now know that chest pain in women can be caused by a range of problems not typically seen in men. Younger and middle-aged women, unlike men of the same age, are subject to a wide variety of other heart conditions that can cause chest pain, dizziness, and shortness of breath—symptoms to be acknowledged with respect and given credence, but which are only rarely life threatening.*
>
> *What was also missed in this early study is that women do get heart attacks, but their heart attacks strike some ten to twenty years later in life than do a man's, generally after menopause. The participants in Framingham ranged in age from thirty-six to sixty-eight. So the heart disease that afflicted women, the same deadly variety men get, was virtually left out of the picture. (Healy 1995:333)*

Chest pain in women is not benign as the Framingham study taught doctors, but rather is more common and important for a woman because the "first sign of coronary disease is apt to be chest pain" (Healy 1995:339).

The Framingham study encouraged researchers to exclude women as subjects in heart research because it so firmly established the myth that only men suffered lethal heart attacks. That myth made studying heart disease with a 100 percent male sample seem logical, and many researchers proceeded accordingly. A fifteen-year, multimillion dollar study of heart-risk reduction, the Multiple Risk Factor Intervention Trial ("MR FIT"), included 13,000 men and no women. Studies of cholesterol intake and its possible effects on the heart were based on men (Rosser 1994:75). A major study of the effect of aspirin in decreasing the risk of heart attacks included no women (Healy 1991). One study used only men as subjects in an effort to ascertain the risks and benefits of estrogen for the heart (Healy 1995:190). The results of that study suggested that estrogen had no beneficial effect on heart disease, thereby postponing a later, and very important finding that arrived at the opposite conclusion—that estrogen appears to protect premenopausal women from heart disease.

The exclusion of women from heart-related research also resulted from other policies and procedures. Through the early 1990s, the Food and Drug Administration (FDA) excluded women from drug trials testing the efficacy, safety, and dosages of new drugs. These regulations were based on a protectionist policy designed to eliminate the possibility of inadvertently including pregnant women in pharmaceutical research. That the relevant female target group for heart medication was postmenopausal (definitely not "potentially pregnant") did not matter. The result is that most research (75 percent of the randomized clinical trials) on cholesterol-lowering drugs has been conducted on men, even though half of the prescriptions are for women (Mastroianni, Faden, and Federman 1992:113).

These post-Framingham studies extended the myth of heart disease as a male problem. Because the research was done on men, the textbooks were written with male symptoms. As Healy notes, the symptoms are different for a woman. Thus, using their textbook knowledge made it unlikely that a doctor would consider heart disease in a woman. If a doctor did make the connection between a woman's symptoms and possible heart problems, the doctor had a hard time properly diagnosing the woman's heart problems because men had been used in the development of diagnostic tests. For example, the exercise stress test (a monitoring of the heart while on a treadmill or stationary bicycle) remains less accurate for women, possibly because a woman's breast casts a shadow and makes it difficult to read the test results (Healy 1995:351).

If the doctor ended up diagnosing a woman with heart disease, her care faced other obstacles based on her gender. First, if treatment was recommended, it was often inappropriate for women because studies of effectiveness (such as drug dosages) had been based on men, or because surgical devices (such as the balloon used in angioplasty) were based on a male physique. Secondly, doctors are less likely to suggest state-of-the-art treatment options for women. Several research studies in the early 1990s drew attention to the sex differences in heart treatment (e.g., Steingart et al. 1991; Ayanian and Epstein 1991; Beery 1995; and Iezzoni et al. 1997). Although some of the treatment differences are due to the fact that women with heart problems are older than men and are more likely to have other problems that complicate the diagnosis, the studies reported a gender bias exists as well. One study controlled for differences by asking doctors to evaluate videotaped patients accompanied by relevant medical data. Unknown to the doctors, the patients were actors following a script, and the medical data were fabricated. With controls for "patient's" insurance and occupation, age, level of coronary risk, type of chest pain, and results of an exercise stress test, researchers found that sex and race had an effect on the doctors' recommendations for cardiac catheterization. Women were less likely to receive such a recommendation, and black women were particularly disadvantaged (Schulman et al. 1999).

An ironic aside on this body of research is that the sexism in the less aggressive treatment for women may not in fact mean that women are receiving lower-quality treatment. The findings merely show that doctors are more likely to provide the state-of-the-art treatment to men, but in fact it may be that men are overdiagnosed and overtreated, and women are treated more appropriately (Ayanian and Epstein 1991).

We now know not only that heart disease is not restricted to men, but that it is the leading cause of female mortality. We also know that black and white women have a similar prevalence of heart disease, but that black women suffer a higher mortality rate. Women are not just "moaning and groaning" about nothing. But the differences between men and women do not stop at the hospital. If women are treated and returned home, their prognosis is less favorable than it is for men. A woman's return to the domestic status quo does not necessarily translate into lots of bed rest, because she is likely to have dependents to care for and housework to do (Bower 1991).

PROBLEMS WITH THE BIOMEDICAL MODEL

Semantically speaking, the United States does have a "health care" system, although in reality Americans have recourse only to disease–cure options. In brief, care providers search for diagnosable problems—diseases—and prescribe cures. Our system has a sophisticated arsenal of high-tech drugs, devices, and procedures to rescue people from acute diseases (diseases of relatively short duration). Although this emphasis on cures for acute diseases is problematic for people of all ages (as noted throughout this book), it is particularly inappropriate and harmful for aging women. Older women have a variety of problems and health needs that do not fit into the traditional acute-disease paradigm. As longevity increases, so does the chance of chronic diseases—diseases of long duration that are unlikely to be cured.

Arthritis and osteoporosis (thinning of the bones) are two good examples of chronic conditions that affect many elderly women. Both greatly diminish the quality of one's life by limiting mobility and participation in activities. A cure is not possible, but an improvement in daily living is not only possible, it is often a relatively easy process. Health care providers can minimize the impact of these problems by recommending adaptive gadgets, such as touch-sensitive light switches and special kitchen utensils. These will make the act of lifting, turning, and switching much easier. Although exercise increases one's dexterity, doctors are likely to recommend against any movement they may view as "excessive," which includes exercise. Thus when a woman complains of pain while walking, "the doctor says, 'Then don't do it, don't walk,' instead of giving exercises that would strengthen her muscles so it wouldn't hurt so much" (Friedan 1993:429). Doctors are more likely to suggest such activity restrictions for women than for men (Safran et al. 1997).

Back pain is a common complaint of older women. Since its sources may be varied, an emphasis on an exact diagnosis is often ill-advised. Even a careful diagnosis would have no bearing on what treatment to recommend. Yet this is the approach that tends to be taken by the biomedical model. A much more helpful alternative would be a palliative approach—to mitigate the back pain by recommending a certain set of exercises and "environmental adjustments tailored to the individual patient" (Friedan 1993:423).

Not only does the biomedical model do poorly when it addresses chronic disease, but it is often just as inept when it comes to treating the loss or diminution of functions, such as sight, hearing, and mobility. As women age, their diminished functions and the fear of falling cause them to restrict their activities, often to the point where their living space is dramatically reduced. They become too afraid to risk walking up and down stairs or venturing out of doors. Health care providers need to adopt a new approach, an approach that helps the elderly anticipate the loss of certain functions, and encourages the use of assistive devices, such as walkers, hearing aides, lift chairs, and glasses. Providing knowledge of the availability of these devices must be accompanied by discussions with the elderly to help them accept the value of their use. People resist eyeglasses in their forties and fifties, and later on they resist canes, walkers, and hearing aids. Recommending such devices doesn't fit well with the prevailing biomedical cure model, nor does the investment of time that is required to demonstrate to the patient the value of using such devices.

Preventive health care should be a main focus when dealing with the elderly. Since accidents and falls are a major problem for the elderly and often lead to hospitalization, a more proactive stance is needed from health care providers. Rather than wait until the damage is done (such as a hip fracture), falls in the home can be minimized by the installation of hand rails, the removal of throw rugs, or by offering Tai Chi instruction to the elderly to improve their sense of balance.

The biomedical model has been slow to adopt preventive strategies for the elderly regarding accident prevention. In addition to this oversight, medical schools have not emphasized communication training for doctors (though this is changing), and the relative lack of effective social interaction between the doctor and patient has especially hurt the elderly. Doctors are likely to spend less time with older patients than with those who are younger which, given the complexity of the problems of the older generation, is totally contrary to what should occur (Adelman, Greene, and Charon 1991; Sharpe 1995).

But chronic disease and loss of function suggest a need beyond better communication with health care providers. There is a need for care such as emotional support, nurturing assistance, and sensitivity to the life-world of the patient—none of these types of care have been valued in our system. Doctors are not paid to think holistically about a patient's health (Adelman, Greene, and Charon 1991), but instead focus on specific, limited problems. To place a woman in a hospital and focus narrowly on her treatment (such as a hip replacement) is to provide inadequate care. Not only must health care providers consider her other health problems that may complicate rehabilitation, and recognize the potential for social isolation resulting from difficulties that same-aged friends have in visiting, but also they need to pay careful attention when planning to discharge an elderly woman, since older women have a higher death rate after hospitalization than do men (Rosser 1994:82).

Curative approaches do have a place with the elderly, but they can be ineffective, impossible, or harmful if health care providers do not assess the person's situation. For example, in-home dialysis for the elderly is possible only if a strong, reliable support system exists. For many women, this simply does not exist. Women are more likely to age alone, and thus not have in-home family members available to help.

Our health care system, with its variety of specialists, often leaves no one to supervise the overall care of the patient. This lack of leadership often causes serious problems regarding the dispensation of potentially harmful combinations of prescription drugs. Despite the symptom and pain relief they can provide, drugs are a main reason for the hospitalization of the elderly (Cooper 1994). Adverse drug reactions may result from their improper use due to confusion on the part of the patient concerning drug regimens. This confusion is sometimes caused by the drugs themselves (Hanlon et al. 1998). Doctors may make mistakes in prescribing drugs due to the manufacturer's poor or nonexistent calibration of the appropriate dosage for elderly people, and women in particular. Elderly women are more likely to be taking many drugs to treat a variety of medical problems. Multiple drugs have the potential of interacting in harmful ways. These interactions are often unanticipated because they are little studied, or drugs are prescribed by different doctors without their knowledge of each other's actions. In these ways, the potential for a harmful drug interaction may not even be taken into consideration (Barry 1987).

An unfortunate aspect of aging is the tendency of the old to take a less public role in the everyday hustle and bustle of life. They simply are not as visible as teenagers and families, for instance. This "invisibility" impacts the populace's perception of the elderly and often is the cause for stereotypical notions about the aged. Doctor–patient interaction, especially with older patients, suffers from the doctor's tendency to see only the infirm elderly. Doctors are constantly communicating with younger people in everyday life, but their contact with the elderly is usually limited to office hours. In this way, ageism becomes an "occupational hazard" for doctors (Adelman, Greene, and Charon 1991:133). They tend to dismiss many patients' symptoms as "normal," inevitable aspects of the aging process and either do not seek remedies or do not attempt to prevent the problem. Thus, incontinence is seen as "normal" and is rarely diagnosed and treated, although it is a major reason for institutionalization of women because it is difficult to manage at home (Rosser 1994:78).

Depression is another condition that is often not treated because doctors assume this is a "normal" mental state for the elderly (Bower 1991). Osteoporosis is seen as an inevitable consequence of aging, so exercise, calcium, and Vitamin D are not recommended as they should be (Bockman 1997; Prince 1997). Sexuality is yet another issue that is ignored by health care providers because they assume that older women "are not sexually active, do not wish to become so, and should not be, even if they wish to be" (Rosser 1994:77).

Finally, pain is prevalent among the very old. Researchers estimate that 25 to 50 percent of community-dwelling elders and 45 to 80 percent of nursing-home residents experience chronic pain (Roberto 1997). Yet pain is understudied and undertreated (Roberto 1997; Strother 1995). The medical professionals have been slow to acknowledge the importance of pain management because they did not consider pain a disease; were not trained in pain management; and fear the legal problems associated with prescribing addictive medications. One study of elderly cancer patients found only one-fourth of the patients who had daily pain received pain medications (Cleeland 1998). Much more attention needs to be given to the issue of pain management and the importance of discussing how much medication a patient wants. There is a delicate balancing act between pain reduction on the one hand and mental alertness on the other. Some people prefer maximum pain relief, whereas others, in their personal calculus, value mental alertness so much that they would choose to endure a certain level of pain (Strother 1995).

HEALTH CARE COVERAGE AND CARE SETTINGS

At all stages of life in the United States, a woman's health and access to health care is an issue of class and ethnicity. The likelihood of having insufficient income or sinking below the poverty line is increased as women grow older. The precipitous economic decline of many aging women is the legacy of a gendered workforce. Employers have paid them less and are less likely to have given them a private or public pension, or to have provided them with the means to accumulate assets. In 1997, 13.1 percent of women over 65 were in poverty (nearly twice the 7 percent rate for men); among African American women the percentage was 28.9 percent (Hitt 1999, quoting Social Security Administration figures). Although poverty among the elderly has been greatly reduced by programs such as Social Security (a monthly income provided to individuals who have worked ten years or more in eligible jobs), many are still forced to rely on marginal incomes. Their near total dependence on Social Security is one indication of financial marginality. Among white elderly households, 39 percent of household income comes from Social Security benefits. This figure is 51 percent for Hispanic households, and 56 percent for black elderly households (Villa, Wallace, and Markides 1997).

The advent of Medicare in the mid 1960s greatly increased access to health care for the elderly. Medicare is the federal government insurance program available to all people who qualify for Social Security benefits (other eligibility criteria such as disability also exist). Part A Medicare covers hospital costs, posthospital rehabilitation in skilled nursing homes, and some services provided by home health agencies and hospices. Coinsurance and deductibles exist, meaning that there are out-of-pocket costs for participants. By paying a monthly premium, older women and men can purchase Part B Medicare, which provides coverage for seeing a doctor and having some other health services.

Despite Medicare's effectiveness in increasing the availability of health insurance to the elderly, access to doctors and health care facilities is still very much tied to one's economic status. By international standards, it is a harsh and stingy package of benefits (Reinhardt 1999:210–211). Medicare does not cover many needed services and items. Most prescription drugs are not covered, nor are routine physical examinations, dental services, hearing aids, eye examinations, eyeglasses, or long-term care. People must purchase costly "Medigap" insurance to cover out-of-pocket expenses for these items. Obviously, many people cannot afford this supplemental insurance, so these items remain uncovered by insurance and sometimes too costly to purchase. In addition, poor people with Medicare have less access to health care because of shortages of physicians in their communities, possible language barriers, and racial discrimination (Trude and Colby 1997:67).

Although Medicaid was originally conceived as a health care program for women and children in the ranks of the deserving poor, many elderly women must turn to Medicaid to cover their health costs—to help pay the insurance premium for Part B Medicare, to assist in covering out-of-pocket expenses for deductibles, and to cover some services that Medicare does not (such as prescription drugs and long-term care). Medicaid now spends nearly three-fourths (72 percent) of its budget on the elderly and people with disabilities (Kronebusch 1997:842). Medicaid, not Medicare, provides the primary public funding for nursing homes (Tanenbaum 1995:941).

The use by the elderly of Medicaid is a sign that as women age, differences between rich and poor women grow. Many elderly Medicaid recipients were not poor enough to qualify for Medicaid when they were younger. As women age, a segment of them become impoverished. If a woman's spouse or partner ends up with a long and costly illness, or if her own illness necessitates significant long-term care, then that woman's financial status may quickly spiral down below the poverty line, and thus adversely affect both her health and her health care. The difference in the situation of poor, elderly women and that of more privileged women is striking. A financially secure woman can hire home health care aides, afford Medigap and supplemental insurance, and otherwise purchase whatever her health insurance does not cover. Her standard of living can remain virtually the same throughout her lifetime. In contrast, a poor woman in ill health must navigate an unbelievably complex bureaucracy to get Medicaid coverage and to remain eligible. (Only half of the eligible elderly poor do sign up for Medicaid, in part because it is so complicated [Rowland, Feder, and Keenan 1998].) The elderly poor may have great difficulty affording transportation to get to medical appointments, and they may not be able to afford things to make their lives easier, safer, and healthier, such as walkers, eyeglasses, or regular health examinations, which are not covered by Medicare or Medicaid. The poor and near-poor elders spend nearly a third (29 percent) of their income on out-of-pocket costs for health care (Villa, Wallace, and Markides 1997:15).

The health care coverage of the elderly is changing dramatically as managed care comes to define health care delivery. The 1990s saw many attempts to push Medicare and Medicaid under the managed care umbrella (Rowland, Feder, and Keenan 1998). The results have been mixed, at best. Proponents have felt that managed care could deliver care more efficiently, and managed care groups have contracted with the federal government to enroll Medicare recipients in their health care plans, and thus receive a per-patient payment from the government. After months of experience with Medicare patients, several large managed care groups found that the needs of the elderly were greater than expected, and rather than making money on them, they were losing money. They abruptly terminated their contracts. Thus, in Massachusetts in September of 1998, 17,000 seniors found out that as of January 1, 1999, Aetna would no longer provide their health care. These seniors had to return to traditional Medicare or find a new managed care group (Pham 1998). Such a termination severed the relations these older patients had with their doctors and forced them to find new ones.

LIVING ARRANGEMENTS

Living independently or with relatives is an option for many women for much of their lives. Notable differences by class and ethnicity exist, such as the likelihood of dwelling with one's children (Sokolovsky 1997). For the elderly who are frail, infirm, or incontinent, living in a home setting may become impossible. As they age, therefore, women and their loved ones are concerned about their future living arrangements, which can vary dramatically in cost and quality. Because women live longer than men, institutionalized care is more of a woman's issue. A third of all older women will spend some time in a nursing home, rehabilitation facility, or other care facility (Kemper and Murtaugh 1991). The occupants of these facilities are about three-quarters female (Strahan 1997).

The quality of institutionalized care to which one has access is determined by one's economic class. For instance, nursing homes are expensive, making it necessary for some people to "spend down" in order to gain admittance. To spend down is to use up nearly all of one's assets in order to qualify for Medicaid, which will then cover the costs. However, some nursing homes will refuse Medicaid patients, and others have tried to evict patients on Medicaid in order to increase the number of more profitable, private-pay patients. The Nursing Home Residential Security Act of 1999 made such eviction illegal, although nursing homes can still exercise their right to refuse to accept Medicaid patients (Graham 1999).

High-quality nursing homes provide good conventional health care, an environment of respect, and participation in a variety of activities. Living in such an institutional environment is directly related to longevity (Friedan 1993:87; Spector and Takada 1991). On the other hand, observers of nursing homes have noted problems in some facilities, including disrespectful baby talk (Sharpe 1995:13), overuse of tranquilizers (Svarstad and Mount 1991), and physical abuse of female residents (McDaniel 1997). State and national standards for nursing homes and reasonable oversight could reduce these abuses. Although two-thirds of nursing homes are operated on a for-profit basis (Strahan 1997), most come under government regulation because they accept Medicare or Medicaid patients. But the regulation of nursing homes disappoints many consumers because the nursing home industry has weakened the standards. The American Health Care Association, which represents nursing homes, has at times successfully lobbied the U.S. Health Care Finance Administration and shaped regulations in its own favor. Thus, in 1997, after strong pressure from the industry, new federal regulations *limited* the use of fines (Edelman 1997). In December of 1999, the political winds blew in a different direction, and the federal government was able to impose stiff fines for violations, mandating immediate penalties for abuse and neglect even if only one resident was affected.

SUCCESSFUL AGING

Our society has long accepted the decline of the elderly as an inevitable process. The mass media characterizes the old as disabled, disoriented, or diseased. Our social sciences have advanced similar theories to explain the inevitable segregation and uselessness of the elderly. Most notably, disengagement theory, which was introduced in the 1960s and remains popular, argues that older people inevitably withdraw from mainstream society and that this withdrawal is necessary for the individual to age successfully and for society to have an orderly transfer of power (Cockerham 1997:53).

We now know that disengagement is not an inevitable characteristic of the elderly. A major reason why social scientists came to accept such theories was due to using a faulty methodology. Most of the studies of the elderly have employed a cross-sectional methodology (Friedan 1993:76). Researchers examined data from one point in time when comparing individuals of various ages. Whatever differences they found in function were attributed to the aging process. Such an evaluation was later discovered to be inaccurate, because cohorts (groups born about the same time) have different life experiences, which affect function. For instance, our mothers and grandmothers had fewer cognitive skills at every age of their lives than we do, because they were less likely to have finished high school or gone to college, not just because of cognitive deterioration over time. A cohort comparison thus tells us more about societal change than individual deterioration. When a different methodology is practiced, such as the use of longitudinal studies (following individuals or cohorts over time), the findings are very different. Researchers doing longitudinal studies, notably those in K. Warner Schaie's group (Schaie 1996), show that the expected decline occurs later than previously thought and can be delayed through active use of cognitive abilities.

Once researchers realized that notions of inevitable decline were unsound, they turned their attention to what elderly people did. Elders displayed a remarkable continuity through the years in their participation in voluntary organizations, religious events, political groups, and gatherings with friends and relatives. This activity appeared quite stable until one's eighties. Interestingly, men showed more of a decline than women did (Friedan 1993:81).

The types of activities in which elders engage are obviously shaped by their economic resources. We don't know a lot about these differences because researchers tend to study women with similar economic backgrounds (George 1999:58). The possibility that aging can be a successful process is reaffirmed by anecdotal reports of elders traveling internationally or domestically, residing at elder hostels, playing weekly tennis, and enjoying leisure time in a vacation home. Although these pursuits are obviously not possible for women with limited incomes, they too are engaged in their own pastimes, such as working on hobbies, enjoying relatives and friends, and participating in church and other voluntary organizations. The experiences of these women, despite their class differences, clearly establish that the golden years are not just a time of disability, depletion, and mortality. They are also a time to enjoy the fruits of one's labor, to rest and relax, to take up hobbies one previously had no time for, and perhaps most importantly, to simply "hang out" with friends and loved ones. In short, most of one's elder years can be spent engaging in activities and contributing to family and society.

Any crippling disability typically occurs only in the last few months of life. As a society, we have only begun to examine that period or to try to understand the impact of a catastrophic illness or disability on a person. The Patient Self-Determination Act of 1990 was an important first step toward recognizing end-of-life issues in patient care (Galambos 1998). The Act stipulated that health-care facilities receiving Medicare and Medicaid funding must provide written information to patients on treatment options, right-to-die options, and advance directives (living wills and durable power of attorney). For the elderly, this Act opened up a discussion of end-of-life possibilities doctors had typically avoided. It mandated respect for patient involvement in care decisions, allowing elderly people to make decisions about end-of-life medical interventions, do not resuscitate orders, and how they wished to die. Such personal choices require an openness on the part of the health care providers, who may disagree with some of the decisions patients make, and even sabotage them (Support 1995; Miles and August 1990), and these decisions require family support to implement them (Ahronheim 1997; Ratcliff and Luschei 1998).

The first steps in a transformation of the view of older women have been taken. We are moving from seeing old age as pathology and problems to acknowledging continued activity, respecting autonomy, and envisioning the possibility of further self-actualization. The women in the baby boom generation who did so much for changing their own childbearing experiences in the 1960s and 1970s are now loud advocates for this changed view of themselves and their aging peers.

JANE FONDA, BARBARA BUSH AND OTHER AGING BODIES: FEMININITY AND THE LIMITS OF RESISTANCE

MYRA DINNERSTEIN AND ROSE WEITZ

Although separated by only half a generation, Jane Fonda and Barbara Bush present us with almost diametrically opposed images of how women can age. Fonda, born in 1937, boasts a "relentlessly improved" body—muscular and nearly fat-free, with dyed hair and surgically enhanced face and breasts. In contrast, Bush, born in 1925, exhibits a "resolutely natural" look, with her matronly figure, white hair, and wrinkled countenance.[1]

The striking contrast between the appearances of these two, highly visible, women led us to select them for a study of how women manage their aging bodies. Their dissimilar appearances seemed to reflect two different approaches to aging and to the prevailing cultural discourse which equates femininity with a youthful appearance (Sontag 1972; Freedman 1986, 200; Seid 1989; Woodward 1991, 161). Moreover, both describe their behavior and appearance as forms of resistance to these cultural pressures. As we will show, however, their lives testify more to the limits of individual resistance than to its possibilities.

As public figures, with sufficient financial resources to employ all that the beauty and fashion industries can offer, Fonda and Bush differ in important ways from most women. In addition, as white heterosexuals, issues of beauty and aging might have different cultural meanings for them than for many lesbians and minority women. Nevertheless, the narratives of their aging reveal a dilemma that most American women confront as they age: how to handle an aging body in a culture in which aging challenges acceptable notions of femininity....

AGENCY, SOCIAL CONTROL, AND THE FEMALE BODY

Part of the problem women face in resisting cultural definitions of femininity is that these definitions influence us in ways that we do not fully recognize. While many women are aware of the barrage of messages from the media about appropriate feminine appearance, few realize how insidiously these notions have entered our individual psyches or think to question their legitimacy.

Our analysis of Fonda and Bush [highlights] the interplay between agency and social control in the reactions of heterosexual white women to their aging appearance, demonstrating how Fonda and Bush simultaneously have attempted to resist the dominant discourse on aging and have been constrained by it. Their experiences delineate the difficulties of resistance and underscore the struggle required to establish oppositional discourses.

For this article, we draw on all articles written about Bush and Fonda in women's magazines (including fashion magazines) indexed in the *Readers' Guide to Periodical Literature* beginning in 1977, when Fonda turned forty.[2] Expectations about women's aging bodies are well-articulated in these magazines, making them a useful source of data....

AGING FEMALE BODIES: A BRIEF HISTORY

What constitutes a culturally appropriate appearance for aging women has changed considerably over time (Banner 1983; Schwartz 1986; Seid 1989). Until the mid-twentieth century, American society expected older women to have what was termed a "mature figure" and to a wear "mature" fashions. Beginning in the 1950s, however, this demarcation between youthful and aging appearances began to break down. The emphasis on youth accelerated in the 1960s and early 1970s, as both medical and fashion experts, bolstered by the highly visible youth culture, declared the youthful, slim body the standard for all (Seid 1989, 116–123, 175–176). By the late 1970s, as the baby boomers who had fostered the youth culture aged, the struggle to maintain a youthful appearance had fostered a nationwide fitness craze.

The admonition to become slim and fit, which intensified in the 1980s, ignored the biological realities of aging—the typically unavoidable weight gain, increased ratio of fat to muscle, and, for women, thickening waists and sagging breasts (Seid 1989, 265). Instead, both medical and popular experts redefined "mature figures" as symbols of self-indulgence and irresponsibility. Failure to take up the new ethic of fitness became a sign of social or even moral failure, with the unfit deemed the secular equivalent of sinners and the fit promised youth and health (Zola 1972; Crawford 1979; Waitzkin 1981; Stein 1982, 168–169, 174; Turner 1984, 202; Tesh 1988).

This new ethic has had greater repercussions for women than for men, for appearance always has formed a more central aspect of how women evaluate themselves and are evaluated by others (Chernin 1981, 145–161; Bartky 1988, 65). Attractiveness often translates not only into feelings of self-esteem but into success in obtaining heterosexual affiliation and professional jobs (Freedman 1986, 98–99; Morgan 1991, 35).

The increased cultural focus since the 1970s on controlling women's bodies has led several critics to label it a "backlash" to the rising power and visibility of women. These commentators suggest that keeping women involved with controlling their bodies diverts their energies from striving to achieve more control in the public arena (Bordo 1989, 14; Bordo 1990, 105; Faludi 1991, 203–204; Wolf 1991, 9–12). An analysis of Jane Fonda, who both rode the wave of the new fitness craze and helped to create it and who promotes women's control of the body as a form of "liberation," illuminates the contradictions of preoccupation with the body.

MANAGING THE AGING BODY

Jane Fonda: Relentlessly Improved

Jane Fonda has undergone many metamorphoses in her lifetime, summarized by one magazine writer as "a sex kitten in the 50s, antiwar radical in the late 60s, feminist in the 70s, successful entrepreneur in the 80s," and someone who focused on "personal fulfillment" in the 90s (Ball 1992, 96). Throughout, however, Fonda, has worked diligently to maintain a shapely body.

Ever since she turned forty, Fonda has garnered particular attention and admiration as a woman who has aged yet retained her beauty. With each successive year, the women's magazines have marked Jane Fonda's chronological aging by announcing her age and marveling at how well and, specifically, how young she looks (e.g., Davis 1990, 165; Andersen 1989, 112). Fonda fascinates aging women, one journalist suggests, "because she has a great body, an over-40 body that offers hope and promise. Along with each book and tape comes convincing evidence that it's possible...to remain beautiful and sexy in midlife" (Levin 1987, 27).

Ironically, for those who recall her 1968 film role as the sex machine "Barbarella" and her pleasure-filled lifestyle as the wife of French film director Roger Vadim, by the 1970s, Fonda had begun describing herself as a feminist role model (e.g., Robbins 1977). Fonda began this new phase of her life—as not only a feminist but also an anti-Vietmam war activist—at about the time that her marriage to Vadim was ending and shortly before meeting and marrying political activist Tom Hayden (Andersen 1990, 214–265). Looking back on her early years from a feminist perspective, Fonda described to interviewers how she had come to reject the cultural stereotypes that formerly oppressed her. In a 1976 magazine story, for example, Fonda bemoaned how she had spent her twenties wearing falsies and declared herself now free from such constraints. She sat before the interviewer "clutching her breasts to make sure the offensive things weren't still around" (*Lear* 1976, 145).

In the same article, she described how her feminist awareness had grown when Hayden showed her pictures of Vietnamese women who had plastic surgery to make their eyes round and enlarge their breasts. Fonda was "stunned and I thought my God that same phony Playboy image that made me wear falsies for ten years, that made billions of American women dissatisfied with their own bodies, has been transported thousands of miles to another culture and made these women too hate their bodies, made them willing to mutilate themselves" (*Lear* 1976, 15)....

In the 1980s, as Fonda emerged as an exercise guru, she at first extolled the virtues of intervening only minimally in the aging process. At age 47, writing about aging skin and cosmetic surgery in *Women Coming of Age* (1984, 71), her book on midlife, she advised, "The course I prefer: making peace with the growing numbers of fine (and some not so fine) lines you see on your face.... Wrinkles are part of who we are, of where we've been. Not to have wrinkles means never having laughed or cried or expressed passion, never having squinted into the sun or felt the bite of winter's wind—never having fully lived!"...

Despite this rhetoric, however, most of Fonda's pronouncements even during these years centered on changing and controlling rather than accepting the body. Yet in these statements as well, Fonda used feminist rhetoric such as "freedom" and "liberation" to frame this bodily control as a form of resistance to traditional expectations of female emotional and physical weakness. Bodily control, she has argued, "gives me a sense of freedom" (Kaplan 1987, 417), for "discipline is freedom" (*Mademoiselle* 1980, 38). Similarly, she has described herself as "liberated" from the cultural pressures that led her to engage in binge/purge eating until age 35.

Magazine writers, too, have described Fonda's life in feminist terms. One reporter, for example, comments that "There is a sense she's on the right side, making a political statement in warm-ups and running shoes. On one level, her tapes are about women taking control of their bodies, gaining physical confidence in front of their VCRs, then striding out of their homes to flex their new power" (Kaplan 1987, 417).

As she began to promote her fitness methods, Fonda also argued that working to develop bodily control empowers women by improving their health....

The benefits of a reasonable exercise program as a way to enhance emotional and physical health, maintain a healthy body weight, and protect against osteoporosis and heart disease have been well established and should not be minimized.[3] What Fonda and her admirers have overlooked, however, in their litany of the benefits of exercise, is the contrast between the obsessive and punitive self-control and self-surveillance implicit in the exercise and beauty regimens she advocates and the liberation she claims to derive from them. In the same quote in which she encourages women to accept wrinkles, for example, she also urges "doing your best through nutrition, exercise, proper cleansing, moisturizing, sleep, and healthy living habits to avoid aggravated and premature wrinkles" (Fonda 1984, 71). This lengthy list of tasks suggests the level of work needed to age "properly" and not "prematurely."

Similarly, since her twenties, Fonda has controlled her shape through daily exercise. Only recently has she allowed herself to skip exercise for even a few days (Ball 1992, 97, 143). In one interviewer's words, Fonda is "an exercise addict, like few others" (Levin 1987, 28). Her language of war, struggle, and labor indicate the amount of effort and self-surveillance she devotes to bodily control: "I have a constant weight problem... It's just a constant struggle" (*Mademoiselle* 1980, 40). Similarly: "I constantly fight against weight, and I don't necessarily have a good figure. I have to work for it, and I do work for it" (Harrison 1978, 40)....

It seems, then, that Fonda's desire for a culturally appropriate body has tyrannized rather than liberated her. Fonda's life demonstrates that maintaining an "acceptable" body requires constant vigilance. As feminist critics have pointed out, such constant demands for self-surveillance keep women in line (Faludi 1991; Wolf 1991).

At the same time, Fonda's insistence on the importance of bodily self-control can lead to denigrating those who appear to lack control. In Fonda's worldview, care of the body is not only a personal responsibility but also a moral one. Bodily control signifies self-control, and hence moral superiority. This belief, which permeates the health and fitness movement, has been labeled a "new asceticism" or "new Puritanism" (Turner

1984; Kilwein 1989, 9–10). If in the past individuals disciplined the body to control their passions and submit to God, nowadays individuals discipline the body to extend their lives and increase their pleasures (Turner 1984, 156, 161–163, 172). Yet the value placed on self-discipline continues to resonate with its religious origins, for a fit body still announces a good character.

In Fonda's secularized world, personal "salvation" (of the character and body, if not the soul) is possible through self-abnegation—denying oneself food and exercising even to the point of pain (cf., Bordo 1990, 83). She has waxed lyrical about the physical benefits of denying herself food: "Going to bed on an empty stomach and waking up hungry is the greatest thing you can do for yourself. If you go to bed hungry and wake up hungry, you've got unbelievable energy" (*Mademoiselle* 1980, 40). She speaks in similarly positive tones about the benefits of fasting (*Mademoiselle* 1980, 38–40). In both her exercise and eating regimens, then, the body becomes a locus of work, something to be subdued....

By extension, those who do not take responsibility for their bodies have only themselves to blame for their problems. In pressing this philosophy, Fonda both reflects and contributes to the prevailing discourse of the health and fitness movement, which stresses individual accountability for healthy behavior and harshly condemns those who do not take responsibility for their bodies (Crawford 1979; Tesh 1988; Nichter and Nichter 1991, 253). Despite Fonda's rhetoric of empowerment, therefore, her emphasis on self-control disheartens and disempowers more women than it empowers.

A similar disempowerment results from Fonda's stance on sexuality. Fonda appears to be rescuing aging women from their usual portrayal as asexual by arguing that is possible for aging women to remain active, sexual beings. "I think," she says, "that when you're healthy, no matter what age you are, you have more sexual stamina and desire and flexibility and the things that go into an active sex life" (Orth 1984, 416). In Fonda's worldview, however, a woman can retain sexuality only by retaining a youthful body. No alternative vision of aging sexuality is presented or considered. All that remains is the impossible goal of remaining young.

An emphasis on youth is not the only drawback to Fonda's ideal of femininity. Despite her emphasis on fitness, Fonda has not created a new and liberating model of femininity so much as she has adopted a model that unrealistically combines stereotypically masculine and feminine elements. Fonda began her fitness quest by arguing for the virtues of a muscled and virtually fat-free body. When asked why she added bodybuilding exercises, Fonda remarked "I didn't have any muscles. I like to see muscle, I like to see sinews, and after taking this class, I could see definition in my arms, shoulders, and back. There's no fat anywhere, not anywhere" (*Mademoiselle* 1980, 38)....

Fonda's body thus has come to symbolize the duality of current femininity: tight muscles but with large breasts.[4] The desire for a more masculine body, Bordo argues, appeals to some women because it symbolizes power in the public arena and a revolt against maternity and restrictive definitions of femininity (Bordo 1990, 105). Simultaneously, the inflated breasts serve as a reminder that a woman's body is there for male desires. Mainstream American culture idealizes women who are both supermen (in their muscles) and superwomen (in their breasts). These women, their bodies suggest, won't be dependent but will continue to seek the "male gaze" to affirm themselves. Fonda's enthusiastic embrace of this dual-function body represents not resistance but submission to the demands of femininity.

Fonda's use of cosmetic surgery (which did not end with her breast implants) suggests that the value she places on having a culturally acceptable body overrides any philosophical commitment to achieving a fit body through hard work. As one magazine asked rhetorically, "Doesn't cosmetic surgery contradict everything she advocates?" (Messina 1993, 65). As Fonda now argues, "If you're trying to buy yourself a few years, especially if you're in the business of looks the way an actress is, then why not?... What the hell is the big deal, as long it's done carefully and with thought?" (Ball 1992, 97). In making these decisions, Fonda turns her body into a commodity that can be used, in her words, to "buy" her a few years....

Over the years, Fonda has expressed the desire to construct a new image for aging women, saying "You can be big and still be in proportion and well-toned" (Bachrach 1989, 82) and that the point is to be the best you can be (Messina 1993, 65). Ultimately, however, she has not done so. Her fit and muscled body and her unwrinkled face offer a standard that few women can attain, suggesting that only by remaining young and fit can women be sexual, strong, and good. As one writer observed, Fonda, "at every age...has managed to sell her youth. And, most important, we have bought it" (Bachrach 1989).

Not surprisingly, as purveyors of the prevailing discourse on femininity, women's magazines uphold Fonda's body as a standard to which women should aspire. Many of the writers demonstrate both the wish to imitate her and their despair of ever doing so by their barely disguised envy—"her enviable long legs" (Fair 1990, 39), "her enviable body" (Glasser and Decatur 1982, 22), a body that is "frightenly firm" (Jong 1984, 35). As one writer acknowledged, "most of us would be pleased to look at 34 the way she looks at 54, especially in Lycra" (Ball 1992, 96). By continuing to run layouts featuring her exercises (eg., *Redbook* 1990; Messina, 1993) the magazines offer hope to their readers that they too can look like her. There is little acknowledgement that Fonda's body represents an unrealistic goal for most aging women.

Barbara Bush: Resolutely "Natural"

In contrast to Jane Fonda, Barbara Bush at least appears to resist and reject the cultural ideal of femininity that valorizes youthfulness. Bush's white hair and wrinkles seem to challenge the prevailing feminine ideal and signal her rejection of technological "fixes" for aging (Morgan 1991, 28).

Even more than Fonda, Bush frames her appearance as resistance to cultural strictures about women's bodies. In Bush's worldview, her unwillingness to change her appearance beyond dressing well, using light makeup, and exercising regularly and moderately underscores her interest in focusing on what she considers important rather than frivolous and narcissistic concerns. She thus draws on a spiritual tradition that disregards the body and looks to the state of the soul for moral value (Turner 1984, 164)....

...Bush appears not only to present aging positively but also to scorn and mock those who seem more concerned about their looks.

Bush appears to counterpose the value of "naturalness" against the contrivances of anti-aging technology. "What you see is what you get" (*Vogue* 1988, 442) is one of her favorite self-descriptions, implying that her relative lack of artifice in appearance means that she stands revealed for who she is without the "disguises" of cosmetics, plastic surgery, or even a diet-improved shape. One writer quotes her remark that all she owes to the public is "to look nice and have a clean mind and a clean head of hair" (Adams 1988, 151).

Bush's discourse reflects an older view of aging that made allowances for the weight gain and other changes that can accompany aging and that excused women above a certain age from the burdens of maintaining sexual attractiveness (Banner 1983; Schwartz 1986; Seid 1989). Despite Bush's rhetoric, however, a close reading of her interviews reveals the great efforts she makes to meet standards of feminine attractiveness and to show herself as reasonably concerned about her appearance. In doing so she reveals her exquisite awareness of the demands of femininity and of her need at least partially to comply. She wears contact lenses and her well-known three strands of false pearls because, she says, she's "too vain" to wear glasses and needs to cover her "sagging neck" (Avery 1989, 191). Moreover, although she does not engage in the kind of obsessive exercising Fonda prefers, Bush regularly walks and rides a stationary bicycle to maintain her weight (Avery 1989, 192)....

Bushes use of self-deprecating humor further indicates her felt need to explain her deviation from cultural expectations. Self-deprecating humor, in which individuals mock themselves for not meeting social expectations, allows individuals both to demonstrate their commitment to those expectations and to frame their deviations as humorous rather than serious flaws (Coser 1960; Goffman 1963, 100–101; Ungar 1984; Haig 1988; Koller 1988; Walker 1988). As a result, such humor, which is most common among relatively powerless groups, "is ingratiating rather than aggressive; it acknowledges the opinion of the dominant culture—[and] even appears to confirm it."[5]

Despite her high status, it is this form of humor which Barbara Bush seems to rely upon most often. For example, after photos appeared showing her in a matronly swimsuit, one interviewer reported that Bush "jokingly pleaded with photographers not to take any more: 'My children are complaining'" (Avery 1989, 294). She often explains why she does not dye her hair (e.g., Adams 1988, 150), by joking about the time the heat caused her hair dye to run all over her during a campaign trip, and she frequently comments that "fat ladies everywhere" love her (e.g., Reed 1989, 314). Or, speaking of her wardrobe, she comments: "One of the myths is that I don't dress well. I dress very well—I just don't look so good" (Cook 1990, 230).

It seems, then, that Bush, like many women, uses self-deprecating humor to try to turn her departures from appearance norms into an unimportant, humorous matter.[6] At least one reporter has recognized this, describing her humor as "a preemptive strike" (Cook 1990, 230), in which Bush makes comments about her appearance before interviewers can. Thus, Bush is not, despite her protests, rejecting femininity standards, but is acknowledging their power and her failure to meet them....

Bush's treatment by women's magazines demonstrates the reaction women can expect when, like Bush, their aging appearance seems not to conform to cultural dictates on normative femininity. When Bush first appeared on the scene in the late 1980s, the magazines, whose pages are filled with articles devoted to improvement and whose income derives largely from advertisements for fashions, diet aids, and cosmetics, were at a loss. How could they deal with a woman who seemed to transgress ideas about what was acceptably feminine and whose stance seemed to challenge the economic structure which supports and defends their version of femininity, particularly when their readers seemed to like and admire her? Bush's appearance was something that the magazines felt had to be explained.[7]

To "normalize" Bush's appearance, the magazines, like Bush, have stressed her grandmotherly qualities, labeling her "every American's favorite grandmother" (Mower 1992) and an honorific grandmother of us all. They have focused on her work with children and her role as the matriarch of the large Bush clan (Reed 1989, 314). In this role as super-grandmother, the magazines allow Bush to remain outside the normal discipline of femininity, a disembodied maternal archetype.

The magazines also deal with Bush's appearance, as she does herself, by highlighting and praising her apparent "naturalness." For example, in an article entitled "The Natural," the headline notes that "Barbara Bush Remains Doggedly Herself" (Reed 1989, 312), while another article proclaims "Barbara Bush is Real" (*Vogue* 1988, 218). Like Bush, the magazines assume that such an entity as a "natural body" exists and disregard the considerable role that culture plays in the construction of this "naturalness." Focusing on her "naturalness" as indicative of a praiseworthy inner self allows the magazines to downplay her body, while underscoring for readers how very noteworthy and thus "unnatural" it is.

Despite these efforts to normalize Bush's appearance, the magazines continue to demonstrate considerable ambivalence toward her looks. For example, in an article published in *Ladies Home Journal* (Avery 1989), the author praises Bush for her apparent acceptance of aging but suggests that other women should hesitate before adopting Bush as a role model, citing the numerous studies that show that attractive women do better in the job market. The writer concludes with the admonition that even "exceptional women" like Bush need to recognize the benefits of attractiveness, and predicts that "perhaps after she's had a year or two squarely in the public eye, we'll begin to notice subtle changes—a wrinkle smoothed here, a pound or two dieted off there." Bush, in other words, will see the light and conform to cultural standards of femininity.

The author and magazine reveal their real attitudes in two full-length pictures of Bush which dominate the article's first two pages (Avery 1989, 120–121). On the first page is the actual Barbara Bush. Attached to various parts of her in balloon-like fashion are boxes advising her how to deal with her wrinkles, her clothes, and her shape. On the opposite page stands a re-touched Bush with all the suggestions put into practice: slimmer, with fluffed out hair, wrinkles surgically removed, wearing cosmetics, and fashionable clothes. It is the ultimate make-over! This desire to change Bush so that she fits in with prevailing notions of femininity is a frequent theme in women's magazines.

WOMEN'S POWER AND WOMEN'S BODIES

The treatment of Jane Fonda and Barbara Bush by women's magazines explicates the discourse on femininity and illustrates the difficulties women face in resisting cultural dictates regarding their aging bodies. Women's magazines praise Fonda only because she conforms to cultural ideals. The magazines' more ambivalent attitude toward Bush reflects their consternation and ultimate disapproval of those who do not appear to comply with appearance norms, even when such individuals in various ways acknowledge their deviance.

Women do not have to be film stars or political wives to feel the pressures imposed by cultural definitions of femininity. Those pressures are everywhere, and it is the rare woman who can evade them. Although the research is not clear-cut, evidence suggests that even those groups we have looked to for alternative visions of body size and aging cannot effectively resist—let alone change—the pressures of femininity standards. While, for example, we may respect those lesbian communities where appearance is downplayed and celebrate the success of large-sized, middle-aged African-American blues singers who exude a down-to-earth sexuality, these alternatives to the prevailing fashion in aging bodies have not affected the broader society. Nor do these alternative visions seem likely to survive even within these communities. For example, as African-Americans rise on the social-economic scale, they appear to adopt the same body goals as white women (Schwartz 1986), and at least some lesbians have become involved in what one writer has termed "style wars," rejecting the casual and unisexed appearance standards of the past (Stein 1992). Fat lesbians, meanwhile, describe the same difficulties in attracting sexual partners as do fat heterosexual women (e.g., Schoenfielder and Wieser 1983).

The pressures to conform to cultural standards of femininity disempower women in insidious ways—insidious because we have internalized them in ways we are hardly aware of and at costs we have not calculated. Cultural standards encourage women's sense of inadequacy and promote frantic use of expensive, time-consuming and sometimes dangerous technologies in a futile effort to check aging and increase one's "femininity." Furthermore, such a focus on the body as a privatistic concern turns people away from focusing on social issues (Stein 1982, 176–177). This is particularly relevant during this current period of backlash to the feminist movement in which many women now find it easier to focus on their individual selves than to continue struggling for the social betterment of women. As Fonda herself admits about exercising, "in a world that is increasingly out of control, it's something you can control" (Ball 1992, 143). Thus an emphasis on the self diverts women from resisting current power relations.

Moreover, as women get older and attempt to move into senior ranks in business, government, and the professions, their employers, clients, and colleagues expect them to maintain norms of femininity. These norms create barriers to advancement for aging women. While on men, gray hair, wrinkles, even a widening waist signify experience, wisdom, maturity, and sometimes sexiness (as in the cases of Clint Eastwood and Sean Connery, for example), on women they denote decline and asexuality. Women's power is diminished, therefore, at the very moment when they might otherwise begin to move into more powerful positions.[8]

Given the difficulties of contesting the discourse on women's bodies, many of which are explicated in the experiences of Fonda and Bush, can we still conclude that effective resistance is possible? We would argue, perhaps optimistically, that it is, but only if women become more aware of the insidious, internalized ways that the discipline of femininity disempowers women and join together to fight it.

The successes of the feminist movement have depended on the movement's ability to question received "wisdom" about women and to expose both the cultural construction and harmfulness of that "wisdom." Feminists have challenged pay inequities, inadequate child care arrangements, restrictions on reproductive freedom, and a host of other problems. But the issue of obsessiveness about body size and appearance is a virtually untouched arena for concerted feminist political action, despite the pioneering work of such individuals and groups as Orbach (1982), Wolf (1991), Bordo (1989, 1990, 1991), Faludi (1991), and the fat acceptance and anti-diet movements (Millman 1980; Kano 1989; Hirschmann and Munter 1988). Their efforts to help women accept their bodies and abandon perpetual dieting have failed to affect large numbers of women, despite the increasing medical evidence that body, shape stems largely from genetic factors and that frequent dieting is unhealthy and does not necessarily result in a leaner body[9] and despite increasing coverage of this evidence in popular magazines (e.g., Brownell 1988; *Good Housekeeping* 1993; Kaufman 1992; Seligmann 1992).

Changing cultural standards of femininity will not be easy, and we concur with Bordo that it would be a mistake to minimize the power that the discourse on femininity has to regulate women's lives. To do so is to underestimate the amount of struggle that is required for change and to minimize the difficulty women experience when they try to accomplish change (Bordo 1989, 13). Yet, as the history of women has shown, it would also be a mistake to dismiss the possibility of resistance. The experiences of Barbara Bush and Jane Fonda demonstrate how difficult it is for any woman, struggling alone, no matter how visible, respected, and in some ways powerful, to fight against entrenched cultural notions. The history of women has taught us that, even in the face of seemingly implacable hegemonic discourses, women can make change when they join together. Perhaps now, with the graying of the feminist movement, feminists will begin to devote more energy to challenging the cultural construction of women's aging bodies. At the same time, the increasing if slow movement of women in their forties and above into positions of power may help a new cultural construction to evolve.

Making changes in our attitudes toward our bodies will not be easy, but it will surely be an important step in empowering women. In such a world, Jane Fonda might be able to moderate her painful and obsessive regimens and Barbara Bush would not have to be so defensive about her appearance.

NOTES

1. We have borrowed the terms "resolutely natural" and "relentlessly improved" from an article by Avery (1989) on Barbara Bush. Bush is referred to as "resolutely natural" while, in this article, it is Cher and not Jane Fonda who is referred to as "relentlessly improved."
2. Bush does not appear to any extent in the magazines until the late 1980s when her husband begins his presidential campaign.
3. See, for example Carlucci, Goldfine, Harvey, Ward, Taylor, Rippe 1991; O'Brien and Vertinsky 1992; Doress and Siegal 1987; and Shangold, 1990.
4. We are grateful to Susan Bordo for this suggestion.
5. In contrast, other forms of humor typically serve as demonstrations of aggression and of power (e.g.,

Coser 1960; Fine 1983; Zillman 1983; Ungar 1984; Haig 1988; Koller 1988; Walker 1988).

6. Bush's self-deprecating humor cannot be dismissed simply as "ice-breakers," designed to put reporters as their ease, for self-deprecating humor is rarely used in this way. Moreover, Bush uses self-deprecating humor not at the beginning of interviews, but scattered throughout whenever the subject of her body appears.

7. Similarly, Bush's 1989 biography, *Simply Barbara* (Radcliffe 1989), written with her cooperation, found it necessary to devote much of its first chapter (entitled "Wrinkles and All") to describing and explaining her appearance—surely a startling introduction to the life story of someone whose fame is unrelated to her looks.

8. We do not mean to suggest, however, that it is morally or politically wrong for women to pay attention to their bodies. Maintaining a reasonable weight and exercising and eating moderately offer substantial health benefits. In addition, it would be foolish to ignore the rewards given to those who conform to cultural values, such as the significantly better chance of obtaining work in many fields (Wolf 1991, 27–57). And, too, women enjoy looking good, for there is a pay-off in embodying culture. Women can gain not just emotional rewards but power from being attractive, including the power that comes from heterosexual affiliation with higher status men. What is sad, and ultimately destructive for women, however, is to be caught in an obsessive ritual of body monitoring where the scale determines moral worth, where foods are "good" and "bad," and where we are judged—and judge ourselves—by our body size.

9. See, for example, Brownell (1991, 307–308), Brownell and Wadden (1992, 505–508), Dulloo and Girardier (1990, 418–419), Rodin, Radke-Sharpe, Rebuffe-Scrive and Greenwood (1990, 307), and Wadden, Bartlett, Letizia, Foster, Stundkard, and Conill (1992, 206s).

REFERENCES

Adams, Cindy. 1988. "Talking with the New First Lady." *Ladies Home Journal,* October.

Andersen, Christopher. 1990. *Citizen Jane.* New York: Henry Holt.

Andersen, Christopher P. 1989. "Jane Fonda: I'm Stronger Than Ever." *Ladies Home Journal,* October.

Avery, Caryl S. 1989. "How Good Should You Look?" *Ladies Home Journal,* June.

Bachrach, Judy. 1989. "Feel the Burn." *Savvy Woman,* October.

Ball, Aimee Lee. 1992. "How Does Jane Do It?" *McCall's,* March.

Banner, Lois W. 1983. *American Beauty.* New York: Alfred A. Knopf.

Bartky, Sandra Lee. 1988. "Foucault, Femininity, and the Modernization of Patriarchal Power." In *Feminism and Foucault,* ed. Irene Diamond and Lee Quinby, 61–86. Boston: Northeastern University Press.

Bordo, Susan. 1989. "The Body and the Reproduction of Femininity: A Feminist Appropriation of Foucault." In *Gender/Body/Knowledge,* ed. Alison M. Jaggar and Susan R. Bordo, 13–33. New Brunswick, New Jersey: Rutgers University Press.

———. 1990. "Reading the Slender Body." In *Body/Politics: Women and the Discourses of Science,* ed. Mary Jacobus, Evelyn Fox Keller, and Sally Shuttleworth, 83–112. New York: Routledge.

———. 1991. "'Material Girl': The Effacements of Postmodern Culture." In *The Female Body,* ed. Laurence Goldstein, 653–677. Ann Arbor: The University of Michigan Press.

Brownell, Kelly D. 1989. "Yo-Yo Dieting." *Psychology Today* 22 (January):20–23.

———. 1991. "Personal Responsibility and Control Over Our Bodies." *Health Psychology* 10(5): 303–310.

———. and Thomas A. Wadden. 1992. "Etiology and Treatment of Obesity: Understanding a Serious, Prevalent, and Refractory Disorder." *Journal of Consulting and Clinical Psychology* 60(4): 505–517.

Carlucci, Daniel, Harvey Goldfine, Ann Ward, Pamela Taylor and James Rippe. 1991. "Exercise: Not Just for the Healthy." *The Physician and Sports Medicine* 19(7):46–56.

Chernin, Kim. 1981. *The Obsession: Reflections on the Tyranny of Slenderness.* New York: Harper & Row.

Cook, Alison. 1990. "At Home with Barbara Bush." *Ladies Home Journal,* March.

Coser, Rose Loeb. 1960. "Laughter Among Colleagues." *Psychiatry* 23:81–95.

Crawford, Robert. 1979. "Individual Responsibility and Health Politics." In *Health Care in America: Essays in Social History,* ed. Susan Reverby and David Rosner, 247–268. Philadelphia: Temple University Press.

Davis, Sally Ogle. 1990. "Jane Fonda Bounces Back." *Cosmopolitan,* January.

Doress, Paula Brown and Diana Laskin Siegal. 1987. *Ourselves, Growing Older.* New York: Simon and Schuster.

Dulloo, Abdul G. and Lucien Girardier. 1990. "Adaptive Changes in Energy Expenditure During Refeeding Following Low-Calorie Intake: Evidence for a Specific Metabolic Component Favoring Fat Storage." *American Journal of Clinical Nutrition* 52:415–420.

Farr, Louise. 1980. "Jane Fonda." *Ladies Home Journal,* April.

Faludi, Susan. 1991. *Backlash: The Undeclared War Against American Women.* New York: Crown.

Fine, Gary Alan. 1983. "Sociological Approaches to the Study of Humor." In *Handbook of Humor Research, Vol. 1,* ed. Paul E. McGhee and Jeffrey H. Goldstein, 138–157. New York: Springer-Verlag.

Fonda, Jane. 1984. *Women Coming of Age.* New York: Simon and Schuster.

Freedman, Rita. 1986. *Beauty Bound.* New York: D. C. Heath and Company.

Glasser, Dorothy Ann and Stephen Decatur. 1982. "Jane Fonda." *Ladies Home Journal,* February.

Goffman, Erving. 1963. *Stigma: Notes on the Management of Spoiled Identity.* Englewood Cliffs, NJ: Prentice-Hall.

Good Housekeeping. 1993. "I was a Yo-Yo Dieter." February.

Haig, Robin A. 1988. *Anatomy of Humor.* Springfield, IL: Charles C. Thomas.

Harrison, Barbara Grizzuti. 1978. "Jane Fonda: Trying to be everywoman." *Ladies Home Journal.* April: 27.

Hirschmann, Jane R. and Carol H. Munter. 1998. *Overcoming Overeating.* New York: Ballantine.

Jong, Erica. 1984. "Jane Fonda." *Ladies Home Journal,* April.

Kano, Susan. 1999. *Making Peace with Food.* New York: Harper and Row.

———. 1987. "The Fitness Queen." *Vogue*, November.

Kaufman, Pamela. 1992. "Rethinking Diets." *Vogue,* March.

Kilwein, John H. 1989. "No Pain, No Gain: A Puritan Legacy." *Health Education Quarterly* 16(Spring):9–12.

Koller, Marvin, R. 1988. *Humor and Society: Explorations in the Sociology of Humor.* Houston: Cap and Gown Press.

Lear, Martha Weinam. 1976. "Jane Fonda: A Long Way from Yesterday." *Redbook*, June.

Levin, Susanna. 1987. "Jane Fonda: From Barbarella to Barbells." *Women's Sports and Fitness,* December.

Mademoiselle. 1980. "Fitness." March.

Messina, Andrea. 1993. "Fonda's Workouts That Really Work." *Family Circle,* January 12.

Millman, Marcia. 1980. *Such a Pretty Face.* New York: Norton.

Morgan, Kathryn Pauly. 1991. "Women and the Knife: Cosmetic Surgery and the Colonization of Women's Bodies." *Hypatia* 6(3):25–53.

Mower, Joan. 1992. "What Kind of First Lady Do We Want?" *McCall's,* September

Nichter, Mark and Mimi Nichter. 1991. "Hype and Weight." *Medical Anthropology* 13(3):249–294.

O'Brian, Sandra J. and Patricia A. Vertinsky. 1991. *The Gerontologist* 31(June):347–357.

Orbach, Susie. 1982. *Fat Is a Feminist Issue*. New York: Berkley.

Orth, Maureen. 1984. "Fonda: Driving Passions." *Vogue,* February.

Radcliffe, Donnie. 1989. *Simply Barbara Bush.* New York: Warner Books.

Redbook. 1990 "Relax with Jane Fonda." March.

Reed, Julia. 1989. "The Natural." *Vogue,* August.

Robbins, Fred. 1977. "Jane Fonda, the Woman." *Vogue,* November.

Rodin, Judith, Norean Radke-Sharp, Marielle Rebuffe-Scrive and M. R. C. Greenwood. 1990. "Weight Cycling and Fat Distribution. *International Journal of Obesity* 14:303–310.

Schoenfielder, Lisa and Barb Weiser, eds. 1983. *Shadow on a Tightrope: Writings By Women on Fat Oppression.* San Francisco: Spinsters/Aunt Lute.

Schwartz, Hillel. 1986. *Never Satisfied: A Cultural History of Diets, Fantasies and Fat.* New York: The Free Press.

Seid, Roberta Pollack. 1989. *Never Too Thin.* New York: Prentice Hall.

Seligmann, Jean. 1992. "Let Them Eat Cake." *Newsweek,* August.

Shangold, Mona M. 1990. "Exercise in the Menopausal Woman." *Obstetrics and Gynecology* 75(4, Supplement):53s–58s

Sontag, Susan. 1972. "The Double Standards of Aging." *Saturday Review,* October.

Stein, Arlene. 1992. "All Dressed Up, But No Place to Go? Style Wars and the New Lesbianism." In *The Persistent Desire: A Femme-Butch Reader,* ed. Joan Nestle, 431–439. Boston: Alyson Publicants.

Stein, Howard F. 1982. "Neo-Darwinism and Survival Through Fitness in Reagan's America." *The Journal of Psychohistory* 10(2):163–187.

Tesh, Sylvia. 1988. *Hidden Arguments: Political Ideology and Disease Prevention Policy.* New Brunswick, NJ: Rutgers University Press.

Turner, Bryan S. 1984. *The Body and Society: Explorations in Social Theory.* New York: Basil Blackwell.

Ungar, Sheldon. 1984. "Self-Mockery: An Alternative Form of Self-Presentation." *Symbolic Interaction* 7(l):121–133.

Vogue. 1989. "First Ladies, First Impressions." October.

———. 1988. "Winning Style: Kitty Dukakis and Barbara Bush on First Lady Dressing." November.

Wadden, T. A., S. Bartlett, K. A. Letizia, G. D. Foster, A. J. Stunkard, and A. Conill. 1992. "Relationship of Dieting History to Resting Metabolic Rate, Body Composition, Eating Behavior, and Subsequent Weight Loss." *American Journal of Clinical Nutrition* 56(1 Supplement:203s–208s).

Waitzkin, Howard. 1981. "The Social Origins of Illness: A Neglected History." *International Journal of Health Services* 11: 77–103.

Walker, Nancy A. 1988. *A Very Serious Thing: Women's Humor and American Culture.* Minneapolis: University of Minnesota.

Wolf, Naomi. 1991. *The Beauty Myth.* New York: William Morrow.

Woodward, Kathleen. 1991. *Aging and Its Discontents.* Bloomington, IN: Indiana University Press.

Zillmon, Dolf. 1983. "Disparagement Humor." In *Handbook of Humor Research, Vol. 1,* eds. Paul E. McGhee and Jeffrey H. Goldstein, 85–108. New York: Springer-Verlag.

Zola, Irving K. 1972. "Medicine as an Institution of Social Control." *Sociological Review* 20(4): 487–504.

Chapter 11

CONTRACEPTION AND ABORTION

Contraception and abortion are necessarily intertwined. Although they raise fundamentally different health and medical questions, they are both concerned with the ways in which the reproductive process can be controlled, and who will exercise that control.

Over the centuries, individual women have attempted to control their own conception and birth using many different means. The methods have varied greatly in effectiveness and in the health dangers they posed, but these realities were usually faced only by those directly involved. Throughout most of history, birth control was relegated to the private sphere, where it was an issue faced by women as a personal choice, or between men and women in a relationship.

It is only in the last century or so that birth control has involved debates over broad social and political questions that reached far beyond the direct medical questions of how pregnancies are prevented or ended. Major struggles have occurred over issues such as who should be encouraged or discouraged to have children, whether it should be public policy to shape population trends through birth control, what birth control education should occur, and if contraception and abortion should even be legal. During the past four decades, these struggles have intensified as they have become centered on efforts to get the state, through legislative, judicial, or executive action, to either restrict or increase opportunities available for individuals to exercise control over their own reproductive choices.

BIRTH CONTROL IN THE NINETEENTH AND EARLY TWENTIETH CENTURIES

In the nineteenth century, birth control was introduced into the public sphere by feminists who advocated for "Voluntary Motherhood." They supported abstinence as a woman's right of refusal (Gordon 1976: Chapter 5). This early version of "just say no" gradually took a back seat to the emergence of medical and technological breakthroughs; doctors and others developed improved abortion practices and products to end early pregnancy. The commercial availability of pills for "blocked menstruation," a common euphemism for unwanted pregnancy, is evidenced by newspaper advertisements of the time (Luker 1984:19). This open availability of birth control techniques did not create much controversy, and abortion usually became an issue only when a woman was injured or died as a result.

Doctors eventually began to speak out against abortion for a variety of reasons. Sometimes their concern was sincere, since abortion still posed many health hazards for women. Often, their protests were aimed to attack rival health care providers, such as midwives. Sometimes they argued against abortion because they did not believe that women should control their own fertility. In 1871, an American Medical Association report spoke of a woman who wanted an abortion as "unmindful of the course marked out for her by Providence.... She yields to the pleasures—but shrinks from the pains and responsibilities of maternity" (quoted in Tribe 1992:33). This pejorative evaluation of women conveniently overlooks the male's role in the sexual act.

In the latter half of the nineteenth century, doctors and their allies were successful in making abortion illegal in most states except to save the life of the mother, and they asserted themselves as the arbitrators of when an abortion could occur. Although abortion at this time was not much of a religious concern, it did carry with it moral issues, especially since it was perceived as an option practiced by single women who needed to conceal their "socially deprecating" sexual behavior (Tribe 1992: Chapter 3; Luker 1984:20–23).

Coinciding with this development, the high rates of immigration into the United States after 1850 contributed to the emergence of birth control as an issue that reached beyond individual behavior and choice. Social critics, drawn by developments in science into questioning birth rates and genetics, became alarmed with the possibilities that immigrants would numerically dominate citizens of English and northern European background. These early eugenicists believed in the betterment of humankind by improving hereditary qualities through, for instance, restricting mating to "superior types," and they talked ominously of "race suicide."

Of immediate concern to the eugenicists was the perception that birth control was practiced mainly by the "superior class," namely "native born" Protestants, including married middle- and upper-class women. They were alarmed at the possibility that immigrants, notably the predominately Roman Catholic Irish and Italians, would soon overwhelm the "native" population. As a result, they opposed all such birth control practices.

Evidence of the growing opposition to birth control came with the passage of the federal Comstock Laws in 1873, an amendment to the Postal Code prohibiting shipment of obscene materials, and defining birth control as obscene. The laws did not destroy public knowledge of birth control, and abortions continued to be available, but these practices assumed an aura of illegality and impropriety. Nevertheless, the controversy and disapproval that were associated with birth control was still muted; neither advocates nor opponents made a public issue. Even in extreme cases, such as those involving criminal abortionists, prosecutions were few, and public comment was limited (Luker 1984:53).

Between 1890 and 1950, abortion remained a medical issue, and was not framed in terms of the individual's rights versus the state, although it was now clearly out of the jurisdiction of the individual. Having been successful in getting abortion declared illegal except to save the life of the mother, doctors proceeded to claim the right to determine what circumstances were legitimate reasons for an abortion. These reasons grew to include poverty, rape, the preservation of health even when the woman's life was not threatened, and "for social reasons to prevent disgrace" (Luker 1984:47).

The one person perhaps most responsible for bringing birth control out of the private and into the public sphere was Margaret Sanger, a public health nurse. Sanger saw women's entire lives as literally defined and limited by their repeated pregnancies, the physical dangers of multiple births, and the crushing burdens of child rearing. Her own mother died at the age of forty-eight, weakened by bearing and raising eleven children. Sanger envisioned birth control as a means for women's emancipation.

In 1916 Sanger initiated a major political controversy when she opened a birth control clinic in New York City, despite threats that she would be arrested. A committed socialist, Sanger drew freely from the socialist tradition, which had long talked of "voluntary motherhood," with a particular concern for the lives of poor women who were entrapped by the prevailing social and religious policies that led to their large families.

Sanger's experience as a public health nurse gave her firsthand exposure to the dangers and life-defining consequences of repeated pregnancies and the often desperate, last resort of self-abortion. Attending to a woman who had attempted a self-abortion, Sanger heard the doctor's response to the woman's request for advice on birth prevention—namely, to tell her husband to "sleep on the roof." The woman was in absolute despair, and when the doctor left she pleaded with Sanger: "He can't understand. He's only a man. But you do, don't you? Please tell me the secret, and I'll never breathe it to a soul. Please!" (quoted in Davis 1986:246). Attesting to the terrible desperateness of the times, this woman died three months later from yet another self-induced abortion. Margaret Sanger vowed to herself that she would make the "secrets" of birth control available to all women.

Sanger's opening of the first birth control clinic in the United States marked the beginning of nearly fifty years of struggle, in which her efforts were central, to make birth control information and methods available to women (Ward 1986). During this period, Sanger developed connections with eugenicists, which continues to mire her work in controversy. Some claim she authored the quote "More children from the fit, less from the unfit—that is the chief issue of birth control," whereas others dispute such authorship (Roberts 1997:80; Chesler 1992:215–222). Her effort to provide birth control for poor women surely walks the fine line between providing, on the one hand, something desperately desired by individual women and, on the other, coercively and disingenuously promoting a technique because of population-altering potential that served the interests of the upper classes. Regardless of such unresolved controversy, Sanger was clearly a passionate advocate for women of limited means who greatly influenced the availability of birth control and the understanding of the emancipatory effects of birth control (Roberts 1997:57–58, 72–81, 88).

Sanger's work and that of others led to a number of organizations that merged into the Planned Parenthood Federation in 1942. At first Planned Parenthood's policies were substantially watered-down versions of Ms. Sanger's vision of women's emancipation; for example, they provided birth control information and assistance only to married women. However, the organization continued to play an important role in disseminating birth control information and devices, and in keeping related issues alive in political and legal arenas.

BIRTH CONTROL IN THE LAST HALF OF THE TWENTIETH CENTURY

The post–World War II years have brought wide-ranging transformation in birth control in the United States. Changes in the legal environment, medical discoveries, the growth of a modern women's movement, shifts in marriage and sexual norms, and revitalized religious and conservative political forces have all influenced the position of birth control in society. The result has been a fundamental improvement in terms of birth control options and freedoms, but also the emergence of political, legal, and social pressures that limit and threaten these options and freedoms.

As noted earlier, doctors in the nineteenth century effectively medicalized abortion, and, as a result, abortion waned as a public issue during the first several decades of the twentieth century. However, as inroads in medical science lessened the personal threat of a continued pregnancy to the expectant mother, doctors became more divisive over what now constituted an "acceptable" reason for approving an abortion. Hospitals responded by creating therapeutic abortion review boards to consider requests on an individual basis. Rather than establishing a standardized protocol to their policy formation, the boards' decisions seemed to lack any consistency, or appeared arbitrary or biased. Some hospitals, for example, formed a quota system, or considered the wealth of the woman in making decisions (Luker 1984:56–57). Public knowledge of the inner workings of such boards became widespread in 1962 when Sherri Finkbine, a married mother of four, realized that the sleeping pill she was taking contained Thalidomide, known for its embryo-deforming potential. Her doctor recommended a therapeutic abortion to the review board. Subsequent publicity over her situation coerced the board to deny her application, and she was forced to go out of the country to abort what was a seriously deformed fetus (Luker 1984:62–65; Tribe 1992:37–38).

The Finkbine incident only served to highlight the extreme degrees to which pregnant women would resort to end an unwanted pregnancy. Worried that the board might not approve their requests, pregnant women who were connected, and who were economically well-off, often either sought out sympathetic doctors who would subvert hospital rules and perform abortions, or left the country to obtain an abortion. In contrast, pregnant women of modest means often were forced to resort to extreme measures, such as attempting to abort themselves with a coat hanger, or by seeking out the services of a criminal abortionist. These "back-alley abortions" were dangerous and sometimes fatal. Botched abortions led to desperate trips to the emergency room (BWHBC 1998:408–416).

Women's groups struggled to find alternatives, and networked to sympathetic doctors. Between 1969 and 1973, a collective in Chicago known simply as "Jane" provided safe and affordable, although illegal, abortions. At first Jane employed the services of doctors, but it soon perceived that early-stage abortion was not a difficult procedure. In order to further bring down the cost of abortion, the Jane staff taught themselves how to do it (Kaplan 1995; Bart 1987; King 1993).

Abortion became a public issue as a result of the Finkbine case, the growing awareness of and subsequent attempts to reform the abortion review boards, and the horrors of illegal abortions. The acceleration and polarization of the abortion debate was exacerbated by both the increased involvement of the Catholic Church, and the burgeoning women's movement, which stressed in part its desire for women to reclaim control over their bodies. Beginning in 1967, several states liberalized their anti-abortion statues. Abortions were now permitted in cases where serious fetal defects were suspected, if the mental and physical health of the pregnant woman was endangered, and if the pregnancy was due to rape or incest (Tribe 1992:42). In 1970, Hawaii became the first state to decriminalize abortion. This bill, legalizing all abortions undertaken before the twentieth week of pregnancy, was signed by a Catholic governor who argued that "it was best for laws to be silent on abortion both to prevent the maimings and deaths caused by dangerous illegal abortions and to respect the separation of church and state" (Tribe 1992:47). Similar legal reforms in New York, California, and other states were followed in 1973 by the famous *Roe v. Wade* Supreme Court decision, which established the freedom of women to exercise their right to an abortion everywhere in the country.

These court decisions were noteworthy in their extension of individual rights to privacy regarding contraception and abortion. Although legal controversy has not ended, especially regarding abortion, the United States Supreme Court has thus far resisted efforts to revoke these newly established freedoms. In the years following *Roe v. Wade,* a well-organized conservative reaction against these freedoms emerged, which was rooted in the Catholic Church as well as in Protestant fundamentalist movements. Although these forces have not outright reversed the landmark Supreme Court decision, they have enjoyed some success in constraining abortion rights. Subsequent court decisions approved laws requiring parental notification in cases of underage teens, and mandatory waiting periods. Furthermore, in the policy arena, the anti-abortion forces succeeded in severely restricting government funding of abortions. These restrictions have primarily affected those in the lower economic brackets who depend on government support for their health care, such as those on Medicaid. The Hyde Amendment in 1976 banned Medicaid funding for abortion unless the woman's life is in danger.

The anti-abortion forces have also been successful at the grassroots level. Abortion center violence has physically harmed and even killed doctors and others, and has restricted access by women. The freestanding clinic, originally designed with the hope of making abortion more accessible, is an easier target than hospitals for anti-abortion forces and the clinic minimizes the breadth of medical participation in and support for abortion issues (Garrow 1999). Some argue that abortion rights have regressed since 1973, to the point that it is as hard now to obtain an abortion as it was before 1973 (Michelman 2000). Part of the access problem results from the large number of residency programs that fail to train new doctors in abortion procedures. By the early 1990s, only 12 percent of U.S. residency programs in obstetrics and gynecology required training in abortions (Westhoff 1994), a statistic that should improve because the Accreditation Council for Graduate Medical Education voted in 1995 to require such training (www.acgme.org).

While abortion was in the spotlight at the end of the twentieth century, the legal system was also attending to contraceptive issues. Well into the 1960s and 1970s, glaring restrictions on contraception were omnipresent. Not until a Supreme Court decision in 1965 were married couples allowed to obtain contraceptives in every state (*Griswold v. Connecticut*), and not until 1972 could a birth control activist hand a woman a package of vaginal foam without fear of a felony conviction (*Eisenstadt v. Baird*). The growing legality of contraception was made more significant as medical innovations increased the choices women had. The development in the 1960s of oral contraceptives—followed by new IUDs, injectables, implants, and morning-after pills—gave women the means to gain more effective personal control over pregnancy and greater sexual freedom. Such new developments were not without their problems. Some caused serious health problems overlooked by a system excited with new technology and anxious to make a profit. Problems with early birth control pills became a rallying point for women's health activists (see Chapter 16 in this book), and the dangers of the Dalkon Shield exposed the callousness of corporations and the absence of government protection (see Chapter 5).

POWER, RACE, AND EUGENICS

Contraceptive innovations have raised other issues. The sexism in contraceptive technology is conspicuous given the nearly exclusive focus in medical research and development on contraceptive drugs aimed at women, as opposed to men. When nearly all contraceptive techniques are for women, women are exposed to a disproportionate share of the risks and the related burdens with regard to birth control. Some have portrayed a largely male medical establishment as showing relative indifference to the potential harm to which women are exposed. Even as some attention has been given to new male contraceptives, the interventions aimed at women tend to be more invasive and health threatening.

The history of birth control is very much the story of disproportionate burdens on, and forced and coercive actions against, minority and poor women. Birth control pills, of unknown safety and effectiveness, were tested on minority women and done so without their consent. Some poor and minority women were tricked into taking placebo pills when they thought they were getting birth control (see Chapter 16). Attempts to limit the births of "undesirables" by sterilization focused on Puerto Rican, African American, Native American, and poor women in general. By 1968, in Puerto Rico, an estimated one-third of women of childbearing age had had "la operacion" (Rodriquez-Trias 1980:123). The coercive sterilization of African American women was so common in the South that it became referred to as a "Mississippi appendectomy" (see Chapter 16). Doctors would threaten women with the loss of welfare benefits or refuse to deliver a baby unless the woman agreed to a sterilization (Roberts 1997:93). A sterilization campaign on Native American reservations left one quarter of the women infertile, and for some of the tribes, the policy was genocidal. One physician claimed "that [a]ll the pureblood women of the Kaw tribe of Oklahoma have now been sterilized. At the end of the generation the tribe will cease to exist" (quoted in Roberts 1997:95).

More recently, efforts to discourage poor women and women of color from becoming pregnant have been more subtle. The promotion of the contraceptive Norplant is a prime example. Norplant consists of six matchstick-like silicone capsules that are implanted in a woman's arm and release progestin over a five-year period. Once in, it requires no action by the woman, but a doctor is needed for its removal. This method may seem to be a triumph for women's freedom since it allows a woman to choose a hassle-free method of preventing pregnancy. However, it has stirred considerable controversy (see the reading by Roberts in this chapter). Norplant has been most aggressively pushed by those who have interests and agendas reaching far beyond the free choice of individuals.

Norplant has been aggressively marketed among poor women and women of color, with a special emphasis on high school–aged girls in the inner city. Advocates for such focused use of

Norplant are a diverse group. Some are fiscal conservatives, seeing a need to limit the welfare rolls, whereas others are antagonistic to welfare recipients. Some are racists promoting a modern form of eugenics. Some are searching for an end to poverty and are attracted to a "magic bullet" that they think will transform the lives of the poor by limiting the number of children they have. Others see themselves protecting unborn children, and perhaps society, from the afflictions that mothers who are drug users or afflicted with AIDS would impose on them. Still others claim to speak in the interests of the mothers themselves, whom they see as needing to be protected from a first or subsequent pregnancy that could hold them back from educational, occupational, and life opportunities. Viewing this complex array of advocates, the interests of women's freedom are hard to disentangle from motivations, often tinged with racism and class bias, to use birth control to make society more comfortable for already advantaged groups.

These conflicting forces, which shape women's access to contraceptives and abortion, are only the most recent expressions of 150 years of social and medical agendas that have impacted women's health and lives. For women to control their own lives and work to undo the gender organization of society, they need to have reasonable control over when they might bear children. Birth control must be safe and offered noncoercively, and responsibility for contraception needs to be shared with men. Even if these goals are achieved, those who have their own agendas are likely to continue to work to influence the options women have and their individual freedom.

FROM NORPLANT TO THE CONTRACEPTIVE VACCINE: THE NEW FRONTIERS OF POPULATION CONTROL

DOROTHY ROBERTS

. . .

TESTING THE WATERS— THE *INQUIRER* EDITORIAL

Norplant's potential to enhance women's reproductive freedom was quickly overshadowed by its potential for reproductive abuse. The new contraceptive was instantly embraced by policymakers, legislators, and social pundits as a way of curbing the birthrate of poor Black women. On December 12, 1990, only two days after the FDA's approval, the *Philadelphia Inquirer* published a controversial editorial entitled "Poverty and Norplant: Can Contraception Reduce the Underclass?"[1] Deputy editorial-page editor Donald Kimelman began the piece by linking two recent news items: one announced the approval of Norplant, and the other reported the research finding that half of Black children live in poverty. Kimelman went on to propose Norplant as a solution to inner-city poverty, arguing that "the main reason more black children are living in poverty is that people having the most children are the ones least capable of supporting them."[2] No one should be compelled to have Norplant implanted, Kimelman conceded. But he endorsed giving women on welfare financial incentives to encourage them to use the contraceptive.

The Norplant editorial sent off shock waves across the country. Black leaders were quick to express their outrage at the editorial's racist and eugenic overtones. Norplant's creator, Dr. Sheldon J. Segal, shot off a letter to the *New York Times* unequivocally opposing the use of Norplant for any coercive purpose: "It was developed to improve reproductive freedom, not to restrict it."[3] Black reporters and editors at the *Inquirer* protested the editorial. An emotional meeting brought Black staff members to tears—was their boss implying that those who grew up in large, poor families should never have been born?[4] The *Inquirer*'s Metro columnist, Steve Lopez, issued a stinging rebuttal the following Sunday. "What we have, basically, is the *Inquirer* brain trust looking down from its ivory tower and wondering if black people should be paid to stop having so many damn kids," Lopez fumed. "By combining contraception and race, the voice of the *Inquirer* calls to mind another David. David Duke."[5] (Lopez was referring to the editorial-page editor, David Boldt, who okayed the editorial.)

The public outcry moved the *Inquirer* to print an apology eleven days later. Admitting that the piece was "misguided and wrongheaded," the paper said it now agreed with critics that the incentives it proposed were tantamount to coercion and that other strategies for eliminating poverty should be explored. As further evidence of America's racial cleavage, David Boldt later wrote that he was astonished by the adverse reaction.[6] He was unaware of Blacks' fear of genocide and had no idea that readers might be angered by the Norplant proposal. A telephone call from Jesse Jackson, he says, cleared things up.

The *Inquirer*'s apology did not put the idea of Norplant incentives to rest. Far from it. Journalists immediately came to the *Inquirer*'s defense. Within days of the apology, *Newsweek* offered careful praise of Kimelman's proposal: "However offensive the editorial, Kimelman was clearly on to something.... The old answers have mostly failed. After the shouting stops, the problem will remain. It's too important to become taboo."[7] The *Richmond Times-Dispatch* gave an even stronger endorsement, arguing that Norplant "offers society yet another way to curb the expansion of an underclass most of whose members face futures of disorder and deprivation."[8] A year later Matthew Rees, writing for the *New Republic,* similarly defended Norplant incentives on the ground that "the current threat to children in our inner cities makes it an option that the morally serious can no longer simply dismiss."[9] ("Our inner cities" and "the underclass," of course, are another way of referring to the *Black* urban poor.) Although Rees acknowledged the need to treat poverty's "deeper roots," as well as constitutional objections to interfering with a woman's reproductive decisions, he concluded that "right now, Norplant may be the only practical option we've got."

More ominously, people in positions to steer public policy followed the media's lead. David Frankel, director of population sciences at the Rockefeller Foundation, made light of tensions at the *Inquirer,* writing to the *Washington Post,* "Despite the infantile reaction of some black staffers,...birth control incentives would not be genocide. Such incentives would be a humane inducement to social responsibility."[10] Backers of the Norplant scheme were not uniformly white, as reflected by Washington, D.C., mayor Marion Barry's support of mandatory Norplant for women on welfare. "You can have as many babies as you want," Barry stated. "But when you start asking the government to take care of them, the government now ought to have some control over you."[11]

MARKETING NORPLANT TO POOR WOMEN

The *Inquirer* episode inaugurated a new wave of birth control politics, with Norplant at the center. What appeared to be an expensive contraceptive marketed to affluent women through private physicians soon became the focus of government programs for poor women. Lawmakers across the country have proposed and implemented schemes not only to make Norplant available to women on welfare but to pressure them to use the device as well.

At a time when legislatures nationwide are slashing social programs for the poor, public aid for Norplant became a popular budget item. Without financial assistance, the cost of Norplant would be prohibitive. The capsules cost $365 and the implantation procedure can run from $150 to $500. Removal costs another $150 to $500, or more if there are complications. The government sprang into action. Every state and the District of Columbia almost immediately made Norplant available to poor women through Medicaid. Tennessee passed a law in 1993 requiring that anyone who receives AFDC or other forms of public assistance be notified in writing about the state's offer of free Norplant. Women in Washington State who receive maternity care assistance also get information about Norplant.

By 1994, states had already spent $34 million on Norplant-related benefits.[12] As a result, at least half of the women in the United States who have used Norplant are Medicaid recipients. When Planned Parenthood surveyed its affiliates it discovered that, although only 12 percent of its clients are Medicaid recipients, 95 to 100 percent of women implanted with Norplant at some of its clinics were on Medicaid.[13]

There were also efforts to provide Norplant to low-income women ineligible for Medicaid. California governor Pete Wilson allocated an extra $5 million to reimburse state-funded clinics for Norplant going to women without Medicaid or Medi-Cal coverage. North Carolina's budget similarly set aside a "Women's Health Service Fund" to pay for Norplant for the uninsured. The Norplant Foundation, a nonprofit organization established by Norplant's distributor, Wyeth-Ayerst, devotes $2.8 million a year to donate Norplant kits to low-income women.[14]

Simply making Norplant more accessible to indigent women was not enough for some lawmakers. Within two years thirteen state legislatures had proposed some twenty measures to implant poor women with Norplant.[15] A number of these bills would pressure women on welfare to use the device either by offering them a financial bonus or by requiring implantation as a condition of receiving benefits. In February 1991, only a couple of months after Norplant was approved, Kansas Republican state representative Kerry Patrick introduced legislation that would grant welfare recipients a one-time payment of $500 to use Norplant, followed by a $50 bonus each year the implants remained in place. Patrick touted his plan as having "the potential to save the taxpayers millions of their hard-earned dollars" by reducing the number of children on the welfare rolls.[16] He suggested that women needed an extra incentive to get them to take advantage of the state's free supply of Norplant, pointing to a study indicating that only one out of eight women currently used birth control. Republican representative Robert Farr echoed these sentiments when he proposed a similar bill in Connecticut: "It's far cheaper to give you money not to have kids than to give you money if you have kids."[17]

In short order, Louisiana state representative and former Ku Klux Klan Grand Wizard David Duke proposed paying women on welfare $100 a year to use the device. Duke's bill was an attempt to fulfill his campaign promise to enact "concrete proposals to reduce the illegitimate birthrate and break the cycle of poverty that truly enslaves and harms the black race."[18] The scheme also reflected his earlier support for what he called "Nazism," when he claimed in 1985 that "the real answer to the world's problems" was "promoting the best strains, the best individuals."[19] Arizona, Colorado, Ohio, Florida, Tennessee, and Washington have considered similar Norplant bonuses. In addition to these financial incentives, a North Carolina bill would have required that all women who get a state-funded abortion be implanted with Norplant unless it is medically unsafe.

Several states have considered even more coercive means to ensure the infertility of women receiving welfare. In his 1993 State of the State address, Maryland governor William Schaefer suggested that the state should consider making Norplant *mandatory* for women on welfare. Similarly, bills introduced in Mississippi and South Carolina would require women who already have children to get Norplant inserted as a condition for receiving future benefits. Legislation proposed in other states would deny increases in AFDC payments to women who declined the device.

The notion of requiring women on welfare to use birth control had circulated decades earlier. In his 1973 book *Who Should Have Children?* University of Chicago physiologist Dwight J. Ingle advocated selective population control as an alternative to the growing welfare state.[20] Ingle proposed that individuals who could not provide their children with a healthy environment or biological inheritance—including people with genetic defects or low intelligence, welfare recipients, criminals, drug addicts, and alcoholics—should be encouraged, or forced if necessary, to refrain from childbearing. "By this I mean that millions of people are unqualified for parenthood and should remain childless," Ingle explained in the book's foreword. One of Ingle's proposals was the mandatory insertion of pellets containing an "antifertility agent" under the skin of every woman of childbearing age. Women would be required to apply for a license to have the pellet removed; only those who qualified for parenthood would be allowed to become pregnant. William Shockley made a similar proposal in a 1967 letter to the editor of the *Palo Alto Times*.[21] Norplant has the potential to fulfill these eugenicists' fantasies.

WHAT'S RACE GOT TO DO WITH IT?

If these proposals apply to all welfare recipients, what is the relevance of race? Clearly, welfare policy, which concerns how America deals with its poor, is governed by capitalist economics and class politics. Class divisions within the Black community also create differences in Blacks' attitudes toward welfare. Although we should not underestimate this class dimension of programs that regulate welfare mothers, it is crucial to see that race equally determines the programs' features and popularity. Because class distinctions are racialized, race and class are inextricably linked in the development of welfare policy. When Americans debate welfare reform, most have single Black mothers in mind.

Some Norplant proponents—Kimelman and Duke, for example—have explicitly suggested distributing the contraceptive to *Black* women. After the commotion over the *Inquirer* editorial, however, few politicians are likely to link birth control specifically to Black poverty, even if that is their intention. But race lurks behind proposals to induce poor women in general to use Norplant. Not only will these incentives disproportionately affect Black women, but they may be covertly targeted at these women as well.

Part of the reason has to do with numbers. Although most families on welfare are not Black, Blacks disproportionately rely on welfare to support their children. Black women are only 6 percent of the population, but they represent a third of AFDC recipients.[22] The concentration of Black welfare recipients is even greater in the nation's inner cities, where Norplant has primarily been dispensed. For example, in Baltimore, the site of a government campaign to distribute Norplant, 86 percent of women receiving welfare are Black.

It is also true that a larger percentage of Blacks than whites are poor. One-third of all Blacks and half of all Black children live in poverty. Black women are five times more likely to live in poverty, five times more likely to be on welfare, and three times more likely to be unemployed than are white women.[23] Welfare programs, then, have a greater direct impact on the status of Black people as a whole. Any policy directed at women on welfare will disproportionately affect Black women because such a large proportion of Black women rely on public assistance. These policies, in turn, affect all Blacks as a group because such a large proportion of Blacks are poor.

The second reason has to do with perceptions. Although most people on welfare are not Black, many Americans think they are. The American public associates welfare payments to single mothers with the mythical Black "welfare queen," who deliberately becomes pregnant in order to increase the amount of her monthly check. The welfare queen represents laziness, chicanery, and economic burden all wrapped up in one powerful image. For decades, the media and politicians have shown pictures of Black mothers when they discuss public assistance. Now the link between race and welfare is firmly implanted in Americans' minds.

When conservative activist Clint Bolick called Lani Guinier, President Clinton's repudiated Justice Department nominee, a "quota queen," he counted on the public's immediate association of the label with the pejorative "welfare queen."[24]

The title automatically linked the Black Guinier to negative stereotypes of Black women on welfare, helping to shut off reasoned debate about her views. Similarly, it is commonplace to observe that "welfare" has become a code word for "race." People can avoid the charge of racism by directing their vitriol at the welfare system instead of explicitly assailing Black people.

In addition, poor Blacks pose a far greater threat to white Americans than do poor whites. The word "underclass" refers not only to its members' poverty but also to a host of social pathologies such as crime, drug addiction, violence, welfare dependency, and illegitimacy. Although poverty may be relatively race-neutral in people's minds, these other depravities are associated with Black culture. Contemporary welfare rhetoric blames Black single mothers for transmitting a deviant lifestyle to their children, a lifestyle marked not only by persistent welfare dependency but also by moral degeneracy and criminality.

White Americans resent the welfare queen who rips off their tax dollars, but even more they fear the Willie Horton she gives birth to. These images are distinctly Black; they have no white counterparts. As I showed in the Introduction, many whites hold deeply embedded beliefs about the dangers of Black reproduction that infect any scheme to solve social problems through birth control. This panic is exacerbated by the predicted end of white numerical supremacy in the United States within decades.[25] Proposals designed to reduce the number of children born to poor parents are an attempt to fend off this threat to white people's welfare, a threat that is specifically Black.

Thus, race and class politics work together to propel coercive birth control policies. The impact of these policies, moreover, crosses the boundaries of race and class. Laws aimed at curbing Black women's fertility restrict poor white women's liberties as well. Programs that apply only to Black women who are poor help to devalue Black people as a whole.

To date, no state legislature has passed a bill offering bonuses for or mandating the use of Norplant. But the numerous proposals for Norplant incentives and the defense of the *Inquirer* editorial show that the idea is alive and well. Commentators and politicians have tested the waters and found growing support for the use of birth control as a solution to the Black underclass. As the social climate becomes increasingly hostile toward welfare mothers and supportive of drastic cuts in welfare spending, there is a good chance that these proposals could become a reality—unless people committed to racial equality, economic justice, and reproductive liberty fight back....

NORPLANT MAY BE HAZARDOUS TO YOUR HEALTH

Nearly all Norplant users experience at least one of a variety of side effects ranging from annoying inconvenience to potentially serious conditions. The hormone in Norplant can cause the same long list of bodily disruptions as the pill: headaches, depression, nervousness, change in appetite, weight gain, hair loss, nausea, dizziness, acne, breast tenderness, swelling of the ovaries, and ovarian cysts. Norplant has also been linked to rare instances of stroke and heart attack, although a causal connection has not been definitively proven.

Because Norplant does not contain estrogen, it is thought to present less of a risk for heart attack, stroke, and certain cancers than oral contraceptives. But Norplant's continuous release of progestin produces the side effect that is most bothersome to women: it upsets the menstrual cycle. Some women have no period for months at a time; others experience spotting or irregular bleeding; the worst off suffer from prolonged, heavy bleeding that can last for months on end.

Excessive bleeding should not be dismissed as a mere annoyance: it can require costly expenditures for sanitary napkins, it can dramatically interfere with a woman's employment and lifestyle, and it can mask serious gynecological conditions such as ovarian cancer. Anthropologists tell us that menstruation has powerful consequences in many cultures, affecting everything from religious ceremonies to cooking procedures. Some

Native American women, for example, have been excluded from certain community functions because of tribal taboos against women's involvement while they are menstruating.[26] Other women have lost their jobs when they were absent too many times owing to constant bleeding. One woman complained that Norplant defeated its own purpose by destroying her sex life: "If they want to know why people don't get pregnant, it's because they are bleeding all the time!"[27] One in four women in a California study said that their sex life worsened with Norplant.

There are yet other dangers peculiar to Norplant's design. Some women have experienced pain and infection at the site where the tubes were inserted. Some claim that the silicone in Norplant capsules caused debilitating immunological reactions similar to those alleged in the silicone breast implant litigation.[28] Two doctors reported in a 1995 issue of *Toxicology and Industrial Health* the case of a twenty-two-year-old patient who suffered severe complications when the Norplant capsules burst in her arm.[29] Not only did her arm swell to three times its normal size, but she was plagued by persistent headaches, gastrointestinal bleeding, asthma, fatigue, muscle aches, and weakness in her arms. The doctors concluded that these ailments were caused by two consequences of the ruptured device—the excessive release of hormones into her bloodstream and a silicone-induced immunological disease. Norplant inserts that are not removed after five years may cause ectopic pregnancy, which could be fatal owing to massive internal hemorrhaging. The possible adverse effects of the lingering hormone on a fetus are unknown.

These are not isolated cases. The severity and prevalence of Norplant's side effects are reflected in the numbers of women who return to get the implants removed. Almost 20 percent of women in test studies had Norplant extracted within one year, most commonly because of bleeding problems. After three years, over half had it taken out.[30]

Women suffering from certain illnesses are at extra risk of harm and should be advised not to use the implant at all. Many of these health conditions disproportionately affect Black women—high blood pressure, heart disease, kidney disease, sickle-cell anemia, and diabetes, for example. Norplant is less effective in women who weigh more than 150 pounds, another concern for Black women, who are more prone to obesity.

Norplant's side effects are especially troubling for poor minority women who rarely see a doctor. Women who do not get regular health care may not know whether or not Norplant is safe for them. There may be delays in treatment of serious side effects or in detection of more dangerous health conditions such as ovarian cancer masked by irregular bleeding.[31] Unlike women who use the pill, Norplant users need not return to the doctor for prescription refills. There is no guarantee, then, that poor patients will return two months after the procedure to discuss any side effects or will maintain regular annual checkups, as recommended. Norplant use requires immediate and regular access to high-quality health care—a privilege most poor Black women do not enjoy.

It is even more likely that physicians will lose track of teenagers once they graduate from the school that dispensed Norplant to them. One study of 136 Baltimore adolescents using Norplant found a high incidence of failure to make routine gynecologic health maintenance visits.[32] The same Texas study that concluded that Norplant was "especially suitable" for teens also found that almost a fifth of the patients did not visit a clinic at all in the six months after Norplant insertion, despite their increased risk of cervical dysplasia and STDs.[33] Other studies of inner-city patients have found similar follow-up rates of only 25 to 40 percent.[34] Rather than making Norplant the perfect teenager contraceptive, teenagers' ignorance and irresponsibility may make Norplant especially dangerous for them.

These are the side effects that women on Norplant have already experienced. But what about Norplant's long-term consequences? Health advocates argue that we do not know enough about the implant's potential for harm because the clinical testing was terribly inadequate. Norplant's developer, the Population Council, points to research collected over fifteen years from 170 clinical trials involving some 55,000 women. Despite the large numbers of women tested, however, there are concerns about the methods the researchers used and the length of time the women were studied.

Most of the testing occurred not in the United States but overseas, in countries such as Brazil, Indonesia, and Egypt. Ethical breaches in administering Norplant to poor, illiterate Third World women place the research findings in question. Researchers in some countries lost track of large numbers of Norplant users (29 percent in Indonesia, for example), jeopardizing both study results and the women's health.[35]

In addition, there has been no research on whether the increases in cholesterol levels experienced by some Norplant users will lead to higher risk of stroke or cardiovascular disease.[36] Nor has research addressed the concern that the long-term administration of the hormone in Norplant may significantly increase women's risk of breast and cervical cancer.[37] Norplant's long-term effects on teenagers are even less certain because all of the clinical trials were conducted on women over the age of eighteen. Some women's health organizations, including the National Women's Health Network and Health Action International (a network of one hundred organizations from thirty-six countries), formally opposed FDA approval of Norplant until its long-term safety could be assured through follow-up studies.

The case of testing in Bangladesh raises serious doubts about both the ethics and the reliability of the Norplant research. An investigation conducted by UBINIG, a Bangladeshi monitoring group, discovered alarming problems with the Norplant clinical trial conducted in Bangladesh between 1985 and 1987 on 600 urban slum women. The organization found that procedures followed by the Bangladesh Fertility Research Program, the national family-planning and biomedical research organization, were marred by gross violations of medical ethics, inadequate methodology, and disregard for the health of the female subjects.[38]

Clinic workers did not give clients a prior medical examination or obtain their informed consent to participate in the testing. Participants were not told about all of Norplant's side effects or that the drug was still in its experimental stage. They did not understand how the device worked or even know its name—nearly everyone referred to the implants as "the five-year needle." Many women were breast-feeding at the time of insertion even though the hormones can travel to a baby through breast milk. The research results were further tainted by giving women monetary incentives for the insertion and then discouraging them from reporting health problems.

Similar methodological errors, ethical lapses, and health complications marked the tryouts in other Third World countries.[39] Under pressure from women's groups, the Brazilian government rescinded its authorization for Norplant testing in 1986. Activist Deepa Dhanraj produced a film entitled *Something Like a War,* which documents abusive testing of Norplant-2, the forerunner of the current version, on thousands of women in India during the 1980s.

Health advocates are also concerned that use of Norplant may increase the risk of STDs. Unlike condoms, Norplant does not provide protection against AIDS and other STDs. Once the implants are in place, women may take fewer precautions against contracting an STD, such as requiring their partner to wear a condom. Studies are already confirming this fear. Although 42 percent of women in a Texas survey used condoms before Norplant, 48 percent of these same women reported that they would rarely or never use them in the future.[40] Therefore, the researchers concluded, "almost one-quarter of the implant acceptors in our sample may be at increased risk of contracting an STD."[41] Of course, the pill and other birth control methods also provide no protection against STDs. But Norplant may be riskier because its users need not check in with a health care provider who might remind them about the importance of using condoms. It also appears that Norplant users are not receiving the necessary counseling about the importance of continuing protection against STDs. For women and teens at risk for both unwanted pregnancy and STDs, the increased potential for contracting AIDS and other diseases may very well outweigh Norplant's enhanced protection against pregnancy.

Norplant proponents seem to have ignored this calculation. For example, Douglas Besharov, a scholar at the American Enterprise Institute, believes that the scales easily tip in favor of Norplant. Besharov acknowledges criticism that Norplant may lead to a marginal increase in teen sex and to a concomitant increase in STDs, but he is willing to trade off these disadvantages to teenagers for what Norplant has to offer society. "Which is worse: the possibility of a marginal increase in sexual activity," Besharov queries, "or losing the opportunity to reduce abortions and out-of-wedlock births by 10, 20, or even 30 percent? To ask the question is to answer it."[42] The peddlers of Norplant curiously minimize the serious health risks from the implants themselves, as well as the increased possibility of disease that comes with them. They also leave out of the equation strategies for improving the availability and effectiveness of less risky birth control methods.

In many cases prescribing Norplant to teenagers is like using a bazooka to kill a gnat. Most young teens engage in sex only sporadically, with sexually active boys reporting no sex at all for an average of six months each year.[43] Yet Norplant is only appropriate for women who have sex regularly: it is expensive and intrusive; and it supplies a constant dose of powerful contraceptive hormones. As one commentator pointed out, "A teenage girl cannot simply stop at the drugstore on the way to a date to pick up Norplant."[44] Adolescent girls who have sex a few times a year do not need such drastic pregnancy prevention. The diminished risk of pregnancy for these teens cannot justify Norplant's grave risk to their health. Government officials who press for mass Norplant distribution to teenagers apparently have not bothered to engage in this sort of cost-benefit analysis.

Why the rush to forfeit women's health for the good of society? Perhaps the answer lies in the poverty and race of the women being sacrificed. Let us think about the hypothetical scheme proposed by Isabel Sawhill, an economist at the Urban Institute in Washington, to insert Norplant in the arm of every girl in the country when she reaches puberty. One reason this suggestion sounds so ludicrous is that it would be unthinkable to inflict such a risky device on the daughters of affluent white parents....

NOTES

1. Donald Kimelman, "Poverty and Norplant: Can Contraception Reduce the Underclass?" *Philadelphia Inquirer,* Dec. 12, 1990, p. A18.
2. Ibid.
3. Sheldon J. Segal, "Norplant Developed for All Women, Not Just the Well-to-Do," *New York Times,* Dec. 29, 1990, p. A18.
4. David R. Boldt, "A 'Racist Pig' Offers Some Final Thoughts on Norplant," *Philadelphia Inquirer,* Dec. 30, 1990, p. F7.
5. Steve Lopez, "A Difference of Opinion," *Philadelphia Inquirer,* Nov. 16, 1990, p. B1.
6. Boldt, "A 'Racist Pig' Offers Some Final Thoughts on Norplant," p. F7.
7. Jonathan Alter, "One Well-Read Editorial," *Newsweek,* Dec. 31, 1990, pp. 85, 86.
8. "Journalistic Thought Police," *Richmond Times-Dispatch,* Dec. 27, 1990, p. A12.
9. Matthew Rees, "Shot in the Arm: The Use and Abuse of Norplant; Involuntary Contraception and Public Policy," *New Republic,* Dec. 9, 1991, p. 16.
10. David Frankel, Letter to the Editor, *Washington Post,* Dec. 29, 1990, p. A18.
11. Quoted in Sally Quinn. "Childhood's End," *Washington Post,* Nov. 27, 1994, p. C1.
12. Deborah L. Shelton, "Complications of Birth; Norplant Contraceptive," *American Medical News* 38 (Feb. 20, 1995), p. 15.
13. Planned Parenthood Federation of America, *Survey of Planned Parenthood Affiliates on Provision of Norplant* (December 1992).
14. Smith and Easton, "Dilemma of Desire."
15. Ibid.
16. Rees, "Shot in the Arm," p. 16.
17. Quoted in Alan Harper, "Racism Suggested in Payments to Poor for Norplant Implants," *New York Beacon,* March 4, 1994 (available on Ethnic News Watch, Softline Information, Inc.).
18. Quoted in William H. Tucker, *The Science and Politics of Racial Research* (Urbana: University of Illinois Press, 1994), p. 294.

19. Quoted in Craig Flourney, "Duke Says He's Proud of Years as Klan Chief," *Dallas Morning News,* June 17,1992, pp. A1, A16.
20. Dwight J. Ingle, *Who Should Have Children? An Environmental and Genetic Approach* (Indianapolis and New York: Bobbs-Merrill, 1973).
21. Tucker, *Science and Politics of Racial Research,* p. 193.
22. Staff of House Committee on Ways and Means, House of Representatives, *Overview of Entitlement Programs 1994 Green Book,* 103d Cong., 2d sess., 1994, pp. 402, 444; Teresa L. Amott. "Black Women and AFDC: Making Entitlements Out of Necessity," in Linda Gordon, ed., *Women, the State, and Welfare* (Madison: University of Wisconsin Press: 1990), p. 280.
23. Nadja Zolokar, *The Economic Status of Black Women* (Washington, D.C.: U.S. Commission on Civil Rights, 1990), p. 1.
24. Clint Bolick, "Clinton's Quota Queens," *Wall Street Journal,* April 30, 1993, p. A12.
25. William Henry, "Beyond the Melting Pot," *Time,* April 9, 1990, pp. 28–31.
26. *Skin Deep* (September 1994), a documentary produced by Deb Ellis and Alexandra Halkin.
27. Bill Sloat and Keith Epstein, "Many Find Side Effects of Norplant Intolerable; Contraceptive Often Removed, but Its Defenders Maintain Implants Still Safe," *Plain Dealer,* June 18, 1995, p. A1.
28. Gina Kolata, "Will the Lawyers Kill Off Norplant?" *New York Times,* May 28, 1995, p. C1; "American Home Faces Suits by Users of Norplant Device," *Wall Street Journal,* July 28, 1994, p. B14.
29. Andrew Campbell and Nachman Brautbar, "Norplant: Systemic Immunological Complications—Case Report," *Toxicology and Industrial Health* 11 (1995), p. 41.
30. G. W. Bardin, "Norplant Contraceptive Implants," *Obstetrics and Gynecology Report* 2 (1990), pp. 96, 98, and tab. 2.
31. "For High School Girls, Norplant Hits Home," *New York Times,* March 7, 1993, p. A28.
32. Vanessa Cullins et al., "Comparison of Adolescent and Adult Experiences with Norplant Levonorgestrel Contraceptive Implants," *Obstetric Gynecology* 83 (1994), pp. 1026, 1031.
33. Abbey B. Berenson and Constance M. Wiemann, "Patient Satisfaction and Side Effects with Levonorgestrel Implant (Norplant) Use in Adolescents 18 Years of Age or Younger," *Pediatrics* 92 (1993), p. 260.
34. Margaret L. Frank et al., "One-Year Experience with Subdermal Contraceptive Implants in the United States," *Contraception* 48 (1993), p. 229; Vanessa E. Cullins, "Preliminary Experience with Norplant in an Inner-City Population," *Contraception* 47 (1993), p. 193.
35. Anita Hardon and Lenny Achthoven, "Norplant: A Critical Review," *Women and Pharmaceuticals Bulletin* 14 (Nov. 1990), pp. 14, 17.
36. "Norplant Approval for U.S. Near; Surveillance Study Planned to Investigate Safety, Delivery Issues," *Network News,* Nov.–Dec. 1989, p. 4.
37. *Letter of Dr. Judith Weisz and Dr. Paul D. Stolley to Frank Young, Commissioner, Food and Drug Administration,* Aug. 4, 1989.
38. Janice G. Raymond, *Women as Wombs: Reproductive Technologies and the Battle over Women's Freedom* (San Francisco: HarperCollins, 1993), pp. 16–18; "Norplant: 'The Five-Year Needle'; An Investigation of the Bangladesh Trial," *Radical Journal of Health,* March 1988, p. 101; "Bangladesh: Norplant on Trial?" *HAI News,* April 1989 (available from the National Women's Health Network, Washington, D.C.).
39. Carmen Barroso and Sonia Correa, "Public Servants, Professionals, and Feminists: The Politics of Contraceptive Research in Brazil," in Ginsburg and Rapp, *Conceiving the New World Order,* p. 292; Raymond, *Women as Wombs,* pp. 15–16.
40. Margaret L. Frank et al., "Characteristics and Attitudes of Early Contraceptive Implant Acceptors in Texas," *Family Planning Perspectives* 24 (1992), pp. 208, 212.
41. Ibid.
42. Douglas J. Besharov, "A Moral Choice: Would Norplant Simply Stop Unwanted Pregnancies—or Increase Destructive Teen Sex?" *National Review* 45 (Aug. 9, 1993), p. 50.
43. Ibid.
44. Ibid.

ILLEGAL ABORTION IN THE UNITED STATES: A PERILOUS HISTORY

DANIELLE MARQUIS CURRIER

In the year 2000, most American women do not worry about the availability of an abortion. But not so long ago, a legal abortion was unavailable to everyone but the rich or socially well-connected. In the twentieth century, up through the 1973 passage of *Roe v. Wade,* legal abortion was solely the purview of medical doctors. It was they who could decide which women could have abortions—first as individual doctors, then as doctors serving on hospital abortion committees determining which women could have a "therapeutic abortion." The only abortions sanctioned by the state at that time were those in which the life of the woman was in danger, although other reasons (such as psychological distress) sometimes came to be accepted by the committees. The procedure of petitioning the hospital abortion committee was humiliating and exhausting for women, with the result never guaranteed, and biased in favor of well-to-do women (Solinger 1993; 1998). The whole process infantalized women, treating them as if they could not make their own, rational, adult decisions. Even worse,

> *many women who were "successful" with the committee found out, to their horror, that they could have the abortion only if they agreed to be sterilized at the same time. One doctor explained, "A serious effort is made to control the need for dealing with the same problem in the same patient twice."... Studies conducted in the early 1950s showed that, indeed, sterilization had become a fairly common practice. Over 53 percent of teaching hospitals made simultaneous sterilization a condition of approval for abortion, and in all U.S. hospitals, the rate was 40 percent. One doctor...observed that the practice was driving women to illegal abortionists because dealing with law-abiding physicians was likely to entail the permanent loss of their fertility. (Solinger 1998:24)*

In addition, many women applied for but were denied the legal right to have an abortion, while others did not want to go through the painful process of applying to the hospital abortion committees. These women turned to illegal abortion as a way out of their dilemmas. Thus, the doctor-control of abortions contributed greatly to the large number and diversity of women who turned to an illegal method of abortion. In the mid twentieth century, between 200,000 and 1.3 million women annually had illegal abortions in the United States (Solinger 1998:xi).

Before legalization, many groups and communities organized to help women gain access to safe, though illegal, abortions. The most well-known of these was the Jane Collective, a group of women in Chicago who organized in 1969 to provide women with safe and effective abortions. Although they were not trained medical doctors, they taught themselves to perform abortions so as to help other women in an empowering and supportive way. Until abortion was legalized in 1973, Jane helped over 11,000 women obtain safe and successful abortions, and quite importantly, ones which respected the psychological and emotional components of this procedure. Often, the women themselves were active participants.

> *When a woman came to Jane for an abortion, the experience she had was markedly different from what she encountered in standard medical settings. She was included. She was in control. Rather than being a passive recipient, a patient, she was expected to participate. Jane said, "We don't do this to you, but with you." By letting each woman know beforehand what to expect during the abortion and the recovery stage, and then talking with her step by step through the abortion itself, group members attempted to give each woman a sense of her own personal power in a situation in which most women felt powerless. (Kaplan 1995:x)*

Our approach gave her a sense of control over her abortion and helped her shed society's judgments of guilt and self-blame. We saw an abortion as a potential catalyst for personal growth, an opportunity for a woman to take stock of her life. (Kaplan 1998:33)

Some traditional medical personnel were actively involved in illegal abortions. There were doctors, nurses, and midwives who put their lives and careers on the line to help women in need of an abortion: those who would perform abortions in safe, sanitary environments; those who would provide the service at minimal or no cost; those who believed in a woman's right to control her own reproductive capacities and sexuality and were willing to help them in any way possible; those who wanted to protect these women and give them the best health care available; and those who worked for the legalization of abortion on the social and political level. Doctors involved in illegal abortion included those who took care of their own private practice patients only; those who would provide abortions to all who came to them for help, based partly in their political activism and beliefs; and those who did abortions to provoke legal action and so as to help change the laws (Joffe 1991). Most of them performed abortions because they believed it was right:

The first abortion I performed was for a seventeen-year-old high school student. She told me, as I talked to her before the operation, that she wanted to be a doctor and an anesthesiologist. I was terrified, and so was she. She cried after the operation in sadness and relief. Her tears and the immensity of the moment brought on my tears. I had helped her change her life. I was relieved that this young woman was safe to go on with her life and realize her dreams. (Hern 1998:307)

And then there were those doctors who would not perform the abortions themselves but were willing to provide post-operative care or refer women to doctors who would perform safe abortions.

But a safe, though illegal, abortion was not available to many women, mostly because of economic or racial factors. Many women seeking an illegal abortion had neither the money nor the social connections to have a safe abortion. One option for women unable to obtain a legal abortion or a safe, illegal one was to turn to a "butcher" doctor (someone claiming abortion expertise) in a "back alley." Countless people born before 1960 know a woman who had obtained, and some who had died from, an illegal abortion. The statistics are grim:

In 1930...abortion was the official cause of death for nearly 2,700 American women, representing 18 percent of all maternal deaths, though it is generally agreed that unreported deaths from illegal abortion make the actual number much higher. In 1965, illegal abortion still accounted for almost 17 percent of all deaths related to pregnancy and childbirth, and 55 percent of those who died were women of color. (Bonavoglia 1991:xxiii)

And additional statistics on women of color are even more devastating:

When contraceptives were unavailable and abortion was illegal, septic abortions were a primary killer of African-American women. One study estimated that 80 percent of deaths caused by illegal abortions in New York in the 1960s involved Black and Puerto Rican women. In Georgia between 1965 and 1967 the Black maternal death rate due to illegal abortion was fourteen times that of white women. (Ross 1998:161)

Back-alley abortionists took advantage of scared, poor, minority, or otherwise vulnerable women. Many of these abortionists were not actually doctors but wanted to earn some extra money doing procedures they knew nothing about. Sometimes they said they performed abortions but actually did nothing but take money and physically scar the women. They demanded exorbitant amounts of money to perform the surgery, and they frequently let women bleed to death in alleys, garages, or cars, or sent them home to die in their own homes. Some even sexually molested or emotionally humiliated the women they were operating on. Some of the methods used were terrifying, life-threatening, and ineffective:

I was told to undress and lie in the bathtub, which I did...there was no anesthetic of course. She jammed something through my cervix. It was incredibly painful. I was screaming and crying; I had no idea what was happening to me. Then she used what looked like a douche to shoot some sort of solution up through my cervix.... I began to go into labor, incredibly horrific pain for I don't know how many hours—ghastly, ghastly pain...and yet we had made a pact that under no condition would we go to a hospital; we felt we should honor it, for her sake.... Finally, John said, 'I don't care what happens to us; we're going to the hospital'.... when I came to—a doctor and a nurse came in, and they looked very scornfully at me, the nurse with a bit of pity. I was told that I had almost died, that the woman had filled me full of Lysol. (Kidder 1991:98)

Some women had to go through a procedure in which they took an active, albeit uneducated and dangerous, part. Vance (1991) describes how her mother had her abortion in a

> *dim, dingy room, single exposed light bulb hanging from the ceiling, table covered with newspaper, unrecognizable "surgical" instruments. They put a catheter inside her body and packed her with gauze. Then she came home and waited for "it" to happen. In those days the pregnancy was eventually terminated by the woman herself. She had horrible pains, then maneuvered herself to the bathroom. She pushed and pushed and pushed out clot after clot, squeezing and forcing and pressing with all her strength. When she thought her body had recovered enough to return to bed, she rose, glanced down, and saw the umbilical cord dangling between her legs. (93)*

Some women did not want to go to an abortionist, whether it was a doctor or not. These women would attempt self-abortions, using coat hangers, drinking various combinations of toxic substances, or by intentionally causing themselves physical trauma, such as throwing themselves down the stairs, punching themselves in the abdomen, or taking baths in scalding hot water.

> *I panicked. I sat in hot baths. I drank these strange concoctions girls told me about—something like Johnny Walker Red with a little bit of Clorox, alcohol, baking soda—which probably saved my stomach—and some sort of cream. You mixed it all up. I got violently ill. (Goldberg 1991:116)*
>
> *You heard all kinds of stories about folks drinking turpentine, kerosene, doing almost anything to keep from being pregnant. (Avery 1991:150)*

As with stories about back-alley abortions, the descriptions of the self-inflicted attempts are horrific and gruesome. This is testimony to how truly desperate the women were and the lengths to which a woman will go to obtain an abortion for an unwanted pregnancy. In a theater production, Whoopi Goldberg describes the looping of a clothes hanger to reduce the chances of perforating the uterus:

> *In the show, I do it very slow because I want the audience to understand what we're talking about: We're talking about a wire metal hanger with one end that is looped and twisted and then inserted in the vagina, up into the uterus, and moved around. Being the space cadet that she [the girl I portray] is, she loops it but doesn't twist the end all the way down. That's why she has so much trouble with it; she in fact just tears out the interior of her uterus and hemorrhages. (Goldberg 1991:117)*

One thing that must be noted is that many of these women did use birth control. Unfortunately, it failed them—they were not just being irresponsible or using abortion as a form of birth control. As Whoopi Goldberg stated,

> *I think I went to Planned Parenthood for the abortion. They gave me birth control, the Pill, and I started to use it, but I'm one of these people they haven't made contraception strong enough for. Always, I'm pregnant: you look at me and I'm having your kid. Three times, I got pregnant using birth control. My daughter, who I had when I was eighteen and married, was a Pill baby. I had taken the Pill religiously,* religiously.... *I met a new man who had, like, sperm of doom. Every time this sperm of doom got near me, we were having kids. I got pregnant with him using a diaphragm and an IUD at the same time. (Goldberg 1991:119)*

And in fact, it is worth noting that even today, failures in birth control "account for an estimated 3.6 million pregnancies per year in the United States" (Bonavoglia 1991:xxxi).

It is also important to note that many of the women were much more ashamed of having had sex than they were of being pregnant and needing an abortion.

> *The immorality was if you got pregnant...it wasn't if you had an abortion. You were pretty damned immoral if you went and got yourself—as they used to say—knocked up. (Janeway 1991:13)*

The personal stories of women who had to seek out illegal abortions have a unique and individual flavor because each woman's experience was rooted in her own perspective and life experiences (Bonavoglia 1991). Strong emotions are evident in all the stories. Some women felt fear. Others felt humiliation. Others felt profound relief or a physical and emotional numbness. But all of them had to make a personal decision that was difficult, and they lived, or died, with the consequences.

The horror stories of women who suffered through or died from illegal abortions are an important part of our medical and social history, and they should not be forgotten, just as the women themselves should not be forgotten. Forgetting the nightmares of the past often allows them to recur in the present. One does not have to be willing to have an abortion oneself to recognize the need to keep abortion legal, for the physical and mental health of all women. We cannot take the legality of abortion for granted. It is constantly threatened by segments of our population who do not believe in a woman's right to control her own body, her own destiny.

> *There are new risks, as forces within the anti-abortion movement pursue strategies of harassment, terrorism, violence, and murder. Recently our local abortion rights fund received a piece of hate mail enjoining "pro-lifers" to "attack" abortion providers and other "peddlers of death."... When we shoot, we should aim for the lower spine and the buttocks.... Two hundred clinics were bombed in the 1980s.... Anti-abortionists have personalized and broadened their targets to include anyone who has* anything *to do with abortion, anyone at an abortion clinic. In Brookline, Massachusetts, it was the receptionists who were killed. (Fried 1998:209–210)*

The United States is one of the few industrialized countries in which abortion laws are becoming more restrictive (Hodgson 1998); even with legal abortion, access remains an issue. At this point in time, less than half of obstetrics/gynecology students in American medical schools learn how to perform abortions, even though it is one of the safest and most frequently performed medical procedures in the United States. This lack of medical training is frightening when one looks at the statistics on death-due-to-abortion before and after *Roe v. Wade.* Whereas "[t]oday, deaths from abortion are extremely rare. In 1973, the risk was 3.4 deaths per 100,000" (Bonavoglia 1991:xxiii).

We must maintain legal abortion in this country. Returning to the days of illegal abortion would not diminish the number of abortions being done. It would just increase the number of women dying from the procedure.

REFERENCES

Avery, Byllye (1991). Personal essay. Pp. 147–154 in Bonavoglia, ed., *The Choices We Made.*

Bonavoglia, Angela, ed. (1991). *The Choices We Made.* NY: Random House.

Fried, Marlene Gerber (1998). "Abortion in the United States: Legal but Inaccessible." Pp. 208–226 in Solinger, ed., *Abortion Wars.*

Goldberg, Whoopi (1991). Personal essay. Pp. 115–122 in Bonavoglia, ed., *The Choices We Made.*

Hern, Warren M. (1998). "Life on the Front Lines.' Pp. 307–319 in Solinger, ed., *Abortion Wars.*

Hodgson, Jane E. (1998). "The Twentieth-Century Gender Battle: Difficulties in Perception." Pp. 290–306 in Solinger, ed., *Abortion Wars.*

Janeway, Elizabeth (1991). Personal essay. Pp. 11–16 in Bonavoglia, ed., *The Choices We Made.*

Joffe, Carole (1991). "Portraits of Three 'Physicians of Conscience': Abortion before Legalization in the United States." *Journal of the History of Sexuality* 2(1):46–67.

Kaplan, Laura (1995). *The Story of Jane: The Legendary Underground Feminist Abortion Service.* NY: Pantheon Books.

Kaplan, Laura (1998). "Beyond Safe and Legal: The Lessons of Jane." Pp. 33–41 in Solinger, ed., *Abortion Wars.*

Kidder, Margot (1991). Personal essay. Pp. 95–100 in Bonavoglia, ed., *The Choices We Made.*

Ross, Loretta J. (1998). "African-American Women and Abortion." Pp. 157–160 in Solinger, ed., *Abortion Wars.*

Solinger, Ricki (1993). "A Complete Disaster: Abortion and the Politics of Hospital Abortion Committees, 1950–1973." *Feminist Studies* 19(2):241–268.

Solinger, Ricki, ed. (1998). *Abortion Wars: A Half Century of Struggle, 1950–2000.* Berkeley, CA: University of California Press.

Vance, Danitra (1991). Personal Essay. Pp. 89–94 in Bonavoglia, ed., *The Choices We Made.*

CHAPTER 12

THE MEDICALIZATION OF CHILDBIRTH AND THE MIDWIFERY ALTERNATIVE

The struggle over birth control, discussed in the last chapter, was defined early on as an issue of control over one's own body and one's own destiny—when and if one would bear children and assume the responsibility of motherhood. Early feminist groups and the women's health movement have seen such control as a central issue in achieving equality. This chapter, on the medicalization of childbirth, as well as Chapters 13 and 14, on the new technologies of reproduction, continue the theme of women's control of their bodies. History quite clearly demonstrates a loss of women's control over reproduction; doctors replaced midwives, and laboring women went from being active decision makers to passive recipients of care determined by experts in a technologically sophisticated profit-making setting. The ascendancy and dominance of the medical model has supported these important changes.

The medicalization of childbirth has been dramatic. The centuries-old model of women providing psychological and emotional support while helping other women birth their own children at home ended relatively abruptly. In the space of fifty years, doctors largely replaced midwives by claiming that childbirth was better seen as a pathological event, not as a natural process, and it needed to be carefully managed by trained personnel, not "ignorant" midwives.

DOCTORS MEDICALIZE CHILDBIRTH

In the mid 1800s doctors were attempting to build their profession by establishing the American Medical Association (AMA) and by decreasing competition from other health care providers. Midwives, among others, were competitors because they had access to an important clientele—pregnant women. Pregnant women represented steady work and an entree to the family for other medical needs (Scully 1994). In their effort to drive the midwives out of the birthing rooms, doctors began a vicious, racist, sexist, and classist campaign against them. They called midwifery a "relic of barbarism," and claimed that midwives were "filthy and ignorant and not far removed from the jungles of Africa, with its atmosphere of weird superstition and voodooism" (quoted in Sullivan and Weitz 1988:11; and see Rooks 1997:22–26).

The doctors' attempts to take over childbirth was successful. Their success came in part because the doctors were organized, whereas midwives were not and did not want to be. Midwives were typically connected to their women clients and their local community, not to other midwives. Doctors proposed training schools for midwives and volunteered to organize and run them. The midwives were not interested; they had valued experiential knowledge, having learned their techniques from their aunts, mothers, or grandmothers. The success of the doctors also came because of the conditions of childbirth at that time. It was an exhausting and risky event. Norms of the day, from corset wearing and passive life styles to multiple pregnancies, made women ill-prepared physically for childbirth. The possibilities that doctors promised became an attractive alternative: They were seen as "modern" and "scientific." Even a doctor's ignorant methods, which caused women to die—for example, from childbirth fever caused by his failure to wash his hands as he went from the autopsy room to the delivery room—did not stop women from assuming a doctor's methods were better than a midwife's care (Mitford 1992:30; Wertz and Wertz 1977:Chapter 4; Rooks 1997:Chapter 2).

Despite the rhetoric of the doctors' campaign, the choice to use a midwife was, at the time, a good choice for a pregnant woman. A 1914 report concluded that a pregnant woman was better off with midwifery care "than in the care of many of the physicians who compete with her" (Rooks 1997:27), and a 1925 White House Conference concluded that "untrained midwives approach, and trained midwives surpass, the record of physicians in normal deliveries" (quoted in Rooks 1997:29). But with the power of the state behind them, doctors took over, relegating midwives to the role as obstetrical backup, or limiting their practice to poor women. Midwife-assisted births declined from over half of the births just prior to the turn of the century, to 11 percent in 1935, and to only 3 percent by 1953 (Sullivan and Weitz 1988:14).

CHILDBIRTH AS PATHOLOGY REQUIRING INTERVENTION

For doctors, birth was only normal in retrospect, and, more ominously, was viewed as pathological. Dr. Joseph DeLee, the author of the most popular obstetrics textbooks of the early decades of the twentieth century, declared that childbirth was a "pathological process from which 'only a small minority of women escape damage'" and wondered "whether nature may have intended women, like salmon, to be 'used up in the process of reproduction'" (quoted in Rooks 1997:25). Such views of the pathology of pregnancy persist in statements using more modern medical jargon, as in the claims of a doctor who said in 1971 that "pregnancy should be viewed as a disease which has an 'excellent prognosis for complete, spontaneous recovery if managed under careful medical supervision'" (Rothman 1991:157). Such a view of pregnancy as a disease needing careful medical monitoring led medical schools to teach students to look for pathology, not to understand the minor discomforts of pregnancy or the normal processes of childbirth (Klass 1984; reproduced as a reading in this chapter).

As part of the required monitoring of the "disease of pregnancy and childbirth," the use of the electronic fetal monitor (EFM) became routine, despite the lack of evidence that its benefits outweighed its risks. The EFM was specifically developed for high-risk women, but due to aggressive marketing by the manufacturer (Kunisch 1989) and liability concerns of doctors and hospitals, EFM use increased so that, by 1994, 80 percent of all birthing women were monitored (Gabay and Wolfe 1997). The use of the EFM is not innocuous. It can cause fetal problems by increasing the anxiety of the woman, and it can falsely detect a fetal problem, leading to an unnecessary cesarean section (Rooks 1997:314–315).

Doctors' monitoring of labor also involved consulting the "Friedman curve," which defined the "safe" length of labor in each stage. It became dogma, and women were artificially speeded up (using, for instance, oxytocin to strengthen labor contractions) if they were too slow, which meant falling outside the so-called normal range of time. Although useful for doctors whose own time was precious, the adherence to a fixed schedule denied individual variability and meant a dramatic increase in the use of artificial rupturing of the membranes (ARM), chemical induction of labor, pain control, and cesarean sections. Between the late 1960s and the late 1980s, cesarean sections increased from 5 percent of all births to nearly 25 percent (Notzon, Placek, and Taffel 1987), making the cesarean section the most frequent surgery performed (Flamm 1993). Widespread criticism of its overuse appeared in medical and popular literature, but the overuse of cesareans was a predictable result of believing in the medical model and placing childbirth in the hands of obstetrics, a surgical specialty (Scully 1994). In contrast to England, which has a strong midwifery history and where 80 percent of birthing mothers were attended by midwives through the 1980s (Ratcliff 1994), by the 1970s, over 80 percent of American births were attended not just by doctors but by obstetrical specialists (Guillemin 1981).

The medicalization of childbirth also embraced pain as central to childbirth and increased the likelihood pain would occur (Rothman 1991:80–94). Left unsupported and sometimes alone in labor, placed in an inefficient position on her back, and exposed to interventions—repeated examinations and drugs to induce labor, which increase the strength of contractions—the woman was literally put in pain. The wisdom of Grantly Dick Read, who argued that "modern" techniques increased fear, which in turn amplified pain for the woman, was not heard in the hospitals of America. Even the recent "doula" studies (Kennell et al. 1991) have not transformed the hospital scene. These studies suggest that emotional support during childbirth by a caring person can reduce the number of interventions and produce equally good outcomes for the mothers and babies.

Instead, through the decades, various models of pain relief have become central to the birthing of babies. From about 1915 to the mid 1950s, Twilight Sleep, providing sleep, pain relief, and amnesia, was popular. As a result of the amnesia, women had no recollection of the birthing process (Mitford 1992:53–56). By the early 1960s, nearly all women (92 percent of white women and 74 percent of African Americans) were anesthetized during childbirth. "Groggy and stupefied during labor and asleep or sleepy at delivery, women as cognizant individuals were no longer involved in the process of giving birth" (Rooks 1997:53). When doctors realized that systemic painkillers were not good for the baby, general anesthesia was abandoned, replaced by a spinal anesthesia. This, too, had its problems, slowing the contractions, rendering the woman unable to actively push, and necessitating forceps for over half of the deliveries. The end of the twentieth century saw a turn to a new pain reliever—regional epidurals. Their use more than doubled between 1981 and 1992, until one-half (51 percent) of the women delivering in large hospitals were given an epidural (American Society of Anesthesiologists 1999). Epidurals increase the likelihood of induced labor, forceps, and cesarean sections (Rooks 1997:316).

Pain relief has not always been pushed on unsuspecting women. Rather, women have sometimes actively demanded pain relief options. The popularity of Twilight Sleep came not from doctors promoting it, but rather from women who learned about it and then began a campaign to demand its availability (Mitford 1992; Caton 1999:Chapter 8). Some argue that one of the reasons for the extensive use of artificial pain relief is that we have lost our cultural knowledge of normal childbirth (Rooks 1997:463). Neither doctors nor women have the personal experience with normal childbirth that women a hundred years ago did. Fear of the process and the pain have become the common understanding, and, as a result, we ask for pain relief.

As the self-proclaimed experts on childbirth, doctors made many assertions unsupported by scientific evidence. Perineal shaving and giving laboring women an enema, begun as a misguided attempt to control the sanitation of the birthing room, became routinized procedures. Even in relatively recent years, doctors have used procedures without evidence of their safety or effectiveness. Drugs have been prescribed during pregnancy because doctors viewed the womb as a protective, impenetrable container for the fetus. Thus DES for pregnant women (later found to cause cancer in offspring) seemed reasonable to prevent miscarriages (Chapter 16), and X rays to determine fetal position were done as late as the 1980s. During the 1950s and 1960s, doctors strictly limited weight gain during pregnancy—even prescribing diet pills to women—because doctors decided arbitrarily on an optimal weight gain. Studies now show that the restriction of weight gain can be detrimental to the baby. Until quite recently, episiotomies (an incision to enlarge the vaginal opening) were routine, again despite lack of evidence of their effectiveness; recent evidence contradicts the practice (Woolley 1995).

CRITICS OF THE BIOMEDICAL MODEL

Critics of the medicalized view argue that the resulting high-tech, high-intervention treatment distorts the human experience of pregnancy and childbirth; exposes women and babies to many unnecessary, intrusive, and potentially dangerous medical procedures; and takes control over pregnancy and birth away from women (Davis-Floyd 1992; Rothman 1991). The most cohesive and comprehensive critique comes from midwifery proponents. The midwifery model views births as a natural process in which normalcy and variation are to be expected. A midwife must remain vigilant for indications of problems requiring intervention and medical assistance, but must be wary of the false positive—assuming problems when there are none. Midwifery challenges hospital routines developed from tradition, not evidence; and designed for the convenience of the doctor, not the woman. A good midwife knows the woman and discusses relevant social and psychological issues with the woman. The midwife supports the laboring woman as central to the birth of her child and as an active decision maker.

Though midwives were largely driven out of practice early in this century, individual lay midwives who depended on experiential knowledge from an apprenticeship persisted in rural and poor areas, especially in the south and in African American communities where doctors did not want to provide care (Davis and Ingram 1993). In addition, organizations of midwives established early in the twentieth century became the foundation for the new midwifery—direct-entry midwifery (midwives without a nursing degree), nurse-midwifery, and then, more formally, certified nurse-midwifery (CNM). Mary Breckenridge brought British nurse-midwives to the Frontier Nursing Service to provide care in poor mountainous areas of Kentucky, and the Maternity Nursing Center Association in New York City used public health nurses to serve the inner city poor. Both represented a more acceptable form of midwifery that embraced nursing. The Maternity Nursing Center Association founded the first American nurse-midwifery program in 1931. Twenty years later, the American College of Nurse Midwifery was incorporated (Rooks 1997).

The late 1960s and 1970s began the real transformation of American midwifery. The women's health movement, the increasing dissatisfaction of middle-class women with technologically intrusive, interventionist births, and the successful midwifery models of other countries created a demand for alternative birth attendants. This demand fostered a growth in direct-entry midwifery and home birth. Direct-entry midwifery changed as many states established licensing requirements for practitioners, other states merely tolerated midwives who had no nursing background, and still others considered it illegal. Direct-entry midwifery was successful in many communities and was an important part of care not just for poor and rural mothers, but also for middle-class women. Although nurse-midwifery has thrived in the United States more than direct-entry midwifery, attempts to build a community among all midwives regardless of training have been successful; the Midwives Alliance of North America (MANA) was founded in 1982.

Nurse-midwifery was more acceptable to the establishment because the midwife received her training in a conventional medical setting, first as a nurse, then as a midwife. In 1971, CNMs were approved by the American College of Obstetricians and Gynecologists. CNMs practice in a variety of settings. Some became glorified obstetrical nurses in hospital settings, specializing in the care of birthing mothers, but relinquishing care to the doctor at the point of birth and allowing him to deliver the baby. In hospital settings, organizational rules inhibit midwives in other ways from implementing a true midwifery model. Midwives realize these constraints if they move from the hospital setting to a home setting. For example, attending a home birth allows a midwife to ignore the dictates of the Friedman curve. Using her experiential knowledge of the woman and normal birthing, a midwife can interpret a woman's slowness in the birthing process as her taking a rest (a good idea), rather than her having "arrested labor" (a problem). Acting on such an interpretation, a midwife can wait and do nothing other than provide support and encouragement, and then allow nature to take its course. Such an experience becomes radicalizing, because it provides empirical evidence that the hospital schedules are not needed (Rothman 1983; Davis-Floyd and Davis 1997). Some nurse–midwives have practiced in birth centers, which free the nurse–midwife from many of the hospital routines, though this setting may still constrain the midwife (Turkel, 1995, reproduced as a reading in this chapter).

SAFETY AND OPPOSITION

Study after study indicates that midwifery is safe. Several national groups have attested to the benefits of midwifery care. In 1985 the Institute of Medicine encouraged the use of CNMs; in 1986 the Congressional Office of Technology Assessment cited the benefits of CNMs with a normal pregnancy; the National Committee to Prevent Infant Mortality called on state universities to increase training for CNMs (Rooks 1990); and in 1989 the *New England Journal of Medicine* said that the birthing centers staffed by midwives were safe and acceptable (Rooks et al. 1989). There were even reports of the benefits of direct-entry midwifery: The *American Journal of Public Health* reported in 1992 that the home birth service in rural Tennessee, The Farm, provided a birthing setting as safe as a physician-attended hospital delivery (Durand 1992).

Yet despite this recognition of a safe alternative model for childbirth, and despite the fact that it is a successful model in other industrialized countries, midwifery has remained a contested practice in the United States. Many doctors will not accept the pregnancy-as-normal model and instead see midwives as a threat to their practice. Physicians' organizations have formally opposed midwifery, as, for example, in the case of the American Academy of Family Physicians, which declared, "The use of nurse–midwives is not in the best interests of quality patient care" (quoted in Rooks 1997:83). Attacks against direct-entry midwifery are particularly vicious (Sullivan and Weitz 1988), but midwives in the hospital meet considerable resistance, causing some to leave and others to practice a modified form of midwifery, accepting more of the hospital routine than they would like (Langton 1994). Independent CNMs need to find obstetricians to work with them as backup, but may find that "[p]hysicians have many effective ways to 'resist' midwives, including denial of CNM applications for hospital privileges, demands for unreasonable levels of professional liability insurance...and professional ostracism of doctors who work with midwives" (Rooks 1997:78). Midwives working in freestanding birth centers may have problems obtaining physician backup (Turkel 1995, reproduced here).

This opposition from doctors is not surprising. The midwifery model embodies a totally different perspective on childbirth. It says that childbirth is a natural process that rarely goes wrong, that the woman should be an active person who births her child, and that medical doctors, technology, and interventions are rarely needed. Both the midwifery philosophy of birth as normal and the statement of who is the appropriate health care person for most births run counter to the beliefs and self-interests of doctors.

Despite physician opposition, nurse-midwifery has established itself legally in all states in the United States. Acceptance of midwifery came in part from the shortage of physicians in the mid 1960s. At that time, training programs began for a number of "midlevel health care providers," including nurse practitioners and physician assistants. State and federal initiatives supported this new category of providers, greatly benefitting nurse–midwives. Their greater acceptance is evident in most states' regulations (39 states in 1995), which grant them permission to write prescriptions, as well as in federal law, which requires state Medicaid programs to pay for nurse–midwife care (Rooks 1997:161). The number of in-hospital births attended by midwives has increased from less than 1 percent in 1975 to just over 5 percent in 1994 (Gabay and Wolfe 1997). Some analyses of this growth suggest that managed care will create even more new openings for nurse–midwives (Hartley 1999).

Attention to the appropriate care of pregnant and laboring women is long overdue. Infant mortality statistics place the United States far behind comparable countries. The primary response to the unhealthy statistics of childbirth has been to follow the biomedical model's dictate of finding a cure: The United States has invested in Neonatal Intensive Care Units, which save low-birth weight babies much more successfully than other countries. We have failed to make a comparable investment in prevention of high-risk births, by providing prenatal care for all women and adequately supporting the safe and empowering model of childbirth represented by midwifery.

BEARING A CHILD IN MEDICAL SCHOOL

PERRI KLASS

One day last year, I sat with my classmates in our reproductive medicine course in Amphitheater E at the Harvard Medical School, listening to a lecture on the disorders of pregnancy. The professor discussed ectopic pregnancy, toxemia, spontaneous abortion and major birth defects. I was eight months pregnant. I sat there, rubbing my belly, telling my baby: "Don't worry, you're O.K, you're healthy." I sat there wishing that this course would tell us more about normal pregnancy, that after memorizing all the possible disasters, we would be allowed to conclude that pregnancy itself is not a state of disease. But I think most of us, including me, came away from the course with a sense that pregnancy is a deeply dangerous medical condition, that one walks a fine line, avoiding one serious problem after another, to reach the statistically unlikely outcome of a healthy baby and a healthy mother.

I learned I was pregnant the afternoon of my anatomy exam. I had spent the morning taking first a written exam and then a practical, centered on 15 thoroughly dissected cadavers, each ornamented with little paper tags indicating structures to be identified.

My classmates and I were not looking very good—our hair unwashed, our faces pale from too much studying and too little sleep. Two more exams and our first year of medical school would be over. We all knew exactly what we had to do next: go home and study for tomorrow's exam. I could picture my genetics notes lying on my desk, liberally highlighted with pink marker. But before I went home, I had a pregnancy test.

My period was exactly one day late, hardly worth noticing—but the month before, for the first time, I had been trying to get pregnant.

Four hours later, I called for the test results. "It's positive," the woman at the lab told me.

With all the confidence of a first-year medical student, I asked: "Positive, what does that mean?"

"It means you're pregnant," she said. "Congratulations."

Somewhat later that afternoon, I settled down to make final review notes for my genetics exam. *Down's syndrome,* I copied carefully onto a clean sheet of paper *the most common autosomal trisomy disorder, one per 700 live births.* I began to feel a little queasy. Over the next 24 hours, I was supposed to memorize the biological basis, symptoms, diagnosis and treatment of a long list of genetic disorders. Almost every one was something that could conceivably already be wrong with the embryo growing inside me. I couldn't even think about it; I would have to pass the exam on what I remembered from the lectures.

Over the following months, as I went through my pregnancy and my second year of medical school, I became more and more aware of two aspects of my life influencing each other, and even sometimes seeming to oppose each other. As a medical student, I was spending my time studying everything that can go wrong with the human body. As a pregnant woman, I became suddenly passionately interested in healthy physiological processes, in my own, normal, pregnancy and the growth of my baby. And yet pregnancy put me under the care of the medical profession—my own future profession—and I found myself rebelling as a mother and "patient" against the attitudes the profession conveyed, particularly that pregnancy was somehow a perilous, if not pathological state.

My pregnancy and the decisions I had to make about my own health care changed forever my feelings about the science of medicine and its view of emergency and intervention. My pregnancy became for me almost a rebellion against this view, a chance to do something healthy and normal with my body, something that would be a joyous event, a complex event but not necessarily a medical event.

Medical school lasts four years, followed by an internship and residency program—three years for medicine and five to seven for surgery—and then maybe a two-year fellowship for those pursuing a specialty.

"The fellowship years can be a good time to have a baby," advised one physician. She was just finishing a fellowship in primary care. "Not internship or residency, God knows—that's when your marriage breaks up since you're working 80 hours a week and you're so miserable all the time."

I was 25 years old. After college, I hadn't gone straight to medical school, but had spent two years doing graduate work in biology and one living abroad. I would probably reach the fellowship stage by around 33. It seemed a long time to wait.

The more I thought about it, the more it seemed that there was no time in the next seven or so years when it would be as feasible to have a baby as the present. As a medical student, I had a flexibility that I would not really have further on, a freedom to take a couple of months off or even a year if I decided I needed it, and without unduly disrupting the progress of my career. Larry Wolff, the baby's father, was also 25 and was finishing his doctoral dissertation on Polish–Vatican relations in the late 18th century for a Ph.D. from Stanford. He was also teaching at Harvard, which allowed him a great deal of flexibility. Both our lives frequently had a slightly frantic quality, but we didn't foresee a less complicated, less frantic future.

I decided against taking a leave of absence right away. Instead, Larry and I started the juggling games that, no doubt, will be a major feature of the years ahead; I took extra courses so I might manage a comparatively light schedule the following spring and stay with the baby two days a week while Larry worked at home the other three. Perfect timing was, of course, of the essence; happily, we'd managed to conceive the baby so it would be born between the time I took my exams in December 1983 and the time I started my hospital course work the following March.

There was one other factor in my decision to have a baby when I did. All through my first year of medical school, in embryology, in genetics, even in public health, lecturers kept emphasizing that the ideal time to have a baby is in the mid-20s—safest for the mother, safest for the baby. "Do you think they're trying to tell us something?" grumbled one of my classmates after a particularly pointed lecture. "Like, why are we wasting these precious childbearing years in school? It almost makes you feel guilty about waiting to have children."

Ironically, I knew no one else my age who was having a baby. The women in my childbirth class were all in their mid-30's. "Having a baby is a very 1980's thing to do," said a friend who is a 27-year-old corporate lawyer in New York. "The only thing is, you and Larry are much too young." In medical school one day, when I was several months along, a lecturer mentioned the problem of teen-age pregnancy, and half the class turned to look at me.

In theory, medical education teaches first about normal anatomy and normal physiology, and then it builds upon this foundation by teaching the processes of pathology and disease. In practice, everyone—students and teachers alike—is eager to get to the material with "clinical relevance," and the whole thrust of the teaching is toward using examples of disease to elucidate normal body functions; specifically, what happens when such functions fail. For example, we understand sugar metabolism partially because of studies on diabetics, who can't metabolize sugar normally. "An experiment of nature" is the phrase often used.

Although we learned a great deal about disease, we did not, in our first year of medical school, learn much about the nitty-gritty of medical practice. As I began to wonder more about what was happening inside me and about what childbirth would be like, I tried to read my embryology textbook but, again, the pictures of various abnormal fetuses upset me. Instead, I read some books written for pregnant women, not medical students.

Suzanne Arms's *Immaculate Deception: A New Look at Childbirth in America,* for instance, was a passionate attack on American childbirth which argues that many routine hospital practices are psychologically damaging and medically hazardous. In particular, the author protested the "traditional birth," a euphemism for giving birth while lying down, a position that is less effective and more dangerous than many others, but convenient for the doctor. An intravenous line is often attached to the arm or an electronic fetal heart monitor strapped to the belly. "Traditional" almost always means a routine episiotomy, a surgical incision to allow the baby's head to emerge without tearing the mother.

Whose "traditions" are these, incorporating interventions designed for problem births into each and every birth? They are traditions developed and perpetuated by doctors trained to define a normal birth as a "negative" event—one with the fortuitous absence of complications. I did not want that kind of traditional birth. I found myself nervously reviewing my own risk factors: I was the perfect age to be having a baby, I had no diabetes or heart disease, I had "a completely negative family history"—none of my close relatives have suffered from obstetrical problems or birth defects. I actually expected to discover some horrendous, lurking source of danger. I reassured myself that I would accept intervention if things went wrong; I just resented the idea that it might be routine.

I decided I would have to shop for a doctor. By this time, I had begun to wonder whether I wanted to have the baby in a hospital at all; when I was a graduate student in California, I knew several people, all biologists like me, who had given birth at home. In the Netherlands, home birth is the norm, and infant mortality rates there have consistently been lower than in the United States.

In our reproductive medicine course last fall, the issue of home birth came up exactly once, in a "case" for discussion. "B B is a 25-year-old married graduate student," the case began. B B, who showed no unusual symptoms and had no relevant past medical problems, had a completely normal pregnancy. When the pregnancy reached full term, the summary concluded, "No factors have been identified to suggest increased risk." Then, the first question: Do you think she should choose to deliver at home?

The doctor leading our discussion section read the question aloud and waited. "No," chorused the class.

"Why not?" asked the doctor.

"Well, there's always the chance of a complication," said one of the students.

B B went two and a half weeks past her due date, began to show signs of fetal distress and was ultimately delivered by Caesarean section after the failure of induced labor. Clearly, B B's case was supposed to teach us something. It was hard for me to read the case without getting the impression that all of B B's problems were a kind of divine retribution for even considering a home birth.

When Larry and I looked into a home birth, we found other problems. For one thing, although it is much cheaper than a hospital birth, my insurance would pay only for the latter. For another, I was frankly not sure I had the moral strength to go ahead with a home birth in a situation in which

I would meet with nothing but disapproval from the people around me. As a woman who had given birth at home told me, "You have to accept that if anything goes wrong—even if it's something that would have gone wrong in a hospital, even if it's something like a birth defect—if you have the baby at home, everyone will blame you."

We eventually decided on a hospital birth with a doctor whose inclination was clearly against intervention except when absolutely necessary. In our interview with him, he volunteered the Caesarean and episiotomy figures for his practice. He also regarded the issue of what kind of birth we wanted as an appropriate subject for our first meeting. "A low-tech birth?" he said, sounding amused. "You're at Harvard Medical School and you want a low-tech birth?"

Our doctor suggested we inspect several hospitals at which he performed deliveries. We toured a large teaching hospital where I would probably spend part of the next two years. The labor and delivery floor is usually busy, often with five or six women in labor at one time, and residents and interns and medical students all trying to get the "clinical experience" that is the real stuff of medical training. Inevitably, in such a busy place, some regimentation develops. And perhaps also inevitably, with so many people eager to get their hands on patients, the regimentation may be biased in the direction of more procedures, more interventions. The nurse leading the tour told us exactly what would happen to us, and, if we questioned a procedure, referred us to our doctors in a tone of surprised disapproval.

We chose another hospital, a smaller one near our home. The nurse who took us around referred decisions to us as well as to our doctor and suggested we send a "wish list" to the hospital a few weeks before our due date, specifying any particular requests we had for the birth.

At the beginning of my eighth month, we went to the hospital for the first meeting of a childbirth class. I had great hopes for this class; I was tired of feeling like the only pregnant person in the world. My medical school classmates had continued to be extremely kind and considerate, but as I moved around the school I was beginning to feel like a lone hippopotamus in a gaggle of geese. I wanted some other people with whom Larry and I could go over the questions we discussed endlessly with each other: How do we know when it's time to leave for the hospital? What is labor going to feel like? What can we do to make it go more easily?

At the first meeting it became clear that that class's major purpose was to prepare people to be good patients. It was like that first hospital tour. The teacher exposed us to various procedures so that we would cooperate properly when they were performed on us. Asked whether a given procedure was absolutely necessary, she said that it was up to her doctor.

I found a childbirth class that met at a local day-care center; we sat on cushions on the floor, surrounded by toys and children's work. Many members of the class were fairly hostile toward the medical profession; once again I was greeted with the odd remark: "A medical student and you think you want a natural birth? Don't you get thrown out of school for that?" This class was, if anything, designed to teach people how to be "bad patients." The teacher explained the pros and cons of the various interventions, and we discussed under what circumstances we might or might not accept them.

The childbirth classes not only prepared me well for labor, but also provided that feeling of community I wanted. Yet they also left me feeling pulled between two poles, especially when I went to medical school during the day to discuss deliveries going wrong in one catastrophic way after another ("C-section, C-section!" our class would chorus when the teacher asked what we would do next) and to childbirth class in the evening to discuss ways to circumvent unwanted medical procedures. As a medical student, I knew I was being trained to rely heavily on technology, to assume that the risk of acting is almost always preferable to the risk of not acting. I consciously had to fight these attitudes when I thought about giving birth.

In our reproductive medicine course, the emphasis was on the abnormal, the pathological.

The only thing said about nutrition, for example, was in passing—nobody knows how much weight a pregnant woman should gain, but "about 24 pounds" is considered good. In contrast, the other women in my childbirth class and I were very concerned with what we ate; we were always exchanging suggestions about how to get through those interminable four glasses of milk a day. We learned nothing in medical school about exercise, though exercise books and classes aimed at pregnant women have proliferated.

Will we, as doctors, be able to give valid advice about diet and exercise during pregnancy?

We learned nothing about any of the problems encountered in a normal pregnancy. All we learned about morning sickness was that it could be controlled with a drug, a drug some women were reluctant to take because some studies had linked it to birth defects. (The drug, Bendectin, which had been on the market 27 years, was withdrawn last year.) We learned nothing about the emotional aspects of pregnancy, nothing about helping women prepare for labor and delivery. In other words, none of my medical-school classmates would have been capable of answering even the most basic questions about pregnancy asked by the people in my childbirth class. The important issues for future doctors simply did not overlap with the important issues for future parents.

I mentioned this to my doctor, explaining that I was tormented by fears of every possible abnormality. "Yes," he said, "normal birth is not honored enough in the curriculum. Most of us doctors are going around looking for pathology and feeling good about ourselves when we find it because that's what we were trained to do. We aren't trained to find joy in a normal pregnancy."

I tried to find joy in my own pregnancy. I am sure that the terrors that sometimes visited me in the middle of the night were no more intense than those which visit most expectant mothers. (Will the labor go well? Will the baby be O.K.?) But I probably had more specific fears than many, as I lay awake wondering about atrial septal heart defects or placenta previa and hemorrhage. And perhaps I did worry more than I might once have, because my faith in the normal had been weakened. In my dark moments, I, too, had begun to see healthy development as less than probable, as the highly unlikely avoidance of a million abnormalities.

I knew that many of my classmates were worrying with me; I cannot count the number of times I was asked whether I had had amniocentesis, the procedure by which fluid is drawn from the amniotic sac and tested for chromosomal abnormalities, particularly Down's syndrome. When I pointed out that we had been taught that amniocentesis is not generally recommended for women under the age of 35, my classmates tended to look worried and mutter something about being *sure.*

The height of the ridiculous came when a young man in class asked me: "Have you had all those genetic tests? Like for sickle-cell anemia?"

I looked at him. He is white. I am white. "I'm not in the risk group for sickle-cell," I said gently.

"Yeah, I know,' he said, "but if there's even a one in a zillion chance…"

My class in medical school was absorbing the idea that when it comes to tests, technology and interventions, more is better. No one in reproductive medicine ever talked about the negative aspects of intervention, and the one time a student asked about the "appropriateness" of fetal monitoring, the question was cut off with a remark that there was no time to discuss issues of "appropriateness." There was also no time to discuss techniques for attending women in labor—except as they related to labor emergencies.

We were also absorbing the attitude, here as in other courses, that most decisions were absolutely out of the reach of nonphysicians. The risks of catastrophe were so constant—how could we let patients take chances like this with their lives? Dangers that could be controlled by pregnant women—cigarettes, alcohol and drug use—were de-emphasized. Instead, we were taught to think in terms of medical emergencies. Gradually, pregnancy itself began to sound like a medical emergency, a situation in which the pregnant woman, referred to as "the patient," must be carefully guided to a safe delivery, almost in spite of herself. As we spent more and more time absorbing the vocabulary of medicine, we became less inclined to think about communicating our knowledge to those lacking the vocabulary.

Some aspects of having a baby while in medical school were very positive. My courses in anatomy, physiology and embryology deepened my awe of the miracle going on inside me. When I looked ahead to the birth, I thought of what we learned about the incredible changeover taking place during the first minutes of life, the details involved in the switch to breathing air, changes in circulation. I appreciated pregnancy in a way I never could have before.

Another wonderful thing about having a baby in medical school was the support and attention I got from my classmates. Perhaps because having a baby seemed a long way off to many of them, there was some tendency to regard mine as a "class baby." My classmates held a baby shower for Larry and me, and presented us with a fabulous assortment of items for infants. At the end of the shower, I lay back on the couch with five medical students feeling my abdomen, finding the baby's bottom, the baby's foot.

I want to believe that I will be a better doctor because I have combined medical school with this experience of having to choose and control medical care for myself. I want to believe that the classmates who were feeling my abdomen, all people I like very much, will also be good doctors. I want to believe that we will take away the important factual knowledge from our courses, but without absorbing all the attitudes that come with it. I also want to believe that obstetrical medicine will change, but I do not really believe that it will change from within.

And so, in the end, I find myself hoping most of all that expectant parents and others will continue to pressure the medical profession to change, to relinquish some of its control over childbirth, to take a more fair-minded attitude toward the risks of intervention versus the risks of nonintervention, to provide more options and more information and, above all, to stop regarding pregnancy and childbirth as exclusively "medical" events.

Our son, Benjamin Orlando, was born on Jan. 28. Naturally, I would like to be able to say that all our planning and preparing was rewarded with a perfectly smooth labor and delivery. But, of course, biology doesn't work that way. The experience did provide me with a rather ironic new wrinkle on the whole idea of interventions. Most of the labor was quite ordinary. "You're demonstrating a perfect Friedman labor curve," the doctor said to me at one point. "You must have been studying!"

At the end, however, I had great difficulty pushing the baby out. After the pushing stage had gone on for quite a while, I was absolutely exhausted, though the baby was fine. There were no signs of fetal distress, and the head was descending steadily. Still, the pushing had gone on much longer than is usual, and I was aware that two doctors and a number of nurses were now in the birthing room.

Suddenly, I heard one of the doctors say something about forceps. At that moment, I found an extra ounce of strength and pushed my baby out.

As I lay back with my son wriggling on my stomach, the birthing room was suddenly transformed into the most beautiful place on earth. I heard one of the nurses say to another, "You see this all the time with these birthing-room-natural-childbirth mothers—you just mention forceps and they get those babies born."

FREE-STANDING BIRTH CENTERS

KATHLEEN DOHERTY TURKEL

Free-standing birth centers (FSBCs) are nonhospital birthing facilities which are geographically and, usually, administratively separate from hospitals. It is important to distinguish free-standing birth centers from alternative birth centers (ABCs) which are in-hospital facilities which provide family-centered maternity care. Although ABCs may have a more homelike appearance than standard hospital labor and delivery facilities, all the high-tech equipment which has come to characterize hospital birth is at hand. Such equipment is hidden behind curtains or screens or in drawers, or it may be wheeled in as needed (Klee, 1986).

Primary care in free-standing birth centers is usually provided by nurse-midwives. The National Birth Center Study (Rooks et al., 1989) reported that certified nurse-midwives and students of nurse-midwifery provided the care during 78.6 percent of the labors and 80.6 percent of the births which occurred at the centers participating in the study. But birth centers are not always owned by nurse-midwives. In the summer of 1984 the National Association of Childbearing Centers (NACC) surveyed those birth centers known to them at the time. Questionnaires were mailed to 130 centers. Of these, 93 centers responded. Only 15 percent of the centers responding were owned by nurse-midwives alone. Physicians owned 32.2 percent. In a few cases centers were co-owned by nurse-midwives and physicians. Other centers were owned by a hospital, business group, community agency, or religious order (*NACC News,* fall/winter 1984–85). More recent research indicates that the trend toward physician ownership has continued and is increasing (Mathews and Zadak, 1991).

Care in birth centers reflects the assumptions that pregnant women are healthy as a rule and that pregnancy is a healthy process. Ideally birth takes place within the context of the family, and control rests with the family. There is a focus on prevention, of which education is an important part. When women have information about pregnancy they can care for themselves in ways which help to insure healthy outcomes. Ernst maintains that the model of care at birth centers is the midwifery model. Most nurse-midwives practicing in birth centers embrace the woman-centered approach which this model implies. Care is involved and intimate. Importance is attached to a close relationship between clients and caregivers, rooted in a sharing of information and mutual respect. There is a commitment on the part of caregivers that responsibility and control should rest with clients (Ernst, 1985).

At the same time that birth centers challenge the medical model, they are part of the system of health care delivery. Eunice Ernst, former executive director of the National Association of Childbearing Centers, has said that the birth center is "a first level of entry into an interdependent system for providing comprehensive care which requires providers to bring together their individual knowledge, skills, and services to form a unified whole" (Ernst, 1985). To this end nurse-midwives working in birth centers usually work in collaboration with physicians who provide consultation and backup. If complications arise during a birth which require a hospital transfer, a backup physician will take over in the hospital setting. In many cases, nurse-midwives can accompany their clients to the hospital and remain with them throughout the labor and birth.

Births at birth centers generally involve little intervention. Women are encouraged to labor at home until they are in active labor. Once they arrive at the centers in labor, they are encouraged and supported to give birth without painkilling medication or augmentation. Episiotomies are not done routinely. Most women continue to eat or drink during labor. Women can take showers or baths for relaxation. Most women at birth centers are accompanied by family and friends, often including other children, who are encouraged to be involved during labor and birth. Family and friends are also welcome at prenatal visits.

Although routine intervention is avoided at birth centers, birth center births involve more intervention than home births. In the 11,814 birth center births studied by Rooks et al. (1989) 1.3 percent involved artificial rupture of the membranes or oxytocin to induce labor. Intravenous infusions were used in 14.7 percent of the cases and 9.3 percent of the women in the sample had enemas. Twenty-four percent of women giving birth for the first time had an analgesic, tranquilizer, or sedative during labor, compared with 6.2 percent of the women who had had one or more previous births. Vacuum extraction was used in 0.4 percent of the births and forceps in 0.2 percent. Episiotomies were done in 17.6 percent of the cases.

Women seeking care in an FSBC must be judged to be at low risk for obstetrical complications. The criteria for judging risk are generally the same as those used by obstetricians. Birth center care is provided in a comfortable, homelike atmosphere. Centers differ quite a bit one from the next, but they share some similarities. The birthing rooms look like bedrooms which might be found in a typical home. Many birth centers have other rooms which can be used by birthing women, their families, and friends. There might be a kitchen for preparing meals or snacks, a place for watching TV, and spaces where children can play. The birth center which I studied has, among other amenities, a Jacuzzi which can be used for relaxation during labor.

BIRTH CENTERS AND THE MEDICAL MODEL: ISSUES OF POWER AND CONTROL

The first birth centers were formed to serve rural populations. In 1975, the Maternity Center Association of New York City (MCA) established the first free-standing birth center in an urban area (Rooks et al., 1989). The initiative to do so came from a new determination in some childbearing couples to stay out of the hospital for birth. According to Lubic (1981), these families needed three things from their childbirth experience—safety, satisfaction, and economy—which the medical model was not supplying. The Maternity Center Association had four possible options in trying to meet the needs of disaffected childbearing couples: (1) try to humanize the hospital setting; (2) establish a freestanding, full-scale maternity hospital; (3) return to a home birth system similar to one which they had operated from 1931 to 1959; or (4) open a free-standing birth center.

They chose the last option, believing that it best met the three criteria. In January 1974, MCA's board of directors filed an application with the state of New York for permission to establish a center. MCA was required to demonstrate both the need for and the feasibility of the project they were proposing. They were expected to provide evidence of the qualifications of future staff along with backup letters of support from obstetricians, pediatricians, and public health physicians. The model for the center was the home, not the hospital. Care was to be provided by a team consisting of obstetricians, nurse-midwives, pediatricians, and public health nurses. Client families would be directly involved in decision making. Four nearby hospitals agreed to provide emergency backup, and the Visiting Nurse Service of New York agreed to do follow-up home visits.

There was, of course, opposition to the project from some members of the medical community, particularly obstetricians and pediatricians. A well-known neonatologist suggested that those involved with the project would "kill babies" (Lubic, 1981, p. 232). There were meetings held to answer criticisms launched by the medical community, including the following objections: (1) that the MCA birth center would be too far from a hospital to be safe (the closest backup hospital was seven blocks away) and (2) that the MCA staff would be unable to define "normal" in a way that would avoid risk to babies. One recommendation which came out of the discussion was that MCA should try to formalize backup arrangements with one hospital rather than four.

There were some minor confrontations with the city of New York and some difficulties over third-party reimbursement, but the MCA Childbearing Center did open in September 1975. Some problems continued after the center's opening. The state notified MCA that it required a formal written agreement with the backup hospital. When the center opened in 1975, they had four such agreements. In June 1976, MCA received word from one of their backup hospitals that they were canceling the agreement because they were going to become self-insured. Several months later another backup institution canceled the arrangement, citing disapproval of the project by the obstetrical profession as the reason. A short time later, the health department began to insist on an updated formal agreement and one of the original four hospitals did agree to update its arrangement. Other problems soon surfaced. One of the backup physicians was told that he would have his hospital admitting privileges revoked if he continued his work with the Childbearing Center.

While the MCA Childbearing Center was established and continues to operate, some of the same problems which plagued Nurse-Midwifery Associates were also evident here. Problems with physician backup and institutional support were most critical. MCA was able to work out arrangements which made it possible for them to remain in operation, but as the Nurse-Midwifery Associates case demonstrates, that is not always possible.

Lubic (1981) argues that childbearing centers threaten both medical control and the fee-for-service model of health care. Interestingly, however, Lubic also argues that childbearing centers also pose a threat to some nurse-midwives who have been practicing in a hospital setting and have become dependent upon physicians and hospital-based technology. Such centers also threaten those nurse-midwives who emulate the economic aspects of the medical model and whose primary goal is making more money. For them, the salary structure of birth centers may be unacceptable. Lubic states: "In our experience and opinion midwifery in CbC [childbearing centers] offers satisfactions which cannot be approached in the hospital setting. Essential to the viability of such centers will be the nurse-midwife's understanding that the costs of normal childbirth must be reduced and the extraordinary monetary rewards of physician specialists cannot be considered an approachable standard" (Lubic, 1981, p. 245).

According to Lubic, the only way to avoid high-tech obstetrics is to remove birth from the hospital setting. Despite strong opposition MCA did establish a low-cost facility where nurse-midwives can practice free of the constraints which hospitals impose (Edwards and Waldorf, 1984, pp. 183–185). Since 1975, at least 240 other birth centers have opened in the United States, although many of these have since closed, primarily as a result of the malpractice insurance crisis (Rooks et al., 1989). As of 1995, NACC in conjunction with the ACNM, an insurance administrator, and insurance companies, have put together an insurance package specifically for birth centers. The package covers all members of the birth center staff including nurses, nurse-midwives, and consulting physicians. At present, part-time staff members are not covered by the package but such coverage may be available in the future.

Rothman (1989, 1983, 1982) has argued that when nurse-midwives work in the physician-controlled environment of the hospital, they are not free to develop their own knowledge or to train incoming nurse-midwives according to their own standards and criteria. Professional autonomy for nurse-midwives may require that they opt out of the medical system. As pointed out earlier, however, this is not easy to do. Nurse-midwives are dependent upon physicians for backup services. Ideally, the relationship between nurse-midwives and their backup physicians is trusting and collegial, but this is not always the case. This is particularly a problem for nurse-midwives who attend home births.

Attending home births also presents some other problems for nurse-midwives. Physician backup is sometimes difficult to come by. Often nurse-midwives are not permitted to accompany home birth clients to the hospital when a transfer occurs. Nurse-midwives who provide home birth services find themselves on call most of the time. If they practice alone they have the constant worry about what to do if two clients go into labor at the same time. The time demands of a home birth practice make it necessary to limit the number of one's clients. This, in turn, means that it is sometimes difficult to support oneself on the income from a home-birth practice (Rothman, 1983).

Free-standing birth centers can provide a compromise for nurse-midwives between the hospital environment and a home-based practice. Free-standing birth centers may provide as ideal a work setting for nurse-midwives as they are likely to find (Rothman, 1983). Centers can provide for nurse-midwives the advantages which hospitals provide for practitioners. In birth centers, for example, there is often a shared responsibility with other nurse-midwives. This is, of course, dependent upon how many nurse-midwives are on staff. It is typically the case that nurse-midwives practicing in birth centers have an agreement with a physician or physicians who will provide consultation and backup services. Within the setting of the birth center, nurse-midwives are usually free from the legal vulnerability which often plagues home birth practitioners.

Birth centers also usually provide nurse-midwives with a high degree of professional autonomy to make decisions and set policy. It is important to note, however, that the degree of autonomy over policy depends upon the kind of administrative relationship which birth centers have with hospitals. Annandale (1988), for example, writes about nurse-midwives practicing in a birth center licensed through an adjacent hospital. Although Annandale characterizes this birth center as free-standing, the administrative connection to the hospital gives the hospital a great deal of control over the practice of the nurse-midwives at the center. Annandale's study demonstrates this point. During the first four years of operation at the center, there were no formal restrictions put on the timing of labor or on when a backup obstetrician should be consulted. In the middle of the fourth year, however, new protocols were introduced which required (1) that pelvic examinations be done every three hours once a woman was in active labor and (2) that a physician be called if a woman had been pushing for two hours, if she had been fully dilated for two hours, or if she was in active labor and had made no progress for three hours. The changes were made as a result of pressure from the hospital administration and obstetricians.

Annandale (1988) argues that nurse-midwifery practice in a free-standing birth center actually represents an interaction between the medical and midwifery models. The midwives Annandale studied saw birth as an instinctual process. Birthing women were encouraged to follow their "natural instincts" and "take responsibility" for the birth. Women were expected to be active participants in their own care. At prenatal visits they were expected to weigh themselves and do their own urinalysis and then enter this data on their medical charts. There was also the stated expectation that women could "run their own labor" (Annandale, 1988, p. 96). However, pressure from obstetricians that births conform to particular patterns and standards often ran directly contrary to the values of the nurse-midwives. In addition, they found that in many cases they had led women to expect a "patient-directed" birth which they could not provide. Nurse-midwives often found themselves in the position of having to balance obstetrical authority and demands, the hopes and anxieties of clients, and their own birth ideology. At the same time that these nurse-midwives were trying to provide an alternative to the medical model, they found themselves engaged in it.

Maurin (1980) also demonstrates the problems associated with trying to negotiate an out-of-hospital birthing service within a structural context of medical control. Maurin studied a free-standing birth center, Western Birth Center, which opened in 1975. She identifies some of the same problems which MCA experienced, and she stresses the power of the gatekeeping position which physicians occupy with regard to gaining access to needed services and resources. Initially, a physician was appointed as medical director of Western Birth Center. He was not an obstetrician and, at the time of his appointment, he was in a full-time residency program. Having very little direct involvement with the center, he served mainly "as a figurehead whose signature was valuable on occasion" (Maurin, 1980, p. 321). At the end of his residency, he decided to try to establish himself as the person in charge at the center. The nurse-midwife who had been acting in that capacity challenged him. It was she who was, in fact, providing the services which clients were seeking and, beyond this, she owned the building in which the center was housed. During this conflict, the medical director asked the board of directors to fire the nurse-midwife. She, in turn, threatened not to renew the lease on the building. In the end, the medical director resigned, and the board of directors eliminated his position.

The resignation proved costly to the birth center because they lost their insurance reimbursement as a result. While serving as medical director, the physician had negotiated for third-party reimbursement for a portion of the services provided by the center. Since services were not being provided in a hospital, the insurance company would not pay the institutional fee. They did agree to pay the professional fee as long as there was a physician's signature on the insurance forms. Once the insurance company learned of the director's resignation, they informed Western Birth Center that they would no longer honor claims from the center. It was their policy only to reimburse physician services. The nurse-midwife tried to explain that services at the center had never been provided by physicians but was unable to convince the insurance company to resume reimbursement to anyone but a physician.

While the nurse-midwives at Western Birth Center experienced many setbacks, they were able to keep the center going. Maurin credits the success of the birth center to the ability of nurse-midwives to negotiate arrangements with individual physicians which allowed official rules to be circumvented. It was the nurse-midwives who actually provided all the care for birthing women who came to the center, yet they did so in a way that left the power of physicians intact. As Maurin notes, "When these actions are performed by a non-physician, however, they are done within the context of a negotiated relationship between physician and non-physician whereby one party is persuaded or manipulated to consent to the exception. At this level of negotiation in the workplace almost anything is negotiable, but the institutionalized role definitions remain unchanged. Thus, while permitting exceptions, these negotiations protect and preserve the overall structure" (Maurin, 1980, p. 328). As Maurin points out, to actually change institutionalized roles means changing power relations. In the case of Western Birth Center, negotiated arrangements made it possible for services to be provided at the same time that the overall power structure was left unchanged, contributing to the vulnerability of the birth center.

Annandale and Maurin identify the crux of the problems faced by birth centers. They attempt to offer a nonhospital alternative to the physician-controlled medical model at the same time that they are defined and constrained by this model.

Rothman (1983) argues that while free-standing birth centers often meet the needs of nurse-midwives as a work environment, they do not necessarily meet the needs of clients, particularly those who "see birth as a fully normal and healthy occurrence and want to integrate birth into family life" (1983, p. 7). Rothman argues that as an alternative to home birth, birth centers have some disadvantages. They require travel both during labor and shortly following birth. While birth centers may be pleasant and comfortable and look "like home," they are not home. Free-standing birth centers appear safer than hospitals, but there is no evidence that they are safer than the home as an environment for birth.

It is important to consider that FSBCs have a cultural advantage over home birth. Most people in our society view birth as requiring hospitalization, and very few choose home birth. While there may be no scientific evidence supporting the choice of hospital over home, the cultural beliefs surrounding birth make it very difficult to reject the medical model of birth. Some women who would not consider home birth are willing to consider birthing at an FSBC. Free-standing birth centers do challenge the medical model and they do provide an environment where birthing women can experience much more power over birth than a hospital experience would allow. Birth center clients who express satisfaction with their birth center experiences express a greater willingness to consider a home birth for subsequent births. Rothman (1983, p. 7) suggests that this can be viewed as a success on the part of birth centers in "resocializing their clients to think of birth in nonmedical ways."

It is true that birth centers are not home, but they are vastly different from hospitals. The atmosphere is homelike, not institutional. The philosophy which guides the practice of nurse-midwives practicing in birth centers is one which sees birth as a healthy process. When women enter hospitals to give birth, they may be going to a place they have never been to before. If they have been there before, it may have been to visit a patient or maybe to take a tour offered to prospective parents who are planning a birth at the hospital. Women who go to birth centers to give birth are going to a place which is familiar to them, where they will be cared for by people (nurse-midwives, nurses, sometimes doctors) who are familiar to them. They will have gone to the birth center for their prenatal care. They may have attended prenatal classes and childbirth classes at the Center. Centers also sometimes host social events, public lectures and workshops, and classes for prospective and new parents. Many women who have gone to birth centers describe very warm feelings for the place as well as the people at the centers....

DISCUSSION

Free-standing birth centers are an important option for birthing women and their families. They offer an out-of-hospital location for birth which is nurturing and supportive. Nurse-midwives in free-standing birth facilities usually practice according to the midwifery model, offering intimate, involved care to women and families.

Birth is not viewed narrowly as a medical event. Rather, it is seen as an important event which changes the lives of all the participants—family members, friends, and even the nurse-midwives themselves. As the Morris Heights example demonstrates, the empowerment that comes from the kinds of positive birth experiences which birth centers facilitate can extend far beyond birth and parenting. It can extend to the workplace and to the community at large.

As many of the examples in this chapter show, however, birth centers challenge the medical model at the same time that they are to some extent defined and constrained by it. The case study which follows discusses the establishment and operation of a free-standing birth center. It presents the important birthing option which the birth center brings to the community in which it is located. It also discusses the difficulties which the birth center has faced over its years of operation and which result mainly from its ambiguous location and status. The center poses a challenge to the medical model but is dependent upon established medical-legal interests for physician and hospital backup, for third-party reimbursement, and for malpractice insurance.

REFERENCES

Annandale, Ellen C. 1988. "How Midwives Accomplish Natural Birth: Managing Risk and Balancing Expectations." *Social Problems* 35, no. 2 (April): 95–109.

Edwards, Margot, and Mary Waldorf. 1984. *Reclaiming Birth: History and Heroines of American Childbirth Reform.* Trumansburg, N.Y: Crossing Press.

Ernst, Eunice K. M. 1985. "NACC Presentation at ICEA/NIH [International Childbirth Education Association/National Institutes of Health] Forum" *NACC News* (National Association of Childbearing Centers, Perkiomenville, Penn.) fall.

Klee, Linea. 1986. "Home Away from Home: The Alternative Birth Center." *Social Science and Medicine* 23, no. 1: 9–16.

Lubic, Ruth Watson. 1981. "Alternative Maternity Care: Resistance and Change." In *Childbirth: Alternatives to Medical Control,* edited by Shelly Romalis. Austin: University of Texas Press.

Mathews, Joan J., and Kathleen Zadak. 1991. "The Alternative Birth Movement in the United States: History and Current Status." *Women and Health* 17, no. 1.

Maurin, Judith. 1980. "Negotiating an Innovative Health Care Service." *Research in the Sociology of Health Care* 1.

NACC News (National Association of Childbearing Centers, Perkiomenville, Penn.). 1984–85. Vol. 2, nos. 3 and 4 (fall/winter).

Rooks, Judith P., Norman L. Weatherby, Eunice K. M. Ernst, Susan Stapleton, David Rosen, and Allan Rosenfield. 1989. "Outcomes of Care in Birth Centers: The National Birth Center Study." *New England Journal of Medicine* 321 (December 28): 1804–1811.

Rothman, Barbara Katz. 1982. *In Labor: Women and Power in the Birthplace.* New York: W. W. Norton.

———. 1983. "Anatomy of a Compromise: Nurse-Midwifery and the Rise of the Birth Center." *Journal of Nurse-Midwifery* 28, no. 4 (July/August): 3–7.

———. 1989. *Recreating Motherhood: Ideology and Technology in Patriarchal Society. New York: W. W. Norton.*

CHAPTER 13

TECHNOLOGY-ASSISTED CONCEPTION

In October, 1999, former exercise video mogul and current fashion photographer Ron Harris announced plans to offer his models' eggs for sale. Commentators latched onto many aspects of the story, from the commodification of human body parts and, perhaps, lives, to the pernicious culture of beauty and perfection in which we live. Practical and ethical questions aside, a jarring aspect of the story was the price tag. Harris expected bids of up to $150,000 for the eggs of models on his website, www.ronsangels.com. Whatever the price, buyers can expect only the model's egg, and perhaps not even that. The website confirms that no medical costs or services are associated with the purchase, and experts note that verification of any egg's origins is unlikely. The only sure conclusion to be drawn is that someone will make a lot of money. We shop for, buy, and sell eggs, sperm, and embryos, and we lease wombs. The "stork market" has arrived.

MARKETING AND CULTURAL ACCEPTANCE

It is no surprise that expensive advertising has coincided with the technology-assisted conception industry's rapid expansion: The industry promises to be very profitable, selling an expensive service to willing, often desperate, customers. Infertility treatments have been heavily advertised from their inception, promoted by people whose careers and pocketbooks benefit from high demand and increased medical options. Billboards, newspapers, and newsletters advertise infertility treatments. A full-page ad in the *New York Times* invites readers "to attend free educational seminars on infertility and the advances in assisted reproductive technology" ("IVF America" 1992). The newsletter of the Saddleback Center for Reproductive Health pictures a woman kissing a baby—accompanied by the caption, "Some women may never know this joy...without your help"—and encourages women to donate ovarian eggs, a complex process. Student newspapers at Stanford, Yale, and other elite universities publish advertisements offering $50,000 for an egg donor who is at least 5-feet, 10-inches tall, athletic, and has a score above 1,400 on the Scholastic Aptitude Test (Greenberg 1999). Companies advertize their sperm bank collections in catalogs allowing women and their partners to shop for the perfect sperm: "When 35-year-old Roxane Helstrom was shopping for sperm a year ago, she and her husband turned to their trusty catalog and, after some debate, selected Sperm Donor No. 522—a blond, blue-eyed student whose interests include filmmaking and writing" (Uzelac 1992).

Publicity for the growing assisted-conception industry is not limited to paid advertising. As the industry has become big business, it has also become big news. Sperm banks, some limited to gifted donors, proliferate; infertility clinics grow into chains and become full-fledged capitalistic enterprises as their stock goes public. For example, IVF America held a stock offering in 1992 to raise $19 million. The media coverage began by saying, "Think of it as *Brave New World* meets Wall Street," noting that the company plans to "become the McDonald's of the baby-making business" (Cowan 1992).

MEDICAL ENTHUSIASM

The rapid expansion of profits and expectations, coupled with the overexuberance of advertising, has inevitably resulted in clinics promoting procedures to women and couples who do not need them. This is exemplified by an advertisement from an assisted reproductive technology program that pictures a fireplace, cozy rug, and two glasses of red wine with the caption: "It's one way to make a baby. But there's a lot to be said for gamete intrafallopian transfer" ("Mount Sinai" 1994). Gamete intrafallopian transfer (GIFT) is a complex procedure. It is not the next step after a failed fire-rug-wine-assisted attempt, even though the ad suggests otherwise.

The increasing use of technology to assist conception is driven by more factors than just the profit motive. The enthusiasm of doctors and specialists has contributed greatly to the technological imperative in the assisted-conception field. For doctors, the ability to understand reproduction more completely and to control the process has been motivating. To those devoted to learning about reproduction, how can this new knowledge about the egg and the sperm, and this growing control over nature, not be thrilling? A reproductive endocrinologist commented, "we can only be overjoyed and exhilarated and consider ourselves extremely fortunate to be working during a period of time when such paramount advances have been made. How thrilling it must have been to be Chaucer writing when Gutenberg invented the printing press, or be a physicist working on the Manhattan Project" (quoted in Scritchfield 1989:89). This researcher's unbridled enthusiasm, paired with his comparison of research in conception to the invention of the printing press and the atomic bomb, suggests a tunnel vision that sees only the positives in the progress of science.

Brave New World—a 1932 novel that portrays the state manipulating the genetic quality of babies, providing an artificial uterine environment, and reinforcing the social structure by predetermining the number of elites and workers—once seemed like science fiction. It no longer does. A scientist titles his book *Designing Babies: The Brave New World of Reproductive Technology* and states matter of factly, as though a common good were described, "If the twentieth century was notable for fertility control, in the twenty-first the emphasis of research will switch to producing a baby that is *free of defects and attractive and arrives with perfect timing*" (Gosden 1999:5, italics mine). Such scientific enthusiasm propels the development of technology.

The effects of this enthusiasm are evident in the ways doctors have accepted their role in diagnosing and treating infertility, even though infertility is not a disease in the conventional sense of the word. Infertility is diagnosed in an unusual way. Patients aren't tested for symptoms; rather, a couple reports an inability to conceive after twelve months of unprotected sex. For some women and men, a pathological condition is identified (e.g., blocked fallopian tube), but for many, no specific pathology is found. Regardless, lack of success at conceiving is taken as a positive indication that medical treatment is required, and nonmedical options are neglected.

The assumption of a physical problem is an improvement over the old medical insistence that infertility resulted from a woman's inability to accept her proper maternal role (Laurence and Weinhouse 1994). However, now that infertility has been medicalized, practitioners with medical-model mind sets are, by definition, in charge. Sex itself has become medicalized: A third party joins what had been the most intimate act between two people, and transforms it into a medical procedure controlled by the physician. In the early evaluation of infertility, the doctor defines when sex will occur and requires women to submit to post-coital examinations. One woman reported, "I had an endless process of post-coitals which became more and more degrading. I felt nothing much at all at first, but lately it has become demeaning, just going in and opening my legs and going through all that again" (quoted in Rowland 1992:21).

With medicalization, nonmedical options such as adoption (Bartholet 1992; Bartholet 1993) are forgotten. The infertile couple are on the seductive cure bandwagon driven by the doctor, with science providing ever more dazzling options. These options are a result of the dramatic expansion of technology-assisted conception in the final two decades of the last century. What began as methods to provide minor assistance in the movement of a partner's sperm to an egg—by simple artificial insemination in the doctor's office, or, even more primitively, with the use of a turkey baster at home (Wikler and Wikler 1991)—has become a confusing avalanche of options. These options include where the conception could occur—in the woman or outside her body; whose sperm and egg are joined—the partners' or that of strangers or friends; whether the egg, sperm, or fertilized egg were frozen; and whether particular genetic qualities are chosen. Even the simplest in vitro fertilization (IVF) typically requires many steps: hormonal stimulation of egg production ("superovulation"), egg "harvesting," sperm retrieval, fertilization, and careful timing of implantation. Women naturally seek their doctor's advice amidst this confusing barrage of highly technical choices, not realizing that their doctor's priorities may differ sharply from their own.

FOR-PROFIT MOTIVATION AND AN UNREGULATED INDUSTRY

Once in the treatment process, women report that the pressures to try every possible procedure can be extreme. A sign in one infertility clinic reads, "You never fail until you quit trying" (Powledge 1988:207). Doctors do little to discourage the belief in the miracle of technology (Scritchfield 1989:80; Bonnicksen 1989:7). Since success rates decrease for each successive attempt, Dr. Edward Kaplan of Yale suggests that doctors *not* encourage people to keep on trying. But he notes, "When you make your money off couples who say 'Do what's possible,' there's quite an incentive to encourage patients to do [still] more" (Quoted in Verhey 1997:141). There are no incentives to encourage women to "say no to yet another attempt,...to begin to write the next chapter of their lives without children of their own" (Verhey 1997:141). The incentives in this for-profit industry are to continue the process, not end it.

The process is also pushed along by the general attitude of a society with a "technological imperative," a drive to develop and use more and more technology. Enthusiasm abounds with few voices of caution, even though there is good reason for caution. The immediate physical risks of many infertility treatments are not well understood or evaluated, a particularly disturbing situation for women because the risks of the assistive technologies are largely risks for the woman due to superovulation drugs, the greater invasiveness of egg harvesting in comparison to sperm retrieval, and the fact that women take most of the risks associated with male infertility (Becker and Nachtigall 1994:511). Rather than stopping to consider such risks, the practitioners of the new technology push to perform the procedures, aided enthusiastically by for-profit companies.

The growth of for-profit aspects of medical practice has led some doctors to protest that medical decisions seem to be increasingly determined by the bottom line. Dr. Carl M. Herbert, a practitioner in a San Francisco clinic, describes the expansion-oriented clinic in which he had practiced as "a place where administrators are saying we have to do this many cases of IVF in order to financially survive, where we have to produce a 20 percent profit above my salary and everyone else's, and above the cost of running the clinic" (Kramon 1992). A clinic's concern for money-making may generate new services. For instance, adding sperm and egg freezing as an option for infertility treatments "enhances a program's prestige, attracts patients, sets the stage for research, and brings in fees that can be channeled back into the program" (Bonnicksen 1989:7).

A clinic's desire to appear successful not only influences the procedures offered, but also leads many to shape treatment accordingly. The implantation of multiple embryos increases the likelihood of a pregnancy, a key to the appearance of clinic success. Unfortunately, multiple implants also lead to multiple fetuses with the iatrogenic (doctor-caused) result that necessitates either "selective reduction" (not called abortion in an attempt to avoid the politics of that term) or acceptance of the multiple pregnancy and its increased risk for short- and long-term health problems for the babies and the mother.

Another way for clinics to increase the appearance of their success—aside from these legitimate, if dangerous, procedures—is to restrict the publication of clinic-specific data on success rates. In fact, published data have not been accessible to peer review, and were often inaccurate and misleading (Sher and Feinman 1997:154). In 1992, the Federal Trade Commission cracked down on clinics, filing charges against five suspected of misrepresenting their success (Pear 1992). One of the founding members of the relevant professional medical society, the Society for Reproductive Technology (SART), commented, "It is unconscionable that, in an area of medicine in which the outcome under specified conditions is so clearly definable, as in the field of IVF, after a decade of empty promises our professional representative, SART, has failed to establish a system of true accountability in our field" (Sher and Feinman 1997:155).

The government has stepped aside and allowed for-profit interests and market values to define what medical treatments are available, who has access to them, and under what conditions babies are conceived. This unregulated environment has greatly speeded the development of technology at the same time that it has precluded public accountability and delayed the discussion of moral and ethical issues (Powledge 1988).

INEQUITIES IN ACCESS

A basic issue in infertility treatment is who has access to reproductive technologies. Without regulation, the industry, rather than any public body, has made the determination. Early practitioners refused services to older women and women who were not in a heterosexual marriage. In 1986, the Ethics Committee of the American Fertility Society declared, "Other things being equal, the Committee regards the setting of heterosexual marriage as the most appropriate context for the rearing of children" (quoted in Scritchfield 1989:72). The appropriateness of lesbian pregnancy continues to be debated.

The more intractable problem is the role of class and race in gaining access. That inequities of race and class in technology-assisted reproduction mirror those of the larger health system should not surprise us. But they do offend many. First, they reveal the eugenic roots of these technologies (Stanworth 1987:28; Rothman 1987:33) as a desire to assist births by the upper classes and limit those of the "less fit." Certainly the spotty coverage of infertility treatments by insurance companies, where typical costs are over $10,000, has restricted such treatments to the financially secure. The newer reproductive technologies require not just money, but also "a privileged lifestyle that permits devotion to the rigorous process of daily hormone shots, ultrasound examinations, blood tests, egg extraction and implantation, travel to and from a fertility clinic, and often multiple attempts—a luxury few Black people enjoy" (Roberts 1997:254), and a luxury that few other women of color or economically disadvantaged women enjoy. Within fertility treatments, there are class distinctions: "Fertility drugs seem to be the poor person's remedy, while IVF is reserved for those with means or very good insurance" (Klotzko 1998:7). Whereas poor people and minorities are at the center of discussions of birth control, they are far removed from the discussions of new reproductive technologies (Roberts 1997).

Inequities surrounding childbearing seem particularly cruel. Some commentators argue that among the basic human rights is a procreative right. According to this logic, the government could mandate that insurance companies provide coverage for a reasonable level of infertility treatment: coverage after several years of infertility, for specific causes of infertility such as endometriosis or DES exposure, or for a single treatment, for example. Persuasive arguments against such a policy question the use of limited health resources for treatments with such low success rates (still about 20 percent). Our society's approach could move from the curative mode advocated by the medical model and consider investing in prevention. We could reduce environmental toxins, better educate young people about sexually transmitted disease, improve the early diagnosis of endometriosis, and promote workplace changes to alter the current incentives that delay childbirth and hence decrease fertility (Woliver 1989:51). If the goal is to maximize the health of women and young children, targeting prevention of infertility and improving prenatal care are much more effective ways to channel money than providing fancy technologies to the few.

EXPLOITATION AND ABUSES OF TECHNOLOGY

Although the government's proper role in providing for widespread access to reproductive technologies is unclear, the need for regulation to prevent abuses of these technologies is apparent. Technology-assisted conception is not only denied to many low-income groups in society, but it also has the potential to exploit these less powerful groups. Advertising for egg donors at colleges puts tempting monetary incentives in front of temporarily poor women, without making it clear that agreeing to be an egg donor may compromise a woman's own future fertility. The *Handmaid's Tale* portrays a breeder class assigned the life role of carrying the fetuses for the more privileged class. Far short of that image of a breeder class, but similar to it, are existing arrangements in which women carry the babies of more economically advantaged women. A woman or couple contracts with a "surrogate mother" who becomes pregnant either by artificial insemination (the surrogate mother's egg combined, usually, with the sperm of the contracting male) or by IVF (eggs and sperm from contracting parties or donors). The contract typically specifies payment for expenses, time, and services. Certain behavioral expectations (no drugs, good prenatal care) are also usually part of the contract. Such arrangements became possible in our society because individual people wanted them and agencies emerged to join the parties together. Rather than establishing rules at the outset or regulating the process in any way, our legal and legislative system stood back and let this happen.

The potential for the exploitation of women of lesser means was evident in the first litigation over surrogacy. In 1985, the Baby M controversy became a high profile court case in which a surrogate mother (Mrs. Mary Beth Whitehead) of modest means sought to retain custody of her genetic child conceived by artificial insemination using the sperm of a wealthy married man (Mr. William Stern), whose wife chose not to become pregnant due to her health. The Supreme Court of New Jersey invalidated the contract finding it "illegal and perhaps criminal" and in conflict with laws that prohibit "paying or accepting money in connection with any placement of a child for adoption" (quoted in Wilentz 1998:791). Yet the court proceeded to grant custody to the Sterns after considering the child's best interests as determined by the "family life of the Whiteheads and Sterns and the personalities and characters of the individuals" (quoted in Wilentz 1998:796). House size, resources for athletics and music lessons, and other correlates of upper-class status determined the fate of Baby M. The potential for exploitation of women of modest means is clear. Despite the court's decision that the contract is illegal, and despite the genetic and gestational contribution of Mrs. Whitehead, she was clearly deemed less worthy.

Although the public policy implications of these new technologies appear widespread and confusing, the ethical and philosophical questions posed by the same are of no less import. Most fundamentally, these new technologies raise the question of what parenthood is, and the degree to which it can be divided and shared.

REDEFINING PARENTHOOD

The development of technology-assisted reproductive options has made the meaning of parenthood ambiguous. Although the long history of adoptive arrangements suggests an ability to separate biological and social parenthood, the alarming new ways in which eggs and sperm are joined and children are birthed has opened unanticipated territory.

A baby with eight potential parents (a genetic mother and her husband, a genetic father and his wife, a gestational mother and her partner, and a married couple contracting for a baby) is found by a California court to have no legal parents (Capron 1998); a woman bears fraternal twins only to learn that during the IVF process one of the embryos implanted was not hers; a woman mourning the death of her husband has his sperm electroejaculated and has herself inseminated; a mother agrees to provide the womb for the implantation of her grandchildren; a 16-month-old baby greets his newly born identical twin; a divorced couple litigates the fate of frozen embryos; and a child is born of a woman who has been a ventilated cadaver for weeks. Such reproductive scenes at the end of the twentieth century suggest worrisome possibilities, both legal and ethical, for the twenty-first century.

Not everyone sees danger in this technological explosion. For some, these developments are exciting, opening up new opportunities, and allowing us to control the vagaries of nature. The options represent what women have long struggled for: reproductive rights and increased choices. Some even envision greater use of surrogacy arrangements and the development of artificial gestational environments. This logic suggests that women should applaud the new conceptive technologies as giving us hope for an even greater severing of the obligations of reproduction from womanhood.

For others, these developments are frightening; without discussion, we have allowed medicine to tamper with the facts of life, to play God with the future of humanity. Although some voice concerns about the loss of the natural state of conception and gestation, it is important to remember that a purely natural state of pregnancy and childbirth has been the atypical event for centuries. Herbal concoctions, mechanical devices, dietary restrictions, behavioral adjustments (timing, position), and the use of experts (midwives and others) have been in use for centuries (Stanworth 1987:34). Even artificial insemination by donor has a longer history than most realize: in 1884 a medical doctor impregnated a "woman whose husband was infertile with a sperm donated by 'the best-looking medical student' in his class" (Cohen 1996:xi). Thus, to judge the current developments against a nostalgic standard of what is "natural" is inaccurate.

Yet clearly, the new ways of making babies are hugely different from the traditional methods. What has dramatically changed is the ideological underpinnings of pregnancy and childbirth. As noted in Chapter 12, viewing childbirth as a natural process that at times needs assistance is very different from seeing it as a pathological process for which medical management is necessary. With technology-assisted conception, it is difficult to find anything but medical management—in the removal of eggs and sperm, fertilization, and implantation. With such medicalization, women are increasingly marginalized from conception. Disturbing questions about the social meaning of parenting and the human ties among family members arise; maternity seems "dismembered," and a source of power is lost (Arditti 1985). A surrogate mother is asked to alienate herself from intimate and emotional processes: conception, carrying a child, childbirth, and the child, itself.

The new technologies have also led to the commodification of children. As noted earlier in this chapter, couples can shop for genetically appealing egg and sperm donors. Some practitioners, such as Gosden, the author of *Designing Babies* (quoted earlier), feel we are properly on the road to the perfect, defect-free, and attractive baby who arrives exactly on schedule. This ability to choose some traits and reject others may alter the parental relationship. Before, parents "took responsibility for the children they bore. When fate dealt them a child with imperfections, largely they accepted it and coped as well as they could. Today, within the context of the expanding selection of intervention possibilities, many persons are no longer satisfied with a child viewed as less than the best. Even the average does not seem good enough for many parents" (Blank 1990:89). Where this trajectory of designer babies might take us is impossible to predict, though experiences with prenatal testing, fetal surgery, and the surveillance of the behavior of pregnant women do suggest some disturbing possibilities. The next chapter examines these three arenas of fetal quality control.

REPRODUCTIVE TECHNOLOGY AND THE COMMODIFICATION OF LIFE

BARBARA KATZ ROTHMAN

The issues that confront us in reproduction these days are indeed complex. They involve new technology, old technology and no technology at all. We confront the newer questions raised by prenatal diagnosis and selective abortion, by *in vitro* fertilization, by something we are calling "surrogate" motherhood, and we face the older questions raised by adoption. It is a bewildering, frightening, challenging array.

Is there any way of organizing our thoughts about these issues, of seeing connections between the disparate techniques and questions? I believe that medicine has, this time unwittingly, supplied us with a key to all of this. The key is not another technology, but a phrase, a bit of language, words that open up and lay bare the underlying ideology which unites our reproductive technology. The phrase is "the products of conception." It is medical language for what you get when sperm joins egg—in a loving waiting mother, in a frightened teenager, in a hired woman, or in a petrie dish—the results are "the products of conception."

Interesting phrase, that. It is really a fine term for what we're talking about. Because in fact we are talking about products and a production process. We are facing the expansion of an ideology that treats people as objects, as commodities. It is an ideology that enables us to see not motherhood, not parenthood, but the creation of a commodity, a baby. We are involved now in the fixing of price tags to the separate parts of the reproductive process. We are negotiating the prices for bodily parts, bodily fluids, human services, energy and lives, as we produce "valuable" babies, "precious" babies.

This is the theme that I see running through all of the issues in the new, and in the old, reproductive technology. Sometimes the theme comes right up to the surface, and we hear and read actual dollar figures: so many thousands of dollars for each *in vitro* attempt, $10,000 as the current market rate for a "surrogate" mother-for-hire, $20,000 to adopt a baby from one country, $15,000 from another. Sometimes the language of commodification, of pricing, goes back under again, and we talk vaguely about the "costs" and the "burdens" of rearing people with disabilities, how much we are "spared" with selective abortion. The talk of money and dollars comes to the fore and recedes to the background, but always, through it all, when we talk about reproduction these days we are talking about the commodification of life. It is not altogether surprising in this society at this time, that this is indeed the approach we take to reproduction: some would claim that this is the approach we take to virtually everything in the United States. We talk about costs and prices, bottom lines and net gains, what things are worth.

This commodification process is very clearly seen in the notion of "surrogate" motherhood. There we talk openly about buying services and renting body parts—as if body parts were rented without the people who surround the part, as if you could rent a woman's uterus without renting the woman. We ignore our knowledge that women are pregnant with our whole bodies, from the changes in our hair to our swollen feet, with all of our bodies and perhaps with our souls as well. We make it "simple," we make it " straightforward" and we make little jokes about "wombs for rent."

But the commodification process is not uniquely seen in surrogacy arrangements: it was there long ago when we first began to experience some "shortage" of babies for adoption. While babies are not for sale in the United States, at least not openly, we all know perfectly well that the availability of a baby for adoption has a lot to do with the amount of money in the hands of the potential adopters. And we know that adoptable babies are themselves sorted as commodities: the whiter, younger and healthier carry the highest price tags; others—the wrong color, damaged, too long on the shelf, the "seconds" of the production process—go cheaply, go begging.

And now we see the commodification process enter all pregnancies, as society encourages the development of prenatal diagnostic technology. This process, the genetic counseling, the screening and testing of fetuses, serves the function of "quality control" on the assembly line of the products of conception, separating out those products we wish to develop from those we wish to discontinue. And we see the commodification process not only in technological developments but in legal developments as well. The "wrongful life" suits, the suits claiming that a particular fetus should never have been conceived, or never brought to term, are a form of "product liability" litigation. Once we see the products of conception as just that, as products, we begin to treat them as we do any other product, subject to similar scrutiny and standards.

One concern raised by the use of this developing ideology is what it does to the "products of conception" to be dealt with in this way. And so, we worry about the effects of artificial insemination with the use of sperm from paid donors, or "surrogate" motherhood and other purchasing agreements, on the children thus created. Certainly, some worry about the fetus and its "right to life," with or without disabilities. But my chief concern lies elsewhere: I want us to think about what this commodification process does to all of us, to us as a society, to us as individuals, and most particularly what it does to women as mothers.

Let me take as an illustration of my concern what has happened in another area of life with the process of commodification. It is not only reproduction that has been commodified, not only eggs and sperm that we sell. Consider what we have done with blood. In the United States we buy and sell blood. In Richard Titmuss' fine book *The Gift Relationship* (1972), the author explores the consequences of the commodification of blood, of turning blood into a purchasable product, and compares American and British blood banking systems. In the United States blood needs to be purchased. One gives blood either for cash, in the most straightforward, crass example of commodification, or in the slightly round-about way of donating blood for blood insurance. In England, by contrast, blood is freely available: one is not charged for its use and not paid for its donation. Thus the giving of blood is a purely altruistic act. The payment of blood-money removes from us as blood donors the right to be altruistic, the right to give freely.

The argument that Titmuss makes does not draw upon the "rights of blood," does not concern itself with the moral value of the blood per se, but rather with the moral value of the giving and selling—what it does to *us,* not to the blood, to commodify blood.

When we look at slides of the products of conception, when the new technology shows us what those newly formed pre-embryo cells look like, we see cells: one, two, four, eight cell clusters, looking as if they lie on a bed of sand before us in their magnified banality. To the non-scientists among us, we might just as well be looking at blood cells, at plant cells, at anything and at nothing. Let us look not at the cells, and not even at the people those cells might become, but rather let us look at the society that prices those cells, and most especially at the women in whose bodies those cells must grow.

I will conclude by briefly considering two of the groups of women most directly affected by the commodification process in reproduction: first, the mothers awaiting prenatal diagnostic testing; and secondly, the women hired as "surrogates."

What happens to women who are undergoing the quality control process of prenatal diagnosis, women who do not yet know if they are mothers, or if they are carriers of something we are going to call a defective fetus and ask them to abort? In my interviews with women caught in this process (Rothman 1986), I saw the development of the "tentative pregnancy," the condition in which a woman acknowledges her wanted pregnancy, accepts the roles and rituals of pregnancy, but knows she may not be having the baby she wants, but the abortion she dreads. I have seen how these women suffer, how they recoil from the movement of fetuses slated for abortion, begging of their bellies, "Baby please, please don't move." I have seen how they cannot maintain the medical language, the needed distancing, but feel the baby within as a baby, as their baby, and when they know they have to end the pregnancy—for good and strong reasons—they use not the language of abortion and termination, but the language of infanticide, of murder and killing, of grief and responsibility. Motherhood resists commodification.

And what does it do to women who "rent" their wombs, to the women we ask to carry within them a baby they are to believe is not theirs? Some women seem to adapt well to the situation: they stand there large with child and say, "This is not my baby. This is someone else's baby. I will birth it and give it up without a qualm." These women have accepted the alienation of the worker from the product of her labor: the baby like any other commodity does not belong to the producer but to the purchaser. But some women do not adapt so well. Some women, like Mary Beth Whitehead, say they agreed to sell an egg, to rent a womb, but in the course of pregnancy and birth realize that that was not what was required. What was required was that they sell a child, sell their baby. That they cannot do. Those are the women who refuse to be workers, who find that they cannot commodify their motherhood, cannot fix price tags on their babies. As Whitehead said, "I looked at $10,000 and I looked at my daughter, and there's no question. This child is my child just like my other children."

So what are we doing to ourselves as we commodify reproduction, create it in the image of all production, aim for "state of the art" babies? We put a price tag on our lives and our love, learn, as they say, "the price of everything and the value of nothing."

Here we are, actively pricing motherhood—it costs about $1,000 to purchase a spare embryo, another $10,000 to "rent a womb," and there we have it. What is the meaning, what the value of motherhood? $11,000 on the open market. And once the priceless is priced, market considerations take over. How long before the brokers in this business, the men who have books of women's pictures to show prospective purchasers, follow the cattle industry in seeking higher profits? With cattle, profits have been increased by planting more valuable embryos in less valuable breeders. Can we look forward to baby farms, with white embryos grown in young and poor Third-World mothers? Price goes down, labor costs are saved, and profit goes up.

But who profits here? In whose interests are we developing our technology? Where is the profit in commodifying life?

REFERENCES

Titmuss, R. 1972. *The Gift Relationship: From Human Blood to Social Policy.* New York: Vintage.

Rothman, B. K. 1986. *The Tentative Pregnancy: Prenatal Diagnosis and the Future of Motherhood.* New York. Viking/Penguin.

THE RISE AND FALL OF OVUM TRANSFER: A CAUTIONARY TALE

JUDITH N. LASKER AND SUSAN BORG

In January 1984, the first baby to have been carried by two mothers was born. This young boy was the product of an unusual partnership of medical researchers, financiers, and a livestock breeder. He was conceived inside one woman who had been inseminated with the sperm of the other woman's husband. Five days after conception, the tiny embryo was removed without surgery and transplanted into the uterus of the second woman. This woman, who was infertile, then carried the baby to term and gave birth to him. His birth, and that of a girl born several months later, represented the first—and almost the only—successes in the United States of a method called ovum transfer (OT).[1]

OT was highlighted in major media outlets, including *The New York Times Magazine,* the Phil Donahue show, and *People* magazine, as another breakthrough for infertile people. It was heavily marketed to the public and to investors, and it continues to be the basis for articles appearing in the medical literature about its past success and future promise. Yet OT was a monstrous failure, both medically and financially. Its story is important because it illustrates some of the ways in which women have been used as guinea pigs in questionable scientific experiments and misled by profit-driven entrepreneurs who see infertility treatment as just one more commodity from which to make money.

Ovum transfer was presented at the outset as having the potential to create major changes in the process of reproduction that could affect fertile as well as infertile women. First, the procedure presumably offered infertile women a nonsurgical alternative to IVF. Second, the commercialization of the OT program departed from the usual medical approach at the time. In addition to being financed by investors buying shares through the stock exchange, the program also operated out of profit-making clinics, and sought to patent the entire procedure as well as the instruments. Third, OT was envisaged from the beginning and continues to be viewed by some of its advocates as the basis for diagnosing the genetic makeup and potential health problems of embryos very early in their development.[2]

OT was not a new concept; it had been widely used in the cattle industry for many years in order to increase the number of offspring of genetically superior cows. These high-quality cows are inseminated with the sperm of prize bulls. Their embryos are then removed, to be carried by more common cattle, so that the superior cow can be inseminated again very quickly. Beginning in the late 1970s, superovulation was introduced to maximize the number of high-quality embryos and ensure the profitability of this method of breeding.[3]

Richard Seed, a consultant to the livestock industry, had a vision of saving Western civilization by increasing the number and quality of American babies. Together with his physician brother Randolph, Richard began a corporation in 1978 named Fertility and Genetics Research (FGR). Its purpose was to apply ovum transfer to humans. Their grant to Drs. John Buster, John Marshall, and colleagues at Harbor UCLA Medical Center made it possible to carry out the first experimental phase in 1983 and 1984.

The developers of this new method for humans called it "ovum transfer," even though it is a five-day-old embryo that they tried to transfer. The avoidance of the term "embryo transfer" in the OT program appears to have been designed to allay public worries about scientists playing with embryos. Dr. John Buster, the professor of OB/GYN who directed the original OT research, talked about the careful selection of a name for the program:

> *We chose the word "ovum" because, in 1980 when we prepared the protocol, we were concerned that there would be people parading with signs outside that we were transplanting things with arms and legs and eyes that we called an embryo.*

OVUM TRANSFER AS AN INFERTILITY TREATMENT

The developers of OT presented it as an ideal solution for women who cannot produce their own eggs, either because they have had their ovaries removed or experienced premature menopause. In addition, they considered it the best method for women who are not infertile but who do not want to take the chance of passing a genetic disease to their children; these women might welcome the chance to be pregnant by carrying another woman's egg fertilized by their own husband's sperm.

FGR, in its promotional literature, listed these as the types of problems that would bring couples to OT, but the research had either not included, or not been successful with, women in most of these categories. Only one OT baby, born in Milan in 1986, had a mother without ovaries. The mothers of the two OT babies born in California did not fit any of these groups. They both had normal ovaries but scarred fallopian tubes, the type of condition for which IVF was first developed. In fact, the owners of FGR expected a major portion of their customers to come from the growing ranks of women who may have tried other methods such as IVF and failed. As FGR president Twerdahl told us:

> *If a couple can afford it and they have their own sperm and eggs, we presume they would prefer IVF. But perhaps they can no longer afford IVF or they failed at IVF a couple of times. Perhaps the patient can't tolerate surgery and anesthesia anymore, whether she can't physically or psychologically. Then ovum transfer becomes a method for them.*

The OT program recruited its first donors by putting a small ad in the newspaper: "Help an infertile woman have a baby. Fertile women age 20–35 willing to donate an egg. Similar to artificial insemination. No surgery required. Reasonable compensation." Of the four hundred women who answered the ad, many lost interest after their initial contact, and others were screened out. Only forty-six were finally accepted. Dr. Buster talked about the donors:

> *To answer that ad was a pretty cavalier thing to do and so we got a large number of people that had high psychopathic scores. After screening out a bunch of them that weren't suitable, we were left with a few great ladies.*

Those "few great ladies" were selected on the basis of psychological stability, medical suitability, proven fertility, and compliance. They and their husbands were questioned at length to make sure they could handle the procedure and any possible side effects. Infertile couples who applied were also carefully screened to be sure they would fully cooperate with the program.[4]

Public relations were, from the very beginning, a key concern. As Dr. Annette Brodsky, the psychologist in charge of screening, explained:

> *You need people who are going to be stable enough to handle the fact that OT is a new procedure, that there might be publicity around it, that they won't get completely overwhelmed or thrown by the fact if something goes wrong. We didn't want them to be so invested in having a baby that, should prenatal testing reveal that the baby is deformed, they'd say they would want it anyway. Then the first baby in the project is deformed and the whole world stops wanting to think about it again.*

After being matched with a recipient woman, a donor arrived at the clinic at the time of ovulation, to be inseminated by the sperm of the infertile woman's husband. The sperm had already been carefully examined for genetic information and the possibility of venereal disease. Five days after the insemination, the donor returned. With a specially designed catheter, about two ounces of fluid were flushed into her uterus. In a procedure called "lavage," the fluid was then removed again through the catheter. If an embryo was growing in the woman's uterus, it was unlikely to have attached itself yet to the uterine wall and therefore should have emerged with the fluid. One woman who was a donor described her experience:

> *It's a simple procedure and doesn't take very long, about fifteen minutes from start to finish. You get undressed, get up on the table, put your feet in the stirrups. They use a speculum and then the catheter. There's a little bit of cramping; you feel a little tug for a second. It's pretty much like a regular exam.*

The fluid that was taken from the donor's uterus was checked for embryos. If one was found, the recipient woman was called, and the embryo was transferred, again by a catheter inserted through the cervix, into her uterus. If everything went as planned, the embryo that started in another woman's body then implanted in the infertile woman's uterus and grew there normally.

While the endless waiting and lack of success were undoubtedly harrowing for the couple, the major physical risks of OT were for the donor. She was exposed to the possibility of infection from the insemination. She also took the risk of remaining pregnant if the "lavage" process did not work. This happened at least three times in OT research, and one of the donor women had to have an abortion. The other two aborted spontaneously. Ectopic pregnancies were also a possibility, since the fluid could wash an embryo back up into the tubes.

In its second phase, in addition to putting ads in local newspapers to recruit donors, the OT program asked infertile couples to help find their own donors. If a couple brought a friend or relative into the pool of donors, they were promised a priority position on the waiting list. Since there were 2,900 names on the list by the time the Long Beach clinic opened, this was an incentive that put a great deal of pressure on couples and their families.

In FGR's plans to establish OT clinics nationwide, there was the possibility that donors and couples would be matched through a central computer. In a few collection centers around the country, "professional" donors would have numerous embryos washed out of them every month. These embryos would be frozen and shipped out to OT centers elsewhere in the country to waiting couples and their physicians. A collection center could even be in the basement of a high-rise office building in the center of a large city. Thousands of women working upstairs could easily descend during their lunch hour for a quick insemination or lavage.

THE COMMERCIALIZATION OF OVUM TRANSFER

Once the "research phase" was completed, FGR sought financing to expand its operations. In December 1985 the company's stock was offered over the counter under the symbol BABYU. The company made plans to create OT clinics in joint ventures with hospitals and physician groups in California, Chicago, and other major population areas.

When the OT procedure was first publicized, and FGR made known its intention to seek patents for the catheter and the process, there was a great deal of criticism. Jeremy Rifkin, a leading opponent of genetic engineering, threatened to bring a lawsuit to contest the patent, claiming it "reduces the process of human reproduction to a commercialized product to be bought and sold in the marketplace." The medical community was equally opposed to FGR's approach to research. An attorney for the American Medical Association explains: "It's always been the view of the medical profession that you should have as widespread dissemination as possible of anything that would be beneficial to patients."[5]

"We're a technology company, just like any other.... We're no different from Polaroid or any other company that invents a new process and wants a patent to protect it."[6] This comment came from Lawrence Sucsy, an investment banker who did much of the fund-raising for FGR. For him and many others in the financial field, infertility is a growth business, a booming market aimed at highly motivated and affluent consumers.

FGR was hardly the only infertility company to offer shares on the stock market and set up joint ventures for profit. Private infertility clinics offering a wide range of treatments have followed the same path. Franchise operations and IVF chains have appeared throughout the United States and many parts of the world.[7]

What difference does the form of organization make for infertile people? From the point of view of FGR's John Buster and James Twerdahl, it could only make things better. They believed that central control guarantees high quality, a large enough pool of donors, and uniformity of performance from one place to another. According to Dr. Buster:

> *The financial issues and the patient care issues and the quality issues are usually about the same. The company does well by contracting only with first-class organizations. It will do well only if it serves the people well, if it is perceived as taking good care of the women. If not, it will fail.*

Of course there are many corporations that have done extremely well financially by treating their customers, workers, and neighbors very badly. If ovum transfer had had any success, FGR would not *have* to have treated people well, because infertile people would come to it anyway; it failed because it simply did not work.

Buster also claimed that, without private financing, the research for OT would never have been possible. He describes himself as having been driven into the arms of Wall Street types by the unavailability of funding:

> *The alternative is to do nothing at all. Wall Street will never help you unless they get their money out. It's kind of analogous to going swimming with sharks. I mean, the sharks are pretty vicious, but their behavior is predictable and if you do exactly what they want and understand that predictable behavior, it is fine. You have to understand that getting money out of it is what makes their system work for them, even though that relationship compromises some of the dear academic principles we've always espoused.*

Centralized control might be an advantage, especially when compared to the very uneven performance of different IVF centers that have been started independently. Profit-making health programs, however, are not necessarily any more efficient or cost-effective than nonprofit ones. The incentives for them to cut corners and to concentrate on the most profitable activities are very strong. As Dr. Buster himself admits:

> *There is a very delicate balance between keeping the Wall Street crew happy, keeping the physicians happy, and keeping the patients happy.*

THE FALL OF OT

The second phase of OT started in the fall of 1986 in Long Beach, California, at a private medical center. Ultimately, according to James Twerdahl, a former electronics executive who became president of FGR, the intention was to have thirty to fifty such OT centers in North America. Once the first clinics proved successful, FGR planned to develop new ones in almost every metropolitan area in the United States, all under the corporation's control.

Yet within a few short months, all of these plans were abandoned. The Long Beach clinic suspended its operation, and the dozens of people who were on waiting lists to be either recipients or donors for OT were informed that they should look elsewhere.[8]

Why did this project, with such great ambitions and media hype, fail so completely and so rapidly? Investors and potential patients were all sent letters early in 1987 informing them of the development of the GIFT procedure at a nearby medical center. GIFT's apparently greater success rate, compared with IVF, made it unlikely that OT could compete effectively for patients for whom IVF was an undesirable option. Investors were told that this "competing technology…could adversely affect the company's operations." Patients were informed about the GIFT procedure and told, "While we strongly believe in Ovum Transfer, we nevertheless want only what is in your best interest."[9]

The reality, however, was that OT had never worked well at all for infertile women, and that it was causing risks for the donors as well. Despite the claims that this method would solve a wide range of infertility problems, the research results were so poor that they could in no way justify marketing the procedure as proven. Dr. Buster spoke expansively of a 60 percent success rate, but his published reports of the first trials are considerably more cautious. It is true that 60 percent of the blastocysts (the most developed fertilized ova) that were transferred resulted in pregnancies. However, only *five* blastocysts were recovered after eighteen months and fifty-three inseminations of ten donor women. Three pregnancies resulted (hence the claim of 60 percent success, or three out of five blastocysts), but one ended in a miscarriage. It is striking that four of the five blastocysts came from only one donor, although all ten donor women had been carefully screened for fertility. Twenty less-developed embryos were also transferred, but only one produced a pregnancy. This was an ectopic pregnancy, and the woman's tube had to be removed.[10]

During the first eighteen months that OT was attempted by Buster and his colleagues, thirteen women received embryos. Thirteen women, two babies. This may sound pretty good for a first trial. But ten donors had been inseminated fifty-three times. Two babies after fifty-three attempts is hardly 60 percent; it should more accurately be represented as less than 4 percent. In addition, recipient women experienced a miscarriage and an ectopic pregnancy, and one of the donors retained two pregnancies after lavages, resulting in a miscarriage and an induced abortion. Most disturbing perhaps is that the only women who had babies became pregnant within the first six months of the program. For another year until the research ended, and in subsequent trials at the Harbor campus, no additional births were reported.[11]

Similar trials were carried out in Milan, Italy, between May 1984 and February of 1986, but with better results. Of forty-two couples in the research, eight became pregnant; two of these had spontaneous abortions and four had given birth at the time of the researchers report. One donor out of forty-two retained a pregnancy after lavage.[12]

Further experimentation resulted in more complications for donors. A report of 265 lavages between 1982 and 1987 claims a "rare (3%)" complication rate, but this is figured on the basis of the number of procedures. Since there were only twenty donors, four instances of infection or retained pregnancy means that 20 percent of donors were adversely affected by the experience.[13]

The developers of the OT method pointed out that the initial trials were only the experimental phase. With more donors, more drugs to eliminate retained pregnancies in the donors, and more money, they hoped to limit the losses and improve the rates considerably. Yet subsequent research at the University of Southern California Medical School in 1987 and 1988 attempted, with dismal results, to overcome the failures of OT. The problem of very few embryos retrieved was addressed by superovulating the donors with hormone treatments; the drawback of retained pregnancies was to be averted by giving all donors an endometrial curettage and contragestive drugs after each lavage. Despite these procedures, which presented more risks for the donors, twenty-eight lavages of six donors resulted in only one embryo transfer, but no pregnancies for recipients and two retained pregnancies in donors.[14]

Clearly this is a method that had moderate success in Milan but very poor results in California, with problems for the donors severe enough to lead even OT's strongest proponents to conclude that the risks were too great to proceed. The subsequent development of ovum donation combined with IVF eliminated any indication for using lavage, as it meant that egg donors no longer have to be inseminated.[15]

On the basis of his very limited and mostly unsuccessful experience with thirteen women, Dr. Buster had proclaimed in 1985 that "the research is completed, the success of the procedure is proven," and the plans for a national marketing campaign were launched. Good medical research, however, requires a much larger sample, trials by other researchers, and better evidence of safety and effectiveness before making a procedure available to the general public. The American Fertility Society's ethics committee concluded in 1986 that, because of reservations about the procedure, OT should be carried out only under carefully controlled experimental conditions.[16]

OVUM TRANSFER FOR PRENATAL DIAGNOSIS

Human ovum transfer was first used with infertile couples. Long before it failed, however, John Buster already had other plans for using the ovum transfer technology, but this time with all pregnant women. He has long since moved on to this new research. His concern now is not with making babies but with improving their "quality." He described the embryo to us as a "little microchip," a package containing an incredible amount of information. Now he is researching that package, decoding the information to discover defects in the chip. In an interview carried out in 1985, Dr. Buster told us:

> *In another five years infertility will be a nonissue, when there's an abundance of human ova available. Women are going to be much more concerned about the quality of life than they are about whether or not they can have babies.*

More than five years have passed. Today infertility is hardly a nonissue, and OT has failed to live up to any of the promises. Yet John Buster continues to be optimistic. In recent publications he describes uterine lavage as "safe," and in 1991 he was quoted as saying that in ten more years it would be perfected enough to give all women the possibility to diagnose their embryos even before they implant in the uterus. Women who are now advised to have prenatal testing must wait at least until late in the first trimester and then agonize over the possibility of an abortion. With the lavage method (that worked so poorly for OT), they could have a newly fertilized egg washed out of their wombs after five days, checked out in a laboratory, and reinserted only if it is healthy.[17]

Thus a new field has developed, called preimplantation genetics. Eggs that are fertilized and grow in a laboratory as part of IVF are already being biopsied to detect sex and genetic disease; Buster's proposal is that uterine lavage should be used to remove embryos from women who conceive naturally, before they implant in the uterus, so that they can be diagnosed for genetic "quality."

Scientists claim that very soon they will be able to detect not only genetic diseases in new embryos but also even tendencies to diabetes, heart disease, and other disorders. Will all of the embryos with these problems be discarded? Will future children with the wrong color hair or shape of nose be tossed out, with the woman trying again the next month for a more perfect "package"? According to the scientists, no embryos will be discarded; instead, they will be frozen until methods are developed to repair the defects. We wonder, though, how many people would go to the expense and trouble of genetic repair—when it becomes feasible—of an embryo if it is relatively easy to produce new ones.

All of the reproductive technologies have this potential for applying eugenics to human procreation. They all will eventually allow parents to pick their children's characteristics. OT may be unique in that one of its founders, Richard Seed, became involved with it in the first place because he considered it a means of improving the number and quality of American babies. According to journalist Martin Stuart-Harle, Seed believed that "there has always been a shortage of humans in Western civilization" and that OT could be a key to "the success of Western civilization."[18]

OT is not likely to contribute very much toward achieving this racist vision. It is more likely to be used by fertile women who are worried that they might have handicapped children and who are able to monitor the possibility of a pregnancy from the very beginning. These would tend to be more affluent and educated women with access to the most advanced medical resources. They are the people who, if they have handicapped children now, push hard for better services. When only poor and uneducated women have children with serious problems, how much influence will they have over the allocation of resources to help such children?

The history of OT is a disturbing one. It demonstrates the worst of science and business combined, with women the experimental subjects paying for their own subjection to unproven and risky procedures, and no outside body empowered to provide any oversight or regulation. The media also played an important role in promoting the program, just as they have consistently highlighted the very few successes of other reproductive technologies and ignored the many negative dimensions for those involved. If GIFT, whose success is also overplayed, and oocyte donation had not been developed around the time when FGR was beginning its operations, it is likely that the program would have continued on hype and hope for several more years before its failure brought it down. But lack of success both scientifically and commercially has hardly discouraged the promoters. This is evident from the current attention in both the press and scientific journals to the use of uterine lavage with "preimplantation genetics." It would not be surprising to find FGR, which is still in the infertility business, setting up franchised embryo check-ins around the world in a few years.

NOTES

1. Information about possible reasons for using OT and about the research on OT is derived from the following sources: Harris Brotman, "Human Embryo Transplants," *The New York Times Magazine,* January 8, 1984; John E. Buster and Mark V. Sauer, "Nonsurgical Donor Ovum Transfer: New Option for Infertile Couples," *Contemporary OB/GYN,* August 1986, 39–48; John E. Buster, Maria Bustillo et al., "Biologic and Morphologic Development of Donated Human Ova Recovered by Nonsurgical Uterine Lavage," *American Journal of Obstetrics and Gynecology,* 153, September 15, 1985, 211–17; Maria Bustillo, John E. Buster et al., "Nonsurgical Ovum Transfer as a Treatment in Infertile Women," *Journal of the American Medical Association,* 251, March 2, 1984, 1171–73; FGR Information Packet, Fertility and Genetics Research, Inc., Los Angeles, CA; Grace Ganz Blumberg, "Legal Issues in Nonsurgical Human Ovum Transfer," *Journal of the American Medical Association* 251, March 2, 1984, 1178–81; Transcript #08223, "Donahue Show," Multimedia Entertainment, Inc., Syndication Services, Cincinnati, OH.

2. Fern Chapman, "Going for Gold in the Baby Business," *Fortune,* September 17, 1984, 41–77; Hal Lancaster, "Firm Offering Human Embryo Transfers for Profit Stirs Legal and Ethical Debates," *Wall Street Journal,* March 7, 1984, 33; Martin Stuart-Harle, "Making a Buck on Babies," *Globe and Mail,* Toronto, April 19, 1984, L1.

3. "Breeding Bonanza: Embryo Swaps Yield Cows Many Calves Each Year," *Wall Street Journal,* May 9, 1979, 1, 39.

4. Anne Marie C. Kelly, "Psychological Interviews with Ovum Transfer Candidates," typescript, paper presented at the American Psychological Association meetings, Anaheim, CA, 1983; David J. Martin, "MMPI Profiles of Ovum Transfer Donors and Recipients," paper presented at the American Psychological Association meetings, Anaheim, CA, 1983.

5. George J. Annas, "Surrogate Embryo Transfer: The Perils of Parenting," *Hastings Center Report,* June 1984, 25–26; Brotman, "Human Embryo Transplants."

6. John Jenkins, "Fertility Rights," *TWA Ambassador,* January 1985, 60–62.

7. Glenn Kramon, "Infertility Chain: The Good and Bad in Medicine," *New York Times,* June 19, 1992, D1; Alison Leigh Cowan, "Market Place; Can a Baby-Making Venture Deliver?" *New York Times,* June 1, 1992, D1.

8. Mona Field, "On the Demise of a Research Project: A Case Study," Glendale Community College, Glendale, CA.

9. *Ibid*

10. Buster and Sauer, "Nonsurgical Donor Ovum Transfer: New Option for Infertile Couples"; Buster et al., "Biologic and Morphologic Development of Donated Human Ova Recovered by Nonsurgical Uterine Lavage"; Bustillo et al., "Nonsurgical Ovum Transfer as a Treatment in Infertile Women."

11. Brotman, "Human Embryo Transplants"; Buster and Sauer, "Nonsurgical Donor Ovum Transfer"; Buster et al., "Biologic and Morphologic Development of Donated Human Ova Recovered by Nonsurgical Uterine Lavage"; Bustillo et al., "Non-surgical Ovum Transfer as a Treatment in Infertile Women"; FGR Information Packet.

12. Leonardo Formigli, Graziella Formigli, Carlo Roccio, "Donation of Fertilized Uterine Ova to Infertile Women," *Fertility and Sterility* 47 (Jan. 1987): 162–65.

13. Mark V. Sauer, M. Jan Gorrill, John R. Marshall, and John E. Buster, "An Instrument for the Recovery of Preimplantation Uterine Ova," *Obstetrics & Gynecology* 71 (1988): 804–06.

14. Mark V. Sauer, Robert E. Anderson, Richard J. Paulson, "A Trial of Superovulation in Ovum Donors

Undergoing Uterine Lavage," *Fertility and Sterility* 51 (Jan. 1989):131–34.

15. Mark V. Sauer, and Richard J. Paulson, "Human Oocyte and Preembryo Donation: An Evolving Method for the Treatment of Infertility," *American Journal of Obstetrics and Gynecology* 163 (Nov. 1990): 1421–24.

16. Ethics Committee of the American Fertility Society, "Ethical Considerations of the New Reproductive Technologies," *Fertility and Sterility Supplement* 46 (Sep. 1986): 15–92.

17. John E. Buster and Sandra A. Carson, "Genetic Diagnosis of the Preimplantation Embryo," *American Journal of Medical Genetics* 34 (1989): 211–16; Ronald Kotulak and Peter Gorner, "Babies By Design," *Chicago Tribune,* March 3, 1991, Sunday Magazine, 14.

18. Stuart-Harle, "Making a Buck on Babies."

Chapter 14

FETAL QUALITY CONTROL

Technology-assisted methods of conception employ novel methods to join the egg and sperm and gestate the embryo. These methods also hold out the possibility of increasingly sophisticated attempts at the genetic evaluation of the egg, sperm, and embryo. Such fetal quality control exemplifies proactive attempts to shape the characteristics of offspring. However, technology already allows for fetal quality control in arenas that are decidedly more reactive. Three of these will be discussed in this chapter: prenatal testing leading to abortion, prenatal testing leading to fetal surgery, and surveillance of pregnant women's behavior. Each of these represents a medical response to existing fetal characteristics that are negatively evaluated.

Fetal quality control is a women's health issue because of the decisions required of women, and the pressures on women to make particular decisions; the physical intrusions on women's bodies occasioned by abortion, surgery, and cesarean sections; the alteration of the pregnancy experience; and the potential for a decrease in a woman's rights as her fetus gains rights. The discussion that follows of these and other issues is organized into the three arenas because each, from the perspective of the woman experiencing them, is strikingly different in terms of risks to the woman, her obligations and required behaviors, and the type of control exerted over her.

PRENATAL TESTING LEADING TO ABORTION

Prenatal testing was developed in the 1960s by a doctor interested in diagnosing and treating Rh incompatibilities (a red blood cell problem) of pregnant women and their fetuses. Doctor A. William Liley's techniques of amniocentesis (sampling of the amniotic fluid surrounding the fetus) and fetal transfusions speeded the development of other prenatal testing and (ironically, because he was antiabortion) of abortion options. Now women can learn of a variety of physical problems affecting the fetus—including Tay Sachs disease, sickle cell anemia, neural tube defects such as spina bifida, and chromosomal disorders such as Downs syndrome—using not just amniocentesis but also ultrasound (high-frequency sound waves to obtain an echo-visual image), and, more recently, biopsies of the placenta (chorionic villus sampling), cameras inserted through an incision in the mother's abdomen (fetoscopy), and sophisticated blood testing (maternal serum alpha-fetoprotein testing, or AFP).

Although prenatal test information can be used to better prepare for the birth of a child with atypical problems, the primary reason for most prenatal testing has been to discover whether a fetus has characteristics deemed "undesirable," with the goal of aborting those fetuses. When first introduced in America, tests were primarily used to identify life-threatening or severely life-limiting physical conditions. But prenatal testing can and has done more. In Asia, the early use of ultrasound and amniocentesis has led to the differential abortion of female fetuses in what is described as the "largest effort ever to suppress the birth of a particular demographic group" (Rothblatt 1997:12).

The process of declaring which characteristics are "undesirable" is an unambiguous example of social construction. Society can define anything as undesirable or handicapping. Being a girl is a clear handicap in most societies—if handicap is measured by possible educational or economic standing, potential power, respect, or status. It is not absurd to suggest that the number of characteristics deemed undesirable will increase and may include very trivial cosmetic features, or that attempts may be made to influence personality predispositions. Parents seem eager to have such control over their potential offspring. "Survey data indicate that many parents would consider termination of a pregnancy for even moderate defects in the unborn child, such as a heightened risk of early heart disease or criminal tendency" (Blank 1990:89). The exponential growth of the knowledge of human genetics resulting from the Human Genome Project, coupled with an apparent belief that the important things in life have a genetic basis (Browner and Press 1995:307), will lead to an expanded number of tested characteristics, even if the genetic information is inexact or wrong (Hubbard 1995).

Designer babies raise serious moral and social issues, including the commodification of babies and the devaluing of individuals with undesirable traits. The commodification argument suggests that the language of industrial processes may have come, unfortunately but accurately, to describe the process of conception and childbirth. The "screening and testing of fetuses serves the function of 'quality control' on the assembly line of the products of conception, separating out those products we wish to develop from those we wish to discontinue" (Rothman 1988:97, reproduced as a reading in Chapter 13). Children are seen "as objects or products chosen on the basis of their qualities, like products in a shop window" (Robertson 1994:150). The images in Huxley's *Brave New World* may be prophetic: "A worst-case scenario envisages repressive political regimes using these techniques ot create a government-controlled Brave New World of genetically engineered social classes" (Robertson 1994: 150).

Fetal quality control not only leads to the commodification of our children, but also encourages a negative perception of individuals with "undesirable" characteristics. It is easy to see how it would make people less tolerant of difference. Indeed, most observers suggest that

> *prenatal diagnosis, genetic screening and characteristic selection will heighten discrimination of children born with congenital or genetic disorders.... In this atmosphere, affected individuals increasingly will be viewed as unfit to be alive, as second-class humans, at best, or as unnecessary persons who would not have been born if only someone had gotten to them in time. (Blank 1990: 91)*

Although prenatal testing leading to abortion is sometimes described as a humanitarian option to reduce the pain and anguish of parents and children, such a view fails to recognize that it is society that makes differences matter, and society that creates much of the pain and anguish. Many people, in spite of being "different," live good and happy lives, which are made even better when society removes barriers to participation and reduces discriminatory practices. Before the 1980s, children with Down syndrome were warehoused, and parents were discouraged from bonding with them. Many thought the children had no chance of a meaningful life. However, when loved by family and friends, these children demonstrated a potential that doctors had thought impossible. Many people live richer lives because of their relationships with people who are "different." Stated at the societal level, one "conception of a just world is one in which there is greater acceptance of individual difference, variation, and deviance—and this is what would be eliminated with greater genetic engineering" (Rothman quoted in Silver, Rifkin, and Rothman 1998:50).

The issues around prenatal testing are central issues of women's health. For many women, such testing is emotionally taxing, though it is rarely recognized as such. Rather than being a cause to celebrate, a woman's pregnancy becomes tentative: "(S)he cannot ignore it, but neither can she wholeheartedly embrace it.... (S)he is a pregnant woman, but she knows that she may not be carrying a baby but a genetic accident, a mistake. The pregnancy may not be leading to a baby, but to an abortion" (Rothman 1987:101). Thus, prenatal testing alters the meaning of the pregnancy, even if the results of the test are "good." When, on the other hand, testing reveals a problem, making and going through with a decision to abort is agonizing for many (Kolker and Burke 1993). Pregnant women undergoing abortion after prenatal testing report how "psychologically and physically horrible" it is (quoted in Kolker and Burke 1993: 516). "Unlike other perinatal losses, in this case the parents must take active steps to bring about the death of their baby; they 'play God'" (Kolker and Burke 1993:520).

Women are often ill prepared to make decisions based on prenatal test results. Prenatal testing has become routinized—accepted as the standard of care for all women and suggested to women not as an option, but as what pregnant women should do. This routinization has resulted in women not being informed of the full significance of the test. For instance, California actively promotes AFP prenatal testing, not just by subsidizing all costs, including follow-up and therapeutic abortion, and by mandating that all providers must offer it to their clients, but also by obscuring the purpose of the test. The nine-page official booklet describes the AFP test as a simple test that can detect, among other things, the presence of twins and give information on the due date. Only on the last page is there a discussion of options if a defect is found. A mere four lines of text tells the woman that "she will be provided with 'information...about what treatments would be available' and that 'different options will be discussed.' The words *abortion* or *pregnancy termination* do not appear at any point" (Browner and Press 1995:313).

The rapid growth of prenatal testing, combined with its careful separation from the socially distasteful label of eugenics, its identification as an individual decision rather than as a state mandate, and its association with reproductive rights and the socially sanctioned abortion alternative (Browner and Press 1995:308) have all allowed prenatal testing to become an accepted practice. Although seeming to be a new reproductive choice, some observers argue that prenatal testing unnecessarily constrains women's choices. "Currently, there is an *imperative* to do anything possible to avoid disability" (Casper 1998:226). Genetic counselors may try to be nondirective in their counseling of women, but their training teaches them that genetics is important. Not surprisingly, many counselors report that they themselves would have an abortion for most abnormalities and suggest that at times they cannot be nondirective. Said one, "Just what kind of person would...[a counselor be] if she saw someone heading off a cliff and sat back 'nondirectively'?" (Rothman 1987:47). At the individual level, women are not given information about raising a child with atypical problems, and thus they do not make truly informed decisions (McDonough 1999:149). Given adequate information, "(s)ome women might still choose *not* to raise a disabled child for a variety of reasons. But the decision to seek fetal treatment for or to abort a potentially defective fetus would be directly related to the specific conditions of a woman's life rather than mandated by the broader social context in which she lives" (Casper 1998:226).

PRENATAL TESTING LEADING TO FETAL SURGERY

Although a major force in the origins of prenatal testing was, as noted earlier in this chapter, a doctor who developed techniques intended to treat babies with problems (Rh incompatibility with the mother), not to abort them, the surgical treatment of fetuses was eclipsed in the 1960s and 1970s by prenatal testing that led to an abortion (Casper 1998). Not until the 1980s did fetal surgery as a speciality begin to develop seriously. Fetal surgery began in utero, with surgeries performed with the fetus still in the woman's uterus, and developed to include extra-utero procedures, which required a surgeon to open up the woman's abdomen and uterus, lift the fetus out, perform fetal surgery, replace the fetus, and sew the woman back up. For doctors "the drama of penetrating the uterus and its contents with needles and catheters, fully *intervening* in pregnancy and fetal life" (Casper 1998: 51), was clearly more exciting than prior hormonal treatment of the fetus delivered by way of the mother and the umbilical cord.

Fetal surgery was not only exciting, but it was also controversial from the beginning. Doctors fully recognized the revolutionary change that fetal surgery involved: "The concept that the fetus is a patient, an individual whose maladies are a proper subject for medical treatment as well as scientific observation, is alarmingly modern.... Historically, we approached the fetus with a wonder bordering on mysticism.... Only now are we beginning to view the fetus seriously—medically, legally, and ethically" (as quoted in Kolata 1990:77–78). Recognizing the controversial nature of their work, the first American doctors who attempted to learn about the possibilities of fetal surgery and develop a proficiency, did so secretly. In 1979, an all-male group formed a club informally referred to as the "Fetal Invaders," with membership by invitation only (Kolata 1990:4).

For doctors, it was a new world. One commented on the extraordinarily exciting nature of the work of being able to "define diseases that no one had seen before" (Kolata 1990:87). Doctors jumped in, knowing little about fetal physiology and the maternal–fetal connection. Reported one fetal surgeon, "We were operating on this organ that nobody understands, flat out, nobody understands it. We thought we were doing what was right: relax the uterus, do the operation, close the uterus, and get out. We didn't know what we were doing...with the placenta" (quoted in Casper 1998:78). There was much to learn and few successes, with a fetal mortality rate of 65 percent for operations repairing congenital defects, and with some operations having fetal mortality rates as high as 80 percent (Casper 1998:6).

Its low success rate, novelty, expense, and maternal risk made recruiting appropriate women a difficult task. As a result, some doctors pressured women to have fetal surgery. One doctor's approach involved telling a woman that she was in a desperate situation in which doing nothing would mean the baby would have a "very tiny chance of surviving," and permitting the fetal surgery would mean the "baby has quite a good chance," although he later admitted that with fetal surgery so new "there's no evidence" for its effectiveness (Kolata 1990:106–107). Such a sales pitch minimizes maternal risk. Even if more fully discussed, maternal risk is hard to communicate to women who are mainly thinking about the fetus. Said one pregnant woman, "I was so focused on the fetal surgery and her [the fetus's] operation and what it entailed, that I don't think it dawned on me that *I* was going to go through major surgery" (quoted in Casper 1998:174).

One important consequence of fetal surgery is the rise of fetal rights and the consequent diminution of the rights for the pregnant woman. The early pronouncements by Liley, the father of prenatal testing, although extreme because of his anti-abortion politics, foreshadowed this erasure of women. Liley privileged the fetus with amazing powers:

> *Our new human has in hand even grander designs and undertakings than simply his own internal organization and development. He also develops his own life-support system, his placenta, and his own confines.... But even the organization of his own confines does not exhaust the list of achievements of our new individual. His own welfare is too important to permit leaving anything to the chance cooperation of others, and therefore* he must organize his mother to make her body a suitable home. *(quoted in Casper 1998:60–61)*

The fetus was so powerful, it controlled the mother. Mothers lost their agency and significance. Doctors continued this trend in a variety of ways, including failing to consider maternal risk during fetal surgery (Casper 1998:145–146,183,185).

The increasing focus on the fetus as the patient set up a situation in which a woman's selfhood was diminished as her fetus's selfhood was constructed. The rights of a fetus developed as the prerogative of the medical world. First, doctors developed expertise to treat a fetus, and then they began to routinely refer to them as people, humanizing them with terms such as *Junior, he, baby,* and *kid* (Casper 1998: 214). This gradual metamorphosis of the fetus from patient to person has led some to assume associated fetal rights independent of the pregnant woman. Given the geography of pregnancy, such rights are often in opposition to those of the woman.

In addition to subtle pressures from doctors for pregnant women to "do all you can do" for the fetus, some observers suggest that the ethics of maternity may *require* fetal diagnosis and treatment (Jonsen 1988), and that even drastic measures involving major surgery will become a duty, a new obligation of potential motherhood. "Presently, women do not face governmental intervention when making a decision about whether or not to undergo prenatal screening. But some legal commentators suggest that a pregnant woman who is at risk of delivering a baby with a disability and refuses screening should be liable for 'prenatal abuse'" (Henifin 1993:69). A legal and procreation specialist has stated that "a woman has an obligation to accept established therapies for the fetus' sake" (Henifin 1993:70). The success of some suits brought on behalf of an infant, claiming the child would have been better off never to have been born ("wrongful life" tort) (Blank 1990:93–101), provides worrisome reinforcement of the implied duty of mothers and health care providers to respond to signs of problems and not to just let nature take its own course.

SURVEILLANCE OF MATERNAL BEHAVIOR

The trajectory of reasoning that obligates women to undergo surgical procedures for the benefit of a fetus is in conflict with the prohibition in our legal system of ordering men or women to donate an organ or replaceable bone marrow that could save a relative. The law even protects cadavers from court-ordered intrusions. Apparently a pregnant woman has fewer rights than a dead person. This set of rules obligating women to risk their lives to ensure fetal health is not limited to prenatal testing and fetal surgery and has moved beyond moral suasion into the courtroom. Two important arenas are court-ordered cesarean sections after the diagnosis of pregnancy difficulties, and the criminalization of women's lifestyles said to be injurious to the health of the fetus.

The first court-ordered intrusion on a pregnant woman was in 1964 when, in two separate cases, courts compelled pregnant women to undergo blood transfusions that they had refused on religious grounds (Condit 1995:38). Since that time, courts have ordered pregnant women to be detained in hospitals and to have cesarean sections. These court orders have included cases in which the cesarean section was later found unnecessary for the fetus (the woman delivered a healthy baby vaginally before the cesarean section could be attempted—see Blank and Merrick 1995:158–159) and a case in which the cesarean section had no benefit for the baby (she died) and speeded the death of a woman with terminal cancer. This latter case, *Carder v. George Washington University Hospital,* gained prominence as one of the few cases to be appealed to a higher court. The appeals court posthumously overturned the decision to impose a cesarean section, and in so doing recognized that "every person has the right, under the common law and the Constitution, to accept or refuse medical treatment" (Terry 1998:755).

Though having the decision overturned and hearing a reaffirmation of bodily integrity seemed like a victory, the appellate decision gave "cold comfort to those concerned with forced treatment of pregnant women" (Condit 1995:40). The court went on to suggest that there could be cases in which the state's interests would prevail over those of the pregnant woman: "We do not quite foreclose the possibility that a conflicting state interest may be so compelling that the patient's wishes must yield, but we anticipate that such cases will be extremely rare and truly exceptional" (Terry 1998:756–757). So far, the statistically rare cases have been predominately nonwhite. Eighty percent of the early cases involved women who were African American, Asian, or Hispanic (Kolder, Gallagher, and Parsons 1987).

Courts have also actively intervened in pregnancies by declaring that certain lifestyles are injurious to the fetus. They place the offending woman under close supervision, which may involve putting her in prison to control her behavior, or making her subject to postdelivery criminal consequences. Criminalization of behavior deemed not in the fetus' best interests has gone so far as to include a woman's behaviors that are legal, but happen to be against medical advice. "Women have been charged or sued for a growing list of legal behaviors that others allege could prove harmful to their fetuses, including taking a prescription drug, smoking cigarettes, having sexual intercourse, drinking alcohol, failing to follow doctors' orders, and not eating properly while pregnant" (Condit 1995:42). But the main reason for prosecution has been drug use.

Such a focus is clearly discriminatory. First, it is discriminatory because poor women are subjected to "greater governmental supervision—through their association with public hospitals, welfare agencies, and probation officers—[so] their drug use is more likely to be detected and reported" (Roberts 1998:765). Thus, one study found that a black woman was nearly 10 times more likely than a white woman to be reported for substance abuse while pregnant, even though the actual incidence of abuse in black women appeared to be the same as in white women (Chasnoff, Landress, and Barrett 1990:1204). Second, it is discriminatory because of all the behaviors that could potentially have a physical effect on the fetus, doctors and courts have chosen to focus on illegal drug use, a substance-abuse behavior that is more typical of disadvantaged and minority women.

Media coverage has also focused on fetal abuse associated with drug use. An analysis of *New York Times* articles from 1989 to 1991 found thirty-four on fetal abuse. Twenty-seven discussed drug use (Schroedel and Peretz 1995:88). Underrepresented were articles on maternal alcohol or tobacco abuse (more of a middle-class problem). Totally missing were articles on paternal abuse: the effect of substance abuse on sperm, occupational or environmental hazards, and wife-battering (Schroedel and Peretz 1995). Furthermore, the particular focus of prosecutors has become crack use, which is predominately a problem in lower-income and minority neighborhoods.

Increases in court-ordered intervention destroy the mother–doctor relationship. No longer can the pregnant woman trust that information given to the doctor will be used in her own best interests. Instead of reporting drug use to the doctor and asking for help, the pregnant woman may fear that she will be reported for fetal abuse.

The focus on "bad" mothers also has important social consequences. "In addition to legitimizing fetal rights enforcement, the prosecution of crack-addicted mothers diverts public attention from social ills such as poverty, racism, and a misguided national health policy" (Roberts 1998:767). We could talk of "poverty babies"; instead we speak of "crack babies" (Murphy and Rosenbaum 1999:141). The focus is on the individual as the source of the problem, not on societal patterns. And at the individual level, women are blamed and punished instead of given help to find treatment for their addiction behavior. In fact, many treatment centers will not accept them because they are pregnant (Chavkin 1996). Such practices embolden the "pregnancy police," ordinary people who have decided that they need to control the behavior of pregnant women. They refuse to serve pregnant women alcohol in restaurants, and comment on what they feel is inappropriate for someone in "that condition."

In the last two decades of the twentieth century, medical science transformed the pregnancy experience. Pregnant women now face new obligations to determine if their child-to-be has any imperfections, and a growing obligation to act on their knowledge. While the pregnant woman's duty to her child-to-be has grown, so has the tendency to see her as irresponsible. Fetal patienthood came in the backdoor as science allowed the world to see the developing fetus on ultrasound, and doctors to operate on it outside the uterus. With the growth of fetal rights, maternal rights are being eclipsed. Pregnant women have become embroiled in an adversarial relationship not of their own making, and the fetus seems to be winning.

THE CASE OF THE DISAPPEARING MOMS: FETAL SURGERY AND WOMEN'S HEALTH

MONICA J. CASPER

In 1963, in Auckland, New Zealand, Dr. William Liley operated on Mrs. E. MacLeod and her thirty-two-week old fetus using a procedure called intrauterine transfusion technology. The fetus, which suffered from a potentially lethal Rh incompatibility, survived the operation, as did the maternal patient. The baby, Grant Liley McLeod, made headlines around the world both at the time of the operation and upon his birth three weeks later. So, too, did the surgeon responsible for breaching the womb and treating a fetus for the first time as a medical patient in its own right. Liley, who would later be knighted by Queen Elizabeth, was celebrated as a medical pioneer and is now widely recognized as the father of fetal surgery. Mrs. E. MacLeod, whose picture had appeared twice in the *New Zealand Herald,* quickly receded from public view.

In 1981, in San Francisco, California, a team of doctors and nurses peeled back the layers of a pregnant woman's womb to operate on her impaired fetus. Both mother and fetus survived that operation and, like the McLeods two decades earlier, entered the media spotlight as biomedical miracles. Unlike Liley's "closed" technique in which needles and catheters were used to access the fetus, in open fetal surgery the fetus was directly exposed and made accessible to the surgeons for treatment. The unborn patient had arrived, bringing with it altered expectations about the inviolability of pregnant women. The 1981 procedure was followed by hundreds more cases, with radically mixed results. Some fetuses lived and many others died; while maternal health was often at risk during and after these operations, no pregnant women died. Yet the innovative procedures of the late twentieth century profoundly challenged taken-for-granted notions of pregnancy, fetal status, and the limits of maternal–fetal medicine.

Forty years after Liley's efforts, and twenty years after the experimental work in California, fetal surgery has become a recognized feature of the biomedical landscape. Not yet considered routine, but no longer as shockingly new as it once was, fetal surgery exists in an ambiguous zone of medical practice somewhere between "experiment" and "standard of care." It is being pursued at several hospitals around the world both within experimental protocols and as a fee-for-service procedure. For example, one of these institutions is Vanderbilt University Medical Center, where fetal surgery is being used—not without controversy—to treat *nonlethal* cases of spina bifida. As the specialty of fetal surgery has evolved, so, too, have conceptions of pregnant women, fetuses, and medicine itself. For several decades, this cutting-edge practice has contributed to the increasingly accepted notion of the unborn patient, fueling debates about fetal status and its social and political consequences.

Often lost within these debates, and within the practice itself, is the pregnant woman. Although she is a key player, discussions of fetal surgery—whether in medicine or the media, in law or ethics—routinely erase her. Fetal surgery is overwhelmingly framed, both by practitioners and by commentators, as a *pediatric* issue. Many of fetal surgery's practitioners are pediatric surgeons who have retooled their skills to work on smaller bodies (the "real" patients) in a more constrained environment. Obstetricians, historically focused on pregnant women, often find themselves sidelined in fetal surgery as maternal patients are deemed peripheral to the main event. The sole purpose of these operations is, after all, to attempt to fix an impaired fetus. In almost all cases, there is nothing whatsoever wrong with the pregnant woman. She is configured by doctors either as "the best heart-lung machine available" to support the unborn patient, or as a flesh-and-blood barrier to be opened surgically in order to access the fetus. Doctors' generic identification of the pregnant women as "moms" can be read as part of an overall effort to manage complicated maternal patients as objects while erasing their role as subjects.

Women are made invisible in the practice of fetal surgery in a variety of ways, despite their obvious material presence. The cultural imagery of fetal surgery often represents only the fetus. For example, the logo of one fetal treatment center features a tiny fetal image nestled in the healing hand of a doctor, with no pregnant woman present at all. The names of the hospital-based clinical programs erase women, too: Fetal Treatment Center, Fetal Surgery Unit, and so on. Almost none mention that there is also a *maternal* patient involved. It is also somewhat ironic, and telling, that "fetal surgeons" operate on both pregnant women and the unborn patient. In addition, while women and their partners attend some preoperative meetings with practitioners, at many fetal treatment meetings the woman is represented only by an ultrasound image, her subjectivity and presence reduced to the grainy black and white picture of her insides. In a particularly compelling example of how women are erased, fetal surgeons at one institution videotape each surgery; taping begins after the pregnant woman has been cut open, continues during the operation on the fetus, and ends before the woman's body has been resealed. Clearly, the maternal patient is not as visually interesting or important as is the fetal patient in this specialty.

The "moms" are disappeared beyond the walls of the operating room, as well. Ethical discourses typically focus on fetal status alone, or on maternal–fetal conflict; rarely do these perspectives take up broader social and political issues such as cost, justice, quality of life, reproductive rights, and so on. Legal scholars also wrestle with the question of maternal–fetal conflict and attempt to strike a balance between maternal autonomy and fetal rights. In these framings, it is pregnant women who are often seen as a threat to their unborn children whether because of drug and alcohol use or refusal to submit to reproductive care such as cesarean sections. With the exception of feminist perspectives, most commentators fail to address the many ways in which fetal surgery, in fact, threatens women's health and autonomy. Media analyses, too, have failed to consider the women's health aspects of fetal surgery. Enamored of modern biomedicine, print and television journalists have emphasized the miraculous and celebrated the successful. In these largely uncritical stories, fetal surgery is positioned as a heroic, cutting-edge last-ditch effort chosen by brave families for whom abortion is not an option. By focusing only on success stories in which the fetus lives, such media coverage perpetuates the deeply-held notion that modern medicine can indeed save us. The mainstream media have been especially lax about calling attention to the broader context of fetal surgery and to its social and political consequences.

But what constitutes the social and political context of fetal surgery? Why is this emergent practice a women's health issue par excellence, and not simply a pediatric concern? How are women configured in fetal surgery, and with what consequences? And how might women be written into the story of fetal surgery to better reflect their crucial role? To answer these questions, I employ a women's health framework to address various features and consequences of fetal surgery. A women's health framework foregrounds the experiences of women, including their desires and needs in selecting medical intervention; the consequences of intervention on their own health; and the social structures that shape health and illness, including gender, race/ethnicity, class, and age.

Pregnant women have been crucial participants in the making of the unborn patient, actively choosing a range of interventions for the sake of their fetuses. In making sense of fetal surgery from a women's health perspective, a feminist intervention is needed that does not claim to know better than the women who opt for fetal surgery. This means finding a way to critique fetal surgery and the social relations that sustain it without criticizing the women who choose it. It also means attending to the many contradictions in reproductive medicine of which fetal surgery is a part. Reproductive medicine both heals and harms women; it both produces and destroys fetuses; it is both palliative and iatrogenic; it both opens and closes reproductive possibilities; it is both a consumer good women choose and a form of social control; and it both shapes cultural meanings and is a product of culture. Fetal surgery contains within it many of these paradoxes, with multiple consequences for women and their fetuses.

CLINICAL SAFETY

Fetal surgery is often portrayed in the media and by doctors themselves as a "successful" intervention, one that produces miracle babies. However, fetal mortality statistics remain quite high (at one institution they ranged from 40 percent to 80 percent, depending on the condition being treated), and maternal morbidity may also be threatened. A women's health perspective should insist that fetal surgery be made safer clinically before being defined as a routine procedure available to all women. Preterm labor is an ongoing problem, as are potential threats to subsequent reproduction after surgery. All additional maternal risks should be identified and, if possible, alleviated. The solution is *not* intensified management of pregnant women's bodies as if they were inert technologies, but rather a search for ways to diagnose and treat fetuses using methods that are safer and better for pregnant women. If it is not possible to perform fetal surgery without jeopardizing women's safety, then it should not be done at all.

Of course, ensuring clinical safety may also mean *not* intervening in situations where fetuses are at risk, instead recognizing that other techniques may be equally viable. The overall aim of fetal surgery should be the safety of pregnant women and their fetuses, and not an idealistic, heroic vision of rescuing fetuses at any cost. Nor should the burden of risk-assessment fall primarily on women, many of whom are likely to disregard their own safety on behalf of their fetuses. Medical workers themselves must take responsibility for assuring that their practices safeguard women's health.

REORGANIZATION OF MEDICINE

Fetal surgery is characterized by considerable conflict between and among its specialist practitioners, jockeying for control of this flashy new domain. In addition, professional and lay perspectives often chafe against each other in a clinical setting, as "experts" are positioned above patients in medical hierarchies. These dynamics are especially pernicious given the clinical and ethical magnitude of operating on fetuses inside living women's bodies. For fetal surgery to be a viable option *for women,* the specialty would have to be reorganized so that it is less competitive and nonhierarchical. Fetal surgery should not proceed as if it were a battle, with "mom docs" and "baby docs" lined up against each other. This kind of conflict certainly does not serve women's needs or those of their vulnerable fetuses. This may mean giving women and their advocates—social workers, nurses, obstetricians—a much-expanded role in fetal surgery. Every effort should be made to incorporate women's perspectives into treatment plans, as well as to provide detailed and adequate informed consent, whether a procedure is experimental or not. Patients in routine medicine should be protected to the fullest extent possible, even if they are not participants in formal protocols and are thus not technically considered to be research subjects.

ACCESS TO HEALTH SERVICES

This is an issue that extends far beyond access to fetal treatments to encompass all of medicine. If fetal surgery is to be part of the arsenal with which clinicians strive to ensure healthier babies, then it should not be limited to a select group of mostly white, mostly middle- to upper-class women who can afford it. All women, regardless of race, ethnicity, class, or citizenship status, should have access to all available health care. Poor women should have just as much opportunity to get the "best" treatment for their fetuses as women of privilege. This will mean addressing class relations and broader issues of social and economic justice. Strategies for increasing health care access for all pregnant women should be part of efforts to build a national health program in general. If we cannot ensure that all pregnant women who desire it will be able to obtain diagnosis and treatment of their fetuses if needed, then we must seriously reconsider the wisdom of investing public funds in research on fetal surgery and related procedures.

POLITICS OF PRENATAL CARE

This is related to access to services, but goes beyond economic issues to encompass broader social and political concerns. From a women's health perspective, it is difficult to see fetal surgery as heroic when infant mortality rates in the United States remain astonishingly high compared to other industrialized nations (in 1989, nineteen countries had lower rates) and when millions of children remain uninsured. Fetal interventions raise the profoundly important question of what types of prenatal care should be and currently are available and to whom. Which fetuses, for example, are worth saving? Whose fetuses are valued? Which women are able to choose certain procedures and not others given the constraints of their lives? Until *all* women have access to basic prenatal care, perhaps there should be a moratorium on expensive, high-tech procedures such as fetal surgery.

Also, a narrow, reductionist focus on surgically fixing extant problems precludes comprehensive preventive strategies. It would be far more heroic for clinicians, communities, and the nation at large to work collectively to ensure that all pregnant women have access to good nutrition, regular physician or midwife visits, and clean, safe places to live. Activities could include efforts to create a national health program that does not allow citizens to fall through the cracks in coverage; the promotion of community-based health activism that recognizes the collective effort required to foster healthier mothers and babies; better attention to the health needs of women in marginalized groups and enhanced public assistance for those without economic resources; language-specific and culturally sensitive health education programs that emphasize both women's health and community health aspects of prenatal care; and limitations on high-tech procedures. Fetal surgery could be reinstituted after the U.S. infant mortality rate has dropped substantially, the number of low-birth-weight babies has decreased, and many pregnant women are no longer deprived of basic prenatal care.

REPRODUCTIVE POLITICS

Most discussions of fetal surgery fail to connect it to reproductive politics. Such politics refer to all of the ways in which women's reproductive experiences are embedded and contested in broader social and political relations. Fetal surgery poses several distinct threats to pregnant women's autonomy, including the reaffirmation of maternal–fetal conflict issues and the erasure of women in frameworks celebrating fetal personhood. Within a women's health agenda, a different kind of maternal–fetal relationship must be realized. The pregnant women in fetal surgery accept an extraordinary amount of risk on behalf of their fetuses, so much so that surgeons refer to them as "heroic moms." A fetal surgery that is part of a women's health agenda must begin with pregnant women's experiences, and not with the fetus. It is women's bodies and lives that will be fundamentally transformed by fetal interventions of all kinds, including treatment and abortion.

For fetal surgery to continue, its practitioners must be accountable to women's needs. This means taking women's agency seriously, respecting women's decisions in clinical settings, providing as much information as possible about a given fetal treatment trajectory, not treating women like "heart-lung machines," de-emphasizing fetal personhood, working to ensure greater clinical safety for women, enhancing access to prenatal care, and recognizing that all reproductive decisions and choices are difficult. The broader social context of choice matters a great deal. A variety of factors, such as a woman's economic situation, her social support network, or her proximity to clinics, may impinge on her reproductive decisions. Making fetal surgery responsive to a women's health agenda may require improving the conditions of women's lives such that fetal surgery is seen as just one of many possible options for ensuring healthier babies.

ABORTION RIGHTS

We cannot make sense of fetal surgery without recognizing the broader context in which the fetus has become a major cultural icon. A women's health framework would insist that women have access to both abortion *and* fetal surgery (and a range of other reproductive options), despite increasingly popular claims of fetal personhood. Yet fetal patienthood feeds into popular notions of fetal personhood, posing distinct threats to abortion rights. If fetal surgery proceeds in a manner that undermines women's right or access to abortion, then it should be eliminated or radically reframed. A reproductive rights perspective is consistent in its recognition of women's agency in all reproductive decisions—including the right *not* to have an abortion. If we accept women's capacity to choose fetal surgery, then we must also accept other choices and build that recognition directly into the social organization of reproductive health care and government policies about reproduction.

FETAL WELL-BEING

Within a women's health framework, we should also care a great deal about what happens to fetuses who are operated on prenatally. Although fetal surgery is often touted as a rescue mission, it may contribute to fetal disability and demise. There are both immediate and long-term effects, on fetuses as well as on women, of removing a fetus from the womb before it is viable, operating on it, and replacing it for continued gestation. Fetuses may also be affected by the inevitable preterm labor, birth by cesarean section, and then more surgery after birth. It is of great consequence that *none* of the surviving babies are ever fully healthy after fetal surgery; all require additional treatment and care, ranging from more surgery to placement in neonatal intensive care units. Practitioners of fetal surgery should make every effort to minimize trauma to the fetus, as well as to gather as much information as possible about the fate of fetuses who survive. Data can include "objective" measures such as function, size, and disability status, as well as qualitative data obtained from parents about their childrens behavior.

We do not, in fact, have to be "pro-life," in the current political political meanings of that term, to care about fetal well-being and the implications of prenatal interventions. In fact, some pro-life individuals and groups advocate fetal surgery because it propagates notions of fetal personhood. But such celebratory discourse elides some of the worst hazards of these procedures, including high fetal mortality rates and the potential for increased disability. There is instead much room in women's health frameworks, where many women are "pro-life" in various ways, for concern about the fate of fetuses.

DISABILITY POLITICS

Much of the impetus for fetal surgery stems from the desire for healthy, nondisabled babies. It is likely that many reproductive decisions, from prenatal diagnosis to abortion to fetal treatment, are made in relation to contexts in which disability matters. For example, which women have the resources necessary to raise a disabled child? What are the cultural and economic implications of bearing a disabled child? For fetal surgery to be viable in terms of women's health, these complicated politics need to be addressed at a societal level. This means working to minimize the stigma attached to disability, as well as broadening social support for the disabled. Currently, there is an imperative to do anything possible to avoid disability, and women's choices may be constrained. Changing the social relations in which such decisions are made requires a rethinking of disability and its place in social life. Some women might still choose not to raise a disabled child for a variety of reasons. But the decision to seek fetal treatment for, or to abort, a potentially defective fetus would be directly related to the conditions of a woman's life, rather than mandated by the broader social context in which she lives.

In sum, understanding fetal surgery requires examining its meanings and consequences in terms of women's health. Making a fetal surgery *for women* would likely involve social and political change on a number of different fronts. For quite some time now, reproductive politics have been dominated by an abundant concern for fetuses, and fetocentric politics have been shaped and enacted by nonfeminist activists, doctors, bioethicists, lawyers, and others. At the same time, pregnant women have been marginalized, criminalized, and stigmatized for their actions. Whether or not fetal surgery itself becomes more routine—and that remains to be seen—it seems clear that the unborn patient is here to stay. Feminists and others interested in women's health should be cautious about the supposed "promise" of fetal surgery. Without negating women's decisions to seek intervention, we might certainly want to ask, Is fetal surgery the kind of medicine we want? Is it the kind of reproductive politics we want? Those of us who care about women's health need to boldly enter this new reproductive frontier and reclaim the terrain of fetal politics—both in and beyond the operating room—from those who may not have women's best interests at heart. If fetal stories are human stories, then let us rewrite the story of fetal surgery so that women are principal authors and actors.

PRENATAL SCREENING AND DISCRIMINATORY ATTITUDES ABOUT DISABILITY

MARSHA SAXTON

"I'm very sorry to tell you, Mrs. Smith, that the fetus you're carrying has been identified as having a defect. Fortunately, we've caught it in time and you can have an abortion."

This statement is a paraphrase of the one that thousands of U.S. women will hear from their doctors this year. With the advent of the new reproductive technology (including blood testing, amniocentesis, and ultrasound), the means to identify a fetus with Down Syndrome, spina bifida, sickle cell anemia, and a growing number of other conditions, allows early detection, usually in the twelfth to sixteenth week of pregnancy. The technologies are heralded by the medical system as a triumph for modern science, a means to control the incidence of disability, and to improve the quality of life for families and society.

But there is another point of view, one that challenges the notion that Mrs. Smith will necessarily choose to abort her fetus, and that also contradicts the assumption that the world would be a better place without another disabled person.

I write as a person with spina bifida, the major target of prenatal screening and abortion. I am also a disability rights activist, a former director of a center for persons with disabilities, where I've had the opportunity to meet and get to know closely many hundreds of disabled people. As a disabled person myself, I would like to challenge the rarely examined assumptions that underlie the current trend to screen prenatally and to abort fetuses identified as disabled.

I have been speaking, writing, and leading workshops on this topic for three years.[1] It raises complex emotional, moral, and political questions, but most people have so little information or exposure to the issues of disability that their overriding reaction is: "I've never thought about this!" This response is common to audiences of physicians, nurses, genetic counselors, college professors, parents, and students. (Ironically, disabled people are one of the largest minority groups in the U.S., approximately 40 million people, or over 10 percent of the population, a group that cuts across all gender, ethnic, racial, class, and age lines.)

The assumptions I challenge include these: that having a disabled child is wholly undesirable; that the quality of life for people with disabilities is less than that for others; that we have the means to humanly decide whether some are better off never being born.

These assumptions are pervasive in a society oriented toward rigid standards of beauty and athletic prowess. Disability triggers much fear in our culture. Our pioneer history has led us to revere rugged self-reliance and stalwart productivity; we are not comfortable with the reminder of our vulnerability brought us by disabled people.

The disabled person in our society is the target of attitudes and behaviors from the more able-bodied world that range from gawking to avoidance, pity to resentment, or from vastly lowered expectations to awe. Along with these attitudes, disabled persons confront a variety of tangible barriers: architectural inaccessibility, lack of sign-language interpreters for deaf people, insufficient taped or braille materials for blind persons. In addition, disabled people confront less tangible barriers: discrimination in employment, second-class education, and restricted opportunities for full participation in the life of the community.

As with any kind of oppression, the attitudes are self-perpetuating, and the stereotypes are reinforced in the popular media. The isolation of disabled persons limits the larger culture's exposure to their life experiences, needs, and common humanness. A child's natural curiosity and inquisitiveness in encountering a disabled person for the first time is often met with a parent's embarrassed, "Hush, don't ask and don't stare." This child's simple wonder is thus replaced with mistrust and fear, to be handed down the generations. As recently as the 1950s, laws remained on the books in some states prohibiting the public presence of persons "diseased, maimed, mutilated or in any way deformed so as to be an unsightly or disgusting object." This fear of vulnerability, this flight from physical limitation (perhaps from death) is at the root of such phenomena as the Eugenics Movement in the early 1900s. By 1937, 28 states had adopted Eugenics Sterilization laws aimed at persons with epilepsy, mental retardation, mental illness, and other kinds of differences where "procreation was deemed inadvisable." Such attitudes are still with us.

Where do these attitudes come from? Many women are familiar with the widespread advice physicians give to parents who give birth to a disabled child: "Put him away in a home with others like himself." Institutionalization is an outgrowth of the assumption that neither the parents nor the community could cope with the child at home. Such an assumption becomes a self-fulfilling prophecy: the family, friends, and community are never exposed to the child and its actual needs, so dreaded fantasies reinforce stereotypes. The child, as a result of being institutionalized, does indeed become a social outcast, ill-prepared to cope with community life, exhibiting many of the asocial behaviors and extreme dependencies which the parents had feared.

How do the oppressive attitudes about disability affect the woman considering prenatal screening? Very often prospective parents have never faced the issue of disability until it is raised in relation to testing. What comes to the minds of most prospective parents at the mention of the term "birth defects"? Our exposure to disabled children has been so limited because of their isolation that most people have only stereotyped views, which include images derived from telethons and displays on drugstore counters soliciting our pity and loose change. The image of a child with Down Syndrome elicits an even more intense assumption of eternal parental burden.

The fear that a handicapped child will be a burden seems to be a prominent issue in the decision to abort. How much reality is there to the "burden of the disabled"?

In a popular women's magazine, I read "a young mother's story" about a family with a severely disabled child. The mother's description of her struggle to care for the child and another non-disabled sibling in their suburban home struck me: this woman, the sole caretaker of the children, had no assistance from her working husband and none also from any extended family, or from neighbors, or community. She mentioned no contacts with associations for parents in her situation, or community services, only contacts with the child's physician. Of course, she was lonely and overwhelmed; she was isolated by the limitations of the nuclear family.

I do not mean to imply that it's easy to raise a disabled child, emotionally or logistically, even where there *are* additional resources and support systems. But I do suggest that the common assumptions which place the primary blame for the parents' difficulties on the child's disability vastly distort the picture.

A few years ago I attended a weekend conference for families involved in a program called "Project IMPACT" (Innovative Matching of Parents And Children Together). This program arranges adoptions for "hard to place" children, many with multiple handicaps such as mobility impairments, hearing or vision loss, or mental retardation. Having previously led workshops and support groups for parents of disabled children, I was familiar with the many issues such families face: feelings of guilt, and resentment at the limited social services and practical resources. I arrived curious about the parents I would meet there. Unlike most of the parents I had counseled, these parents had *chosen* to raise disabled children. I met with about forty of these families and learned of their experiences and feelings, their ways of dealing with their situations. What struck me was that the usual feelings of "burden" seemed consistently to be replaced with a sense of challenge to find solutions, to meet with others who had found new answers to this or that question, or to share what they had learned. Absent was the attitude "Why me?" or "What did I do to deserve this?" so common among the many other parents of disabled children. To the IMPACT parents, their disabled children served as a source of enrichment, growth, challenge, and joy.

I was reminded of the many mothers of disabled children whom I have seen grow and change over the years. One in particular, Emily, had struck me as especially timid and passive when she first came for training and support to advocate for her disabled child's rights in the school system. Through the course of the work she did on behalf of her child in the six years I knew her, she blossomed, she grew, she became a leader of others, she became triumphant in her new strength as a fighter against discrimination. Her disabled child, originally perceived as the source of her difficulty, had become the impetus for her transformation.

So often *disability is perceived as the problem,* when in fact the disability becomes *the arena* to play out deep-seated distress, disappointment, losses. When seen with clarity and infused with adequate support, the disability becomes the motivation to re-evaluate old attitudes and formulate a more meaningful and satisfying life.

Another of the stereotypes affecting prospective parents concerns "suffering"; it is assumed that disabled persons' lives are filled with pain.

In my work as a therapist, trainer, and former director of a counseling center, I've gotten to know closely the lives of severely disabled people: people with quadriplegia, multiple sclerosis, muscular dystrophy, cerebral palsy, people who are blind or have hearing impairments, "hidden" chronic diseases such as epilepsy and diabetes. Just as the larger population, some of these individuals experience considerable difficulty in their lives while others do fine, have jobs, and enjoy a full and satisfying life with their friends and families. Most disabled people have told me with no uncertainty that the disability, the pain, the need for compensatory devices and assistance can produce considerable inconvenience, but that very often these become minimal or are forgotten once the individual makes the transition of living everyday life. But it is the discriminatory attitudes and thoughtless behavior that make life difficult. These are the source of the real limits; the oppression, the architectural barriers, the pitying stares or frightened avoidance, the unaware assumptions that "you couldn't do the job," couldn't order for yourself in a restaurant, couldn't find a mate or direct your own life. The *oppression,* as I have heard many other disabled people say, in one way or another, is what's disabling about disability.

There is no doubt that there are disabled people who "suffer" from their physical conditions. There are even those who may choose to end their lives rather than continue in pain or with severe limitations, but this is obviously also true for nondisabled people who suffer from emotional pain and limitation of resources. As a group, people with disabilities do not "suffer" any more than any other group or category of humans. Our limitations may be more outwardly visible, our need for help more apparent, but like anybody else, the "suffering" we may experience is primarily a result of not enough human caring, acceptance, and respect.

Often when I speak at conferences, a participant will comment that they know of a disabled person who has suffered greatly: a child who has become the guinea pig in a series of experimental operations to keep her alive; a middle-aged person in constant pain from cancer; an aged person on life support machines. "Wouldn't these people be better off dead?" is the question the participant is really asking.

In advocating that the disabled fetus be allowed to live (and be accepted and loved as any child), I also advocate that terminally ill people be allowed to die, and with dignity. It is often the case that aging, dying individuals in medical institutions are suffering as much from the loss of power over their own affairs, disorientation at being away from home, and objectification as a diseased body, as they are from their illness. Regarding these extreme cases of suffering, the point is that here again, we attempt to *control* life from a vantage point distorted by our own confusions and erroneous attitudes.

I advocate that people be allowed to live and die according to their *own* volition. Above all I challenge the assumption that we as a culture and as individuals have the essential and profound clarity to assess the quality of life for others and to humanely determine their fate.

The medical system wishes to fix, to cure, to control, to perfect, reinforcing the ideal and the possibility of the "perfect baby." Physicians exert strong influence over consumers regarding prenatal screening and they often function as the primary counsel to prospective parents. Because physicians are under pressure to encourage prenatal screening and even abortion out of fear of malpractice suits, they may lobby for enforced screening and will certainly encourage more screening. But physicians, by the very nature of their work, often have a distorted picture of disability. By working in hospitals, with sick people, doctors generally see only those cases of disability where there are complications, where patients are poorly managed, or patients in terminal stages. Many physicians never have the opportunity to see disabled individuals living independently, productively, enjoyably.

If I could counsel to a woman considering prenatal screening with possible intent to abort a disabled fetus, I would ask her: Was she satisfied that she had sufficient knowledge about disability, an awareness of her own feelings about it so that she could make a rational choice? Did she personally know any disabled adults or children? What was she taught about disability by adults when she was young? Was she aware of the distorted picture of the lives of disabled people presented by the posters, telethons, and stereotyped characters in the literature and media? I would ask her to consider the opportunities for herself in taking on the fears and prejudice, the expectations and pressures of her family and friends.

I would suggest that the major factors to consider in decision making are the *resources* of the parents, the family, the community, to care for and love and encourage the child to its fullest potential, and that accurate assessment of those resources can come only with greater clarity about the real nature of disability. By confronting our human vulnerability rather than denying or attempting to take flight from it, we achieve the deepest experience of our humanness.

We will most likely never achieve the means to eliminate disability: our compelling and more profound challenge is to eliminate oppression. Our achievement of acceptance of all people with differences will bring the greatest enhancement of the quality of our lives.

NOTE

1. "Born and Unborn: Implications of the Reproductive Technologies for People with Disabilities" by Marsha Saxton, in *Test Tube Women: What Future for Motherhood?* edited by Rita Arditti, Renate Duelli-Klein and Shelly Minden. Boston: Routledge and Kegan Paul, 1984.

BIBLIOGRAPHY

"The Implications of 'Choice' for People with Disabilities" by Marsha Saxton, in *Women Wise,* The N.H. Feminist Health Center Quarterly, Winter 1984.

CHAPTER 15

WOMEN AS HEALTH CARE PROVIDERS

To mention that women dominate the workforce in health care would be understating the case. Three out of every four workers in the health care industry, as well as three-quarters of those who provide informal health care, are women (Emanuel et al. 1999). Obviously, health care is an important area of employment for women, and particularly for poor and minority women (Himmelstein, Lewontin, and Woolhandler 1996). Health care in the United States has always been a strongly gendered activity that has been stratified along class and ethnic lines as well. This chapter will examine those lines of stratification among formal health care providers, and the gendering and devaluing of care activities that women have provided. Then the focus turns to informal caregivers, to understand what they do and why the current political economy of medicine is requiring them to do even more.

FORMAL HEALTH CARE PROVIDERS

Gender, Class, and Ethnic Stratification

In colonial times, women provided most of the health care (Starr 1982:49). Their medical skills were handed down orally from generation to generation. Elder kin, such as mothers, aunts, or grandmothers, typically apprenticed the younger women. Working as midwives and nurses, they assisted in childbirths and tended to the sick and dying, most of whom were relatives and friends. This work took place in the home, since hospitals were nonexistent. In some ways, little has changed in the last three hundred years. Women still provide most of the care, and that care increasingly takes place in the home, with home health care the second fastest growing industry in the entire U.S. economy in 1994 (El-Askari and DeBaun 1999).

In other ways, however, the changes are dramatic. With the establishment of the hospital, the sick were taken out of their homes and were cared for by strangers who charged them for their treatment. Women's health work became part of a huge employment industry, an industry consisting of a complex hierarchy of primary care doctors, surgeons, anesthesiologists, midwives, physician assistants, registered nurses, licensed practical nurses, nurses aides, and physical therapists, to name but a few.

In addition to size and complexity, a dominant characteristic of health care is the pervasive stratification by gender, class, and ethnicity. Doctors (73 percent male) sit atop the wage and prestige scale, and nurses aides (91 percent female) lie near the bottom of the hierarchy (Bureau of the Census 1999). As one moves down the pay and prestige scale, the percent who are minority increases (Manley 1995:307). The rapidly growing area of home health care is female, minority, dangerous (see Chapter 6 in this book) and very poorly paid, with job security and employee medical benefits rarely provided (Feldman, Sapienza, and Kane 1990).

The salary differential between three sample categories, doctors, nurses, and home health aides, is substantial. The median annual salary of doctors is $160,000, in contrast to a median salary of $34,850 for registered nurses (based on 50 weeks) and $14,450 for home health aides (Bureau of Labor Statistics 1999). And even within each category, salary disparities stubbornly remain. In 1997, male doctors had a median income of $175,000 in contrast to $120,000 for female doctors (Gonzalez 1999). Although some of these differences in doctors' salaries are due to one's area of speciality, hours worked, and years of experience, gender remains a factor. The differences are less for younger doctors, but are still not eliminated (Baker 1996).

Gender stratification takes many forms other than differences in the size of paychecks. Within occupational groups, women and men have different job titles. Female physicians are overrepresented in pediatrics, obstetrics and gynecology, psychiatry, and family practice, while they are underrepresented in surgery, anesthesiology, and radiology (Roback, Randolph, and Seidman 1993). Male nurses are more likely to be in administrative positions than are female nurses.

Maintaining Gender Stratification

A principal way in which stratification in health care has been maintained is to declare some work appropriate for women, and other work more suitable for men.

Caring as a Woman's Duty. Women in health care are, and always have been, disproportionately engaged in "caring" work, while men do "curing" work. The major division of labor in health care, which has men populating medicine and women dominating nursing, is a telling example of this gendered definition of work.

The linking of women, caring, and nursing has been obvious throughout history. In colonial America, with nursing seen as "[e]mbedded in the seemingly natural or ordained character of women, it became an important manifestation of women's expression of love of others, and was thus integral to the female sense of self" (Reverby 1987:5). Florence Nightingale, Britain's prominent nineteenth century nursing visionary who greatly influenced American nursing, felt that nursing training required the "honing of womanly virtue" (Reverby 1987:7). This vision of the special appropriateness of women for nursing has endured to the present, even as the work of nurses has become more diversified and as more men have entered the field. When male Vietnam vets returned from the war with their considerable medical experience, "[r]ather than encouraging veterans to become nurse practitioners, a new category of health care provider was created" (Manley 1995:308). Becoming a physician assistant allowed men to avoid a career of "nursing."

Caring is not only gendered, it is also devalued. Such devaluation is reflected in the pay of those engaged in such work. Controlling for relevant occupational characteristics, studies find strong evidence that "there is a pecuniary penalty for working in a caring occupation" (England and Folbre 1999:43). Simply put, nurses have been expected to provide quality care "in a society that refuses to value caring" (Reverby 1987:5). However important and worthy the work of caring is held to be, it is typically not seen as skilled. The more gendered it is viewed, the less it is seen as involving the exercise of skills (Steinberg and Figart 1999).

Caring as women's work is seen not just in the domination of men in medicine and women in nursing, but also within medicine. Here a gendered organization of medical specialities is evident. The specialities at the top of the prestige and salary hierarchy, such as surgery, are dominated by men and characterized by masculine images of technology, activity, and invasiveness. At the bottom of the hierarchy, where women are found, specialities such as family medicine, psychiatry, and pediatrics are characterized as more caring—more personal, passive, and emotional (Hinze 1999).

Keeping Women Out of Medicine, or Making It Uncomfortable to Be in Medicine. An important mechanism used to perpetuate the dominance of men in medicine was fairly simple in its directness: Women were denied admittance to medical school (Starr 1982:50, 124). Although women had been allowed in some medical schools in the 1800s, as medicine grew more respectable the hostility toward women in medical schools increased. Women in America have always been labeled the "weaker sex," and perhaps more so during the Victorian era than at any other time. In keeping with the prevailing beliefs of the day, doctors developed theories on why women shouldn't be in higher education. Dr. Clarke of Harvard University (whose views are discussed in Chapter 9 of this book) stated that a woman's reproductive ability would be recklessly endangered if she were not freed from the drain of intellectual activity. Clarke's own medical school made sure that women were spared such suffering. Harvard refused to admit women until 1945, and then did so only because Harvard was plagued by intern and resident shortages. The first African American woman was not admitted until 1951 (Langone 1995:139, 154). Harvard alumni were not pleased with the change, as noted by their less-than-welcoming comments in the alumni bulletin: "Each place taken in the Harvard Medical School by a woman represents a lost opportunity to a potential male physician, which is later wasted if, a few years after her graduation, the woman abandons medicine to raise her family" (quoted in Langone 1995:155). The local press had its own evaluation: "As you look them over, they seem girls with better than average looks" (quoted in Langone 1995:155).

The women who did manage to enter medical school faced a wide variety of gender discrimination and sexual harassment. They soon discovered that they were excluded from their schools' medical fraternities, which offered the benefit of cheap rent and connections to other students. In one instance, female students were listening to the department chair's orientation speech on the supportiveness of the faculty, only to find it illustrated with a "slide of a woman (student) on the lap of a man in a white coat (professor)" (Jones 1996:66).

Countless other cases of harassment have been recorded which show a systematic hostility toward female medical students persisting until they either dropped out of school or managed to turn a deaf ear to the hectoring and eventually graduated. In classes, women learned anatomy in lectures interspersed with "pinup" slides. At several schools, the female students discovered that the so-called doctor's lounge was actually the men's bathroom, and that they had to change clothes in the nurses' locker room (Berrien 1992; Perrone, Stockel, and Krueger 1989).

In some cases, the harassment of women reached levels of hostility that made remaining at the medical school a nearly impossible task, given that female students had no one to whom they could address their concerns or complaints. Their education was impaired to the point that they were kept from learning critical aspects of medical treatment. One woman, a student at Georgetown University School of Medicine in the late 1980s, recalled that

> *on the first day of an emergency medicine rotation in our senior year, students were asked who had had an experience placing a central line (an intravenous line placed into a major vein under the clavicle or in the neck). Most of the male students raised their hands. None of the women did. For me, it was graphic proof of inequity in teaching; the men had had the procedure taught to them, but the women had not. (Fugh-Berman 1992:54)*

In addition to this silent form of ostracism, instructors were known to publically disparage their female students' abilities to perform. One example of this occurred at a major midwestern medical school in the early 1980s. With the patient and nurses in attendance, a staff surgeon commented: "I've never known a woman who was a decent surgeon, but I guess we have to give you a crack at it" (Grant 1988:116). Instructors showed a marked favoritism toward the male students when selecting students for further training, with women less likely to be assigned to the prized residencies.

Some of the old practices have changed with the passage of time, but discrimination and sexual harassment have certainly not disappeared, even though the percentage of female medical school students has increased dramatically during the last forty years. In 1968, only 9 percent were women; in 1978, female enrollment nearly tripled to 24 percent; by 1988, 35 percent of students were women, and by 1998, 43 percent of the total class enrollment at medical schools were women (Barzansky, Jonas, and Etzel 1999).

Recent surveys estimate that one-fourth to one-third of female medical students are sexually harassed (Lenhart et al. 1991; Mangus, Hawkins, and Miller 1998; Frank, Brogan, and Schiffman 1998). With increased litigation concerning issues such as job discrimination and sexual harassment, the amount of abuse women take at the hands of men should decline in the years to come.

Once outside of school, however, women do not walk into their professional lives with all the hazing and hectoring behind them once and for all. Gender continues to define the world of practicing doctors (Frank, Brogan, and Schiffman 1998; Lenhart et al. 1991). The following is indicative of the persistence of such events. One female doctor reported,

> *At an office Christmas party I received a present: a sepia photograph of a bare-breasted woman on a do-not-disturb sign, purportedly for my examining room door. Did I confront the colleague who presented it? No, I laughed along with the rest of the guests (who wants to be a party pooper?). (Berrien 1992: 2616)*

Although scenes such as this may be dismissed as the result of too much drink or the boorishness of a single male, the following story created shockwaves throughout the country. A prominent neurosurgeon, Frances Conley, resigned from the prestigious Stanford Medical School faculty, stating that she was tired of the "pervasive sexism" (Conley 1998). Her action unintentionally galvanized many other women holding top medical or academic positions to speak up over what they identified as the same "pervasive sexism."

Keeping Nurses in Their Place. Doctors reinforce their position of power and maintain the stratification by keeping nurses in their places in their everyday interaction with them. For years, the so-called doctor–nurse game defined many interactions (Stein, Watts, and Howell 1990). The nurses' script was to cleverly recommend care regimens to doctors without appearing to do so, for nurses were not supposed to possess the necessary knowledge and certainly did not have the permission to make recommendations. Their roles were to be the "handmaidens" to the doctors. The game has changed with time, because nurses are becoming increasingly less willing to blindly follow doctor's orders. However, vestiges of the game clearly remain. In one regionalized perinatal system this author has studied, nurses placed relevant academic articles on the table in the conference room, hoping that doctors would read them, learn, and not repeat their mistakes with the next patient.

In less subtle ways, doctors have tried to make it clear to the nurses and to the public who's in charge. In the mid 1980s, doctors tried to force nurses to wear badges that identified their supervising physician (Reverby 1987). In the late 1980s, the AMA tried to strengthen the lines of stratification by proposing a new speciality that would operate under its aegis—the registered care technologist (RCT). Their attempt failed, in part because they insulted potential female supporters by suggesting that the new speciality would appeal to minorities "who don't have the financial wherewithal or the intellectual expectation to pursue baccalaureate programs" (quoted in Mallison 1989:161). This statement inadvertently revealed their overriding concern, that women were becoming too educated for comfort.

In other ways, doctors were vocal when they felt threatened with the increasing professionalization or specialization of nursing. They were particularly unhappy with the 1923 Goldmark report recommending an upgrading of nursing. In a poorly veiled response to the report, "Dr. Charles Mayo of the Mayo Clinic actually advocated lowering nursing educational requirements and recruiting 100,000 country girls 'born' to nurse" (Manley 1995:303). Fifty years later, when nurse practitioners and clinical nurse specialists began practicing, doctors again feared that these new occupations, staffed primarily by women, would provide direct competition with, and thus undermine, their secure position at the top of the medical hierarchy. They lobbied extensively to limit the responsibilities of nurse practitioners. When certified nurse midwives started to deliver babies on their own, obstetricans vehemently objected.

Class and Ethnic Stratification within Nursing

Stratification in health care is evident not just in the hierarchy that puts doctors on top and others below, but it is also evident within the nursing profession. Nursing began as a working-class profession. When industrialization and the growth of the waged economy moved nursing out of the private home and into the hospital, it was a "menial occupation taken up by women of the lower classes, some of whom were conscripted from the penitentiary or the almshouses" (Starr quoted in Manley 1995:301). Attempts to recruit more middle-class women were often unsuccessful (Manley 1995:301), but early in the twentieth century, the institutionalization of a "two-tiered system of education and licensing" (Manley 1995:303) laid the foundation for the class and ethnic divisions within nursing that persist to this day. At the top of the nursing profession are the registered nurses (RNs) whose educational credentials (2- or 4-year undergraduate degrees) contrast with the high school education of the licensed practical nurses (LPNs), and lower requirements of the nurses aides. The racial divisions one would expect in an occupational hierarchy such as this are readily apparent. Whereas African Americans constitute only 7 percent of RNs, they make up 18 percent of LPNs and 31 percent of nurses aides (Manley 1995:307).

The desire for nurses to professionalize their occupation has ironically caused factionalism among their ranks. In creating a hierarchy of job levels, those at the top are in essence deskilling those underneath. On the one hand, RNs' attempts to further professionalize themselves can be seen as important and appropriate. On the other hand, "advancements," such as their push in 1970 for a four-year university degree requirement, have marginalized LPNs and nurses aides. The National Black Nurses Association opposed this move because it discriminated against them (Barbee 1993:357–358).

When threatened with competition by LPNs and nurses aides, RNs have fought to restrict and limit their development and growth. "They sought a narrow job description for LPNs and nurses aides, much as physicians did for RNs, and refused to allow these nursing personnel to learn a core nursing knowledge" (Glazer 1991:365). Some argue that RNs have been less than sensitive in their treatment of their nursing colleagues: "Discussions in journals, books, and reports by leaders about training, job differences, and ranks show no recognition of how creating barriers to training for poor women means that those latter are frozen in dead-end low-wage jobs" (Glazer 1991:367).

The ethnic and class lines within nursing have also been supported by the actions of professional nursing organizations that for years largely excluded minority nurses from membership by requiring applicants to be nurse educators, a status few minorities had (Manley 1995:305).

However, nurses and their professional associations alone did not create or maintain the class and ethnicity lines in nursing (Hine 1989). The lines were also supported by a hospital system that was racially segregated until the 1950s (Manley 1995:304), and by hospitals that established limited quotas for minority students. The New England Hospital for Women and Children in Boston "enforced a quota system permitting the admission of one black student per year" (Manley 1995:306). Justification for the quotas used cruel racist stereotypes: Nursing leaders declared black women "deficient in the qualities needed to be good nurses: they lacked executive skills, intelligence, strength of character, and the ability to withstand pressure" (Glenn 1992:26). Further, the government reinforced the class and ethnicity lines in nursing through the War on Poverty and Community Action Programs, which recruited women from poor neighborhoods into only the lower echelons of nursing (Glazer 1991:364). The seriousness of these class and ethnicity divisions is indicated in a historian's comment that "class so divided nurses historically that gender could not unite them" (Reverby 1988:22).

The Importance of Caring

Despite working amid the tensions that accompany such class and ethnic stratification, and in a system that devalues care, nurses have proven that the kinds of relationships they have with patients and the tasks they perform are critical aspects of health care. By attending not just to the physical needs of patients but also to their emotional and social needs, nurses improve the health outcomes of patients. The evidence comes from varied settings. Nurses who do home visits of single mothers and educate them on nutrition and prenatal care improve the outcomes of the women's children (Olds and Eckenrode 1997). Having more nurses available after major surgery reduces the number of patient deaths as well as the chances of infections and pneumonia (Kovner and Gergen 1998). In an intensive care unit, the better the communication between doctors and nurses, the greater the nurse's independence and felt respect, and the more favorable the outcomes for patients (Knaus et al. 1986).

INFORMAL AND OTHER HEALTH CARE PROVIDERS

Informal health care—that is, unpaid care provided mainly inside the home—has always been a major, albeit invisible, aspect of health care in general. Mothers, daughters, wives, sisters, female partners, and female friends provide three-fourths of informal health care, whether it's for their own acutely sick family members, for their children with disabilities, for the terminally ill, or for their elderly parents or relatives. The burden is greater among female minorities because fewer women of color are in nursing homes (Olesen 1997:399), and also because AIDS victims are disproportionately minorities (Schiller 1993).

If health care is conceived of more broadly, as not only tending those with disease, but also providing the "material conditions for health" (Graham 1985:30), then housecleaning; food preparation; and emotional work that provides for the social, psychological, and emotional health of family members need to be included, too. Clearly, women dominate in these areas. Despite the importance of such work, the following discussion is limited to care for people with health problems.

Informal health care, an essential yet underrecognized form of care, has been increasing during the last decade due to the shift in population demographics, the recent arrival of new diseases, and the changes in hospital discharge policies. The number of elderly persons, especially those over the age of 85, has increased dramatically. Some families cannot afford to send a parent to a nursing home and must care for them at home; others choose to "take their parents in," as an option that they feel is more humane.

The recent epidemic of AIDS, a long-term illness that was virtually nonexistent more than twenty years ago, places new demands on informal health care. Those with AIDS are frequently not sick enough to warrant constant hospitalization, but do require a great deal of care at home. Another recently identified illness is Alzheimer's, and those who are afflicted with this slow and painful loss of memory require constant home care for years before they need professional help.

Perhaps the biggest reason for the increased demand on women to provide health care in their homes is the change in health care policy. Patients are routinely being released into the community before they are well enough to leave the hospital under their own power. These shorter hospital stays are a result, in part, of federal cost consciousness in the Medicare and Medicaid programs. In an effort to reduce health care costs, the federal government chose to provide incentives to hospitals for efficient handling of Medicare and Medicaid patients by codifying the "efficient handling of patients" into a book of guidelines called the *Diagnostic Related Groups,* or DRGs. The DRGs established expected lengths of hospital stay categorized by illness. The government paid hospitals a set amount for each Medicare or Medicaid patient based on the admitting doctor's diagnosis. Thus, long hospital stays became costly for the hospitals in question, since they weren't being reimbursed for anything beyond the DRG-mandated length of stay. Their response was to send patients home as early as possible in order to avoid losing money.

In a similar move, managed care organizations seeking to limit expenditures and maximize profit began to discharge patients earlier than they previously had. In large part, government, insurance companies, and hospitals were able to adopt these policies without too much of a public outcry because they could depend on the free labor of women (Graham 1985:33). They all banked on the assumption that each patient had a woman at home who could pick up where the insurance left off, and they apparently guessed right.

Often, providing health care for another goes beyond providing tender love and emotional support. Increasingly, informal health care providers are asked to do rather complex technical procedures: operate a home dialysis machine and irrigate the patient; clean and change dressings on surgical areas; give shots; and monitor drug reactions (Kaye and Reisman 1991). These tasks are often accompanied by a small "how to do it" brochure, and the promise of one house call by a nurse to see that things are proceeding as planned. The demands on caregivers are considerable. Speaking of elderly patients discharged shortly after cardiac surgery, one doctor comments,

> *Most of them are scared to go home after four days. But they end up doing fine.... There's nothing else we really do for them at that stage of recovery. It's just babysitting and helping them walk up and down the hall a few times. Their wives can do that for them at home. (quoted in Gordon 1997:77)*

This doctor clearly understands that wives will bear a huge burden taking care of patients who are physically unstable and psychologically terrified. His statement also clearly trivializes that work (Gordon 1997:77).

As is true with many experiences, providers of health care find both burdens and joys. The burdens at times can be emotionally, financially, and socially overwhelming (Mezey, Miller, and Linton-Nelson 1999). Caring for another means giving up one's valued activities, cutting back on one's own waged labor, and sometimes engaging in unpleasant medical procedures. Some caregivers experience serious levels of stress (Gordon 1997), especially when they are tending to those who have lengthy illnesses that seemingly have no end; or if they are themselves elderly and caring for a spouse, they are more likely to die due to the stress of caregiving (Schulz and Beach 1999). Caring for an elderly parent may require an uncomfortable change in roles, including toileting assistance (wiping three generations of bottoms in the same week), placing restrictions on one's parents (taking away the car), making decisions to move a mother or father to a nursing home, and "coming to terms with the course of a human being's life" (quoted in Abel 1991:73). Caring for a parent with Alzheimers puts one in the heartbreaking position of loving and helping someone who no longer recognizes you. For daughters who are also mothers, helping one's elderly parents has doubled the demands put on them, and as a result they earn the dubious distinction of being called the "sandwich" generation.

Caring for a child with disabilities is a long-term commitment that requires the constant alternation of social roles. One may be the loving mother in the morning, and in the afternoon she is the vocal advocate, in frequent contact with bureaucracies that exist ostensibly to help. In actuality, these bureaucracies often hinder one's access to relief, whether it be financial or otherwise, and fail to understand the emotionally and logistically complex lives families must construct (Wickham-Searl 1994).

But along with the burdens are joys and personal benefits. Being able to connect with and relate to people who have needs makes the experience profoundly humanizing for some. "You gain a lot of wisdom and insight and compassion for other people's suffering and problems," commented one woman (quoted in Abel 1991:96–97). Knowing that a loved one is getting the best possible care is an added benefit.

In addition to the formal and informal health care providers we have discussed, many women serve in other health care capacities, such as in public health, nutrition, mental health, and maternal and child health care, and some women serve as midwives and doulas (see Chapter 12). Women are also practitioners of alternative healing, such as herbalists, manual healers (massage therapists and chiropractors), mind–body practitioners (utilizing hypnosis, biofeedback, yoga, dance, music, and art) and ethnic folk healers, such as curanderas.

Most alternative health approaches explicitly critique the interventionism of the biomedical model and its rejection of mind–body connectedness. As evidence grows that some alternative healing approaches have positive health consequences (Fugh-Berman 1996), and as women and others increasingly demand use of such methods (Goldstein 1999), traditional health practitioners, medical schools, and the NIH (with its Office of Alternative Medicine) are beginning to embrace it.

FROM BOTH ENDS OF THE SPECULUM: REFLECTIONS ON WOMEN'S HEALTH CARE IN AMERICA

ALICE ROTHCHILD

When I finished medical school in 1974, my fantasy of providing healthcare without society, sexism, and economics battering at the door was long gone. And while many of my male colleagues and friends were joining the medical establishment and developing a sense of loyalty and belonging, I was becoming a feminist and a permanent outsider, thanks to my medical school training. I wanted to change society rather than help women adjust to the existing oppression in their lives. Medicine, it appeared, would be my battleground.

This was a time of protest on many fronts. The Vietnam War was front page, the women's movement and other self-help movements were growing, the civil rights movement was being fought in the workplace, schools, and streets. I lived in a commune and struggled with the issues of sexism, relationships, and community in many a consciousness-raising group where women could learn, listen and try to imagine a different kind of future. Even the medical students in my class underwent radicalizing changes: our class proudly sent our free stethoscopes from Eli Lilly to the North Vietnamese. We refused to sign our bimonthly exams and created a defacto pass/fail system at the medical school.

Meanwhile, the Playboy bunny pictures intermixed with the microbiology slides, the surgeons who discussed their cases in the (male) Doctors' Change Room and expected me to sit patiently outside, and the constant barrage of low-level hostility took their toll. The first year psychiatry course was based on a textbook entitled *The Person,* which spent an entire chapter on the importance of work in the life of men, mentioning women in a short paragraph at the end. One psychiatrist lectured us that the women were in medical school only because of our "unresolved penis envy." Our gynecology text advised women that their role in sexual intercourse was primarily to satisfy the husband. One edition of our obstetrics text had an entry in the index listing "male chauvinism" and cited the entire book—I have always wondered what brave and subversive secretary slipped that in!

Although I had wanted to be a psychiatrist since the age of six, I found my first obstetrics and gynecology course profoundly important. The esteemed department chairman gave a famous lecture entitled something like, "What is a woman?" The handout consisted of a useful list of answers: "a woman is a man's wife, a man's competitor, a man's mistress. . . ." This provoked protest signs and a vigil during the lecture which ultimately brought an end to this yearly offense. Nonetheless, women were always referred to as "girls"; one frequent comment by the chairman was, "The only good uterus is a uterus on the table!"; middle-aged women were referred to as "the three F's" (forty, fat, and fertile). These things, and watching inadequately supervised City Hospital residents struggle through their surgical education, practicing on the poor and powerless, left me with an intense sense of outrage and a need to respond.

My exposure to obstetrics and gynecology, in particular, revealed a field so politically backward and oppressive to women that I felt that I could have my greatest impact as a physician in just this speciality. At a hospital in Brooklyn, I watched in horror while a woman strapped to her guerney screamed, smeared feces, and labored under the influence of twilight sleep. I turned to her doctor and asked, "Why do you do this?" He replied that this is what women want and that if you don't give them heavy sedation, you can't get patients. At that moment I was reborn as an avid believer in natural childbirth. I went into the field to change it—not because I identified with my mentors, or was intellectually interested in research or the technical challenges of surgery. Contrary to the usual process of identification, I joined the Fellows as a permanent and often angry outsider.

I did my internship at a city hospital in New York. There, the issue of sexism paled beside the obvious impact of poverty, drug abuse, alcoholism, and homelessness. I got to live the two-class health care system in action—walking down the open wards with beds lined up in every corner, bagging (manually breathing for) comatose patients when the electricity failed, running out of essential items like IV tubing and penicillin. While there was intense community involvement in the hospital, it was clear that major changes in society were needed if the lives of these people were to improve. My ob-gyn residency, in a well-run, well-funded hospital, was a striking institutional contrast. Records arrived with the patient, women planned their surgery, and once again the impact of economics on how well health care could be provided was apparent. As I became more independent, it was also a very positive experience to support women through pregnancy and childbirth in a more empowering environment.

Nonetheless, the culture of the specialty did little to change my perception that this was still a battlefield. Few women physicians had gone before me, and I always felt I had to prove myself, particularly in the OR [operating room]. The attitudes of the attendings towards both their patients and the small but ever-increasing number of female residents, who did unheard-of things, from changing in the "Doctors' Lounge" to getting pregnant, left much to be desired.

Later I participated in establishing a non-profit group practice in the inner city, with another woman obgyn, a midwife, and a pediatrician. Ideologically, our practice was what I wanted, but despite our immense popularity, we constantly came up against the status quo. The midwife couldn't get hospital privileges; health centers went bankrupt, leaving large debts; our former attendings were unwilling to share coverage.

We were the only private physicians who accepted Medicaid, who worked with midwives, and later a nurse practitioner, and saw ourselves as having a feminist mission regarding the care of women and their families. We worked in the office, in neighborhood health centers, a woman's health center, and at the hospital where we trained. We were on the "fringe" in this mostly male and often quietly hostile environment. Our allies were the nurses, midwives, nurse-practitioners, and women patients who were both the users of health care and prime negotiators for their children and their elderly parents. For these people, being a woman doctor was finally an asset.

Our practice consciously set out to do things differently. Besides the warmed speculums, potholders over the stirrups, and endless supplies of mirrors and *Our Bodies, Ourselves,* we emphasized education, making health care a joint venture with the woman, her family and her support system. We tried to be attuned to the fact that there is no such thing as a "routine pelvic," since approximately one in four women has experienced sexual assault. We welcomed lesbians and people with disabilities; we supported home births and alternative approaches. In short, we saw the patients no other private MD wanted, and we learned exactly what it means to be outside the "old boy network." Our hospital colleagues were friendly, but finding coverage during our maternity leaves was almost impossible. They told me, "I'm too stressed." "Your patients are too difficult." "Your patients expect too much from their doctors." The translation was that whether we took care of pushy educated feminists or poor, non-English speaking Medicaid patients, we were on our own. What kept us going was our popularity in the communities we worked, our passion about our work, and our political committment to provide feminist health care. After eight and a half years, having had two babies each, while being on call almost every other night, with little financial success (Medicaid paid $5 per office visit) or cooperation from other hospital staff, we gave up.

Since then all of my old partners and I are working in a pre-paid nonprofit HMO. The struggles are obviously different because of the massive chaos and constant restructuring of health care. I am lucky that I work in a group with many women, and men who treat me as an equal, although sometimes different, colleague. I am lucky that there are now many women in this specialty who are beginning to be in positions of power. Much of the current challenge comes from the economics of medicine—the previously unimagined power and control of insurance companies, the squeeze on resources and staff, and intense pressure to shorten hospital stays, while learning new gynecological procedures and technologies and the desire to use them for the benefit of the patients and not only the bottom line.

My challenge in this "system" is to save the ideals that have evolved in me over the last quarter century: to treat each woman with respect; to make no assumptions about sexual preference or safety; to provide surveillance, guidance, expert advice, emotional support; and to honor each woman as the ultimate judge of her own body. I try to pay attention to the whole context of a woman's life—is she 45 and pregnant, or menopausal? I see every exam as an opportunity to educate and empower a woman about her body and her healthcare, and to give her a sense of validation about her perceptions. Also, I focus on menopause, PMS, and sexual dysfunction, areas in which women have been classically dismissed. During pregnancy, despite the availability of technology and women's unquestioning belief in it, I see my role as to support and educate, to "love someone through their pregnancy." I see women increasingly tending not to trust their bodies, and my role is to remind women of their immense power and strength, and of the normalcy of childbirth.

In the OR my personal struggle has been to learn to be decisive, aggressive, and calm. When the OR is no longer a man-surgeon's fiefdom and the usual yelling and temper tantrums of the past are unacceptable, what are the rules? I am constantly learning how to deal with the enormous stress, anxiety, and insecurity (which surgeons rarely admit to), while needing to be the leader of the team and to command respect.

The other struggle is the physican-wife-mother balancing act. There are days when I feel like I am the woman who has everything and I'm doing all of it badly, and on those days it is critical to redefine the meaning of a successful career in medicine. My medical training told me that a good doctor is an academic, with few limits on work hours, and a magical ability to read every pertinent journal. In 1997, a good doctor can be a clinician, can limit hours and still be a "serious player," can take off all school vacations, and be respected for her devotion to her work. The more difficult redefinition for me is the good mother. I wanted to really parent my daughters and not feel like a visiting dignitary between the yearly au pairs. I used to rush home in between office and surgery to breast feed because I had a child who would not take a bottle. I now rush from office to school, lugging canvas bags of paperwork to be done after bedtime. How many other surgeons get paged during a case because their child has a fever at school and needs to be picked up immediately, or the kid forgot her trumpet or can't find her socks? Being a good wife is also an ongoing, constantly-being-invented state of affairs. My husband is a cabinetmaker—I work more hours than he does, I have a more inflexible schedule, make more money, have more social status. These are all loaded and complicated issues. Our relationship is anchored on a respectful kind of equality of value as individuals who are sharing the tasks of life in nontraditional ways. We really have to make up the rules as we go along.

In the world of work, managed care has always existed. Before, care was secretly managed by a patient's socioeconomics, power, and ability to speak English. Now the battles are clearer and more vicious and more dangerous to everyone. This is a battle we did not foresee. As a clinician, I work at the lowest level of the medical food chain. As a feminist physician, I see the future as fighting the battles on the ground while keeping a close eye on defending reproductive rights and options, working for national health insurance, respecting family diversity, defending preventive services. I worry that with all the corporate manuevering and the complete absence of responsible national leadership and vision, that the changes that are happening will have very little to do with healthcare.

I feel that like-minded people must remain agitators, both from the inside and the outside of the systems in which we work. Just the fact that there are more of us women is a reason for great expectation and possibility. Clearly the innocence of the past is lost forever.

WHAT IT MEANS TO BE A NURSE

DANIEL F. CHAMBLISS

So what, then, does it mean to be a nurse?...[For the nurse], the hospital is a normal place, and with routinization even traumatic events that occur there appear normal. What once was a frightful emergency to the novice has become, more and more, just the "same ol' same ol'." The nurse now casually handles naked bodies, measures output of stool, suctions fluid from patients' lungs, passes knives to surgeons, and, just as routinely, cares for the dying. None of this, once she has made the "leap" into a routine, disrupts her daily life or causes her any special concern.

This attitude radically separates nurses and other health workers from the rest of us, and the separation is *morally* relevant, a distance between what nurses and laypersons see as "the right way to behave." Patients are regularly subjected to events no one outside the hospital would willingly undergo. Invasive procedures, humiliating exams, and radical surgery are considered not only acceptable but even in a sense good; the staff rarely gives them a passing thought. Not only is there a shift in what is thought good and what is thought bad; some very serious matters are not much thought about at all. Routinization means that once-crucial issues have been set aside: "These," it declares, "need not concern us."

Of course, routinization of hospital life is not peculiar to nursing. Physicians undergo a similar process, becoming bored with routine physical exams, hurrying through colonoscopies, pelvic exams, and assorted consultations; so too, in varying degrees and in their own activities, orderlies, blood technicians, and respiratory therapists find their work taking on the rhythm of everyday life. Occupational therapists may work every day with children who have cerebral palsy, surgeons quickly get used to removing gall bladders, aides get used to wiping bottoms, and hospital secretaries learn to comfort crying relatives and guide wandering geriatric patients back to their rooms. In all of the health care professions, repeated encounters with messiness, confusion, and tragedy dull the senses a bit, professional jargon softens the hard edges, and jokes become genuinely funny. All hospital workers experience routinization; nursing is not special in this.

But some things *are* special about nursing. The nurse is a particular kind of hospital worker, one with at least three difficult and sometimes contradictory missions. The hospital nurse is expected, and typically expects herself, to be simultaneously (1) a caring individual, (2) a professional, and (3) a relatively subordinate member of the organization. Nurses will argue, even among themselves, just what these directives require, or even that they should exist. (Many nurses will say, for instance, that they should not be subordinates.) Regardless, these three principles tell us who nurses really are and what they really do.

The inherent conflict of these demands makes nursing a prototype case for a dilemma of many workers in an organizational society: I want to do good, but my boss won't let me. The directives conflict: be caring and yet professional, be subordinate and yet responsible, be diffusely accountable for a patient's total well-being and yet oriented to the hospital as an economic employer. Perhaps no other occupation suffers so great a conflict between the practical requirements of the job—and nursing is, rhetoric aside, still fundamentally a job, a paid assignment—and the explicitly moral goals of the profession. Perhaps these are dilemmas of all the "caring" professions (teaching, social work, nursing). Or perhaps they somehow typify predominantly female professions. With more women entering the labor force, with the caring professions growing, and with an increasing proportion of all Americans working under the control of large organizations, increasing numbers of Americans may face conflicts such as those faced by nurses.

In this chapter, these three requirements of the nurse's role will be examined—the directives of caring, being a professional, and being a subordinate. Then the difficult theoretical issue of nursing as a "female" profession will be considered. Finally, I will suggest why nursing ethics should matter to the rest of us. In nursing, I think, we can see how morally concerned but subordinate people in organizations handle moral problems in their work.

NURSES CARE FOR PATIENTS

"Care" is the key term in nursing's definition of itself, and crucially defines what nurses believe is their task.... Care, some nurses say, distinguishes nursing from medicine: "Nurses care, doctors cure"; and while physicians might dispute the moral connotations of that slogan, few would completely deny its message.... It may be true, as historian Susan Reverby says, that "a crucial dilemma in contemporary American nursing" is "the order [to nurses] to care in a society that refuses to value caring,"[1] but among nurses, the willingness to care when that is difficult is the distinguishing mark of the nurse.

As nurses use the term, "care" seems to include four meanings: face-to-face working with patients, dealing with the patient as a whole person, the comparatively open-ended nature of the nurse's duties, and the personal commitment of the nurse to her work. All of these are included in what nurses mean by "caring." To a moderate degree, "caring" describes what nurses actually *do;* to a great degree, it describes what nurses believe they *should* do.

1. *Nursing care is hands-on,* a face-to-face encounter with a patient. Unlike in medicine, in nursing there can be no quick review of lab reports, a scribbling of orders, and then a fast exit down the hall. Nurses carry out the scribbled orders, deliver the medications, pass the food trays, monitor the IVs and the ventilators. Nurses give baths, catheterize patients, turn patients who cannot move themselves, clean bedsores, change soiled sheets, and constantly watch patients, writing notes on their patients' progress or deterioration. Close patient contact, with all five senses, is nursing's specialty. ("I could never be a nurse," says one unit clerk. "I couldn't stand all those smells.") Nurses are constantly talking with, listening to, and touching their patients in intimate ways; the prototypical, universal dirty work of nursing is "wiping bottoms...."

Physicians visit floors to perform major procedures (inserting tubes into the chest, bronchoscopies); but most of what is said and physically done to patients is said and done by bedside nurses.

The nurse works primarily in a contained space, on one floor or unit; if the patients are very sick, she stays in one or two rooms. She is geographically contained and sharply focused, on this room, this patient, perhaps even this small patch of skin where the veins are "blown" and the intravenous line won't go in.... So nurses have close contact with their patients over time, hour by hour if not minute by minute, for an extended period of time—"around the clock," they say, and sometimes this is precisely true. This close contact, over time, in a confined space, can give nurses the sense that they know better than anyone else what is happening with their patients; and they may resent any other view:...

No doubt, the "continuity of care" by nurses can be exaggerated by nurses themselves. In fact, with rotating nursing schedules, shifting assignments, the short turnaround time of many nursing tasks, and the constant turnover of nursing personnel, it is not clear that nurses provide continuity at all. Few nurses are actually on the scene "around the clock," and only occasionally is one nurse responsible for the total care of a particular patient. Nevertheless, the geographical restriction of a nurse to one area does enhance her knowledge of the condition of those patients, even when she isn't personally caring for them.

To care for patients, then, first means that one works directly, spatially and temporally, with sick people.

2. *Care means that the patient should be treated not merely as a biological organism* or the site of some disease entity, but as a human being with a life beyond the hospital and a meaning beyond the medical world. Nurses certainly handle the physiological treatment of disease, but they also spend time teaching patients (on dialysis units, e.g., this may be their major task), answering the family's questions, listening to the patient's worries, calling for social service consultations, helping fill out insurance forms, or even, to use a fairly common example, helping an old person find a pair of glasses lost somewhere in the sheets or under the bed. In caring for AIDS patients, nurses often manage negotiations between families and lovers, or among relatives and friends, when families often don't know the true diagnosis. In all these ways, nurses seem focused on the personal experience of illness:

> *[N]ursing appears to be directed to more immediate and experiential goals than medicine: a compassionate response to suffering is more closely identified with nursing than with medicine. Nurses also more often express an interest in disease prevention and health maintenance than physicians. Nurses are less wedded to the physiological theories and diagnostic modes of medical practice. And nursing has a more global and unified science approach to health care.*[2]

"Care," then, includes a broad range of the patient's concerns, not just the physical disease itself.

3. *The nurse's duties are open-ended.* Perhaps because of the nurse's sheer physical availability, her job often expands to fill the gaps left by physicians, orderlies, or even families. Some duties are prescribed, but many are not. "To care" for a nurse comes to mean that the nurse will handle problems that arise, whether or not they are part of her official tasks. This occurs for practical reasons. "The nurse," in the words of Anselm Strauss, "comes and stays while others come and go...*The role of the nurse is profoundly affected by her obligation to represent continuity of time and place.*"[3] Being on the scene, around the clock, means that nurses are there to integrate the different aspects of hospital work: "Since there's no general agreement about what a nurse is, there are no obvious limits to the job."[4]

Thus the nurse takes on more and more tasks, cleaning up the physical and social messes left by others. When doctors don't explain a diagnosis to the patient, when a unit clerk isn't there to answer the phone, when housekeeping has left a sink unwashed or a floor unmopped, when administration hasn't provided the staff to cover the unit, when chaplains aren't around to listen to a family, when the transportation aide hasn't shown up to take a patient to X-ray—then, often, nurses take over and do these jobs themselves, probably grumbling in the process but realizing that it must be done and that nurses will have to live with the results if they don't:

> *Everybody else says: "What do you do as a nurse?" And I say, "I do everything that nobody else wants to do." [Interview]*

Nurses might say they do this work *because* they "care"; but here there is no distinction between doing and caring. To care is to *do* the leftover work, to take that responsibility, whether ordered to or not.[5]

4. *Caring requires a personal commitment of the nurse to her work.* It requires a commitment of the nurse herself, as a person, to her work. There is an intertwining of professional skills and personal involvement; in a sense, the involvement is the work, in a way not true of more technical occupations. Nurses would say that some excellent surgeons are horrible human beings; but perhaps it is not theoretically possible to be simultaneously an excellent nurse and a despicable person.[6] The job itself seems to call for decency.

In practice, nursing often elicits a deep personal involvement. In the best cases, nurses give and receive with their patients, first giving of themselves and then receiving, in turn, an unusual intimacy and personal satisfaction from helping another person in his or her most difficult time. Patients can be more open with nurses than with their own families, for a variety of reasons: to spare loved ones the truth of suffering, to maintain the dignity of one's body with a spouse, or to protect children from the reality of their mother's imminent death. The caring professional hears of these things without falling apart, so patients often tell nurses what they wouldn't tell anyone else.

> *It's the nurse who's there when the patient is upset and crying, especially on those long, dark nights. It's also the nurse who develops a day-to-day rapport with the patient. Patients can feel comfortable sharing their physical and emotional pain. There is a lot of intimacy involved; it's the same intimacy found with anyone who is terminal. For some reason, people who are dying tend to lessen their barriers. It's a sad phenomenon that we wait until that time to establish those relationships. But it's a privilege for nurses to work in this area [with AIDS patients and dying pts generally], because in no other type of work, are you invited into another's soul.*[7]

So the first imperative of nursing is to give care—direct, person-to-person, relatively open-ended care. When nurses tell of their best moments in nursing, they tell of giving such care—not of their technical expertise, or their ability to follow complicated orders without bungling, but of care. This is what nurses identify as the meaningful heart of nursing.

Obviously "caring" is also an ideological term, an idealized way of talking about nursing. It is openly used as a weapon in nurses' conflicts with physicians, to distinguish what nurses do ("care") from what doctors do ("cure"), and to assert the nurse's moral superiority. The more challenging "care" is, the greater the moral prestige of the nurse. So when nurses say they "care," this is more than an empirical description of duties; it is a defense of their own importance.

Nurses don't live up to this high ideal of caring all the time. Not at all. But they do accept it as the ideal, and enjoy achieving it now and then, and talk about it as the noblest mission of nursing. Perhaps this is changing with the increasing emphasis on professionalism, a somewhat different principle; but nursing is still, at its center, about caring.

NURSES ARE PROFESSIONALS

So nurses care—but others care as well. Parents care for their children, lovers for their beloved, children for their pets. For nurses, though, caring is a *job,* an economically rewarded task. And it is a certain *kind* of job, one with high demands for education and responsibility and a claim to a special status, commonly called "professional." The first imperative of nursing is to care; the second imperative of nursing is to behave like a *professional....*

Being a professional means (1) doing a job (2) that requires special competence and (3) that deserves special status.

1. *Most basically, a profession is a job*—and a good one at that. The most accurate generalization about nurses is not that they care for patients; it is that they are *paid* to care for patients. For many, ideology aside, this is the primary motivation. Nurses typically have little trouble find-

ing work in America, or almost anywhere in the world. It is easy to move in and out of the nursing workforce, taking time out for raising a family, pursuing other careers, or just taking vacations. The unemployment rate for nurses in the United States is typically close to zero, and nurses' salaries rose significantly during the 1980s in the United States, so that by 1990 their typical starting income was close to $30,000.…

Since nursing is a job, the nurse is frequently required to deal with unpleasant colleagues, uncooperative patients, frustrating bureaucracies, and the routine difficulties of paid work. Even when nurses hate their patients or disapprove of their identities (casualties of gang wars, drug dealers shot in a deal gone bad), or feel that patients are to blame for their own predicament (smokers with emphysema, or alcoholics with gastrointestinal bleeding), they claim to care for them fully. In a sense, I believe, nurses' talk about disliking certain patients reinforces the pride of professionalism. Whoever the patients are, the nurse still goes to work, delivers meal trays, fills out forms, listens to supervisors, delivers medications, and cleans up messes. She can't just walk away, as a volunteer could, or care only for loved ones, as a mother could. Professionalism, then, first means performing the job.

2. Second, *professionalism requires special competence.* Nursing work is often neither simple nor easy; it can be intellectually, emotionally, and physically demanding. So sheer competence is a value, perhaps the central value in nursing.[8] Some people just can't do the work, aren't organized or responsible enough, lack the manual dexterity to insert IVs or give injections, or don't understand the necessary physiology. Nurses can quickly differentiate the good nurses from the bad based on their ability to do the job, finish the assigned tasks, and not make the disastrous mistakes that can so easily happen. They know which nurses can be trusted and which ones can't:

> *"If my baby comes in here," said one pregnant neonatal nurse to her colleague, "swear to me that you'll take care of him. I don't want R—— [another nurse] taking care of my kid." [Field Notes]*

Professional competence is most challenged in those emergencies when routines break down. Normally, the professional cares for her clients in the form of a "detached concern"[9]—holding her personal feelings in check while remaining open to the feelings of the patient. A special effort is required for a nurse to keep this "professional" detachment when a critically ill patient, after coming close to recovery, suddenly codes and dies.

> *Right after the code had started, Madge, laughing nervously as the team worked on Mrs. B——, said to me, "Oh, God, I'd just written her assessment" [saying she was improving].*
>
> *After Mrs. B.'s code was over, and they'd declared her dead, Madge (who had nursed her for the past week) immediately sat at the rolling desk outside the room and wrote notes for at least ½ hour, very persistently, almost through tears—her face was flushed—when people said anything to her, she answered only vaguely, kept her head down writing. [Field Notes]*

"Being professional" here may mean, as it often does, going into a bathroom to cry, then cleaning up and coming back out to continue working for the rest of the shift, trying to act as if nothing happened. "Competence" includes technical expertise as well as the personal fortitude to maintain that expertise under pressure.

3. *A professional deserves special status.* A professional, nurses feel, deserves respect. Nurses typically feel that they deserve more respect than they receive, from their colleagues (especially physicians) and from laypersons. They are paid for their work, but good pay is not sufficient.

> *No amount of money is worth what you have to do and what you have to put up with. That's it: what you have to put up with...patients throwing full urinals at you, slapping you, biting, fighting, swearing. [Interview]*

As professionals, nurses feel they deserve an improved status and better treatment: polite treatment by doctors, the listening ear of administrators, the respect of outsiders who too often treat nurses like maids or waitresses.

In trying to be professionals, nurses strive to differentiate themselves in the public eye from other occupations. A nurse, they emphasize, is *not* a maid, *not* a waitress, *not* a servant. Nurses commonly mention these "antiroles" in talking about their work, to distinguish nursing from those jobs, even if the tasks themselves may sometimes be similar: answering patient call bells, changing sheets, emptying bedpans, helping patients dress or turn over. Nurses do some things maids do. How then does one change sheets "professionally"? The public, they feel, doesn't understand:

> *It bothers me, the chronic stupid image of the nurse, the handmaid-to-the-doctor thing. I don't take well to people who kiddingly say, "You just empty bedpans all day long." The public has no idea what nursing really is all about. They can see you giving baths, carrying bedpans, taking blood pressures, temperatures, whatever. And they think that's all nurses do. [Interview]*

A major part of nursing's effort to improve its status has come in changing the educational requirements for becoming an R.N. Initially, such requirements were more vocational than academic. From the late nineteenth century until the middle of the twentieth, most nurses were trained by hospitals, often the Catholic hospitals run by religious orders of nuns, and after three years they were awarded a diploma. These nursing students worked as poorly paid apprentices and received, in turn, the skills to go out and practice on their own. The training was rigorous, often notoriously so, and very applied. The nurses received training, the hospitals had cheap labor.[10]

But since the 1960s, many of the hospital schools have closed down, replaced by academic university or community-college programs. With this change, the tone of nursing has changed.

> *Nursing is no longer the calling it once was, says P.W.; the influence of nuns, so pervasive when she was younger, is now fading, being replaced by the university-trained academic model of nursing. [Interview]*

The collegiate nurse has come, perhaps unfairly, to represent the ascendance of education, of science, of classroom training, and of the increased social status of higher education. By comparison, the older, hospital-trained nurse represents more traditional values, the more ready subservience to doctors, the hands-on experience, the "school of hard knocks." As can easily be imagined, this split in the profession, and in what counts as a "real" nurse's education, makes a truly unified effort to improve nursing's status difficult. In addition, social class divisions in nursing between the typically middle-class B.S.N. nurses and the more working-class A.A. or diploma nurses are themselves the basis of much contention.[11] Even nurses' caps, which once symbolized a nurse's status, are now considered by most to be outdated and symbolic of lesser prestige; nurses are abandoning the traditional white uniform dress in favor of scrub suits or even civilian clothes.[12]

Many younger nurses see such changes as good; they mark the path to professionalism. Their formal education is longer, their occupational class is higher, their pay is greater, and their expectations for respect and individual initiative have increased. Professionalism is an ideal, but one which, especially through increased education, can improve their social standing.

NURSES ARE SUBORDINATES

Finally, nurses are subordinates in the hospital hierarchy. Not surprisingly, nurses see this feature of nursing less positively than the injunctions toward care and professionalism. Nurses want to care, and they want to be professionals. They don't always want to be subordinates but without doubt they are, and for the most part they accept this as part of their role. The old hospital-based nursing schools actively taught this: "under the dominance of male doctors and administrators, schools of nursing grew; and they were not noted for their development of independent, thoughtful nurses. Students entered nursing schools already expecting that women would defer to men, and, therefore, that nurses would defer to doctors."[13] Nurses' daily work is guided by others: by administrators, some of whom come from nursing; by head nurses who assign them patients; and by physicians, whose detailed orders structure their medical tasks. Nurses arrive at work at an ordered time, on an ordered shift, on specified days. They report at rounds when scheduled, read reports according to custom, answer beepers, fill out charts, and deliver medications as ordered. It is nurses who prepare the patients before procedures and who clean up afterward, changing the sheets, mopping blood, counting sponges, and calming the patients....

Nurses aren't always directly under the orders of others, of course. In ICUs, nurses frequently make quick decisions on their own, when no physician is available; in dialysis units, it is nurses who teach patients how to dialyze themselves, who write the manuals for patients to use at home, who decide how long dialysis will continue, and who evaluate the patient's tolerance of the side effects. The nurse's subordination, then, is situational: it is almost total in the operating room, where the entire staff is under the command of a surgeon; in long-term nursing home care, by contrast, nurses are in charge. Nurses often supervise other workers, such as aides, orderlies, and therapists of various sorts. And as nurses climb the status hierarchy, other workers fill the lower positions and are subject to the abuse nurses themselves have long known:

> *A nurse made a passing comment to L——, a respiratory therapist (and an older, black woman), about how she, the nurse, would have to do some procedure; as a therapist, L. wasn't supposed to do it. Over the next ten minutes, L. kept saying when spoken to, "Don't talk to me, I'm just a therapist," or "You don't want to ask me anything, I'm just a therapist," or "You asking me? A therapist???" etc. [Field Notes]*

If there is a single dominant theme in nurses' complaints about their work, it is the lack of respect they feel, from laypersons, from coworkers, and especially from physicians. It is nearly universally felt and resented. "The docs never listen to us" they say, "you don't get any recognition from doctors"; doctors don't read the nurse's notes in the patients' chart, don't ask her what she has seen or what she thinks, they don't take her seriously. The daily evidence for this is truly pervasive; I was genuinely surprised at how common the obvious disrespect is. One day I was talking with several staff nurses in a conference room when a young male physician—probably an intern—walked in and asked what a drug was for. Immediately, the assistant head nurse explained quickly and in detail. "Oh yeah," said the doctor, "that's right," and walked out. The nurses began to laugh, and one said to the advisor, "You get an A." And doctors also often ignore nurses' opinions:

> *Attending not present today, so the Fellow took charge of doc's rounds in the ICU. In discussing one patient, a resident asked the nurse taking care of this pt if she had anything to add. Before the N finished her first sentence, the Fellow was looking away, visibly uninterested; by the second sentence he had started talking with the other intern. [Field Notes]*

Sometimes such ignoring of the nurse's view can have serious consequences:

> *At Tuesday's conference on Geriatric floor, with residents, attending, social workers, etc., all present, Asst HN said repeatedly, "You should look at Mr. F.'s foot, it will be a big problem," etc. She didn't seem to make an impression on the docs.*
>
> *They did nothing about it. Saturday morning, the residents called an emergency surgery consultation because the foot was badly necrosed. Surgeon looked, said had to amputate above the ankle, maybe even above the knee, to check the sepsis. The Asst Head Nurse, who had warned them on Tuesday, was standing off to one side during this discussion, visibly exasperated. [Field Notes]*

Even medical students put down nurses in small ways.

> *In psychiatry unit: during nursing rounds, one nurse reads aloud, written on chart, as doctor's order: "Make sure patient voids [urinates]."*
>
> *"Who wrote that?"*
>
> *"Doctor R.'s little med. student." A good laugh about this, as if the nurse would overlook something so obvious. Getting no respect from docs—even future docs—is a source of aggravation and sometime laughs. [Field Notes]*

Here, then, may begin a cycle: doctors don't trust nurses; nurses, not trusted even when they are correct, slack off. The mutual lack of respect shows in various ways. Some nurses complain that doctors doing research projects try to recruit nurses as unpaid research assistants—"You're charting this anyway, can't you just keep another copy of it for my data, too?"—and then become angry if the nurse misses six hours of this charting and the data are lost. Generally, nurses' time is considered less valuable, her work less pressing, her opinions less worthy of consideration.

Outside the door of a middle-aged woman patient, with a steady stream of visitors going in, two nurses and the resident are arguing about acidosis and ventilator settings and what Respiratory Therapy should be doing to suction the patient, all in very technical jargon, decreasing this and increasing that. The nurse who takes care of this patient is very angry, with a constant forced smile she puts on in these situations, and repeating, "I don't really want to discuss it anymore," and "It's obvious what we should do. Just sedate her, that's all you need to do." But the resident isn't sure at all, and the nurses are at the end of their rope. [The patient died within days.] [Field Notes]

There are, then, pervasive problems in nurses' work relationships with doctors.[14] In part, the difficulty results from different views of what the nurse's task actually is. To doctors, the nurses are there to carry out physicians' orders.[15] Indeed, many doctors (and many nurses) regard nursing as a sort of "lesser" medicine, with the subordination of nursing dictated by the shorter period of training.

Dr. M., explaining why he should make the DNR decisions—and why the nurses should not—explains that the difference between him and the nurses is "years of training—I have 6 or 10, depending on how you count, and they have 2 or 4—I just understand things better." [Interview]

Dr. M. here assumes that nursing is essentially the same as medicine but with less training. He assumes that nurses share medicine's basic theory of disease (a physiological disturbance with psychosocial ramifications) and share medicine's ideas of the goals of treatment. For many physicians, laypersons, and even nurses, nursing is basically second-tier medicine, and nursing education consists of watered-down physiology courses, using textbooks written by physicians, teaching nurses how to be "the doctor's helper."

In recent years, this position is formulated in a description of nurses as "physician extenders," a cost-effective substitute in areas where there aren't enough physicians—a kind of "Hamburger Helper"[16] who does the same work for less money. So the nursing viewpoint is not merely subordinated; indeed, it is often invisible as a distinct approach....

Some nurses feel this notion that they simply practice introductory medicine is insulting....

But many, if not most, staff nurses accept the assumption that medicine is superior and that nursing is simply a lesser form of medicine. They try to enhance their own prestige by a kind of "drift to medicine": by going into the more "medical" areas of nursing, like emergency work, or ICUs; by appropriating the scientific and pathophysiological model of disease; and by getting into the "medical macho" of high technology, invasive procedures, and massive pharmacological interventions, all the while setting aside the lower status "dirty work" of nursing. Although nursing as a profession tries to distance itself from medicine, establishing its own expertise, the typical nurse takes respect where she finds it, from her close association with doctors.[17]

To some extent, nurses' subordination lessened, or at least changed its character, during the period of my research from the late 1970s to the early 1990s. Nurses now more often will openly confront physicians rather than practice subterfuge; they have more ready support from independent nursing schools; perhaps because of the women's movement, nurses are somewhat more likely to expect to be treated with respect, if not really as equals. Still, despite some movement in these directions, nurses remain fundamentally unequal to doctors in their power and status. They are clearly subordinates, much more than their professional leaders or even staff nurses would like to believe. They do important work, and many of them do it with deep personal commitment and a high degree of skill. Yet their subordinate position, more than professionalism and perhaps even more than "caring," is a crucial component of most hospital nursing.

Here we see the dilemma of the nurse's role. On the one hand, she would like to raise her status by both differentiating her work from medicine ("we care, doctors cure") and by claiming to be a professional. On the other hand, by being a necessary member of the medical team she can borrow some of the prestige of medicine. The three components of the nurse's role—caring, professionalism, subordination—all represent in some degree what nurses empirically do and how they interpret what they do. In some ways they are conflicting requirements, fortified by conflicting parties: nursing schools with their admonition to professionalism, administrators with their efforts at controlling nurses, journals with their calls to "care." In some ways, managing these conflicts is inherent in the job of being a nurse....

...We have already seen that nurses treat their work in the hospital routinely and experience the hospital as a relatively normal place. Nurses understand their work as falling under the sometimes conflicting imperatives of caring for patients, behaving as professionals, and working as subordinates in the hospital organization. These imperatives are simultaneously *prescriptive*—saying what nurses should do—and somewhat *descriptive*—that is, actually reflecting what nurses in fact do. Nursing is basically a female occupation, with low visibility of its work and moderate prestige accorded to it. All of these components of the nursing role are suffused with moral implications: they carry moral judgments about who the nurse is and how she should do her work.

That role has implications for the ethics of nurses and for the rest of us. The nurse's position is not so unusual. Many Americans work in the "helping professions," broadly defined, and many more would characterize their work as serving others. While most do not consider themselves professionals, they do take their work seriously. And a growing number of workers are female. The ethical challenges of nurses may suggest the ethical challenges of any caring but subordinate person working in a large organization today. In trying to understand the ethics of nursing, then, we can begin to understand the ethical problems of the rest of us as well....

NOTES

1. Reverby, Susan M., 1992. *Ordered to Care: The Dilemma of American Nursing. 1850–1945.* (New York: Cambridge University Press), p. 1.
2. Jameton, *Nursing Practice: The Ethical Issues,* p. 256.
3. Anselm Strauss, "The Structure and Ideology of American Nursing: An Interpretation," in Davis, *The Nursing Profession: Five Sociological Essays,* pp. 117, 120; italics in the original.
4. Anderson, *Nurse,* p. 31.
5. For further elaboration, see Hughes, *Men and Their Work,* p. 74.
6. "The one-caring, in caring, is present in her acts of caring. Even in physical absence, acts at a distance bear the signs of presence: engrossment in the other, regard, desire for the other's well being." Nel Noddings, *Caring: A Feminine Approach to Ethics and Moral Education* (Berkeley: University of California Press, 1984), p.19.
7. Janet Kraegel and Mary Kachoyeanos, *"Just a Nurse"* (New York: Dell Publishing, 1989), p. 16.
8. Jameton, *Nursing Practice,* chap. 6.
9. Robert K. Merton, *Sociological Ambivalence and Other Essays* (New York: Free Press, 1976)...
10. Jo Ann Ashley, *Hospitals, Paternalism, and the Role of the Nurse* (New York: Teacher's College Press, 1977). See also Barbara Melosh, *The Physician's Hand: Work Culture and Conflict in American Nursing* (Philadelphia: Temple University Press, 1982); and Reverby, *Ordered to Care.*
11. "[C]lass divisions within the nursing culture made a feminist politics difficult to achieve," Reverby, *Ordered to Care,* p. 6.
12. The shift in number of registered nurses coming from diploma programs versus associate and baccalaureate (college-based) programs is dramatic: "More than 90 percent of the nurses [practicing in 1984] who graduated before 1960 were graduates of diploma schools... During the period 1980 to 1984, only 17 percent of all registered nurse graduates were graduated from a diploma program." *Facts about Nursing* 86–87, p. 21.
13. Benjamin and Curtis, *Ethics in Nursing,* p. 79.
14. The classic article on how the nurse "plays the game" is C. K. Hofling et al., "An Experimental Study in Nurse-Physician Relationships," *Journal of Nervous and Mental Disorders* 143 (1966), pp. 171–180.

15. Crane, *The Sanctity of Social Life;* Anderson, *Nurse,* pp. 246–248.
16. I borrow the characterization from Gretchen Aumann, R.N.
17. Perhaps to the long-term detriment of nursing's effort to independent status. See W. Glasen in Davis, *The Nursing Profession,* p. 27.

A MOTHER'S RESPONSIBILITY

ANONYMOUS

I have a daughter, Sally, who is now 22. She has Down syndrome and is moderately mentally retarded. It is difficult to describe Sally. To say that she is unique is an understatement and an actual disservice to her. She is a person of many abilities and disabilities. First of all, Sally is a person with a great sense of humor, a superior vocabulary, and excellent discourse skills. She can make you laugh by finding the humor or incongruity in a situation and stating it. She also has a severe articulation disorder which makes her difficult (at times) for others to understand. Sally is talented in many ways. She is an astute observer of emotions, zeroing in on other people's emotions, especially those of sadness. She has an enormous capacity to freely give solace and the best hugs in the world. Friends often comment, "When you've been hugged by Sally, you've really been *hugged.*" She is a wonderful person, independent and mastery motivated, and we love her.

Sally has learned many complicated tasks (cooking lasagna, writing a check, repairing a shredding machine, running a copier) by observation. She is independent in most home care situations, yet she can lose all her skills if it suddenly thunders during a spring storm. At the same time, Sally has very significant challenges. Sally also has a significant seizure disorder and mild autism. She is rooted in her routine. If the TV remote is in a different place in the morning, or her line of pens is awry, she can become difficult, sometimes defiant or stubborn, frightened or noncommunicative. If a favorite show is on, she will refuse to go bowling. She is afraid to try new social situations. I have learned to read her nonverbal behavior and to employ strategies (unique to Sally) that work to allay her fears and regain her cooperation. There is simply no one who can do this better than I (for good or bad). Even her father David is unable to accomplish this as well as I. Therefore, Sally, while very capable and wonderful, remains a responsibility for my husband and myself. In fact, she is today as much a responsibility as she was the day she was born.

Once upon a time, I had the "law" on my side, and there were funds under the Individuals with Disabilities Education Act (IDEA) to ensure that Sally would receive some services. Under IDEA, Sally had to be included in the least restrictive environment possible, which in her situation meant that she was enrolled in public school, included in school and community activities, and had a right to be with her nondisabled peers. The school was held accountable for how that was done. Although there are regulations and procedural safeguards that guide the process, we found that having mandated services is not simple at all from the parent's perspective. Parents must be active parts of the teams that deliver services to their children. For me, that meant meeting once a month and making frequent telephone calls, arranging for transportation to and from activities, and supervising at activities. There were also many informal contacts: coming to the school to bring in clean clothes (Sally could have a seizure requiring clean clothing), or coming to discuss her behavior (which could be inconsistent and challenging) or stopping by to provide an insight into a peculiar behavioral expression, or assisting the school to devise ways to help Sally build relationships. Although my contacts with the school were many, disrupting my days in unpredictable ways, I always had a safe feeling that the school was responsible for her from 7:10 in the morning until 3:00 in the afternoon. It was a positive environment for her. Most importantly, it meant that each day Sally would have opportunities to interact with people who were not disabled. She was able to participate in many activities with her nondisabled peers, take a computer class, and join school-based sports and clubs, such as the social justice club, blood drives, chorus, and the art club. She went to school dances and enjoyed being a spectator at sports events. In addition, Sally worked at various jobs in the community to prepare her to assume employment after graduation. One was a part-time job working the noon shift at a local restaurant, Friendly's, from 11:00 to 1:00. Her job coach was paid by the school (using funds from IDEA). Within this framework of supportive services, Sally thrived, and I was able to work a consistent forty-hour week, without constant fear about her safety or happiness.

At 22, Sally is no longer in school. She is now an adult. There are no federally mandated services for adults with disabilities. Often you must take what is available. Sometimes, that means less in terms of opportunities for a self-determined quality of life for her and for us, her parents.

When Sally transitioned from school, the Bureau of Rehabilitation Services continued supportive training and provided funding for the job coach position for 90 days. At the end of this time, Sally was deemed employable but needing continued support. However, the Bureau of Rehabilitation Services did not have any more money for her training. Instead, the Department of Mental Retardation (DMR) became the service coordinator. Funding promised in June, 1998, to high school graduates finally materialized two months later. DMR would continue to pay for a job coach for 15 hours a week and provide transportation to Sally to her job site. During this time, I was expecting to see the job coach develop natural supports among Sally's coworkers, Sally's hours to increase, and Sally's need for a job coach to fade. Somehow this did not happen. I mistakenly assumed that I would not need to supervise what happened. I thought that DMR and the agency it contracted with had a plan that would result in full-time employment for Sally, allowing me to commit to my work with the intensity of most other professionals in my field. Sally never received more hours, nor did she learn to work without her job coach.

The lack of a plan was a significant issue, but less pressing than the more immediate concern about how to provide for Sally during the morning and afternoon hours she was at home when I was scheduled to be at work. Providing for Sally is not easy because of her long history of seizure disorder. During her senior year in high school, the seizures became a major problem, with seizures occurring almost every week. Her seizures required me to leave work frequently. I left my full-time position, realizing that I could not commit to being on my work site eight hours a day, and accepted another full time position where I could have flexible hours. Still there were problems. I would often be in the middle of a meeting (often in another city), when Sally would call because she was ill or scared. As frequently as I could, I allowed her to come to work with me and even became her informal job coach. Under my tutelage, Sally learned how to run a shredder, use our copying machine, use our pamphlet folder and stapling machine. She learned how to catch a nearby bus to go to Friendly's and then how to come back to my office. She also decided that she would like to work in an office.

I continued to be the person in Sally's life who assumed the responsibilities of helping her with her finances as her conservator, transporting her to work, planning social activities (pottery classes, bowling), and coordinating trips with DMR. I continued (as I had always done) to coordinate her medical visits to our family practitioner, the geneticist, endocrinologist, neurologist, and dentist. Since having seizures, she no longer allowed the dentist to give her nitrous oxide prior to filling cavities. The laughing gas made her feel dizzy, a feeling associated with seizures, so I held her hands as she cried and screamed through dental work. I continued to assist people working with her by providing insights into her behavior. Later in 1998, I was in need of help myself. After being in severe depression and trying to cope with exhaustion, I committed myself to a psychiatric hospital.

During my hospitalization, I found out that *now* I could garner more support from DMR. I had moved up in their priority list from a 3—child in home, family needs minimal support—to a priority 1 "crisis," placement must be made within one year, and in-depth services are required. DMR immediately placed Sally in its community support program. We had an emergency meeting looking for in-home supports. Two months later, DMR was able to provide a woman to come in three days a week from 2:00 until 5:00. She came a few times, but I really didn't need her because, after my release from the hospital, I was on partial disability from my job and I was home by 2:00. The psychologists recommended that I work only part-time because Sally occupied so much of my time. They suggested that I put her in a group home if I were to continue full-time work.

I worked for several months to help her dad see that a group home was the right thing to do, not only for us, but also for Sally. She needed to be with other young people developing independent living and social skills. We wanted her to be in a group home nearby, so that we could maintain a close relationship with her. At the beginning of May, 1999, David and I sat down with several individuals from DMR to discuss placement in a group home. I was back to work about half time.

Ironically, David and I have done *too good* a job raising Sally. She now functions with such a high range of skills, she is probably overqualified for a group home. New groups homes are being constructed slowly, and they are being saved for individuals with significant emotional, physical, and behavioral needs. Sally did not fit any of these categories. We were told that Sally would not be eligible for a group home in our region. She would be more likely to fit into a supervised apartment model or in independent living. David left the meeting saying that he was just as happy for her to stay with us. He could not support her move into either a supervised apartment or into independent living. David expressed a fear that Sally's safety could not be assured, that she would not receive the supports that she needed, and that she would end up lonely and isolated.

I began anew to work on procuring Sally steadier work that would include longer days. In June, Sally's hours at Friendly's were reduced from 15 to 9 hours per week, due to the lack of business at the particular Friendly's restaurant. We scrambled for a few weeks. Sally found a job as a dishwasher at a camp for children with disabilities. The length of day was better, and a member of the staff could transport her to work. This new arrangement worked out very well, and I was able over the summer to increase my work load back to 60 percent time. I had to take a week off during the break in July for the two summer sessions of camp, and my boss was gracious about this. This fall, I decided that we needed more support during the day. We asked DMR to focus on developing employment skills with the goal of increasing Sally's ability to work a typical week. The change was accomplished by a DMR contract with Sally's support agency. From September to February, Sally was picked up each morning and driven 25 minutes to the site of the agency serving her. She then joined a workgroup of other persons with disabilities who were sent into community settings to do kitchen or maintenance work until 2:00, after which she took Dial-A-Ride home. Sometimes the site of the job was back in our community, which meant that she would ride fifty minutes only to end up back in town. In addition, the scheduling of transportation was inconsistent, and required me to start my day anywhere from 8:00 to 9:30 in the morning.

It is February, 2000, now. I look back to see where we are. What changes have been made? I am still the major advocate for Sally: monitoring employment, teaching her community skills, teaching her money skills and how to use a checkbook, facilitating her social life, planning for her future, and prompting her in daily living tasks (bathing, washing hair, cutting nails, when to shower, how much money to spend, nutrition, exercise, meal preparation). I still make and transport her to all medical appointments. She just started a full-time job (which I transport her to), and she continues to live at home. She is part of a workcrew of other individuals with disabilities. While gaining a more stable work schedule, she has lost contact with nondisabled coworkers in her community. I have gained the ability to commit more consistently to my work and have sacrificed some of Sally's quality of life. There are other parents in the same position as I am. We would like to get together, but we have not found time to do this. I am back to work at 80 percent time, but I struggle with this schedule each day. David works long hours, and we are both too exhausted at the end of the day to go out. We have been to dinner twice this year, and took one overnight trip to Vermont. We went with Sally to a couple of movies.

Any day can become a major challenge. Two weeks ago, Sally and I went to a local store for a long-awaited shopping trip. She purchased several items, including a new watch. When we went to pay, we both found that we had left our IDs at home and could not write checks. There were two cashiers and we asked them to total the purchase, and said that we would come back with cash. Our bank is nearby in the mall. Sally took $125.00 out of her account to pay for a $103.00 purchase. I sent her back to the store to pay while I did my banking. She returned to the bank with her purchases and two dollars in change. I suggested that we go back to the store to talk with the two cashiers because she had been shortchanged. Sally, feeling shy, did not want to go, but I insisted that she accompany me, mostly to help her become empowered to advocate for herself. Several times, the cashier insisted that Sally had lost the money. I was sure that she hadn't because Sally is very careful with her money. The manager was called. She promised to call us when the registers were closed and the money counted. We left the store at 12:00.

When we arrived home, we opened the bag to find *no watch.* We called the manager, who interviewed each of the cashiers separately. Each claimed that the watch had been placed in the bag and suggested that Sally must have lost the watch. At 2:00, the manager called to say that the watch and change had been found hidden under the personal belongings of one of the cashiers. The store apologized and returned Sally's watch and change. The entire episode lasted from 10:00 a.m. until 2:30 p.m., leaving us both upset and with little time left in our day.

When I look back over the year, I realize that not much has changed. Many of my hours are still spent in advocating for my daughter, monitoring her employment, overseeing her entitlements and financial matters, promoting her social development. The job is tougher now. The school used to have individuals to assist with planning for Sally. Now I am the main advocate. I realize that my advocacy for my daughter will continue for many years in diverse situations. It is often emotionally and physically exhausting. There is no way I would urge a return to institutionalizing children and adults like my daughter. Her life now has freedoms and a richness that is to be protected. But the burdens and challenges parents like myself face are formidable. Sometimes I reflect that when my friends retire and start to enjoy their later years, I will remain responsible for another.

Chapter 16

HEALTH CARE ACTIVISTS

A distinct women's health care movement began in the late 1960s and early 1970s and has persisted with many of the same faces, long-lived organizations, and enduring issues, despite great changes in the health care arena. Participants in the movement have criticized the health care provided to women; voiced frustration with the traditional paternalistic doctor–patient relationship; challenged professional authority and expertise; objected to the medicalization of childbirth, menopause, and other natural processes in women's lives; criticized the privileging of technology and intervention over prevention and self-care; educated each other; provided alternative forms of care; and effectively lobbied for changes in the health and health care of women (Ruzek 1978; Zimmerman 1987).

Although this chapter provides an overview of the women's health movement that emerged in the last third of the twentieth century, women's activism around health issues predates that time. The current movement owes a considerable debt to the broader women's liberation movement, as well as to the many women who previously fought for changes in diverse health arenas. These activists include the turn-of-the-century, industrial-hygiene activists such as Alice Hamilton, who exposed the dangers to women from occupational lead poisoning and from radium poisoning incurred through painting luminous watch dials (Bale 1990). Also included are the early birth control proponents such as Margaret Sanger, jailed in 1917 for distributing contraceptives to immigrant women. Other pioneers are writers such as Rachel Carson, whose 1962 book, *Silent Spring,* on ecological degradation forced the government to acknowledge the tremendous damage caused by pesticides and insecticides. Still others are granny midwives who provided care to poor, rural, and minority women (see Davis and Ingram 1993); and government workers, such as Dr. Frances Kelsey, who in the 1960s refused to give FDA approval for Thalidomide because of its potential harm to the fetus, and thereby precluded its open marketing in the United States (Zimmerman 1987).

It is useful to identify three overlapping centers of activity that were the foundation for the current women's health movement. One was the group of women in Boston (noted in Chapter 3) who, after gathering in 1969 at a conference workshop, decided that greater knowledge of women's bodies was empowering. The resulting Boston Women's Health Book Collective (BWHBC) thrives to this day, publishing ever-revised editions of their ambitious *Our Bodies, Ourselves,* and serving as a center of health education, advocacy, coalition building, and outreach (see www.ourbodiesourselves.org). Members of the collective examine their history and accomplishments in the article included in this chapter (Norsigian et al. 1999).

The second center of activity grew out of investigative work done by Barbara Seaman who, as a writer for *Ladies Home Journal* and *Brides Magazine,* made the connection between women's complaints about weight gain, blood clots, depression, and decreased sex drive and their use of the birth control pill. Her 1969 book *The Doctor's Case Against the Pill* was the impetus for U.S. Senate hearings the following year, which mandated the inclusion of patient information with birth control pills (so-called PPIs, or Patient Package Inserts). Her work made people more aware of the paternalistic attitudes of doctors who wished to keep such information from their patients, and of the dangers of the hormonal dosage in the early birth control pills.

Fortuitously, Alice Wolfson, who believed that women too often kept their health problems private, attended those hearings. When the hearings excluded any testimony from women who had had experiences with the pill, Wolfson jumped up from the audience and demanded to know why. Seaman and Wolfson then organized other women to protest outside the hearings. The resulting media attention transformed women by making their private troubles into public issues (Bloom 1995). This activism by Seaman and Wolfson—and their collaboration with Phyllis Chesler, Belita Cowan, and Mary Howell—led to the founding of the National Women's Health Network (NWHN), which endures as an effective protest and lobbying organization for women's health [www.womenshealthnetwork.org; and see Berglas (1995) for the story of a successful protest spearheaded by the NWHN].

The third center of activity was self-help gynecology promoted by Carole Downer and Lorraine Rothman. On April 7, 1971, Downer "inserted a speculum in her vagina and invited the other women present to observe her cervix" (Ruzek 1978:53). The resulting self-help and self-examination gynecology encouraged women to understand their bodies empirically and to find female support and assistance at women's health centers, rather than from traditional medical caregivers. A Feminist Women's Health Center model emerged and became influential nationally and even internationally. The evolution of this radical idea is discussed in an article included with this chapter (Pearson 1996).

In addition to these three points of organized collective activity, many individual women were simultaneously facing situations that led them to become health activists. For instance, in the early 1970s, Karen Silkwood became a health care activist when, as a technician at a plutonium plant in Oklahoma, she grew suspicious of the safety of the plant and her own exposure to plutonium there. She became a whistle-blower and was on her way to provide evidence of radiation hazards to a reporter and union activist when she was mysteriously killed, and the documents she was carrying were lost. Shortly thereafter, in 1978, Lois Gibbs became a health care activist when she realized that her child was attending a school located on top of a huge, toxic chemical dump at Love Canal. Activists around local environmental issues have primarily been women. They have often struggled with those who would dismiss their concerns as being based on "housewife's" data (see Brown and Ferguson 1995 and Camp 1991, both reprinted as readings in this chapter).

At the same time that this occupational and environmental health activism was occurring, the general public was shocked to learn of several women's health tragedies. Those who had been skeptical of the women's health movement, and its critique of the paternalistic medical treatment of women, were put on the defensive. In a brief, five-year period, from 1970 to 1975, documentation of the abuse of women within the health care system pushed the limits of what the movement had claimed was happening. Several revelations stand out as having documented particularly devastating health consequences.

First, in 1970 and 1971, reports of a rare form of vaginal cancer in adolescent girls began appearing in the literature. The cancer was soon traced back to their mothers who had taken DES (diethylstilbestrol, a synthetic estrogen) to prevent miscarriage and premature labor while pregnant with these daughters. DES was on the market because the enthusiasm of drug companies and doctors for the latest scientific breakthrough had silenced those who urged caution in its use, based on decades of evidence of the potential carcinogenic effects of estrogenic drugs. So strong was the enthusiasm, that the Federal Drug Administration (FDA) failed in its mission to protect the public (Dutton 1988).

The DES tragedy was compounded by the failure of public health agencies, hospitals, and doctors to contact women and inform them of their exposure. In addition, most university health services "carelessly and casually" gave DES for another purpose—as a morning-after contraceptive (Ruzek 1978:40)—producing another class of potentially harmed women. The dangers of hormonal prescriptions did not end there. Shortly thereafter, in 1975, research reports discussed the risks of menopausal estrogens (see Chapter 9), forcing the FDA to take these concerns seriously (Berglas 1995).

Second, reports of unnecessary operations on women were surfacing at about the same time. A study at the Columbia University School of Public Health suggested that as many as 66 percent of hysterectomies were not medically justified (Ruzek 1978:49). Unnecessary hysterectomies were sometimes performed so doctors in training could learn techniques (see Chapter 3), a practice which placed women of color and economically disadvantaged women at particular risk. "One Boston City Hospital medical student reported that a common joke was that the only prerequisite for a hysterectomy was to not speak English" (Ruzek 1978:52). Other unnecessary operations, such as cesarean sections and radical mastectomies, were performed for the convenience of the doctor, or because the procedures had evolved into the standard of care, despite a lack of evidence that they should be. Thus, "once a c-section, always a c-section" became routine, until someone suggested the possibility of a vaginal birth after c-section. And the radical Halsted mastectomy—the removal of the entire breast, lymph nodes and underlying chest wall muscle—usually immediately after a biopsy, was routine despite a lack of evidence that it had to be performed immediately and that it was the best option for the woman. Diagnosed with cancer, Rose Kushner questioned the logic of this standard procedure, and the exclusion of the woman from the decision making. *Why Me?,* her 1975 book, led to a reevaluation of the Halsted procedure, and it quickly fell out of favor (Eagan 1994).

Third, a series of contraceptive disasters were revealed in the early 1970s. In 1971, a gynecologist presented a paper at an American Fertility Society conference, reporting a double-blind study of the birth control pill, in which he gave women either birth control pills or a placebo. "The subjects, mostly poor Mexican-American women, were enrolled in the experiment when they came to the clinic for contraceptives. They were neither told of the experiment nor informed that some of them would receive a dummy pill rather than a contraceptive" (Ruzek 1978:45). Feminists were infuriated by the absence of any ethical concerns over what the researcher did, or any regard for the women who came seeking birth control, and by the fact that not only did subjects not receive contraception, but they were *not aware* that they did not recieve it. Close on the heels of this evidence of callous disregard for women were reports of "Mississippi appendectomies": the sterilization of poor black women without obtaining their consent (Ruzek 1978:46). And in the early 1970s, the horrors of the Dalkon Shield became widely known (see Chapter 5). Women's health activists were seeing an unbelievable string of horrifying abuses of women.

Fourth, the late 1960s and early 1970s was a time of major debate, activism, and tragedy surrounding abortion. Prior to the 1973 *Roe v. Wade* decision legalizing abortion, women desiring an abortion had to go "underground" or, if they had the money, abroad. Illegal, "back-alley" abortions were scary, degrading, and sometimes fatal. Many women's health activists, such as those involved in the Jane Collective in Chicago, ingeniously worked to provide safe abortions. Then, once abortion was legalized, many health activists continued in the struggle for safe access to abortion facilities (see Chapter 11).

In the 1970s, the women's health movement concentrated on reproductive issues, due in part to the childbearing ages of the women who were most active, and in part to the frequency of reproductive tragedies, as noted, to which they responded in that decade. The primary activists in those early years were white, middle-class women. Since that time the women's health movement has diversified both in membership and in issues. Several of the articles reproduced here discuss the broadened base of women's health groups as women of color, women with disabilities, lesbian women, older women, and others formed their own organizations.

With the membership diversification has come increased activism on more varied issues. The National Black Women's Health Project (Avery 1990, reproduced as a reading in this chapter), the National Latina Women's Health Organization, and other ethnically defined organizations have focused attention on diseases and conditions disproportionately affecting their members, on racism, and on health and health care for economically disadvantaged women. Similarly, the Older Women's League, the Lesbian Health Agenda, and DisAbled Women's Network have encouraged serious examination of health issues relevant to their constituencies. With the "naming" of rape and domestic violence, rape centers and battered women's shelters became centers of women's health activity. The agenda of women's health activists has expanded enormously since the early 1970s.

The evolution of the women's health movement is also seen in other characteristics. As noted by Ruzek, the movement has changed from grassroots groups to the greater involvement of professional organizations, and from groups proposing a broad critique of the health system to more groups organizing around single issues. This "disease du jour" orientation has generated monies for long-neglected problems, but it has the negative potential of pitting one disease against another (Ruzek and Becker 1999, reproduced as a reading in this chapter). In addition, corporate America has become a major player in single-disease activism. Breast cancer, which has become the "darling" of corporate America, is a prime example. Corporations realized that cause-related marketing could make a good impression on consumers and generate product loyalties. Avon spent $20 million supporting community-based mammogram screening programs for underserved women, generating an estimated 700 million "media impressions.... That's what this is all about," says a member of Avon's marketing staff—"making a good and a lasting impression for our company" (quoted in Belkin 1996:52). The corporate booths lining San Francisco's Race for the Cure included Genentech, JCPenney, American Airlines, Ford, Vogue, and Wells Fargo, as well as representatives from the fitness, nutrition, beauty, and fashion industries (Klawiter 1999). Such corporate sponsorship does not challenge the perspectives and priorities of the medical and research establishments; rather, it conveys the message that breast cancer survival is about individual choice and responsibility—early detection and appropriate treatment. Such an approach contrasts dramatically with feminist, radical, and environmentally based breast cancer activists who target corporate polluters, the tobacco industry, and even the American Cancer Society (Klawiter 1999; Myhre 1999).

Despite all these changes in the women's health movement, it is notable that many faces and organizations active in the 1970s have endured. The BWHBC and the NWHN have continued to follow the missions they set for themselves in the 1970s, and many of the women active at the beginning remain involved. The women's clinic movement has perhaps changed the most, due to abortion center violence and to co-optation and competition from for-profit health groups who have established women's clinics bearing almost no resemblance to the strong feminist organizations of the 1970s. Few women-controlled clinics now exist, yet here, too, there is reason for continued celebration because the "spark is still alive." Self-help groups across the country continue to meet and to influence the care women receive (Pearson 1996, reproduced as a reading in this chapter).

The achievements of the women's health movement are many, at both the policy level and the individual level. Annually, NWHN produces an impressive list of some of the accomplishments of the movement, and many diverse, community-based organizations continue the struggle for better health care for women.

THE BOSTON WOMEN'S HEALTH BOOK COLLECTIVE AND *OUR BODIES, OURSELVES*: A BRIEF HISTORY AND REFLECTION

JUDY NORSIGIAN, VILUNYA DISKIN, PAULA DORESS-WORTERS, JANE PINCUS, WENDY SANFORD, AND NORMA SWENSON

This article offers a brief history of Our Bodies, Ourselves, *the landmark book about women's health and sexuality first published in 1970, as well as the Boston Women's Health Book Collective, its author and sponsor of numerous women's health initiatives. The organization's transition from a small, grass-roots collective to a non-profit organization working at both the domestic and international levels is briefly discussed, including the development of a more diverse board and staff. Past accomplishments and current concerns of the global women's health movements are described including some of the larger advocacy organizations now active in the women's health field. Collaboration with feminist physicians over the past two decades is also noted.*

OUR EARLY HISTORY

The history of *Our Bodies, Ourselves* (*OBOS*) and the Boston Women's Health Book Collective (BWHBC) began in the spring of 1969 at a women's liberation conference held in Boston. At a workshop on "Women and Their Bodies," we discovered that every one of us had a "doctor story," that we had all experienced feelings of frustration and anger toward the medical maze in general, and toward those doctors who were condescending, paternalistic, judgmental, and uninformative in particular. As we talked and shared our experiences, we realized just how much we had to learn about our bodies, that simply finding a "good doctor" was not the solution to whatever problems we might have. So we decided on a summer project: we would research our questions, share what we learned in our group, and then present the information in the fall as a course "by and for women." We envisioned an ongoing process that would involve other women who would then go on to teach such a course in other settings.

In creating the course, we learned that we were capable of collecting, understanding, and evaluating medical information; that we could open up to one another and find strength and comfort through sharing some of our most private experiences; that what we learned from one another was every bit as important as what we read in medical texts; and that our experiences frequently contradicted medical pronouncements. Over time these facts, feelings, and controversies were intertwined in the various editions of *OBOS.*

When we began this work, our ages ranged from 23 to 39, and we focused heavily on reproductive health and sexuality, new issues in the second wave of feminism. As we revised subsequent editions of *OBOS,* we included more material on such topics as environmental and occupational health, menopause and aging, often at the behest of readers and with outside help. At this writing, those of us in the original group range in age from our late 40s to our mid-60s, and one of our original members, Esther Rome, has died of breast cancer.

In the 1970s, we worked together in "cottage industry" mode at home or in libraries, often meet-

All authors of this article are also authors of *Our Bodies, Ourselves* and founders of the BWHBC.

ing together around our kitchen tables. In 1980 we consolidated our books, articles, and correspondence in a rented office and began to hire women not part of the original Collective to do cataloging and to help with other tasks. This effort marked the beginning of our Women's Health Information Center (WHIC) and two decades of networking and information sharing that has extended beyond the publication of *OBOS* to a number of women's health education, activist, and advocacy projects involving us locally, nationally, and internationally. We supported the founding of the National Women's Health Network—the first national women's health advocacy membership organization. We were also among the few women's organizations calling for universal health care in the 1970s, and we supported Congressman Ron Dellums' National Health Services Act, a visionary bill that included provisions for contraceptive, sexually transmitted disease, and abortion services, and access to midwives and out-of-hospital childbearing options. Internationally, we served on the Advisory Board of ISIS (an information and communication service focused on women in developing countries), distributed packets and books to health workers and groups overseas, attended global women's health meetings, and ensured, when possible, that women's groups translating *OBOS* would be able to reap royalties to support their work.

The founders of the BWHBC were all college educated, but a significant number of us were from working class backgrounds and were the first in our families to attend college. Some of us had professional degrees, but none of us were in health fields. Many of us had been active in the social protest movements of the 1960s, particularly the civil rights movement, the anti-war movement, movements for women-centered childbirth and legal abortion. Some of us came from families with histories of struggle for social justice. Others of us came of age during a time of social change and found our own way to political activism. When we came together as part of a larger women's liberation movement, we were thrilled by the realization that working for social justice could affect the conditions of our lives as women. We believed that with our new found freedom and solidarity as feminists, we could be more effective advocates on behalf of ourselves and other women, as well as other progressive causes.

RECENT GROWTH AND DEVELOPMENT

Over the nearly three decades since the first edition of *OBOS,* we have continued to develop our awareness of the injustices that prevent women from experiencing full and healthy lives. As we approach the millennium, such causes of poor health as poverty, racism, hunger, and homelessness continue to disproportionately affect black and brown populations in this country and around the world. We continue to believe that effective strategies for mitigating these problems require all of us to reject the assumptions that so often have hurt women of color and women who are poor. Over the years we have collaborated with women's groups both in the United States and abroad to ensure that the priorities for the women's health movement reflect the needs and concerns of all women. We also recognize the importance of supporting the leadership of women of color and low-income women within our own organization as well as in the larger women's health movements. Although this is a difficult challenge for many groups founded originally by white women, we believe that our ultimate success as a movement depends on respectful collaboration at many levels.

BWHBC's own structure has evolved over the years. We began as a collective, a circle of 12 women who met weekly and grew together both personally and politically, raising our own consciousness about health and sexuality as we reached out to inform others. We took no profits from sales of the books, using the royalties to support women's health projects and eventually to start our own WHIC and advocacy work. As soon as we hired staff who were not authors of the book, the BWHBC was not formally a collective any more, although the board (mostly original authors for many years) and the paid staff each worked in a largely collaborative manner.

As the staff grew, so did organizational tensions and the need to develop a different model of management. For the past four years, the board of directors—now a more diverse group than it was originally—worked closely with a variety of consultants to shape a structure for the BWHBC that would introduce mechanisms of accountability that are consistent, dependable, and consonant with feminist principles. The organization now has a unionized staff (including a signed union contract) and formally designated leadership positions that operate in quite a different manner from the earlier years.

During the past few years a major revision of *OBOS* was also produced, *Our Bodies, Ourselves for the New Century* (May 1998). For this edition we expanded even more our efforts to include other women whose backgrounds and experiences are different from the original coauthors in terms of race, class, ethnicity, geographic origin, and sexual/gender identity. This experience helped us to develop an even greater appreciation for the challenges facing any organization working across differences, many of which have the potential to separate us.

BWHBC'S ROLE IN THE GLOBAL WOMEN'S HEALTH MOVEMENT

Within five years of its first publication, *OBOS* became a best seller first in the United States, and then internationally (more than 4 million copies have been sold to date). Almost 20 foreign-language editions have been produced, including Japanese, Russian, Chinese, Spanish, French, Italian, and German versions. Women in Egypt produced an Arabic book modeled after *OBOS,* as women are now doing in French-speaking Africa. More projects are underway today in Asia, Eastern Europe, and Armenia. At the 1995 NGO Women's Forum in Beijing, many of the women working on these translation/adaptation projects came together to compare notes and to share strategies for dealing with problems such as government censorship and fundraising.

In all editions of *OBOS,* we have encouraged women to meet, talk, and listen to each other as a first step toward bringing about needed change. Over the years, we have developed a number of fruitful collaborations with women's groups in different countries and have attended almost all the international women and health meetings that have been convened since the first "International Conference on Woman and Health" held in Rome in 1977. The activism of women's health groups across the globe has been spurred by the advent of e-mail and the Internet, and we are excited to be a part of a growing web of organizations working on issues such as breastfeeding, maternal mortality, and environmental health hazards.

One continuing concern of the current global women's health movement has been the growing trend, especially among environmental groups, to label population growth as a primary cause of environmental degradation. It would be a serious step back if this trend were to lead to more overly zealous family planning programs[1] driven by demographic goals rather than by women's reproductive health needs. We believe that the unethical and growing use of quinacrine, a sclerosing agent, as a means of nonsurgical sterilization in countries such as Indonesia, India, Pakistan, and Vietnam, represents the very "population control" mentality that has so often been destructive to women's health. Thus, we have joined activists around the globe in protesting the use of quinacrine.[2]

We also collaborated with such other groups as the Women's Global Network for Reproductive Rights (Amsterdam), the International Reproductive Rights and Research Action Group (IRRRAG), and WomanHealth Philippines to sponsor "The Double Challenge," a well-attended workshop series at the Beijing NGO Forum in September 1995. The brochure for this series stated:

> *Women from around the world face a formidable challenge. On one side are the fundamentalists led by the Vatican; on the other is the population establishment. Both are vying for control over women's sexual and reproductive lives. While the*

fundamentalists outlaw contraception and abortion, the populationists push new reproductive and contraceptive technologies.

THE CONTINUED NEED FOR A WOMEN'S HEALTH MOVEMENT[3,4]

The concerns that brought women together several decades ago to form women-controlled health centers, advocacy groups, and other educational and activist organizations largely remain. Women are still the major users of health and medical services, for example, seeking care for themselves even when essentially healthy (birth control, pregnancy and childbearing, and menopausal discomforts).[5] Because women live longer than men, they have more problems with chronic diseases and functional impairment, and thus require more community and home-based services. Women usually act as the family "health broker": arranging care for children, the elderly, spouses, or relatives, and are also the major unpaid caregivers for those around them.[6]

Although women represent the great majority of health workers, they still have a relatively small role in policy making in all arenas. Despite increases in the number of women physicians, they also have a limited leadership role in US medical schools, where women represent less than 10% of all tenured faculty.[7] Women face discrimination on the basis of sex, class, race, age, sexual orientation, and disability in most medical settings. Many continue to experience condescending, paternalistic, and culturally insensitive treatment. Older women, women of color, fat women, women with disabilities, and lesbians routinely confront discriminatory attitudes and practices, and even outright abuse.[8]

Women usually find it difficult to obtain the good health and medical information necessary to ensure informed decision making, especially for alternatives to conventional forms of treatment. This problem is intensified for poor women and for those who do not speak English, in part because their class, race, and culture increasingly differ markedly from those of their health care providers.[9]

Many women are subjected to inappropriate medical interventions, such as overmedication with psychotropic drugs (especially tranquilizers and antidepressants), questionable hormone therapy, and unnecessary cesarean sections and hysterectomies, although managed care has reduced the rates of unnecessary surgery in some places.[10] The medical care system has been slow to recognize the importance of preventive and routine care, as well as the need for more rigorous study of alternative (nonallopathic) approaches to women's health problems that have not responded well to conventional forms of treatment.[10]

Despite enormous advances for women over the past two decades, ongoing gender bias in public and private settings continues to relegate women to a separate and unequal place in society. We must have a strong community of women's organizations to assist women individually, to articulate women's needs, to advocate for policy reform, and to resist the more destructive aspects of corporate medicine. Organizations such as the National Women's Health Network, the National Black Women's Health Project, the National Latino Health Organization, the National Asian Women's Health Organization, and the Native American Women's Health Education Resource Center, to name just a few, could play a key role in ensuring that lay and consumer voices are part of any larger women's health debate. The inclusion of such groups by the Office of Women's Health Research at the National Institutes of Health already has enriched discussions concerning research affecting women.

Ironically, except in a handful of states, poor women on Medicaid can obtain a federally funded sterilization but not a federally funded abortion. This limitation has led some women to "choose" sterilization because they have so few options. As the women's health movement continues to emphasize, without access to all reproductive health services, there can be no real choice in matters of childbearing.

Over the years, the BWHBC has collaborated with physicians who have shared the feminist perspective represented in *OBOS*. One such colleague, Mary Howell, MD, (more recently known as Mary Raugust), died from breast cancer in February 1998. The author of a popular 1972 book entitled *Why Would A Girl Go Into Medicine?* and the first woman dean at Harvard Medical School, Mary contributed to the research that resulted in a legal ruling forcing medical schools to eliminate female quotas. These informal quotas had kept the female presence in medical schools well below 20% of the total number of students since the turn of the century. She remains for us one of the finest role models for women in medicine, and we hope that her speeches and writings will be published to inspire the younger generations of female physicians. Another physician, Alice Rothchild, MD, has written and spoken eloquently about her experience as a feminist obstetrician-gynecologist, and we have made her 1998 AMWA speech[11] available at our website (www.ourbodiesourselves.org).

Members of the media often ask us if we think that progress has been made in addressing the concerns women have had about medicine. We believe that physician awareness of condescending and paternalistic behaviors that are now generally regarded as disrespectful elsewhere in society has been heightened. It also appears that more women feel that their physicians take their concerns seriously, rather than dismissing complaints with "it's all in your head." But other problems have been exacerbated, and although not unique to women, women's more frequent contact with the medical care system means that women confront these issues much more regularly than men do.[5]

Many managed care plans have contributed to reductions in access to care, especially good quality care, for some women. They have, for example, not allowed some physicians to provide needed treatments. Sometimes, physicians have not had the time to adequately assess the plethora of new drugs and medical technologies that they regularly recommend to patients. Cutbacks in local community services and public health programs make it harder to sustain an emphasis on preventive health care.

The BWHBC has a special interest in such problems as the increasing influence of right-wing organizations over public policies affecting women's health, the explosion of health and medical technologies marketed primarily to women, the objectification of women's bodies in the media, the exclusion of consumers from policy setting and oversight functions in many managed care plans, and the relatively few sources of noncommercial information about women and health, especially with a well-informed consumer perspective. We recognize institutional racism as a continuing problem exacerbated by the fact that most caregivers and health care administrators come from economic, social, racial, and ethnic backgrounds quite different from those of the people they are serving. Finally, we believe it is critical to challenge the tendency to over-"medicalize"[12] women's lives and turn normal events such as childbearing and menopause into disabling conditions requiring medical intervention.

As the women's health movement moves into the next century, the ability to build broad coalitions will largely determine the political effectiveness of women's health care advocates. We can learn much, for example, from the passage of the Americans with Disabilities Act, which succeeded in large part because the disability rights community reached out to form broad alliances with other groups not initially aware of the universal impact of this legislation. Finding common ground and ways to bridge racial, ethnic, and class differences in particular, will be among the great challenges we face.

REFERENCES

1. Hartmann B. To vanquish the hydra. *Political Environments.* Spring 1994:1.

2. Berer M. The quinacrine controversy one year on. *Reproductive Health Matters.* November 1994:105.

3. Swenson N. Women's health movement. In: Mankiller W, et al, eds. *Reader's Companion to U.S. Women's History.* New York, NY: Houghton-Mifflin; 1998:648.

4. Norsigian J. Women and national health care reform: A progressive feminist agenda. *Women's Health.* 1993;2:91.

5. *Managed Care Consumer Protections and Women's Health: The Balanced Budget Act.* Washington, DC: Women's Legal Defense Fund; 1997:1.

6. Horton J, ed. *The Women's Health Data Book: A Profile of Women's Health in the United States.* Washington, DC: Jacobs Institute of Women's Health. 1992:93.
7. *The Blue Sheet.* Washington, DC: F-D-C Reports; 1996:5.
8. Scully D, *Men Who Control Women's Health: The Miseducation of Obstetrician/Gynecologists.* New York, NY: Teacher's College Press; 1994.
9. *Health Care Reform: What Is at Stake for Women?* New York, NY: The Commonwealth Fund Commission of Women's Health; 1994:13.
10. Ruzek S. Access, cost, and quality medical care: Where are we heading? In: Ruzek S, Oleson V, Clarke A, eds. *Women's Health: Complexities and Differences.* Columbus, Ohio: Ohio State University Press; 1997:197.
11. Rothchild A. From both ends of the speculum: A feminist analysis of health care. Paper presented at the American Medical Women's Association meeting, New York City, March 8, 1998.
12. Zola IK. Medicine as an institution of social control. In: Zola IK. *Socio-Medical Inquiries.* Philadelphia, Pa: Temple University Press; 1983.

THE WOMEN'S HEALTH MOVEMENT IN THE UNITED STATES: FROM GRASS-ROOTS ACTIVISM TO PROFESSIONAL AGENDAS

SHERYL BURT RUZEK AND JULIE BECKER

The grass-roots women's health movement grew rapidly during the 1970s and 1980s, but contracted by the end of that decade. Surviving organizations must now negotiate roles and relationships with newer women's health organizations that burgeoned in the 1990s and that are typically professionalized and disease specific. They differ from grass-roots groups through: (1) their relationships to broader movements for social change; (2) leadership; (3) attitudes toward biomedicine; (4) relationships to corporate sponsors; (5) educational goals; and (6) lay versus professional authority. There is little overlap between women's health advocacy organizations identified by the National Women's Health Network and two Internet search engines. The proliferation of newer organizations dilutes the role of grass-roots groups as information brokers for women in the United States and raises questions about who will speak for women in the electronic age. (JAMWA. *1999;54:4–8)*

Women's health activists have generated public debate and spearheaded social action in a number of waves throughout US history, waves that Carol Weisman views as part of a women's health "megamovement" that has spanned two centuries.[1 p. 37–93] The US women's health movement grew rapidly through the 1970s; broadened its base with women of color and others in the early 1980s; and contracted, was co-opted, and became institutionalized during the late 1980s and 1990s. Surviving grass-roots organizations are now negotiating roles and relationships with newer, more professional women's health support and advocacy organizations. While both older and newer women's health organizations seek improvements in women's health care, their focus and priorities vary.

In this article, we analyze the historical development of the grass-roots women's health movement in the United States, note key contributions, and differentiate surviving movement organizations from the newer, professionalized women's health advocacy groups. Distinguishing between grass-roots and more professional women's health groups becomes particularly important as we move into the global "information age." Because public trust of mainstream medical institutions is eroding, as evidenced by the growth of alternative and complementary medical practices[2–4] and the increasing distrust of managed care organizations,[5] both grass-roots and professionalized health advocacy groups are likely to play key roles in defining the quality and trustworthiness of health information.[6–8] Growing calls for accountability and improved patient satisfaction create windows of opportunity for health advocates to use their influence and authority to shape how the quality of health information and services will be defined.[9]

SOCIAL MOVEMENTS AND SOCIAL CHANGE

The women's health movement's very success makes differentiating surviving grass-roots movement organizations from professionalized ones that are historically, ideologically, and strategically aligned with this episode of activism particularly challenging. For concept clarity, it is important to note that social scientists have long distinguished between general social movements and specific social movements. Theorists of social movements are particularly careful to differentiate between grass-roots movements and professionalized movements that emerge from within established institutions.[10–13] General social movements affect the public's consciousness of many issues and bring about social change in many arenas. The general feminist movement of the 1960s and 1970s spawned dozens of specific movements and hundreds of movement organizations.[14–17] As specific social movements gain momentum, they, like general social movements, shape public consciousness beyond the smaller world of movement organizations.

It is also crucial not to confuse formally constituted movement organizations with social movements themselves, although these groups represent the active components of a movement.[18] As health activists differentiated themselves within the broader feminist movement and developed an identity as a specific grass-roots feminist movement, they founded organizations such as the Boston Women's Health Book Collective, the Federation of Feminist Women's Health Centers, DES Action, and the National Women's Health Network.[19–21]

RISE AND DEVELOPMENT OF THE WOMEN'S HEALTH MOVEMENT

More than three decades ago, when access to medical information was restricted almost exclusively to physicians (who were mostly men), laywomen's insistence on access to medical research was truly "revolutionary." Few books on women's health could be found in bookstores, except for books on childbirth. The assumption was simply that physicians were the experts and women were to do as instructed. Breaking open this closed system, laywomen asserted that personal, subjective knowledge of one's own body was a valid source of information and deserved recognition, not scorn.[22,23]

The women's health movement grew rapidly through the leadership of several grass-roots groups with strong ties to other social change movements, particularly the abortion rights, prepared childbirth, and consumer health movements. As the general feminist movement of the 1960s and 1970s sought equal rights and the full participation of women in all public spheres, many believed that without control over reproduction, all other rights were in jeopardy. Thus in the early years, reproductive issues defined many branches of the movement and shaped group consciousness and social action.[16, 24] Reproductive rights remain central to feminist health agendas worldwide.[25]

Feminist health writers such as Barbara Seaman,[26] Barbara Ehreinreich and Deirdre English,[27] Ellen Frankfort,[28] Gena Corea,[29] Claudia Dreifus,[30] and columnists for prominent feminist newspapers galvanized women to explore their own health, providing critical momentum for the emerging grass-roots movement. The Boston Women's Health Book Collective produced the enormously popular *Our Bodies, Ourselves,* which has gone through numerous US and many other language editions worldwide.[31] The Federation of Feminist Women's Health Centers "invented" and championed gynecological self-help and woman-centered reproductive health services.[23] The National Women's Health Network (NWHN) linked a wide array of local groups to provide a voice for women in Washington. Monitoring legislation, Food and Drug Admistration actions, and informing the public about women's health issues continue to be central to this organization's mission.[32] A few nationally prominent groups focused on specific diseases or condition (eg, DES Action, the Endometriosis Association). Members of pivotal groups and other health activists traveled, spoke, and published widely, and used contacts with the media effectively, becoming spokespeople for the rapidly growing movement.

An important achievement of the women's health movement was transferring women's health from the domain of largely male experts to women themselves. Developing in parallel with self-help medical care movements, consciousness-raising and gynecological self-help became strategies for empowering women to define their own health and create alternative services. Local movement groups in all 50 states were providing gynecological self-help, women-controlled reproductive health clinics, clearinghouses for health information, and referral services and producing their own health educational materials. Advocacy ranged from accompanying individual women seeking medical care to advising and influencing state and local health departments. By the mid-1970s, more than 250 formally identifiable groups provided education, advocacy, and direct service in the United States.[19(p. 245–265)] Nearly 2,000 informal self-help groups and projects provided additional momentum to the movement (B. Seaman, unpublished data, 1998). Although ideologically committed to being inclusive, the leadership of the women's health movement remained largely white and middle class in North America during the early years. Sterilization abuse mobilized women of color to seek government protection during the 1970s, and groups such as the Committee to End Sterilization Abuse (CESA) were founded.[33]

The women's health movement grew increasingly visible globally, with groups such as ISIS in Geneva creating opportunities for worldwide feminist health activism.[34–35] By the mid-1970s, there were more than 70 feminist health groups in Canada, Europe, and Australia.[19(p. 241–245)] Today, there are growing efforts to make connections with feminist health activists worldwide, both in industrialized and developing countries.[36–38]

As the women's health movement evolved in the United States, the distinct health needs of diverse women emerged, and women of color formed their own movement organizations such as the National Black Women's Health Project, the National Latina Women's Health Organization, the Native American Women's Health Education and Resource Center, and the National Asian Women's Health Organization. Women of color health organizations gained national recognition and developed agendas to protect women against racist sterilization and contraceptive practices; to widen access to medical care for low-income women, including abortions no longer covered by Medicaid; and to focus on diseases and conditions affecting women of color such as lupus, fetal alcohol syndrome, hypertension, obesity, drug addiction, and stress related to racism and poverty that were ignored or misunderstood by largely white movement groups.[39] By the late 1980s, the National Black Women's Health Project had established local chapters with more than 150 self-help groups for African-American women.[40]

Other women added distinct health agendas. Lesbians, rural women, and women with disabilities joined older women's groups and women with specific health concerns to direct attention to their particular needs. Groups such as the Dis-Abled Women's Network, the Older Women's League, and the Lesbian Health Agenda broadened constituencies and issues. With the rise of environmental health concerns, groups such as the Women's Environmental Development Organization (WEDO) built bridges between feminist health activism and other movements for social change.

Like other social movements, the women's health movement has gone through periods of emergence, rapid growth, decline, and institutionalization. Grass-roots feminist health organizations declined in the 1980s, apparently as a result of changes in movement adherents and the social context in which movement groups operated. For example, many founders of movement organizations returned to school, began families, or entered the paid labor force, as have the next generation of women who increasingly juggle careers and families, thus reducing the traditional volunteer labor pool. Much of organized feminism, as it evolved both in media imagery and academe, came to be seen as distant or disconnected from ordinary women's lives.[41–43] The success of single-issue groups, particularly acquired immune deficiency syndrome (AIDS) organizations, to secure funding for direct services, education, and research presented new models for health activism.[44–46] And the discovery of mainstream health institutions that "marketing to women" could increase profits[47] led to the designation of a wide array of clinical services as "women's health clinics." By the 1990s, women's health services were widespread, although most were now part of larger medical institutions. In a recent national survey of women's health services, most centers founded in the 1960s and 1970s claimed a commitment to a feminist ideology; those founded later or sponsored by hospitals were significantly less likely to report this commitment.[48]

By the end of the 1980s, most alternative feminist health clinics had ceased to exist, and the survivors had broadened their range of services and affiliated with larger health systems.[49] Gynecological self-help has virtually disappeared. The surviving grass-roots movement advocacy and education groups such as the NWHN face declining support from both individuals and foundations as they compete with newer organizations for members and resources. Thus, grass-roots groups contracted internally as they were diluted externally by the growing prominence of both mainstream women's support groups (on a wide array of health issues ranging from alcohol problems to breast cancer) and disease-focused health advocacy groups whose efforts supported the growing federal initiatives for greater equity in women's health research (S.B. Ruzek, unpublished data, 1998).

FROM GRASS-ROOTS IDEOLOGIES TO PROFESSIONAL INSTITUTIONAL AGENDAS

The success of the women's health movement is reflected in the extent to which mainstream organizations and institutions, particularly federal agencies, have incorporated or adopted core ideas and created new opportunities for women's health advocates. By the 1990s, the reform wings of feminism had made significant claims for gender equity in all social institutions. With a growing number of women in Congress, in the biomedical professions, and in health advocacy communities, organizations that had pursued very different paths to improving women's health coalesced around the 1989 General Accounting Office (GAO) report showing that the National Institutes of Health (NIH) had failed to implement its policy of including women in study populations. The GAO report proved to be a catalyst for pressuring Congress and the NIH to take action, and by the end of 1990, the Women's Health Equity Act was passed, and the NIH established the Office of Research on Women's Health. In 1991, the NIH undertook the Women's Health Initiative, the largest project of its kind, seeking data on prevention and treatment of cancer, cardiovascular disease, and osteoporosis.[1(p. 77–89)] Although grass-roots women's health groups have criticized many aspects of the research and have attempted to rectify perceived problems in consent procedures and inclusion criteria, they have largely supported greater federal funding of biomedical research into women's health.[50] Thus the women's health movement critique of biomedicine and the call for demedicalizing women's health care[51] was reframed into a bipartisan agenda for equity. Scientific and professional interest in women's health burgeoned in the early 1990s. Spurred by growing federal investment in women's health and by the "cold-war dividend" funding of women's research through the Department of Defense, health activists saw opportunities to collaborate with scientists and professionals who were eager to take advantage of these new research priorities.

To maximize the likelihood of obtaining federal funding for research on women's health, scientists and their consumer allies focused on specific diseases. This narrowing of focus was critical for navigating federal funding streams that are tied to specific diseases and organ systems. The new "disease-oriented" organizations reflect the interests of women who expect a high level of professionalism. Facing dual roles as workers outside the home and traditional caretakers inside the home, the highly educated women who support the new single-issue groups may find that their interests lie in organizations that dispense professionally endorsed information, solicit donations, and carry out advocacy efforts on behalf of women. Thus the success of women's entry into the labor force, changes in cultural ethos, and women's own commitment to specialization and professionalism may explain why the narrower, highly professionalized women's health equity organizations attract women who do not identify either with broader movements for social change or with feminism per se.

AIDS advocacy groups also raised a new standard of effectiveness for health activists. They not only successfully increased funding for education and research, but gained a voice in how these added appropriations from government and foundations would be spent. Thereafter, breast cancer advocates[52,53] and others (ovarian cancer advocates, Parkinson patients and their families, etc.) adopted many of the AIDS organizations' strategies, albeit with a more professional and less confrontational style. A growing willingness to own illness and become "poster people" for cancer, as people with AIDS had done effectively, put a face on diseases that women privately and pervasively feared. Creating strong alliances between consumers, medical professionals, and researchers, breast cancer advocates rallied behind a specific cause that affected many of them directly or through family and friends. Many local support and advocacy organizations joined larger, well-funded organizations such as the National Breast Cancer Coalition, leaving behind older-style support groups and feminist health organizations with broader agendas.

Using well-established letter-writing and advocacy strategies, breast cancer activists testified at hearings, held press conferences, and took their case to the NIH. In collaboration with growing bipartisan support in Congress and the scientific community, advocates succeeded in increasing federal funding for breast cancer research from $84 million to more than $400 million in 1993.[53 (p. 315–325)] Breast cancer advocates also insisted that survivors be involved in shaping research agendas and educational efforts and aligned themselves more consistently and collaboratively with scientists than some AIDS activists or earlier grass-roots movement leaders had.

The success of breast cancer advocacy quickly created a "disease du jour" climate, where professionals rallied people directly or indirectly affected by particular diseases to lobby for increased funding. Ovarian cancer was the next women's disease to achieve national prominence. While this approach secures more resources for particular groups in the short run, it pits diseases against each other, turning research funding into a "popularity contest" or war of each against all—to be won by the group that can make the most noise or wield the greatest political pressure. A result may be overfunding some diseases without regard for their prevalence, contribution to overall population health, or likelihood of scientific value. In this environment, orphan diseases will join orphan drugs as the unfortunate, but unavoidable downsides of market-driven research and medicine.

DIFFERENCES OF GRASS-ROOTS AND PROFESSIONALIZED WOMEN'S HEALTH ORGANIZATIONS

In a market-focused society, identifying differences is important for establishing a niche, and like other organizations, movement groups emphasize their unique features. Grass-roots women's health movement groups see themselves as different from what they perceive the more professional, mainstream organizations to be, although these differences are not always clearly articulated. After observing a wide range of groups for three decades, we have found that surviving grass-roots advocacy groups are differentiated from most professionalized, disease-focused groups in the following six ways.

Social Movement Orientation

The founders of many grass-roots feminist groups had ties to progressive or radical social movements that emphasized social justice and social change, to which many remain committed. In contrast, the newer professionalized support and advocacy organizations are typically more narrowly focused on a single disease or health issue, and except for environmentally focused groups such as WEDO, few are integral to broader social movements for social change (although some individual members may have such commitments).

Leadership

Although some women physicians who were critical of medical education, training, and practice were leaders of the grass-roots women's health movement, lay leadership was the norm. The role of physicians relative to others remains a point of contention.[54–55] In contrast, the professionalized support and advocacy groups formed in the 1990s had a growing pool of women physicians, scientists, and other highly trained professionals to turn to for leadership.

Attitude toward Biomedicine

A recurring theme in the grass-roots women's health movement has been the demand for "evidence-based medicine," long before this term came into vogue. Major feminist advocacy groups aligned themselves with scientists and physicians who sought to put medical practice on a more scientific basis at a time when it was resisted by many clinicians. Grass-roots health activists were critical of the side effects of inadequately tested drugs and devices, particularly early high-dose oral contraceptives, diethylstilbestrol, and the intrauterine device.[5] They also questioned the number of unnecessary hysterectomies and radical mastectomies performed. In short, consumer groups sought to protect women from unsafe or unnecessary biomedical interventions.[21,56] The professionalized advocacy groups founded in the 1990s focus more on ensuring women an equitable share of biopsychosocial science and treatment. The growing number of women physicians and scientists also facilitates alliances with women consumers because perceived interests in safety and effectiveness make these relationships seem mutually beneficial.

Relationships with Corporate Sponsors

Older grass-roots advocacy groups remain deeply concerned about the effects of drug and device manufacturers sponsoring journals and organizational activities. In fact, this issue is a pivotal source of strain between grass-roots groups and professionalized women's health organizations. While organizations of women physicians and professionalized advocacy groups rely heavily on corporate sponsorships, older grass-roots groups avoid such relationships on grounds that financial ties affect the willingness of groups to criticize sponsors, promote competitors' products, or address alternative or complementary therapies that might undermine conventional prescribing patterns. Refusing support from corporate sponsors remains a hallmark of grass-roots movement groups, but they struggle financially as a result. Because professionalized groups accept corporate support, they have more resources for education and advocacy.

Goals of Education

Both older and newer women's health organizations share the goal of educating women to improve their own health and make decisions about their own care. A central feature of grass-roots feminist groups, particularly through the 1970s, was to demystify medicine and to encourage women to trust their subjective experience of their own health. Having access to larger numbers of women physicians may have reduced the perceived need to demystify medicine, and professionalized organizations appear largely concerned with making their highly educated constituencies aware of medical and scientific information.

Lay versus Professional Authority

Grass-roots health groups remain committed to substantial lay control over health and healing and to expanding the roles of such nonphysician healers as midwives, nurses, and counseling professionals. They would involve consumers in all aspects of health policy making, not simply transfer legitimate authority from male to female physicians. In professionalized organizations, women physicians become the primary societal experts on women's health matters.

The grass-roots women's health movement organizations leave a legacy of making health an important social concern and educating women to take responsibility for their own health and health care decision making. The movement as a whole has made substantial efforts to influence powerful social institutions—organized medicine, the pharmaceutical industry, and regulatory agencies. In partnership with newer, professionalized equity organizations, health movement activists have taken up mainstream reform efforts that will become increasingly important as medical care is dominated by market forces. Thus the current episode of women's health activism overlaps with, but is, in many ways, different from the activism of the 1960s and 1970s. These distinct episodes of women's health activism need to be differentiated and understood in the specific historical contexts in which they emerged, recognizing the distinct roles that their history may lead them to play in the future.

THE NEXT CHALLENGE: WHO WILL SPEAK FOR WOMEN IN THE ELECTRONIC AGE?

The electronic communication technologies foster a climate in which researchers and consumers expect to find information instantaneously and effortlessly. The reliability of information in electronic media is often questionable, however. Until data can be transformed into useable knowledge that can shape human action, the information age will not fulfill its promise.[57] Neither grass-roots women's health movement organizations nor newer professionalized disease agenda groups have adequately grappled with how to communicate with their constituencies effectively. Both types of groups as well as government and mainstream health organizations will have to assess, manage, and distribute what each sees as "reliable" health information. Organizational survival may depend increasingly on teaching both "customers" and staff how to use reliable information effectively.[57]

Because of the role of advocacy groups in health policy making in the United States,[1] how they present themselves and are perceived are important. As electronic media provide all-comers the opportunity to claim organizational status in an increasingly "virtual" world, and the number of groups claiming to speak for women increases, how will the public differentiate among them? As we navigate the uncharted "information age," the ability of the grass-roots women's health movement to remain viable appears somewhat precarious because the technology allows anyone with a computer and minimal skill to "create" an organization with worldwide visibility. Most movement organizations have not moved beyond hard copy resource centers and clearinghouses, in part because they have well-established communication networks that have served them well in the past (S.B. Ruzek, J. Becker, unpublished data, 1998). Newer professionalized advocacy groups are better funded and more attuned to technological advancements. As electronic communications gain prominence, those who position themselves in this media will be perceived as speaking for women. In an effort to address the complexity of electronic media, the Boston Women's Health Book Collective is including a section on how to assess the adequacy of electronic sources of information in the 1998 edition of *Our Bodies, Ourselves.*[58]

To assess the complexity of the environment in which grass-roots activist groups find themselves at the close of this century, and to determine the array of groups that present themselves as speaking for women, we compared the number of national women's health advocacy organizations easily identified through two worldwide web search strategies with those identified by the National Women's Health Network in 1994 as meeting their criteria: national, women-controlled or a women-controlled project of a larger organization, feminist outlook, mostly consumer controlled, and primary advocacy, not just engaged in service or education. In an effort to identify organizations that might easily be identified by the public, Yahoo, a common Internet search engine, was used along with Healthfinders, the electronic database that the Department of Health and Human Services unveiled for public use in May 1997. Using the term "women's health organizations," 339 groups were located on the two Internet sources. After coding them for meeting two of the five NWHN criteria (being national and having an advocacy agenda beyond service or education), and removing duplications, 223 women's health advocacy organizations were identified, 46 by the NWHN, 53 by Healthfinders, and 124 by Yahoo.

When we cross-tabulated the data, it became clear that there is little overlap in the women's health advocacy organizations identified by these three sources. Only the Society for the Advancement of Women's Health Research was identified by all three. Six organizations were identified by both the NWHN and DHHS Healthfinders; 9 were identified by both DHHS and Yahoo, and 13 were identified by both NWHN and Yahoo. Thus, "who speaks for women's health" in the electronic age very much depends on where one looks—and how willing one is to sort through hundreds of self-characterized "women's health organizations." In this environment it is unclear how the women's health movement will continue to be perceived as a key information broker in an increasingly complex sea of women's health information.

Grass-roots health movement groups remain important forces for increasing awareness of women's health issues and are viewed as trustworthy sources of information by feminist groups in the United States and worldwide. Newer, professionalized equity organizations, too, face competition from a growing array of institutions that claim expertise in matters of women's health. The challenge for both types of women's health groups will be to differentiate themselves from others whose interests lie more in marketing than in meeting diverse women's health needs. Both types of groups need to be allies for widening access and equity in health care for all women,[59, 60] not just some women, in the next century.

REFERENCES

1. Weisman C. *Women's Health Care. Activist Traditions and Institutional Change.* Baltimore, Md: The Johns Hopkins University Press; 1998.

2. Fugh-Berman A. *Alternative Medicine: What Words. A Comprehensive, Easy-to-read Review of the Scientific Evidence, Pro and Con.* Tucson, Ariz: Odonian Press; 1996.

3. Northrup C. *Women's Bodies, Women's Wisdom.* New York, NY: Bantam Books; 1994.

4. Weil A. *Spontaneous Healing.* New York, NY: Knopf; 1995.

5. Anders G. *Health Against Wealth. HMOs and the Breakdown of Medical Trust.* Boston, Mass: Houghton Mifflin; 1996.

6. Ruzek SB. Communicating with patients: Linking managed care and women's health advocacy organizations. In: *Proceedings of the Conference on Healthcare Technology Choices under Managed Care: Communicating Directly with Patients and Their Clinicians.* Plymouth Meeting, Pa: ECRI/WHO Collaborating Center for Technology Transfer; 1997:81–85.

7. Parrott RL, Condit CM, eds. *Evaluating Women's Health Messages. A Resource Book.* Thousand Oaks, Calif: Sage; 1996.

8. Proctor RN. *Cancer Wars.* New York, NY: Basic Books; 1995.

9. Stabiner K. *To Dance with the Devil.* New York, NY: Delacorte Press; 1997.

10. McCarthy JD, Zald MN. Resource mobilization and social movements: A partial theory. *American Journal of Sociology.* 1977;82:1212–1241.

11. Zald MN. The trajectory of social movements in America. *Research in Social Movements, Conflicts and Change.* 1988;10:19–41.

12. Ash R. *Social Movements in America.* Chicago, Ill: Markham; 1972.

13. Tarrow S. *Power in Movement: Social Movements, Collective Action and Politics.* Cambridge: Cambridge University Press; 1994.

14. Buechler SM. *Women's Movements in the United States.* New Brunswick, NJ: Rutgers University Press; 1990.

15. Freeman J. *Social Movements of the Sixties and Seventies.* New York, NY: Longman; 1983.

16. Staggenborg S. *The Pro-Choice Movement.* New York, NY: Oxford University Press; 1991.

17. Ferree MM, Hess BB. *Controversy and Coalition: The new Feminist Movement Across Three Decades of Change.* Boston, Mass: Twayne; 1994.

18. Zald MN, Ash R. Social movement organizations. *Soc Forces.* 1966;44:327–41.

19. Ruzek SB. *The Women's Health Movement. Feminist Alternatives to Medical Control.* New York, NY: Praeger; 1978.

20. Rodriguez-Trias H. The women's health movement: Women take power. In Sidel VW, Sidel R, eds. *Reforming Medicine: Lessons of the Last Quarter Century.* New York, NY: Pantheon;1984:107–126.

21. Zimmerman M. The women's health movement: A critique of medical enterprise and the position of women. In: Hess B, Ferree MM, eds. *Analyzing Gender: Social Science Perspectives.* Beverly Hills, Calif: Sage; 1987.

22. The Boston Women's Health Book Collective. *Our Bodies, Ourselves—A Book By and For Women.* New York, NY: Simon and Schuster; 1973.

23. Federation of Feminist Women's Health Centers. *A New View of a Woman's Body.* New York, NY: Simon and Schuster; 1981.

24. Gordon L. *Woman's Body, Woman's Rights: Birth Control in America.* New York, NY: Penguin; 1990.

25. Cottingham J, Norsigian J, Guzman C, et al. The personal is political: Beginnings and endings in an ongoing history. *Reproductive Health Matters.* November 10, 1997;9–28.

26. Seaman B. *The Doctors' Case Against the Pill.* New York, NY: Avon; 1969.

27. Ehreinreich B, English D. *Complaints and Disorders. The Sexual Politics of Sickness.* Old Westbury, New York, NY: The Feminist Press; 1972.

28. Frankfort, E. *Vaginal Politics.* New York, NY: Quadrangle Books; 1972.

29. Corea G. *The Hidden Malpractice. How American Medicine Mistreats Women.* New York, NY: Harper & Row; 1985.

30. Dreifus C, ed. *Seizing Our Bodies.* New York, NY: Vintage Books; 1978.

31. The Boston Women's Health Book Collective. *The New Our Bodies, Ourselves, Updated and Expanded for the '90s.* New York, NY: Simon & Schuster; 1992.

32. The National Women's Health Network. *1997 Annual Report.* Washington, DC: National Women's Health Network; 1997.

33. Rodriguez-Trias H. Sterilization abuse. In: Hubbard R, Henifin MS, Fried B, eds. *Biological Woman: The Convenient Myth.* Cambridge, Mass: Schenkman; 1982:147–160.

34. The Boston Women's Health Book Collective and ISIS. *International Women and Health Resource Guide.* Boston, Mass: Boston Women's Health Book Collective; 1980.

35. Ruzek SB. Feminist visions of health: An international perspective. In: Mitchell J, Oakley A, eds. *What is Feminism: A Re-examination.* New York, NY: Pantheon; 1996:184–207.

36. Guzman C. Planting the seeds of a Latina women's health movement. *Reproductive Health Matters.* November 10, 1997:13–16.

37. Berer M. Editorial. The international women's health movement. *Reproductive Health Matters.* November 10, 1997:6–8.

38. Doyal L. Campaigning for women's health rights worldwide. *Nurs Times.* 1995;91:27–30.

39. Ruzek SB, Clarke AE, Olesen VL. What are the dynamics of differences? In: Ruzek SB, Olesen VE, Clarke AE, eds. *Women's Health: Complexities and Differences.* Columbus, Ohio: The Ohio State University Press; 1997:51–95.

40. Avery BY. Breathing life into ourselves: The evolution of the National Black Women's Health Project. In: White EC, ed. *The Black Women's Health Book.* Seattle, Wash: Seal Press; 1994:4–10.

41. Sommers CH. *Who Stole Feminism?* New York, NY: Touchstone; 1994.

42. Wolf N. *Fire with Fire. The New Female Power and How to Use It.* New York, NY: Fawcett Columbine; 1994.

43. Fox-Genovese E. *Feminism Without Illusion: A Critique of Individualism.* Chapel Hill, NC: University of North Carolina Press; 1991.

44. Epstein S. *Impure Science: Aids, Activism, and the Politics of Knowledge.* Berkeley, Calif: University of California Press; 1996.

45. Shilts R. *And the Band Played On.* New York, NY: Penguin Books; 1987.

46. Schneider BE, Stoller NE. *Women Resisting AIDS.* Philadelphia, Pa: Temple University Press; 1995.
47. Alpern BB. *Reaching Women: The Way to Go in Marketing Healthcare Services.* Chicago, Ill: Pluribus Press; 1987.
48. Weisman CS, Curbow B, Khoury AJ. The national survey of women's health centers: Current models of women-centered care. *Women's Health Issues.* 1995;5: 103–117.
49. Weisman CS, Curbow B, Khoury AJ. *Case Studies of Women's Health Centers: Innovations and Issues in Women-Centered Care.* New York, NY: Commonwealth Fund; 1997.
50. Narrigan D, Zones JS, Worcester N, Grad MJ. Research to improve women's health: An agenda for equity. In: Ruzek SB, Olesen VE, Clarke AE, eds. *Women's Health: Complexities and Differences.* Columbus, Ohio: The Ohio State University Press; 1997: 551–579.
51. Reissman CK. Women and medicalization: A new perspective. *Soc Policy.* 1983;14:3–18.
52. Batt S. *Patient No More.* Charlottetown, Canada: Best Gagne; 1994.
53. Altman R. *Waking Up/Fighting Back. The Politics of Breast Cancer.* Boston, Mass: Little, Brown; 1996.
54. Wallis LA, Donoghue GD, Fourcroy JL, Editorial. Feminists and women physicians. *Women's Health.* 1994;3:6.
55. Cousins O, Fugh-Berman A, Kasper A, et al. Letter to the editor. *Women's Health.* 1994;3:6.
56. Ruzek SB. Technology and perceptions of risks: Clinical, scientific and consumer perspectives in breast cancer treatment. In: *Executive Briefings. Health Technology Assessment Information Service.* Plymouth Meeting, Pa: ECRI-WHO Collaborating Center for Technology Transfer; 1995:1–6.
57. Davis S, Botkin J. *The Monster Under the Bed. How Business is Mastering the Opportunity of Knowledge for Profit.* New York, NY: Touchstone Books; 1995.
58. The Boston Women's Health Collective. *Our Bodies, Ourselves for the New Century: A Book by and for Women.* New York, NY: Simon & Schuster. In press.
59. Ruzek SB. Rethinking feminist ideologies and actions: Thoughts on the past and future of health reform. In: Olesen VL, Clarke AE, eds. *Revisioning Women's Health and Healing.* New York, NY: Routledge. In press.
60. Kasper AS. *The Making of Women's Health Public Policy.* Chicago, Ill: University of Illinois Center for Research on Women and Gender; Spring 1996.

BREATHING LIFE INTO OURSELVES: THE EVOLUTION OF THE NATIONAL BLACK WOMEN'S HEALTH PROJECT

BYLLYE Y. AVERY

I got involved in women's health in the 1970s around the issue of abortion. There were three of us at the University of Florida, in Gainesville, who just seemed to get picked out by women who needed abortions. They came to us. I didn't know anything about abortions. In my life that word couldn't even be mentioned without having somebody look at you crazy. Then someone's talking to me about abortion. It seemed unreal. But as more women came (and at first they were mostly white women), we found out this New York number we could give them, and they could catch a plane and go there for their abortions. But then a black woman came and we gave her the number, and she looked at us in awe: "I can't get to New York...." We realized we needed a different plan of action, so in May 1974 we opened up the Gainesville Women's Health Center.

As we learned more about abortions and gynecological care, we immediately started to look at birth, and to realize that we are women with a total reproductive cycle. We might have to make different decisions about our lives, but whatever the decision, we deserved the best services available. So, in 1978, we opened up Birthplace, an alternative birthing center. It was exhilarating work;

I assisted in probably around two hundred births. I understood life, and working in birth, I understood death, too. I certainly learned what's missing in prenatal care and why so many of our babies die.

Through my work at Birthplace, I learned the importance of being involved in our own health. We have to create environments that say "yes." Birthplace was a wonderful space. It was a big, old turn-of-the-century house that we decorated with antiques. We went to people's houses and, if we liked something, we begged for it—things off their walls, furniture, rugs. We fixed the place so that when women walked in, they would say, "Byllye, I was excited when I got up today because this was my day to come to Birthplace." That's how prenatal care needs to be given—so that people are excited when they come. It's about eight and a half or nine months that a woman comes on a continuous basis. That is the time to start affecting her life so that she can start making meaningful lifestyle changes. So you see, health provides us with all sorts of opportunities for empowerment.

Through Birthplace, I came to understand the importance of our attitudes about birthing. Many women don't get the exquisite care they deserve. They go to these large facilities, and they don't understand the importance of prenatal care. They ask, "Why is it so important for me to get in here and go through all this hassle?" We have to work around that.

Through the work of Birthplace, we have created a prenatal caring program that provides each woman who comes for care with a support group. She enters the group when she arrives, leaves the group to go for her physical checkup, and then returns to the group when she is finished. She doesn't sit in a waiting room for two hours. Most of these women have nobody to talk to. No one listens to them; no one helps them plan. They're asking: "Who's going to get me to the hospital if I go into labor in the middle of the night, or the middle of the day, for that matter? Who's going to help me get out of this abusive relationship? Who's going to make sure I have the food I need to eat?" Infant mortality is not a medical problem; it's a social problem.

One of the things that black women have started talking about regarding infant mortality is that many of us are like empty wells; we give a lot, but we don't get much back. We're asked to be strong. I have said, "If one more person says to me that black women are strong I'm going to scream in their face." I am so tired of that stuff. What are you going to do—just lay down and die? We have to do what's necessary to survive. It's just a part of living. But most of us are empty wells that never really get replenished. Most of us are dead inside. We are walking around dead. That's why we end up in relationships that reinforce that particular thought. So you're talking about a baby being alive inside of a dead person; it just won't work.

We need to stop letting doctors get away with piling up all this money, buying all these little machines. They can keep the tiniest little piece of protoplasm alive, and then it goes home and dies. All this foolishness with putting all this money back into their pockets on that end of the care and not on the other end has to stop. When are we going to wake up?

THE NATIONAL BLACK WOMEN'S HEALTH PROJECT

I left the birthing center around 1980 or '81, mostly because we needed more midwives and I wasn't willing to go to nursing school. But an important thing had happened for me in 1979. I began looking at myself as a black woman. Before that I had been looking at myself as a woman. When I left the birthing center, I went to work in a Comprehensive Employment Training Program (CETA) job at a community college and it brought me face-to-face with my sisters and face-to-face with myself. Just by the nature of the program and the population that I worked with, I had, for the first time in my life, a chance to ask a nineteen-year-old why—please give me the reason why—you have four babies and you're only nineteen years old. And I was able to listen, and bring these sisters together to talk about their lives. It was there that I started to understand the lives of black women and to realize that we live in a conspiracy of silence. It was hearing these women's stories that led me to start conceptualizing the National Black Women's Health Project.

First I wanted to do an hour-long presentation on black women's health issues, so I started doing research. I got all the books, and I was shocked at what I saw. I was angry—angry that the people who wrote these books didn't put it into a format that made sense to us, angry that nobody was saying anything to black women or to black men. I was so angry I threw one book across the room and it stayed there for three or four days, because I knew I had just seen the tip of the iceberg, but I also knew enough to know that I couldn't go back. I had opened my eyes, and I had to go on and look.

Instead of an hour-long presentation we had a conference. It didn't happen until 1983, but when it did, 2,000 women came. But I knew we couldn't just have a conference. From the health statistics I saw, I knew that there was a deeper problem. People needed to be able to work individually, and on a daily basis. So we got the idea of self-help groups. The first group we formed was in a rural area outside of Gainesville, with twenty-one women who were severely obese. I thought, "Oh this is a piece of cake. Obviously these sisters don't have any information. I'll go in there and talk to them about losing weight, talk to them about high blood pressure, talk to them about diabetes—it'll be easy."

Little did I know that when I got there, they would be able to tell me everything that went into a 1200-calorie-a-day diet. They all had been to Weight Watchers at least five or six times; they all had blood-pressure-reading machines in their homes as well as medications they were on. And when we sat down to talk, they said, "We know all that information, but what we also know is that living in the world that we are in, we feel like we are absolutely nothing." One woman said to me, "I work for General Electric making batteries, and, from the stuff they suit me up in, I know it's killing me." She said, "My home life is not working. My old man is an alcoholic. My kids got babies. Things are not well with me. And the one thing I know I can do when I come home is cook me a pot of food and sit down in front of the TV and eat it. And you can't take that away from me until you're ready to give me something in its place."

So that made me start to think that there was some other piece to this health puzzle that had been missing, that it's not just about giving information; people need something else. We just spent a lot of time talking. And while we were talking, we were planning the 1983 conference, so I took the information back to the planning committee. Lillie Allen (a trainer who works with NBWHP) was there. We worked with her to understand that we are dying inside. That unless we are able to go inside of ourselves and touch and breathe fire, breathe life into ourselves, that, of course, we couldn't be healthy. Lillie started working on a workshop that we named "Black and Female: What is the Reality?" This is a workshop that terrifies us all. And we are also terrified not to have it, because the conspiracy of silence is killing us.

STOPPING VIOLENCE

As we started to talk, I looked at those health statistics in a new way. Now, I'm not saying that we are not suffering from the things we die from—that's what the statistics give us. But what causes all this sickness? Like cardiovascular disease—it's the number one killer. What causes all that heart pain? When sisters take their shoes off and start talking about what's happening, the first thing we cry about is violence. The violence in our lives. And if you look in statistics books, they mention violence in one paragraph. They don't even give numbers, because they can't count it: the violence is too pervasive.

The number one issue for most of our sisters is violence—battering, sexual abuse. Same thing for their daughters, whether they are twelve or four. We have to look at how violence is used, how violence and sexism go hand in hand, and how it affects the sexual response of females. We have to stop it, because violence is the training ground for us.

When you talk to young people about being pregnant, you find out a lot of things. Number one is that most of these girls did not get pregnant by teenage boys; most of them got pregnant by their mother's boyfriends or their brothers or their daddies. We've been sitting on that. We can't just tell our daughters, "just say no." What do they do about all those feelings running around their bodies? And we need to talk to our brothers. We need to tell them, the incest makes us crazy. It's something that stays on our minds all the time. We need the men to know that. And they need to know that when they hurt us, they hurt themselves. Because we are their mothers, their sisters, their wives; we are their allies on this planet. They can't just damage one part of it without damaging themselves. We need men to stop giving consent, by their silence, to rape, to sexual abuse, to violence. You need to talk to your boyfriends, your husbands, your sons, whatever males you have around you—talk to them about talking to other men. When they are sitting around womanizing, talking bad about women, make sure you have somebody stand up and be your ally and help stop this. For future generations, this has got to stop somewhere.

MOTHERS AND DAUGHTERS

If violence is the number one thing women talk about, the next is being mothers too early and too long. We've developed a documentary called "On Becoming a Woman: Mothers and Daughters Talking Together." It's eight mothers and eight daughters—sixteen ordinary people talking about extraordinary things.

The idea of the film came out of my own experience with my daughter. When Sonja turned eleven, I started bemoaning that there were no rituals left; there was nothing to let a girl know that once you get your period your life can totally change, nothing to celebrate that something wonderful is happening. So I got a cake that said, "Happy Birthday! Happy Menstruation!" It had white icing with red writing. I talked about the importance of becoming a woman, and, out of that, I developed a workshop for mothers and daughters for the public schools. I did the workshops in Gainesville, and, when we came to Atlanta, I started doing them there. The film took ten years, from the first glimmer of an idea to completion.

The film is in three parts. In the first part all the mothers talk about when we got our periods. Then the daughters who have their periods talk about getting theirs, and the ones who are still waiting talk about that. The second part of the film deals with contraception, birth control, anatomy and physiology. This part of the film is animated, so it keeps the kids' attention. It's funny. It shows all the anxiety: passing around condoms, hating it, saying, "Oh no, we don't want to do this."

The third part of the film is the hardest. We worked on communication with the mothers and daughters. We feel that the key to birth control and to controlling reproduction is the nature of the relationship between the parents and their young people. And what's happening is that everybody is willing to beat up on the young kids, asking, "Why did you get pregnant? Why did you do this?" No one is saying to the parents, "Do you need some help with learning how to talk to your young person? Do you want someone to sit with you? Do you want to see what it feels like?" We don't have all the answers. In this film, you see us struggling.

What we created, which was hard for the parents, is a safe space where everybody can say anything they need to say. And if you think about that, as parents, we have that relationship with our kids: we can ask them anything. But when we talk about sex, it's special to be in a space where the kids can ask *us,* "Mama, what do you do when you start feeling funny all in your body?" What the kids want to know is, what about lust? What do we do about it? And that's the very information that we don't want to give up. That's "our business." But they want to hear it from us, because they can trust us. And we have to struggle with how we do that: How do we share that information? How do we deal with our feelings?

REALIZING THE DREAM

The National Black Women's Health Project has ninety-six self-help groups in twenty-two states, six groups in Kenya, and a group in Barbados and in Belize. In addition, we were just funded by the W.K. Kellogg Foundation to do some work in three housing projects in Atlanta. We received $1,032,000 for a three-year period to set up three community centers. Our plan is to do health screening and referral for adolescents and women, and in addition to hook them up with whatever social services they need—to help cut through the red tape. There will be computerized learning programs and individualized tutorial programs to help young women get their General Equivalency Degrees (GED), along with a panel from the community who will be working on job readiness skills. And we'll be doing our self-help groups—talking about who we are, examining, looking at ourselves.

We hope this will be a model program that can be duplicated anywhere. And we're excited about it. Folks in Atlanta thought it was a big deal for a group of black women to get a million dollars. We thought it was pretty good, too. Our time is coming.

SELF HELP CLINIC CELEBRATES 25 YEARS

CINDY PEARSON

On April 7, 1971, thirty women met together to talk about "breaking through" the abortion issue by working on women having control over their reproduction, rather than continuing previous efforts aimed at influencing hospitals, doctors and legislators. Twenty-five years later, the movement started that evening has not only had an enormous impact on abortion care in the United States, but has also affected the manner in which routine health care is provided to millions of women and the relationship that thousands of women have with their own bodies.

What happened at that meeting? Self Help Clinic began. Like many others at the 1971 meeting, Carol Downer was a reproductive health activist in her local NOW chapter. After a visit to a clandestine abortion clinic, she had gone home with a plastic vaginal speculum. At the 1971 gathering, she demonstrated how women could use speculums with mirrors and flashlights to see their own and each other's cervixes. Women took turns doing self exam and talked about the importance of doing self exam in a group setting where they could see the range of normal, healthy women's experiences. The group also talked about the new abortion equipment in use at some clinics—a flexible plastic cannula attached to a syringe—and one member of the group, Lorraine Rothman, volunteered to modify it for safe use by non-professionals.

The techniques eventually developed by Rothman and Downer were entitled menstrual extraction, to differentiate them from abortion in the medical setting. Menstrual extraction was never envisioned as a service that lay women practitioners would provide to other women who needed an abortion. Rather, the early self helpers advocated that women join self help groups and practice extracting each other's menses around the time they expected their periods. If a pregnancy happened to be present, it would be extracted along with the contents of the uterus. The self helpers believed that their experience with each other, the modified nature of the equipment they were using, and the fact that they were ending pregnancies far earlier than was typical during an abortion would make menstrual extraction safe.

In order for self help and menstrual extraction to be the strategy that allowed women to "break

This is the ninth in a series of articles commemorating the history of the women's health movement.

through" the abortion issue, women everywhere would need to know about it. Helped along by the presence in Los Angeles of thousands of women attending a NOW convention in August, 1971, self help began to spread across the nation. After distributing a flyer announcing just one hour-long meeting about self examination, the original self help group found themselves sharing self help with small groups of women non-stop throughout the entire conference. Leaving the meeting room with their speculums in brown paper bags, these women went back home to their local NOW chapters and started spreading the word. In October, Downer and Rothman went on a six-week cross country tour (via Greyhound bus!), sharing self help and menstrual extraction with women everywhere from Wichita to New York City. Many long-lasting groups resulted.

Back in Los Angeles, a core group of about a half a dozen women had been working together throughout 1971. They had space at the Los Angeles Women's Center and held a self help clinic on Wednesday nights that was open to everyone. They also shared self help with women who dropped by during the week. At the same time, they began a program of referring women for abortions, which gave them the power to negotiate with physicians for better quality abortions—women were awake and supported by an advocate while a physician performed a suction abortion on an out-patient basis.

In the meantime, the authorities were investigating the self helpers. Using infiltrators, investigators hoped to catch the self helpers performing abortions. In fact, when they finally raided the Self Help Clinic, the only evidence of criminal activity they could gather was a container of yogurt used for vaginal yeast infections, leading to the movement's lasting description of this episode as the Great Yogurt Conspiracy. In December, 1972, Carol Downer was acquitted by a jury of charges that she was practicing medicine without a license. Many years later, author Linda Gordon described this decision as establishing the precedent that women's genitals were no longer territory reserved for men.

Shortly after, as a result of the *Roe v. Wade* decision, abortions could be provided openly and independent of hospitals. The self helpers quickly established the Los Angeles Feminist Women's Health Center, a women-controlled clinic. Doctors were hired by the self helpers to perform abortions, and many other services were provided, including "well-woman" care. A self help attitude permeated the health care offered, and the health center served as a base from which to continue spreading Self Help Clinic. By 1975, there were nearly 2000 grassroots women's health projects across the country and it had spread internationally. Though these projects ranged from book-writing groups to women fighting against sterilization abuse, many were women-controlled clinics influenced by self-help, some explicitly in the Feminist Women's Health Center model, others similar, but less closely aligned with the FWHCs.

During this period, the women's health movement was at a high point of its influence. Abortion was as widely available and accessible as it has ever been, before or since. Information about women's bodies and the drugs, devices and procedures used on women became available to women through books and an enormously expanded market for feminist health journalism. Medical schools and individual physicians began to realize that the callous and insensitive treatment many women received had to stop and took steps to reform medical training (not to mention abolishing the unwritten quotas that had severely limited the number of women allowed to enter medical school.) Dangerous drugs and devices were improved or taken off the market as a result of women's protests. Curbs were placed on sterilization abuse. Challenges were posed to the US practice of funding foreign birth control programs strictly for the purposes of population control, not to empower women to control their fertility. Many women came to believe, in a way almost inconceivable during the heyday of physician control, that their bodies were their own to understand *and* to control.

Along with all the other strands of the women's health movement, Self Help Clinic played a key role in these gains. Like other elements of the movement, though, by the late 1970s Self Help Clinic began to experience backlash. The strategy of establishing clinics to offer women good health care and to serve as bases from which to spread self help led many groups to spend endless hours fighting regulatory battles about clinic licensing and the definition of "medical" services and who was allowed to provide them. In smaller communities, local physicians sometimes banded together to boycott the clinic. The economic hard times of the 1980s, followed quickly by anti-abortion violence, left many clinics unable to continue providing services. Midway through the 1990s, relatively few women-controlled clinics exist.

However, the spark of Self Help Clinic is still alive. Several Feminist Women's Health Centers worked together to create three women's health books, *A Woman-Centered Pregnancy and Birth, A New View of a Woman's Body,* and *How to Stay Out of the Gynecologists Office.* These books are available from the FWHCs in addition to basic materials on self examination (including, of course, speculums!). Menstrual extraction, which had receded into the background during the years in which abortion was relatively available, was widely discussed in the mainstream press in connection with *Casey* and *Webster,* the Supreme Court abortion cases. Self helpers even reprised the 1971 tour around that time, sharing self examination and menstrual extraction with groups of women interested in maintaining control over their reproduction regardless of the Supreme Court rulings. Self help groups are continuing to meet, particularly on college campuses and in cities with direct-action women's groups. Self Help Clinic is very much alive in the lasting impact the women's health movement has had upon women, their sense of their bodies, and the way in which health care provided to women has improved over the past twenty-five years.

"MAKING A BIG STINK": WOMEN'S WORK, WOMEN'S RELATIONSHIPS, AND TOXIC WASTE ACTIVISM

PHIL BROWN AND FAITH I. T. FERGUSON

Grassroots activists who organize around toxic waste issues have most often been women, led by women....

Despite high levels of participation by women in toxic waste activism, gender and the fight against toxic hazards are rarely analyzed together in studies either on gender or on environmental issues. The absence of rigorous analysis of gender issues in toxic waste activism is particularly noticeable, since many scholars of toxic waste activism often note in passing that women predominate in this movement. Little work to date systematizes the overall characteristics of women toxic waste activists despite several case studies of the organization and activities of women in local toxic waste activist groups (Cable 1992; Garland 1988; Hamilton 1990; Krauss 1993) and many accounts of these groups in the popular media. Some work on toxic waste site organizing includes substantial discussion of women's roles (Brown and Mikkelsen 1990; Cable 1992; Edelstein, 1988; Levine 1982); moreover, scholarly work concerning gender and environment is focused mainly on ecofeminism and on economic development issues in the Third World and not on the consequences of class, gender, and race that characterize the experience of local toxic waste activist groups (Freudenberg and Steinsapir 1992; Nelson 1990; Taylor 1989). This article analyzes women's toxic waste activism by examining case studies and attitude surveys and then tracing the sources of this activism through a "ways of knowing" perspective (Belenky et al. 1986)....

In their toxic waste activism, these women challenge the political and economic power structure as well as the gendered boundaries of behavior in their communities and in their families. Most of these women activists are housewives, typically from working-class or lower middle-class backgrounds, and most had never been political activists until they discovered the threat of toxic contamination in their communities.

Although grassroots women activists have not necessarily seen themselves as descendants of prior movements, especially the women's movement (Cable 1992), they follow in the steps of generations of women activists who fought for occupational health and safety concerns throughout this century and who more recently have become involved in the women's health movement. Bale (1990) has noted some clear connections between various forms of "women's toxic experience." For example, early labor organizing around health issues often stemmed from women's workplaces and often involved specific women's health hazards. Women Strike for Peace, starting in 1961, was central to the movement against nuclear testing. Women's health activism concerning drug and contraceptive side effects, another set of technological hazards akin to toxic waste, is also a significant predecessor to current toxic waste struggles. Minority women active in toxic struggles do sometimes come out of a civil rights movement orientation (Bullard 1993; Taylor 1993).

In their efforts to understand the hazards and to draw attention to the consequences of toxic exposure, these women activists come up against power and authority in scientific, corporate, and governmental unwillingness to consider their claims or address their concerns. As activist Cathy Hinds of Gray, Maine, said about her initial efforts to get her contaminated water supply tested, "It almost seemed as if they were angry with us—as if we had done something wrong, and how dare we inconvenience them this way. It was like talking to someone with no ears" (Garland 1988, 94). Authorities typically deny the need for action, largely on the basis that as women, particularly as housewives, activists cannot possibly know or understand the issues.

Women activists have a different approach to experience and knowledge. We view their different, gendered experience as based on their roles as people who center their worldview more on relationships than on abstract rights and on their roles as the primary caretakers of the family. These roles lead women to be more aware of the real and potential health effects of toxic waste and to take a more skeptical view of traditional science. This article examines these women's transformation of self, with an emphasis on Field Belenky et al.'s (1986) concept of "ways of knowing." That perspective traces the ways that women come to know things, beginning with either silence or the acceptance of established authority, progressing to a trust in subjective knowledge, and then to a synthesis of external and subjective knowledge.

We define *toxic waste* as the residue of toxic substances that are human-made or human-generated and known or suspected to be injurious to health....

We define *activists* as people who take some public action in legislative, judicial, political, or media arenas to cause prevention or remediation of known or suspected toxic waste hazards. Activists usually act at the local level, by which we mean individual or joint action in specific locations....

Toxic waste activism frequently takes the form of *popular epidemiology* (Brown and Mikkelsen 1990) whereby laypeople gather scientific data and also marshal the knowledge and resources of experts to understand the epidemiology of disease. To some degree, popular epidemiology parallels scientific epidemiology, such as when laypeople conduct community health surveys; yet, popular epidemiology is more than public participation in traditional epidemiology, since it emphasizes social structural factors as part of the etiology. Furthermore, it involves social movements, uses political and judicial approaches to remedies, and challenges basic assumptions of traditional epidemiology, risk assessment, and public health regulation. Popular epidemiology is, as we shall illustrate, largely a women's effort.

Lay attempts to do science or to use science, as in the case of popular epidemiology, are frequently subject to dismissal—if not ridicule—by professional scientists, mainly because of the practitioners' lay status. Because of their gender, women's attempts to use science for their own goals, rather than for normal goals of the scientific mainstream, are further disparaged by scientists in the service of government or industry. For example, when community activists in Los Angeles organized to prevent construction of a toxic waste incinerator, "the contempt of the male experts was directed at professionals and the unemployed, and Whites and Blacks—all the women were castigated as irrational and uncompromising" (Hamilton 1990, 220)....

EXPERIENCE, KNOWLEDGE, AND GENDER IN WOMEN'S TOXIC WASTE ACTIVISM

Gender Issues Found in Case Studies

In each case study we have found, there are remarkable similarities in the women activists' transformation from housewives to activists. Although there are differences in time, in region, in the particular circumstances of each woman's life and the cause of the toxic waste nearby, overall there is a consistency of theme and of experience. Each woman who becomes a toxic waste activist first suspects that there may be a health problem in her neighborhood when her children become ill. Outreach to her neighbors leads to the discovery of a pattern of illness in the community. Local public health authorities respond to the suspected problem with evasion or denial and only after an organized community presents its demands strongly and publicly is there an effort at cleanup or resolution by the government. When the original source of the pollution is industry, as is usually the case, the activists' efforts to hold the industrial interests accountable is difficult because of unequal resources. One of industry's main strategies to resist activists is the use of expert science to discount or minimize the communities' claims of risk and harm. Rather than working with the results or data from "housewife surveys" (Nelson 1990), scientists in the service of polluting industry or the government challenge them on the basis of their right to even be called evidence.

This challenge is made using objectivity as the standard against which lay work is judged, and objectivity debates are central to the gender-and-science question. We view this phenomenon in light of an awareness that science is historically, culturally, and structurally shaped very strongly by embedded beliefs about gender and women's role in science as well as about lay forms of knowledge and the value of subjective everyday experience. The women toxic waste activists' struggle not only is about the material conditions that have led to their exposure, but is centrally about the uses of knowledge and the validity of claims to recognition and authority as knowers....

Case studies of women toxic waste activists support Sara Ruddick's assertion that women's work and perceptions tend to be rooted, at least initially, in the concrete and the everyday. Bale suggests that the upsurge in environmental action in the 1970s, and toxic waste activism in particular, was for women "an attempt [by women] to attach meaning to their fears and pain" (1990, 421) resulting from exposure to toxic waste. Among toxic waste activists, this assertion is reflected in the following quote from a local activist: "The real issues came down to the human level. What we have seen in this community is kids die. When that happens, go for it" (Brown and Masterson-Allen 1994, 276).

The traits and experiences of women who become toxic waste activists are not theirs simply because they are women who live in proximity to toxic waste hazards; rather, they conceptualize their action, both for themselves and a wider public, out of the meaning of womanhood, and especially of motherhood, in our culture....

Despite the centrality of gender and emphasis on mothering in our analysis, as Morgen points out, much of the literature on women and community organizing tends to begin with the presupposition that a sexual division of labor determines that women activists work primarily out of their conventional private-sphere responsibilities (i.e., family service and motherhood) and that this presupposition limits our understanding of women's activist work within the community. She notes, however, that "women's community-based political activism is a conscious and collective way of expressing and acting on their interests as *women,* as *wives and mothers,* as *members of neighborhoods and communities,* and as *members of particular race, ethnic and class groups*" (1988, 111). Rather than making an essentialist argument about women's nature as the determinant of this particular kind of activism, it is in this sense of distinctive identity rooted in gendered experience, especially the encounter with scientific expertise and the activists' growing belief in their own knowledge as authoritative, that we approach the work of women toxic waste activists....

How the Gendered Position of Women Influences Toxic Waste Activism

When women who define themselves primarily as housewives become involved in activism and work against local toxic waste hazards, they must find the resources to organize their communities, challenge local political systems, and hold corporate interests accountable. They find or develop many of these resources within themselves as they struggle and succeed in learning about science (e.g., epidemiology, hydrogeology, medicine, engineering), about politics and influencing public opinion, and about community organizing. These women also learn to cultivate external resources: they gain mentors in both scientific and political processes and become skilled in media relations. The women activists transform their everyday experiences, most typically their own and their neighbors' children's illness, into knowledge that they can use in the struggle against toxic waste, and they insist on its validity as knowledge. Such validity is contested by scientific experts and professionals, whose cultural beliefs about women and science lead them to refuse to accept the women activists' claims about the consequences of toxic exposure.

Women toxic waste activists encounter deeply held beliefs about women and science on many levels. In light of this, it is critical to understand that science itself, our perceptions of it, how and where and by whom it gets done, and what kinds of problems get selected for study all are highly gendered social constructions (Harding 1986; Merchant 1980). The prevalence of Baconian metaphors in our culture's beliefs about science—female nature, male science—complicate responses to women's attempts to do science or to use it in pursuit of other goals. This association has a profound impact especially on nonexpert women, trying to use science to achieve social justice. As Fox Keller (1986) suggests, our culture takes for granted the association of science and objective rational thought with masculinity and masculine ways of thinking. She notes that scientific thought is commonly held to be a masculine quality, although objectivity itself is held by definition to be gender neutral....

Popular epidemiology is the method of choice for women facing toxic hazards. Women are generally denied access to scientific information, and their attempts at gaining access are trivialized as subjective and antiscientific. They therefore turn to approaches they develop themselves, such as informal health surveys and "lay mapping" of disease clusters. In some situations where sympathetic professionals are available and where the data are sufficient, activists collaborate with professionals in rigorous health surveys. A good example of women practicing this approach is the annual conference of EHN. Leaders and members of local toxic groups spend several days sharing their experience in investigation and action with other activists, physicians, epidemiologists, social scientists, and lawyers. These lay epidemiologists share health questionnaires, methods of data gathering and analysis, and other scientific issues.

EHN acts as a national clearinghouse to assist local groups, but not to turn them into organizational branches. EHN staff work to develop alternatives to long and costly epidemiology studies. For example, they are correlating disease clusters with existing, accessible EPA data on toxic releases at the zip code level....

Ways of Knowing

To understand what Bale terms the "evolution of women's consciousness of the toxic experience" (1990, 431), we have adapted the model developed in *Women's Ways of Knowing* (Belenky et al. 1986) as a framework for analyzing women toxic waste activists' epistemological development. Through transformations in their ways of knowing, women toxic waste activists come to terms both with the nature of the toxic contamination and with denial or evasion by public officials and industry. Women tend to take up the side of "cultural rationality" in opposition to "technical rationality." That is, they are centrally concerned with individual suffering, impaired relationships, ordinary daily experience, and direct perception of health effects. Just as in the larger case of popular epidemiology, approaching a problem from subjective experience rather than from a stance of perceived rational objectivity (i.e., conventional science) gives the activists' claims greater legitimacy in their own eyes.

Local toxic waste activists typically describe the discovery of the truth about their communities' contamination as a developmental process. Their convictions about their government, their communities, and their own abilities follow a characteristic series of changes. Their self-development in understanding and using knowledge of science in defense of their children and communities conforms in many key ways to feminist relational psychology's descriptions of women's ways of knowing. Among women toxic waste activists, ways of knowing strongly affect the capacity for effective action. Activists' knowledge evolves from an initial trust in larger institutions—assumptions that government and businesses know and do what is morally right—to the discovery in their own neighborhoods of, for example, common incidence of rare childhood illness, to the ability to act on these discoveries. The process of coming to understand themselves as knowers is an important means by which women toxic waste activists empower themselves to act as forces for change in their communities.

This perception of knowledge and its uses, and also of activists basing their claims in subjective experience, is associated with a type of moral and psychological development that involves an orientation to an ethic of specific care rather than abstract rights (Gilligan 1982). Toxic waste activists argue that the quantitative risk assessment approach ignores personal and community experience in favor of global calculations of financial accounting, potential psychological response, and, most importantly, probability of hazards at toxic sites. The "rights" of corporations are thus placed on an (allegedly) objective plane, as contrasted with the subjective plane of local response. The conflict between these two is seen clearly in Love Canal, New York, where Hooker Chemical Company gave land to the town for a school with the proviso that the company would never be liable for chemical injuries. While Hooker relied on a legal document to protect itself from a lawsuit, Lois Gibbs's efforts on behalf of her own family and her community to solve the problem for everyone were based on a more personal notion of responsibility (Levine 1982). There is a tension between objective (public, governmental, corporate, rational, male) and subjective (private, familial, emotional, female) that resembles in many ways the opposition between women toxic waste activists as claimants to science and the authority of experts to judge those claims.

We are not arguing that women toxic waste activists pursue their goals merely or solely because, as women, they experience a specific psychological developmental path; rather, we suggest that given social and material constraints that largely stem from gender and class, these activists find creative and effective ways to generate change in their communities. These creative forms grow out of a self-articulated ethic of responsibility and connection. In addition to clearly voicing a call to action based on justice, women toxic waste activists give credence to their claims based on a belief in the necessity and importance of caring and a recognition of interdependence. They find the actions of nonresponsive polluters and agencies wrong and requiring redress not simply because these actions violate their rights as citizens and members of a larger polity, but also because these actions violate a moral imperative of caring and responsibility....

The two stages that Field Belenky et al. label *silence* and *received knowing* are often merged in women toxic waste activists. Although they generally express a perspective characteristic of received knowers, in the particular case of the scientific issues, they more closely resemble silent knowers. Such a perspective is illustrated by a quote from a victim of the Velsicol dumping in Hardemann County, Tennessee: "I took a water sample to the health department; they said nothing's wrong with it. I thought they was good people, smarter than I was. But they wasn't" (Brown and Mikkelsen 1990, 145). Many narratives about women toxic waste activists describe how they were "just plain" housewives at the start who did not have anything to say about toxic contamination or its associated issues. For example, Gibbs relates her initial reaction to a news story about her neighborhood: "The problem didn't affect me, so I wasn't going to do anything about it, and I certainly wasn't going to speak out about it" (1982, 9–10).

Subjective knowing, the turn in attention to the inner voice, comes with recognition of the validity of self-determined truths. Gibbs recounts what she was thinking when she tried to start collecting signatures at the very beginning of her activism:

> *When I got there, I sat at the kitchen table with my petition in my hand, thinking "Wait, What if people do slam doors in your face? People may think you're crazy." But what's more important—what people think or your child's health? Either you're going to do something or you're going to have to admit you're a coward and not do it. (1982, 13)*

Hearing an "inner voice" of "self-protection, self-assertion, and self-definition" (Belenky et al. 1986, 54) leads to the beginning of activism. This is the point at which Anne Anderson in Woburn, Massachusetts, Hinds in Gray, and Gibbs in Love Canal began to believe that something was wrong in their communities, despite the denials of local authorities. As Gibbs said, "I used to have a lot of faith in officials, especially doctors and experts. Now I was losing that faith—fast!" (1982, 23). Field Belenky et al. state that as women "began to think and to know, they began to act" (1986, 77). Many subjective knowers come to this position as a result of an encounter with "failed authority," usually male. In the lives of many women toxic waste activists, the disillusionment comes from repeated encounters with officials in which their assumptions about the value of human safety over profits or convenience are violated by the officials.

Further stages designated by Field Belenky et al. include *procedural knowing,* a reasoned attempt at resolving the conflicts between external and subjective knowledge, and *constructed knowing,* which emerges in a voice that integrates the preceding voices of reason, intuition, and expertise of others. Among women toxic waste activists, procedural knowing evolves often out of contacts with a mentor in the role of scientific expert, since these mentors are able to help the activists in learning ways to use scientific expertise for their own goals. Constructed knowing is often focused on an attempt to transcend local issues and address larger concerns. Both Gibbs and Hinds moved beyond their tight-knit communities to work on toxic waste issues at a national level. In Hinds's words,

> *[A young boy] looked at the EPA officials and said, "I don't want to die." That boy, and the loss of my own first baby son, and hearing all the stories of people like us around the country—all that's been a fuel to me. It makes me think that, damn it, this is America, this stuff shouldn't be happening. (Garland 1988, 105)*

Experience and Knowledge

Although scientific experts and government officials typically view mundane experience as insufficient or unhelpful in finding or interpreting unusual health patterns, often the toxic waste activists' knowledge derives directly from their daily experience and from their relational orientation within the community. Ruddick notes that

> *the physical home and the social household are usually part of a larger socio-physical community. There is nothing romantic about the extension of mother's activity from keeping a safe home to making their neighborhoods safe.... If children are threatened, mothers join together, in all varieties of causes, to protect the neighborhoods they have made. (1989, 80)*

Women toxic waste activists' motivation to force changes in their communities seems to be rooted initially in personal and familial experiences—in the subjective experience of the everyday world (Krauss 1993). This aspect of their experience marks it not only as culturally female but also as maternal thinking and action....

Housewife data, housewife studies, and housewife movements embody aspects of the everyday world; consequently, they are easily marginalized. A close relationship between thought, emotion, and action compounds the class and political disadvantages of women toxic waste activists, because the experts whom they challenge rest their authority on scientific rationality. As Smith notes:

> *In relation to men (of the ruling class) women's consciousness did not, and most probably generally still does not, appear as an autonomous source of knowledge, experience, relevance, and imagination. Women's experience [does] not appear as the source of an authoritative general expression of the world. (1987, 51)*

Women whose approach to knowledge is intensely or primarily subjective conform most closely to cultural stereotypes about female thinkers and thinking as subjective, intuitive, and nonrational. As Ruddick describes maternal action:

> *Rather than separate reason from feeling, mothering makes reflective feeling one of the most difficult attainments of reason. In protective work, feeling, thinking, and action are linked; feelings demand reflection, which is in turn tested by action, which is in turn tested by the feelings it provokes. (1989, 70)*

In studying women's approaches and relationship to knowledge, Field Belenky et al. (1986) found that women often rejected science, seeing it as a form of alien expertise; nevertheless, toxic waste activists claim science and use it in their activism, even as they reformulate it into means of reaching their own goals. They deliberately use science as a tool for social justice, bringing their activism into the practice of science, thus going beyond pure knowledge seeking; indeed, their use of science is essential. The results of lay scientific studies of contamination in their communities confirm their intuitive and subjective knowledge, rooted in daily experience about the origins of their families' illnesses.

The consequences of living in proximity to a toxic hazard affect many members of the local community. Once residents learn that they share these risks, the consequences also become shared and viewed as a community-wide problem. The realization that each family is not alone with its problems is an important step toward forming a grassroots coalition, and it is a pivotal point in the involvement of blue-collar women in community activist groups. Learning of the commonality of their situation helps them realize that their health problems are tied to geography, and they begin to look for causes nearby. As national activist leader Gibbs reflected on a community meeting:

> *The meeting had one good effect: it brought people together. People who had been feuding because little Johnny hit little Billy are now talking to each other. They had air readings in common or a dead plant or a dead tree. They compared readings, saying, "Hey, this is what I've got. What have you got?" The word spread fast, and the community became close-knit. (1982, 26)*

The sense of connection is important on a national or regional level as well as locally. When Hinds found out about the situation at Love Canal, she said the experience of toxic exposure she shared with residents there made it more possible to bear her own fears and moved her to work in her community: "I was so relieved. Not to see others suffering, but to realize there was someone else we could talk to about this who would know what we were talking about, who would understand how we felt" (Garland 1988, 96).

Connectedness, the state of sharing, also makes the activists feel that they are accomplishing something real, and it bolsters their beliefs that their actions are right both morally and as a response to a real threat. In Los Angeles, white middle-class women came together with the poor minority activists to work against construction of an incinerator for toxic waste. As Charlotte Bullock explained, "We are making a difference.... When we come together as a whole and stick with it, we can win because we are right" (Hamilton 1990, 219). The women relied on each other for support and encouragement, both despite and because of their ridicule by white male experts....

Public Boundaries, Private Dilemmas

Prior to beginning their activist careers, most women toxic waste activists centered their lives in the private, or domestic, sphere of home and family. It is not only that they were not previously political activists; they had not been active participants in shaping the course of events in the public sphere. They approach the political realm as an area of power that has always excluded them. This encounter involves crossing the boundaries between the traditionally female private domain and the traditionally male public world of politics and policy determination....

The work of women toxic waste activists illustrates this challenge. Their efforts at mobilizing local communities to combat toxic hazards are often dismissed initially as mere collections of "housewife data" gathered by "hysterical housewives." As housewives, they cannot do science (in the eyes of expert professionals), nor can they challenge the local political and corporate power structures. As their efforts gain support, however, both the activists themselves and the community at large usually redefine their activism as work appropriate for mothers, thereby moving it conceptually into a normatively female domain. As Smith writes, "Experiences, concerns, needs, aims and interests arising among people in the everyday and working context of their living are given expression in forms that articulate them to the existing practice and social relations constituting its rule" (1987, 56). Even though the work may remain the same, as an extension of mothering it becomes normatively appropriate for housewives to be doing it. This work also represents a challenge along class lines to the authority to define appropriate kinds of behavior.

Institutions in the public domain are supposed to protect elements within the private sphere. When activists discover that local industry values its bottom line or national reputation more highly than it does the health of children in the community, this realization violates the trust that the women toxic waste activists have placed in the ideal of corporate good citizenship and governmental protection. It represents a breech in the implicit societal contract between the private world—their children's health and safety—and the public world of governmental public health policy and industrial regulation. One of the mothers in Woburn phrased it this way:

> *I think we all think, somehow we are all very comfortable thinking that industry just wouldn't do this to us, government wouldn't allow industry to do this to us even if industry wanted to, and it is a very difficult thing to grasp in the first place. (Brown and Mikkelsen 1990, 60)*

The problems occur inside the home, but they are consequences of actions taken outside of it.

Images and Ideologies of Motherhood

The images and reality of both social and biological mothering are basic to the experience of women toxic waste activists. These images are manipulated both by the activists and by their opposition. A politics of mothering is at the root of the activists' own claim to legitimacy, and to their rights to take action within the community. Mothering a sick child is most often the experience that motivates these activists to action. These women nearly always use their own maternal identities in public relations to gain attention to toxic waste issues. The image of a mother rising to the defense of her children is an extremely powerful one, and it is skillfully used to great advantage by women toxic waste activists.

Industry and government frequently use negative beliefs about mothers to discredit the activists' claims of connections between toxic waste and health consequences, since "housewife data" are not real science to the experts. Women who are upset by growing knowledge of the consequences of toxic waste exposure in their homes are easily labeled hysterical. The labeling gives government and industry permission not to take the activists' claims seriously, by playing on cultural beliefs about women's temperament and science. Each case study of a grassroots toxic waste fight led by women includes some anecdote about authorities and experts claiming that the activists could not possibly know what they were talking about because they were only housewives and mothers. For instance, Bullock recounted,

> *I did not come to the fight against environmental problems as an intellectual, but rather as a concerned mother. People say, "But you're not a scientist. How do you know it's not safe?" I know if dioxin and mercury are going to come out of an incinerator stack, somebody's going to be affected. (Hamilton 1990, 215)*

The view of women as hysterical housewives is a contemporary example of a form of oppression that has been used throughout history to psychopathologize women for their particular forms of experience and perception. Just as "scientific" psychiatry has so often supported traditional gender roles and punished women who rebel, so too do organized professional and governmental bodies involved in environmental hazards. Activists turn this to their own use, as in Gibbs's frequent claim to be hysterical and proud of it. Otherwise, she adds, women's fear of publicizing personal toxic waste experiences will silence them. Capek's (1987) study of activists at the Jacksonville, Arkansas, Vertac site found that women experienced a tension between "issues of the head" and "issues of the heart." The issues of the head, manifested in sympathetic expert research and testimony, could be defeated in court and other official locations. "So," leader Patty Frase recounted, "we kept it an emotional issue because an emotional issue you can't beat."...

It is ironic that women's involvement in toxic waste organizing is an outgrowth of one of their chief domestic responsibilities—family health. Women are the organizers of health surveillance and medical care for themselves and their children and often their husbands as well. Again, from Cannon:

> *All these social issues as well as political and economic issues are really intertwined. Before, I was concerned only about health and then I began to get into the politics, decision making, and so many things. (Hamilton 1990, 221)*

Since health concerns are the root of most toxic waste activism, women organizers are actually fulfilling an important traditional role, albeit in an untraditional and sometimes controversial fashion....

CONCLUSION

In this article, we have examined a significant phenomenon of our time—a burgeoning social movement concerned with toxic wastes and their known or feared health effects. We have seen that this movement is largely populated by women, especially by women without prior scientific and political experience. These women, as well as most of their men co-participants, share an approach to knowledge that is democratic, collective, and a synthesis of subjective and objective features. Attitude surveys and case studies have provided us with a picture of women's toxic waste activism that is concerned with local problems, especially when they threaten health. This differs from the larger environmental movement where women's attitudes are not necessarily more pro-environment than those of men and where women do not predominate as leaders and members....

We do not wish to essentialize ways of knowing as only a women's phenomenon. Indeed, there is a large number of men activists who also take the popular epidemiology approach. Both men and women share in these efforts a dislike of the hierarchical and remote structure of most national environmental organizations that have failed to address environmental health effects. Both share a distrust of government and corporate structures that keep citizens at a distance. They have also experienced the failure of most mainstream science to come to their assistance. In response, they have relied on networks of trust, associations of collective research, and shared empathy over sickness and death of family and friends; hence, they have gravitated to a way of knowing and a method of action that centers on democratic participation and relational logic.

Yet, since women predominate in this activism, and since they play particular roles in relating to environmental health, we have focused on women's ways of knowing. Women toxic waste activists change their relationship to their known world—their families and communities and the corporate and political institutions that guide them—and, in the process, transform themselves as knowers. The changes reinforce one another. Women toxic waste activists experience knowledge and authority—especially scientific knowledge and political authority—in a way that is strongly determined by their gender as well as by social class. The activists' relationship to knowledge and their belief in themselves as knowers play a central role in their experience of activism.

Such belief in themselves and in the moral, as well as scientific, foundation of their activism is hard won. Women toxic waste activists create within themselves the abilities to organize and to lead the process of change in their communities, despite opposition or evasion by local public health authorities, by industry experts, and often even by their neighbors and families. This is a remarkable transformation, and they deserve recognition not only for their efforts to protect their families and communities, but also for the courage to change themselves in the process.

REFERENCES

Bale, Anthony. 1990. Women's toxic experience. In *Women, health, and medicine in America: A historical handbook,* edited by Rima Apple. New York: Garland.

Belenky, Mary Field, Blythe McVicker Clinchy, Nancy Rule Goldberger, and Jill Mattock Tarule. 1986. *Women's ways of knowing: The development of self, voice, and mind.* New York: Basic Books.

Brown, Phil, and Susan Masterson-Allen. 1994. Citizen action on toxic waste contamination: A new type of social movement. *Society and Natural Resources* 7:269–86.

Brown, Phil, and Edwin J. Mikkelsen. 1990. *No safe place: Toxic waste, leukemia, and community action.* Berkeley: University of California Press.

Bullard, Robert D. 1993. Anatomy of environmental racism and the environmental justice movement. In *Confronting environmental racism: Voices from the grassroots,* edited by Robert D. Bullard. Boston: South End.

Cable, Sherry. 1992. Women's social movement involvement: The role of structural availability in recruitment and participation processes. *Sociological Quarterly* 33:35–47.

Capek, Stella M. 1987. *Toxic hazards in Arkansas: Emerging coalitions.* Paper presented at annual meeting of Society for the Study of Social Problems, Chicago, August.

Edelstein, Michael R. 1988. *Contaminated communities: The social and psychological impacts of residential toxic exposure.* Boulder, CO: Westview.

Freudenberg, Nicholas, and Carol Steinsapir. 1992. Not in our backyards: The grassroots environmental movement. In *American environmentalism: The U.S. environmental movement, 1970–1990,* edited by Riley E. Dunlap and Angela G. Mertig. Philadelphia: Taylor & Francis.

Garland, Anne Witte. 1988. *Women activists: Challenging the abuse of power.* New York: Feminist Press.

Gibbs, Lois Marie. 1982. *Love Canal: My story.* Albany: State University of New York Press.

Gilligan, Carol. 1982. *In a different voice: Psychological theory and women's development.* Cambridge, MA: Harvard University Press.

Hamilton, Cynthia. 1990. Women, home, and community: The struggle in an urban environment. In *Reweaving the world: The emergence of ecofeminism,* edited by Irene Diamond and Gloria Feman Orenstein. San Francisco: Sierra Club Books.

Harding, Sandra. 1986. *The science question in feminism.* Ithaca, NY: Cornell University Press.

Keller, Evelyn Fox. 1986. Gender and science: Why is it so hard for us to count past two? *Berkshire Review* 21:7–21.

Krauss, Celene. 1993. Women and toxic waste protests: Race, class and gender as resources of resistance. *Qualitative Sociology* 16:247–62.

Levine, Adeline Gordon. 1982. *Love Canal: Science, politics, and people.* Lexington, MA: Lexington Books.

Merchant, Carolyn. 1980. *The death of nature: Women, ecology, and the scientific revolution.* San Francisco: Harper & Row,

Morgen, Sandra. 1988. "It's the whole power of the city against us!": The development of political consciousness in a women's health care coalition. In *Women and the politics of empowerment,* edited by Ann Bookman and Sandra Morgen. Philadelphia: Temple University Press.

Nelson, Lin. 1990. The place of women in polluted places. In *Reweaving the world: The emergence of ecofeminism,* edited by Irene Diamond and Gloria Feman Orenstein. San Francisco: Sierra Club Books.

Ruddick, Sara. 1989. *Maternal thinking: Towards a politics of peace.* Boston: Beacon.

Smith, Dorothy E. 1987. *The everyday world as problematic: A feminist sociology.* Boston: Northeastern University Press.

Taylor, Dorceta E. 1989. Blacks and the environment: Toward an explanation of the concern and action gap between Blacks and whites. *Environment and Behavior* 21:175–205.

———. 1993. Environmentalism and the politics of inclusion. In *Confronting environmental racism: Voices from the grassroots,* edited by Robert D. Bullard. Boston: South End.

NUMBERS, NUMBERS, NUMBERS...

LOIS CAMP

I'm a third generation farm wife, and I've lived and worked in the country all my life. One morning in the fall of 1986, I found myself preparing to do something quite out of the ordinary for me. I was driving to Richland, Washington to testify before the Hanford Health Effects Panel, appointed by the Center for Disease Control (CDC) to hear public testimony and review 19,000 pages of recently released classified documents regarding the Hanford Nuclear site.

My mind bubbled over with questions. Would those experts listen to what I had to say? Would my testimony be effective? Would I present enough convincing information? Was I dressed appropriately? I reassured myself; I did not want to project an image which differed from who I really am—a rural woman who feels a deep obligation to defend her principles and who suspects that her people and her land had been grievously harmed. I never let my self-doubts stop me from relentlessly searching for the facts, and I would not let those doubts stop me now from telling the truth as I know it.

My story really begins many years ago when more than one million curies of radiation were released from the Hanford Nuclear Reservation between 1944 and 1956.[1] The truth about the radioactive emissions from Hanford did not surface until early in 1986, and, in fact, the whole truth is still seeping out piece by piece. Those of us living in the area knew that we were having more cancers—and other health problems—than other parts of the country. But we didn't know why.

I lived about fifty miles from the Hanford Reservation during my early childhood. In those early years I experienced health problems which I now believe can be attributed to my being dosed with radioactive emissions. My first hint of physical harm was a minor skin rash when I was eight or nine years old. But the rash didn't disappear as I had expected it to; it rapidly worsened, and within hours I became one mass of blisters which covered every inch of my body except for the soles of my feet. I ended up in the hospital, where for weeks I slid in and out of consciousness. My doctor was baffled.

I was given test after test, but all my doctor could say was that I had evidently come into contact with something so toxic that it had nearly killed me; he could not, however, determine what that toxic substance was. Ever since that time I have continued to have unusual skin disorders. I have a near-zero sun tolerance. My skin is easily irritated and infected, and it takes a very long time to heal.

The eruptions on my skin were only the beginning. I seem to have no resistance to infections, viruses, and fungi. At the age of forty-eight I have the energy level of an eighty-four-year-old; I've been recently diagnosed with cardiomyopathy (meaning that a major portion of my heart has been irreversibly damaged), and my doctor, one of the top cardiologists in the state, is stumped because he can't determine a cause for it. I had endometrial cancer in 1980 and then uterine cancer in 1983. Several members of my family have had cancer. Many of my friends have had (and died from) cancer. In fact, where we live cancer as prevalent as the common cold.

I first learned about the Hanford emissions from a newspaper article in the spring of 1986. Needless to say, I was stunned by the implications—for me and for my community—of this disclosure. I had a term paper due for a class I was taking, a perfect motive to find out more. I read articles and studies and statistics written by experts and specialists. But the more I read, the more muddled the "official" picture became.

The research I had done for my term paper provided me with enough information to seriously question many of the statistics I came across concerning numbers and percentages of cancer incidence and death, as well as the data on many other illnesses. Even at the very beginning of my study, I was amazed to learn that there were no actual 1986 population numbers available for local counties or school districts. The data from the 1980 census count was obtainable at the courthouse, but no one had any figures more current. I had hoped to find a baseline number of the actual population count so that the figures I had gathered about illnesses and deaths in those areas would yield fairly accurate percentage rates. It was curious, I thought, that so many other studies claimed to be accurate when the researchers couldn't have had recent population counts, either.

More reliable demographic data, however, doesn't insure officially sanctioned results. One example is the epidemiological study which was done in Garfield County (downwind of the Hanford plant). That county is largely agrarian with a relatively small population and low mobility, making its residents ideal for a study of long-term exposure to environmental hazards. Some health care providers in Pomeroy, the county seat, became concerned about the "very high"[2] cancer rate there, particularly the number of cases of pancreatic cancer in their area. In the early 1980s they had directed a study which verified causes of death, including examination of death certificates. In an effort to uncover what might lie behind the elevated cancer statistics for this community, Garfield County officials conducted a detailed analysis of numerous water sources in the county because water was the one element they could isolate as being common to all the people in the county. They found no significant levels of the pesticides or herbicides which had been the most widely suspected contaminants. This inconclusive investigation left the question of environmental factors in the pancreatic cancer rate unanswered. When the report about the Hanford emissions became public in 1986, it seemed evident that the area in which the cancers had occurred had undoubtedly received exposure to the radiation. The county had not had access to the equipment necessary to identify radioactive isotopes when the water analysis was done, and nobody was looking for radioactive isotopes, anyway. So the presence of this obvious carcinogenic agent remained unknown.

When legislators learned about the unresolved Garfield County study, they called a special public meeting. Officials from the Epidemiological Section of the Department of Social Health Services in Washington state, along with other high officials, were invited to attend. At the meeting, a Garfield County Health Department employee who had assisted in the earlier study of pancreatic cancer incidence was challenged by state health officials, as was the entire study.[3] The state officials insinuated the entire study lacked credibility. They implied that death certificates used may have been inaccurate as pancreatic cancer is difficult to diagnose, and the deceased may not have even had cancer!

The conjecture by health officials that death certificates might be imprecise intrigued me. What if they were right, and the death certificates really didn't accurately reflect the causes of death? If there was any doubt that death certificates were unimpeachable sources for information about causes of death, then certainly studies which depended upon them for any statistical analysis were seriously flawed. But what if the inaccuracy were the opposite of the accusation implied by the skeptics of the Garfield study? What if, in fact, some death certificates were inaccurately attributing causes of death to reasons other than cancer when cancer was the cause?

I began my own very unscientific and informal survey of illnesses and deaths in my rural school district area. One of my friends provided valuable information as she was a former city employee, and as part of her job had kept data on deaths for the last twenty-five years. In our school district alone, there had been an approximately 600 percent increase in stillbirths from 1961 to 1968. The actual numbers of total cases of stillbirths are considered "insignificant numbers" by the expert scientific researchers. I have often wondered if that's what they told the parents who are still suffering from their loss.

Another friend who was helping me compile a list of cancer deaths told me that she knew cancer was not listed on her father's death certificate, even though he had had cancer. He had died of organ failures which were listed on the death certificate form, but the cancer which had caused those organ failures was never mentioned. Time after time we encountered similar discrepancies between what people knew about a death and what appeared on the death certificate. But when I finally realized the full import of what we were accidentally discovering, I had no actual numbers to present to the panel. I had read numerous statistical studies about cancer and other disease incidence and deaths which were based on random selection of death certificates. If the death certificate omissions which my friend and I were uncovering represented even only a fraction of the death certificates used by other researchers, then their statistical conclusions would have to be skewed.

I recently spoke with a home health care nurse from our county who agrees with my rough estimate that cancer is evident in approximately 80 percent of the deaths in this area. In comparison, 22 percent of deaths nationally in 1987 were attributed to cancer. She is convinced that this area, at least, has a much higher number of cancer cases per capita than is statistically "normal." Not only are death certificates a questionable source on which to base a statistical study; another difficulty lies in the way in which data are gathered. Official statistics are "age-adjusted" so that, in essence, if a person is diagnosed with cancer after a certain age (such as seventy-five years), that cancer isn't included in the statistics. Presumably, the statisticians figure that the person would have died anyway from old age, and therefore the death is not statistically significant. So if eight out of ten of the cases which the nurse cared for were cancer, but three of those cancer cases were in older people, maybe only five of those would be credible statistical numbers. Many cancers take more than twenty years to develop after exposure to a carcinogenic substance. Discounting the cancer-related deaths of people over a certain age undermines the probability of statistics demonstrating that a particular area might suspect a specific contamination as being responsible for an abnormal increase in cancer cases. At best, these statistical maneuvers simply cloud the issue; at worst, they forestall people's efforts to understand and prevent the causes of a terrible disease.

Even with all the information I had at my command, I felt my knees quaking when my name was called to testify before the Hanford Health Effects Panel. After all, these people were the recognized experts in their fields; how could I expect them even to listen to an ordinary farm wife?

I had prepared my presentation much like I always did for a typical Sunday School or Bible School class. I had an enlarged map of eastern Washington on which I had highlighted all the areas I had lived in, and I had indicated the places where there were geographical clusters of illnesses. As I nervously moved into my testimony, I observed subtle changes in the panel members. Some sat up straight. Pencils stopped tapping. A few panel members began jotting notes. They were beginning to listen.

When I finished speaking, I turned to go back to my chair, still suspecting that there would be no response from the panel. To my surprise, one of the physicians began questioning me. First he requested that I provide him with more information about the study I had done. Then, almost defensively, he stated that he had never heard of a disease not being listed on a death certificate. I just shrugged my shoulders. I told him I didn't know about all death certificates, but I did know that the record of cancer as a primary cause for death had been left out of some death certificates here, and that if I could discover such omissions, there sure could be a chance that they happened elsewhere.

With a deep sigh of relief, I finally, sat down. To my surprise, two newspaper reporters hurried to my side and began questioning me. At last it began to sink in; this farm gal just might have a story to share.

The slippery statistics, the cover-ups, and the deceptions which have historically provided a safety net for government agencies are sufficient reason to challenge the credibility of our official experts. A classic example of such bureaucratic duplicity appeared in an agricultural publication recently. The article hailed the studies done by a program of the United States Department of Agriculture (USDA) to measure erosion levels on the steep farm hills in our area. The USDA has given our local farmers an ultimatum to retard erosion unless they want to risk becoming ineligible for government programs like crop insurance, but many farmers have not been able to afford the expensive equipment and techniques required to prevent soil erosion. Now it appears that the USDA has a way of checking up on us. According to the article, they can measure the amount or depth of cesium-137 (Cs-137), which is a by-product of radioactive fission, in the soil at the top of a hill or from a flat area, and then measure the Cs-137 levels at the bottom of the hill. If there is more Cs-137 found in the soil samples from the bottom of the hill, they can conclude that there has been soil erosion. After nearly fifty years of being told that there was no "significant" contamination of radionuclides in our earth, that same authority (the U.S. government) can now announce that Cs-137 is not only present, but the presence is vast enough and consistent enough to be useful in a soil research program.[4]

The same article is careful not to implicate Hanford by maintaining that the Cs-137 in our area comes from the Nevada Test Site, despite the fact that we are behind the prevailing winds from the Test Site. But it doesn't really matter where the radioactive poison comes from. What's important is the fact that it's there at all. Cs-137 tends to travel to the bones when it enters a human body, and my first son has already had one bone tumor. Now I have learned that the soil on which he played as a child contains Cs-137, though all our questions about safety had only brought us emphatic reassurances that any contamination was so low that there could not be any ill effects on the population.

The personal and scientific data I have accumulated leads me to only one conclusion. I believe there has been a very real attempt, in the face of overwhelming evidence to the contrary, to discount environmental hazards as possible causes of cancer. The question we need to ask is: why? Is it possible to expect the "experts" even to understand or care about our concerns? Can they imagine what it is like to learn that Cs-137 has been present in the dust that we have breathed all these years? Is this the price of progress? Is this what we are expected to pay for a strong defense?

I am no longer willing to let others answer these questions for me. My family has suffered from unusual cancers and other illnesses. I've had cancer twice myself. In frustration and desperation I pray that this insanity—the deceptions, contradictions, and denials—will stop. Since the 1986 acknowledgment of the Hanford releases, I have been on a merry-go-round; I always end up at the beginning instead of gaining any ground. No matter what information I present, there is always some "expert" with a briefcase full of numbers ready to contradict what I say. I have been reassured over and over again that our government will do everything they can and use every bit of information known in their assessment of health problems in our area, but nothing is ever specific. Generalizations and evasive double talk prevail.

I want to get off my merry-go-round. All of us have to climb down from our revolving horses and look at reality if we are to force government agencies, presumably designed to protect us and care for our best interests, to finally be accountable.

Until the full extent of what has actually happened to us in the Hanford area and in many other parts of the country is finally admitted and examined, all nuclear facilities should halt production. It is critical that political expediency not play a part in this issue, for if we can't make our world safe we won't have to fear being destroyed by the Soviets or anyone else. We'll destroy ourselves, and our cemeteries will be "hot" for centuries.

NOTES

1. Schumacher, Eloise, "Radioactive release is remembered in Fremont exhibit," *Seattle Times,* December 3, 1989, p. B-1.
2. Bingman, Teresa, "Cancer rate alarms health officials," *East Washingtonian,* January 2, 1986.
3. Cecil, Nelta, "Water supply scheduled for cancer testing," *East Washingtonian,* February 5, 1986.
4. Veseth, Roger, "Radioactive Fallout Provides Estimator for Soil Erosion," *Growers Guide,* May/June, 1990, pp. A12–A15.

CHAPTER 17

FINDING RESOURCES

TERRY PLUM AND EVAN SABATELLI

Recent years have seen a massive expansion of information resources: online databases, electronic books, electronic journals, and the Internet. Never before have so many facts been so widely available. Yet at times, the supply of information seems so vast that finding exactly what you are seeking can appear to be a daunting, if not impossible, task. Becoming intimidated may be a common response, but it is not a productive one. Instead, one should understand different types of available resources, the best strategies for finding information, and what questions to ask knowledgeable people. This chapter will help the reader tackle this new world of information gathering.

The most frequently used resources for academic research can be divided into three main categories: libraries with their collections of print books, journals, and other physical objects; computerized databases of collected information often about a particular subject; and the protean Internet.

LIBRARIES

Libraries stocked with massive stores of books, academic journals, popular magazines, government documents, newspapers, and other periodicals still thrive, despite the new emphasis on computer-based resources. Libraries allow hands-on browsing of materials, serendipitous searching of bookshelves, and access to reference librarians. Determining the contents of a library has now been made more convenient, because many library catalogs are searchable via computer. At the end of this chapter is a section specifically on searching libraries for books via the computer and the Internet.

DATABASES

Computerized databases number in the hundreds, each with particular strengths and weaknesses. Many databases, such as *InfoTrac Expanded Academic ASAP*, *Contemporary Women's Issues*, and *Academic Universe* (formerly known as *Lexis-Nexis*), organize recent articles from a broad array of commonly read publications. Another, MEDLINE, as its name suggests, indexes medical literature. Some databases provide the full text of some or all of the resources they index; others offer only a short abstract, or just a citation. Databases cover different academic journals and periodicals, vary in the extent of their subject linkages to similar articles, differ in the inclusion of backfiles, and vary in the search strategies and rules they use. Some databases allow you to email an article to someone, which is a useful feature because printing the article at a library can be expensive or time-consuming. Some allow you to search for other articles that cite the one you have found (e.g., the *Web of Science* citation search), allow you to limit your search to refereed articles, allow a search by author or journal, or provide access to the table of contents of many journals (e.g., UnCover). With the help of a librarian, you can determine the databases most appropriate for a search on your topic and also any special features. Although most of these databases are available only through libraries that have paid for a subscription, some (e.g., UnCover and MEDLINE) are offered for free, without restriction.

THE INTERNET

The Internet can now be accessed from nearly anywhere on the planet; most typically, it is accessed from a home, office, or library computer. The most commonly used part of the Internet is known as the World Wide Web (www), or more simply, the Web. The Web consists of "pages," which can be in nearly any format, including text, pictures, sounds, and videos. Anyone can create a website. Whereas information in refereed journals has gone through a peer-review process intended to ensure the quality of information, and reputable news magazines and newspapers conform to journalistic standards, no such quality controls exist on the Internet. The mere existence of official-looking web information does not mean that it is factually correct, or even that the author has made any attempt to ensure the validity of his or her work. Carefully consider the source of any resources you use, and the extent to which you trust the information. Internet addresses end with top-level domain names, or extensions, which broadly identify them as educational (.edu), government (.gov), organizations (.org), or commercial (.com), which may help you to evaluate the information. The old adage "don't believe everything you read" has never been more important than in the Internet information age.

When using any tool to search for information, it is important to be a creative and flexible detective. It is highly unlikely that whoever cataloged the information you are looking for will divide up the content area exactly as you do, or that all the people writing about a topic will use the same words. Thus, while you may be looking for "domestic violence," they may have been thinking of or writing about "family violence." A beginning and continuing task in searching is to think of synonyms and related phrases for your topic. For example, for domestic violence, it may also be important to search for information on "battered women," or "abused women," or "acquaintance rape." The more ways you can phrase a topic and think about it, the more complete your results will be.

SEARCHING A DATABASE

There are two main methods of searching a database. In the world of reference librarians, these are known as searching by subject and by keyword. If a database allows a *subject search,* this means that each and every article in the database was assigned to a set of subject headings by a living, breathing human being using that database's predetermined set of subject words. Although the results you get with a subject search are likely to be pertinent to your topic in some way, you are limited in your retrieval to materials that someone else decided was relevant to the subject area. If your search produces too much, the database subject search may allow you to combine subject areas to limit your search.

Performing a *keyword search* will return articles that contain any word or set of words that you designate. The keyword can be a topic, an author's name, or other words of your choice. Most databases allow you to restrict the keyword search to only titles or abstracts, or you can search entire articles for the keyword. This approach is considerably more flexible than subject searching, since it does not depend on the controlled vocabulary of subject searching. However, it is also more prone to return results that have little or nothing to do with your intended research topic. Just because someone uses the word "battering" in a particular article does not mean that the article has anything to do with battered women—it may be about battering rams instead.

Using a subject and a keyword approach together can improve the quality of your results. After doing a keyword search, look over the full display of the results. Many databases will tell you the subject(s) assigned to each item you have identified. You may find other useful articles by following the links to articles with a similar subject heading. Similarly, a subject search may alert you to a new term to use in a subsequent keyword search to broaden your results.

Like the Internet, databases are rapidly changing. New ones become available and old ones change their features. You need to ask a professional what electronic resources are appropriate for your search, and what special features are important. Give yourself sufficient time to play around with the databases.

Searching the Internet is surprisingly similar to searching library databases. Unfortunately, because of the sheer quantity of information available on the Internet, the chance of getting search results that have nothing to do with your intended topic increases greatly. Rather than finding hundreds of sources, you may get a hundred thousand. It is easy to feel overwhelmed.

SEARCHING THE WEB

There are two main methods of searching the Web. Instead of searching by subject and keyword, you can use search directories and search engines. *Search directories* are websites with established categories, although some do allow keyword searching. Search directories include www.yahoo.com and www.looksmart.com. Again, like the subject designations in databases, the websites found by a search directory have been organized by people who feel their categories are useful. A web directory looks like a sequence of menus: You choose a broad category, such as "Health and Medicine" and gradually narrow the category until you reach the heading you are looking for. For example, one could follow a path of categories from "Health" to "Reproductive Health" to "Pregnancy and Birth" and finally to "Midwifery." While the sites found under "Midwifery" will almost definitely have something to do with the topic, many web sites on midwifery will not be connected to the search directory you used, so you might want to try several different search directories.

Using *search engines*, on the other hand, is very similar to keyword searching, mentioned earlier. Search engines use a variety of methods to search the web for new sites and typically make no attempt to categorize them. A search engine will give you a list of Web sites that contain the words or phrases you're searching for, often sorted into relevance order. Of course, this can yield hundreds, thousands, or even tens of thousands of results, most of which will have nothing to do with your intended topic. Examples of search engines include www.altavista.com, www.google.com, www.alltheweb.com, and www.northernlight.com. Some of the search engines now include directory features. For instance, after a keyword search at www.northernlight.com, your results will be listed and grouped into categories. Thus, a search on domestic violence may provide you with categories such as family law, emergency medicine, hotlines, and current news.

Every search engine will give you different results. Not only do they use different strategies for searching and listing results, but they do not necessarily "know about" the same web sites. Some search engines cover more of the Web than others, and some will invariably return more useful sites than others. In order to try to get the best results from many search engines at once, a new breed of Web searching tool was created. Known as *metasearch engines,* these tools do not actually perform any searching of their own. They merely forward your search to a number of search engines and combine the results for you. Since no one search engine is the best, it is sometimes to your advantage to use the power of a metasearch engine when performing a Web search, because this will allow you to cover a greater amount of the Web. However, any unique or special features available in a specific search engine are lost when doing a metasearch. Examples of metasearch engines include www.dogpile.com, www.infind.com, and www.metacrawler.com.

The challenge in writing any guide to the Web is that it is an ever-changing environment. Web sites come and go, and new features appear on websites. To learn about other features, use the help option on the particular site. To check out general information on the Web, try www.searchenginewatch.com, www.notess.com/search/ and <www.learnthenet.com/english/index.html>. In addition, there are tutorials available on line, such as one prepared by the University of California at Berkeley titled "Finding Information on the Internet," available at <www.lib.berkeley.edu/TeachingLib/Guides/Internet/FindInfo.html>.

DATABASE SEARCH TECHNIQUES

Almost any search you perform, whether in a database or on the Internet, will allow you to use a wide variety of options to narrow or expand your search. The goals of using such options are to increase the relevance of your search results and to make your search easier. The most important of such options are known as wildcards, or truncation; Boolean operators, or logical operators; and phrase searching.

Using *wildcards,* or *truncation,* allows you to search for a set of words with some spelling in common, rather than for a single word, which makes the search more inclusive. A wildcard is a special character used at the end, or in the middle, of a word. For instance, if you are interested in contraception, rather than using the full word, you could truncate it and, assuming your database uses the special character asterisk as a wildcard, you could search for contracept*. Such a search would return results for "contraceptive," "contraceptives," "contraception," and any other words starting with "contracept." Or you might be interested in obtaining results for both "woman" and "women." If the wildcard in your data base is the pound sign, by specifying "wom#n," you will obtain results for both words. Searching with wildcards may give you results you did not intend, because truncation means any ending to the word becomes valid. The special wildcard characters vary by database or Internet site. Experiment with popular ones (the symbols *, $, #, and?), use the Help guide to identify the appropriate symbol, or ask a knowledgeable person.

Boolean, or logical, operators allow you to combine words in your search in ways that expand or limit the search. George Boole was a nineteenth-century mathematician who explored the use of the operators AND, OR, and NOT. These operators can be extremely useful, especially when you are performing a keyword search or using an Internet search engine. For example, combining terms, as in "women AND breast AND cancer" will limit retrieval to items containing all three words. Or "labor NOT unions" might put you in the realm of health instead of the work site. Some of the Internet search engines have a default Boolean operator in which all searches are the limiting AND searches, or they are the more inclusive OR searches.

Sometimes searching with Boolean operators does not sufficiently limit your search. You may wish to search a specific phrase. Using a Boolean operator and searching on "Down AND syndrome" will give you resources discussing how the incidence of some other *syndrome* is *down,* rather than taking you to sites about Down syndrome. *Phrase searching* will solve this problem. Some searches use quotation marks to indicate that a set of words is to be considered a phrase, making "Down syndrome" the proper way to ask for this information.

Many additional ways to refine your search are available. Some common, currently used techniques are to request a search for words that appear *next* to each other in a text (often with "adj" for adjacent), which would be another way to obtain appropriate references for Down syndrome, or to ask for words that are *near* each other. More advanced options include using combinations of Boolean operators and nesting. Thus, you might specify

> (wom#n or female*) and (work or occupation*) and (health or illness or disease)

to maximize your results in your search on women and occupational health. Some searches are *case sensitive* either for the keywords used (e.g., "Down" is different from "down"), or for Boolean operators (e.g., requiring "AND" in capital letters). As always, be aware of the possibilities, experiment, or ask someone to determine exactly how the search works.

SEARCHING LIBRARIES ONLINE

Most libraries have converted the physical card catalog to an online version, often referred to as the OPAC (Online Public Access Catalog). It allows the same author, title, and subject searching as traditional card catalogs, but in addition, it offers keyword searching.

Different libraries use different subject heading systems to catalog books. In a university library, the Library of Congress Subject Headings (LCSH) are usually used, and in a health sciences library, Medical Subject Heading (MeSH) are used. Each book is assigned to subject headings to describe its content. When you are performing a subject search, you will retrieve all the books assigned to that subject heading. Subject headings have to be searched *exactly* as they appear in the thesaurus; thus, you would search for *"fertilization, in vitro"*—the correct subject heading in MeSH and LCSH—not *"in vitro fertilization."* Title searches include book titles, journal titles, government document titles, and more.

Keyword searching for books allows the searcher to do many types of searches that are impossible with subject searching, for example, combining author and title searches, searches on publishers, searches on dates, or any combination of these.

For books not in your library, you can consult WorldCat (OCLC), an online catalog of the holdings of many libraries, which contains over 40 million records of books, journal titles, sound recordings, audiovisual materials, manuscripts, and maps—with the locations of these materials. *Books in Print,* available in paper and online, lists books currently printed in the United States. Some of the commercial online bookstores, such as www.Amazon.com or www.bn.com, may provide a more useful search approach for books, since many of the citations contain interesting reviews. If your search leads you to a book your library does not have, find out if your library can obtain it for you using the interlibrary loan system.

Whenever you start looking for more information, whether it be in a broad subject range or a very narrow field, be assured that the information you are looking for probably exists. It may not be easy to find, but with a little perseverance and creativity, success is likely. Remember to be innovative when doing a search. Do not expect that your original query will yield the results you want; be prepared to change your approach and ask for help. Think of different ways to reach the same goals, and think of ways that people might have indexed that information. Keep in mind that, especially with the advent of the Internet and its vast resources, there is no one way to find information.

The following is a short and selective list of websites that have listings of, and links to, women and health sites:

<www.ourbodiesourselves.org/annotate.htm> organized by the Boston Women's Health Book Collective

<www.library.wisc.edu/libraries/WomensStudies/core/coremain.htm> core lists prepared by the Women's Studies Section of the Association of College and Research Libraries

<aztec.lib.utk.edu/~shrode/wss_health.htm> organized by the Women's Studies Section of the Association of College and Research Libraries.

umbc7.umbc.edu/~korenman/wmst/links_hlth.html> organized by the Center for Women and Information Technology at the University of Maryland

<www.lii.org> a librarian's index to the Internet, organized by the California State Library

References

Abel, Emily K. 1991. *Who Cares for the Elderly? Public Policy and the Experiences of Adult Daughters.* Philadelphia: Temple University Press.

Abel, Emily K., and C. H. Browner. 1998. "Selective compliance with biomedical authority and the uses of experiential knowledge." Pp. 310–326 in *Pragmatic Women and Body Politics,* ed. Margaret Lock and Patricia A. Kaufert. Cambridge: Cambridge University Press.

Abraham, Laurie Kaye. 1993. *Mama Might Be Better Off Dead: The Failure of Health Care in Urban America.* Chicago: The University of Chicago Press.

Adams, Carol J. 1993. " 'I just raped my wife! What are you going to do about it, Pastor?': The church and sexual violence." Pp. 57–86 in *Transforming a Rape Culture,* ed. Emilie Buchwald, Pamela R. Fletcher, and Martha Roth. Minneapolis: Milkweed Editions.

Adams, Diane L., ed. 1995. *Health Issues for Women of Color: A Cultural Diversity Perspective.* Thousand Oaks, CA: Sage Publications.

Adelman, Ronald D., Michele G. Greene, and Rita Charon. 1991. "Issues in physician–elderly patient interaction." *Aging and Society* 11:127–148.

Ahronheim, Judith C. 1997. "End-of-life issues for very elderly women: Incurable and terminal illness." *JAMWA* 52:147–151.

Ainsworth-Vaughn, Nancy. 1998. *Claiming Power in Doctor–Patient Talk.* New York: Oxford University Press.

Allman, Richard M., William C. Yoels, and Jeffrey Michael Clair. 1993. "Reconciling the agendas of physicians and patients." Pp. 29–46 in *Sociomedical Perspectives on Patient Care,* ed. Jeffrey Michael Clair and Richard M. Allman. Lexington: University Press of Kentucky.

American Heart Association. 1999. "Tobacco industry's targeting of youth, minorities and women." Retrieved September 30, 1999, from the World Wide Web: www.americanheart.org/Heart_and_Stroke_A_Z_Guide/tobta.html

American Society of Anesthesiologists. 1999. "OB services shrinking in smaller hospitals." Retrieved November 15, 1999, from the World Wide Web: www.asahq.org/PublicEducation/Alert_0797.html

Anders, George. 1996. *Health Against Wealth: HMOs and the Breakdown of Medical Trust.* New York: Houghton Mifflin Company.

Angell, Marcia. 1996. *Science on Trial: The Clash of Medical Evidence and the Law in the Breast Implant Case.* New York: W. W. Norton.

Arditti, Rita. 1985. "Review essay: Reducing women to matter." *Women's Studies International Forum* 8:577–582.

———. 1998. "Tamoxifen: Breast cancer prevention that's hard to swallow." *Sojourner: The Women's Forum* 23:32.

Arditti, Rita, and Tatiana Schreiber. 1999. "Breast cancer: The environmental connection. A 1998 update." Pp. 463–473 in *Reconstituting Gender,* 2d ed., ed. Estelle Disch. Mountain View, CA: Mayfield Publishing.

Arenson, Karen W. 1995. "In cancer fight, a $100 million bullet." *New York Times,* 3 October: A12.

Austin, S. Bryn. 1999. "Fat, loathing and public health: The complicity of science in a culture of disordered eating." *Culture, Medicine and Psychiatry* 23:245–268.

Avery, Byllye. 1990. "Breathing life into ourselves: The evolution of the National Black Women's Health Project." Pp. 4–10 in *Black Women's Health Book,* ed. Evelyn C. White. Seattle: Seal Press.

Ayanian, John A., Betsy A. Kohler, Toshi Abe, and Arnold M. Epstein. 1993. "The relation between health insurance coverage and clinical outcomes among women with breast cancer." *NEJM* 329:326–331.

Ayanian, John Z., and Arnold M. Epstein. 1991. "Differences in the use of procedures between women and men hospitalized for coronary heart disease." *NEJM* 325:221–225.

Bachman, Ronet, and Linda E. Saltzman. 1995. "Violence against women: Estimates from the redesigned survey." *Bureau of Justice Statistics Special Report.* NCJ-154348 (August): 1–7.

Baker, Laurence C. 1996. "Differences in earnings between male and female physicians." *NEJM* 334:960–964.

Bale, Anthony. 1990. "Women's toxic experience." Pp. 411–439 in *Women, Health, and Medicine in*

America: A Historical Handbook, ed. Rima D. Apple. New York: Garland Publishing.

Banta, H. David, and Annetine Gelijns. 1987. "Health care costs: Technology and policy." Pp. 252–274 in *Health Care and its Costs,* ed. Carl J. Schramm. New York: W. W. Norton.

Banta, H. David, and Clyde J. Behney. 1981. "Policy formulation and technology assessment." *Milbank Memorial Fund Quarterly* 59:445–479.

Barbee, Evelyn L. 1993. "Racism in U.S. nursing." *Medical Anthropology Quarterly* 7:346–362.

Barbre, Joy Webster. 1993. "Meno-boomers and moral guardians: An exploration of the cultural construction of menopause." Pp. 23–35 in *Menopause: A Midlife Passage,* ed. Joan C. Callahan. Bloomington: Indiana University Press.

Barry, Patricia P. 1987. "Older women's health: Contemporary and emerging health issues. Appropriate health care for older women." *Public Health Reports Supplement* 102:71–73.

Bart, Pauline. 1987. "Seizing the means of reproduction: An illegal feminist abortion collective—how and why it worked." *Qualitative Sociology* 10:339–357.

Bart, Pauline B., Patricia Y. Miller, Eileen Moran, and Elizabeth Anne Stanko. 1989. "Guest editors' introduction." *Gender & Society* 3:431–436.

Bartholet, Elizabeth. 1992. "In vitro fertilization: The construction of infertility and of parenting." Pp. 253–260 in *Issues in Reproductive Technology I: An Anthology,* ed. Helen Bequaert Holmes. New York: Garland Publishing.

———. 1993. "Blood knots: Adoption, reproduction, and the politics of family." *American Prospect* 15:48–57.

Barzansky, Barbara, Harry S. Jonas, and Sylvia I. Etzel. 1999. "Educational programs in U.S. medical schools, 1998–1999." *JAMA* 282:840–846.

Bass, Alison. 1984. "Defining toxic exposure: A battle of semantics." *Technology Review* (May/June):25, 31.

Batt, Sharon. 1994. *Patient No More: The Politics of Breast Cancer.* Charlottetown, P.E.I., Canada: Gynergy Books.

Batt, Sharon and Liza Gross. 1999. "Cancer, Inc." *Sierra* 84:36–41,63.

Bayne-Smith, Marcia ed. 1996. *Race, Gender, and Health.* Thousand Oaks, CA: Sage Publications.

Becker, Gay, and Robert D. Nachtigall. 1994. "'Born to be a mother': The cultural construction of risk in infertility treatment in the U.S." *Social Science and Medicine* 39:507–518.

Beckman, Howard B. and Richard M. Frankel. 1984. "The effect of physician behavior on the collection of data." *Annals of Internal Medicine* 101: 692–696.

Beery, Theresa A. 1995. "Gender bias in the diagnosis and treatment of coronary artery disease." *Heart and Lung* 24:427–435.

Belkin, Lisa. 1996. "Charity begins at…the marketing meeting, the gala event, the product tie-in." *The New York Times Magazine,* 22 December:40–46, 52,55,57.

Bell, Susan. 1979. "Political gynecology: Gynecological imperialism and the politics of self help." *Science for the People* (Sept/Oct):8–14.

Berglas, Nancy. 1995. "The first FDA protest: The Network's first action." *The Network News* (Nov/Dec):1, 4–5.

Berrien, Roberta. 1992. "Outside in." *JAMA* 268:2616.

Bertin, Joan E. 1989. "Women's health and women's rights: Reproductive health hazards in the workplace." Pp. 289–301 in *Healing Technology: Feminist Perspectives,* ed. Kathryn Strother Ratcliff, Myra Marx Ferree, Gail O. Mellow, Barbara Drygulski Wright, Glenda D. Price, Kim Yanoshik, and Margie S. Freston. Ann Arbor: University of Michigan Press.

Bickell, Nina A., Jo Anne Earp, Joanne M. Garrett, and Arthur T. Evans. 1994. "Gynecologists' sex, clinical beliefs, and hysterectomy rates." *AJPH* 84:1649–1652.

Binder, Arnold, and James Meeker. 1992. "The development of social attitudes toward spousal abuse." Pp. 3–20 in *Domestic Violence: The Changing Criminal Justice Response,* ed. Eve S. Buzawa and Carl G. Buzawa. Westport, CT: Auburn House.

Birdwell, Brian G., Jerome E. Herbers, and Kurt Kroenke. 1993. "The patient's presentation style alters the physician's diagnostic approach." *Archives of Internal Medicine* 153:1991–1995.

Blank, Robert, and Janna C. Merrick. 1995. *Human Reproduction, Emerging Technologies, and Conflicting Rights.* Washington, DC: Congressional Quarterly Press.

Blank, Robert H. 1990. *Regulating Reproduction.* New York: Columbia University Press.

———. 1993. *Fetal Protection in the Workplace: Women's Rights, Business Interests, and the Unborn.* New York: Columbia University Press.

Bleier, Ruth. 1985. "Biology and women's policy: A view from the biological sciences." Pp. 19–40 in *Women, Biology, and Public Policy,* ed. Virginia Sapiro. Thousand Oaks, CA: Sage Publications.

———. 1988. "*Science* and the construction of meanings in the neurosciences." Pp. 91–104 in *Feminism within the Science and Health Care Professions: Overcoming Resistance,* ed. Sue V. Rosser. New York: Pergamon Press.

Bloom, Amy. 1995. "The pill hearings: Alice Wolfson breaks the silence." *The Network News* (Jan/Feb). Retrieved February 4, 2000, from the World Wide Web: www.womenshealthnetwork.org/NN%20articles/phearing

Bockman, Richard Steven. 1997. "Osteoporosis and its management in older women." *JAMWA* 52:121–126.

Bonnicksen, Andrea L. 1989. "Human embryo freezing and public policy: Patterns and directions." Pp. 3–19 in *Biomedical Technology and Public Policy,* ed. Robert H. Blank and Miriam K. Mills. New York: Greenwood.

Boston Women's Health Book Collective (BWHBC). 1998. *Our Bodies, Ourselves for the New Century.* New York: Simon & Schuster.

Bowen, Deborah J., Nicole Urban, David Carrell, and Susan Kinne. 1993. "Comparisons of strategies to prevent breast cancer mortality." *Journal of Social Issues* 49:35–60.

Bower, Bruce. 1991. "Marked questions on elderly depression." *Science News* 140:310–312.

Bowler, Rosemarie M., Donna Mergler, Stephen S. Rauch, and Russell P. Bowler. 1992. "Stability of psychological impairment: Two year follow-up of former microelectronics workers' affective and personality disturbance." *Women & Health* 18:27–48.

Britton, Brandy M. 1997. "The battered women's movement." Pp. 486–492 in *Women's Health: Complexities and Differences,* ed. Sheryl Burt Ruzek, Virginia L. Olesen, and Adele E. Clark. Columbus: Ohio State University Press.

Brody, Jane E. 1995. "Even moderate weight gain can be risky, a study finds." *New York Times.* September 14:A1, B13.

Brown, E. Richard. 1979. *Rockefeller Medicine Men: Medicine and Capitalism in America.* Berkeley: University of California Press.

Brown, Phil, and Faith I. T. Ferguson. 1995. " 'Making a big stink': Women's work, women's relationships, and toxic waste activism." *Gender & Society* 9:145–172.

Browner, Carole H., and Nancy Ann Press. 1995. "The normalization of prenatal diagnostic screening." Pp. 307–322 in *Conceiving the New World Order: The Global Politics of Reproduction,* ed. Faye D. Ginsburg and Rayna Rapp. Berkeley: University of California Press.

Brozan, Nadine. 1991. "Health risks rise with close of gynecological clinics." *New York Times.* March 25:B1, B2

Brumberg, Joan Jacobs. 1997. *The Body Project: An Intimate History of American Girls.* New York: Random House.

Buchwald, Emilie, Pamela R. Fletcher, and Martha Roth. 1993. "Preamble." Pp. vii in *Transforming a Rape Culture,* ed. Emilie Buchwald, Pamela R. Fletcher, and Martha Roth. Minneapolis: Milkweed Editions.

Bullough, Vern, and Martha Voght. 1973. "Women, menstruation, and nineteenth-century medicine." *Bulletin of the History of American Medicine* 47: 66–82.

Bureau of Labor Statistics. 1997. "Injuries to caregivers working in patient's homes." *Issues in Labor Statistics* Summary 97:4.

———. 1999. "1998–99 Occupational Outlook Handbook." Washington, DC: Bureau of Labor Statistics.

———. 2000. "Table 1: Union affiliation of employed wage and salary workers by selected characteristics." Retrieved January 14, 2000, from the World Wide Web: http://stats.bls.gov/news.release/union2.t01.htm

Bureau of the Census. 1999. "Table 11. Employed persons by detailed occupation, sex, race, and Hispanic origin." Retrieved August 2, 1999, from the World Wide Web: ftp.bls.gov/pub/special.requests/lf/aat11.txt

Burke, Carol. 1997. "Dames at sea: Life in the Naval Academy." Pp. 146–150 in *Gender Violence: Interdisciplinary Perspectives,* ed. Laura L. O'Toole and Jessica R. Schiffman. New York: New York University Press.

Bush, Corlann Gee. 1983. "Women and the assessment of technology: To think, to be; to unthink, to free." Pp. 151–170 in *Machina ex Dea: Feminist Perspectives on Technology,* ed. Joan Rothschild. New York: Pergamon Press.

Bush, Trudy L., and Maura K. Whiteman. 1999. "Hormone replacement therapy and risk of breast cancer." *JAMA* 281:2140–2141.

Buzawa, Eve S., and Carl G. Buzawa. 1993. "The impact of arrest on domestic violence: Introduction." *American Behavioral Scientist* 36:558–574.

———, eds. 1996. *Do Arrests and Restraining Orders Work?* Thousand Oaks, CA: Sage Publications.

Cahn, Naomi R. 1992. "Innovative approaches to the prosecution of domestic violence crimes: An overview." Pp. 161–180 in *Domestic Violence: The Changing Criminal Justice Response,* ed. Eve S. Buzawa and Carl G. Buzawa. Westport, CT: Auburn House.

Camp, Lois. 1991. "Numbers, numbers, numbers." Pp. 97–103 in *1 in 3: Women with Cancer Confront an Epidemic,* ed. Judith Brady. Pittsburgh: Cleis Press.

Caplan, Paula J. 1995. *They Say You're Crazy: How the World's Most Powerful Psychiatrists Decide Who's Normal.* New York: Addison-Wesley.

Capron, Alexander Morgan. 1998. "Too many parents." *The Hastings Center Report* (September):22–24.

Carlson, Karen J., and Susan E. Skochelak. 1998. "What do women want in a doctor? Communication issues between women and physicians." Pp. 33–38 in *Textbook of Women's Health,* ed. Lila A. Wallis. New York: Lippincott-Raven.

Cash, Thomas F., and Patricia E. Henry. 1995. "Women's body images: The results of a national survey in the U.S.A." *Sex Roles* 33:19–28.

Casper, Monica J. 1998. *The Making of the Unborn Patient: A Social Anatomy of Fetal Surgery.* New Brunswick: Rutgers University Press.

Cassell, Eric J. 1986a. "The changing concept of the ideal physician." *Daedulus* 115:185–208.

———. 1986b. "Ideas in conflict: The rise and fall (and rise and fall) of new views of disease." *Daedalus* 115:185–208.

Caton, Donald. 1999. *What a Blessing She Had Chloroform: The Medical and Social Response to the Pain of Childbirth from 1800 to the Present.* New Haven: Yale University Press.

Centers for Disease Control (CDC). 1995. "Update: AIDS among women—United States, 1994." *Morbidity and Mortality Weekly Report* 44:81–84.

Chaney, Carole Kennedy, and Grace Hall Saltzstein. 1998. "Democratic control and bureaucratic responsiveness: The police and domestic violence." *American Journal of Political Science* 42: 745–768.

Chang, Sophia W., Karla Kerlikowske, Anna Napoles-Springer, Samuel F. Posner, Edward A. Sickles, and Eliseo J. Perez-Stable. 1996. "Racial differences in timeliness of follow-up after abnormal screening mammography." *Cancer* 78:1395–1402.

Charney, William. 1999. "An epidemic of health care worker injury." Pp. 1–9 in *The Epidemic of Health Care Worker Injury: An Epidemiology,* ed. William Charney and Guy Fragala. New York: CRC Press.

Charney, William, and Guy Fragala. 1999. *The Epidemic of Health Care Worker Injury: An Epidemiology.* New York: CRC Press.

Chasnoff, Ira J., Harvey J. Landress, and Mark E. Barrett. 1990. "The prevalance of illicit-drug or alcohol use during pregnancy and discrepancies in mandatory reporting in Pinellas County, Florida." *NEJM* 322:1202–1206.

Chavkin, Wendy. 1996. "Mandatory treatment for pregnant substance abusers: irrelevant and dangerous." *Politics and the Life Sciences,* March:53–54.

Chavkin, Wendy, Paul H. Wise, and Deborah Elman. 1998. "Topics for our times: Welfare reform and women's health." *AJPH* 88:1017–1018.

Chesler, Ellen. 1992. *Woman of Valor: Margaret Sanger and the Birth Control Movement in America.* New York: Simon & Schuster.

Choi, Precilla Y. L. 1995. "The menstrual cycle and premenstrual syndrome: What is this news on the menstrual cycle and premenstrual syndrome?" *Social Science and Medicine* 41:759–760.

Chrisler, Joan C., and Karen B. Levy. 1990. "The media construct a menstrual monster: A content analysis of PMS articles in the popular press." *Women & Health* 16:89–104.

Cleeland, Charles S. 1998. "Undertreatment of cancer pain in elderly patients." *JAMA* 279:1914–1915.

Cleland, Richard, Dean C. Graybill, Van Hubbard, Laura Kettel Khan, Judith S. Stern, Thomas A. Wadden, Roland Weinsier, and Susan Yanovski. 1997. "Commercial Weight Loss Products and Programs: What Consumers Stand to Gain and Lose. A Public Conference on the Information Consumers Need To Evaluate Weight Loss Products and Programs. Report of the Presiding Panel." Washington, DC: Federal Trade Commission.

Cockerham, William C. 1997. *This Aging Society.* Upper Saddle River, NJ: Prentice Hall.

Cohen, Cynthia B, ed. 1996. *New Ways of Making Babies: The Case of Egg Donation.* Bloomington: Indiana University Press.

Cohen, Stuart J., Deirdre Robinson, Elizabeth Dugan, George Howard, Patricia K. Suggs, Katherine F.

Pearce, Dena D. Carroll, Paul McGann, and John Preisser. 1999. "Communication between older adults and their physicians about urinary incontinence." *The Journals of Gerontology* 54:34–37.

The Collective. 1997. "Feminist strategies: The terms of negotiation." Pp. 83–93 in *Feminists Negotiate the State: The Politics of Domestic Violence,* ed. Cynthia R. Daniels. New York: University Press of America.

Collins, Barbara S., Roberta B. Hollander, Dyann Matson Koffman, Rebecca Reeve, and Susan Seidler. 1997. "Women, work, and health: Issues and implications for worksite health promotion." *Women & Health* 25:3–30.

"The commodification and advertising of infertility treatment." 1997. *Women's Health Issues* 7:149–152.

Condit, Deirdre Moira. 1995. "Fetal personhood: Political identity under construction." Pp. 25–54 in *Expecting Trouble: Surrogacy, Fetal Abuse, and New Reproductive Technologies,* ed. Patricia Boling. San Francisco: Westview Press.

Conley, Frances. 1998. *Walking Out on the Boys.* New York: Farrar, Straus, and Giroux.

Connolly, Heidi M., Jack L. Crary, Michael D. McGoon, Donald D. Hensrud, Brooks S. Edwards, William D. Edwards, and Hartzell V. Schaff. 1997. "Valvular heart disease associated with fenfluramine-phentermine." *NEJM* 337:581–588.

Cooper, James W. 1994. "Drug-related problems in the elderly patient." *Generations* (summer):19–27.

Cooper-Patrick, Lisa, Joseph J. Gallo, Junius J. Gonzales, Hong Thi Vu, Neil R. Powe, Christine Nelson, and Daniel E. Ford. 1999. "Race, gender, and partnership in the patient–physician relationship." *JAMA* 282:583–589.

Corea, Gena. 1985. *The Hidden Malpractice.* New York: Harper and Row.

Cowan, Alison Leigh. 1992. "Can a baby-making venture deliver." *New York Times* (June 1):D1, D6

Crawshaw, Ralph. 1983. "Technical zeal or therapeutic purpose: How to decide?" *JAMA* 250:857–859.

Crenshaw, Kimberle. 1991. "Mapping the margins: Intersectionality, identity politics, and violence against women of color." Pp. 625–629 in *Women and the Law,* ed. Judith G. Greenberg, Martha L. Minow, and Dorothy E. Roberts. New York: Foundation Press.

Dalaker, Joseph. 1999. "U.S. Census Bureau, Current Population Reports, Series P60-207," *Poverty in the United States: 1998.* Washington, DC: U.S. Government Printing Office.

"The Dalkon Shield story: A company rewarded for its faulty product." 1996. *Health Facts* 21:1–2.

Daniels, Cynthia. 1997. "Introduction: The paradoxes of state power." Pp. 1–4 in *Feminists Negotiate the State: The Politics of Domestic Violence,* ed. Cynthia Daniels. New York: University Press of America.

Darby, Jan. 1992. "Sex and punishment: The politics of cervical cancer." *Healthsharing* (summer/fall):24–26.

Davies, Kevin, and Michael White. 1996. *Breakthrough: The Race to Find the Breast Cancer Gene.* New York: John Wiley & Sons.

Davis, Angela Y. 1986. "Racism, birth control, and reproductive rights." Pp. 239–255 in *All American Women: Lines That Divide, Ties That Bind,* ed. Johnnetta B. Cole. New York: The Free Press.

Davis, Devra Lee, and H. Leon Bradlow. 1995. "Can environmental estrogens cause breast cancer?" *Scientific American* 273:166–170.

Davis, Devra Lee, Deborah Axelrod, Michael P. Osborne, and Nitin T. Telang. 1999. "Environmental influences on breast cancer risk." Retrieved July 7, 1999, from the World Wide Web: www.wri.org/wri/health/med-e-br.html

Davis, Shiela P., and Cora A. Ingram. 1993. "Empowered caretakers: A historical perspective on the roles of granny midwives in rural Alabama." Pp. 191–201 in *Wings of Gauze: Women of Color and the Experience of Health and Illness,* ed. Barbara Bair and Susan E. Cayleff. Detroit: Wayne State University Press.

Davis-Floyd, Robbie. 1992. *Birth as an American Right of Passage.* Berkeley: University of California Press.

Davis-Floyd, Robbie, and Elizabeth Davis. 1997. "Intuition as authoritative knowledge in midwifery and home birth." Pp. 315–349 in *Childbirth and Authoritative Knowledge: Cross Cultural Perspectives.* ed. Robbie Davis-Floyd and Carolyn F. Sargent. Berkeley: University of California Press.

De la Torre, Adela, Robert Friis, Harold R. Hunter, and Lorena Garcia. 1996. "The health status of US Latino women: A profile from the 1982–1884 HHANES." *AJPH* 86:533–537.

Dearing, Ruthie H., Helen A. Gordon, Dorolyn M. Sohner, and Lynne C. Weidel. 1987. *Marketing*

Women's Health Care. Rockville, MD: Aspen Publishers.

Delaney, Janice, Mary Jane Lupton, and Emily Toth. 1988. *The Curse: A Cultural History of Menstruation.* Chicago: University of Illinois Press.

Dew, Mary Amanda, Evelyn J. Bromet, David K. Parkinson, Leslie O. Dunn, and Christopher M. Ryan. 1989. "Effects of solvent exposure and occupational stress on the health of blue-collar women." Pp. 327–345 in *Healing Technology: Feminist Perspectives,* ed. Kathryn Strother Ratcliff, Myra Marx Ferree, Gail O. Mellow, Barbara Drygulski Wright, Glenda D. Price, Kim Yanoshik, and Margie S. Freston. Ann Arbor: University of Michigan Press.

Dickson, Geri L. 1993. "Metaphors of menopause: The metalanguage of menopause research." Pp. 36–58 in *Menopause: A Midlife Passage,* ed. Joan C. Callahan. Bloomington: Indiana University Press.

Dobash, R. Emerson, and Russell P. Dobash. 1988. "Research as social action: The struggle for battered women." Pp. 51–74 in *Feminist Perspectives on Wife Abuse,* ed. Kersti Yllo and Michele Bograd. Beverly Hills: Sage Publications.

Donat, Patricia L. N., and John D'Emilio. 1992. "A feminist redefinition of rape and sexual assault: Historical foundations and change." *Journal of Social Issues* 48:9–22.

Dorin, Maxine H. 1998. "Hysterectomy and adnexectomy." Pp. 955–959 in *Textbook of Women's Health,* ed. Lila A. Wallis. Philadelphia: Lippincott-Raven.

Doyal, Lesley. 1995. *What Makes Women Sick: Gender and the Political Economy of Health.* New Brunswick: Rutgers University Press.

Dresser, Rebecca. 1992. "Wanted: Single, white male for medical research." *Hastings Center Report* (January–February): 24–29.

Dujon, Diane, and Ann Withorn. 1996. "'Buked and scorned: Beyond ending welfare as we know it." Pp. 155–161 in *For Crying Out Loud: Women's Poverty in the United States,* ed. Diane Dujon and Ann Withorn. Boston: South End Press.

Dull, Diana, and Candace West. 1991. "Accounting for cosmetic surgery: The accomplishment of gender." *Social Problems* 38:54–70.

Durand, A. Mark. 1992. "The safety of home birth: The Farm study." *AJPH* 82:450–452.

Dutton, Diana B. 1988. *Worse than the Disease: Pitfalls of Medical Progress.* Cambridge: Cambridge University Press.

Eagan, Andrea Boroff. 1994. "The women's health movement and its lasting impact." Pp. 15–27 in *An Unfinished Revolution: Women and Health Care in America,* ed. Emily Friedman. New York: United Hospital Fund of New York.

Edelman, Toby S. 1997. "The politics of long-term care at the federal level and implications for quality." *Generations* 21:37–41.

Ehrenreich, Barbara. 1992. "Stamping out a dread scourge." *Time* (17 February):88.

El-Askari, Elaine, and Barbara DeBaun. 1999. "The occupational hazards of home health care." Pp. 201–213 in *The Epidemic of Health Care Worker Injury: An Epidemiology,* ed. William Charney and Guy Fragala. New York: CRC Press.

Elderkin-Thompson, Virginia, and Howard Waitzkin. 1999. "Differences in clinical communication by gender." *Journal of General Internal Medicine* 14:112–121.

Eley, J. William, Holly A. Hill, Vivien W. Chen, Donald F. Austin, Margaret N. Wesley, Hyman B. Muss, Raymond S. Greenberg, Ralph J. Coates, Pelayo Correa, Carol K. Redmond, Carrie P. Hunter, Allen A. Herman, Robert Kurman, Robert Blacklow, Sam Shapiro, and Brenda K. Edwards. 1994. "Racial differences in survival from breast cancer." *JAMA* 272:947–954.

Elias, Marilyn. 1993. "Mind and menopause." *Harvard Health Letter* 19:1–3.

Elmore, Joann G., Carolyn K. Wells, Carol H. Lee, Debra H. Howard, and Alvan R. Feinstein. 1994. "Variability in radiologists' interpretations of mammograms." *NEJM* 331:1493–1499.

Emanuel, Ezekiel J., Diane L. Fairclough, Julia Slutsman, Hillel Alpert, DeWitt Baldwin, and Linda L. Emanuel. 1999. "Assistance from family members, friends, paid care givers, and volunteers in the care of terminally ill patients." *NEJM* 941:956–963.

Engel, George L. 1988. "How much longer must medicine's science be bound by a seventeenth century world view?" Pp. 113–136 in *The Task of Medicine,* ed. Kerr L. White. Menlo Park, CA: The Henry J. Kaiser Family Foundation.

England, Paula, and Nancy Folbre. 1999. "The cost of caring." *The Annals of the American Academy of Political and Social Science* 561:39–51.

Epstein, Samuel S. 1999. "American Cancer Society: The world's wealthiest 'nonprofit' institution." *International Journal of Health Services* 29:565–578.

Epstein, Samuel. 1998. "Winning the war against cancer?... Are they even fighting it?" *The Ecologist* 28:69–80.

Equal Employment Opportunity Commission (EEOC). 1997. "Facts about sexual harrassment." Retrieved on October 19, 1999, from the World Wide Web: www.eeoc.gov/facts/fs-sex.html

Erickson, Judith. 1987. "Women in the workplace." *Professional Safety* (Feb):30–37.

Estrich, Susan. 1991. "Sex at work." *Stanford Law Review* 43:813–861.

Families-USA. 1999. "Welfare-Medicaid Links: What Every Welfare Advocate Should Know about Medicaid." Retrieved September 21, 1999, from the World Wide Web: http://www.familiesusa.org/whatwelf.htm

Farmer, Paul. 1996. "Women, poverty, and AIDS." Pp. 3–38 in *Women, Poverty, and AIDS: Sex, Drugs, and Structural Violence,* ed. Paul Farmer, Margaret Connors, and Janie Simmons. Monroe, ME: Common Courage Press.

Fausto-Sterling, Anne. 1985. *Myths of Gender: Biological Theories about Women and Men.* New York: Basic Books.

Feldman, Penny Hollander, Alice M. Sapienza, and Nancy M. Kane. 1990. *Who Cares for Them? Workers in the Home Care Industry.* New York: Greenwood Press.

Ferraro, Kathleen J. 1989. "Policing woman battering." *Social Problems* 36:61–74.

Figert, Anne E. 1996. *Women and the Ownership of PMS: The Structuring of a Psychiatric Disorder.* Hawthorne, NY: Aldine De Gruyter.

Finkel, Elizabeth. 1998. "Phyto-oestrogens: The way to postmenopausal health?" *The Lancet* 352:1762+.

Fisher, Sue. 1988. *In the Patient's Best Interest: Women and the Politics of Medical Decisions.* New Brunswick: Rutgers University Press.

Flamm, Bruce L. 1993. "America's most common operation." *Medical Interface* (October):71–81.

Food and Drug Administration (FDA). 1998. "Breast Implants: An Informational Update." Retrieved July 16, 1999, from the World Wide Web: www.fda.gov/cdrh/breastimplants/

Fossett, James W., Janet D. Perloff, John A. Peterson, and Phillip R. Kletke. 1990. "Medicaid in the inner city: The case of maternity care in Chicago." *The Milbank Quarterly* 68:111–141.

Fouts, Gregory, and Kimberley Burggraf. 1999. "Television situation comedies: Female body images and verbal reinforcements." *Sex Roles: A Journal of Research* 40:473–481.

Fox, Steve. 1991. *Toxic Work: Women Workers at GTE Lenkurt.* Philadelphia: Temple University Press.

Frank, Erica, Donna Brogan, and Melissa Schiffman. 1998. "Prevalence and correlates of harassment among U.S. women physicians." *Archives of Internal Medicine* 158:352–358.

Frankel, Richard M., and Howard B. Beckman. 1993. "Teaching communication skills to medical students and house officers: An integrated approach." Pp. 211–222 in *Sociomedical Perspectives on Patient Care,* ed. Jeffrey Michael Clair and Richard M. Allman. Lexington: The University Press of Kentucky.

Freedman, Rita. 1986. *Beauty Bound.* Lexington, MA: Lexington Books.

Freund, Peter E. S. and Meredith B. McGuire. 1995. *Health, Illness, and the Social Body.* 2d ed. Englewood Cliffs, NJ: Prentice Hall.

Friedan, Betty. 1993. *The Fountain of Age.* New York: Simon & Schuster.

Friedman-Jimenez, George, Ricky Lee Langley, Lynn V. Mitchell, and Kathryn L. Mueller. 1994a. "Lung and skin disorders." *Patient Care* 28:48–50, 55, 58, 61–62, 69–73.

———. 1994b. "Radiation, repetitive motion, and other job hazards." *Patient Care* 28:77–88.

Frohmann, Lisa. 1997. "Convictability and discordant locales: Reproducing race, class, and gender ideologies in prosecutorial decisionmaking." *Law & Society Review* 31:531–555.

Fugh-Berman, Adriane. 1992. "Tales out of medical school." *The Nation.* January 20:1, 54–56

Fugh-Berman, Adriane. 1996. *Alternative Medicine: What Works.* Tucson, AZ: Odonian Press.

Fugh-Berman, Adriane, and Samuel Epstein. 1992. "Tamoxifen: Disease prevention or disease substitution?" *The Lancet* 340:1143–1145.

Furey, Darlene. 1997. "Foreword." Pp. vii–viii in *Feminists Negotiate the State: The Politics of Domestic Violence,* ed. Cynthia R. Daniels. New York: University Press of America.

Gabay, Mary, and Sidney M. Wolfe. 1997. "Nurse-midwifery: The beneficial alternative." *Public Health Reports* 112:386–394.

Galambos, Colleen M. 1998. "Preserving end-of-life autonomy: The Patient Self-Determination Act and the Uniform Health Care Decisions Act." *Health and Social Work* 23:275–281.

Garrow, David J. 1999. "Abortion before and after *Roe v. Wade:* A historical perspective." *Albany Law Review* 62:833–852.

Gazmararian, Julie A., Suzanne Lazorick, Alison M. Spitz, Terri J. Ballard, Linda E. Saltzman, and James S. Marks. 1996. "Prevalence of violence against pregnant women." *JAMA* 275: 1915–1920.

Geiger, H. Jack. 1984. "Community Health Centers: Health care as an instrument of social change." Pp. 11–32 in *Reforming Medicine: Lessons from the Last Quarter Century,* ed. Victor W. Sidel and Ruth Sidel. New York: Pantheon Books.

George, Linda K. 1999. "Social perspectives on the self in later life." Pp. 42–66 in *The Self and Society in Aging Processes,* ed. Carol D. Ryff and Victor W. Marshall. New York: Springer.

Gifford, Blair. 1997. "Obstetricians' receptiveness to teen prenatal patients who are Medicaid recipients." *Health Services Research* 32:265–282.

Gilman, Charlotte Perkins. 1935. *The Living of Charlotte Perkins Gilman: An Autobiography.* New York: D. Appleton-Century Company.

Glazer, Nona Y. 1991. "'Between a rock and a hard place': Women's professional organizations in nursing and class, racial, and ethnic inequalities." *Gender & Society* 5:351–372.

Glazer, Sarah. 1993. "Violence against women: The issues." *CQ Researcher* 3:171–178.

Glenn, Evelyn Nakano. 1992. "From servitude to service work: Historical continuities in the racial division of paid reproductive labor." *Signs: Journal of Women in Culture and Society* 18:1–43.

Goff, Barbara A., Howard G. Muntz and Joanna M. Cain. 1997. "Is Adam worth more than Eve?: The financial impact of gender bias in the federal reimbursement of gynecologic procedures." *Gynecologic Oncology* 64:372–377.

Goldstein, Jan. 1987. *Console and Classify: The French Psychiatric Profession in the Nineteenth Century.* New York: Cambridge University Press.

Goldstein, Michael S. 1999. *Alternative Health Care: Medicine, Miracle, or Mirage?* Philadelphia: Temple University Press.

Golub, Sharon. 1992. *Periods: From Menarche to Menopause.* Newbury Park, CA: Sage Publications.

Gonzalez, Martin L. 1999. "Median unadjusted net income among non-federal physicians (excluding residents)." Chicago: AMA Center for Health Policy Research.

Gordon, Linda. 1976. *Woman's Body, Woman's Right: A Social History of Birth Control in America.* New York: Grossman Publishers.

Gordon, Linda. 1988. *Heroes of Their Own Lives: The Politics and History of Family Violence. Boston 1880–1960.* New York: Viking Penguin.

Gordon, Suzanne. 1997. "The impact of managed care on female caregivers in the hospital and home." *JAMWA* 52:75–80.

Gortmaker, Steven L., Aviva Must, James M. Perrin, Arthur M. Sobol, and William H. Dietz. 1993. "Social and economic consequences of overweight in adolescence and young adulthood." *NEJM* 329:1008–1012.

Gosden, Roger. 1999. *Designing Babies: The Brave New World of Reproductive Technology.* New York: W. H. Freeman.

Graham, Bob. 1999. "Anti-dumping law is good for residents and facilities." *McKnight's Long-Term Care News* 20:43–44.

Graham, Hilary. 1985. "Providers, negotiators, and mediators: women as the hidden carers." Pp. 25–52 in *Women, Health, and Healing: Toward a New Perspective,* ed. Ellen Lewin and Virginia Olesen. New York: Tavistock Publications.

Grant, Linda. 1988. "The gender climate of medical school: perspectives of women and men students." *JAMWA* 43:109–119.

Greenberg, Brigitte. 1999. "Wanted: Tall, smart, fertile." *Hartford Courant,* 28 February:B4.

Greenberg, Judith G., Martha L. Minow, and Dorothy E. Roberts. 1998a. "Sexual harassment: Legal regulation of sex in the workplace." Pp. 284–286 in *Women and the Law,* ed. Judith G. Greenberg, Martha L. Minow, and Dorothy E. Roberts. New York: Foundation Press.

———. 1998b. *Women and the Law.* New York: Foundation Press.

Griffith, Pamela J. 1997. "Medical and social dynamics of college women's interactions with their gynecologists." *Sociological Inquiry* 67: 397–408.

Grisso, Jeane Ann, Amy R. Wishner, Donald F. Schwartz, Barbara A. Weene, John H. Holmes, and Rudolph L. Sutton. 1991. "A population-based study of injuries in inner-city women." *American Journal of Epidemiology* 134:59–68.

Guillemin, Jeanne. 1981. "Babies by cesarean: Who chooses, who controls?" *Hastings Center Report* 11:15–18.

Guo, How-Ran, Shiro Tanaka, William E. Halperin, and Lorraine L. Cameron. 1999. "Back pain prevalence in U.S. industry and estimates of lost workdays." *AJPH* 89:1029–1035.

Gurevich, Maria. 1995. "Rethinking the label: Who benefits from the PMS construct?" *Women & Health* 23:67–98.

Haas-Wilson, Deborah. 1993. "The economic impact of state restrictions on abortion: Parental consent and notification laws and Medicaid funding restrictions." *Journal of Policy Analysis and Management* 12:498–511.

Haiken, Elizabeth. 1997. *Venus Envy: A History of Cosmetic Surgery.* Baltimore: The Johns Hopkins University Press.

Hamburg, Paul. 1996. "Body weight and mortality among women." *NEJM* 334:732.

Hand, Roger, Stephen Sener, Joseph Imperato, Joan S. Chimel, JoAnne Sylvester, and Amy Fregman. 1991. "Hospital variables associated with quality of care for breast cancer patients." *JAMA.* 266: 3429–3432.

Hanlon, J. T., R. D. Horner, K. E. Schmader, G. G. Fillenbaum, I. K. Lewis, W. E. Wall Jr., L. R. Landerman, C. F. Pieper, D. G. Blaze, and H. J. Cohen. 1998. "Benzodiazepine use and cognitive function among community-dwelling elderly." *Clinical Pharmacology and Therapeutics* 64:684–692.

Harding, Sandra. 1991. *Whose Science? Whose Knowledge? Thinking from Women's Lives.* Ithaca, NY: Cornell University Press.

Harrington, Michael. 1997. *The Other America: Poverty in the United States.* New York: Simon & Schuster.

Hartley, Heather. 1999. "The influence of managed care on supply of certified nurse-midwives: An evaluation of the physician dominance thesis." *Journal of Health and Social Behavior* 40:87–101.

Haskins, Katherine M., and H. Edward Ransford. 1999. "The relationship between weight and career payoffs among women." *Sociological Forum* 14:295–318.

Hayes, Dennis. 1989. *Behind the Silicon Curtain: The Seductions of Work in a Lonely Era.* Boston: South End Press.

Hayt, Elizabeth. 1999. "Vanity goes to the doctor." *New York Times.* 14 November:9:1–2.

Healy, Bernadine. 1991. "The Yentl Syndrome." *NEJM* 325:274–276.

———. 1995. *A New Prescription for Women's Health.* New York: Penguin Books.

Heaney, Robert P. 1998. "Osteoporosis." Pp. 445–454 in *Textbook of Women's Health,* ed. Lila A. Wallis. New York: Lippincott-Raven.

Henefin, Mary S. 1993. "New reproductive technologies: Equity and access to reproductive health care." *Journal of Social Issues* 49:61–74.

Hennekens, Charles H., I-Min Lee, Nancy R. Cook, Patricia R. Hebert, Elizabeth W. Karlson, Fran LaMotte, JoAnn E. Manson, and Julie E. Buring. 1996. "Self-reported breast implants and connective-tissue diseases in female health professionals." *JAMA* 275:616–621.

Hesse-Biber, Sharlene. 1996. *Am I Thin Enough Yet?: The Cult of Thinness and the Commercialization of Identity.* New York: Oxford University Press.

Himmelstein, David U., James P. Lewontin, and Steffie Woolhandler. 1996. "Medical care employment in the United States, 1968 to 1993: The importance of health sector jobs for African Americans and women." *AJPH* 86:525–528.

Hine, Darlene Clark. 1989. *Black Women in White: Racial Conflict and Cooperation in the Nursing Profession, 1890–1950.* Bloomington: Indiana University Press.

Hinze, Susan W. 1999. "Gender and the body of medicine or at least some body parts: (Re)constructing the prestige hierarchy of medical specialities." *The Sociological Quarterly* 40:217–239.

Hitt, Greg. 1999. "Old women's hope fades for Social Security overhaul." *Wall Street Journal.* September 24: A16.

Hochschild, Arlie Russell. 1983. *The Managed Heart: Commercialization of Human Feeling.* Berkeley: University of California Press.

Hoffman, Catherine. 1998. *Uninsured in America: A Chart Book.* Washington, DC: Kaiser Commission on Medicaid and the Uninsured.

Horton, Jacqueline A., ed. 1992. *The Women's Health Data Book.* New York: Elsevier.

Houppert, Karen. 1999. "You're not entitled! Welfare reform is leading to government lawlessness." *The Nation.* October 25:11–13,15,17–18.

Hubbard, Ruth. 1990. *The Politics of Women's Biology.* New Brunswick: Rutgers University Press.

———. 1995. *Profitable Promises: Essays on Women, Science and Health.* Monroe, ME: Common Courage Press.

Hubbard, Ruth, and R. C. Lewontin. 1996. "Pitfalls of genetic testing." *NEJM* 334:1192–1194.

Hulley, Stephen. "Randomized trial of estrogen plus progestin for secondary prevention of coronary heart disease in post-menopausal women." *JAMA* 280:605–613.

Iezzoni, Lisa I., Arlene S. Ash, Michael Shwartz, and Yevgenia D. Mackiernan. 1997. "Differences in procedure use, in-hospital mortality, and illness severity by gender for acute myocardial infarction patients." *Medical Care* 35:158–171.

"IVF America." (Advertisement) 1992. *New York Times.* November 19:BQLI.C9.

Jackson, Donald Dale. 1994. "The art of wishful shrinking has made a lot of people rich." *Smithsonian* 25:147–156.

Jeffress, Charles N. 1999. "Work-related musculoskeletal disorders." Speech at the *National Coalition of Ergonomics,* April 29, Washington, DC. Retrieved January 27, 2001, from the World Wide Web: www.osha-slc.govOshDocSpeech_data/SP19990429.html

Jones, Ann. 1994. *Next Time, She'll be Dead: Battering and How to Stop It.* Boston: Beacon Press.

Jones, Deborah L. 1996. "Father knows best...?" Pp. 59–80 in *Women in Medical Education: An Anthology of Experience,* edited by Delese Wear. Albany: State University of New York Press.

Jonsen, Albert R. 1988. "Women's choices—the ethics of maternity." *Western Journal of Medicine* 149:726–728.

Kaplan, Laura. 1995. *The Story of Jane: The Legendary Underground Feminist Abortion Service.* New York: Pantheon Books.

Kapsalis, Terri. 1997. *Public Privates: Performing Gynecology from Both Ends of the Speculum.* Durham: Duke University Press.

Kasper, Anne S. 1985. "Hysterectomy as social process." *Women and Health* 10:109–127.

———. 1994. "A feminist, qualititative methodology: A study of women with breast cancer." *Qualitative Sociology* 17:263–281.

Kassirer, Jerome P., and Marcia Angell. 1998. "Losing weight—an ill-fated New Year's resolution." *NEJM* 338:52–54.

Kaw, Eugenia. 1993. "Medicalization of racial features: Asian American women and cosmetic surgery." *Medical Anthropology Quarterly* 7:74–89.

Kaye, Lenard W., and Susan I. Reisman. 1991. "Life prolongation technologies in home care for the frail elderly: Issues for training, policy, and research." *Journal of Gerontological Social Work* 16:79–91.

Keller, Evelyn Fox. 1983. *A Feeling for the Organism: The Life and Work of Barbara McClintock.* San Francisco: W. H. Freeman and Company.

Kemp, Alice Abel, and Pamela Jenkins. 1992. "Gender and technological hazards: women at risk in hospital settings." *Industrial Crisis Quarterly* 6:137–152.

Kemper, Peter, and Christopher M. Murtaugh. 1991. "Lifetime use of nursing home care." *NEJM* 324:595–600.

Kennell, John, Marshall Klaus, Susan McGrath, Steven Robertson, and Clark Hinkley. 1991. "Continuous emotional support during labor in a U.S. hospital." *JAMA* 265:2197–2201.

King, Charles R. 1993. "Calling Jane: The life and death of a women's illegal abortion service." *Women & Health* 20:75–93.

Klass, Perri. 1984. "Bearing a child in medical school." *New York Times Magazine* November 11:120–125.

Klawiter, Maren. 1999. "Racing for the cure, walking women, and toxic touring: Mapping cultures of action within the Bay Area terrain of breast cancer." *Social Problems* 46:104–126.

Klotzko, Arlene Judith. 1998. "Medical miracle or medical mischief? The saga of the McCaughey septuplets." *The Hastings Center Report* 28:5–8.

Knaus, William A., Elizabeth A. Draper, Douglas P. Wagner, and Jack E. Zimmerman. 1986. "An evaluation of outcome from intensive care in major medical centers." *Annals of Internal Medicine* 104:410–418.

Kolata, Gina. 1990. *The Baby Doctors: Probing the Limits of Fetal Medicine.* New York: Delcorte Press.

Kolder, Beronika E. B., Janet Gallagher, and Michael T. Parsons. 1987. "Court-ordered obstetrical interventions." *NEJM* 316:1192–1196.

Kolker, Aliza and B. Meredith Burke. 1993. "Grieving the wanted child: Ramifications of abortion after prenatal diagnosis of abnormality." *Health Care for Women International* 14:513–526.

Kovner, Christine, and Peter J. Gergen. 1998. "Nurse staffing levels and adverse events following surgery in U.S. hospitals." *Image: Journal of Nursing Scholarship* 30:315–321.

Kronebusch, Karl. 1997. "Medicaid and the politics of groups: Recipients, providers, and policy making." *Journal of Health Politics, Policy and Law* 22:839–878.

Kunisch, Judith R. 1989. "Electronic fetal monitors: Marketing forces and the resulting controversy." Pp. 41–60 in *Healing Technology: Feminist Perspectives,* ed. Kathryn Strother Ratcliff, Myra Marx Ferree, Gail O. Mellow, Barbara Drygulski Wright, Glenda D. Price, Kim Yanoshik, and Margie S. Freston. Ann Arbor: The University of Michigan Press.

Kurz, Demie, and Evan Stark. 1988. "Not-so-benign neglect: The medical response to battering." Pp. 249–266 in *Feminist Perspectives on Wife Abuse,* ed. Kersti Yllo and Michele Bograd. Beverly Hills: Sage Publications.

Laine, Christine, and Frank Davidoff. 1996. "Patient-centered medicine: A professional evolution." *JAMA* 275:152–156.

Langone, John. 1995. *Harvard Med: The Story Behind America's Premier Medical School and the Making of America's Doctors.* Holbrook, MA: Adams Media.

Langton, Phyllis A. 1994. "Obstetricians' resistance to independent private practice by nurse-midwives in Washington, D.C. hospitals." *Women and Health* 22:27–48.

Laurence, Leslie, and Beth Weinhouse. 1994. *Outrageous Practices: The Alarming Truth About How Medicine Mistreats Women.* New York: Ballantine Books.

Lavizzo-Mourey, Risa J., and Jeane Ann Grisso. 1994. "Health, health care, and women of color." Pp. 47–63 in *An Unfinished Revolution: Women and Health Care in America,* ed. Emily Friedman. New York: United Hospital Fund of New York.

Lawrence, Susan C., and Kae Bendixen. 1992. "His and hers: Male and female anatomy in anatomy texts for U.S. medical students, 1890–1989." *Social Science and Medicine* 35:925–934.

Lazare, Aaron, Samuel M. Putnam, and Mack Lipkin Jr. 1995. "Three functions of the medical interview." Pp. 3–19 in *The Medical Interview: Clinical Care, Education, and Research,* ed. Mack Lipkin Jr., Samuel M. Putnam, and Aaron Lazare. New York: Springer.

Lee, Felicia R. 1990. "Needless breast cancer deaths reported among New York's poor." *New York Times.* October 30: B1, B5.

Legato, Marianne J. 1992. "Reaching across the gender gap." *The Female Patient* 18:11–12.

Lenhart, Sharyn A., Freda Klein, Patricia Falcao, Elizabeth Phelan, and Kevin Smith. 1991. "Gender bias against and sexual harassment of AMWA members in Massachusetts." *JAMWA* 46:121–125.

Lillie-Blanton, Marsha, Rose Marie Martinez, Andrea Kidd Taylor, and Betty Garman Robinson. 1993. "Latina and African American women: Continuing disparities in health." *International Journal of Health Services* 23:555–584.

Lipkin, Mack Jr., Samuel M. Putnam, and Aaron Lazare. 1995. *The Medical Interview: Clinical Care, Education, and Research.* Ann Arbor: Springer.

Love, Susan. 1993. "Confronting breast cancer: An interview with Susan Love." *Technology Review* (May/June):45–53.

Lucky Cigarettes advertisement. 1930. *Literary Digest* (April 5):26.

Luker, Kristin. 1984. *Abortion and The Politics of Motherhood.* Berkeley: University of California Press.

Macklin, Ruth. 1993. *Enemies of Patients.* New York: Oxford University Press.

MacPherson, Kathleen I. 1993. "The false promises of hormone replacement therapy and current dilemmas." Pp. 145–159 in *Menopause: A Midlife Passage,* ed. Joan C. Callahan. Bloomington: Indiana University Press.

Mahoney, Martha R. 1991. "Legal images of battered women: Redefining the issue of separation." Pp. 678–681 in *Women and the Law,* ed. Judith G. Greenberg, Martha L. Minow, and Dorothy E. Roberts. New York: Foundation Press.

Mallison, Mary B. 1989. "The gang that couldn't listen straight." *American Journal of Nursing* February:161.

Mangus, R. S., C. E. Hawkins, and M. J. Miller. 1998. "Prevalence of harassment and discrimination among 1996 medical school graduates: A survey of eight U.S. schools." *JAMA* 280:851–853.

Manley, Joan E. 1995. "Sex-segregated work in the system of professions: The development and stratification of nursing." *The Sociological Quarterly* 36:297–314.

Manson, JoAnn E., Walter C. Willett, Meir J. Stampfer, Fraham A. Colditz, David J. Hunter, Susan E. Hankinson, Charles H. Hennekens, and Frank E. Speizer. 1995. "Body weight and mortality among women." *NEJM* 333:677–685.

Marcus, Isabel. 1994. "Reframing 'domestic violence': Terrorism in the home." Pp. 11–35 in *The Public Nature of Private Violence: The Discovery of Domestic Abuse,* ed. Martha Albertson Fineman and Roxanne Mykitiuk. New York: Routledge.

Martin, Emily. 1987. *The Woman in the Body: A Cultural Analysis of Reproduction.* Boston: Beacon Press.

———. 1991. "The egg and the sperm: How science has constructed a romance based on stereotypical male-female roles." *Signs: Journal of Women in Culture and Society* 16:485–501.

Martin, Margaret E. 1997. "Double your trouble: Dual arrest in family violence." *Journal of Family Violence* 12:139–155.

Marvel, M. Kim, Ronald M. Epstein, Kristine Flowers, and Howard B. Beckman. 1999. "Soliciting the patient's agenda: Have we improved?" *JAMA* 281:283–287.

Marwick, Charles. 1991. "Desirable weight goes up in new guidelines." *JAMA* 265:17.

Mastroianni, Anna C., Ruth Faden, and Daniel Federman, eds. 1994. *Women and Health Research. Ethical and Legal Issues of Including Women in Clinical Studies. Volume 1.* Washington, DC: Institute of Medicine.

McCann, Una D., Lewis S. Seiden, Lewis J. Rubin, and George A. Ricaurte. 1997. "Brain serotonin neurotoxicity and primary pulmonary hypertension from fenfluramine and dexfenfluramine: A systematic review of the evidence." *JAMA* 278:666–672.

McCrea, Frances B. 1983. "The politics of menopause: The 'discovery' of a deficiency disease." *Social Problems* 31:111–123.

McCurdy, Stephen A., Marc B. Schenker, and Steven J. Samuels. 1991. "Reporting of occupational injury and illness in the semiconductor manufacturing industry." *AJPH* 81:85–89.

McDaniel, Christine L. 1997. "Elder abuse in the institutional setting." *KELN Bibliography.* Retrieved February 7, 2001, from the World Wide Web: http://www.keln.org/bibs/mcdaniel2.html

McDonough, Peggy. 1999. "Congenital disability and medical research: the development of amniocentesis." *Women & Health* 16:137–153.

McKinlay, John B. 1981. "From 'promising report' to 'standard procedure': Seven stages in the career of a medical innovation." *Milbank Memorial Fund Quarterly* 59:374–411.

McKinlay, John B., and Sonja M. McKinlay. 1977. "The questionable effect of medical measures on the decline of mortality in the United States in the twentieth century." *Milbank Memorial Fund Quarterly* 55:405–428.

McWhorter, William P., and William J. Mayer. 1987. "Black/white differences in type of initial breast cancer treatment and implications for survival." *AJPH* 77:1515–1517.

Mercer, Kobena. 1990. "Black hair/style politics." Pp. 247–264 in *Out There: Marginalization and Contemporary Cultures,* ed. Russell Ferguson, Martha Gever, Trinh T. Minh-ha, and Cornel West. Cambridge: The MIT Press.

Mergler, Donna, Carole Brabant, Nicole Vezina, and Karen Messing. 1987. "The weaker sex? Men in women's working conditions report similar health symptoms." *Journal of Occupational Medicine* 29:417–421.

Messing, Karen. 1997. "Women's occupational health: A critical review and discussion of current issues." *Women & Health* 25:39–68.

Meyer, Cheryl L. 1997. *The Wandering Uterus: Politics and the Reproductive Rights of Women.* New York: New York University Press.

Mezey, Mathy, Lois L. Miller, and Lori Linton-Nelson. 1999. "Caring for caregivers of frail elders at the end of life." *Generations* Spring:44–51.

Michelman, Kate. 2000. "Who decides? A state by state review of abortion and reproductive rights." National Abortion and Reproductive Rights Action League (NARAL). Retrieved February 23, 2000, from the World Wide Web: www.naral.org/mediaresources/press/pr011300_whodecides.html.

Mignon, Sylvia I., and William M. Holmes. 1995. "Police response to mandatory arrest laws." *Crime and Delinquency* 41:430–442.

Miles, Steven H., and Allison August. 1990. "Courts, gender and 'the right to die'." *Law, Medicine & Health Care* 18:85–95.

Mintz, Morton. 1985. *At Any Cost: Corporate Greed, Women, and the Dalkon Shield.* New York: Pantheon Books.

Mitford, Jessica. 1992. *The American Way of Birth.* New York: Dutton.

Mizrahi, Terry. 1984. "Coping with patients: Subcultural adjustments to the conditions of work among internists-in-training." *Social Problems* 32: 156–165.

———. 1986. *Getting Rid of Patients: Contradictions in the Socialization of Physicians.* New Brunswick: Rutgers University Press.

Montini, Theresa, and Sheryl Ruzek. 1989. "Overturning orthodoxy: The emergence of breast cancer treatment policy." *Research in the Sociology of Health Care* 8:3–32.

"Mount Sinai Assisted Reproductive Technologies Program." 1994. (Advertisement.) *New York Times Magazine.* April 3:10.

Mumford, Emily, Herbert J. Schlesinger, and Gene V. Glass. 1982. "The effect of psychological intervention on recovery from surgery and heart attacks: An analysis of the literature." *AJPH* 72:141–151.

Munsick, Robert. 1979. "Comment on 'A controlled trial of the differential effects on interpartum fetal monitoring' by Haverkamp and others." *American Journal of Obstetrics and Gynecology* 134:409–411.

Murphy, Sheigla, and Marsha Rosenbaum. 1999. *Pregnant Women on Drugs: Combating Stereotypes and Stigma.* New Brunswick: Rutgers University Press.

Muth, Jennifer L., and Thomas F. Cash. 1997. "Body-image attitudes: What difference does gender make?" *Journal of Applied Social Psychology* 27:1438–1453.

Myhre, Jennifer R. 1999. "The breast cancer movement: seeing beyond consumer activism." *JAMWA* 54:29–31.

Naranch, Laurie. 1997. "Naming and framing the issues: Demanding full citizenship for women." Pp. 21–34 in *Feminists Negotiate the State: The Politics of Domestic Violence,* ed. Cynthia Daniels. New York: University Press of America.

National Institute of Child Health and Human Development, Office of Medical Applications of Research, Division of Research Resources, and Food and Drug Administration. 1984. "Diagnostic Ultrasound Imaging in Pregnancy. Report of a Consensus Conference." Washington, DC: U.S. Government Printing Office.

National Women's Health Network. 1993. *Taking Hormones and Women's Health: Choices, Risks and Benefits.* Washington, DC: Desktop.

Nechas, Eileen, and Denise Foley. 1994. *Unequal Treatment: What You Don't Know About How Women Are Mistreated by the Medical Community.* New York: Simon & Schuster.

"The new weight guidelines." 1995. *Harvard Women's Health Watch* III:1.

Nordholm, Lena A. 1980. "Beautiful Patients are good patients: Evidence for the physical attractiveness stereotype in first impressions of patients." *Social Science and Medicine* 14a:81–83.

Norsigian, Judy, Vilunya Diskin, Paula Doress-Worters, Jane Pincus, Wendy Sanford, and Norma Swenson. 1999. "The Boston Women's Health Book Collective and *Our Bodies, Ourselves:* A brief history and reflection." *JAMWA* 54:35–38,40.

Notzon, Francis C., Paul J. Placek, and Selma M. Taffel. 1987. "Comparisons of national cesarean-section rates." *NEJM* 316:386–389.

Novello, Antonia C., Mark Rosenberg, Linda Saltzman, and John Shosky. 1992. "From the Surgeon General, US Public Health Service." *JAMA* 267:3132.

Nsiah-Jefferson, Laurie. 1994. "Reproductive genetic services for low-income women and women of color." Pp. 234–259 in *Women and Prenatal Testing: Facing the Challenges of Genetic Technology,* ed. Karen H. Rothenberg and Elizabeth J. Thomson. Columbus: Ohio State University Press.

O'Hanlan, Katherine A. 1995. "Lesbian health and homophobia: Perspectives for the treating obstetrician/gynecologist." *Current Problems in Obstetrics, Gynecology, and Fertility* 18:100–133.

Olds, David L., and John Eckenrode. 1997. "Long-term effects of home visitation on maternal life course and child abuse and neglect: Fifteen-year follow-up of a randomized trial." *JAMA* 278:637–643.

Olesen, Virginia L. 1997. "Who cares? Women as informal and formal caregivers." Pp. 397–424 in *Women's Health: Complexities and Differences,* ed. Sheryl Burt Ruzek, Virginia L. Olesen, and Adele E. Clarke. Columbus: Ohio State University Press.

Paludi, Michele A., and Richard B. Barickman. 1991. *Academic and Workplace Sexual Harassment: A Resource Manual.* Albany: State University of New York Press.

Paulsen, Monte. 1994. "The cancer business." *Mother Jones* May/June:41.

Pear, Robert. 1992. "Fertility clinics face crackdown." *New York Times.* October 26:B1.

Pearlman, Deborah N. 1998. "Slipping through the safety net: Implications for women's health." *Journal of Health Care for the Poor and Underserved* 9:217–221.

Pearson, Cindy. 1995. "NWHN members act as catalyst for largest study of African American women and breast cancer." *The Network News* 20:2.

———. 1996. "Self-help clinic celebrates 25 years." *The Network News* (March/April):1,2,4.

Pence, Ellen, and Melanie Shepard. 1988. "Integrating feminist theory and practice: The challenge of the battered women's movement." Pp. 282–298 in *Fem-*

inist Perspectives on Wife Abuse, ed. Kersti Yllo and Michele Bogard. Beverly Hills: Sage Publications.

Perloff, Janet D., Phillip Kletke, and James W. Fossett. 1995. "Which physicians limit their Medicaid participation, and why." *Health Services Research* 30:7–26.

Perrone, Bobette, H. Henrietta Stockel, and Victoria Krueger. 1989. *Medicine Women, Curanderas, and Women Doctors.* Norman, OK: University of Oklahoma Press.

Pham, Alex. 1998. "17,000 Massachusetts seniors hit by Aetna pullout." *The Boston Globe.* September 2:D7.

Pleck, Elizabeth. 1987. *Domestic Tyranny: The Making of Social Policy Against Family Violence from Colonial Times to the Present.* New York: Oxford University Press.

Podolsky, Doug. 1996. "The price of vanity." *U.S. News & World Report.* October 14: 22–28.

Pope, Barbara Spyridon. 1993. "In the wake of Tailhook: A new order for the Navy." Pp. 303–309 in *Transforming a Rape Culture,* ed. Emilie Buchwald, Pamela R. Fletcher, and Martha Roth. Minneapolis: Milkweed Editions.

Pottern, Linda M. 1994. "Women in the workplace: Discussion session I." *Journal of Occupational Medicine* 36:848.

Powledge, Tabitha. 1988. "Reproductive technologies and the bottom line." *Women and Health* 13:203–210.

Prince, Richard L. 1997. "Diet and the prevention of osteoporotic fractures." *NEJM* 337:701–702.

Profet, Margie. 1993. "Menstruation as a defense against pathogens transported by the sperm." *The Quarterly Review of Biology* 68:335–386.

Ptacek, James. 1999. *Battered Women in the Courtroom: The Power of Judicial Responses.* Boston: Northeastern University Press.

Public Citizen Health Research Group. 1997. "Hospital Emergency Rooms and Patient Dumping." Retrieved January 17, 2000, from the World Wide Web: www.citizen.org/hrg/publications/dumping.htm

Putnam, Samuel M., and Mack Lipkin Jr. 1995. "The patient-centered interview: Research support." Pp. 530–537 in *The Medical Interview: Clinical Care, Education, and Research,* ed. Mack Lipkin Jr., Samuel M. Putnam, and Aaron Lazare. New York: Springer.

Randall, Teri. 1990. "Domestic violence intervention calls for more than treating injuries." *JAMA* 264:939–940.

———. 1993. "Women need more and better information on menopause from their physicians, says survey." *JAMA* 270:1664.

Ratcliff, Kathryn Strother. 1989. "Health technologies for women: Whose health? Whose technology?" Pp. 173–198 in *Healing Technology: Feminist Perspectives,* ed. Kathryn Strother Ratcliff, Myra Marx Ferree, Gail O. Mellow, Barbara Drygulski Wright, Glenda D. Price, Kim Yanoshik, and Margie S. Freston. Ann Arbor: University of Michigan Press.

———. 1994. "Midwifery in East London: Responding to the challenges." *Women and Health* 22:49–78.

Ratcliff, Kathryn Strother, and Nancy Strother Luschei. 1998. "Choice in dying." *Hemlock News* 48:2.

Register, Charles A., and Donald R. Williams. 1990. "Wage effects of obesity among young workers." *Social Science Quarterly* 71:130–141.

Reinhardt, Uwe. 1999. "The political economy of health care for the elderly population." Pp. 203–229 in *Healthy Aging: Challenges and Solutions,* ed. Ken Dychtwald. Gaithersburg, MD: Aspen Publications.

Relman, Arnold. 1980. "The new medical-industrial complex." *NEJM* 303:963–970.

Rennie, Susan. 1993. "Breast cancer prevention: Diet vs. drugs." *MS* (May-June):38–46.

Reverby, Susan. 1987. "A caring dilemma: womanhood and nursing in historical perspective." *Nursing Research* 36:5–11.

Reverby, Susan, and Health/PAC Interviewer. 1988. "Nursing and caring: Lessons from history." *Health/PAC Bulletin* Fall:20–23.

Rheingold, Paul D. 1998. "Fen-phen and Redux: A tale of three drugs." *Trial* 34:78–83.

Richie, Beth E., and Valli Kanuha. 1993. "Battered women of color in public health care systems: Racism, sexism, and violence." Pp. 288–299 in *Wings of Gauze: Women of Color and the Experience of Health and Illness,* ed. Barbara Bair and Susan E. Cayleff. Detroit: Wayne State University Press.

Rifkind, Basil M., and Jacques E. Rossouw. 1998. "Of designer drugs, magic bullets, and gold standards." *JAMA* 279:1483–1485.

Rittenhouse, C. Amanda. 1991. "The emergence of premenstrual syndrome as a social problem." *Social Problems* 38:412–425.

Roback, Gene, Lillian Randolph, and Bradley Seidman. 1993. "Physician characteristics and distribution in the U.S." Chicago: American Medical Association.

Robbins, James M., and Laurence J. Kirmayer. 1991. "Attributions of common somatic symptoms." *Psychological Medicine* 21:1029–1045.

Roberto, Karen A. 1997. "Chronic pain in the lives of older women." *JAMWA* 52:127–131.

Roberts, Dorothy. 1997. *Killing the Black Body: Race, Reproduction, and the Meaning of Liberty.* New York: Vintage Books.

Roberts, Dorothy E. 1998. "Punishing drug addicts who have babies: Women of color, equality, and the right of privacy." Pp. 765–774 in *Women and the Law.* 2d ed., ed. Judith G. Greenberg, Martha L. Minow, and Dorothy E. Roberts. New York: Foundation Press.

Robertson, John A. 1994. *Children of Choice: Freedom and the New Reproductive Technologies.* Princeton: Princeton University Press.

Rodriquez-Trias, Helen. 1980. "Sterilization Abuse." Pp. 113–127 in *Science and Liberation,* edited by Rita Arditti, Pat Brennan, and Steve Cavrak. Boston: South End Press.

Roetzheim, Richard G., Naazneen Pal, Colleen Tennant, Lydia Voti, John Z. Ayanian, Annette Schwabe, and Jeffrey P. Krischer. 1999. "Effects of health insurance and race on early detection of cancer." *Journal of the National Cancer Institute* 91:1409–1415.

Rogers, Bonnie. 1999. "Health hazards in nursing and health care: An overview." Pp. 11–33 in *The Epidemic of Health Worker Injury: An Epidemiology,* ed. William Charney and Guy Fragala. New York: CRC Press.

Rome, Esther. 1986. "Premenstrual syndrome (PMS) examined through a feminist lens." Pp. 145–151 in *Culture, Society, and Menstruation,* ed. Virginia L. Olesen and Nancy Fugate Woods. New York: Hemisphere.

Rooks, Judith P. 1990. "Nurse-midwifery: The window is wide open." *American Journal of Nursing* 90:30–36.

Rooks, Judith Pence. 1997. *Midwifery and Childbirth in America.* Philadelphia: Temple University Press.

Rooks, Judith P., N. L. Weatherby, E. K. M. Ernst, Susan Stapleton, David Rosen, and Allan Rosenfield. 1989. "Outcomes of care in birth centers: The National Birth Center Study." *NEJM* 321:1804–1811.

Rosenthal, Elisabeth. 1992. "Commercial diets lack proof of their long-term success." *New York Times.* November 24:A1, C11.

Rosser, Sue V. 1994. *Women's Health—Missing from U.S. Medicine.* Bloomington: Indiana University Press.

Rothblatt, Martine. 1997. *Unzipped Genes: Taking Charge of Baby-Making in the New Millennium.* Philadelphia: Temple University Press.

Rothman, Barbara Katz. 1983. "Midwives in transition: The structure of a clinical revolution." *Social Problems* 30:262–270.

———. 1987. *The Tentative Pregnancy: Prenatal Diagnosis and the Future of Motherhood.* New York: Viking Penguin.

———. 1988. "Reproductive technology and the commodification of life." *Women and Health* 13:95–100.

———. 1991. *In Labor: Women and Power in the Birthplace.* New York: W. W. Norton.

Rowland, Diane, Alina Salganicoff, and Patricia Seliger Keenan. 1999. "The key to the door: Medicaid's role in improving health care for women and children." *Annual Review of Public Health* 20:403–426.

Rowland, Diane, Judith Feder, and Patricia Seliger Keenan. 1998. "Managed care for low-income elderly people." *Generations* Summer:43–50.

Rowland, Robyn. 1992. *Living Laboratories: Women and Reproductive Technologies.* Bloomington: Indiana University Press.

Rubenstein, Sharon, and Benjamin Caballero. 2000. "Is Miss America an undernourised role model?" *JAMA* 283:1569–1570.

Ruzek, Sheryl Burt. 1978. *The Women's Health Movement: Feminist Alternatives to Medical Control.* New York: Praeger.

———. 1980. "Medical responses to women's health activities: Conflict, accommodation and co-optation." Pp. 335–354 in *Research in the Sociology of Health Care: Volume 1: Professional Control of Health Services and Challenges to Such Control,* ed. Julius A. Roth. Greenwich, Connecticut: JAI Press.

Ruzek, Sheryl Burt, and Julie Becker. 1999. "The women's health movement in the United States: From grass-roots activism to professional agendas." *JAMWA* 54:4–8, 40.

Safran, Dana Gelb, William H. Rogers, Alvin R. Tarlov, Colleen A. McHorner, and John E. Ware Jr. 1997. "Gender differences in medical treatment: The case of physician-prescribed activity restrictions." *Social Science and Medicine* 45:711–722.

Schaie, K. Warner. 1996. *Intellectual Development in Adulthood: The Seattle Longitudinal Study.* Cambridge: Cambridge University Press.

Schairer, Catherine, Jay Lubin, Rebecca Troisi, Susan Sturgeon, Louise Brinton, and Robert Hoover. 2000. "Menopausal estrogen and estrogen-progestin replacement therapy and breast cancer risk." *JAMA* 283:485–491.

Schechter, Susan. 1982. *Women & Male Violence: The Visions and Strategies of the Battered Women's Movement.* Boston: South End Press.

Schiebinger, Londa. 1986. "Skeletons in the closet: The first illustrations of the female skeleton in eighteenth-century anatomy." *Representations* 14:42–82.

Schiller, Ine Glick. 1993. "The invisible women: Caregiving and the construction of AIDS health services." *Culture, Medicine, and Psychiatry* 17:487–512.

Schroedel, Jean Reith, and Paul Peretz. 1995. "A gender analysis of policy formation: The case of fetal abuse." Pp. 85–108 in *Expecting Trouble: Surrogacy, Fetal Abuse, and New Reproductive Technologies,* ed. Patricia Boling. San Francisco: Westview Press.

Schulman, Kevin A., Jesse A. Berlin, William Harless, Jon F. Kerner, Shyrl Sistrunk, Bernard J. Gersh, Ross Dube, Christopher K. Taleghani, Jennifer E. Burke, Sankey Williams, John M. Eisenburg, Jose J. Escarce, and William Ayers. 1999. "The effect of race and sex on physicians' recommendations for cardiac catheterization." *NEJM* 340:618–626.

Schulz, Richard, and Scott R. Beach. 1999. "Caregiving as a risk factor for mortality: The Caregiver Health Effects Study." *JAMA* 282:2215–2219.

Scritchfield, Shirley A. 1989. "The infertility enterprise: IVF and the technological construction of reproductive impairments." *Research in the Sociology of Health Care* 8:61–97.

Scully, Diana. 1994. *Men Who Control Women's Health: The Miseducation of Obstetrician-Gynecologists.* New York: Teachers College Press.

Scully, Diana, and Pauline Bart. 1973. "A funny thing happened on the way to the orifice: Women in gynecology textbooks." *American Journal of Sociology* 78:1045–1050.

Seid, Roberta Pollack. 1989. *Never Too Thin: Why Women are at War with Their Bodies.* New York: Prentice Hall.

Shapiro, M. C., J. M. Najman, A. Chang, J. D. Keeping, J. Morrison, and J. S. Western. 1983. "Informational control and the exercise of power in the obstetrical encounter." *Social Science and Medicine* 17:139–146.

Sharpe, Patricia A. 1995. "Older women and health services: Moving from ageism toward empowerment." *Women & Health* 22:9–23.

Sher, Geoffrey, and Michael Feinman. 1997. "Accountability, representation, and advertising." *Women's Health Issues* 7:153–161.

Silver, Lee, Jeremy Rifkin, and Barbara Katz Rothman. 1998. "Biotechnology: A new frontier of corporate control." *Tikkun* 13:47–50,63.

Snell, John E., Richard J. Rosenwald, and Ames Robey. 1964. "The wife-beater's wife: A study of family interaction." *Archives of General Psychiatry* 11:107–112.

Sokolavsky, Jay. 1997. "Bringing culture back home: Aging, ethnicity and family support." Pp. 263–275 in *The Cultural Context of Aging: Worldwide Perspectives,* second edition, ed. Jay Sokolovsky. Westport, CT: Bergin and Garvey Books.

Solarz, Andrea L. 1999. *Lesbian Health: Current Assessment and Directions for the Future.* Washington, DC: National Academy Press.

Sparks, Anne. 1997. "Feminists negotiate the executive branch: The policing of male violence." Pp. 35–52 in *Feminists Negotiate The State: The Politics of Domestic Violence,* ed. Cynthia Daniels. New York: University Press of America.

Spector, William D., and Hitomi Adrianna Takada. 1991. "Characteristics of nursing homes that affect resident outcomes." *Journal of Aging and Health* 3:427–454.

Spiegel, David. 1995. "How do you feel about cancer now?—Survival and psychosocial support." *Public Health Reports* 110:298–300.

Spiegel, David, Joan R. Bloom, Helena C. Kraemer, and Ellen Gottheil. 1989. "Effect of psychosocial treatment on survival of patients with metastatic breast cancer." *The Lancet* October 14:888–891.

Sporkin, Elizabeth. 1993. "They met the enemy, and it was food: The body game." *People.* January 11: 80–85.

Stalans, Loretta J., and Arthur J. Lurigio. 1995. "Responding to domestic violence against women." *Crime and Delinquency* 41:387–398.

Stanworth, Michelle. 1987. *Reproductive Technologies: Gender, Motherhood and Science.* Minneapolis: University of Minnesota Press.

Stark, Evan, and Anne Flitcraft. 1996. *Women at Risk: Domestic Violence and Women's Health.* Thousand Oaks, CA: Sage Publications.

Starr, Paul. 1982. *The Social Transformation of American Medicine.* New York: Basic Books.

Stein, Leonard I., David T. Watts, and Timothy Howell. 1990. "The doctor-nurse game revisited." *NEJM* 322:546–549.

Steinberg, Ronnie J. and Deborah M. Figart. 1999. "Emotional labor since *The Managed Heart.*" *Annals of the American Academy of Political and Social Science* 561:8–26.

Steingart, Richard M., Milton Packer, Peggy Hamm, Mary Ellen Coglianese, Bernard Gersh, Edward M. Geltman, Josephine Sollano, Stanley Katz, Lem Moye, Lofty L. Basta, Sandra J. Lewis, Stephen S. Gottlieb, Victoria Bernstein, Patricia McEwan, Kirk Jacobsen, Edward J. Brown, Marrick L. Kukin, Niki E. Kantrowitz, and Marc A. Pfeffer. 1991. "Sex differences in the management of coronary artery disease." *NEJM* 325:226–230.

Steinman, Joan E. 1992. "Women, medical care, and mass tort litigation." *Chicago-Kent Law Review* 68:409–429.

Stevens, June, Jianwen Cai, Elsie R. Pamuk, David F. Williamson, Michael J. Thun, and Joy L. Wood. 1998. "The effect of age on the association between body-mass index and mortality." *NEJM* 338:1–7.

Stevens, Patricia E. 1996. "Lesbians and doctors: experiences of solidarity and domination in health care settings." *Gender & Society* 10:24–41.

Stevens, Patricia E. and Joanne M. Hall. 1991. "A critical historical analysis of the medical construction of lesbianism." *International Journal of Health Sciences* 21:291–307.

Stone, Richard. 1995. "Analysis of a toxic death." *Discover* April:66–75.

Strahan, Genevieve W. 1997. "An overview of nursing homes and their current residents: Data from the 1995 National Nursing Home Survey." *Advance Data* January 23:1–10.

Strother, Charles R. 1995. *One Life: Three Careers.* Mansfield CT: Fenton River Associates.

Suchman, Anthony L., Kathryn Markakis, Howard B. Beckman, and Richard Frankel. 1997. "A model of empathic communicaton in the medical interview." *JAMA* 277:678–682.

Sullivan, Deborah. 2001. *Cosmetic Surgery: The Cutting Edge of Commercial Medicine in America.* Piscataway, NJ: Rutgers University Press.

Sullivan, Deborah A., and Rose Weitz. 1988. *Labor Pains: Modern Midwives and Home Birth.* New Haven: Yale University Press.

Summey, Pamela, and Marsha Hurst. 1986. "Ob/Gyn on the rise: The evolution of professional ideology in the twentieth century—Part II." *Women and Health* 11:103–122.

SUPPORT, Principal Investigators. 1995. "A controlled trial to improve care for seriously ill hospitalized patients: The study to understand prognoses and preferences for outcomes and risks of treatments (SUPPORT)." *JAMA* 274:1591–1598.

Svarstad, Bonnie L., and Jeanine K. Mount. 1991. "Nursing home resources and tranquilizer use among the institutionalized elderly." *Journal of the American Geriatrics Society* 39:869–875.

Swasy, Alecia. 1996. "Rely tampons and Toxic Shock Syndrome: Procter & Gamble's responses." Pp. 278–289 in *Corporate and Governmental Deviance: Problems of Organizational Behavior in Contemporary Society,* ed. M. David Ermann and Richard J. Lundman. New York: Oxford University Press.

Szekely, Eva. 1988. *Never Too Thin.* Toronto: The Women's Press.

Tanenbaum, Sandra J. 1995. "Medicaid eligibility policy in the 1980s: Medical utilitarianism and the 'deserving' poor." *Journal of Health Politics, Policy and Law* 20:933–954.

Tavris, Carol. 1992. *The Mismeasure of Woman.* New York: Simon & Schuster.

Terry, John A. 1998. "In Re A. C." Pp. 751–758 in *Women and the Law,* ed. Judith G. Greenberg, Martha L. Minow, and Dorothy E. Roberts. New York: Foundation Press.

Todd, Alexandra Dundas. 1989. *Intimate Adversaries: Cultural Conflict Between Doctors and Women Patients.* Philadelphia: University of Pennsylvania Press.

———. 1993. "Exploring women's experiences: Power and resistance in medical discourse." Pp. 267–285 in *Social Organization of Doctor-Patient Communication,* ed. Alexandra Dundas Todd and Sue Fisher. Norwood, NJ: Ablex.

Toscano, Guy A., Janice A. Windau and Andrew Knestaut. 1998. "Work injuries and illnesses occurring to women." *Compensation and Working Conditions* Summer:16–23.

Tribe, Laurence H. 1992. *Abortion: The Clash of Absolutes.* New York: W.W. Norton.

Trude, Sally, and David C. Colby. 1997. "Monitoring the impact of the medicare fee schedule on access to care for vulnerable populations." *Journal of Health Politics, Policy and Law* 22:49–71.

Turkel, Kathleen Doherty. 1995. *Women, Power and Childbirth: A Case Study of a Free-Standing*

Birth Center. Westport, CT: Bergin and Garvey Books.

U.S. Department of Health and Human Services. 2000. "2000 HHS Poverty Guidelines." *Federal Register* 65, 31:7555–7557.

Uzelac, Ellen. 1992. "Catalogs assist people shopping for sperm." *Hartford Courant.* January 12:A3.

Vaitukaitis, Judith. 1984. "Premenstrual syndrome." *NEJM* 311:1371–1373.

Vellozzi, Claudia J., Martha Romans, and Richard B. Rothenberg. 1996. "Delivering breast and cervical cancer screening services to underserved women: Part I. Literature review and telephone survey." *Women's Health Issues* 6:65–73.

Verhey, Allen. 1997. "Commodification, commercialization, and embodiment." *Women's Health Issues* 7:132–142.

Villa, Valentine M., Steven P. Wallace, and Kyriakos Markides. 1997. "Economic diversity and an aging population: The impact of public policy and economic trends." *Generations* Summer:13–18.

Virginia Slims advertisement. 1996. *Home Magazine* (June): back cover.

Waitzkin, Howard. 1984. "Doctor–patient communication: Clinical implications of social scientific research." *JAMA* 252:2441–2446.

Wallen, Jacqueline, Howard Waitzkin, and John D. Stoeckle. 1979. "Physician stereotypes about female health and illness: A study of patient's sex and the informative process during medical interviews." *Women & Health* 4:135–146.

Wallis, Lila A. 1998. "Introduction." Pp. xxxvii–xli in *Textbook of Women's Health,* ed. Lila A. Wallis. New York: Lippincott-Raven.

Wallis, Lila A., and Dorothy M. Barbo. 1998. "Hormone Replacement Therapy (HRT)." Pp. 731–743 in *Textbook of Women's Health,* ed. Lila A. Wallis. New York: Lippincott-Raven.

Ward, Martha C. 1986. *Poor Women, Powerful Men: America's Great Experiment in Family Planning.* Boulder, CO: Westview Press.

Warshaw, Carole. 1989. "Limitations of the medical model in the care of battered women." *Gender & Society* 3:506–517.

Warshaw, Robin. 1994. *I Never Called It Rape: The Ms. Report on Recognizing, Fighting, and Surviving Date and Acquaintance Rape.* New York: HarperCollins Publishers.

Waxler-Morrison, Nancy, T. Gregory Hislop, Bronwen Mears, and Lisa Kan. 1991. "Effects of social relationships on survival for women with breast cancer: a prospective study." *Social Science and Medicine* 33:177–183.

Weijer, Charles. 1995. "Our bodies, our science." *The Sciences* May-June:41–44.

Weissman, Joel S., Constantine Gatsonis, and Arnold M. Epstein. 1992. "Rates of avoidable hospitalization by insurance status in Massachusetts and Maryland." *JAMA* 268:2388–2394.

Weitz, Rose, and Deborah A. Sullivan. 1986. "The politics of childbirth: The reemergence of midwifery in Arizona." *Social Problems* 33:163–175.

Welner, Sandra L. 1998. "Caring for the woman with a disability." Pp. 87–92 in *Textbook of Women's Health,* ed. Lila A. Wallis. New York: Lippincott-Raven.

Wermuth, Laurie. 1982. "Domestic violence reforms: Policing the private?" *Berkeley Journal of Sociology* 27:27–49.

Wertz, Richard W., and Dorothy C. Wertz. 1977. *Lying-In: A History of Childbirth in America.* New York: The Free Press.

West, Candace. 1993. "'Ask me no questions…' An analysis of queries and replies in physician–patient dialogues." Pp. 127–157 in *The Social Organization of Doctor–Patient Communication,* 2d ed., ed. Alexandra Dundas Todd and Sue Fisher. Norwood, NJ: Ablex.

Westhoff, Carolyn. 1994. "Abortion training in residency programs." *JAMWA* 49:150–152.

Wickham-Searl, Parnell. 1994. "Mothers of children with disabilities and the construction of expertise." *Research in the Sociology of Health Care* 11:175–187.

Wikler, Daniel, and Norma J. Wikler. 1991. "Turkey-baster babies: The demedicalization of artificial insemination." *Milbank Memorial Fund Quarterly/Health and Society* 69:5–39.

Wilentz, Robert N. 1998. "In the matter of Baby M." Pp. 788–796 in *Women and the Law,* second edition, ed. Judith G. Greenberg, Martha L. Minow, and Dorothy E. Roberts. New York: Foundation Press.

Wilkinson, Sue, and Celia Kitsinger. 1993. "Whose breast is it anyway? A feminist consideration of advice and 'treatment' for breast cancer." *Women's Studies International Forum.* 16:229–238.

Wilson, Robert A. 1966. *Feminine Forever.* New York: M. Evans and Company.

Winslow, Ron. 1998. "Study raises new questions about women's use of estrogen." *The Wall Street Journal* August 19:B1.

Wiseman, Claire V., James J. Gray, James E. Mosimann, and Anthony H. Ahrens. 1992. "Cultural expectations of thinness in women: An update." *International Journal of Eating Disorders* 11:85–89.

Wolf, Naomi. 1991. *The Beauty Myth: How Images of Beauty are Used Against Women.* New York: Doubleday: Anchor Books.

Woliver, Laura R. 1989. "New reproductive technologies: Challenges to women's control of gestation and birth." Pp. 43–56 in *Biomedical Technology and Public Policy,* ed. Robert H. Blank and Miriam K. Mills. New York: Greenwood Press.

Woolley, R. J. 1995. "Benefits and risks of episiotomy: A review of English-language literature since 1980. Part 1." *Obstetrical and Gynecological Survey* 50:806–820.

Worcester, Nancy, and Mariamne H. Whatley. 1992. "The selling of HRT: Playing on the fear factor." *Feminist Review* 41:1–26.

Yllo, Kersti. 1988. "Political and methodological debates in wife abuse research." Pp. 28–50 in *Feminist Perspectives on Wife Abuse,* ed. Kersti Yllo and Michele Bograd. Beverly Hills: Sage Publications.

Zahm, Shelia Hoar, Linda M. Pottern, Denise Riedel Lewis, Mary H. Ward, Deborah W. White. 1994. "Inclusion of women and minorities in occupational cancer epidemiologic research." *Journal of Occupational Medicine* 36:842–847.

Zimmerman, Mary K. 1987. "The women's health movement: A critique of medical enterprise and the position of women." Pp. 442–472 in *Analyzing Gender: A Handbook of Social Science Research,* ed. Beth B. Hess and Myra Marx Ferree. Beverly Hills: Sage Publications.

Zimmermann, Susan M. 1998. *Silicone Survivors: Women's Experiences with Breast Implants.* Philadelphia: Temple University Press.

Zones, Jane Sprague. 1997. "Beauty myths and realities and their impact on women's health." Pp. 249–275 in *Women's Health: Complexities and Differences,* ed. Sheryl Burt Ruzek, Virginia L. Olesen, and Adele Clarke. Columbus: Ohio State University Press.

Zuckerman, Diana. 1998. "Briefing paper: The safety of silicone breast implants." Washington, DC: Institute for Women's Policy Research.

Credits

Emily Martin, "The Egg and the Sperm: How Science Has Constructed a Romance Based on Stereotypical Male-Female Roles." *Signs* 16(3), pp. 485–501, abridged. Published by University of Chicago Press. Copyright © 1991 by The University of Chicago. All rights reserved.

Patricia E. Stevens and Joanne M. Hall, "A Critical Historical Analysis of the Medical Construction of Lesbianism." *International Journal of Health Services* 21(2), pp. 291–307, abridged. Copyright © 1991 by Baywood Publishing Co., Inc.

Terri Kapsalis, "Cadavers, Dolls, and Prostitutes: Medical Pedagogy and the Pelvic Rehearsal." From Terri Kapsalis, *Public Privates: Performing Gynecology from Both Ends of the Speculum* (excerpts from Chapter 3). Copyright © 1997, Duke University Press. All rights reserved. Reprinted with permission.

Laurie Kaye Abraham, "Fitful Primary Care Fails Mrs. Jackson," abridged. From Laurie Kaye Abraham, *Mama Might Be Better Off Dead: The Failure of Health Care in Urban America.* Published by University of Chicago Press. Copyright © 1993 by the University of Chicago. All rights reserved.

Carole J. Sheffield, "Sexual Terrorism," abridged. From Jo Freeman, editor, *Women: A Feminist Perspective,* 5th ed., pp. 3–19 (Mountain View, CA: Mayfield Press, 1994). Copyright by Carole J. Sheffield. Reprinted by permission of the author.

"The 'Rape' of Mr. Smith." Reprinted by permission of Champaign County Women Against Rape.

Ann Jones, "Why doesn't she leave?", abridged. From Ann Jones, *Next Time She'll Be Dead: Battering and How to Stop It,* pp. 129–136. Copyright © 1994 by Ann Jones. Reprinted by permission of Beacon Press, Boston.

Patricia Yancey Martin and Robert A. Hummer, "Fraternities and Rape on Campus," abridged. *Gender and Society* 3(4), pp. 457–473. Copyright © 1989 by Sociologists for Women in Society. Reprinted by permission of Sage Publications, Inc.

Steve Fox, "Health Complaints and the Deaths of Friends." From Steve Fox, *Toxic Work: Women Workers at GTE–Lenkurt,* pp. 49–64. Reprinted by permission of Temple University Press. Copyright © 1991 by Temple University. All rights reserved.

Sharon Batt, " 'Perfect People': Cancer Charities," pp. 213–238, abridged. From Sharon Batt, *Patient No More: The Politics of Breast Cancer.* (Charlottetown, Prince Edward Island, Canada: Gynergy Books, 1994.) Used with permission of Gynergy Books. Copyright © 1994 by Sharon Batt.

Rita Arditti and Tatiana Schreiber, "Breast Cancer: The Environmental Connection. A 1998 Update." Copyright ©1998 by Rita Arditti and Tatiana Schreiber. From Estelle Disch, editor, *Reconstructing Gender,* 2nd ed., pp. 463–473 (Mountain View, CA: Mayfield Publishing). Reprinted by permission of authors.

Denise Anthony, "The Care and Feeding of the Diet Industry: Implications for Women's Health." Copyright © 2000, by Denise Anthony.

Rebecca Wepsic Ancheta, "Discourse of Rules: Women Talk about Cosmetic Surgery." I would like to thank Virginia Olesen, Adele Clarke, and Candace West for their comments and suggestions. I am particularly grateful to the women who shared their cosmetic surgery stories. A version of this paper was presented at the Society for Social Studies of Science 1999 annual meeting in San Diego, California. This project was supported by a Graduate Dean's Humanities Research Fellowship at the University of California, San Francisco. Copyright © Ancheta 2000.

Gloria Steinem, "If Men Could Menstruate—A Political Fantasy." *MS* October, p.110. Copyright © Gloria Steinem. Reprinted with permission.

Anne Fausto-Sterling, "Menopause: The Storm before the Calm," selection from Chapter 5, pp. 110–122. From Anne Fausto-Sterling, *Myths of Gender,* Copyright © 1986 by Basic Books, Inc. Reprinted by permission of Basic Books, a member of Perseus Books, L. L. C.

Leora Tanenbaum, "The Bitter Pill: Bombarded by Propaganda on Premarin, We Can't Trust Our Doctors and We Can't Trust Ourselves," abridged. *On the Issues: The Progressive Women's Quarterly* 7(1), pp. 38–41. Copyright by Merle Hoffman. Reprinted by permission.

Myra Dinnerstein and Rose Weitz, "Jane Fonda, Barbara Bush and Other Aging Bodies: Femininity and the Limits of Resistance." *Feminist Issues* 14(3), pp.3–24, abridged. Copyright © 1994 by Transaction Publishers. Reprinted by permission of Transaction Publishers. All rights reserved.

Dorothy Roberts, "From Norplant to the Contraceptive Vaccine: The New Frontiers of Population Control," abridged. From Dorothy Roberts, *Killing the Black Body,* pp. 106–127. Copyright © 1997 by Dorothy Roberts. Reprinted by permission of Pantheon Books, a division of Random House, Inc.

Danielle Currier, "Illegal Abortion in the United States: A Perilous History." Copyright © 2000 by Danielle Currier.

Perri Klass, "Bearing a Child in Medical School." *New York Times Magazine* November 11, 1984, pp. 120–125. Reprinted with permission of author.

Kathleen Doherty Turkel, "Free-Standing Birth Centers," abridged. From Kathleen Doherty Turkel, *Women, Power, and Childbirth: A Case Study of a Free-Standing Birth Center,* pp. 73–85 (Westport CT: Bergin & Garvey, 1995). Copyright © 1995 by Greenwood Publishing Group, Inc. Reproduced with permission of Greenwood Publishing Group, Inc., Westport, CT.

Barbara Katz Rothman, "Reproductive Technology and the Commodification of Life." *Women and Health* 13(1–2), pp. 95–100. Copyright © 1987 by The Haworth Press, Inc., Binghamton, NY. All rights reserved.

Judith N. Lasker and Susan Borg, "The Rise and Fall of Ovum Transfer: A Cautionary Tale." From Judith N. Lasker and Susan Borg, *In Search of Parenthood: Coping with Infertility and High-Tech Conception, Revised and Updated,* pp. 93–102. Reprinted by permission of Temple University Press. Copyright © 1994 by Temple University. All rights reserved.

Monica J. Casper, "The Case of the Disappearing Moms: Fetal Surgery and Women's Health." Copyright © 2000 by Monica J. Casper. The ideas in this article are elaborated in Monica J. Casper, *The Making of the Unborn Patient: A Social Anatomy of Fetal Surgery.* (New Brunswick: Rutgers University Press, 1998).

Marsha Saxton, "Prenatal Screening and Discriminatory Attitudes about Disability." *Women and Health* 13(1–2), pp. 217–224. Copyright © 1987 by The Haworth Press, Inc., Binghamton, NY. All rights reserved.

Alice Rothchild, "From Both Ends of the Speculum: Reflections on Women's Health Care in America." Based on a speech given at the American Medical Women's Association National Conference, Chicago, November 5–9, 1997. From Boston Women's Health Book Collective, <www.ourbodiesourselves.org/rothchil.htm>. Retrieved February 3, 2000. Reprinted by permission of the author.

Daniel F. Chambliss, "What It Means to Be a Nurse," abridged. From Daniel F. Chambliss, *Beyond Caring,* pp. 61–85. Published by University of Chicago Press. Copyright © 1996 by the University of Chicago Press. All rights reserved.

"A Mother's Responsibility." Copyright © 2000 by Kathryn Strother Ratcliff. Reprinted with permission.

Judy Norsigian, Vilunya Diskin, Paula Doress-Worters, Jane Pincus, Wendy Sanford, and Norma Swenson, "The Boston Women's Health Book Collective and *Our Bodies, Ourselves:* A brief history and reflection." *Journal of the American Medical Women's Association* 54(1), pp. 35–40. Copyright © 1999 by American Medical Women's Association, Inc. All rights reserved. Reprinted with permission.

Sheryl Burt Ruzek and Julie Becker, "The Women's Health Movement in the United States: From Grass-Roots Activism to Professional Agendas." *Journal of the American Medical Women's Association* 54(1), pp. 4–8, 40. Copyright © 1999 by American Medical Women's Association, Inc. All rights reserved. Reprinted with permission.

Byllye Y. Avery, "Breathing Life into Ourselves: The Evolution of the National Black Women's Health Project." From Evelyn C. White, editor, *The Black Women's Health Book.* Copyright ©1994 by Evelyn C. White. Reprinted by permission of Seal Press.

Cindy Pearson, "Self Help Clinic Celebrates 25 Years." *The Network News* March/April, pp. 1–2, 4. Cindy Pearson is the executive director of the National Women's Health Network (NWHN). For more information, see <www.womenshealthnetwork.org>. Copyright © 1996 by NWHN. Reprinted by permission.

Phil Brown and Faith I. T. Ferguson, " 'Making a Big Stink': Women's Work, Women's Relationships, and Toxic Waste Activism," abridged. *Gender and Society* 9(2), pp. 145–172. Copyright © 1995 by Sociologists for Women in Society. Reprinted by permission of Sage Publications.

Lois Camp, "Numbers, Numbers, Numbers …" From Judith Brady, editor, *1 in 3: Women with Cancer Confront an Epidemic* (Pittsburgh: Cleis Press, Inc., 1991). Reprinted by permission of the publisher.

Index